Microcomputer Engineering

Gene H. Miller

GMI Engineering & Management Institute

Flint, Michigan

PRENTICE HALL, Englewood Cliffs, New Jersey 07632

Library of Congress Cataloging-in-Publication Data

Miller, Gene H.
Microcomputer Engineering / Gene H. Miller
   p. cm.
   Includes bibliographical references and index
   ISBN 0-13-584475-4
1. Microcomputers. 2. Assembler language (Computer program
language) 3. 68HC11 (Microprocessor) I. Title.
TK7888.3.M548   1993
004.165--dc20   92-42363
               CIP

Acquisitions editor: Marcia Horton
Production editor: Irwin Zucker
Copy editor: Brenda Melissaratos
Cover design: Design Source
Prepress buyer: Linda Behrens
Manufacturing buyer: David Dickey
Supplements editor: Alice Dworkin
Editorial assistant: Dolores Mars

© 1993 by Prentice-Hall, Inc.
A Simon & Schuster Company
Englewood Cliffs, New Jersey 07632

The author and publisher of this book have used their best efforts in preparing this book. These efforts include the development, research, and testing of the theories and programs to determine their effectiveness. The author and publisher make no warranty of any kind, expressed or implied, with regard to these programs or the documentation contained in this book. The author and publisher shall not be liable in any event for incidental or consequential damages in connection with, or arising out of, the furnishing, performance, or use of these programs.

Material from Motorola manuals, including the MC68HCIIA8/D manual, is reprinted with permission from Motorola.

Printed in the United States of America
10 9 8 7 6 5 4 3 2 1

ISBN 0-13-584475-4

Po 3142

Prentice-Hall International (UK) Limited, *London*
Prentice-Hall of Australia Pty. Limited, *Sydney*
Prentice-Hall Canada Inc., *Toronto*
Prentice-Hall Hispanoamericana. S.A., *Mexico*
Prentice-Hall of India Private Limited, *New Delhi*
Prentice-Hall of Japan, Inc., *Tokyo*
Simon & Schuster Asia Pte. Ltd., *Signapore*
Editora Prentice-Hall do Brasil, Ltda., *Rio de Janeiro*

Dedicated to my father
Herbert L. Miller

Contents

Appendixes

411

Glossary

523

General Index

531

Preface

To the Student

Microcomputer Engineering was written for students studying engineering and related disciplines in a first microcomputers course. Knowledge of microprocessors and single-chip microcomputers is essential to the design of products, manufacturing equipment, and laboratory instrumentation. So, many schools now require at least one microcomputers course that includes laboratory work with these devices. Practicing engineers with some digital systems background can learn this material without an instructor by using this book. The best background includes courses in electrical circuits, electronics, digital systems, and high-level language programming. Digital systems is the most important of these.

This textbook will help you learn the fundamentals of microcomputers; it is not a computer manual. Examples demonstrate conceptual topics, since most people learn examples before they can generalize. Small sections cover only a few details at a time. I introduce the computer instructions only when the topic requires them; a table of the instructions appears only in an appendix.

You should experience the computer by hands-on work with microcomputer training hardware. In using that hardware, you will see all its features simultaneously, and that is a problem. You cannot force parts of the hardware to stop operating until you learn about them; the hardware operates whether you know about it or not. You must learn to ignore those things that you are not yet prepared to comprehend. Similarly, this book ignores unnecessary details until you are ready for them. Implement all the small program examples on trainer hardware as you read.

I recommend the Motorola M68HC11EVB microcomputer trainer hardware for implementing the examples and exercises. The appendixes contain information about this hardware. In the text, boxes enclose material that refers to the Motorola trainer. If you are using other hardware, ignore the boxed text.

I sincerely hope that this book will be useful to students. If the opportunity arises, I will improve it based upon the recommendations and other feedback that I receive. I invite and urge you to write to me to comment on this book; student opinion about books is hardly ever heard, but always appreciated.

To the Instructor

Microcomputer Engineering is a complete course-teaching aid that encourages hands-on laboratory work. The Motorola 68HC11 single-chip microcomputer/microprocessor is the only hardware discussed. I recommend the Motorola M68HC11EVB microcomputer trainer with an IBM PC compatible personal computer system for laboratory work. I also recommend the CTC SPF/PC editor and the 2500AD assembler. Material related to this support equipment and software is in the appendixes. Other equipment and software can be used, although with greater effort. An appendix describes how to set up a complete laboratory.

The text makes teaching easy. The order of the chapters is the order I present the material. I want students working on a trainer as soon as possible, so I deliberately simplified the early topics. Reading assigned by section is possible since the sections are mostly independent of one another. Small laboratory/homework exercises are at the end of each chapter. Larger projects are in Appendix E.

Chapter 1 reviews the digital systems and computer fundamentals required. The section on number systems is essential to understanding later chapters.

Chapter 2 introduces some of the microprocessor registers, the programming model, and the functions of these registers. Following this, some instructions and the addressing modes are introduced with straightforward examples. At the end of this chapter, a section discusses designing and writing a small machine language program.

I encourage laboratory/homework exercises on the trainer that demonstrate the instruction set, addressing modes, and a machine language program.

Chapter 3 changes direction and introduces assembly language. The remainder of the book uses assembly language for all examples.

Motorola notation and terminology are used so you can reference Motorola manuals without confusion. Although the examples came from the SPF/PC editor and the 2500AD assembler, I removed anything specifically related to this software. Exercises in writing simple programs using an editor and assembler are appropriate, but only use the instructions from Chapter 2 at this point.

The student is now beginning to understand what a microcomputer is and how to program it. Since bad habits develop quickly, it is important to discuss program design before people have much programming experience. Chapter 4 concentrates on the established ideas for writing cost-effective and useful programs. Most microcomputer books avoid this topic apparently assuming that good software engineering is unnecessary; this book assumes exactly the contrary.

Chapter 5 introduces most of the remaining instructions using assembly language. Instructions are grouped according to their usual function, such as bit manipulation, comparison, BCD arithmetic, and stack operations. Subroutines and several parameter-passing techniques are covered in detail.

Chapter 6 covers hardware, input/output concepts, and input/output programming. Microprocessor buses, memory and I/O chips, and input/output synchronization techniques are the main topics. The I/O section includes both polling and interrupt techniques. Little electronics knowledge is required.

Chapter 7 covers the I/O hardware capabilities of the 68HC11 chip. Operation in both the single-chip microcomputer and expanded modes, chip versions, chip configuration, and pin connections are first. The next topics include hardware reset and details of the interrupt system. The following I/O hardware sections discuss the real-time clock, programmable timer, pulse accumulator, serial communications interface, and the analog-to-digital converter—all with programming examples. The next section on fail-safe operation discusses the COP timer, clock failure detection, and illegal instruction response. The hardware expansion section covers microprocessor bus extension, the SPI bus, and the port replacement unit. Finally, special hardware operations such as stopping the clock are covered.

Appendix A is an introduction to IBM PC compatible computers for running editor and assembler programs. Appendixes B and C document the use of the SPF/PC editor and the 2500AD assembler. Appendix D explains the Motorola 68HC11 microcomputer trainer and includes a tutorial on its use. Appendix E contains laboratory exercises for use with a microcomputer trainer. Appendix F discusses setting up a laboratory that uses the Motorola trainer. Appendixes G through I document the 68HC11 instruction set in several tables. Appendix J tabulates the internal I/O hardware control registers. Appendix K has answers to selected exercises.

The glossary defines and explains many of the microcomputer terms used in the text. The glossary avoids relying on extensive knowledge of computer hardware and electronics.

Acknowledgments

Special thanks are due to several people who directly helped me during the development of this book. First, I thank my wife, Margo, who continued to encourage me even after I was absent for many hours sitting in front of my personal computer. I also thank Margo for finding my many errors in the page layouts, section headings, page headings, and so on. Next I thank Tim Bozik and Pete Janzow of Prentice Hall for recognizing my ability to produce this book with desktop publishing software. I thank Roy Czernikowski, Rochester Institute of Technology, and Robert Pinteric, Motorola, Inc., for reviewing the book. I also thank Mr. Mark Chuey, Instructor of Electrical Engineering at GMI Engineering & Management Institute. Mark's critique of both the content and the written material in the book was very helpful. And finally, I thank my many students who have made my life both interesting and challenging.

I gratefully acknowledge the information in this book obtained from the manuals published by Motorola, Inc. The reader is encouraged to consult Motorola manuals for further information when needed.

Colophon

I created this entire book on a Dell 310 personal computer containing an Intel 80386 microprocessor, four megabytes of memory, and a 150-megabyte hard disk. An NEC Monograph desktop publishing monitor provided WYSIWYG page displays. The text was composed and spell checked using the WordPerfect word processor. I did the page layout and generated the table of contents and index with Ventura Publisher. Figures were drawn using GEM Draw or the Ventura Publisher table feature. Grammar and style were checked using the Right-Writer, Grammatik, and Correct Grammar programs after stripping the Ventura Publisher codes with a C program written by my son Eric Miller. Frequent backups of the hard disk were made with Fastback Plus. The book was printed to disk as PostScript files which were supplied to Prentice Hall.

Chapter 1

Computer Fundamentals

Microprocessors and microcomputers are so commonplace today that almost everybody, regardless of their education, is aware of them. Elementary school students in most developed countries routinely work with personal computers containing microprocessors. The microprocessor has become a fundamental device for engineering design. It is as common as the resistor, transistor, and circuit board have been in the past.

Studying microcomputers should be fun. Many people play with microprocessors as their hobby. These hobbyists generally are self-taught and have learned to program by trial and error rather than through an organized educational program.

Effort is required to learn the many fundamental concepts covered by this book; the fun comes when you apply them in the laboratory. Since the cost of quite powerful hardware is so low, it is probable that you can experience the microcomputer yourself. Most of the material on microcomputers is very abstract, so working with actual hardware helps you learn the concepts; then the material is easy to learn and, to repeat, fun to learn.

Unfortunately, some people think of computers as trial-and-error devices. They don't think understanding is necessary. They believe that enough tries will result in a working system. Trial and error simply doesn't work when designing sophisticated, complex, and costly systems. Lack of understanding results in subtle bugs in software that testing may not find; some things happen only under obscure circumstances. Such bugs can be catastrophic. They lead to manufacturers recalling products to repair defects. Such recalls usually eliminate any possibility of a profit.

Your emphasis should be on a full understanding of the operation, design, and programming of the microcomputer. Use your hands-on experience to reinforce the concepts rather than to prove that you can make things work by trial and error. And by all means, have fun!

1.1 NUMBERS AND NUMBER SYSTEMS

The fundamentals of number systems are important to the use of computers. You will not need to calculate using binary and other numbers frequently—the machine will do that. The reason to study numbers is to better understand how the various kinds of numbers are formed and the limitations on their use. Binary numbers are especially difficult for humans to use, so a coding scheme is used to isolate us from the actual binary numbers.

Binary, Octal, and Hexadecimal Numbers

Let's begin with a review of decimal numbers, and then we can extrapolate to other number systems. Decimal, or base ten, numbers have digits that have ten different values called 0 through 9. The base is ten because there are ten different digit values.

Decimal numbers are built from the digits by placing them to the left or right of a decimal point. The position relative to the point is important, so the decimal number system is called a *weighted number system*. Each position as you move to the left has a weight or value that is the base ten raised to an integer exponent or power. The first position to the left of the point has weight of the base raised to the power zero, so its weight is always one regardless of the base. The next position to the left has weight of the base raised to the power one, and so on counting to the left. Fractional numbers have weights defined with the base to a negative exponent. For example, the decimal number 123.45 means

$$123.45_{10} = (1 \times 10^2) + (2 \times 10^1) + (3 \times 10^0) + (4 \times 10^{-1}) + (5 \times 10^{-2})$$

which can be written as

$$123.45_{10} = (1 \times 100) + (2 \times 10) + (3 \times 1) + (4 \times \frac{1}{10}) + (5 \times \frac{1}{100})$$

You will most frequently use integer numbers without a fractional part when programming microcomputers. Usually integer numbers are written without the point, which is assumed to be at the right end of the number.

Octal numbers

Next extend the ideas illustrated with the decimal number system to the octal or base eight number system. Octal numbers use the digits 0 through 7.

Let's convert the number 123_8 to its decimal equivalent by using the definition of the number. Therefore,

$$123_8 = (1 \times 8^2) + (2 \times 8^1) + (3 \times 8^0) = 83_{10}$$

One serious difficulty with octal numbers is the lack of English words to describe them. There is no word for octal 100! Therefore, we simply use the words we have with a modifier. For octal 123, say *octal one hundred twenty-three*. Of course, you now must think about two number systems at once to understand the meaning. But decimal is second nature to us, so mixing two systems is easy after a little practice.

Hexadecimal numbers

Now consider the base 16, or hexadecimal, number system. Since our ordinary decimal digits do not have 16 values, we use letters of the alphabet. So the hexadecimal digits are 0 through 9 and A through F.

Hexadecimal numbers have the same language problem as octal numbers. So say the number 123_{16} as *hexadecimal one hundred twenty-three*, or just *hex* one hundred twenty-three. Hexadecimal numbers with letter digits usually are spoken by reciting the digits. For example, say *C three five F* for the number C35F.

Here is the conversion of 123_{16} to the equivalent decimal number:

$$123_{16} = (1 \times 16^2) + (2 \times 16^1) + (3 \times 16^0) = 291_{10}$$

Notice that 123_{16} is a much larger number than 123_{10} because the digits have much bigger weights.

Finally, the word is spelled *hexadecimal*, not hexidecimal; this is a common spelling error found in manuals and textbooks.

Binary numbers

Finally, let's look at the binary, or base 2, number system. The binary digits are very restricted in that they only have the values 0 and 1. Binary numbers also are weighted numbers, so the conversion to decimal is done as with other numbers. For example,

$$101_2 = (1 \times 2^2) + (0 \times 2^1) + (1 \times 2^0) = 5_{10}$$

A problem for humans using binary numbers is the communication of long yet practical numbers. If you try to read the number 1101010110010111 to someone, it would sound like *one one zero one zero one zero one one zero zero one zero one one one*. Reading the number as a decimal number is no better. Clearly normal humans will not easily communicate large binary numbers in spoken, written, or keyboard form by these methods.

Consider an alternative representation of binary numbers. A straightforward approach is to convert the binary number to its equivalent number in the decimal number system. Then people could communicate using the decimal equivalents of the binary numbers. Unfortunately, conversion to decimal is quite difficult, especially with large numbers.

Converting binary numbers to other number systems

Consider both 3-bit and 4-bit binary numbers as Table 1-1 shows. The 3-bit numbers have eight different values ranging from 0 to 7 which match the octal digits. The 4-bit numbers have 16 different values ranging from decimal 0 to 15, or from hexadecimal 0 to F. The 4-bit numbers match the hexadecimal digits.

TABLE 1-1 NUMBER CONVERSIONS

Decimal	Octal	Binary 3-bit	Hexadecimal	Binary 4-bit
0	0	000	0	0000
1	1	001	1	0001
2	2	010	2	0010
3	3	011	3	0011
4	4	100	4	0100
5	5	101	5	0101
6	6	110	6	0110
7	7	111	7	0111
8	10	—	8	1000
9	11	—	9	1001
10	12	—	A	1010
11	13	—	B	1011
12	14	—	C	1100
13	15	—	D	1101
14	16	—	E	1110
15	17	—	F	1111

Let's convert a 16-bit binary number to octal by grouping the digits in bunches of three bits, and then writing the octal digits for the binary bunches.

$$1101010110010111 = 1\ 101\ 010\ 110\ 010\ 111 = 152627_8$$

Similarly, the same binary number can be written in hexadecimal by making bunches of four bits and writing the hexadecimal equivalents,

$$1101010110010111 = 1101\ 0101\ 1001\ 0111 = D597_{16}$$

You may wonder if the binary number was correctly converted to octal or hexadecimal. The conversion is correct, but only because the bases of all these number systems are a power of two.

Now we are mixing three number systems together. A person may refer to a 16-bit binary number by saying *hex one hundred twenty-three*. The pattern is decimal, the representation is hexadecimal, but the number is binary. An example of the conversion of the spoken version to binary is

$$hex\ one\ hundred\ twenty\text{-}three = 0000000100100011$$

The conversion from binary to octal or hex is so easy that you can do it in your head as you read the numbers! Therefore, it is common to represent binary numbers in octal or hexadecimal form. You will easily memorize the bit patterns for 3-bit and 4-bit numbers by using them frequently. When the numbers you work with are 8-bit and 16-bit numbers, the better choice is hexadecimal because the numbers fit better.

The remainder of this book uses hexadecimal number representation of binary numbers. Any exceptions are either obvious or the number base is noted by use of the appropriate subscript. Hexadecimal numbers are printed using the Helvetica typeface for further clarity. Also, hexadecimal representation is used regardless of the meaning of the number—think of hexadecimal as a pattern-matching scheme to make use of binary numbers easier.

Two's Complement Signed Numbers

You will need signed positive and negative numbers for many applications. Several techniques can represent signed numbers. However, the most used is the two's complement number system.

An important restriction

Since you will be writing two's complement numbers on paper, you must heed an important restriction on the use of these numbers. *All the numbers used in a calculation must have the same number of bits.* That is, you must add an 8-bit number to another 8-bit number and get an 8-bit number. You cannot add an 8-bit number to a 6-bit number; instead, you must convert the 6-bit number to the equivalent 8-bit number and then add. Likewise, the sum of two 8-bit numbers is always an 8-bit number.

The size restriction is of no importance in the computer, and textbooks seldom mention it. Without exception, computer hardware will operate on numbers with the same number of bits. For example, 8-bit hardware can add two 8-bit numbers because there are eight adder circuits that work at once. It is not possible to add other sizes of numbers with 8-bit hardware. Of course, you can write a program to use multiple 8-bit numbers to represent bigger numbers, but the hardware still inherently works on 8-bit numbers. So the restriction is only important when you write numbers on paper.

Working with two's complement numbers

Let's begin by looking at the construction of a two's complement number. All two's complement binary numbers have a sign bit and a numerical value. The left bit of the number is the sign bit.

Positive numbers.   Look first at the positive numbers only because they are easier to read. A positive sign is a binary zero in the left bit; the rest of the bits determine the numerical value. So the positive numbers appear to be unsigned binary numbers with at least one leading zero bit. Here are some examples:

$$00000101 = +5_{10} \qquad\qquad 01000100 = +68_{10}$$

Don't be confused by the similarity to unsigned numbers. The zero sign bit makes the number a positive number. When you write the decimal equivalent value of a positive two's complement number, you should always write it with a plus sign to remind yourself that it represents a positive number.

Negative numbers.   The negative numbers in the two's complement number system are more difficult to read. They don't look like ordinary binary numbers. Let's approach the construction of the negative numbers in a strange way by first stating a rule to change the sign of a number.

The rule to change the sign of any two's complement number is a two-step algorithm as follows:

- *Step 1.*   Complement ALL the bits of the number, including the sign bit. That is, change all the zeros to ones and the ones to zeros.

- *Step 2.*   Add one to the result.

Now you can make a negative number by writing the positive number and changing its sign. Let's change the signs of the numbers $+5_{10}$ and $+68_{10}$. Beginning with the number $+5_{10}$,

- *Step 1.*   Complementing 00000101 yields 11111010.

- *Step 2.*   Adding one yields 11111011, or -5_{10}.

The second number is $+68_{10}$, so

- *Step 1.*   Complementing 01000100 yields 10111011.

- *Step 2.*   Adding one yields 10111100, or -68_{10}.

The resulting numbers do indeed have a one in the left bit and thus meet the definition of a negative number. Now look at how strange the rest of the number is. The negative two's complement numbers are difficult to read.

But you probably ask how you can tell if these numbers really are -5_{10} and -68_{10}. Let's see what happens if +5 is added to −5 and $+68_{10}$ is added to -68_{10}. Of course, you would like to get zero:

$$
\begin{array}{rr}
00000101 & +5 \\
+\ 11111011 & -5 \\
\hline
00000000 & 0
\end{array}
\qquad
\begin{array}{rr}
01000100 & +68 \\
+\ 10111100 & -68 \\
\hline
00000000 & 0
\end{array}
$$

As you see, the result of adding these numbers was indeed zero. Of course, getting zero depends upon the restriction that each number must have the same number of bits. Any carry outside the number is lost.

Of course, zero was expected! The rule to change the sign was derived to make this happen. The essence of the derivation is to ask: What number can be added to a positive number so the answer will be zero? When this problem is solved, you get the rule to change the sign.

The rule to change the sign applies to all two's complement signed numbers. Let's apply it to −5:

- *Step 1.* Complementing 11111011 yields 00000100.

- *Step 2.* Adding one yields 00000101, or +5.

Of course, the result is correct—changing the sign of −5 gave +5. Don't make the error of thinking that the rule only applies to positive numbers. It applies equally well to both positive and negative numbers.

Two's complement overflow. Consider adding the following numbers. The first two are large positive numbers and the second two are large negative numbers.

$$
\begin{array}{r}
01000101 \\
+ \ 01000011 \\
\hline
10001000
\end{array}
\qquad
\begin{array}{r}
10000100 \\
+ \ 10111100 \\
\hline
01000000
\end{array}
$$

Notice that the first result is negative and the second is positive! The only appropriate comment is that the answers are wrong. Adding two positive numbers cannot result in a negative sum, and adding two negative numbers cannot result in a positive sum. The problem is caused by answers too big to fit an 8-bit number. The name of this problem is *two's complement overflow error*. A two's complement overflow is really a sign error, although the rest of the answer is also incorrect. Checking only the sign of the answer will always detect this error regardless of what calculation, including changing the sign, you are doing.

The properties of zero. Next let's apply the *change the sign* rule to the number zero, which you should recognize as a positive number.

- *Step 1.* Complementing 00000000 yields 11111111.

- *Step 2.* Adding one yields 00000000.

The result is still positive zero. This exercise illustrates an important property of the two's complement number system; that is, there is only one zero in the number system and it is positive. There is no negative zero. Since zero is an important number that is used frequently, a number system that has only one zero is convenient. Therefore, even though changing the sign of zero caused a two's complement overflow, we choose to ignore the error and define zero as a special number.

One other number is not affected by the change the sign rule; it is the most negative number, 10000000. This number, hex 80, does not change sign, because there is no positive number with a magnitude as large as its magnitude. Consequently, changing the sign of 80 truly causes a two's complement overflow error.

Subtraction. You also can subtract two's complement numbers. A common error is thinking that subtraction must be done by changing the sign of the subtrahend and adding.

Of course, this is a correct solution—but not the only solution. Let's subtract two numbers by both subtracting and by adding the negative number:

$$
\begin{array}{llll}
00000011 & +3 & 00000011 & +3 \\
-\ 00000101 & +5 & +\ 11111011 & -5 \\
\hline
11111110 & -2 & 11111110 & -2 \\
\end{array}
$$

Both answers are correct. However, remember that a two's complement overflow can occur when two's complement numbers are either added or subtracted. Again, if the signs don't make sense, a two's complement overflow has occurred and the answer is wrong.

Sign extension.   It is often necessary to convert an 8-bit two's complement number into an equivalent 16-bit number. The conversion is necessary when you want to add or subtract mixed size numbers. The number with fewer bits must be extended to the same number of bits as the other number. The process of converting a number to the equivalent number with more bits is called *sign extension* because you need only reproduce the sign bit enough times to achieve the required number of bits. The result will always have the equivalent value. For example,

$$01001111_{\text{8-bit}} = 0000000001001111_{\text{16-bit}} = +79_{10}$$

$$10111000_{\text{8-bit}} = 1111111110111000_{\text{16-bit}} = -72_{10}$$

In each case, the sign bit was reproduced eight times at the left end of the number. Eight zeros were put to the left of the positive number and eight ones to the left of the negative number.

Modular number systems

Numbers are usually visualized as points along a line. The line begins at the origin and extends to infinity in both the positive and negative directions. The numbers in a modular number system are visualized as points along a circle that has a fixed size. If you count through these numbers far enough, you come back to your starting point. When using binary numbers with a fixed number of bits, the number of bits determines the size of the circle.

The numbers on the face of an analog clock illustrate a common modular number system. One hour past 12 o'clock is called one o'clock because 12 different hour numbers represent time—the clock is a modulo 12_{10} system. Similarly, many automobile odometers are modulo 100,000 systems because the odometer returns, or rolls over, to zero after the car travels 100,000 miles.

The two's complement number system is a modular number system. Figure 1-1a uses 8-bit numbers to show that half the circle is positive and the other half is negative.

The circular representation also helps you see the effects of changing the sign. An axis is drawn through the circle including the numbers 00 and 80 in Figure 1-1b. Changing the sign of a number flips its location from a position on one side of the axis to the equivalent position on the other side. Notice that flipping the numbers 00 and 80 does not change their signs.

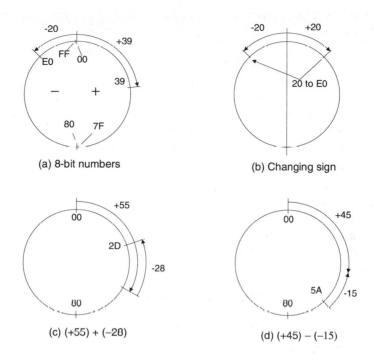

(a) 8-bit numbers

(b) Changing sign

(c) (+55) + (−28)

(d) (+45) − (−15)

Figure 1-1   Circular representation of 8-bit two's complement numbers.

Adding and subtracting can be visualized with line segments placed end to end. However, the line segments must fit on the same circle, which means the numbers must have the same number of bits. Figure 1-1c illustrates the addition of a positive and a negative number by placing the tail of one line segment at the head of the other.

Subtraction is more complicated. Draw the minuend beginning at zero, and then draw the subtrahend with its arrow head at the arrow head of the minuend. Figure 1-1d illustrates the subtraction of a negative number from a positive number.

The problem called two's complement overflow should now be apparent. For example, adding two positive numbers can result in a negative answer because the sum ends up on the wrong side of the circle. You should also see that adding a positive and a negative number can never cause a two's complement overflow.

The reason for two's complement numbers

It's easy to lose sight of the real reason for two's complement numbers as you do all the manipulations discussed above. The ultimate reason is that the computer hardware can treat them just like unsigned binary numbers. For example, adding and subtracting are no different for unsigned binary numbers and two's complement signed binary numbers. In the discussion above, the manipulations of the two's complement numbers treated the sign just like any other bit. In other words, we ADDED the signs! The hardware adds all the bits including the sign bits just as it would do with unsigned numbers. Different hardware is not required for each kind of number.

You should ask how unsigned and signed numbers are distinguished. The answer is that *you* must keep them straight! The computer hardware neither knows nor cares about the difference. The difference is in your interpretation of the numbers.

Don't think that you don't need to understand the differences between signed and unsigned numbers. You will find hardware in the computer specifically designed to work on only one type of number. For example, most computers have hardware to change the sign of a two's complement signed number. Trying to change the sign of an unsigned number results in garbage.

Binary-coded Decimal Numbers

Binary-coded decimal, or BCD, numbers are binary codes for decimal digits. Each digit of a decimal number is represented by four binary bits. For example,

$$73_{10} = 01110011_{BCD}$$

$$91_{10} = 10010001_{BCD}$$

To clarify the point, if each of these numbers is treated as an ordinary unsigned binary number and converted to decimal, the results will not be the same as the BCD value.

BCD coding is very convenient for certain input/output devices that work with decimal numbers. The device makes or uses a 4-bit code for each decimal digit.

The difficult part of using BCD numbers is making calculations with them. Consider the addition of two pairs of BCD numbers,

01110011	73		01110011	73
+ 00000101	5		+ 00011001	19
01111000	78		10001100	8C

The first addition is straightforward, but the second one did not result in a proper BCD number. The least-significant digit is incorrectly greater than 9. The answer is converted to a correct BCD number by a simple rule. Add a number containing zero at each position with a correct BCD digit and six at each position with an incorrect BCD digit. The following examples demonstrate the effect:

01110011	73		01101001	69
+ 00011001	19		+ 01000001	41
10001100	8C		10101010	AA
+ 00000110	06		+ 01100110	66
10010010	92		00010000	10

The result of adding the correct number is that each digit is converted to a correct BCD form for 8-bit numbers. The conversion process works because the group of four bits has 16 values, while the decimal digit has only 10—adding a 6 adjusts for this difference. Of course, any carries that occur are included in the addition.

1.2   DIGITAL SYSTEM FUNDAMENTALS

You need some knowledge of digital systems design to gain full understanding of micro-computers. Later parts of this book refer to the fundamental concepts and other information reviewed in this section.

Signals, Functions, and Hardware

Digital electronic circuits, also called logic circuits, use binary signals. Proper notation to represent these circuits and signals is necessary to communicate ideas correctly. Also, the fundamental logic circuit devices must be understood. Making the logical connection between physical hardware and abstract notation is a very important task.

Binary signals

A *signal* is an electrical quantity that conveys information. Most electronic circuits use voltage as the signal. Usually signals require only very low power levels.

Analog circuits use the size of a voltage to represent a numeric quantity. Analog circuits have the practical problem of maintaining the accuracy of the signal under various circumstances. Changes in circuits due to temperature and aging effects cause inaccurate signal values. Electrical noise pollutes the signals and generally cannot be removed. Inaccurate components also cause incorrect signals.

Digital circuits use only two sizes of voltage to represent numeric quantities, so the signals are called *binary signals*. In digital circuits, close is good enough. If the actual signal voltage is close to the ideal voltage, the electronic circuit treats it as if it were ideal because there are only two ideal voltages. For the same reason, digital circuits have few problems due to inaccurate components and temperature and aging effects. Noise problems are dramatically reduced. Furthermore, digital circuits can be easily manufactured as integrated circuits. Integrated circuit technology is well suited to the manufacture of large quantities of simple circuits. Therefore, digital circuits can be made at very low cost, which makes them very practical.

In many applications, only two signal values cannot accurately represent the information. Then multiple signals are used to represent many more possible values. Of course, each additional signal requires an additional electronic circuit. The use of multiple circuits certainly increases the cost and reduces reliability of the system. Yet the electronic hardware in integrated circuits is simple, is very reliable, does not require great accuracy in the components, and is available at low cost.

Binary signal notation

A binary signal has only two ideal voltages. The electronic circuit with a sensor shown in Figure 1-2 generates such a signal. The sensor is a simple toggle switch. The switch handle can be in either the up position or the down position. It is a binary switch because a mechanism prevents any other position. The mechanism operates switch contacts that operate an electronic circuit. The electronics generates the binary signal; when the handle is changed from one position to the other, the signal changes value.

Different digital circuits use different voltages. Some common DC voltage pairs are −12 and +12 volts, −5 and 0 volts, 0 and +5 volts, and 0 and +10 volts. Repeatedly stating these particular voltages makes it difficult to discuss digital circuits. To avoid this problem, a well-accepted naming convention distinguishes the two voltages without specifying the numerical voltage. The two voltages are called the *high level* and the *low level* and are defined as follows:

- *The high level is the more positive of the two voltages.*

- *The low level is the less positive of the two voltages.*

The words *more* and *less* are used in an algebraic sense—the sign of the voltage is significant. So −12 volts is less positive than 0 volts, though the magnitude is larger. Most people now describe the operation of digital electronic circuits using the words *high* and *low*.

Binary variables

A binary variable is an algebraic variable that can have only two values. Many names are used for the two values: true and false, one and zero, operated and normal, asserted and deasserted, or active and inactive. Although one pair of names may be better suited for a certain application, they all mean the same thing. The words *true*, *one*, *operated*, *asserted*, and *active* are equivalent. Also, *false*, *zero*, *normal*, *deasserted*, and *inactive* are equivalent.

Binary variable notation

A binary variable is usually named by a symbol that reflects its application. For example, the variables SW1, SW2, and LT1 may represent the conditions of two toggle switches and an indicator light. Each of these devices has two useful states. If the switch is a vertical

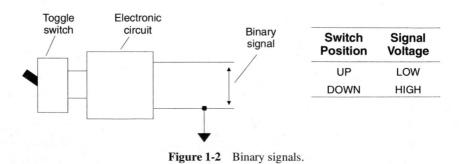

Figure 1-2 Binary signals.

toggle switch, the up position is the asserted condition and the down position is the deasserted condition. A push button switch is asserted when the button is pushed, and deasserted when the spring returns the device to its normal condition. A light is asserted when illuminated and deasserted when dark.

Tying variables to signals

To correctly use digital hardware, abstract binary variables must be related to physical hardware. Several types of notation are used to make this connection. Probably the best notation is *mixed-logic* notation. This notation encompasses all configurations of hardware and the other notations in one simple notation. More restrictive notations only apply correctly to certain hardware, so the logical meaning must be adjusted to fit the hardware.

Mixed-logic notation.   The purpose of logic notation is to describe the binary event that controls a binary signal generated by hardware. A binary variable represents the binary event. A logic level, high or low, represents the binary signal. Mixed-logic notation is a way of labeling signal wires with both the binary variable and the corresponding binary signal level. *The wire is labeled with a binary variable and the voltage level that corresponds to the true or asserted case of the variable.*

Figure 1-3 illustrates the notation. The wire from logic Device 1 carries a signal representing the variable RESET such that a true or asserted RESET variable makes the wire low as designated by the letter L in parentheses. Consequently, a false or deasserted RESET makes the wire high. The wire from logic Device 2 represents START where an asserted START signal makes the wire high as designated by the letter H. Therefore, a deasserted or false START signal makes the wire low. The notation always logically connects the true case of the labeled variable with the corresponding signal voltage.

The example shows that some devices use *high-asserted* signals while others use *low-asserted* signals. There are valid and useful reasons for one circuit to use both high-asserted and low-asserted signals. Usually, it will be easier to design circuits where the assertion level is chosen for convenience. However, the asserted signal level is sometimes chosen for safety or for compatibility with other equipment.

Motorola logic notation.   Motorola product documentation usually does not follow the mixed-logic notation. Sometimes Motorola labels hardware only with a name that describes the function performed. Often, you can interpret a Motorola label as a binary variable.

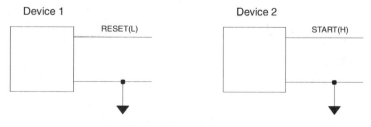

Figure 1-3   Mixed-logic notation.

However, further study of the documentation is often necessary to determine the associated voltage level.

Sometimes Motorola labels binary variables with a bar on top, such as $\overline{PB1}$. Interpret this notation to mean that the true case of the variable is associated with the low voltage. Then, the lack of a bar on a variable implies that the true case is associated with the high level. The notation $\overline{PB1}$ probably means that a signal wire is low if push button switch 1 is pushed. It is easy to mistakenly omit the bar and change the assertion level of the signal with this notation.

Logic functions

The fundamental logic functions are AND, OR, and COMPLEMENT. It is convenient to use the word NOT when describing the complement function. Truth tables for the logic functions are shown in Table 1-2. The table also shows logic equations for the functions using the distinctive notation for the logical operators. Functions of two variables are shown, but these can be expanded to any number of variables. The derived function EXCLUSIVE OR (EOR) is shown because computer programs frequently use this function. If you compare the EOR function to the OR function, you see that EOR excludes the both case—the EOR function is zero when both variables are ones.

Be careful! The bar on top of a variable in a logic equation always means the complement of the variable. However, some companies use a bar to mean that a signal is low-asserted. Don't confuse a binary signal that is low-asserted and the complement of a binary variable.

Logic hardware

Although the fundamental logic hardware is very easy to understand, describing it and drawing circuit diagrams can be confusing because many different notations are used. Probably the best notation available is one that clearly illustrates both the logic function and the hardware levels used. Such notation is compatible with the mixed-logic notation for binary signals. Only IEEE standard symbols are used in this book. However, Motorola manuals sometimes use a different notation, so that variation is also discussed.

TABLE 1-2   LOGIC FUNCTIONS

AND			OR			COMPLEMENT		EXCLUSIVE OR		
X	Y	F1	X	Y	F2	X	F3	X	Y	F4
0	0	0	0	0	0	0	1	0	0	0
0	1	0	0	1	1	1	0	0	1	1
1	0	0	1	0	1			1	0	1
1	1	1	1	1	1			1	1	0

$$F1 = X \wedge Y \qquad F2 = X \vee Y \qquad F3 = \overline{X} \qquad F4 = X \veebar Y$$

Device symbols.   Logic *gates* are electronic hardware devices that perform the fundamental logic functions on binary signals. Distinctive symbols that depend on shape denote the circuits that do the fundamental functions. There is a shape for AND, another for OR, and a third shape for an identity element. The identity element simply passes the signal through from the input to the output. Its logic function is to reproduce its input at its output. Its circuit function may be to reproduce the signal at a higher possible current level or at a different logic voltage level. Here, from left to right, are the most commonly used symbols for AND, OR, and identity function devices:

Note that no input or output signal wires are shown on these symbols. The reason is that the inputs and outputs require binary signals that are asserted or active at a certain voltage level. One device may require a high level to assert an input, while another device requires the low level for assertion. Additional standard symbols can designate which is the asserted level for each input and output wire.

Polarity indicators.   To designate high-asserted inputs or outputs, show a wire connected to the symbol with no additional symbol. To designate low-asserted inputs or outputs, show a wire with a *polarity indicator*. The standard symbol for a polarity indicator is a right triangle. *The presence of the polarity indicator means low-assertion and the absence of the polarity indicator means high-assertion.* Here are examples of devices with high-asserted inputs and low-asserted outputs:

The standard polarity indicator is the triangular symbol. However, many people still use an older symbol described as a *bubble*. The following devices also have high-asserted inputs and low-asserted outputs, but use the bubble notation:

In this book, these two variations of polarity indicators are interchangeable. When circuit drawings are shown, the standard polarity indicator is used simply because it is the standard. However, Motorola manuals use the bubble symbol. Interpret bubbles in Motorola manuals as indicators of low-assertion.

To clarify the notation, Figure 1-4 describes two circuit devices by tables of voltages illustrating the input to output relationships. The figure also shows the corresponding circuit

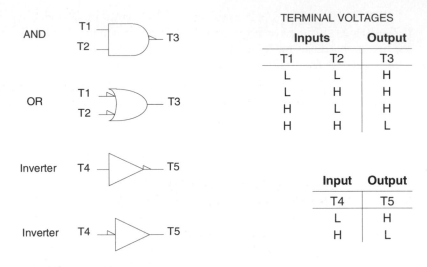

TERMINAL VOLTAGES		
Inputs		**Output**
T1	T2	T3
L	L	H
L	H	H
H	L	H
H	H	L

Input	**Output**
T4	T5
L	H
H	L

Figure 1-4   Two symbols describe each logic gate.

symbols. Two different symbols correctly describe each logic device, as you can see by examining the figure carefully. The first device can be described by these sentences:

- Terminal 3 is low if both terminal 1 AND terminal 2 are high.

- Terminal 3 is high if either terminal 1 is low OR terminal 2 is low OR if both terminals 1 and 2 are low.

Similarly, the identity element has two symbols. The particular device shown in the figure is called an *inverter* or *level changer* because the output voltage level is opposite the input voltage level.

When designing logic circuits, you must select the symbol that conveys the intent of the circuit. If the device is used for ANDing, draw an AND symbol. If it is used for ORing, then draw the OR symbol.

As a final note, if you have learned logic symbols where the bubble is described by the word NOT, carefully consider changing your point of view. You will find the polarity indicator approach to be much better as you work with practical logic circuits. Most companies are using and many new textbooks are written with this better notation.

Combinational Logic Networks

A *combinational logic network* (CLN) makes output signals now that are a function only of the input signals now. A CLN, which is built from a collection of AND, OR, and inverter devices, performs a more complicated logic operation than does a single device. The CLN outputs are determined solely by the combination or pattern of the current input signals. So time is not relevant to combinational logic networks—assume that the circuits respond instantaneously. The response is not instantaneous, but this is a practical assumption for most applications. Combinational logic networks are simpler than the alternative, the synchronous sequential network, which has outputs now that depend on the inputs sometime in the past.

CLN example

The example circuit is a controller for the dome light in a two-door automobile. The purpose is to turn on the dome light if the left door is open or if the right door is open. Consequently, the light is on when both doors are open. A logic equation that describes this problem with binary variables is

$$LIGHT = LDOPEN \lor RDOPEN$$

where the definition of the binary variables should be apparent. This equation describes the logical operation of the circuit without any information about the physical circuit.

Figure 1-5 is a complete circuit drawing of the combinational logic circuit. The designer had a supply of the two hardware devices shown in Figure 1-4 for building the circuit. The hardware uses +5 V_{DC} as the high level and zero volts as the low level. The circuit drawing shows an OR symbol for the logic gate because the problem is described by an equation using OR.

Carefully consider how the door position-sensing switches work. A closed door presses on the push button and operates the switch. The switches are drawn in their normal positions with the doors closed. When a door is opened, the spring in the switch moves the mechanism so the switch terminals are electrically connected. It is strange and not very practical that the two switches are wired differently, but the mixed-logic notation clarifies the wiring difference easily. For example, when the left door is open, the switch connects the signal wire to the common ground making the wire low. When the left door is closed, the switch breaks the connection, so the resistor pulls the wire to the high level. The inverter that controls the light is designed to handle the current required for the light—typical integrated circuit inverters would not have the required current capability.

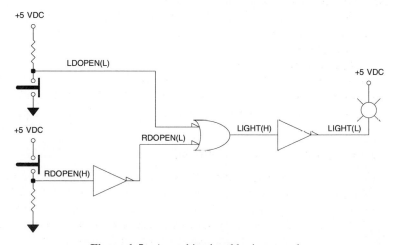

Figure 1-5   A combinational logic network.

Flip Flops and Registers

Complex digital circuits require the ability to remember or store binary information so it can be used later. Flip flops and registers are the basic devices for storing information. The addition of these devices to a circuit makes the circuit much more complex than a CLN because time must then be considered.

Flip flops

A *flip flop* is a 1-bit memory device. It remembers a single binary signal. The most common flip flop in computer systems is the D-flip flop. Figure 1-6 illustrates the symbols for two D-flip flops and the transition table that describes their operation. The input signal that is to be remembered is applied to the D input, and the remembered signal is the output at Y.

The D-flip flop is a *clocked* flip flop. A clocked flip flop can change its output only if a timing signal called the *clock* activates the flip flop. To activate the flip flop, the clock signal must be changed from one level to another—it is not possible to indicate time with a static signal. The transition table in Figure 1-6 shows how the D-flip flop acts when it changes from the current state to the next state at the clock change.

The output of a flip flop responds to its input signal or signals when the clock signal changes from the logic zero level to the logic one level, but does not respond on the opposite change. The change that causes the flip flop to respond is called the *active transition* of the clock signal.

Dynamic indicators. An input to a device, such as a clock signal, is designated as *transition sensitive* by a standard symbol called a *dynamic indicator*. The symbol is a small equilateral triangle as shown on the clock leads in Figure 1-6. The dynamic indicator says the active transition is a change from logic zero to logic one.

In Figure 1-6, the left flip flop clock has both a polarity indicator and a dynamic indicator, so its output responds when the clock lead is changed from high to low. The right flip flop does not have a polarity indicator, so it responds to a change from low to high.

Registers

A *register* is a collection of flip flops that are clocked as a unit. Together, the flip flops remember several binary signals that together represent a binary number. Figure 1-7 illus-

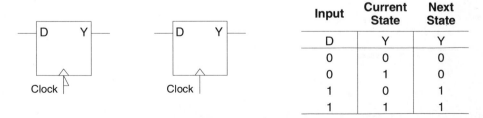

Input	Current State	Next State
D	Y	Y
0	0	0
0	1	0
1	0	1
1	1	1

Figure 1-6   Two D-flip flops and their transition table.

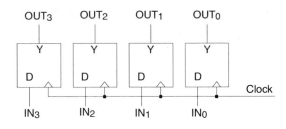

Figure 1-7   4 bit register using parallel transfers.

trates a 4-bit register. This register stores all the bits of the input number at once, and all the bits in the register can be read at once on the output wires. Storing or reading all the bits at once is called a *parallel transfer*.

Shift registers.   Some registers are little more than a collection of flip flops with a common clock lead. Others contain control hardware to enable internal operations on the number stored in the register—a shift register is an example. A *shift register* can move the bits in the register one position at a time. For example, the register may shift all its bits left one position for each active clock transition. Usually, a new bit value is supplied to the hardware to replace the right bit, so a new number can be stored in the register one bit at a time. Similarly, the bits in the register may be read one bit at a time by reading the left bit as the register is shifted left. Loading or reading the register one bit at a time is called a *serial transfer*. There are many varieties of shift registers including some that can shift either left or right according to a control signal. Some can also be parallel loaded or read.

Load-controlled registers.   The register shown in Figure 1-7 does a parallel load anytime that the register is clocked. Sometimes a register has extra control circuitry to allow the register to retain its information and ignore the input number even if it is clocked. This is called a *load-controlled* register and it has an additional input signal called *load*. When the load input is asserted or active, the register loads from the input on an active clock transition; otherwise, the number in the register is unaffected.

Register symbols.   The choice of a symbol to represent a register depends on the amount of detail needed. Sometimes every signal wire must be shown. But more frequently, the symbol need only show the number in the register or whether the data transfer is parallel or serial.

Figure 1-8 illustrates some ways of representing registers. The first drawing shows all the details. The second uses boxes to represent the flip flops and 1s and 0s in the boxes to show the states of the flip flops. The third drawing is simplified by showing a box for the entire register without showing the individual flip flops. And finally, the last drawing is the most common notation where the number stored in the register is labeled as a hexadecimal number with only the outline of the register shown.

The figure also shows a notation for parallel and serial transfers. If a register can do both serial and parallel transfers, both notations may be combined. For example, it is common practice to combine a serial load with a parallel read of a register. Such a register is described as doing a serial to parallel conversion.

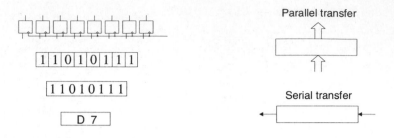

Figure 1-8   Register notation and serial and parallel transfers.

Buses and transfer gates

A *bus* is a group of binary signal wires that collectively carry a binary number. A bus may be used to parallel transfer a number from one register to another. Figure 1-9 shows a 3-bit bus bringing a number to three AND gates and there is a 3-bit bus connected to the outputs of the three AND gates.

A transfer gate is an AND gate used to pass a binary signal to another wire, or to block it. Consider the three AND gates in Figure 1-9. When the input labeled TRANSFER is asserted or true making the wire high, the output of each AND gate is the same as its other input—low in gives low out and high in gives high out. When TRANSFER is not asserted making the wire low, the output of the AND gate is always low, in effect blocking the transfer of the input signal. In this example, use high for logic 1 and low for logic 0 so a deasserted transfer lead causes the outputs of the AND gates to be all 0s. So the three transfer gates together either transfer the number from the input bus to the output bus, or they put the number zero on the output bus.

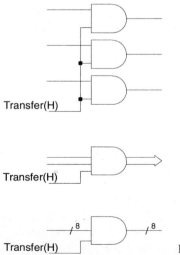

Figure 1-9   Buses and transfer gates.

Figure 1-9 also shows a symbol that represents any number of transfer gates with an input and output bus. The double line is commonly used to represent a bus. Sometimes the double line has a large arrow head to indicate the direction of signal flow if it is not apparent. An alternative bus symbol is a single line labeled with the number of wires in the bus.

Memory

A *memory* is a device that stores many binary numbers that can be accessed electronically. There are many types of memories using a variety of technologies. The numbers may be stored by physical wiring, magnetic fields, electric fields, or the active operation of an electronic circuit. Later chapters discuss some of these technologies further. Therefore, a memory will be defined now as a collection of registers made from flip flops.

Memory signals

The registers within a memory need to be accessed only one at a time. Furthermore, a number may be loaded or written into the register or a number may be read from the register, but it is never necessary to write to the register and read its contents at the same time. Due to these restrictions, the memory hardware is very simple.

Since only one register is accessed at a time, each register is assigned a binary code number by the memory hardware. The number distinguishes each register from the others. The code number is called an *address*. The memory address is similar to the postal address on a mailbox.

A memory is a package that interacts with other devices through several groups of binary signals. The signal wires include those to carry a data number, those to select or address the register, those to determine whether read or write will happen, and a timing signal to tell the memory when to respond to the other signals. The wires that carry the data number to or from the memory are called the *data bus*. The wires that carry the address to the memory are called the *address bus*. Figure 1-10 shows the binary signals on a block diagram.

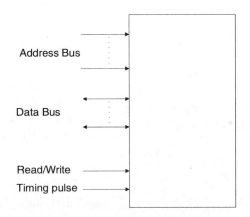

Figure 1-10   Memory signals.

When another device makes signals to write a number into a memory register, we speak of that device as *storing* to the memory. The other device must supply an address on the address bus, the data number on the data bus, a write signal, and the timing pulse to make the memory write. When the other device reads a number from a memory register, we speak of *loading* a number from the memory into the other device. The other device now supplies an address, a read signal, and a timing pulse. During a read operation, the memory unit puts the data number on the data bus. So numbers travel on the data bus in two directions—the read/write signal controls the direction.

Memory model

Initially you will not need to know all the signal details to use a memory. So an abstract picture called a *model* is an adequate representation of a memory. Figure 1-11 shows a memory model. In this figure, each box represents one 8-bit register containing a hexadecimal number. The 16-bit address of each register is the hexadecimal number shown to the left of each register. The memory model shows none of the control signals. Usually a memory model will not show all the registers in a memory and therefore will have breaks.

Words and bytes

When a number is read from or written to the memory, a certain number of bits are transferred at once in parallel. This collection of bits is called a *word* of memory; the word size is the same as the size of a register. So the *word size* is the length of a register measured in bits. In effect, a word is a group of bits that are accessed together.

However, another word is used to denote a contiguous group of bits; the word is *byte*. Originally, the word *byte* meant any size group of bits. Usually, these bits are part of some larger number. The most common size group is eight bits. So, through common usage, the word *byte* has evolved to mean a group of eight bits.

Since many memories are built with 8-bit registers with a word size of 8-bits or one byte, the word *byte* and the word *word* have come to have the same meaning to many people. Be careful! Not everyone uses these words as synonyms. Many memories have 16-bit or 32-bit words.

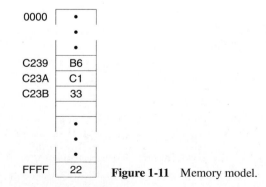

Figure 1-11   Memory model.

Memory length

Each register within a memory has a unique address code. The address is a binary number. The number of combinations of the bits within a number is 2 raised to the power N where N is the number of bits in the number. For example, an 8-bit number has 2^8, or 256_{10}, combinations. A 10-bit number has 1024_{10} combinations. And a 16-bit number has $65,536_{10}$ combinations. Therefore, a memory with a 10-bit address cannot have more than 1024_{10} registers.

The number of registers in a memory device will almost always be a power of two. For example, if a memory is designed for a 10-bit address, it will have 1024_{10} registers. To include fewer registers is to waste some of the capability of the hardware.

The number 1024_{10} is close to the number 1000_{10} which engineers and scientists describe by the prefix *kilo*, so people who work with digital systems have redefined kilo to mean 1024_{10}! The abbreviation for kilo is the capital letter K.

A memory with 1024_{10} 8-bit registers is described as a 1-kilobyte memory. Furthermore, a memory with $65,536_{10}$ 8-bit registers is called a 64-kilobyte memory. The memory shown in Figure 1-11 is a 64-kilobyte memory because the addresses have 16 bits.

Sometimes people also use kilo with bit in describing memories, so a memory device may have 256_{10} kilobits of memory. The abbreviation for kilobyte is KB, and the abbreviation for kilobit is Kb. It is easy to overlook whether the B is capitalized and get the wrong meaning from the abbreviation.

Synchronous Sequential Networks

A *synchronous sequential network* (SSN) is a circuit made from a combinational logic network and clocked flip flops. The output signals from a SSN depend both on current input signals and upon the input signals in the past. Control systems have the same requirements—they must have information about both the past and the present condition of the device being controlled. A mathematical point of view says that this is the essence of differentiation and integration. So, SSNs are essential to the design of digital control systems. Synchronous sequential networks are also interesting because a computer is a very large and sophisticated SSN. Most of the devices connected to computers also contain SSNs.

SSN block diagram

The block diagram shown in Figure 1-12 illustrates the configuration of a synchronous sequential circuit in the most general way. This block diagram represents any SSN including some trivial cases. The essence of it is the combination of a combinational logic circuit with memory devices or flip flops.

State of the network.   The *state* of a synchronous sequential network is the combined states of the flip flops. Together, the flip flops represent stored information. Individually, the outputs of the flip flops are called *state variables* or feedback variables.

External inputs.   The external inputs, or just *inputs*, are the signals used by a network in generating next state and output information. Similarly, the state variables are sometimes

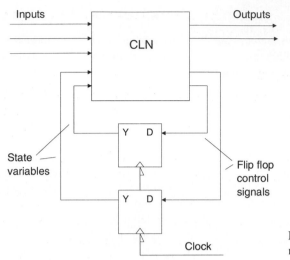

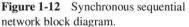

Figure 1-12   Synchronous sequential network block diagram.

called internal inputs because they also affect the next state and outputs. Both are inputs to the combinational logic network.

External outputs.   The external outputs, or just *outputs*, are the control signals generated by the synchronous sequential network; they are the purpose for having the SSN. External outputs clearly are signals that go outside the SSN. The external outputs depend upon the current external inputs and the current state of the network—the inputs and the current condition of the flip flops.

Flip flop control signals.   The combinational logic network generates the *control signals* for the flip flops. The control signals determine the information to be stored at the time of the next active clock transition. Together, the external inputs and the current state of the network determine what information will be stored. Therefore, the next state of the SSN depends on the current inputs and the information stored in the flip flops in the past.

The clock.   The *clock* signal is usually a periodic or repeating pulse or square wave signal. The clock signal provides timing so the sequential network can operate properly.

When the active transition of the clock signal occurs, the outputs of the flip flops can change. Changes will propagate through the CLN to the input side of the flip flops at various speeds. The characteristics of the circuit components at the time of the discussion determine the speed. These characteristics can vary depending upon temperature, replaced parts, or even changed position of adjacent components. All the signal changes must reach steady state before the next active clock transition. If the memory control signals were still changing at the clock transition, incorrect state changes would occur.

There is an upper limit on the clock speed determined by the characteristics of the circuit components. If the clock is changed to a higher frequency, the network will be unreliable because the flip flop control signals may still be changing when the next active clock transition occurs. With an appropriate clock signal, the SSN will reliably change from state to state as determined by the inputs and thus generate the correct output signals.

Notice that the output signals can change at times other than an active clock transition because input changes may change the outputs.

State transition diagram

A graphical tool makes it easy to describe the complicated operation of a SSN. The *state transition diagram* is the most common graphical tool. It shows the input to output relationship of the SSN at each state. It also shows how the states will change at active clock transitions.

Figure 1-13 illustrates a state transition diagram. Circles containing a descriptor represent the states of the network. As the figure shows, the states of the flip flops, which together determine the state of the SSN, are written in the circle. The flip flop outputs are labeled with Ys.

At a given state, the SSN has a certain input to output relationship. The relationship is shown on an arrow that points outward from a state circle. The input condition X is written to the left of a slash. It corresponds to the output condition Z written to the right of the slash. Each input combination requires an arrow, but sometimes the combinations are grouped on one arrow if the output is the same for all the combinations. The input/output relationship is associated with the state at the tail end of the arrow.

The arrows that connect the state circles illustrate the state changes. Which change of state takes place is determined by the inputs at the time of the active clock transition, so each arrow has an associated input condition even if the change is back to the same state. The diagram does not explicitly show the time at which a state transition occurs.

Example SSN

The state transition diagram in Figure 1-13 describes a two-speed light flasher for a light connected to the output Z. If the input X is zero, the output oscillates between zero and one at a slow speed synchronized to the clock. If the input is one, the output oscillates twice as fast making a fast flasher.

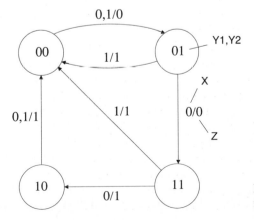

Figure 1-13   State transition diagram for two-speed light flasher.

You can follow the operation by tracing the state transition diagram while the input is kept at a constant value.

Figure 1-14 is a circuit diagram for the light flasher. You can trace the binary signals in the circuit as the circuit changes state on each active clock transition. You will find this much more difficult than reading the state transition diagram.

1.3 DIGITAL SYSTEMS

A *digital system* is a network of registers and CLNs controlled by a synchronous sequential network. The SSN is therefore called the *control unit* since it controls other hardware in the system rather than directly generating the system output signals. The hardware controlled by the control unit may be very simple or very complex.

There are other ways to design digital circuits besides using a control unit with other hardware. Instead, a larger SSN can always do the job. An advantage to the control unit approach is that the system is less complex. Similarly, it is easier to build the hardware, easier to repair, and easier to change if new algorithms are required. On the contrary, the speed of the system may be slower.

Synchronous Serial Communications Example

In many applications of digital hardware, it is necessary to transmit 8-bit numbers from one circuit device to another, or from one printed circuit board to another. Parallel transfers provide the fastest communication because all the bits of a number are sent at once over

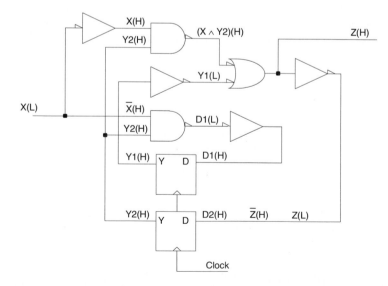

Figure 1-14   Light flasher circuit.

multiple paths. But parallel transfers require many pins and interconnecting wires—one wire for each bit of the number. Simpler serial hardware requiring only a single signal wire can send the number one bit at a time. The serial transfer is inherently slower than an equivalent parallel transfer. However, synchronous serial transfers over a path with little delay achieve high transfer rates, easily making serial transfers practical.

The building blocks

The digital system shown in Figure 1-15 will transmit 8-bit numbers in both directions simultaneously using three signal wires between the two devices. So this circuit does two-directional duplex serial communication. The control unit controls the shift registers, flag, and pulse counter in response to a start signal. Its complexity is similar to that of the light-flashing circuit. Only the master device has a control unit; the serial transfer in the slave device is controlled by the master device. The other hardware does all the significant work.

Here is a description of the building blocks of this digital system shown in Figure 1-15:

- *Shift registers.* These shift-left registers move the contents of the register one bit to the left for each active shift or clock transition. The right bit is an input that comes from the other device and the left bit is the output signal to the other device. The shift registers can also be parallel loaded and parallel read from within the system using the parallel register.

- *Flag.* A flag is a flip flop that indicates the occurrence of something. When a flag is set, information is ready to be used. If it is cleared, it means wait.

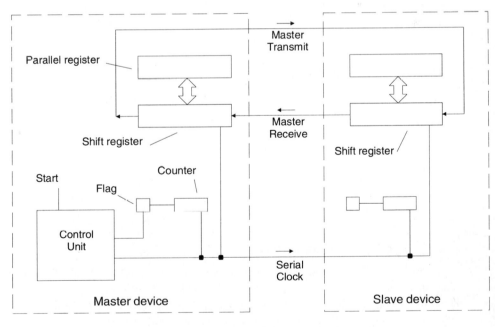

Figure 1-15 Synchronous serial communication system.

- *Pulse counter.* The counter circuits in the master and slave devices count the pulses to determine when an 8-bit transfer is complete. After eight pulses, the counter sets the flag to indicate that a transmission is complete.

System operation

The control algorithm is very simple, only requiring eight pulses on the serial clock line to do an 8-bit transfer. Before a transmission begins, other hardware parallel loads the shift registers in both the master and slave devices. Next, the master device is told to start a transmission. The control unit clears the flag and then makes a string of eight pulses. At the eighth pulse, the counters set the flags indicating the transmission is complete. When other devices respond to the flags, they will parallel read the shift registers and use the transmitted data.

Since the output of one 8-bit shift register is connected as the input of the other, together they effectively make one 16-bit circular shift register. Of course, one register is within the master device and the other is in the slave device.

When the shift leads are pulsed together, all the bits in the two registers move to the left one place. The bit at the left of the master register is transmitted to the slave register and enters the right end of the slave register. The bit at the left end of the slave register is transmitted to the master register and enters the right end of the master register. After eight pulses, the numbers in the two registers have been exchanged. The effect is serial communication between the two systems containing the shift registers with only three signal wires. Only a few details have been omitted from this discussion.

The transmission system sends information in both directions at once one bit at a time, so it is called a duplex serial communication system.

Instruction-controlled Information Processor Example

An information processor is a digital system that manipulates binary numbers according to an algorithm. An instruction-controlled processor can perform more than one algorithm. An instruction code number tells the system which algorithm to perform. In many designs, some parts of the different algorithms will be common to several instructions.

The example that follows is an instruction-controlled digital system. It carries out one of two simple algorithms beginning when a start signal changes to the asserted condition. The instruction number tells the control unit which sequence of states to follow. Each sequence therefore carries out a different algorithm.

The building blocks

A collection of hardware devices can manipulate numbers. Manipulating numbers is information processing, so it is appropriate to call this hardware the *processor*. Figure 1-16 shows the block diagram of a processor with a control unit. The control unit is a synchronous sequential network that controls the processor hardware to carry out each of the possible algorithms.

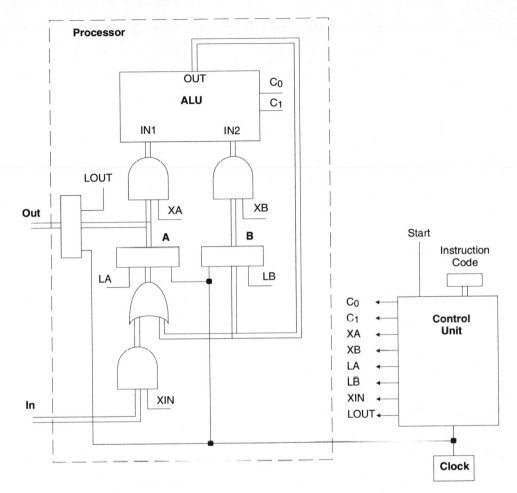

Figure 1-16   Instruction-controlled digital system.

Here is a description of the building blocks that form the processor hardware shown in Figure 1-16:

- *Arithmetic logic unit.*   The ALU is a combinational logic network that does the functions shown in Table 1-3. This ALU performs very simple operations. You could design this one easily if you have some digital design experience. More complex yet practical ALUs perform dozens of operations.

- *A and B registers.*   The A and B registers are load-controlled registers. They parallel load a number from the incoming bus on the active clock transition if the load lead is asserted. Otherwise, the register is unaffected and the number in the register remains the same as it was.

TABLE 1-3   ALU OPERATION

Controls C_0C_1	Operation
00	IN1 + IN2 → OUT
01	IN1 + IN2 + 1 → OUT
10	IN1 + $\overline{\text{IN2}}$ → OUT
11	IN1 + $\overline{\text{IN2}}$ + 1 → OUT

- *Transfer gates.*   These are two-input AND gates that pass the input number to the output when the transfer lead is asserted. If transfer is not asserted, the output is the number zero.

- *Input port.*   The collection of OR gates passes one number or another number to its output. The unwanted number must be zero so it doesn't affect the output. The input port has transfer gates that can output the number zero. So external hardware doesn't affect the output of the OR gates except during input.

- *Output port.*   The output register can capture a number from the bus at an appropriate time and hold the output signals for external devices to respond.

- *Control unit.*   The control unit is the synchronous sequential network that controls all the hardware in the digital system. The control unit interprets the instruction code and generates the proper sequence of control signals.

System operation

The processor hardware proposed here could perform many different operations, but let's consider only two of them. In this discussion, assume that all the numbers are unsigned binary numbers. First, let's input a number and send it directly to the output port. Second, let's input a number, multiply it by two, and then send the product to the output port.

Here are the steps necessary to input a number and output it to the output port. Carefully follow Figure 1-16 as you read these steps.

- *Step 1.*   Pass the input number through the transfer gates and load into the A register.

- *Step 2.*   Load the output register from the bus carrying the contents of the A register.

Here are the steps necessary to input a number, multiply it by two, and send the result to the output port:

- *Step 1.*   Pass the input number through the transfer gates and load it into the A register.

- *Step 2.*   Add the number in the A register to zero and load the result into the B register. To do this, pass the number in the A register through the transfer gates to the ALU; don't assert the B side transfer gates so the number zero goes to the ALU; tell the ALU to add the two numbers; and load the B register.

- *Step 3.*   Add the two numbers and put the answer in A, effectively multiplying the number by two. To do this, transfer the numbers to the ALU; tell the ALU to add; and load the sum into the A register.

- *Step 4.*   Load the output register from the bus carrying the contents of the A register.

Control unit operation

The control unit is a synchronous sequential network that makes all the signals that control the processor hardware. These signals are shown in Figure 1-16 and include C_0, C_1, XA, XB, LA, LB, XIN, and LOUT. The control unit inputs include a start signal and a 1-bit instruction code. The instruction code determines which of two operations the system will perform. An external device will make the start signal change from 0 to 1 to indicate a start of operation.

Instruction code is 0.   Figure 1-17 shows the state transition diagram for the control unit. Let's follow the signals that the control unit generates as it moves through its states. Assume the system user has set the current instruction to 0. The operation will be the transfer of the input number to the output register. Refer to the figure for the inputs and outputs as you follow the states of the control unit. The d's on the state transition diagram are *don't cares*, meaning that the output could be either zero or one. Here are the details:

- *State 0.*   While the start signal is 0, the controller doesn't care what the processor does, provided it does not disturb the output. It can't change the output, because there may be a number in the output register from a previous operation. When the start signal changes to 1, the outputs remain the same and the SSN changes state at the next active clock transition. Note that the clock transition also clocks registers A and B, but they are not important at this point.

- *State 1.*   Since the instruction is 0, the SSN will go to state 2 next. While at state 1, the outputs must transfer the input number to the A register through the OR gates. Therefore, the other number applied to the OR gates must be zero. The control unit deasserts the transfer signals XA and XB to send zeros to the ALU; it sends 00 to the ALU control signals telling it to add; it asserts the A register load lead; and it asserts the XIN transfer gates to bring the input number to the A register. When the active clock transition comes, the A register loads the input number.

- *State 2.*   Regardless of the inputs, the SSN will next go to state 6. At state 2, it transfers the number in the A register to the output register. The control unit asserts the LOUT signal to enable the output register to load on the next active clock transition. Since there are no other useful numbers in the system, the control unit doesn't care about the remaining control signals.

Instruction code is 1.   Now let's consider the operation when the instruction is 1 telling the control unit to send two times the input number to the output. Here are the details:

- *State 0.*   The operation is the same as state 0 described above.

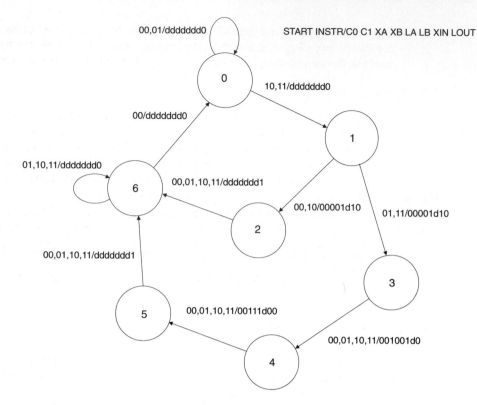

Figure 1-17   State transition diagram for information processor.

- *State 1.*   Since the instruction is 1, the SSN will go to state 3 next. At state 1, the control unit brings the input number into the A register the same as state 1 above.

- *State 3.*   Regardless of the inputs, the SSN will next go to state 4. At state 3, a copy of the number in A is loaded into the B register. To do this, the control unit asserts XA to transfer the A register to the ALU; does not assert XB so zero is sent to the ALU; tells the ALU to add, which makes a copy of the number in A; and asserts LB to load the number into the B register. Notice LA and LOUT are not asserted, so the numbers in these registers are not disturbed.

- *State 4.*   Regardless of the inputs, the SSN will next go to state 5. At state 4, two times the input number is loaded into A. The control unit asserts both XA and XB to transfer two copies of the number to the ALU, tells the ALU to add, and asserts LA to load the output of the ALU into the A register. The control unit no longer needs the B register, so it doesn't care if B is loaded. But it must not assert XIN because it must apply zero to the OR gates so the correct number loads into A. The output register is not loaded, to prevent unwanted changes in the output number.

- *State 5.* The next state will always be state 6 because the operation will be complete. At state 5, the control unit loads the result into the output register by asserting LOUT. No other hardware is used, so all the other outputs are don't cares.

Observations

The information processor discussed here is very simple. Building it in a laboratory is not difficult. But consider making a more complex system; say, one that has eight different instruction codes. If the design of the processor hardware is adequate, only the control unit need be changed. Probably making the changes will be relatively easy compared to constructing a new system. The total complexity of the system will be only slightly greater than that of the example.

It is significant that a complex system can be designed and built with very little extra hardware. The reason is the algorithmic approach used in the system design. The hardware does only small operations at a time and uses relatively simple hardware to do them. Of course, the time it takes to complete the total operation depends on the complexity of the operation. If the hardware is fast enough, this is a good design approach for practical systems.

1.4 STORED PROGRAM PROCESSORS

A *stored program processor* is an instruction-controlled digital system with a memory. The instruction controlled system contains a processor and a control unit. The control unit is a synchronous sequential network, but the complete system is also a SSN. The memory unit is an electronic device that stores numbers. The numbers from the memory are sequentially supplied to the instruction-controlled system as instructions. A computer is one example of a stored program processor. However, many other commercial devices that are stored program processors are not computers.

Practical programmable devices are very similar to the instruction-controlled digital system illustrated in Figure 1-16. However, practical systems are much more complex and their design is beyond the scope of this book. So the discussion of programmable devices will use a block diagram approach.

Block Diagram

Let's examine the major functional pieces of a stored program processor using the block diagram in Figure 1-18. Later sections discuss the hardware that implements these blocks.

The clock

The stored program processor is a large synchronous sequential network that requires a clock signal to synchronize all the memory elements. The signal from the clock is a periodic pulse waveform; you can see it with an oscilloscope. To give meaning to the pulses, let's call them *ticks* to emphasize that they provide timing information. The typical clock will operate at one million ticks per second (1 MHz) or faster.

The clock circuit usually consists of some electronics and a quartz crystal. The crystal is a package containing a thin piece of quartz crystal with wires attached to opposite sides. Quartz is a piezoelectric material; this means that bending the material slightly makes a voltage across it. Similarly, applying a voltage to quartz will cause it to bend. A timing device is made from quartz by cutting a small wafer of it to the proper size so it vibrates at a desired frequency. Since the piece of quartz is small and the material very stiff, the frequency is typically hundreds of kilohertz. This is in the range of frequencies of computer clocks. When the proper electronic circuit uses a crystal, the vibrations of the quartz provide a voltage of known and very stable frequency. The electronic circuit provides energy to the crystal to enable it to continue vibrating. Very accurate watches also use quartz crystals to provide accurate frequencies.

The processor

The central block of the system is called the processor. The principal part of the processor is a combinational logic network, called the ALU, that manipulates binary numbers. Practical ALUs can perform dozens of different operations, but only one at a time. Usually ALUs can add, subtract, complement bits, position bits, and so on.

Registers in the processor hold the data numbers operated on or produced. Usually processors are parallel devices that work on multiple bit numbers. If it helps you understand the discussion, think of 8-bit numbers because this is a common case. Signals from outside the processor control the operation the processor performs on the numbers. Any hardware involved in data transfer into or out of the processor is considered separate from the processor. Use the term *processor* for only the hardware that manipulates numbers.

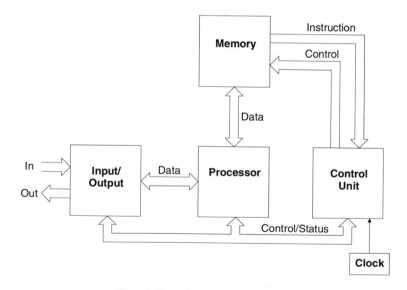

Figure 1-18   Stored program processor.

Some people call the processor the central processing unit, or CPU. Let's avoid the terminology CPU because its meaning differs from person to person. For example, some people also use CPU to refer to the major processing hardware and control panel and display screen on mainframe computers. Unless you carefully define the term, avoid using CPU. Instead, use the term *processor*, since the job of this block in the stored program processor is to process information where that information is in the form of binary numbers.

The control unit

The control unit is a synchronous sequential network that sends control signals to the processor, memory, and other parts of the system. Interpret the bold arrow between the blocks as a path along which information flows from one block to another. This path is rather abstract at this point and may not be unique wires in actual hardware. An arrow head is shown pointing toward the control unit because it gets information on the status of operations performed by the processor.

The clock is shown connected to the control unit to emphasize that the control unit is a SSN, but timing signals are passed to other blocks also. For example, the processor has registers that are clocked.

The signals from the control unit tell the processor to manipulate numbers according to the algorithms built into the SSN. The control unit is instruction controlled, so it can do more than one algorithm based on its design. Typical control units recognize several hundred different instruction codes. This level of complexity is practical because the control unit needs only a few states to control the processor for different operations. But the algorithms are built into the control unit, so only certain instruction operations can be performed by the control unit.

The memory

The addition of a memory device to the instruction-controlled system greatly increases the capability of the system. The memory, which is a collection of registers, holds binary numbers used for two distinct purposes. The first type of number is instruction code numbers used by the control unit. The second type is data numbers that are associated with the processor.

Instruction code numbers.   The memory holds instruction code numbers that are sequentially accessed by the control unit under control of the control unit. The control unit will get an instruction code from the memory, carry out that operation, and then return to the memory for further instructions. Very large, complex algorithms can be carried out as a series of small operations that are built into the control unit. However, the added capability due to the memory increases the complexity of the digital system very little.

Figure 1-18 shows a control path from the control unit to the memory. The control signals select the correct register and control the memory. The path from the memory to the control unit carries instruction code numbers. The block diagram does not specify how many bits this path can carry.

Program.   The sequence of instruction code numbers stored in the memory is called a *program*. Although the word *program* is routinely associated with computer programming, the word is more general. For example, when you go to the theater to see a play, you are given a program. The program describes the first act, the second act, and so on. The instruction codes in memory describe the first action, the second action, and so on.

Software.   If the memory technology allows people to change the numbers in the memory easily, then this electronic machine can be easily redesigned to do different jobs or different sequences. If the code numbers in the memory require only electronic information, the redesign of the unit can be done without any physical wiring changes at all. Since the numbers in the memory are rather abstract as opposed to hardware, the numbers are collectively called *software*.

The ability to change the operation of a digital system without changing the wiring makes stored program processors very important. Identical copies of the hardware can be manufactured under carefully controlled conditions so the reliability and cost are very good. Then the operation of the hardware can be changed for different applications by putting a program into the memory.

Data numbers.   The memory also holds data numbers for the processor. The processor has enough registers to store only the numbers operated on by the ALU. So results generated by the processor are stored in the memory. The processor will later retrieve needed numbers from the memory.

Figure 1-18 shows a two-directional path between the processor and the memory for transferring data numbers. Transferring a number from the processor to the memory is called a *store* operation, and transferring a number from the memory to the processor is called a *load* operation. The control path from the control unit to the memory selects the memory register and controls the memory hardware.

Input/output

The input/output (I/O) block in Figure 1-18 includes any hardware that allows data transfer between the processor and hardware devices external to the stored program processor. People often call the devices outside the computer the real world.

Consider the real world that is the concern of this book. The stored program processor is primarily a control system. It is used inside consumer products, manufacturing machines, or laboratory instruments. The usual input devices are sensors and the output devices are actuators. Common sensors are switches, temperature sensors, and oxygen sensors. For example, oxygen sensors monitor automobile engine exhaust to determine if the proper amount of fuel is being used. Actuators include solenoids, indicator lights, and motor starters. The solenoid may move a valve such as a hydraulic valve or the fuel valve in a gasoline engine fuel injector. A motor starter may turn on the fresh air fans for the building you work in. Some other I/O devices include the switches operated by the keys of a personal computer, or the solenoids that drive the pins in the head of a dot matrix printer.

Most input/output devices need power electronics or signal conditioning electronics to interface to the signals in the computer. The power electronics is not properly part of the computer, but rather is called interface electronics. The computer only uses low power level logic signals.

The data path in Figure 1-18 between the I/O block and the processor is two-directional. Data numbers travel from the processor to output devices and from input devices to the processor over this path. The control unit controls the input/output section using the control path. The control unit selects which input/output device will communicate with the processor.

Instruction Operation

The complete operation of an instruction may require several ticks of the clock. In general, several machine cycles are necessary to complete the operation of an instruction as the control unit proceeds through its states. In the stored program processor, a complete instruction operation happens in two distinct phases or groups of ticks.

Fetch phase

During the *fetch* phase, a copy of the instruction code number is brought out of the memory and transferred to the control unit. In spoken language, say *the control unit goes to the memory to fetch the instruction*. Of course, the word *goes* is figurative—only electrical binary signals travel on wires. The control unit sends binary control signals to the memory to accomplish the fetch.

Usually the control unit will fetch the instructions from the memory in the physical order of the memory registers—one after another. So part of the fetch operation is preparation for the next fetch.

The fetch phase of an instruction requires one or more ticks of the clock. The actual number of clock ticks depends on the design of the electronics.

Execute phase

During the *execute* phase, the instruction operation is carried out or executed. Execution means that the control unit sends signals to other parts of the machine to direct the operations specified by the instruction code. Instruction execution may affect only the processor, but it may also affect data transfers between the memory or I/O section and the processor. The execute phase of an instruction also requires one or more ticks of the clock.

In spoken language, people refer to the *execution* of an instruction, meaning both the fetch and execute phases together. The distinction of fetch and execute phases is most important to an understanding of how a stored program processor works.

The control unit will automatically continue to fetch and execute instructions until something stops it. So people speak of *executing* programs or *running* programs.

In control system applications, usually the program will run forever, as long as the system is powered up and operational. Control programs run in loops so they continuously control devices connected to them.

Definition of the Instruction Set

The control unit of a given stored program processor can carry out only a finite number or set of operations. That is, the control unit cannot do an infinite number of different operations. Therefore, the control unit recognizes only a limited number of instruction code numbers. The group or set of valid code numbers that the control unit and processor, working together, can recognize and carry out is called the *instruction set* of the machine.

In many practical designs, the number of possible numbers that can be sent to the control unit exceeds its capabilities. That is, some of the numbers are invalid because the control unit was not designed to recognize them. The hardware will do something if it fetches an invalid number, but usually you will not know what it was! The instruction set includes only the valid codes recognized by the control unit.

General-purpose Computer

Suppose you set out to design a stored program processor that could be used for many different applications. You might ask this question: What do I put into the processor and control unit to make a system that can do everything? Or more simply: What does everything include? Of course, one design may be better than another because it is cheaper, faster, or smaller. But the question here is, What is necessary to do everything?

The answer is a list of characteristics of a machine called the *general-purpose computer*. Here are the necessary operations that such a machine must have:

- *Arithmetic operations.* The machine must be able to do some arithmetic. It could be very simple and only add, or very complex with hardware floating point operations.

- *Logical operations.* The logical operations AND, OR, and COMPLEMENT are required. Many practical machines that are not computers are built that have these logical operations, but do not have any arithmetic capability.

- *Load and store operations.* There must be the capability to store and retrieve many data numbers. The processor usually stores only a few numbers and does not qualify—a memory device is required. For those interested in computer control systems, this ability is essential to integration and differentiation, which are necessary for control system operation.

- *Testing and branching.* More simply, this means the ability to make decisions. The hardware must first test a number and then respond to the test result. The response will be to change the order in which the instructions are used. This is called branching.

- *Input and output.* The machine must be able to communicate with other devices or it could only churn inside, accomplishing nothing useful.

Most computers that are called computers are general-purpose computers. However, it is useful to note these characteristics because it will help you understand the instruction set of

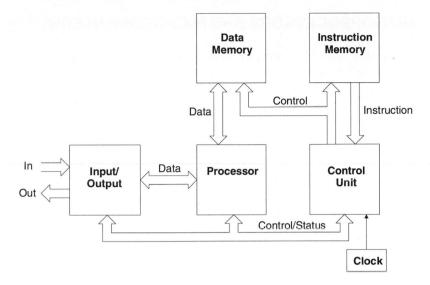

Figure 1-19   A Harvard architecture computer.

a computer. When you are faced with learning several hundred instructions, learning is easier if you group the instructions into categories.

Computer architecture

The term *computer architecture* describes the overall design of a computer. The design shown in Figure 1-18 is often named the *Princeton architecture* or *von Neumann architecture* in honor of the professor who developed this design. One of its principal characteristics is the use of the memory. The memory holds both the instruction codes and the data numbers. This design allows the limited number of memory registers to be used most efficiently. One characteristic of the Princeton machine is seldom used in small computers. It can treat instructions as data numbers. So the program can change itself as it runs. Since microcomputers often use permanent memory to hold the program, it is not possible to use this feature in most microcomputer applications.

The principal alternative design is named the *Harvard architecture*. The Harvard design is diagramed in Figure 1-19. The difference between the Princeton and Harvard architectures is that the Harvard machine has two memories instead of one. One memory holds the instruction codes and the other holds data numbers. The two kinds of numbers are logically separated, but each memory must be large enough for its job. An advantage of this design is that the hardware can be made to operate faster because each memory operates independently.

Most small computers now have the Princeton architecture. However, the computers of the future will include more Harvard architecture machines because of the speed advantages.

1.5 MICROPROCESSORS AND MICROCOMPUTERS

Now let's look at how modern hardware is used to build the parts discussed on the block diagram. The many kinds of hardware in use have led to many terms to describe it. Since so many people and different companies are involved with microcomputer hardware, it is natural to find the terminology used somewhat differently by different people. To avoid confusion, this book consistently uses the terminology introduced here. Usually, this terminology is consistent with Motorola terminology.

Integrated Circuit Technology

The development of integrated circuits has made the microcomputer possible. The integrated circuit may be the most significant technological development of the twentieth century because it makes so many other technologies possible.

Transistors

Let's begin with a brief discussion of transistors, since they are the building blocks of electronic circuits. Transistors are made from very pure silicon, which is a semiconductor material. Regions of the silicon are doped with a few atoms of another element to give it the proper characteristics to form transistors. The transistor is generally used as an electronic switch in digital circuits such as a computer. Tens of thousands of these switches are needed to build a practical computer. The transistors and their interconnections must be very small to be practical. One advantage of the integrated circuit is that many thousands of transistors can be interconnected in a very tiny device.

Integrated circuit construction

The construction of an integrated circuit begins with the manufacture of extremely pure silicon crystals. Wafers are cut from the crystalline silicon that are about one millimeter thick. These wafers are polished so the surface looks much like a black glass mirror. A smooth surface is necessary for the processes that follow to succeed.

The wafer is very pure silicon into which doping atoms must be introduced in microscopic-sized regions that are rigidly controlled. The doping atoms become part of the crystalline structure of the silicon. Doping atoms enter the silicon structure if they are introduced in a gaseous form at a high temperature—the silicon must be very near its melting point. However, doping atoms must only go into the silicon at the correct places.

In the most basic manufacturing process, the doping atoms are controlled by a coating that is placed on the surface of the wafer. The coating resists the entry of the doping atoms into the silicon. The coating is made with windows or openings that allow the atoms to enter at the correct place. The coating is applied as a photosensitive material that is exposed to ultraviolet light through a mask. The mask allows the light to expose only selected areas of the coating. The coating is then developed by a photographic process that removes or retains the coating as required, thus forming the window openings.

After the coating is in place, the wafer is passed through a furnace tube that contains the doping atoms. When the temperature and time of exposure are properly controlled, the doping atoms will enter the silicon and form part of a transistor or other device.

The complete wafer will require many passes through various furnaces with coatings in different patterns and different doping atoms. When all the processing is completed, a tiny area of the wafer will contain a complete electronic circuit. Usually hundreds of copies of this circuit will be made on the wafer simultaneously. When these circuits are separated into individual circuits, they are called *chips*. One process to separate the pieces of the wafer is to scribe the surface of the wafer with diamond-pointed tool and then break it along the score marks—the wafer chips into pieces.

The chips containing complete functional circuits must be mounted in useful packages. The individual chips are usually a square of one to twenty millimeters on a side. The package must provide eight to several hundred electrical connections to the chip. The package also provides mechanical protection for the chip. The completed package is called an *integrated circuit*, or *IC*. The integrated circuit industry has standardized packages and their pin arrangements.

A simple integrated circuit contains a few hundred transistors, and a sophisticated microcomputer chip contains many hundreds of thousands of transistors. The cost of ICs ranges from a few cents each to many hundreds of dollars each.

The Microprocessor and Microcomputer

In the early 1970s, it became practical to implement large portions of a computer in integrated circuits. Certainly ICs were used in computers before then, but only to do small functions. When the technology had progressed so about 7000 transistors could be put in a single low-cost chip, the microcomputer era began. With such a chip, the processor and control unit of a relatively powerful computer can be built in a single integrated circuit called a *microprocessor*.

Be careful with the terminology microprocessor. Unfortunately, the computer business is subject to a wide range of interest and attracts uninformed people who use terminology incorrectly. Newspaper articles often contain errors of terminology in technical areas. The term *microprocessor* has been used to describe almost any computer-related item from a single integrated circuit to a complete computer system.

Definition of microprocessor

In this book, the term *microprocessor* means the electronics in a single integrated circuit that implements the processor and control unit of a computer. Often this integrated circuit contains some minor support electronics for other parts, such as the clock. If the integrated circuit contains other major devices, such as memory, the part of this larger chip that implements the processor and control unit is called the microprocessor. Figure 1-20 shows the microprocessor part of a computer.

The memory used with a microprocessor is also integrated circuits. A single IC is used if the required number of memory registers is small enough. If more memory is required,

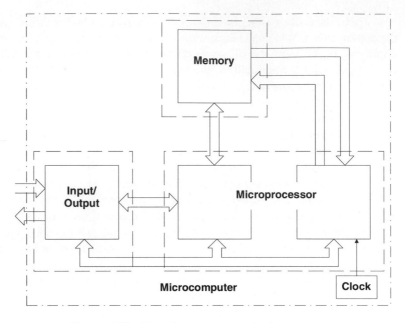

Figure 1-20   The microprocessor and microcomputer.

multiple ICs are used. Memory ICs are designed so many copies of the same part can be added to make a larger memory.

The input/output section of the computer can be a single IC if relatively few I/O signals are required. As with memory ICs, the I/O ICs are designed so many copies of the same IC can be added to make more signals.

The last part of the computer is the clock circuit. Most clock circuits use a quartz crystal as the time base.

Definition of microcomputer

The four major components of the computer—the microprocessor IC, one or more memory ICs, one or more I/O ICs, and the clock—are shown in Figure 1-20. Although a few other minor electrical components such as capacitors may be required, a working computer can be constructed from these four basic components. A single printed circuit board usually connects the ICs, making a computer called a *microcomputer*.

The single-chip microcomputer

As integrated circuit technology manufacturing technology improves, more and more transistors can be made in a single chip. Therefore, there is a great range of choices of how to build computer hardware. One use of the improved technology has been to make bigger and better microprocessors with bigger and better memory chips. However, there are many applications that don't require the greater power of larger microprocessors. An alternate choice is to integrate the microprocessor, memory, I/O, and the clock electronics into the same chip to make a *single-chip microcomputer*.

The single-chip microcomputer is an ideal component for controlling mechanical and electrical devices, and is used inside many consumer products. Because this chip controls the product, it is sometimes called a *microcontroller*. The names *single-chip computer* and *microcontroller* are interchangeable, although some companies prefer one over the other in their literature.

The processor and control unit part of the single-chip computer is called a *microprocessor*. Microprocessor is a reasonable name because the electronics from the microprocessor integrated circuit is incorporated into the single-chip computer. The quickly changing technology makes it difficult to create perfectly clear terminology.

It is impossible to identify the individual parts of the single-chip computer from outside the IC package. Usually, you can identify an IC as a single-chip computer only from the part number printed on the package. People often buy equipment containing microcomputers without realizing that a computer is present.

Microcomputer Applications

The microprocessor and the single-chip computer have affected the design of most electronic devices in the 1980s. The applications of these devices in the 1990s will be so widespread that examples will be unnecessary. All engineers must learn the fundamentals of this technology. Most consumers already make daily use of products with computers embedded in them so they don't need to understand the computer themselves. Other products are more obviously computer based, but the product designers usually try to isolate the user from the details of the hardware and software of the computer.

Embedded control systems

A microcomputer is said to be *embedded* if it is inside a device that is not called a computer. The microcomputer provides a cost-effective and practical implementation of the electronics required by the device. Microcomputers provide sophisticated features to consumer products at low cost. The computer makes the products easy to use by people with a wide range of skills.

The following is a list of some common products that contain embedded microcomputers. Some of these microcomputers may be proprietary chips with limited features to reduce cost. Others use standard off-the-shelf parts that are available to the public.

Cassette tape decks.   Most cassette tape units now have electronic control buttons, digital displays, and automatic tape bias adjustment controlled by a single-chip computer.

Microwave ovens.   Most microwave ovens can be programmed for various cooking times and power levels. Some sense food temperature and change the program accordingly. An internal microcomputer controls these and other features.

Home heating thermostats.   Programmable thermostats control home temperatures and reduce energy consumption.

Automobiles.   Most cars use a microcomputer to control the delivery of fuel and the spark timing for the engine. Microcomputer-controlled transmissions communicate with the engine controller to provide smooth transmission operation. Microcomputer-controlled anti-lock braking systems greatly improve the safety of cars and trucks. Electronic dashboard instruments contain a microcomputer.

Robotics.   The revolution in manufacturing caused by robots and related manufacturing devices is a direct result of the use of microcomputers in the robots. Some robots use a separate microcomputer to control each axis of movement of the robot.

Personal computers

The name *personal computer*, or *PC*, originally described a small desktop or portable computer system intended for business and computation purposes. The name implies that a single person will use the computer system. However, the technology has grown in many directions so the PC is sometimes connected to several terminals for a group of people to use; it may be too large to fit on the desktop or small enough to fit in a briefcase; and it may be used for playing games or for acquiring data from scientific experiments. Some very powerful personal computers are suitable for large computational jobs and are called *workstations* to distinguish them from other lower power devices.

Often people call a personal computer system a microcomputer, which confuses the meaning of the terminology. A personal computer is usually a collection of components that contain many microcomputers. The main computer box contains the central microcomputer, but there are other microcomputers, too. The keyboard usually contains a single-chip computer. The disk drive interface probably contains a microcomputer. The hard disk drive probably contains a microcomputer. The display monitor interface may contain a microcomputer. The printer probably contains a computer. If the printer uses the PostScript language, the computer in the printer may be more powerful than the computer in the main box. So a personal computer system is a collection of many microcomputers as they are defined here.

Distinguishing the types of computers

The personal computer, or the even more powerful minicomputer, is a computer system purchased as a package. Even if some components are bought separately, they will be designed to be compatible with the system components. By contrast, a microcomputer is a collection of one or more integrated circuits on a circuit board that requires other devices such as a power supply to operate.

The personal computer user usually purchases software designed to meet a particular application need. Using the computer is a matter of learning to use the software.

The microcomputer user needs some knowledge of digital systems to apply microcomputer hardware effectively. Programming will probably be done at a level that directly controls the microcomputer hardware. The microprocessor manufacturer or a third party will provide software development tools, but the user will likely develop the applications software.

1.6 REVIEW

A broad range of topics have been overviewed in this chapter. All of these will help you understand microcomputers. However, the section on number systems is the most important. Later chapters will use all the types of numbers introduced here without review.

1.7 EXERCISES

1-1. Do the following calculations by changing the given decimal numbers to 8-bit two's complement numbers and then performing the indicated operation on the two's complement numbers. Were there any two's complement overflows?
(a) $(+3) + (-100) =$
(b) $(-10) + (-12) =$
(c) $(-10) + (+10) =$
(d) $(+75) + (+100) =$
(e) $(+75) - (+100) =$
(f) $(+127) + (-127) =$
(g) $(-1) + (-1) =$
(h) $(-50) - (-100) =$
(i) $(-76) + (-82) =$
(j) $(-2) + (-126) =$

1-2. Find the equivalent numbers.
(a) 11111111 two's complement $=$ _____ Hex
(b) 25 Hex $=$ _____ 2
(c) 01110011 BCD $=$ _____ 2
(d) 01100000 BCD $=$ _____ Hex
(e) 95 Hex $=$ _____ 10
(f) $11000011_2 =$ _____ 8
(g) $60_8 =$ _____ 10

1-3. Change the sign of each of the following two's complement numbers.
(a) 00000001
(b) 11111100
(c) 00001111
(d) 00000000
(e) 10000000
(f) 0111111100000000
(g) 11111111
(h) 11110000
(i) 01010101
(j) 11011100

1-4. Find the decimal equivalent value of each of the following two's complement numbers.
(a) 00000001
(b) 11111100
(c) 0000000000001111
(d) 00000000
(e) 1000000000000000
(f) 01111111
(g) 10000000
(h) 10101010
(i) 01001110
(j) 1111111111111111

1-5. Write each of the following numbers in hexadecimal format.
(a) 11110000
(b) 10100101
(c) 00111100
(d) 0110110100000000
(e) 1110101101111100
(f) 11000011
(g) 10001110
(h) 01110110
(i) 11010000
(j) 0110101011101111

1-6. Add the 8-bit two's complement numbers 01001100 and 01101111 and make observations about the result.

1-7. Subtract the 8-bit two's complement number 00001111 from 11111110.

1-8. Subtract the 8-bit unsigned binary number 00001111 from 11111110.

1-9. Two 8-bit two's complement numbers are called A and B. When B is subtracted from A, there is a borrow from outside the numbers. What is the relationship, if any, between numbers A and B?

1-10. Two 8-bit unsigned numbers are called C and D. When D is subtracted from C, there is a borrow from outside the numbers. What is the relationship, if any, between numbers C and D?

1-11. What is the largest positive 16-bit two's complement number both in hexadecimal and decimal?

1-12. What is the smallest, or most negative, 16-bit two's complement number both in hexadecimal and decimal?

1-13. If you are using 8-bit two's complement numbers represented by hexadecimal numbers, which of the possible hex numbers represent positive numbers and which represent negative numbers?

1-14. Convert the 8-bit two's complement numbers 01001110 and 11001110 to the equivalent 16-bit two's complement numbers.

1-15. If a negative two's complement number is subtracted from a positive two's complement number, a two's complement overflow occurs if the answer is (positive, negative, other).

1-16. Subtract the two's complement number 01101010 from 10010001 and discuss the result.

1-17. The two's complement number for -1 is used frequently. Find the 8-bit, 16-bit, and 32-bit two's complement numbers for -1, and then write them in hexadecimal notation.

1-18. The hexadecimal representation of the 8-bit two's complement number equivalent to -1 is FF. Learn to form the hex numbers for -2, -3, and -4 quickly by counting downward from FF.

1-19. Add the two's complement numbers 11001100 and 1001100110000001.

1-20. Convert the unsigned binary number 01110011 to a BCD number.

1-21. What is the difference between a combinational logic network and a synchronous sequential network?

1-22. How many binary signals are necessary to represent a code for 12_{10} different items?

1-23. A thumbwheel switch generates four binary signals to represent a decimal number. When the switch is set to the number seven, three outputs are low and one is high. Sketch the four signals and label them with mixed-logic notation.

1-24. If a circuit uses binary signals of 0 volts and −10 volts, which of these is the low level and which is the high level?

1-25. A signal wire is labeled RESET(L). Describe the apparent function of each voltage level.

1-26. A 2-input logic gate has low-asserted inputs and a high-asserted output when it performs the AND function. The wires connected to the inputs are labeled A(L) and $\overline{B}$(L). The output is labeled START(H). Should A and B be zero or one to make START true?

1-27. Make an EXCLUSIVE OR circuit using only gates as shown in Figure 1-4.

1-28. Explain the difference between the notation $\overline{PB1}$ used in a logic equation and the same notation on a wire in a Motorola manual.

1-29. Write a word description of each of the logic functions AND, OR, COMPLEMENT, and EXCLUSIVE OR.

1-30. Draw the logic symbol for a 2-input OR gate with low-asserted inputs and a high-asserted output. Also draw the AND symbol for this gate.

1-31. Make a voltage level table that describes a 2-input OR gate with low-asserted inputs and a high-asserted output.

1-32. A 3-input logic gate has low-asserted inputs and a high-asserted output when performing the AND function. Draw the logic symbol for this gate when it performs the OR function.

1-33. Design a new circuit to replace the one in Figure 1-5 with the following hardware changes. The switches both work like the upper switch in the figure, and the new light is high-asserted.

1-34. Why do the outputs of a synchronous sequential network depend on what the inputs were in the past?

1-35. In many applications, the faster a circuit responds, the better it is. Why not increase the speed of the clock for a SSN until the circuit almost stopped working, and then leave it?

1-36. Trace the operation of the synchronous sequential network in Figure 1-14.
(a) Assume the network is in state Y1Y2=11 and the input X=0, and then sketch the circuit and label each wire with high or low to indicate its logic level. Compare your results to the state transition diagram in Figure 1-13.
(b) Next assume that one active clock transition takes place. Label the wires a second time with their new logic levels. Compare your results to the state transition diagram.

1-37. Change the state transition diagram in Figure 1-17 so an instruction of 1 multiplies by three instead of by two.

1-38. Assume that a second input port and a transfer control signal are added to the system in Figure 1-16. The second input will transfer to register B the same way the first input transfers to register A. Modify the state transition diagram in Figure 1-17 so an instruction of 1 inputs two two's complement signed numbers, and then puts the A number minus two times the B number in the output port.

Chapter 2

Instruction Subset and Machine Language

Programming a microcomputer requires knowledge of its internal operation. High-level programming languages try to isolate the programmer from the internal operation of the computer. Most applications of microcomputers require unique hardware configurations that make use of a high-level language difficult. In such cases, microcomputer programming is usually done with a low-level language that requires intimate knowledge of the internal operation of the microprocessor. In particular, you must know and understand the operation of the hardware instructions.

This chapter introduces the fundamental operation of the microprocessor and the instructions that control the hardware. The examples use the Motorola 68HC11 microcomputer, although the fundamental concepts are the same for other devices, including those manufactured by other companies.

This chapter clearly demonstrates that hardware and software are not separate topics when learning microcomputers. Programming cannot be done well without fully understanding the registers in the microprocessor and the memory.

Not all the many instructions available in the 68HC11 are covered here. The advanced instructions are in Chapter 5 after the intervening chapters introduce some helpful programming tools.

> **Motorola Products**
>
> All the material in this chapter except Figure 2-1 and the double-precision instructions applies to the Motorola 6800, 6801, 6802, 6803, 6808, and 68701 chips.

2.1   THE 68HC11 COMPUTER OPERATION

The functions performed by machine instructions can be more easily understood if you understand the operation of the computer hardware. This section introduces the principal registers in the 68HC11 and explains their uses during instruction fetch and execution.

The Programming Model

You would find it very difficult to comprehend all the details of the microprocessor hardware and instructions at once. You must learn the many details a few at a time. To aid your learning, an abstract model of the most important microprocessor registers is used. Since this model provides enough detail to understand the fundamentals of programming, it is called the *programming model* of the computer. Usually a model of the memory registers accompanies the programming model. The programming model is useful only for learning and for writing programs because it does not provide any details of the electronics. Figure 2-1 shows the complete programming model of the 68HC11 microprocessor, although some of these registers will not be discussed until much later. You must think about only the registers discussed and ignore the others to avoid confusion. Remember that the programming model is an abstraction that cannot accurately relate how the hardware is constructed.

The memory model

A computer is a collection of registers and some other hardware that manipulate numbers and move numbers around among those registers. Some of the registers are in memory and others are in the microprocessor.

7	A	0	7	B	0	8-BIT ACCUMULATORS A & B
15			D		0	16-BIT DOUBLE ACCUMULATOR D
15			X		0	INDEX REGISTER X
15			Y		0	INDEX REGISTER Y
15			SP		0	STACK POINTER
15			PC		0	PROGRAM COUNTER
			S X H I N Z V C			CONDITION CODE REGISTER

Figure 2-1   Motorola 68HC11 programming model.

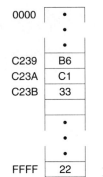

0000	•
	•
	•
C239	B6
C23A	C1
C23B	33
	•
	•
	•
FFFF	22

Figure 2-2   Memory model.

The memory registers will be represented as shown in Figure 2-2. The numbers in the boxes represent the contents of the registers; that is, the bits stored in the flip flops. The numbers to the left of the boxes represent the addresses of the memory registers. Wherever a figure does not have numbers, you should assume that the number is unknown or is of no current interest. All the registers always contain numbers, but if the number is unknown, the box will be blank.

Usually a figure illustrates only a few memory registers, but they may have widely separated addresses. A break in the memory with dots in the register boxes indicates that some registers are not shown.

The size of the hexadecimal numbers represents the Motorola 68HC11 hardware correctly. The numbers in the memory registers are 8-bit numbers requiring two hexadecimal digits. The address numbers are 16-bit numbers shown as four hexadecimal digits. Since the addresses have 16_{10} bits, the 68HC11 can directly address 64-K memory registers.

The memory register with address 0000 is explicitly shown in many figures in this book so you can determine the order of increasing addresses. In Figure 2-2, you can see that increasing addresses go from the top of the figure to the bottom. But this would not be apparent if the addresses C239, C23A, and so on were not shown. The addresses are often not shown, meaning that any address could be used. For certain topics, figures illustrate memory, with increasing addresses going from the bottom to the top of the figure. Computer manuals sometimes have both types of figures on the same page. You can always determine the direction of a figure when address 0000 is shown.

In spoken language, the two ends of the memory are called the *top* and *bottom* of memory. Most people use the word *bottom* to describe the end of memory with address 0000 and the word *top* to describe the end with address FFFF. However, some people use the words *top* and *bottom* in the opposite sense.

An instruction format

Figure 2-3 illustrates one kind of instruction and its associated data number in memory. The example is the *Load Accumulator A* instruction. The mnemonic name of this instruction is LDAA. A *mnemonic* is an abbreviation or symbol designed to make the abbreviation easy

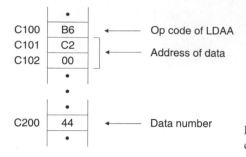

Figure 2-3   Example of an instruction code—Load Accumulator A.

to remember. The LDA means load accumulator and the final A specifies the A accumulator. In spoken language, we often refer to an instruction by spelling its mnemonic name.

The LDAA instruction has two parts. The first is the operation code byte B6 that specifies the operation to be performed by the microprocessor. The term *operation code* is usually shortened to *op code*. All instructions have an op code as the first byte.

The second part of the instruction is the 2-byte address C200 that specifies the memory register containing the data for this instruction. The instruction shown will copy the data number 44 into the accumulator A register in the microprocessor when the microprocessor executes it.

Not all instructions will contain an address like this instruction. Many more details of this instruction and others are covered in later sections.

The operation code of the instruction in the figure is the number B6 located at address C100. The address part of the instruction C200 is located at memory locations C101 and C102. The data value is the number 44 in the memory register with address C200. After the microprocessor executes this instruction, accumulator A will contain 44.

The microprocessor model

Figure 2-4 illustrates four of the microprocessor registers—only those registers needed for a particular discussion are shown. Later sections introduce the remaining registers in the microprocessor.

The size of the boxes in the figure and the size of the hexadecimal numbers correctly represent the number of bits in the registers. So the figure says that the program counter register is a 16-bit register—also called a double-byte register. Drawing the program counter as two joined boxes emphasizes that it holds two bytes. The A accumulator register is an 8-bit register. Figure 2-4 has the same size box for the 8-bit A register as was used for an 8-bit memory register in Figure 2-3.

Accumulators.   A general-purpose register in a microprocessor that holds a data number is called an *accumulator*. The data number in an accumulator may be the result created by an instruction—for example, the sum of two numbers. Also, the number in the accumulator may be operated on by an instruction.

The name *accumulator* may be confusing—the name also applies to the display mechanism on outdated mechanical adding machines that accumulated a total or sum. For now,

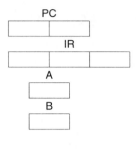

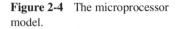

Figure 2-4   The microprocessor model.

just think of the number in the accumulator as a data number. Some people call the accumulator a general-purpose register, which is also not very informative.

The Motorola 68HC11 has two 8-bit accumulators called A and B as Figure 2-4 illustrates.

Caution! People are often inexact in using spoken language. It is common to say *A register* when describing the A accumulator register. Do not confuse the A register with the memory register with address 000A. Similarly, the spoken expression *the registers* refers only to the registers inside the microprocessor, not the memory registers.

Program counter.   The microprocessor register that holds the address of the next instruction to be fetched from memory is called the *program counter.* The Motorola 68HC11 has a 16-bit program counter labeled PC in Figure 2-4. The size of the program counter is the same as the size of the memory address. In spite of its name, the program counter is not a counter and it does not count programs! The program counter is a register that holds addresses for use by the control unit in the microprocessor.

Instruction register.   The register in the microprocessor that holds an instruction code number as it is fetched from memory is called the *instruction register*. The instruction register is said to be *transparent* because its operation cannot be seen. The microprocessor uses the instruction register for its internal operations. Therefore, instructions cannot control the instruction register. Even laboratory test equipment cannot easily access the hardware in this register. The programming model usually does not show the instruction register for this reason.

Figure 2-4 shows the instruction register as a 3-byte register because the instruction in the figure requires three bytes. Remember that the programming model does not give an accurate representation of the electronics in the microprocessor.

Internal Computer Operations

Chapter 1 discussed the operation of a programmable device such as a computer using a block diagram. This section repeats that discussion in greater detail using the programming model. One typical instruction is traced through each step of the fetch and execute phases of its execution.

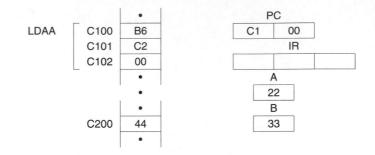

Figure 2-5   Programming model with an instruction in memory.

Figure 2-5 shows the programming model with a Load Accumulator A instruction in memory. Remember that the Load Accumulator A instruction copies the contents of the data location addressed by the instruction into the A accumulator. The number that was originally in the accumulator is lost. This LDAA instruction occupies three bytes of memory.

Following the step-by-step operation of the computer requires a known starting point. Assume that some electronic device put the numbers shown into both the memory and the microprocessor registers—assume that it was done by magic if you prefer.

In Figure 2-5, the address of the op code of the instruction is in the program counter. The numbers in the A and B accumulators are meaningless—they were specified so you can see changes in the numbers. Previous instructions would normally leave their results in the accumulators.

The operation of the computer can now be traced one clock tick at a time. Since the ticks or cycles of the microprocessor clock synchronize the operation of the entire micro-computer, the register transfers are traced at each tick.

The term *tick* is a simplification of the 68HC11 internal clock that runs at one-fourth the crystal clock frequency.

Instruction fetch

The *fetch phase* of the instruction execution brings a copy of the next instruction code from memory into the microprocessor instruction register. The microprocessor enters the fetch phase each time it completes the previous instruction. When the microprocessor is turned on and starts running, the very first operation is a fetch.

The fetch of a Load Accumulator A instruction is traced in the following sections. LDAA was chosen because all programs use it and it is easy to understand. Bold type in the figures directs your attention to the numbers discussed in the text and has no other meaning.

First tick of the instruction operation.   During the first tick or machine cycle of the fetch phase of an instruction:

- *The microprocessor sends the number in the program counter register to the memory as an address and tells the memory to read.* The program counter determines where an instruction will be fetched from, since it supplies the address to the memory. You should say that the program counter is *pointing* to the memory register as you might

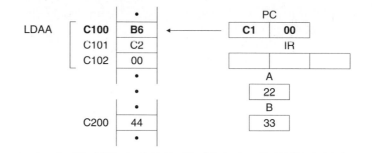

Figure 2-6   Beginning of the fetch phase of an instruction.

do with your finger. Figure 2-6 shows the program counter pointing at address C100.
A hardware signal controls the memory read operation.

- *The memory sends a copy of the number at the specified address to the micropro-*
  cessor and the microprocessor puts the number into the left byte of the instruction
  register. Part of the instruction code has now been fetched from the memory and
  put into the instruction register as Figure 2-7 shows.

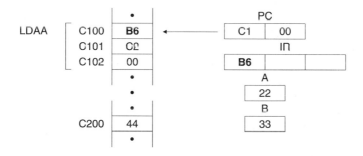

Figure 2-7   First byte of instruction has been fetched.

- *The microprocessor adds one to the number in the program counter and puts the*
  result back into the program counter. The program counter now contains the address
  of the next memory register in order. Figure 2-8 shows the result of this operation.
  Since the microprocessor adjusts the program counter this way, it will automatically
  fetch instruction bytes from the memory in order. When the current instruction is
  finished, the program counter will automatically point to the next instruction in
  order. Using a program counter eliminates the need for the instruction to specify the
  address of the next instruction, greatly simplifying the hardware.

- *The microprocessor determines if fetching should continue by examining the in-*
  struction op code in the left byte of the instruction register. If the instruction is more
  than one byte long, the fetch phase must continue. If not, the execute phase is
  entered. For this example, there are two more bytes to be fetched, so the fetch phase

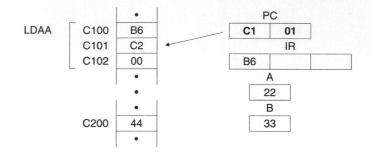

Figure 2-8   The program counter has been incremented after the first clock tick.

must continue. The registers shown in the programming model don't change due to this step.

So far, the fetch phase has brought the first byte of the instruction into the microprocessor and adjusted the program counter to point to the next memory location. The microprocessor has determined that three bytes must be fetched for this instruction.

Second tick of the instruction operation.   Since the example instruction is three bytes long, the fetch phase of the operation continues.
At the second tick of the clock:

- *The microprocessor sends the number in the program counter to the memory as an address and tells the memory to read.*

- *The memory sends a copy of the number at the specified address to the microprocessor and the microprocessor puts the number into the next byte of the instruction register.* Two bytes of the instruction code are now in the instruction register as Figure 2-9 shows.

- *The microprocessor adds one to the number in the program counter and puts the result back into the program counter.* Figure 2-10 shows the registers after the second tick of the clock.

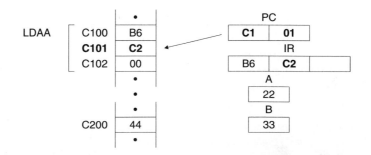

Figure 2-9   The second byte of the instruction has been fetched.

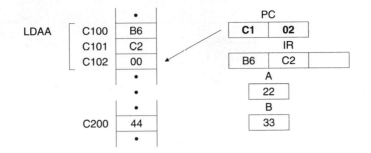

Figure 2-10 The program counter has been incremented after the second clock tick.

After two ticks of the clock, the first two bytes of the instruction are in the instruction register and the program counter is pointing to the next location. Since the microprocessor already knows that a third byte must be fetched, the fetch operation will continue.

Third tick of the instruction operation. The third tick continues the fetch operation getting the last byte of the instruction code in this example:

- *The microprocessor sends the number in the program counter to the memory as an address and tells the memory to read.*

- *The memory sends a copy of the number at the specified address to the microprocessor and the microprocessor puts the number into the next byte of the instruction register. The three bytes of the instruction code are now in the instruction register* as Figure 2-11 shows.

- *The microprocessor adds one to the number in the program counter and puts the result back into the program counter.* Figure 2-12 shows the registers now that the fetch operation is complete.

In summary, during the fetch phase of this instruction, the three bytes of the instruction were put into the instruction register and the program counter was adjusted. Since the entire instruction code has been fetched from memory into the microprocessor, the fetch phase of the instruction operation is complete.

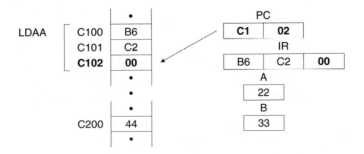

Figure 2-11 The third byte of the instruction has been fetched.

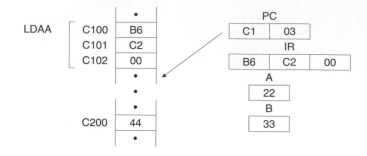

Figure 2-12   The fetch operation is complete after the third clock tick.

The program counter now contains the address of the next location in memory after this instruction code. The next location must contain the next instruction in the program. The design of the computer requires that instructions be in order in the memory.

The program counter register is defined as a register that holds the address of the next instruction. You should understand that the contents of the program counter change during the fetch operation—the definition applies at the completion of the fetch phase of an instruction.

The instruction register holds the instruction code as it awaits the execute phase of the instruction. The fetch phase of an instruction never changes the accumulators or any memory registers.

Instruction execution

The microprocessor automatically enters the execute phase of instruction operation at the completion of the fetch phase. The execute phase carries out the function specified by the instruction code. The function of the Load Accumulator instruction used in the example is to transfer the data number to the accumulator.

Fourth tick of the instruction operation.   The execute phase of the Load Accumulator instruction requires only a single clock tick or machine cycle to do the following:

- *The right two bytes of the instruction register are sent to the memory as an address and the memory is told to read.* The right two bytes of the instruction register contain the address part of the instruction code and thus point to the data number in memory.

- *The memory sends a copy of the number at the specified address to the microprocessor and the microprocessor puts the number into the A accumulator.* Figure 2-13 shows that the single-byte data number for this instruction has been put into the accumulator. The number originally in the accumulator is lost.

During the execute phase, the microprocessor copied the addressed data number into the accumulator, destroying the original number there. The execute phase of this instruction does not affect the program counter. Only a few instructions affect the program counter during the execute phase.

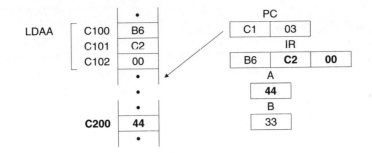

Figure 2-13   The data number has been put into the accumulator.

Both the fetch and execute phases of the instruction operation are now finished. The microprocessor automatically begins a new fetch at the next tick of the clock.

After the instruction operation is finished, the number in the program counter specifies the address of the next instruction to be fetched. The number in the instruction register is no longer useful. The accumulators hold data numbers including the one that resulted from this instruction. Figure 2-14 shows the final state of the registers.

Instruction operation notation

A concise notation can describe the function performed by an instruction. Unfortunately, there are many varieties of notation used in textbooks and computer manuals. Since this book uses Motorola hardware for the examples, it will use Motorola notation. But even this is a problem—the Motorola notation is not only somewhat incomplete and therefore sometimes incorrect, but Motorola has also changed notation from one manual to another. You must be careful when reading Motorola literature with this book. Look for the notation problems to avoid confusion.

A complete notation.   Let us begin the discussion of notation by using the LDAA instruction as an example. A word description of this instruction is: *The Load Accumulator A instruction transfers or copies the contents of the addressed memory register into the A accumulator.* This statement only describes the function performed; it does not explain the

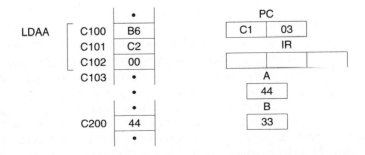

Figure 2-14   The result at the completion of the LDAA instruction after four clock ticks.

Motorola Trainer

All the examples have been designed to work in the Motorola trainer. Single step the instruction discussed. Enter the numbers shown in Figure 2-5. Then use the Trace command to execute just one instruction. The trainer cannot show you each step of the fetch and execute phases. The results should be as Figure 2-14 shows. Only consider the microprocessor registers shown in the figure even though the trainer shows you more registers. Also look at the memory registers to confirm there were no changes.

Appendix D will help you use the trainer.

details of how the function is accomplished. For example, the actions of the program counter are not stated.

The phrase *the contents of* a register, meaning the number in the register, can be written symbolically. A common notation encloses the symbolic name of the register with parentheses; for example, (A) refers to the 8-bit number in the A accumulator. The spoken language for (A) is *the contents of A.*

Describing the contents of a memory register is more complicated. The memory register of interest depends on the address specified by the instruction. We could use the notation M to identify *the memory register addressed by the instruction.* Then the notation M identifies a memory register as the A identified the A accumulator. Adding parentheses gives the notation (M), meaning *the contents of the memory register addressed by the instruction.*

An arrow symbol denotes the transfer or copy operation, so the LDAA instruction is described by (M)→(A). This notation literally means that the contents of the A register becomes the contents of the memory register addressed by the instruction, and that the previous number in the A register is lost. This brief notation describes the function of Load Accumulator completely, but leaves out the details of how the microprocessor does it.

Motorola shortened notation.   The notation introduced so far is an excellent notation, but Motorola seldom uses it in its manuals! Instead, Motorola usually uses a shortened version of this notation. But the shortened version cannot correctly describe all the register transfers that occur.

Motorola solves this problem by returning to the longer notation whenever it is necessary. Therefore, two notation schemes are mixed, sometimes within the same statement, and this may cause confusion. But since this mixed notation is common, this book avoids any additional confusion by following the most used version of Motorola notation. You must understand the notation problems or you will be confused when you read information about the instructions.

Here is the shortened version of the notation—the parentheses are left out! You are to infer from the context of the statement that the parentheses are there when they are needed. Fortunately, most of the time you will need to assume that the parentheses are there.

When using this new Motorola notation, the LDAA instruction is described by M→A. Since you already understand this instruction, it is easy to understand the notation—you may

Source Form	Operation	Boolean Expression	Machine Code		Bytes
			Op Code	Operand	
ADDA	Add Memory to A	A + M → A	BB	hh ll	3
LDAA	Load Accumulator A	M → A	B6	hh ll	3
STAA	Store Accumulator A	A → M	B7	hh ll	3
STOP	Stop program in trainer		3F		1

Figure 2-15   Part of the instruction set table.

even prefer it until a more difficult situation occurs. In the new notation, the M refers to the contents of the memory register addressed by the instruction, and the A refers to the contents of the A accumulator.

There are now three ways to describe the LDAA instruction. They are (M)→(A), (M)→A, and M→A. All these mean the same thing and all are used. Whenever it is reasonable, this book uses the shortest form of the Motorola notation.

The instruction set table.   Let's look at a table that uses the Motorola notation to describe some more instructions that have the same format as the LDAA instruction discussed earlier. Figure 2-15 is a table that describes only a few instructions. A table for all the instructions of a microprocessor is called the *instruction set table*. A complete table for the 68HC11 is in Appendix H. You should avoid any information provided there beyond that in Figure 2-15 until much later.

The columns of the instruction set table are defined as follows:

- *Source Form.*   The mnemonic name of the instruction. A person writing a program on paper would write this name, so it is the source of the program.

- *Operation.*   This column contains a very short word description of the operation performed by the instruction.

- *Boolean Expression.*   This column has the logical description of the register transfers performed by the instruction written in Motorola notation.

- *Machine Code-Op Code.*   This column documents the instruction binary op code in hexadecimal format.

- *Machine Code-Operand.*   This column specifies the additional bytes beyond the op code that the instruction requires. The instruction format used so far requires two bytes for the address of the data. The address of the data is the operand. The hh designates the high byte of the address that is the second byte of the instruction code. The ll designates the low byte of the address that is the third byte of the instruction code.

- *Bytes.*   This column reiterates the total number of bytes of memory required by the instruction code. You can determine this number from the Machine Code column.

The instruction set table is in alphabetical order by mnemonic instruction name.

Motorola Trainer

Programs must end with an instruction to stop the microprocessor from continuing program execution. When you run programs at full speed with the G command, the last instruction in your program must have an op code of 3F. The 3F instruction will be called the *STOP instruction because it stops programs in the trainer by transferring control to the monitor program. The effect is to stop your program from running.*

Caution! The 68HC11 has an instruction named STOP that has quite a different effect. Don't use it.

Now let's look at some details of the instructions shown in Figure 2-15, which are listed in alphabetical order. Then, using only these few instructions, an example program can be written:

- *ADDA.*   The ADDA instruction adds the number in the A accumulator to the number in the addressed memory location and then puts the sum in the A accumulator. The number in memory is unchanged and the original number in A is lost. The numbers are 8-bit numbers. The addition is a binary addition, so the microprocessor does not distinguish two's complement signed numbers from unsigned numbers.

- *LDAA.*   The LDAA instruction was described earlier. However, the word *load* in an instruction name always means to copy a number from a memory register to a microprocessor register. Later you will find load instructions for other registers. The size of the number copied depends on the size of the destination register. Therefore, LDAA transfers an 8-bit number.

- *STAA.*   The STAA instruction copies the number in the A accumulator into the memory register addressed by the instruction. The previous number in the memory register is lost and the accumulator is unchanged. The word *store* in an instruction name always describes the transfer of a number from a microprocessor register to a memory register. You will see many more kinds of store instructions in later discussions. The size of the number copied depends on the size of the source register.

- *STOP.*   The *STOP* instruction is shown in italics, since this is NOT the correct name of the instruction with an op code of 3F. The *STOP* instruction is used in Motorola trainers to stop a program. The 3F instruction will stop a program correctly only when used in a Motorola trainer. The real name and operation of this instruction will be discussed much later, since it is very complicated. The examples that follow use the *STOP* instruction to stop the program.

If you are familiar with the Fortran or Basic programming languages, you recognize the name STOP used here for the *STOP* instruction because those languages have a STOP that has the same purpose.

Instruction similarities

All instructions have fetch and execute phases that are similar. Therefore, you need not learn the detailed hardware operation for every instruction to write programs. The instruction set table does not describe all the hardware operations; it only describes the functions performed by the instructions. Accordingly, this chapter continues at a lesser level of detail describing only the functions performed by the instructions.

Machine language programming

The binary numbers that form a program in the memory of the computer are called *machine language*. Machine language programming is the process of creating a sequence of binary instruction codes and then putting them into the memory to make a program. A program is just a series of instruction codes. A machine language program directly controls the hardware in the computer.

Let's look at a small machine language program that uses the instructions covered so far. This exercise demonstrates the computer operation during a complete program. The program adds two 8-bit numbers from memory registers to form an 8-bit sum that is put into a memory register. The program will do no more than add—nothing else such as error checking will be done. Therefore, the program adds either unsigned numbers or two's complement signed numbers.

Program loading. The phrase *loading a program* means to put the instruction numbers and data numbers into the memory. Loading can be done by a person typing at a keyboard or by a computer program controlling a peripheral device that holds the numbers.

Figure 2-16 shows the add program loaded into memory. The numbers to be added, called N1 and N2, are placed in memory locations C20B and C20C. The program must put the sum, called SUM, into location C20D. The number in location SUM was initially set to FF, so it will be obvious when the program changes the answer. You should always put in an incorrect answer when testing a program—bad luck will cause the correct answer to occur accidentally when the program is incorrect.

Figure 2-16 shows the computer ready to run because the program counter contains C200—the address of the first instruction. The accumulators are blank because the numbers in them are unknown when the computer is started.

The locations—memory addresses—of both the instructions and data numbers in the figure have no significance. Both the instructions and data numbers could be located anywhere in the memory. The example does not use memory location C20A to show that the data numbers do not need to be next to the instructions. The instructions and data numbers may be widely separated in memory. The numbers in all other memory registers and microprocessor registers do not affect this program.

Program operation. Let us follow the operation of the program in detail. The logic of the program is N1 + N2 → SUM.

Assume that the computer started running somehow—a person has pressed some buttons. A trainer computer requires a single command to start the computer. The sequence of the instructions in the program is as follows.

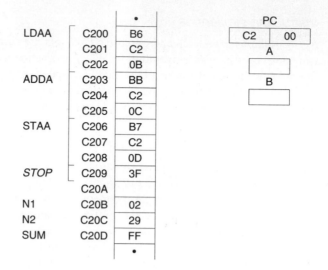

Figure 2-16   The first machine language program.

- *First instruction.* Figure 2-17 illustrates the state of the computer after it has fetched and executed one instruction. The program counter is pointing at the next instruction at location C203. The first data number N1 has been loaded into the A accumulator. Notice that memory location C20B was not affected.

- *Second instruction.* Figure 2-18 illustrates the computer after two instructions. The program counter is pointing at the next instruction at location C206. The two

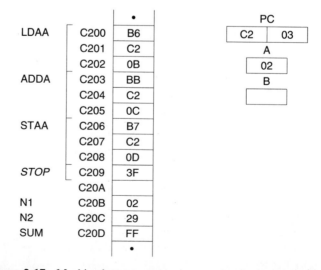

Figure 2-17   Machine language program—one instruction executed.

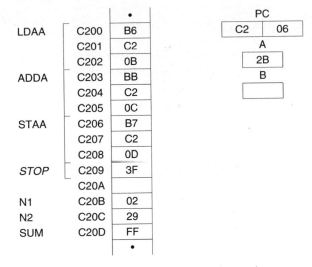

Figure 2-18 Machine language program—two instructions executed.

numbers, N1 in the A accumulator and N2 in a memory register, have been added and the sum is in the A accumulator. Whatever number was in the A accumulator has been lost.

- *Third instruction.* Figure 2-19 shows the result after three instructions. The program counter contains C209, so it is ready for the fetch of the fourth instruction. The sum has been stored into memory and the number in memory location C20D was lost. The STAA instruction did not affect the contents of the A accumulator.

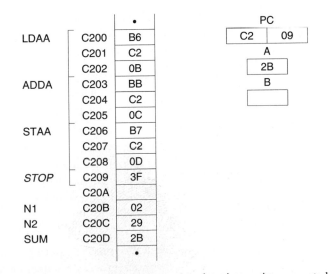

Figure 2-19 Machine language program—three instructions executed.

Motorola Trainer

Enter the numbers shown in Figure 2-16 including the number in the program counter. Using the Trace command, single step the program and look at the contents of the program counter and accumulators after each step. The numbers should follow Figures 2-17 through 2-19. Also look at the contents of memory location C20D when the program counter contains C206. Then trace the next instruction and look at this memory location again.

- *Fourth instruction.* The last instruction, *STOP*, only stops the computer and does not alter any registers in the microprocessor or memory.

Problems and common errors

Many kinds of mistakes could be made in loading and running the example program in Figure 2-16. Here is a list of some of the more likely errors and the kinds of consequences that you should expect. The variety of possible actions that could occur is almost limitless, but learning that so many things could go wrong is valuable.

- *The program counter is loaded with an incorrect address.* The computer will use whatever numbers it encounters as instructions, which will probably lead to chaos. As an example, suppose the program counter was loaded with C201, which is only one binary bit different from the correct value. The first op code fetched will be C2 instead of B6. From here on, it is impossible for the program to operate correctly.

- *The STOP instruction is left out.* Assume further that the numbers in locations C209 and C20A are not 3F. The computer will use the numbers starting at address C209 as instructions—probably executing the data numbers as instructions. What happens will depend upon the numbers encountered, and hence is unpredictable.

  Sometimes the computer will continue using garbage from memory until it accidentally runs into some good program and it starts operating accordingly—this can be very confusing! You intend to run your program and some other program runs instead.

- *An instruction code is entered incorrectly.* Certainly an incorrect code will make the program work incorrectly. But suppose the number at location C208 was entered as 08. Then the address part of the STAA instruction would be C208. When this program is run, the sum of two numbers will be stored at location C208. The incorrect sum FF is left at location C20D. Regardless, the program will run to the *STOP* instruction, giving the impression of correct operation until you find the wrong answer.

  But the problem is more serious than that. The storing of the result at C208 modifies the STAA instruction. So the program will do something different when it is run a second time. After that, the program will do the same thing every time as long as the data numbers are not changed. Usually programs must be run several times before you can have any confidence that they are working correctly. And even then, you should be cautious.

2.2   INSTRUCTIONS AND ADDRESSING MODES

Determining how the instructions will access data is a major consideration in the design of a microprocessor. How the instructions access data significantly affects the use and programming of the microcomputer. In particular, if the data number for an instruction is in memory, the microprocessor will form a memory address to access it. If the data number is in a register inside the microprocessor, a memory address is not needed.

The address formed by the microprocessor as part of the instruction execution is called the *effective address*. The microprocessor uses the effective address to control the memory. In some designs, the effective address may be formed from several different numbers.

Some instructions can tell the microprocessor to form the address of the data several ways. The various ways are called the *addressing modes* of the computer. So an addressing mode is a particular way that the microprocessor forms the effective address of a data number in memory.

The Motorola 68HC11 has six addressing modes. You will find that certain categories of instructions have a subgroup of the possible modes. Learning the instruction set so you can program the computer is simplified by first learning the addressing modes.

This section introduces a few new instructions to illustrate the addressing modes. This section also introduces all the fundamental addressing modes of the Motorola 68HC11 and gives a brief description of their uses. Later you will become aware of the tradeoffs in using various addressing modes. Only the basics are covered here; minor variations are covered later after you have some experience.

Extended Addressing

The Motorola 68HC11 uses 16-bit addresses. *Extended addressing* means that the complete 16-bit address of the data is in the instruction code. The address can be any number from 0000 through FFFF. All instructions with extended addressing have the format Figure 2-20 shows.

The name *extended* that Motorola chose for this mode has little meaning at this point. Some other companies call an identical addressing mode *absolute addressing*. Regardless of the name, the idea is that the complete address of the data is in the instruction code.

All instructions with extended addressing have two distinct parts—an op code and an address. The instruction works the same at any location in memory, so Figure 2-20 does not specify addresses for the instruction. The data number also can be anywhere in the memory; the example shows it at location C133.

Some possible locations for the instruction make no sense, but the hardware won't care and will operate correctly. For example, the op code could be at FFFF and the address

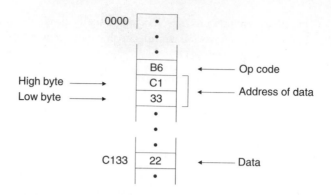
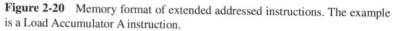

Figure 2-20 Memory format of extended addressed instructions. The example is a Load Accumulator A instruction.

part at addresses 0000 and 0001. Since FFFF is the highest possible memory address, the program counter will wrap around to zero as the instruction is fetched. Certainly this should be avoided.

Another example, although somewhat more devious, is an instruction that addresses its op code as the data number. Both examples are *very bad programming practice*, but the hardware in the computer doesn't care!

Example

The example in Figure 2-16 illustrates extended addressed instructions. Extended addressing is the simplest addressing mode, so it was used for the instructions in the first programming example.

Memory map and address range

A visual technique makes understanding the implications of the addressing modes easier. A *memory map* is a diagram of the whole possible memory that indicates uses of groups of registers. The memory map displays all the possible memory even though hardware may not be installed for all the registers. Individual registers cannot be shown, so only an outline of the memory areas is used. A memory map conveniently shows the range of registers accessible to an instruction with a certain addressing mode. Many instructions cannot access all the memory registers.

Figure 2-21 is a memory map for the extended addressing mode. It shows all the possible locations of the data accessible to a given instruction by bracketing that memory region. The number of bytes the instruction occupies and the location of the instruction are also shown. The address of the instruction is not specified to indicate that the instruction can be anywhere in the memory.

The memory map is very simple for the extended addressing mode because it can access the entire memory. Other addressing modes are more complicated because only portions of the memory can be accessed.

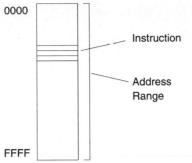

0000

Instruction

Address
Range

FFFF

Figure 2-21 Extended addressing range.

Direct Addressing

Suppose the data numbers for the example in Figure 2-16 were moved to locations 0010 through 0012. Figure 2-22 shows the new program—look carefully at the instruction codes. The address parts of all the instructions that reference memory have 00 as the most-significant byte. This leads one to think that a compromise could be made to shorten the length of the instruction. A shorter instruction would be valuable. It would both use less memory and could be fetched faster. Now we are looking at the performance aspects of the computer. Shorter and faster instructions would improve the performance or apparent speed of the computer without the greater expense of faster hardware.

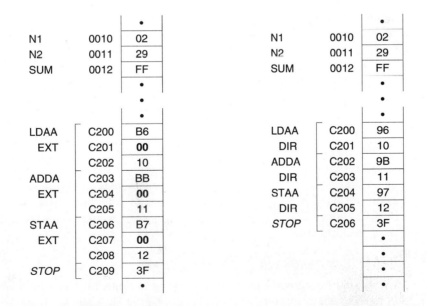

		•
N1	0010	02
N2	0011	29
SUM	0012	FF
		•
		•
		•
LDAA	C200	B6
EXT	C201	**00**
	C202	10
ADDA	C203	BB
EXT	C204	**00**
	C205	11
STAA	C206	B7
EXT	C207	**00**
	C208	12
STOP	C209	3F
		•

Figure 2-22 Modified program with data numbers at new locations.

		•
N1	0010	02
N2	0011	29
SUM	0012	FF
		•
		•
		•
LDAA	C200	96
DIR	C201	10
ADDA	C202	9B
DIR	C203	11
STAA	C204	97
DIR	C205	12
STOP	C206	3F
		•
		•
		•
		•

Figure 2-23 Program using direct addressed instructions.

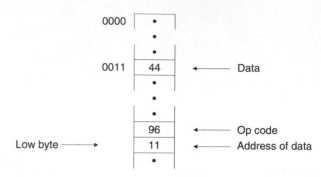

Figure 2-24   Memory format of direct addressed instructions. The example is a Load Accumulator A instruction.

Motorola made a second addressing mode called *direct addressing* to gain these advantages. In this mode, the most-significant byte of the address is 00 by default and can be left out of the instruction code. A new op code is necessary to specify this way of forming the address of the data.

Direct addressed instructions require only two bytes of memory. The first byte is an op code as it is for all instructions. The second byte is the least-significant or low byte of the address of the data. The high byte of the address of the data always defaults to 00.

Figure 2-24 shows the memory format of the direct addressed instructions. Addresses are not shown for the instruction, since it can be anywhere in memory.

Using direct addressed instructions imposes the limitation that the data numbers must be placed in the address range 0000 through and including 00FF. The benefits of this addressing mode outweigh the limitations.

Since direct addressing is very practical, most 68HC11 programs will have some data numbers in the direct addressing range. The instructions will be put elsewhere in the memory to conserve the valuable direct addressing range.

Example

Figure 2-23, shown next to Figure 2-22, shows the program to add two numbers using direct addressed instructions. Compare this program to the equivalent program using extended addressed instructions in Figure 2-22. These figures are shown side by side to make this comparison easy. You will see that the program with direct addressed instructions is three bytes shorter. The program uses less memory and requires three fewer clock ticks for fetching the instructions.

Memory pages and addressing range

The addressing range of direct addressing is limited by its 8-bit address. A 16-bit address is needed to specify the whole address range. The same limitation applies to other addressing modes where there are not enough bits for the address. The limited range of memory that can be accessed is called a *page* of memory.

Motorola Trainer

The trainer has only a limited range of memory available for your programs. Similarly, not all of the direct addressing range can be used in the trainer. See Appendix D for details.

Some people call direct addressing *zero page addressing* because the high byte of all the addresses is 00. You will even find this name in some Motorola manuals.

The memory map in Figure 2-25 shows the direct addressing range and the 2-byte instruction. You can easily visualize the page of memory. The imaginary line between locations 00FF and 0100 marks the end of the page—there is nothing physical about this line.

Direct addressing is a compromise between the size of the addressing range and speed of program execution. The range of addresses for direct addressing is only 0000 through 00FF, not the entire memory as with extended addressing. Now you can see why extended addressing has its name—its range is extended or greater than the direct addressing range.

Inherent Addressing

Some instructions operate on data in microprocessor registers only. There is no need for a memory address, so only the op code part of the instruction is necessary. Instructions requiring only an op code have *inherent addressing*. The op code specifies the operation and the internal microprocessor register or registers. Inherent addressing really designates the lack of a memory addressing mode.

The ABA instruction has inherent addressing. ABA adds the B accumulator to the A accumulator and then puts the sum into the A accumulator. The B accumulator is not changed. The mnemonic name ABA is easier to remember if you read it as *add B to A*.

Look at the instruction set table in Appendix H for more details. A memory map is not appropriate to this addressing mode.

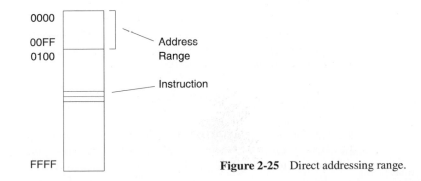

Figure 2-25   Direct addressing range.

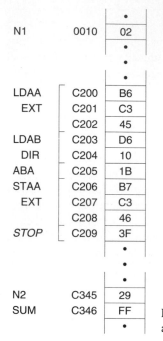

Figure 2-26   Program with inherent addressed instruction.

Example

Figure 2-26 shows a program to add two numbers using the **ABA** instruction. The logic of this program is slightly different from the version in Figure 2-23. You should see that the two accumulators hold the numbers to be added. The program puts the sum into memory and leaves the second number in the B accumulator. Leaving a number in a register at the completion of a program segment is useful in certain programming strategies.

The example also uses some instructions with extended addressing, direct addressing, and inherent addressing. This illustrates that instructions with different addressing modes may be used in the same program.

Implied addressing

The Motorola 68HC11 and many of Motorola's other products have inherent addressing. Strangely, some of Motorola's manuals call inherent addressing *implied addressing*. If you have a manual that uses the name *implied addressing*, just substitute the name *inherent*, since it is referring to the same addressing mode.

Double-byte Data

Some registers in the microprocessor hold 16-bit or double-byte numbers. Therefore, some instructions, such as a load instruction for one of these registers, must address double-byte numbers in memory.

Double-byte numbers in the Motorola 68HC11 *are always stored in two consecutive memory registers with the high byte at the lower address and the low byte at the higher address.*

This ordering convention for the bytes is called the *big-endian* convention. Some computers use the *little-endian* convention where the low byte is at the lower address and the high byte is at the higher address. Still, other computers can use either convention.

An instruction contains only the address of the first or high byte of the data. The microprocessor automatically accesses the second byte of the data at the next address. The instruction op code specifies that the data number is two bytes long. The instruction format for direct and extended addressed instructions is the same for both single- and double-byte data numbers.

A double-byte register

The programming model in Figure 2-27 includes the double-byte register called *index register X*. The instruction register will no longer be shown in the figures because its operation should now be apparent. The index register will be used to demonstrate addressing of double-byte numbers.

The purpose of the X register will be discussed later. At this point, only the functions of the load and store instructions for X will be considered. They are named LDX and STX. In spoken language, say *load X* and *store X*. The X implies an index register even though the type of register is not in the name as it is in the load accumulator instruction. An example of the LDX instruction is in the next section.

More notation

Describing the function of the LDX instruction in spoken language is simple—it loads a double-byte number from memory into the X register. In contrast, describing the function performed by the LDX instruction in precise written notation is difficult. It is difficult because the data number is two bytes long and only one of the bytes has an address in the instruction.

Here is the notation used in the instruction set table in Appendix H. It says that the operation of LDX is M:(M + 1) → X. As discussed earlier, multiple meanings of the notation are used together. The symbols to the left of the arrow designate the double-byte number that will be transferred to register X. The double-byte number is formed from two 8-bit or

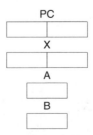

Figure 2-27   Programming model including the X Index register.

single-byte numbers that are *concatenated*—they are placed end to end. The colon indicates concatenation.

The M to the left of the colon designates the contents of the memory register that is addressed by the instruction. This use of M is the same as before. But the M on the right side of the colon designates the address, not the contents of, of the memory register specified by the instruction. On the right side of the colon, one is added to the address to form the address of the next byte higher in memory. Finally, the parentheses around the M + 1 designate the contents of that memory location. The two bytes from the two consecutive memory locations are concatenated and transferred to X. The byte at address M is put in the left half of X and the byte at address M + 1 is put in the right half.

The notation is inconsistent and confusing! Leaving out the necessary parentheses to make the notation shorter causes the problem. The address of the memory register and the contents of that memory register cannot be distinguished properly.

Figure 2-28 illustrates the LDX instruction with extended addressing. The notation M refers to the contents of location C234, which is the number 56. The notation (M + 1) refers to the contents of location C234 plus one, which is the number 78. The index register is loaded with 5678.

Immediate Addressing

To understand immediate addressing, you need the concept of a constant. A *constant* is a data number that never changes unless a new program is written. Running the program will never change the constant number. Constants may relate to physical quantities like the number π, or to data organization within the program such as table spacing.

A constant can be put inside an instruction code. The addressing mode that places a constant data number inside the instruction is called *immediate addressing*. Immediate addressed instructions do not contain an address. Figure 2-29 shows that they have an op code and a data number.

When immediate addressed instructions are fetched, the data number is fetched along with the op code. At the completion of the fetch phase, the data is immediately available. No more clock ticks are necessary to return to memory to get the data number. So immediate addressed instructions require fewer clock ticks than similar extended or direct addressed

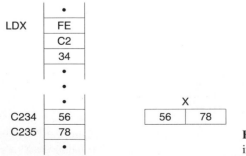

Figure 2-28 Extended addressed instruction with double-byte data.

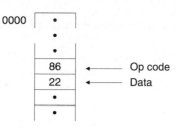

Figure 2-29 Memory format of immediate addressed instructions that have single-byte data numbers.

instructions. Also, the instruction and data numbers together require fewer bytes of memory. So even if a constant is needed many places in a program, immediate addressed instructions will be shorter and faster than equivalent instructions with other addressing modes.

Example

Figure 2-29 shows a Load Accumulator A instruction with immediate addressing that loads the single-byte number 22 into the accumulator. Figure 2-30 shows the **LDX** instruction that loads the number 1234 into the X register. The formats of both instructions should look familiar to you. There is an op code followed by an operand.

The operand for immediate addressed instructions is a data number—the data number is inside the instruction. The **LDAA** instruction has a single-byte data number because the A accumulator holds single-byte numbers. The **LDX** instruction has a double-byte data number because the X register is two bytes long. Because the notation is difficult, you should verify that the **LDX** does the operation M.(M + 1) $\rightarrow$ X.

Self modifying programs

Consider another viewpoint of the constants contained in immediate addressed instructions. Sometimes an instruction must store a number that will be used by another instruction. In this case, immediate addressing will not be useful. Here is the problem. The immediate data value could be changed only by another instruction storing the new number inside the immediate addressed instruction—a very poor programming practice in the microcomputer environment. *A program must never change instruction codes as the program runs.* Self-modifying programs are impractical and very difficult to debug. However, the computer hardware can access the data inside the immediate addressed instruction using other instructions.

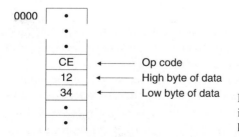
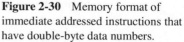

Figure 2-30 Memory format of immediate addressed instructions that have double-byte data numbers.

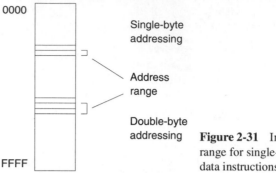

Figure 2-31 Immediate addressing range for single-byte and double-byte data instructions.

To avoid such problems within a single instruction, store instructions don't have immediate addressing. If there were such an instruction, that single instruction would make a self-modifying program—the store immediate instruction would store the data into itself! You can verify that store instructions do not have immediate addressing by scanning the instruction set table in Appendix H.

The discussion above discourages writing programs that change the data within instructions. Similarly, never write programs that modify instruction op codes as they run.

Data ownership

No other instruction can use the data number within an immediate addressed instruction. *The constant within the immediate addressed instruction is owned by that instruction and no other instruction may use it.* Good programming practice requires this viewpoint. By contrast, many different instructions usually reference the data numbers used by direct and extended addressed instructions.

Addressing range

Figure 2-31 illustrates the addressing ranges for immediate addressed instructions. The range is quite limited because it includes only the space in the instruction for data. It is interesting that the data number moves to a different location if the instruction is moved to a new location. In contrast, the data stays in fixed locations when direct or extended addressed instructions are moved to new locations.

Indexed Addressing

Indexed addressing is much more complicated than the addressing modes discussed before. Let us begin by looking at the mechanics of how indexed addressing works. A later section will explain the need for this addressing mode.

Indexed addressed instructions contain an op code and an offset byte. The instruction uses an index register in forming the effective address; that is, the address of the data. Figure 2-32 illustrates the format of these instructions using the **LDAA** instruction and the X index register.

Motorola Trainer

Single step the instruction in Figure 2-32. Use the numbers in the figure and put the instruction wherever in memory you desire. Use the RM command to put the number into the X register. A *STOP* instruction will not be necessary if you Trace only the one instruction. Also change the offset byte to some other reasonable value, such as zero, and single step the instruction again. Also try changing the number in the index register.

An indexed addressed instruction forms the effective address by adding the offset byte from the instruction to the number in the index register—the index register is unchanged. Therefore, the effective address of the data number is the sum of two numbers. The number in the index register is a double-byte number and the offset in the instruction code is a single-byte number. Both are unsigned numbers. Consequently, the lowest address for the data is the same as the number in the index register. The highest address is the number in the index register plus FF. Once again, FF is the largest unsigned number—not minus one!

The offset number inside the instruction is a constant. Changing the offset requires writing a new program that changes the instruction code. On the contrary, other instructions in the program probably will change the number in the index register.

Example

Figure 2-32 shows a way to visualize the indexed addressing mode using a specific LDAA instruction. Think of the index register X as pointing to the memory register with address C200. The index register is a *pointer* because it contains an address.

The data number is in the memory register that is offset in the higher direction by the offset distance, which is 02 for the instruction in the figure. So the instruction in the figure

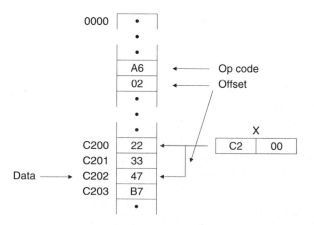

Figure 2-32 Memory format of indexed addressed instructions. The example is a Load Accumulator A instruction.

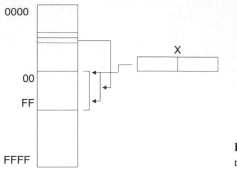

Figure 2-33 Indexed addressing range as offset varies from 00 to FF.

would load the A accumulator with the number 47, which is at address C202. The C202 is formed by adding C200 from the index register to 02 from the instruction.

The LDAA instruction does not change the number in the index register. Other indexed addressed instructions, such as LDX, will change the index register after it has been used to form the address.

Memory pages and addressing range

Indexed addressed instructions access a page of memory, since the offset in the instruction is only eight bits long. The index register determines the location of the page. The page includes those memory registers offset by 00 through FF from the address in the index register. Since the index register is 16 bits long, it can point to any address in the whole possible memory. So indexed addressed instructions can access the entire memory. Figure 2-33 illustrates the indexed addressing range as the offset varies and the number in the index register remains unchanged.

The size of the indexed addressing page is the same as the size of the direct addressing page. One viewpoint of indexed addressing is that it is direct addressing with a movable page. Both instruction formats have an op code and one byte for forming the effective address of the data.

Purpose

Here is a preview of the use of index addressing. Many programs need to change the address part of instructions as the program runs, but the instruction codes must not change. Indexed addressing requires part of the effective address to be in the index register in the microprocessor. The contents of that index register can be changed by the program. The effect of altering the index register is to alter the effective address of the instruction. The instruction code including the offset byte remains unchanged.

Relative Addressing

The 68HC11 branch instructions have only program relative addressing, and only branch instructions have program relative addressing. In the 68HC11, program relative addressing

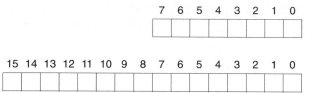

Figure 2-34   Register bit numbers.

and branch instructions go together. You must learn about branch instructions to make sense of program relative addressing—the two topics are inseparable.

The branch instructions make decisions by either altering the program flow or not altering the program flow. The decisions are two-way binary decisions. Information in the condition code register in the microprocessor determines whether a branch will occur. You must understand the condition code register to use the branch instructions correctly.

Condition code register

The 8-bit microprocessor register that holds test results is called the *condition code* register. The individual bits in this register report individual test results. Therefore, it is appropriate to examine the bits of this register one at a time. The other registers in the microprocessor are thought of as containing 8-bit or 16-bit numbers. The condition code register is used bit by bit.

Bit numbers.   The bits within a register are numbered. The numbering scheme is applicable to all registers. However, it is especially useful in discussing the condition code bits and the tests related to them. Figure 2-34 shows the bit numbers for an 8-bit register. The bits are always numbered starting with 0 at the right and continuing to the left while counting in decimal. Therefore, bit 15 is the left bit of a 16-bit register.

The origin of this numbering scheme may help you remember it. If the number in the register is a weighted number, the weights of the positions starting at the right are $2^0, 2^1, 2^2$, etc. The bit numbers are the exponents for these weights.

Bit numbers are particularly useful in verbal communications. If you speak of *bit 1* rather than the *second bit*, there will be no confusion. The second bit could be the second bit from the right or the second bit from the left.

Bit names.   The bits of the condition code register are referenced very frequently, so they have been given word names. Also, the word names are shortened to single-letter names. The instructions in a program will use the bits in the condition code register in many different ways. The word names help to identify the bits in terms of their uses.

Unfortunately, assigning name is difficult because not all the instructions use the bits the same way. A name that is appropriate to one instruction is incorrect for another instruction. However, only one name can be assigned to each bit. So don't assume too much when you learn the names of the bits. You must interpret the names according to the operation performed by the instruction you are considering.

Condition code bits.   Figure 2-35 shows the condition code register with both the bit word names and the bit letter names. Some bits in this register indicate test results while

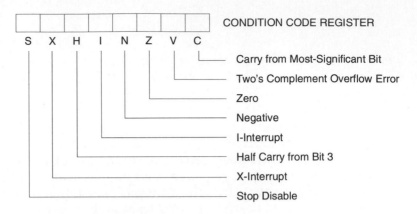

CONDITION CODE REGISTER

S   X   H   I   N   Z   V   C

Carry from Most-Significant Bit
Two's Complement Overflow Error
Zero
Negative
I-Interrupt
Half Carry from Bit 3
X-Interrupt
Stop Disable

Figure 2-35   Condition Code Register bit identifiers.

others control microprocessor hardware. The S, X, and I bits are hardware control bits that will be discussed in later sections. Ignore these three bits when considering branch instructions. The remaining five bits—H, N, Z, V, and C—indicate test results although they may not be those you expect from the bit names.

The microprocessor performs certain tests automatically each time an instruction is executed. The microprocessor does these tests without the need for instructions directing the tests. Programs ignore the test results when they are not needed. Since it takes no extra time for the microprocessor to perform the tests, they cost nothing in terms of performance.

Usually, the test is performed on the result generated by an instruction. When a test is performed, the condition tested for is either true or false. A true test result is indicated by 1 in a condition code bit, and a false test result is indicated by 0.

The names of the condition code bits fit the **ADDA** instruction best, so it will be the example. Figure 2-36 shows the addition of two binary numbers where number N1 is in the A accumulator and number N2 is in memory. The instruction puts the sum in the A accumulator.

```
        C           H
  1     1  1  1
     1  0  1  0  1  0  1  0   ←——— A = N1
 +   1  0  1  1  1  1  0  0   ←——— M = N2
     0  1  1  0  0  1  1  0   ←——— A = SUM
  N
```

x	x	1	x	0	0	1	1	Resultant CCR
S	X	H	I	N	Z	V	C	Unknown = x

Figure 2-36   Condition code bits following **ADDA** instruction execution.

The ADDA instruction affects the five condition code bits that report test results as follows:

- *C—The C bit indicates the result of testing for a carry from the most-significant or left bit.* One indicates a carry occurred; zero that no carry occurred. C is 1 in the example because there was a carry from bit 7. The C bit is not significant if the addition was done on signed numbers. However, for unsigned numbers, the carry means the sum was too big for the register.

- *V—The V bit indicates the result of testing for a two's complement overflow error.* The example had such an error because adding two negative numbers gave a positive sum. So, V is 1 in the example. For the V bit to give significant results, the numbers must be two's complement signed numbers. If your numbers are unsigned, ignore the V bit.

- *Z—The Z bit indicates the result of testing the result of the instruction for zero.* The result must contain all zero bits for Z to be 1 or true. Z is 0 in the example because the result that went to A was not zero. The Z bit confuses many people who expect it to be 0 when the result is zero.

- *N—The N bit indicates a negative result from the instruction.* In effect, it is a copy of the left bit of the result. N is 0 in the example because the sum of the numbers is positive. The N bit is only significant for two's complement numbers. If your numbers are unsigned, ignore the N bit.

- *H—The H bit indicates a carry halfway through the 8-bit number; that is, it indicates a carry from the bit 3 position.* H is 1 in the example. The H bit is generally used only with BCD numbers.

Condition code bit notation.   Not all instructions affect all the condition code bits. Some bits are not meaningful or are not affected during the execution of some instructions. Motorola uses a notation to indicate the effects an instruction has on the condition code bits. Table 2-1 lists this notation. The instruction set table in Appendix H uses the same notation.

The notation - means that the bit is unaffected by the instruction. The instruction does not change the condition code bit under any circumstance. Sometimes an instruction that controls a condition code bit is followed by an instruction that does not affect that bit. Then the next instruction after those two uses the information left in the condition code bit. Therefore, leaving the bit unaffected is useful.

TABLE 2-1   CONDITION CODE NOTATION

Symbol	Operation
-	Bit is unaffected by this instruction.
0	Bit is always cleared to 0 by this instruction.
1	Bit is always set to 1 by this instruction.
↕	Bit is set or cleared depending on instruction.

An instruction may always put a 0 or a 1 in a condition code bit. The most obvious example is an instruction designed to set a condition code bit to 1. Certainly that instruction will put a 1 into the bit.

The notation ↕ means, in informal language, *the bit works like you think it ought to work!* More formally, the bit is affected by the instruction, although you may have to interpret the result. An example is the C or carry bit test for a subtraction instruction. The subtraction cannot cause a carry, but you can extrapolate the meaning carry to the meaning borrow. Indeed, the C bit indicates whether a borrow from outside the number occurred during a subtraction. But the C bit is not given a new name when it is used with a subtract instruction—it is still called the C bit. Look at the SUBA instruction in the instruction set table in Appendix H.

Caution! People often assume they know how the condition code bits work from the name of an instruction. This is dangerous because the condition code bits are complicated and don't work as expected for all instructions. *Always use the instruction set table to determine how the condition code bits work.* Many programming errors occur because people assume too much about condition code bits.

Branch instruction format

The branch instructions make it possible for a program to make decisions. A branch instruction may alter the program flow based on the information the condition code register provides. A branch instruction is always used with another instruction that leaves test results in the condition code bits.

A branch instruction, when it branches, alters the contents of the program counter register. If it doesn't branch, the program counter is not altered and the next instruction follows immediately after the branch instruction. If the program counter is altered, the next instruction is fetched from the effective address created by the branch instruction.

The 68HC11 has many different branch instructions that respond to almost any decision to be made. A later section covers the details of the branch instructions.

The effective address.   Remember that the branch instructions have only program relative addressing which is illustrated in Figure 2-37. A program relative addressed instruction forms the effective address by adding the relative offset byte of the instruction to the program counter. The sum is put into the program counter changing the address that it contains. This addressing mode, unique to the branch instructions, is similar to indexed addressing. Relative addressing uses the program counter as a kind of index register.

The effective address of a relative addressed instruction depends on the location of the instruction in memory. The effective address formed is relative to the location of the instruction—the same instruction code will form different addresses if it is located at different places.

Here are some important details about the effective address. The effective address is formed during the execute phase of the instruction. The program counter will have been incremented during the fetch phase. The program counter already points to the next instruction before the execute phase begins. During the execute phase, the program counter may be altered. If not, the next instruction follows in order because the program counter was

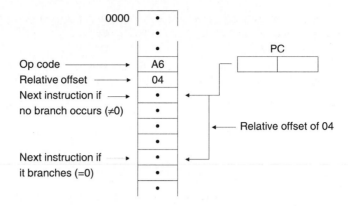

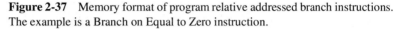

Figure 2-37   Memory format of program relative addressed branch instructions. The example is a Branch on Equal to Zero instruction.

already pointing at it. If it is altered, the relative offset byte is added to the incremented program counter.

To repeat, the program counter is not pointing at the op code of the branch instruction at the time the effective address is formed. Some manuals describe this by referring to the program counter plus a number, such as PC + 2. Don't be confused by this notation.

The BEQ instruction.   Figure 2-37 illustrates the BEQ—branch on equal to zero—instruction and program relative addressing. The BEQ instruction examines the Z bit in the condition code register to determine whether to branch. The condition of the Z bit depends on an instruction executed sometime before the BEQ. If Z = 0, the previous instruction had a result that was not zero, so the next instruction will follow the BEQ. If Z = 1, the last result was zero and the BEQ branches to the location determined by the relative offset.

Look at the BEQ in the instruction set table in Appendix H. The Boolean expression column describes only the use of the condition code bit. The ? Z = 1 means the branch occurs if this question has a true answer.

Branch instruction example

The program example in Figure 2-38 demonstrates the operation of a branch instruction. The program determines if the data number in memory location C444 is zero. If the data number is zero, the program stops at address C208. If the data number is not zero, the program stops at address C205. The program examines the data number by loading it into the A accumulator with a LDAA instruction. The LDAA makes the Z bit respond. The BEQ instruction then either does or does not branch based on the information in the Z bit.

Addressing range and pages

The relative offset byte in a branch instruction is an 8-bit *two's complement signed* number. The offset can be either positive or negative. The examples so far have positive numbers, so you could not detect that the offset is signed.

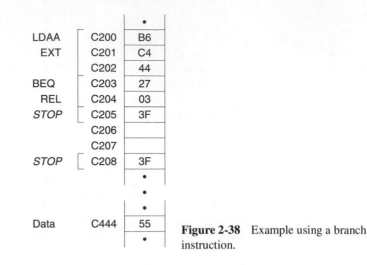

Figure 2-38   Example using a branch instruction.

The 8-bit size of the offset causes a page of memory for the addressing range of the branch instructions. The instruction reaches locations with both higher and lower addresses than that of the instruction. Adding a positive offset generates a higher address. Adding a negative offset generates a lower address.

Figure 2-39 illustrates the memory map for the program relative addressed branch instructions. The page is located with the instruction approximately in the middle—the exact numbers depend on how you count. Some people start counting at the next instruction and others start at the op code of the branch instruction.

Unconditional and long branches.   The branch instructions are called conditional branches because they branch only on the correct conditions. The 68HC11 also has some unconditional branches that don't depend on the condition code bits. One of these is the branch always—BRA—instruction that has program relative addressing. Another is the jump instruction, JMP, that also branches unconditionally, but has extended and indexed addressing. The name *jump* clearly sounds different from *branch*. This helps you remember that JMP does not have relative addressing.

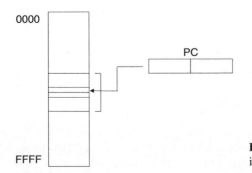

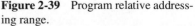

Figure 2-39   Program relative addressing range.

Motorola Trainer

Run the program in Figure 2-38 for several different data numbers including zero. Look at the address in the program counter when the program stops. Also single step the program observing the program counter and condition code register after each instruction. Single step it for both a zero and a nonzero data value. This is tedious work, but it will help you understand the microprocessor better than almost any other technique can.

The JMP can branch to any location in the whole memory. Long conditional branches to any location in memory are accomplished with two instructions, a branch and a JMP.

Relative addressing idiosyncracies

The way the effective address is formed may bother you. Think about adding the 16-bit number in the program counter to the 8-bit relative offset. The address in the program counter is an unsigned number. Addresses increase from 0000 at the low end of memory to FFFF at the high end of memory. Address FFFF is not called minus one!

The relative offset in the instruction is a two's complement signed number. So the microprocessor apparently adds a 16-bit unsigned number to an 8-bit signed number. Normally, you would not expect useful results from such an addition.

However, the microprocessor does calculate the correct effective address. For this purpose only, think of the address in the program counter as a two's complement number. This is possible because the program counter is only 16 bits long—incrementing the program counter when it contains FFFF gives 0000. Next, extend the 8-bit signed offset to a 16-bit signed offset by copying the sign bit eight times. The microprocessor gets the correct address by adding these two 16-bit numbers. Of course, the correct effective address is now interpreted as an unsigned number.

Relative addressing problems

Some effective addresses that can be formed by branch instructions are not useful. For example, a relative offset of FF or minus one is incorrect—it causes a branch to the offset part of the branch instruction. Similarly, an offset of minus two is incorrect because it makes an infinite loop when the instruction branches to itself.

Caution! Be careful to use the correct offset. Errors cause branches to incorrect locations, so errors may crash the program. The error is worse if the program doesn't crash because you may not realize that an error occurred. If you are hand coding a program, you can get the correct offset by counting from the branch instruction to the destination point. Start counting at the next register after the branch instruction with the number zero. If the destination is at a higher address, count in the positive direction. If it is at a lower address, count in the negative direction.

2.3   ADDRESSING MODE SUMMARY

The 68HC11 has six basic addressing modes. The fundamentals of these have been introduced in this chapter. A later chapter introduces some advanced instructions with more complicated addressing that is based on the fundamental modes.

The following summarizes the characteristics and uses of the six fundamental addressing modes. Figure 2-40 is a graphic presentation of the memory formats of each mode.

- *Inherent addressing*—the instruction code has only an op code without an operand such as an address. The instruction operates only on microprocessor registers.

- *Immediate addressing*—the instruction code is an op code and a constant data number. The data number is a single- or double-byte number as needed. The data value should be used only by the immediate instruction.

- *Direct addressing*—the instruction code is an op code and the low byte of the address of the data. The high byte of the address defaults to 00. The instruction can address only memory locations 0000 through 00FF. This range of memory is called the direct addressing page.

- *Extended addressing*—the instruction code is an op code and a double-byte address that can access the whole memory from address 0000 through FFFF.

- *Indexed addressing*—the instruction code is an op code and a single-byte unsigned offset. The offset is added to an index register to form the address of the data. The data is in a page extending from 00 to FF higher than the location pointed at by the index register. The double-byte index register can point to any location in the whole memory. The index register is not changed when the offset byte is added to it.

- *Relative addressing*—the instruction code is an op code and a single-byte signed relative offset. The offset is added to the program counter to alter it if the instruction branches. Program relative addressing is available only to branch instructions. The branch instruction is located approximately at the middle of the addressing page that extends to relatively higher and lower addresses.

You will find it useful to know the memory formats of the various addressing modes because it will help you visualize how a program looks in memory.

2.4   AN EXPANDED REPERTOIRE

You will now see many more instructions that have the basic addressing modes. This section covers many details in a brief discussion. It assumes that you understand the instruction formats and the addressing modes. Once you know these basic categories, you can learn more instructions very quickly. You probably will need to review these instructions several times so you can remember what instructions are available. Then you will be able to write programs using these tools.

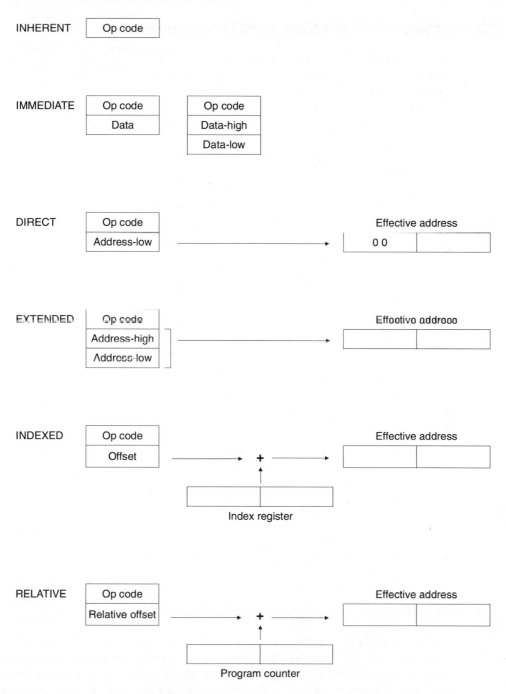

Figure 2-40 Memory formats of instructions with the six fundamental addressing modes.

Motorola 68HC11 Instruction Set

Source Form	Operation	Boolean Expression	Addr. Mode	Machine Code Op Code	Machine Code Operand	Bytes	Cycles	S	X	H	I	N	Z	V	C
•	•	•	•	•	•	•	•	•	•	•	•	•	•	•	•
ABX	Add B to X	X + 00:B → X	INH	3A		1	3	-	-	-	-	-	-	-	-
•	•	•	•	•	•	•	•	•	•	•	•	•	•	•	•
ADDA (opr)	Add Memory to A	A + M → A	A IMM	8B	ii	2	2	-	-	$\updownarrow$	-	$\updownarrow$	$\updownarrow$	$\updownarrow$	$\updownarrow$
			A DIR	9B	dd	2	3								
			A EXT	BB	hh ll	3	4								
			A IND,X	AB	ff	2	4								
			A IND,Y	18 AB	ff	3	5								
•	•	•	•	•	•	•	•	•	•	•	•	•	•	•	•
CLC	Clear Carry Bit	0 → C	INH	0C		1	2	-	-	-	-	-	-	-	0
•	•	•	•	•	•	•	•	•	•	•	•	•	•	•	•
LDX (opr)	Load Index Register X	M:(M + 1) → X	X IMM	CE	jj kk	3	3	-	-	-	-	$\updownarrow$	$\updownarrow$	0	-
			X DIR	DE	dd	2	4								

Figure 2-41   A few rows of the instruction set table.

The Instruction Set Table

You will constantly refer to the instruction set table in Appendix H. That table is the principal tool of the programmer. It documents all the programming details required to write programs. Figure 2-15 showed only some columns of the table. Figure 2-41 is a reproduction of a few lines of the complete table.

The following describes each column of the instruction set table in Figure 2-41.

- *Source Form*—lists the instruction mnemonic and specifies any operands required besides the instruction op code. The operand abbreviation designates the type of operand required as follows:

    (opr)   data or data address for an instruction that references memory

    (rel)   relative offset of program relative addressed branch instruction

- *Operation*—a very short word description of the function performed by the instruction. The description is incomplete for some instructions, so don't depend on it alone. The description for CLC, clear the carry bit, is straightforward.

- *Boolean Expression*—the detailed description of the register transfers that specify the function of the instruction. The ABX instruction adds the 16-bit number in X to 00 concatenated with the 8-bit number in the B accumulator, and then puts the sum in the X register.

- *Addressing Mode*—the first item is the microprocessor register used by the instruction when there is one, or it is blank otherwise. The second item is the memory addressing mode. Some inherent addressed instructions use two microprocessor registers. The registers can be ascertained from the instruction mnemonic and are not listed. The ABX instruction is one of these.

- *Op Code*—the instruction op code for the corresponding addressing mode. Some advanced instructions in the 68HC11 have 2-byte op codes, so there are two columns under this heading. Look at the ADDA instruction with both IND,X and IND,Y addressing in the instruction set table.

- *Operand*—the operand bytes that follow the op code. The abbreviations have the following meaning:

ii	8-bit immediate data
dd	low byte of a direct address
hh ll	high and low bytes of an extended address
ff	unsigned 8-bit offset in indexed addressed instruction
jj kk	high and low bytes of 16-bit immediate data
rr	signed 8-bit relative offset in branch instruction

- *Bytes*—the number of bytes of memory occupied by the complete instruction code. The op code and operand columns specify the bytes required, so the bytes column contains redundant information. For example, the LDX IMM has an op code and two bytes of data for a total of three bytes.

- *Cycles*—the number of E-clock cycles required by the Motorola 68HC11 to fetch and execute the instruction. Other Motorola products have some of the same instructions as the 68HC11, but the number of cycles may differ slightly. The figure shows that the ADDA EXT instruction discussed earlier requires four clock cycles.

- *Condition Codes*—specifies the operation performed on each condition code bit during the execution of the instruction. The instruction has the same effect on the condition code bits regardless of the addressing mode, so the table lists only the condition codes once for each instruction. The condition code notation from Table 2-1 is reproduced here:

-	Bit is unaffected by this instruction.
0	Bit is always cleared to 0 by this instruction.
1	Bit is always set to 1 by this instruction.
↕	Bit is set or cleared depending on instruction.

As the condition codes column shows, the CLC clears the C bit. The LDX affects the N and Z bits, clears the V bit, and does not affect the C bit. For LDX, N is a copy of bit 15 of X.

A Tour through the Basic Instructions

The following is a tour through the instruction set table in alphabetical order. A few comments and examples are included along the way. Only basic instructions that relate to the A and B accumulators, the X index register, and the condition code register are discussed in this chapter. Chapter 5 discusses the other instructions.

As you look through the instruction set table reading the following comments, you should look for inconsistency. The designers of microprocessors make compromises to simplify the hardware and reduce cost. These compromises often lead to inconsistent features in the instructions. The 68HC11 is very consistent, but not completely so. For example, some instructions will not have all the addressing modes. Similarly, an instruction will be available to operate on the A accumulator, but the parallel equivalent for the B accumulator doesn't exist.

You should find each of the following instructions in Appendix H as you proceed through this tour of the instruction set:

ABA
Add B to A. Does binary addition of the accumulators; the addition is correct for either unsigned numbers or two's complement signed numbers. The C bit is meaningless for two's complement numbers, while the V bit is meaningless for unsigned numbers. There is no parallel instruction that puts the result into the B accumulator.

ABX
Add B to X. Add B accumulator to X index register and put the answer in the X register. ABX is only useful for unsigned numbers such as addresses. Notice the condition code bits do not respond to this arithmetic operation. There is no parallel instruction to subtract B from X, nor one to add A to X.

ADCA, ADCB
Add memory with carry to accumulator. Same as the ADD instruction except it also adds the carry bit. These instructions are used for multiple precision addition of either unsigned or signed numbers.

ADDA, ADDB
Add memory to accumulator. These are the fundamental instructions for adding. The condition code bits work as their names suggest. Notice that only the 8-bit add instructions ABA, ADCA, ADCB, ADDA, and ADDB affect the H bit. Any other instruction that affects H only copies it.

BCC
Branch on carry clear. Branch if the C bit is clear (0), and don't branch otherwise. None of the branch instructions affect any of the condition code bits. The branch conditions of BCC are opposite those of the BCS instruction. Each 68HC11 branch instruction has a parallel instruction with the opposite branch condition.

BCS
Branch on carry set. Branch if the C bit is set (1), and don't branch otherwise. BCS is most often used to branch to an error routine when an unsigned number operation gives an incorrect result.

BEQ
Branch on equal to zero. Branch if the result of the previous instruction was zero; otherwise, don't branch. Notice this is not branch if the Z bit is clear (0)! Don't interpret BEQ to mean

> **Motorola Trainer**
>
> To enhance your learning, make up one or two instruction program modules using each of these instructions. Single step or trace your examples confirming all the information on the instruction set table. Try several data values to confirm the operation of the condition code bits.

branch on equal unless you are comparing two numbers. See the section on comparison branches for more discussion.

BMI
Branch on minus. Branch if the result of the previous instruction was minus or negative; otherwise, don't branch. The numbers operated on by the previous instruction must be two's complement signed numbers. Unsigned numbers can't be negative! Using the word minus instead of negative in the name of this instruction is strange. Apparently this name BMI avoids conflict with the name BNE used for another instruction.

BNE
Branch on not equal to zero. Branch if the result of the previous instruction was not equal to zero; otherwise, don't branch. Notice that the branch occurs if Z bit is clear (0). Don't interpret the mnemonic BNE as branch on not equal unless you are comparing two numbers. See the section on comparison branches for more discussion.

BPL
Branch on plus. Branch if the result of the previous instruction was plus or positive; otherwise, don't branch. The numbers operated on by the previous instruction must be two's complement signed numbers. Unsigned numbers can't be positive, because they don't have a sign bit.

BRA
Branch always. Unconditional branch or branch always. A BRA should never follow immediately after a conditional branch, because that just reverses the branch condition. Other branches are available that will do the job in one instruction.

BRN
Branch never. This instruction does nothing except waste time and space! It is effectively a 2-byte NOP instruction.

BVC
Branch on overflow clear. Branch if the V bit is clear (0), and don't branch otherwise.

BVS
Branch on overflow set. Branch if the V bit is set (1), and don't branch otherwise. BVS is most often used to branch to an error routine if a two's complement overflow error has occurred.

CBA	*Compare B to A.* Subtract the B accumulator from the A accumulator and throw the answer away! The name *compare* means that the difference from a subtraction is discarded so the accumulators are not changed. The condition code bits are affected, so this instruction will always be followed by a branch instruction that responds to the comparison. Carefully note the order of subtraction, since the opposite order gives different results.
CLC	*Clear the carry.* Clear, zero, the C bit in the condition code register.
CLR, CLRA, CLRB	*Clear memory or accumulator.* Put the number 00 into the specified register. Zero is used so frequently that an instruction was provided to create it. A LDAA IMM instruction could be used instead of CLRA, but it requires two bytes instead of one. The CLR does not have direct addressing. There are no clear instructions for any other registers.
CLV	*Clear overflow.* Clear, zero, the V bit in the condition code register.
CMPA, CMPB	*Compare accumulator to memory.* Subtract the contents of a memory register from the accumulator and discard the answer so the accumulator is unchanged. Makes the condition code bits respond. See CBA.
COM, COMA, COMB	*Complement memory or accumulator.* Complement all the bits of the specified register by changing 0s to 1s and 1s to 0s. Notice that the operation is done by a subtraction. The carry bit is always set to 1. The COM does not have direct addressing.
CPX	*Compare X to memory.* Subtract a double-byte number in memory from the X index register and discard the answer so the X register is unchanged. Makes the condition code bits respond.
DEC, DECA, DECB	*Decrement memory or accumulator.* Subtract one from the number in the specified register. Very useful because adding and subtracting onc is the essence of counting. Notice that the carry bit is unaffected—this leads to many programming errors, so be careful! The DEC does not have direct addressing—an apparent design compromise because direct addressing would be used frequently if it was available.
DEX	*Decrement X.* Subtract one from the number in the index register X. Only the Z bit is affected; however, the X register usually holds addresses so the other condition code bits are of little use. X is not a data register in the sense of an accumulator, although it is used for some limited data manipulation. Notice that this

instruction is the first one introduced in this book that gives a 16-bit arithmetic result instead of an 8-bit result.

INC, INCA, INCB — *Increment memory or accumulator.*   Add one to the number in the specified register. See DEC.

INX — *Increment X.*   Add one to the number in the index register X. See DEX.

JMP — *Jump.*   An unconditional branch to any location in memory. Does not affect any condition code bits. Does not have direct addressing.

LDAA, LDAB, LDX — *Load accumulator or index register.*   Load a number from memory into the specified register. Although a carry cannot occur, the C bit is unaffected rather than set to 0. See ADCA for an example of why this is so.

NEG, NEGA, NEGB — *Negate memory or accumulator.*   Change the sign of the two's complement number in the specified register. Changing the sign is sometimes called *taking the two's complement of a number*. Notice that the operation is done by a subtraction. Changing the sign of 00 gives the correct result 00 with V set to 0. Changing the sign of 80 gives the correct result 80 with V set to 1. The NEG does not have direct addressing.

NOP — *No op.*   Do no operation, just waste time and space. NOP is not used in final programs, but is helpful while debugging new programs. You can remove an instruction from your program without moving the remaining instructions to new locations. Just replace the undesired instruction by the correct number of NOPs.

SBA — *Subtract B from A.*   Subtract the B accumulator from the A accumulator and put the difference in the A accumulator. There is no parallel instruction to put the result into B.

SBCA, SBCB — *Subtract with carry.*   Subtract memory register and carry bit from an accumulator and put the difference in the accumulator. These instructions are used for multiple precision subtraction of either signed or unsigned numbers. See ADCA.

SEC, SEV — *Set the carry or overflow.*   Set the carry bit C or the overflow bit V to 1. Affects no other condition code bits. May be used to force a test condition to a known value.

STAA, STAB, STX — *Store accumulator or index register into memory.*   Store the contents of the specified microprocessor register into memory.

The carry bit is unaffected rather than made 0 even though a carry cannot occur. These instructions do not have immediate addressing, because it would not be useful—an IMM store would make a self-modifying program.

SUBA, SUBB   *Subtract memory from accumulator.*   Subtract the addressed memory register from the accumulator and put the difference into the accumulator. May be used to subtract either unsigned or two's complement signed numbers. A common misconception is that the two's complement signed numbers cannot be subtracted! When working with 8-bit numbers, a 1 in C indicates an error for unsigned numbers while a 1 in V indicates an error for signed numbers. The H bit is not affected by any subtraction instruction.

TAB, TBA   *Transfer A to B or B to A.*   TAB transfers or copies the A accumulator to the B accumulator, and TBA transfers B to A. After the TAB instruction is executed, both the A and B accumulators contain the number originally in A. The 68HC11 lacks an instruction to exchange accumulators A and B.

TAP   *Transfer A accumulator to condition code register.*   Transfer the A accumulator into the processor condition code register. *Caution!* Don't use this instruction unless you are an advanced programmer. It affects all the condition code register bits including those that control the hardware. The TAP may alter the hardware operation in undesirable ways.

TPA   *Transfer condition codes to A.*   The mnemonic came from "transfer the processor condition code register into the A accumulator." This instruction is rarely needed in programs because the branch instructions respond to the condition code bits adequately. There is no parallel instruction to transfer B.

TST, TSTA, TSTB   *Test memory or accumulator.*   Test the specified register and make the condition code register respond by subtracting 00. The register tested is unchanged. The TST is a convenience that is used with branch instructions. The instruction set table implies that the V and C bits don't work, but they are affected correctly.

   You now know enough instructions to starting writing useful programs in machine language. Chapter 5 will introduce a few more instructions. However, the majority of the instructions in most practical programs are included in this list.
   It will take you some effort to remember all the instructions introduced here. But as you use them to write a few programs, you will learn them easily. Since each instruction has

been designed to do a needed function, it will easily come to mind as you need that function. However, practice at writing programs is necessary.

The Comparison Branch Instructions

The branch instructions covered so far are relatively easy to understand because they involve only a single condition code bit. The comparison branches are more complex because they use two or more condition code bits to decide whether to branch. The microprocessor applies a logic relationship to the bits to determine the branch condition. Generally, you do not need to learn the relationship, because the name of the instruction tells you what the instruction does. The name of the instruction describes the relationship between two numbers that are being compared.

Branch with subtraction

All the branches discussed here require a subtraction operation immediately preceding the branch. Don't try to circumvent this requirement! If you do, the instruction may appear to work correctly for your immediate data numbers, but there are probably other numbers that lead to errors.

The reason that the subtraction is necessary is that these instructions all compare two numbers. The essence of the comparison is the subtraction. The subtraction instructions include the following: CBA, CMPA, CMPB, CPX, SBA, SUBA, and SUBB. For example, SBA subtracts the B accumulator from the A accumulator, so the A accumulator holds the minuend and the B accumulator holds the subtrahend. There are a few more subtraction instructions that will be introduced later.

As you read the descriptions of the comparison branches, think about the words *greater* and *less* versus *higher* and *lower*. Motorola was consistent in the naming conventions for the branch instructions. The consistent names will help you remember whether the instruction relates to two's complement signed numbers or unsigned numbers. The words *greater* and *less* are used with signed numbers; greater means more positive and less means less positive. The words *higher* and *lower* are used with unsigned numbers; higher means bigger and lower means smaller.

Here are the comparison branches:

BGE   *Branch if greater than or equal to.*   Causes a branch if (N is set AND V is set) OR (N is clear AND V is clear). The branch will occur if and only if the *two's complement signed* number represented by the minuend (e.g., accumulator A) was greater than or equal to the *two's complement* number represented by the subtrahend (e.g., M).

                                       Caution! Some Motorola manuals describe this instruction as *branch if greater than or equal to zero.* This name comes from applying the instruction name to the difference from the subtraction rather than the numbers being compared.

BGT

Branch if greater than. Causes a branch if (Z is clear) AND ((N is set AND V is set) OR (N is clear AND V is clear)). The branch will occur if and only if the *two's complement signed* number represented by the minuend (e.g., accumulator A) was greater than the *two's complement* number represented by the subtrahend (e.g., M).

Caution! Some Motorola manuals describe this instruction as *branch if greater than zero.* This name comes from applying the instruction name to the difference from the subtraction rather than the numbers being compared.

BHI

Branch if higher. Causes a branch if (C is clear) AND (Z is clear). The branch will occur if and only if the *unsigned* number represented by the minuend (e.g., accumulator A) was higher (bigger) than the *unsigned* number represented by the subtrahend (e.g., M).

BHS

Branch if higher or same. This is a second name for the BCC instruction. Causes a branch if (C is clear). The branch will occur if and only if the *unsigned* number represented by the minuend (e.g., accumulator A) was higher (bigger) than or equal to the *unsigned* number represented by the subtrahend (e.g., M).

BLE

Branch if less than or equal to. Causes a branch if (Z is set) OR ((N is set AND V is clear) OR (N is clear AND V is set)). The branch will occur if and only if the *two's complement signed* number represented by the minuend (e.g., accumulator A) was less than or equal to the *two's complement signed* number represented by the subtrahend (e.g., M).

Caution! Some Motorola manuals describe this instruction as *branch if less than or equal to zero.* This name comes from applying the instruction name to the difference from the subtraction rather than the numbers being compared.

BLO

Branch if lower. This is a second name for the BCS instruction. Causes a branch if (C is set). The branch will occur if and only if the *unsigned* number represented by the minuend (e.g., accumulator A) was lower (smaller) than the *unsigned* number represented by the subtrahend (e.g., M).

BLS

Branch if lower or same. Causes a branch if (C is set) OR (Z is set). The branch will occur if and only if the *unsigned* number represented by the minuend (e.g., accumulator A) was lower (smaller) than or equal to the *unsigned* number represented by the subtrahend (e.g., M).

BLT   *Branch if less than.*   Causes a branch if (N is set AND V is
                                   clear) OR (N is clear AND V is set). The branch will occur if
                                   and only if the *two's complement signed* number represented by
                                   the minuend (e.g., accumulator A) was less than the *two's com-
                                   plement signed* number represented by the subtrahend
                                   (e.g., M).

                                   Caution! Some Motorola manuals describe this instruction as
                                   branch if less than zero. This name comes from applying the in-
                                   struction name to the difference from the subtraction rather than
                                   the numbers being compared. The BLT instruction is not equiva-
                                   lent to the BMI instruction!

   Do not be concerned by two's complement overflow errors that occur during the subtraction that precedes the branch instruction. The branch instructions will correctly account
for the information in the V bit. To emphasize this point, you should demonstrate to yourself
that a subtraction of two's complement numbers followed by the BGT instruction does not
perform the same function as the subtraction followed by BPL. The numbers that cause two's
complement overflows will not work correctly with BPL.

Using BEQ and BNE for comparisons

   The instructions BEQ and BNE can compare two numbers to see if they are equal or
unequal. These instructions were used earlier to test if one number was zero or not zero. If
they are to do a comparison, they must be preceded by a subtraction operation just like the
other comparison branches. But now the meaning of the instruction will be interpreted as
follows:

BEQ   *Branch on equal.*   Causes a branch if (Z is set). The branch
                                   will occur if and only if the number represented by the minuend
                                   (e.g., accumulator A) was equal to the number represented by
                                   the subtrahend (e.g., M). The two numbers may both be two's
                                   complement signed numbers or they may both be unsigned
                                   numbers.

BNE   *Branch on not equal.*   Causes a branch if (Z is clear). The
                                   branch will occur if and only if the number represented by the
                                   minuend (e.g., accumulator A) was equal to the number repre-
                                   sented by the subtrahend (e.g., M). The two numbers may both
                                   be two's complement signed numbers or they may both be un-
                                   signed numbers.

   The BEQ and BNE instructions cause some confusion because they are used two different ways. To complicate matters, some Motorola manuals describe BEQ as *branch on
equal to zero* and others describe it as *branch on equal* without distinguishing the two different uses.

Applications of Complex Instructions

Many instructions were designed for specific applications. After you have some programming experience, the need for these specialized instructions is obvious. Therefore, the following programming examples demonstrate the uses of some of these instructions.

Multiple precision arithmetic

A program that does multiple precision addition requires the ADCA instruction. The
68HC11 instructions you have seen operate on 8-bit numbers. When larger numbers are
needed, they will be made up of 8-bit single-precision pieces because it is easier that way.
The example program that follows adds two double-precision or double-byte numbers from
memory and stores the double-byte sum in memory. The same technique as used in the
example applies to larger numbers.

Figure 2-42 will help you visualize the algorithm for the example. The numbers all
reside in 8-bit registers, so the figure shows sample 8-bit numbers. The registers are arranged
to appear as if 16-bit numbers are being added. In the figure, the numbers 44 and C1 are
added to obtain 05 and a carry from bit 7. Then the carry, the 82 and the A3 are added to
obtain the sum 26 and a carry.

The program example.   Figure 2-43 shows the program for the double-precision
addition. The LDAB, ADDB, and STAB instructions add the least-significant eight bits. The
STAB instruction does not affect the C bit so the carry information generated by the ADDB
is not lost.

Next, the most-significant eight bits of the numbers and the carry from the least-significant bits are added. Accounting for the carry could be done by branching on carry set to
a program module that adds one, but it's much easier to use the ADCA instruction. The ADCA
adds two 8-bit numbers and the C bit. This one instruction does the job if the carry information is correct.

When the ADCA adds the most-significant eight bits, the N, Z, V, and C bits are affected. The information in these bits describes the 16-bit result. The C bit indicates whether
there was an addition error if unsigned numbers are used. The V bit indicates whether there
was an addition error for two's complement signed numbers. Similarly, the N and Z bits
refer to the 16-bit sum. So a branch instruction that follows this addition correctly responds
to the 16-bit operation.

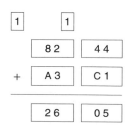

Figure 2-42   Adding two double-precision numbers.

		•
N1	0010	82
	0011	44
N2	0012	A3
	0013	C1
SUM	0014	FF
	0015	FF
		•
		•
		•
LDAB	C200	D6
DIR	C201	11
ADDB	C202	DB
DIR	C203	13
STAB	C204	D7
DIR	C205	15
LDAA	C206	96
DIR	C207	10
ADCA	C208	99
DIR	C209	12
STAA	C20A	97
DIR	C20B	14
		•

Figure 2-43   Double-precision add program module.

Multiple branch conditions

Many programs require multiple decisions. Figure 2-44 illustrates the testing of a two's complement signed number to see if it is negative, zero, or nonzero positive. Remember that zero is positive in the two's complement number system. Be careful to distinguish zero from nonzero positive numbers. This example additionally shows that the branch instructions do not affect the condition code bits for good reasons.

		•
TST	C200	7D
EXT	C201	C5
	C202	55
BEQ	C203	27
REL	C204	03
BPL	C205	2A
REL	C206	02
STOP	C207	3F
STOP	C208	3F
STOP	C209	3F
		•

Figure 2-44   Program module with multiple branch paths for negative, zero, and nonzero positive numbers.

Motorola Trainer

You should thoroughly test the program in Figure 2-43 using the trainer. Single step the program and observe the use of the C bit. Then modify the program to do double-precision subtraction. Also add a branch instruction and two *STOP* instructions to make it compare two double-precision numbers.

The program uses a TST instruction to set the N and Z bits in the condition code register. These bits provide the information needed for the decisions. The BEQ instruction branches to the routine that handles the zero case; the routine is just a *STOP* instruction in the figure. Since the BEQ does not affect the condition code bits, the BPL uses the same condition code results for a second branch. If the BPL does not branch, the number tested must have been negative and a separate test for negative is unnecessary. The example program stops at address C207 for a negative number, at address C208 for a zero number, and at address C209 for a nonzero positive number.

Double-precision Instructions

The 68HC11 has a few instructions that operate on double-byte numbers in a general way. All these instructions require a double-byte accumulator. To accommodate this need, the A and B accumulators are used together as a single 16-bit accumulator called the *D accumulator*. The programming model in Figure 2-1 illustrates the D accumulator with the A accumulator on the left and the B accumulator on the right. The A accumulator holds the most-significant byte and the B accumulator holds the least-significant byte of the double-byte number in D. The D accumulator is not an additional register, but only a different way of using the A and B registers. For example, bit 15 of the D accumulator is bit 7 of the A accumulator. The basic instructions that use the D accumulator are as follows:

ADDD   *Add memory to D.*   Add a double-byte number from memory to the D accumulator.

LDD   *Load accumulator D.*   Load a double-byte number from memory into the D accumulator. Notice that the name is not LDAD.

STD   *Store accumulator D.*   Store a double-byte number from the D accumulator into memory. Notice that the name is not STAD.

SUBD   *Subtract memory from D.*   Subtract a double-byte number in memory from the D accumulator.

All instructions that use the D accumulator make the condition code bits respond to a 16-bit number. The number is always the result obtained from the execution of the instruction. The branch instructions may be used following the double-precision instructions. For example, two two's complement signed 16-bit numbers can be compared using the instruction sequence LDD, SUBD, and BGT.

2.5   MACHINE LANGUAGE PROGRAMMING EXAMPLE

You now have enough background to write a program that does a significant job. This section discusses a program that brings together many instructions, addressing modes, programming techniques, and other concepts. The program will be very small, but it should make you think about how good programs should be written.

Minimum Requirements of a Good Program

You should think about the characteristics that are desirable in a good program. This is easier to do if you have had some programming experience regardless of the kind of computer or language used. The ideas considered here are most basic.

- *The program must do the same thing every time it is run.* There should be no need to reenter any data or instructions to run the program again. It must perform the same function on the same data producing the same results every time.

- *The program must not modify itself.* That is, the instructions cannot be changed by the program. A program that changes itself and then returns itself to the original state before finishing is also unacceptable. Programs that don't change themselves are called *pure procedure* programs.

- *The program must work correctly for all reasonable data values.* For example, a valid data value of zero is often overlooked in program design.

- *The instructions and data numbers should be separated in memory.* Any data that must be entered to run the program or data values that change while the program runs must be separated from the instructions. They should not be mixed in one area of memory so the instructions have to branch over data values. The two areas in memory are called the *program section* and the *data section*.

- *The program should adapt easily to different sets of data.* For example, a program that works on a table of numbers must easily adapt to tables at any reasonable location and of any reasonable length. Writing a new program for each table is not practical.

- *The program should start at the first instruction and stop at the last instruction.* Programs that are scattered around in memory are difficult to understand.

Many more considerations are involved in writing sophisticated programs. The ideas presented here provide a good starting point for the first significant program. Chapter 4 presents more information on good programming practices.

A Classic Example: Copy a Table

A table or list is a series of data numbers grouped together in memory. For example, a manufacturing facility may have many identical automated manufacturing machines. The computer could monitor the number of parts each machine makes by counting the parts as they exit the machine. Each number in a table may represent the number of parts manufactured by a different machine. All the data numbers together represent the production of the manufacturing facility. Microcomputer programs for control and data acquisition applications frequently use tables.

Let's look at a practical and useful program that copies a table of numbers from one place in memory to another. The goal is to have two copies of the same data numbers. For example, these two tables may be used in a machine-monitoring application. The first table may represent production counts for the last hour. At the end of an hour, a copy is made to be used by a report program that prints the data, and the entries in the first table are set to zero. While the printer is printing the data from the second table, the first table is updated with new production data.

Assume that the number of numbers in the tables will be small so the length of the table can be represented by a single-byte number. Similarly, assume that the entries in the tables are single-byte numbers. Figure 2-45 illustrates what the program should do to tables of four entries.

A brainstorming session

The copy-a-table program could be written many different ways. Let's begin with a brainstorming session to evaluate various approaches.

Copy-a-table instruction.   You could browse through the instruction set table until you find an instruction that copies a table! Then the program would consist of that one instruction. Of course, you are not surprised that the 68HC11 does not have such an instruction, although there are microprocessors that do. One reason you would not expect to find such an instruction is that it would at least require two addresses. One address would specify

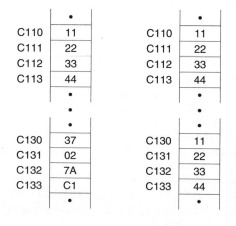

Figure 2-45   Memory contents before (left) and after (right) running the copy-a-table program. The source table is at address C110 and the destination table at address C130.

the location of the first table, and the second address the location of the second table. All the instructions you have seen only have one address. So it is unlikely that such an instruction exists and it doesn't.

Copy a memory byte.   The next approach you may consider is an instruction that copies one number from one memory register to another. This instruction could be used repeatedly to copy the entire table. The 68HC11 does not have this instruction either, for it too would require two addresses. However, more sophisticated microprocessors do have such instructions.

Load and store.   A simpler and practical approach is to use the LDAA and STAA instructions. The LDAA can get a data number from the first table, and the STAA can store it into the second table. It will require the execution of two instructions to move each data number, but the job can be done. Figure 2-46 shows part of a program to copy the table shown in Figure 2-45 using this approach.

Let's evaluate the program. Certainly, the program is very simple and easy to understand. The program also will run very quickly because it does nothing more than the required operations. It also meets most of the minimum requirements discussed earlier. However, it is not very easy to adapt it to different tables. The program must be rewritten if any change, such as length or location, is made to the tables. Also, the length of the program will be unacceptable for long tables. This approach is not very good as a general solution.

A loop.   The next approach uses the LDAA and STAA instructions, but requires that the same two instructions be executed repeatedly once for each entry in the table. Repeating or iterative programs are called *loops*. A loop does its function and then branches back to use the same instructions over and over. In the copy a table program, the loop will copy one table entry each time around the loop. When all the entries have been copied, the program will break out of the loop and stop.

•	•	•
LDAA	C010	B6
EXT	C011	C1
	C012	10
STAA	C013	B7
EXT	C014	C1
	C015	30
LDAA	C016	B6
EXT	C017	C1
	C018	11
STAA	C019	B7
EXT	C01A	C1
	C01B	31
LDAA	C01C	B6
•	•	•

Figure 2-46   Part of a copy-a-table program using LDAA and STAA.

One problem here is that the LDAA and STAA instructions that do the copying contain addresses. The addresses must change each time around the loop or the same entry would be copied each time. That is, the same instructions must copy a different entry each time around the loop. To meet the requirement that the instructions don't change due to program execution, the LDAA and STAA instructions must have indexed addressing. Indexed addressing makes it possible for a program to modify the effective address of an instruction without modifying the instruction code. Indexed addressing makes it possible to write practical looping programs for the 68HC11.

A basic looping program

A looping copy-a-table program has several distinct parts. The parts include a means of keeping track of the next entry to be copied and a means to stop looping when all the entries have been copied. The looping program will be much more complex than the in-line program in Figure 2-46. It also will run much slower, but it will be better in almost every other way.

The pointer.   The index register X will be used to point to the table entry to be copied. It does this by holding the address of the entry in the first table that will be picked up by the program. It also will be used to determine where to store the entry into the second table. As the program copies individual entries, the pointer will be adjusted forward one location each time around the loop.

But the pointer must point at the first location of the first table as the loop begins running the first time. The pointer, the X register, must be initialized to contain this address before the loop starts.

Pointers must always be initialized before they can be used by the program loop. The initialization must be done by the program—not by a person entering a number every time the program is to be run.

The counter.   The loop in the program will repeatedly copy table entries, but it must stop looping when all the entries are copied. The program can do this simply by counting the entries as they are copied. When the number of entries that have been copied equals the length of the table, the loop can exit.

A number called a *counter* will be put into a register before the loop starts. The counter will be tested and adjusted each time around the loop. When the number in the counter reaches a limit, the loop will exit.

The counter can be in any appropriate register. The two basic choices are an accumulator and a memory register. Generally, you have two accumulators and thousands of memory registers, so the memory register is the most common choice. Using a memory register as a counter is easy, since most computers, including the 68HC11, have instructions to increment or decrement a memory register.

A counter must always be initialized before it can be used by a loop. The program must do the initialization; you cannot expect a person to enter a value each time.

The counting method.   Now consider some ways the program could use the counter register. For example, the table in Figure 2-47 has four entries shown. The counter could be initialized to negative four, the program could add plus two each time around the loop, and then stop at a limit of plus four. The counter could be initialized to an unsigned seven and decremented by one to the limit of three. Similarly, the counter could be initialized to an unsigned four and decremented to zero. There are many other ways to count from a starting point to an ending point. However, some ways to use the counter are better than others.

In choosing a counting method, you probably will choose to use an unsigned number in the counter. A signed number doesn't add anything useful over an unsigned number, but it does make the numbers more difficult to read and interpret. Also the range of possible numbers is twice as great if an unsigned number with the same number of bits is used. In addition, a negative counter value doesn't have any obvious physical meaning.

Next, in choosing the counting method, you probably will choose to start the counter at the number of table entries, and then count to zero by ones. It is very easy to detect if a number is zero because the computer hardware automatically detects zero and indicates it with the Z bit. Testing for any other value requires more instructions and more complication. Likewise, it is easy to subtract one from a number because the hardware has a decrement instruction. So counting will not be done by twos or any other number besides one. All microprocessors have decrementing and zero testing capabilities because they are essential to counting.

Furthermore, decrementing an unsigned number by ones makes the number in the counter equal to the number of loops yet to go. When you test the program, this makes interpreting the number in the counter easy.

The code.   Figure 2-48 lists the instructions for a program that copies a table using a loop. The operation and design of the program should be studied carefully. The program has some design problems that can be overcome, but then the program would be somewhat longer. The next section discusses these design deficiencies.

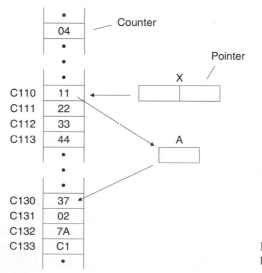

Figure 2-47   Pointer and counter used by copy-a-table loop.

Address	Contents	Instruction	Description
•	•	•	•
0030	C1		Address of first table
0031	10		
0032	04		Table length
0033	xx		Working counter
•	•	•	•
•	•	•	•
C010	DE	LDX DIR	Initialize pointer to first table
C011	30		
C012	96	LDAA DIR	Get initial counter value
C013	32		
C014	97	STAA DIR	Store initial counter value into working counter
C015	33		
C016	27	BEQ REL	Branch to *STOP* if working counter equals zero
C017	0A		
C018	A6	LDAA IND,X	Get next entry from first table
C019	00		
C01A	A7	STAA IND,X	Put entry into second table
C01B	20		
C01C	08	INX	Advance pointer to the next entry
C01D	7A	DEC EXT	Count down the working counter
C01E	00		
C01F	33		
C020	20	BRA REL	Go around again
C021	F4		
C022	3F	*STOP*	Stop the program
•	•	•	•

Figure 2-48   Copy-a-table program.

The data section of the program was put at addresses 0030 through 0033 so it would be in the direct addressing range. This decision leads to good program design that uses the capabilities of the addressing modes well. The program section includes locations C010 through C022. The only consideration in choosing these addresses was to put the program outside the direct addressing range to allow easy program expansion. If more data locations are needed in the direct addressing range when the program is changed, the instructions will not have to be moved.

Here is a step-by-step discussion of the program. Look at the instructions and comments in Figure 2-48 as you read the following:

- *Initialize the pointer.* The LDX instruction at address C010 loads the pointer, the X index register, with the address of the first entry of the first table. The double-byte address is supplied by the data section at locations 0030 and 0031. You can see that the first table is at address C110 because that is the number loaded into X.

- *Initialize the counter.* Since the counter will change as the program runs and will be zero when the program stops, it must be initialized at the beginning of the program. If it were not initialized, the program would copy zero entries the next time it runs. The program must do the initialization. The data section holds the initial value of the counter, the table length, that must be copied to a working counter. The working counter will change as the program runs, but the initial value will not. The LDAA instruction at address C012 gets the initial counter value, 04, and the STAA instruction at address C014 puts it into the working counter. So the example will copy four numbers. Notice that an instruction to copy one number from one memory location to another would be useful here.

- *Break out of the loop if all the entries have been copied.* It is not intuitive to consider breaking out of the loop at this point. Though hindsight is required, consider using the BEQ instruction that branches on equal to zero. The BEQ at address C016 uses the Z bit to determine its actions. The STAA instruction that precedes the BEQ stored a number into the working counter and made the Z bit respond. Check the instruction set table to confirm that STAA affects the Z bit. Since the working counter controls the exit from the loop, this appears correct so far. For example, if the data section said the length of the table was zero entries, the loop would correctly exit before doing anything. If the number of entries is not zero, the program continues in sequence. The relative offset in the branch cannot be determined until the program is completed, because it is doing a forward reference. That is, the instruction must branch to a location farther ahead in memory.

- *Copy one entry.* The LDAA and STAA instructions with indexed by X addressing at addresses C018 and C01A copy the entry. The LDAA gets the entry from the first table into the A accumulator using the X register with an offset of zero as the pointer. The STAA puts the entry into the second table using the X register with an offset of 20 as the pointer. The offset of 20 determines the location of the second table; namely, address C130. The effect of the offset 20 is to allow the X register to point to both tables. A later section discusses the many limitations of this approach. The approach was chosen for this example both to make it simple and to demonstrate some problems.

- *Advance the pointer to the next entry.* The loop must be prepared for the next time around. When it runs again, it must copy the next entry, not the first entry again. So, the pointer must be adjusted by incrementing X with the INX instruction at address C01C. The effect is to advance the pointers to both tables. Notice that the INX must follow the copying of an entry so the initial value in the pointer is the first address of the table. It would be confusing to set the initial address of the table to one lower address and put the INX before the copy.

- *Count off one entry copied.* The working loop counter is decremented by the DEC at address C01D. The Z bit is affected by the DEC instruction, so the Z bit indicates whether the working counter has reached zero. Notice that the DEC instruction that

---

Motorola Trainer

The program in Figure 2-48 should be tested thoroughly using the trainer. Single step the program using the given table for data. Examine the A, X, and Condition Code registers, memory register 0033, and the destination table registers after each step.

---

is used has extended addressing because the DEC instruction cannot have direct addressing.

- *Go around again.* The end of the loop sends control back to the beginning of the loop to test the working counter. Notice that the BRA instruction at address C020 does not affect the condition code bits. After branching back to the BEQ, the Z bit still contains the information from the DEC instruction. The DEC decremented the working counter, so the BEQ will respond to the correct information. Also notice the negative relative offset in the BRA that causes a branch to a lower address. A JMP instruction could be used instead of the BRA, but the BRA is shorter and faster. Since most loops are short, the BRA is almost always used.

- *Stop the program.* The *STOP* instruction at address C022 is reached by the BEQ after the loop is completed.

This program is much more complicated than the one in Figure 2-46. It will run several times slower. Besides copying an entry, it also must adjust a pointer and a counter, test the counter, and loop back.

A slower and complicated program may be considered a disadvantage. In contrast, this program is much better if the table is large, if the table must be moved to different locations, or if the table length is changed. Each of these modifications can be done by relatively minor changes. For practical applications, this program would be far better than the one in Figure 2-46.

Limitations and problems

The copy a table program in Figure 2-48 has many limitations and a major design error. Here are some comments about the program:

- *Location of tables.* The tables may be located anywhere in memory provided the second table starts at an address 20 locations higher than the start of the first table. Changing this spacing between the tables requires changing the offset of the STAA IND,X instruction—the program must be changed! Also, the range of spacings is 00 through FF, which is not a very large range; this range also limits the length of the tables. A long table with a small spacing will cause the second table to overlap the first table. Similarly, the second table must always be at a higher address than the first table because the offset of the STAA IND,X is an unsigned number.

- *Size of the tables.* The maximum length of the tables is FF entries because the working counter is a single-byte number. The minimum table size is zero. Setting the size to zero in effect disables the program from working. This may be useful during the debugging stage, especially if the copy a table program is a small module of a larger program.

- *Insignificant changes in the program will make it malfunction.* The order of the program parts is very dependent on the programming approach. For example, if the pointer was advanced after decrementing the working counter, the program would no longer work. The problem is the dependence of the BEQ instruction on the Z bit condition left by the DEC instruction. Similarly, if the pointer was initialized after the initialization of the working counter, the BEQ would not work correctly for the same reason. Both defects could be remedied by putting a TST instruction immediately before the BEQ to test the working counter. Then the other parts could be arranged in any order without problems. The program would be a better program.

- *Some data is in the program section instead of the data section.* This is a serious conceptual as well as practical problem. The offset 20 in the STAA IND,X instruction determines the spacing between the tables. The number 20 is a data number that should be put in the data section and then used as a data number. Changing the table spacing in the current program requires that the program be rewritten. There are several ways to change the program to correct this problem, but all require a more complex program design.

You should always examine your programs for the kinds of details discussed here. It is easier to correct such defects as a program is written than to change it at a later time. In particular, you should ask yourself what changes are likely to be made to the program some time in the future. Plan ahead for these changes.

An improved program

The program in Figure 2-49 is an improvement over the program in Figure 2-48. It removes the most serious limitation—the data is now all in the data section. Also, the spacing between the tables can be changed without writing a new program. The spacing is now a data value stored in the data section of the program.

Here are some observations about the new program:

- Both the data section and the program section were moved to new locations to encourage you to investigate the changes in the instructions that are necessary.

- The order of the program parts was changed.

- The working counter is tested before the branch instruction so further changes will have no consequence on the BEQ instruction.

- The pointer to the first table must be saved and restored each time around the loop.

Address	Contents	Instruction		Description
•	•	•		•
0020	C2			Address of first table
0021	20			
0022	20			Spacing between tables
0023	04			Table length
0024	xx			Working counter
0025	xx			Save pointer
0026	xx			
•	•	•		•
C100	DE	LDX	DIR	Get address of first table
C101	20			
C102	DF	STX	DIR	Store in save pointer location
C103	25			
C104	96	LDAA	DIR	Get initial counter value
C105	23			
C106	97	STAA	DIR	Store initial counter value into working counter
C107	24			
C108	D6	LDAB	DIR	Get table spacing
C109	22			
C10A	7D	TST	EXT	Test working counter
C10B	00			
C10C	24			
C10D	27	BEQ	REL	Branch to *STOP* if working counter equals zero
C10E	11			
C10F	DE	LDX	DIR	Restore pointer to first table
C110	25			
C111	A6	LDAA	IND,X	Get next entry from first table
C112	00			
C113	3A	ABX	INH	Adjust pointer to second table
C114	A7	STAA	IND,X	Put entry into second table
C115	00			
C116	7A	DEC	EXT	Count down the working counter
C117	00			
C118	24			
C119	DE	LDX	DIR	Get pointer value
C11A	25			
C11B	08	INX		Advance pointer to the next table entry
C11C	DF	STX	DIR	Store in save pointer location
C11D	25			
C11E	20	BRA	REL	Go around again
C11F	EA			
C120	3F	*STOP*		Stop the program

Figure 2-49   An improved copy-a-table program.

The limitations that remain all involve restrictions of instruction addressing modes or the size of the numbers. For example, the maximum spacing between the tables is still FF.

You should trace the operation of this improved program and investigate the limitations that remain.

2.6   REVIEW

You have now seen all the fundamental addressing modes and a subset of the 68HC11 instructions. You have also seen machine language programming where the binary instruction codes are found in the instruction set table and then put into memory.

Programming in machine language is, at least, very tedious. A computer system and an assembler program can help you program by providing the binary numbers. The program will do the work of looking in the instruction set table. The next chapter discusses assemblers and assembly language programming.

2.7   EXERCISES

2-1. Rewrite the program in Figure 2-16 to add three numbers together. The first instruction must be kept at the same address; this means that the data numbers must be moved. The problems that result from this move are common to all computer programming.

2-2. Rewrite the program in Figure 2-16 so the instructions are moved to address C400 but the data numbers remain at the same locations.

2-3. Trace the execution of the program in Figure 2-26 by writing down the contents of the program counter, instruction register, A and B accumulators, and memory register C346 after each instruction is executed.

2-4. Find the values in the H, N, Z, V, and C bits after each instruction in Figure 2-26 is executed.

2-5. Modify the program in Figure 2-26 to add three numbers together. Experiment with different addressing modes and programming approaches.

2-6. What is the machine code for a single instruction that puts zero in memory location C234?

2-7. The BLE instruction is normally used with (signed, unsigned, BCD, other) numbers.

2-8. If a positive number is subtracted from a negative number, the V bit will be 1 if the answer is (positive, negative, other).

2-9. Find all the known condition code bits if an INC instruction operates on the hexadecimal number 7F.

2-10. Find all the known condition code bits if a NEG instruction operates on the hexadecimal number 80 or the number 00.

2-11. List all the branch instructions that must follow a subtraction operation under normal circumstances.

2-12. Under what condition does the BGT instruction branch if it immediately follows a TST instruction?

2-13. Write a program module to exchange the numbers in the A and B accumulators.

2-14. Which instructions set the C bit when a borrow to bit 7 occurs?

2-15. What do the branch instructions do to the condition code bits? Why is this so?

2-16. Compare the meaning of the C and V bits after a subtraction instruction has been executed.

2-17. How does subtracting two two's complement numbers compare to changing the sign of the subtrahend and adding? Do you get the same results in the condition code bits?

2-18. Are the condition codes the same if one is added to the A accumulator with the ADDA instruction versus the INCA instruction?

2-19. If you wanted to branch on the sign of a number in memory, is it better to use LDAA or TST followed by the branch instruction?

2-20. Compare the BHS instruction to the BCC instruction.

2-21. Compare the BLO instruction to the BCS instruction.

2-22. List all the instructions that do addition of any kind.

2-23. List all the instructions that do subtraction of any kind.

2-24. List those instructions that were designed specifically for use with two's complement numbers.

2-25. List all the instructions that have inherent addressing.

2-26. List all the instructions that have direct addressing.

2-27. List all the instructions that have extended addressing but do not have direct addressing.

2-28. Do you get the same results from the NEG instruction as from COM followed by INC?

2-29. Write a program module to increment a double-byte number in the A (high byte) and B (low byte) accumulators.

2-30. Modify the program in Figure 2-43 to subtract two unsigned triple precision numbers. Use the SBCA instruction. Your program must stop at one location if the difference obtained was correct, and at another if incorrect.

2-31. Modify the program in Figure 2-43 to subtract two two's complement double-precision numbers. Use the SBCA instruction. Your program must stop at one location if the subtraction was correct, and at another if incorrect.

2-32. Modify the program in Figure 2-44 to accomplish the same goal with the branch instructions in a different order—put the BPL first. Repeat this exercise with a BMI as the first instruction.

2-33. Modify the program in Figure 2-48 to use the B accumulator as the working counter.

2-34. Consider the program in Figure 2-48. What advantage, if any, is there to copying the table starting at the highest address and working to the lowest address?

2-35. Why didn't the program in Figure 2-48 use direct addressing for the DEC instruction?

2-36. In Figure 2-48, would it make any difference if the LDX DIR instruction were moved to immediately after the STAA DIR instruction?

2-37. Discuss the use of indexed addressing for the LDX instruction that is the first instruction in the program in Figure 2-48.

2-38. What is the length in bytes of the longest table that the program in Figure 2-48 can correctly copy?

2-39. Modify the program in Figure 2-48 by adding a TST instruction immediately before the BEQ instruction.

2-40. Modify the program in Figure 2-48 by moving the DEC instruction ahead of the INX instruction instead of after it, and then make any other necessary changes.

2-41. Modify the program in Figure 2-48 so the table locations are specified by the addresses of their first entries. Then the tables can be anywhere in memory. The data section will contain the addresses of the two tables and the single-byte length of the tables. Use only instructions introduced in this chapter.

2-42. Assume the program in Figure 2-48 is run using the four entry tables in Figure 2-47. After the program stops, find the numbers in the following registers: A, B, X, memory locations 0033 and C133. Assuming the *STOP* instruction does not change the condition codes, what will the values in H, N, Z, V, and C be?

2-43. Consider the program in Figure 2-49. What is the maximum possible spacing from the beginning of the first table to the beginning of the second table?

2-44. Modify the program in Figure 2-49 so the tables contain double-byte numbers. Use only instructions introduced in this chapter.

2-45. Modify the program in Figure 2-49 so it compares two tables and indicates if they are identical. The program must put FF for true or 00 for false in memory location 0010.

2-46. Modify the program in Figure 2-49 so it sums all the negative single-byte numbers in a table and puts the double-byte sum at location 0030.

2-47. Modify the program in Figure 2-49 so it adds one to all the nonzero positive numbers in a table. If a two's complement overflow occurs, the program should set that entry to FF.

2-48. An unsigned minuend is in the B accumulator and an unsigned subtrahend is in the A accumulator. Will the instruction sequence SBA, NEGA put the correct difference in the A accumulator?

Chapter 3

Assemblers and Assembly Language

When writing machine language programs, you must continually refer to the instruction set table to find the instruction codes. The process is quite tedious and mechanical. You first decide what instruction you want and what addressing mode is appropriate. Then you follow the Source Form column in alphabetical order until you find the mnemonic name of the desired instruction. Next you look down the Addressing Mode column to find the row for your desired addressing mode. Now look across the row and finally you have the op code. If you don't remember the operand format, you continue horizontally across the row to find the format. At this point, you probably write the op code on paper and add the required operand. After doing this for all the instructions in your program, you enter the codes into the memory of your computer with some appropriate hardware.

After you perform these steps a few times, you will decide that this work is boring and quite routine. It is a job best done by a computer! This leads us to the idea of assembly language and assemblers.

Assembly language is a symbolic representation of the instructions and data numbers in a program. A program called an *assembler* translates the symbols to binary numbers that can be loaded into the computer memory. The name *assembly language* apparently comes from the operation of the assembler program. The assembler puts together or assembles the

115

Motorola Products

All the material in this chapter applies to the Motorola 6800, 6801, 6802, 6803, 6808, and 68701 chips as well as the 68HC11.

---

complete instruction code from the op code and operand. This chapter discusses the Motorola assembly language for the 68HC11 and the basic operation of an assembler.

The material in this chapter applies to any vendor's assembler that uses Motorola 68HC11 assembly language. When you purchase an assembler, be careful to determine if the assembler is compatible with standard Motorola language. Some assemblers will generate correct binary code, but the syntax and symbolic statements could be quite different from the Motorola language.

3.1   THE ASSEMBLY PROCESS

When you use assembly language to program a microcomputer, the assembler program will usually run on a computer other than the microcomputer. The computer system that runs the assembler program is called the *assembly system*. The assembly system requires sufficient resources, such as printers and disk drives, to carry out all the functions of the assembler program. The computer may be a personal computer system, a minicomputer system, or a mainframe computer system. Although the principles involved are the same in all cases, the way you access each of these systems differs somewhat. To simplify the discussion and yet represent common systems, assume that the assembly system is a personal computer using floppy disks as the storage medium. Assume a direct connection from the assembly computer to the microcomputer.

When the internal machine language of the assembly system computer is different from the language of the microcomputer, the assembler program is called a *cross assembler*. This name recognizes that the two computers are different, and nothing more. Be careful when purchasing an assembler program; you must specify both the computer it runs on and the computer for which it generates code.

The following is an overview of the assembly process. It discusses the process from the development of the symbolic program to loading the binary numbers into the microcomputer. The details of the symbolic language are discussed later in this chapter.

The Editor, Assembler, and Loader Programs

The ultimate goal of the assembly process is to put the binary instruction codes and binary data numbers that are your program into the memory of your microcomputer. The microcomputer is called the *target computer*. All the work that precedes putting the program into memory is aimed at the target computer.

Editor and Assembler Programs

Appendix B explains the use of the SPF/PC editor program that runs on IBM PC compatible computers. Appendix C covers the details of the 2500AD assembler program for IBM PC compatible computers. Other editor and assembler programs have features similar to these programs.

The assembler program reads a symbolic source module that it translates into a binary object module. The *source module* is a physical entity, such as a disk file, that contains all the characters that make a symbolic program. The symbolic program is called the *source code*. The *object module* is a physical entity, such as a disk file, that contains the binary numbers that will be loaded into the memory of the target computer. The binary numbers in the object module are called the *object code*.

The word *source* correctly implies that the source code is the origin or beginning of the program. The object or purpose of the assembly system is to generate the binary codes, so the name *object code* for these binary codes is appropriate.

A *load module* is a physical entity, such as a disk file, that can be read by a loader program. A *loader program* reads the load module and places the binary numbers into the memory of the target computer. Some assembler programs generate object modules that are also load modules, so the name *load module* is sometimes an alternative to the name *object module*. However, other systems may require an intermediate program, sometimes called a *linker*, to convert the object module into a load module.

Creating the source module

Figure 3-1 illustrates the development of the source module. The characters of the source program are coded into some form of memory storage device that is compatible with the assembly system. There are many common devices such as magnetic tape, punched cards, and floppy disks. The examples in this book refer to disks because they are the most common.

The source module is usually created by an editor program. An *editor program* can create, edit, store, and retrieve text characters from a disk file. The programmer will type the symbolic characters for the source program, change them as needed, and then direct the editor to make a disk file and write the characters into the file. The file can be retrieved later by the editor if further changes are needed.

Usually, the editor program will run on the assembly system computer. A programming editor is similar to the more common word processor program. However, the editor has functions devoted specifically to editing computer programs, so it is generally better than a word processor for this job.

Learning to use an editor is easy because you can see the text change on the computer screen as you type. The editor also will print a paper copy of the text.

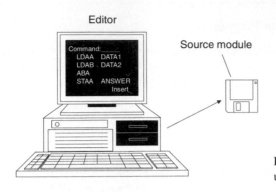

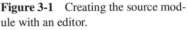

Figure 3-1   Creating the source module with an editor.

You should learn most of the commands available in your editor program. Usually the commands were put there because they are immediately useful to editing programs. Sometimes people are content to learn only how to insert and delete single characters. If you intend to do any serious work with an editor, the time spent to learn most of the editor features will be saved many times over as you use the editor.

Creating the object module, load module, and listing

Figure 3-2 illustrates the development of the load module and listing. The assembler program creates the object module from information contained in the source module. Another program may be required to convert the object module into a load module. The information in both the object module and load module is put into some form of memory storage device such as magnetic tape, punched cards, or floppy disks. The medium must be compatible with the assembly computer system and the loader hardware and software. Assume the use of disks as an example.

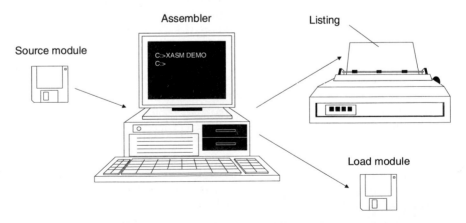

Figure 3-2   Creating the load module and listing with an assembler.

Motorola Trainer

The Motorola trainer has a loader program in permanent memory. A direct connection from the assembly computer to the trainer can be used to send a load module to the trainer. Appendix D explains how to load programs into the trainer.

The printed *listing* shows all the source and object code. Usually, the listing will be printed on paper. However, some assemblers will allow you to print to disk, which saves the listing in a disk file.

Running the assembler program is usually very easy. You tell it the name of the source file and which devices will receive the object code and listing, and it does the work. Generally, any information provided by the assembler will be in the printed listing.

Loading the program

The object code stored in the load module must be loaded into the target computer memory. The physical form of the load module determines how this is done. For example, if the load module is a magnetic tape unit, the target computer must be interfaced to an appropriate tape reader.

It is common to use a direct-wired connection between the assembly computer and the target computer to transfer the load information. A program in the assembly system transmits the binary numbers from the object file over the wires. A program in the target computer, called a *loader program*, receives the numbers and places them into the memory at the proper locations. Of course, this approach requires the proper hardware interfaces in both computers and compatible software. Figure 3-3 illustrates this way of loading a program.

Another common way to transfer the object code to the target computer is the use of a memory integrated circuit. The assembly system will have a device and software to put

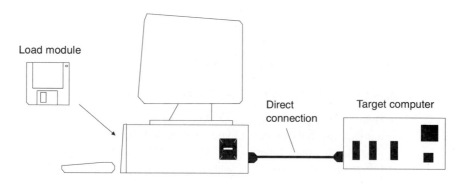

Figure 3-3   Loading the program into the memory of the target microcomputer.

the binary numbers into a permanent memory integrated circuit. The integrated circuit is then plugged into the target computer. One advantage here is that the target computer does not need a loader program and peripheral device. However, the error checking that the loader would do is lost. This approach is very practical for distributing mass market software such as video games. The memory integrated circuit is made into a cartridge that plugs into the video game computer.

The Source Module, Load Module, and Listing

There are three distinct parts to the information associated with the assembler. The source module is the input to the assembler, which then creates the object module and the listing. The assembler may directly create a load module, or another program may convert the object module to a load module.

The information in a source module

The source module contains the entire source program in symbolic form. The format of the information must be compatible with the assembler program that must read it. There are several types of symbolic information as discussed here:

- *Symbolic instructions, data, and addresses.*   Your assembly language program will use the instruction mnemonic names provided in the instruction set table. You will create your own symbols to represent data numbers and addresses.

- *Directives.*   These are symbols that control and direct the operations of the assembler program. Another name for a directive is *pseudo op*; this name comes from the similarity between the symbolic op codes of the target computer instructions and the symbolic control codes for the assembler program.

- *Comments.*   Comments are statements added by the programmer to explain the program. These statements are printed on the listing but do not affect the object code in any way.

The information in a load module

The load module will be read by the loader program to put the binary numbers into the memory of the target computer. The format of the information in the load module must be compatible with the loader program that must read it. Here is what it contains:

- *Binary instructions and data.*   The binary codes for your instructions and data numbers are in the object module. The symbols that were used in the source program are not in the object module, because they have been translated to binary numbers. It is not possible to read the object module and regenerate the source program.

- *Load information.*   Any information needed by the loader program is provided by the assembler program in the load module. For example, the loader is given the beginning load address for a series of binary numbers. The loader program then puts the numbers at consecutive locations beginning at the load address.

- *Error-checking information.*   There are many chances for error from the time the assembler generates binary codes until the loader puts the numbers into memory. For example, exposure of a disk to magnetic fields could change the numbers in the load module. Therefore, a way of assuring correctness for the numbers loaded into the target computer is necessary. The usual method requires a checksum. The assembler program uses an algorithm to create a number from all the other numbers put into the load module. The algorithm may be as simple as adding. Then the checksum number is put into the load module. The loader program will follow the same algorithm as it reads the numbers from the load module. After finishing reading, it compares its result to the checksum in the load module. If the checksums match, the loader assumes no errors. Notice that there could still be errors even if the checksums match because the algorithm will give the same checksum for many different numbers. However, missing an error is very unlikely to happen. If the checksums don't match, the loader indicates an error.

The information on the listing

Sample listings are illustrated later in this chapter, but here is an overview of the information found on the listings made by assemblers:

- *The source code.*   All the characters in the source module are printed on the listing. Some assemblers will automatically adjust spacing so the program is in neat columns. Others print the characters exactly as they were created by the editor.

- *The object code.*   The binary codes created by the assembler program are printed in hexadecimal format. Also, the memory addresses used by those numbers are printed beside them.

- *The symbol table.*   The symbol table lists all the user symbols that the programmer created in the source program. The table usually includes the numerical values of the symbols that the assembler determined. Some assemblers also add a cross-reference table to the symbol table. The cross reference includes the listing line numbers of all lines where each user symbol was used within the source program.

- *Error messages.*   Errors detected by the assembler program are usually indicated within the listing near the place where the error was detected. The error message may be an English statement or a code number that must be found in a manual. The assembler will indicate the number of errors found near the end of the listing. The number of errors is the first item to look at when reading a listing. If there are errors, there is no value in continuing with the load process. The assembler finds syntax errors such as misspelled instruction names. It may also detect incorrect addressing modes, multiple use of the same memory location, and other programming errors. Unfortunately, it cannot determine if your program works as you want it to work!

2500AD Assembler

Appendix C describes the use of the 2500AD assembler program that runs on an IBM PC compatible computer. Read the appendix to learn more about this assembler and its listing format and error messages. Appendix C necessarily includes programming information that has not yet been introduced in the text.

Some assemblers allow the user to suppress various information such as the symbol table or even the entire listing. Usually, you should print all this information and use it to help you write programs.

3.2 THE MOTOROLA ASSEMBLY LANGUAGE

This section lists and describes the characteristics of an assembly language source statement and defines the standard Motorola language. Examples illustrate each statement. Some more extensive and comprehensive examples are in the next section. The information included in this chapter is a subset of all possible source statements because not all the 68HC11 instructions have been presented yet. However, you will easily learn the omitted information in later chapters.

Many companies sell assembler programs for Motorola products. Different assemblers have different characteristics and features—such as the directives that control the assembler. Therefore, one assembler may assemble a source module without error while another may indicate a large number of errors and produce no useful code when assembling the same source.

All useful 68HC11 assemblers accept standard Motorola notation for the instructions. This section covers notation that works with all assemblers for the standard Motorola 68HC11 language. Most assemblers recognize extensions to the language beyond those statements in this section. Therefore, the material covered here is incomplete for any particular assembler.

Source Statement Content

Assembly language programming requires that you create symbolic source statements. An assembly language source statement is a single line of a source program. A source statement may contain various numbers and symbols. The numbers and symbols can be connected by operators to make expressions.

Spaces or blanks in the source program are important. Spaces serve as delimiters or separators between groups of other characters. Therefore, spaces cannot be embedded at arbitrary places in the source statement as in some other computer languages. If you try to

TABLE 3-1   NUMBER EXAMPLES

Number Type	Source Example	Binary Number Formed
Decimal	10	0000000000001010
Decimal	−100	1111111110011100
Hexadecimal	$10	0000000000010000
Hexadecimal	$ACBD	1010110010111101
Binary	%1001	0000000000001001

embed a space, the assembler will treat the characters preceding the space and the characters following the space as two separate items.

Numbers

A source statement may contain numbers specified by several different number bases. The assembler translates all numbers to 16-bit binary numbers, and then other commands determine the number of bits to be used.

The examples in Table 3-1 show the different number types. A hexadecimal number is written with a preceding dollar sign. A binary number has a preceding percent sign. However, the decimal number requires no special character.

A common error is the omission of the dollar sign from a hexadecimal number. If the result is a valid decimal number, the assembler treats it as such. However, if the hexadecimal number begins with a letter, the assembler treats the result as a symbol.

The examples in the table show that the assembler makes negative two's complement signed numbers when a number has a minus sign. No other designation of type of number is needed. Also, leading zeros are not necessary in the source statement.

User symbols

User symbols are groups of characters that represent memory addresses or data values. The assembler assigns numerical values to the user symbols as part of the assembly process. Since you will create the user symbols, you should choose symbols that are useful to the reader of the assembly language source program.

In contrast to user symbols, the assembler has a predefined or known symbol for each instruction. Since these symbols have been chosen to make them easy to remember, they are called *mnemonics*. For example, LDAA is the instruction mnemonic for the load accumulator A instruction.

User symbols must meet the following minimum requirements to be acceptable to the assembler program:

- *A symbol consists of one to six alphanumeric characters.* The first character must be alphabetic. Some assemblers allow longer symbols with other characters, but all assemblers accept symbols as specified here. If a symbol is too long, most assemblers truncate the extra characters, which may cause confusing program errors that are usually not detected by the assembler. For example, an assembler that allows only six character symbols may treat both ABCDEFGHI and ABCDEFXYZ as the symbol ABCDEF.

- *A user-defined symbol may not consist of the single characters A, B, X, or Y.* The assembler has already defined these symbols to represent the microprocessor registers. Although most assemblers allow it, you should not define symbols that are identical to instruction mnemonics. For example, LDAA as a user symbol may be confusing.

- *Each user symbol must be unique.* The assembler will generate an error message for doubly defined symbols. For example, the same symbol cannot refer to the addresses of two different memory locations.

Here are some valid user symbols: TIME, INITCT, TEMP3, and AA. The following are incorrect user symbols: 34ABC, 125, and A.

Expressions

Symbols, numbers, and combinations of symbols and numbers separated by the arithmetic operators +, −, *, and / are called *expressions*. A single number or a single symbol is the simplest expression. Spaces cannot be embedded within an expression. Inexperienced programmers should avoid using complicated expressions.

An example of an expression is ABC+1. It means to add one to the value of the symbol ABC. So, if the value of ABC is 5, the value of the expression is 6. Expressions that add one to a symbol are used frequently.

The meaning of an expression depends upon its application. Good names for the symbols makes it easier to understand the expression.

Source Statement Format

A *field* is a part of a source statement with a particular meaning. Each source statement contains up to four fields of information. These fields—from left to right—are the label, operation, operand, and comment fields. Some fields may be left blank. The fields have variable lengths and are delimited by spaces.

The items within the fields must be separated by at least one space. You may use more spaces without changing the meaning of the statement. Some assemblers print the listing with your spaces included while others arrange columns independent of your spaces.

The maximum length of a source statement in the listing depends on the assembler. If your line length exceeds the assembler limit, the assembler will do something to accommodate the extra characters. Usually the result is not very good. For example, the excess characters may be printed at the beginning of the next line.

In addition, the length of the source statement may cause the listing line to exceed the line length accepted by the printer or to be greater than the paper width. All these problems should be resolved before you make a source program.

Label field

A *label* is a user symbol that represents the memory address of the labeled item. A symbol is called a label when it represents an address. A symbol is made a label by placing its first character in column one of the source statement. The label field extends from column one to the first space character. Placing the symbol at column one tells the assembler to assign the value of the current address to the symbol. The assembler keeps the current address in its location counter.

The EQU directive discussed later overrides the assignment of an address value to the symbol starting in column one by assigning its own value. A symbol defined by EQU is usually not an address and then is not called a label.

Since column one defines the label, the label field is always to the left of the operation column. This arrangement mimics the memory diagrams in Chapter 2 that show the address to the left of the memory registers containing instruction codes.

Column one of the source statement is special in that it defines labels. However, most statements do not need a label. Put a space in column one if no label is required.

Here is an example of a source statement with a label:

            START   CLRA

where the symbol START is the label with the S in column one.

Operation field

The next field to the right of the label field, called the operation field, contains an instruction mnemonic or an assembler directive. The operation field can be any length and starts at any column beyond column one or beyond the label. You can use spaces to align statements.

The allowed instruction mnemonics are defined on the instruction set reference for the microprocessor in Appendix H. The instruction set table therefore is both an assembly language reference and a machine language reference.

In this example of a source statement:

            START   CLRA

the CLRA instruction mnemonic is in the operation field beyond the label START. One space between the T and C is required and the others are ignored.

Operand field

The content of the operand field varies depending on the operator used in the operation field. If the operator is a directive, the operand may be nothing or it may be an expression that is appropriate to that directive. If the operator is an instruction mnemonic, the operand will be nothing, a symbol, a number, or an expression with an addressing mode character. Table 3-2 illustrates the instruction operands and their formats for instructions introduced

TABLE 3-2   INSTRUCTION OPERAND FORMATS

Addressing Mode	Operand Format	Operand Type
Inherent	none	none
Immediate	#operand	data number
Extended	operand	address
Direct	operand	address
Indexed	operand,X	offset
Program relative	operand	address

so far. A few more formats will be covered in later chapters. Table 3-3 is a series of examples of instructions illustrating each addressing mode.

No spaces are allowed in the operand field. Be careful because extraneous spaces may cause your program to be incorrect while the assembler interprets the statement as correct.

Carefully notice that the instruction formats for direct, extended, and relative addressing are the same. The assembler can easily determine that an instruction uses relative addressing, since this mode is only for branch instructions. However, many instructions have both direct and extended addressing. Nothing in the assembly language statement explicitly determines which addressing mode should be used.

The assembler must choose between the direct and extended addressing modes based on the value of the operand. If the operand is an address in the range 0000 through 00FF, the assembler selects direct addressing. If not, the assembler selects extended addressing.

Immediate addressing is indicated by the # character. Since immediate addressing means that a constant number is in the instruction, using the symbol # that means number makes the format easy to remember. Similarly, indexed addressing is indicated by ,X at the end of the operand which is easy to remember. Be careful not to omit the # or ,X because the result will be a correct statement to the assembler that will not cause an error message, but it will change the meaning to a different addressing mode.

TABLE 3-3   INSTRUCTION FORMAT EXAMPLES

Addressing Mode	Example 1	Example 2
Inherent	INCA	TAB
Immediate	LDAB #40	LDX #$0100
Extended	STAA LENGTH	LDAA UPLIMIT
Direct	DEC COUNT	ADDD CORRECT
Indexed	NEG 5,X	LDD FACTOR,X
Program relative	BVS OERROR	BHI NEXT

Comment field

The comment field is the remainder of the line to the right of the operand field. The comment field may be left blank. Otherwise, you will put messages or comments to document the program in this field.

The assembler ignores comments when generating object code—it only prints the comments on the listing. The length of the line that can be printed by the assembler is limited by the assembler, the printer, and the paper width. Long comments will cause problems. You must determine the limits inherent to your assembly system.

Spaces delimit the fields, so the comment field starts after the first space after the operand field. Be careful to avoid putting spaces in the operand field because a space makes the rest of the operand a comment.

As an example of a comment, the statement

```
READY        TST FLAG     CAREFUL! THIS IS TRICKY
```

has a comment to the right of the instruction.

The Basic Assembler Directives

Directives are symbolic commands in the source program that control the operation of the assembler program. Directives are placed in the operation field although they do not direct the assembler to generate instruction codes.

The following sections describe the basic, most frequently used Motorola directives. Most commercial assemblers have many more directives to give the programmer greater control over the assembler. Unfortunately, there is no easy way to standardize the directives among companies, so a given source program cannot be used with all assemblers. The basic directives presented here work with all assemblers that follow the Motorola assembly language format.

In some of the descriptions of directives that follow, square brackets enclose optional quantities. The brackets are not part of the statement—they indicate only that some quantities are optional. Optional items can be omitted entirely. Also, lower-case names distinguish various quantities from the directive name in upper-case letters. Use your values for anything in lower case.

Memory allocation

Specifying how certain areas of memory will be used is called *memory allocation*. Some memory allocation directives determine where numbers, whether they are instructions or data, will be placed in the memory of the target computer. Other directives determine the amount of space or the number of registers allocated for data numbers.

ORG directive. The origin directive, ORG, puts an address into the assembler location counter. The assembler program uses the location counter to track the current address as statements are assembled. The source statements that follow create numbers that are assembled into memory locations at the address specified in the location counter. Each time the assembler generates a new byte, it also adds one to the location counter. Therefore, the original number in the location counter determines the origin or beginning point for loading numbers into the memory of the target computer. The format of the statement is:

ORG   expression

where the expression usually is a hexadecimal address.

Normally, there will be at least two ORG statements in a program listing—one to specify the beginning of the data section and one for the beginning of the program section. For example, the statement

ORG $C800

tells the assembler the following statements will specify numbers to load into consecutive memory registers beginning at address C800.

Most assemblers initialize the location counter to zero if they don't find an ORG directive in a source program. Be careful to avoid having two ORG statements that each cause code to be assembled at the same memory locations. Some assemblers will warn you if this happens. If this error is made, usually the last numbers to be loaded into the conflicting locations will be the final numbers in the memory of the target computer.

RMB directive.   RMB is an acronym for reserve memory bytes. The format of the statement is

[label]   RMB   expression

where the expression determines a number the assembler adds to the location counter. Adjusting the location counter causes the assembler to skip the number of bytes determined by the expression. In effect, RMB reserves a block of memory registers for use elsewhere in the program. The loader does not affect the memory bytes skipped by an RMB. Some assemblers leave the contents column of the listing blank to indicate that nothing happens to these registers during loading.

The label on an RMB refers to the first of the bytes reserved. For example, the statement

WORKCT   RMB   2

reserves a double-byte in memory that probably is a working counter. The instructions that initialize and adjust the counter will use the label WORKCT to access it.

The RMB directive is appropriate here because the working counter must be initialized by running the program. Loading a program into memory should not initialize the working counters.

Number formation

The assembler must be directed to generate a number and put it into memory whenever a data number is required. The directives that generate numbers also determine such details as the number of bits allotted to the number.

Use the number formation directives to generate data numbers only. Never use them to generate instruction code numbers. Always use instruction mnemonics for instructions to avoid confusion.

Assembler Listings

All the assembler listings in this book were made with the 2500AD assembler running on an IBM PC compatible personal computer. All the listings except some of those in Appendix C have been edited to remove unnecessary information such as dates, file names, page numbers, etc.

FCB directive.   FCB is an acronym for form constant byte. The FCB directive creates single-byte numbers and puts them in consecutive memory registers. The format of the statement is

> [label]   FCB   expression[, expression, ...]

where the expressions determine the values of the numbers. The most common expression is a single number. The label refers to the first of the numbers specified by the expressions. For example, the statement

> TABLE   FCB $27,12,LENGTH+1,%10

creates a table of four single-byte data numbers beginning at the address TABLE. An expression with a symbol specifies the third number. The symbol LENGTH was defined elsewhere in the source. Notice there is no way to label any bytes in the table beyond the first. If you need such labels, use separate FCBs for each data number

The FCB truncates each number it creates to its least-significant eight bits. Some assemblers warn you if the most-significant eight bits of the numbers are not all zeros.

FDB directive.   FDB is an acronym for form double-byte. The FDB directive creates double-byte numbers and puts them in consecutive memory registers. The high or most-significant byte is at the lower address and the low byte is at the higher address. The format of the statement is

> [label]   FDB   expression[, expression, ...]

where the expressions determine the values of the numbers. The label refers to the high byte of the first double-byte number specified by the expressions. For example, the statement

> LARGE   FDB $C3D

creates a single double-byte number where LARGE represents the address of the 0C byte. Notice it is not possible to label the low byte of a double-byte number. If you need a label on each byte, use two FCB directives to form the double-byte number. An alternative is the expression LARGE+1 that refers to the low byte of the double-byte number.

Symbol definition

Symbols represent either addresses or data numbers. The assembler cannot distinguish the two types of numbers. The only distinction is the means of defining the symbol. Always define address labels by placing the first character in column one. Always define data symbols with a directive in the Motorola assembly language.

EQU directive.   This directive equates a symbol to a numerical value. The symbol must have its first character in column one. The format of the statement is

symbol   EQU   expression

where the symbol is assigned the value of the expression. The EQU overrides the normal assignment of the symbol by directly specifying its value. In other words, even though the symbol is in column one, it is not assigned a value from the location counter. For example, the statement

PI   EQU   31416

creates a symbol PI and assigns it the value 31416_{10} in the assembler symbol table. Symbols defined by EQU are usually data values rather than addresses or labels.

The value of the expression is always a 16-bit number. The use of the symbol elsewhere in the program determines whether eight or 16 bits are needed.

The EQU directive affects only the assembler symbol table. It does not directly affect the memory of the target computer. If the symbol PI was never used anywhere else in a program, the memory of the target computer would contain no evidence the value 31416_{10} exists.

Assembler control

Some directives control how the assembler program works and therefore do nothing to the object code generated by the assembler. Most such directives are for the convenience of the programmer and can be ignored. However, the following control directives are essential to use of the assembler.

END directive.   The END directive marks the end of the source program and needs no label or expression. The END statement tells the assembler it has reached the last source statement. The assembler will not read any more source lines after the END directive. If there are any additional source statements beyond the END directive, they will be ignored. When the assembler encounters the END, it proceeds to generate the object module.

If the END is omitted, the error recovery action taken depends upon the particular assembler program in use.

The END directive is not the same as the *STOP* instruction in the program. *STOP* is an instruction that controls the target microcomputer. END is a directive that controls the assembler program.

Asterisk directive in column 1.   An asterisk in column one is a directive that tells the assembler the entire line is a comment. The assembler prints the characters following the asterisk on the listing, but ignores them for everything else. The asterisk character has this special meaning only in column one. For example,

* THIS LINE IS A COMMENT

is a line that is entirely comment. The normal meanings of the source statement fields have been overridden.

Asterisk or $ directive.   The assembler treats an asterisk anywhere other than column one or in a comment as another directive that is equivalent to a $ directive. This directive tells the assembler to substitute the current address for the symbol * or $. A common usage is to set a label equal to the current address.

An example of the use of the * directive follows:

```
                ORG     $C100
        FIND    EQU     *
                LDAA    SEARCH
```

The label FIND is assigned the value C100 because that is the number specified by the ORG statement on the previous line. Also, FIND is the label on the LDAA instruction, which is assembled at address C100. This way of labeling the LDAA instruction is useful if the program is changed frequently because the label does not need to move from line to line.

3.3   EXAMPLES FROM THE ASSEMBLER

The first example here includes a source listing and the corresponding assembler listing. The source listing was made with the SPF/PC editor. The assembler listings for all the examples were made with the 2500AD cross assembler, but anything unique to the 2500AD assembler has been removed from the figures. Therefore, the listings are good examples for almost any assembler.

Some Good Assembly Language

The first example in this section is nothing more than a collection of assembly language statements. It is not a useful program! The example includes a variety of statements to show what the assembler does. A realistic program example follows later.

The source listing

A listing of source statements is shown in Figure 3-4. An editor program printed the source listing from the contents of the source module. Refer to the figure as you read the following comments:

- Box 1 points to a comment line. The asterisk directive in column one defines this line as a comment. All program listings should have a title section to identify the program. Comment lines create the title section and separate various parts of the listing. Remember, a comment does not affect the target computer.

- Box 2 points to a line that defines the symbol CONST and assigns it the value 17_{10}. This line does not directly affect the memory of the target computer. EQU statements are usually put at the beginning of the source module so the symbol definitions are easy to find.

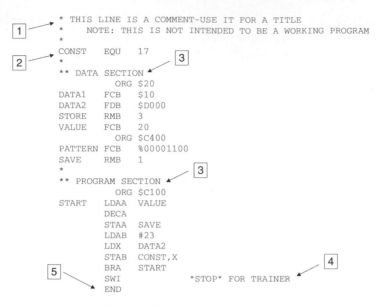

Figure 3-4 Assembly language source listing.

- The lines pointed at by the two Box 3s are comments that are titles for major sections of the listing. The data section is a collection of statements that allocate memory and define data numbers. The program section is the list of instructions in the program. The titles mark the listing to make it easier to read. Sometimes, additional directives tell the assembler to print these parts of the program on separate pages.

- Box 4 points to a comment added at the end of a source statement to clarify that statement. This book calls the SWI instruction the *STOP* instruction because that is its function in a Motorola trainer and some other trainers, but the assembler must be given the correct instruction name. The comment to the right of the instruction should help you recognize the purpose of this instruction. Use the space to the right of instructions for comments that explain unusual or special uses for instructions. This space is not very useful for documenting the function of the program.

- Box 5 points to the END directive that tells the assembler there are no more source statements. All source listings have exactly one END directive and it always is the last statement.

Some statements in this source program have been indented. The instructions were indented to avoid the label defining column one. The ORG statements were indented an extra amount to make the listing easier to read.

The assembler listing

Figure 3-5 shows the listing that the assembler printed. A few lines were removed from the figure. They contained additional titles, disk file identifiers, blank lines, etc.

```
 1                                      * THIS LINE IS A COMMENT-USE IT FOR A TITLE
 2      1              3               *     NOTE: THIS IS NOT INTENDED TO BE A WORKING PROGRAM
 3                                     *
 4      2    0011                      CONST   EQU   17
 5                                     *
 6                      4              ** DATA SECTION
 7    0020                                     ORG   $20
 8    0020   10                        DATA1   FCB   $10
 9    0021   D000                      DATA2   FDB   $D000
10    0023                             STORE   RMB   3
11    0026   14                        VALUE   FCB   20
12    C400                                     ORG   $C400
13    C400   0C                        PATTERN FCB   %00001100
14    C401                             SAVE    RMB   1
15                                     *
16                                     ** PROGRAM SECTION
17    C100                                     ORG   $C100
18    C100   96 26                     START   LDAA  VALUE
19    C102   4A                                DECA
20    C103   B7 C4 01                          STAA  SAVE
21    C106   C6 17                              LDAB  #23
22    C108   DE 21                              LDX   DATA2
23    C10A   E7 11                              STAB  CONST,X
24    C10C   20 F2                              BRA   START
25    C10E   3F                                 SWI         "STOP" FOR TRAINER
26    C10F                                      END

 Defined                 Symbol Name              Value              References      5

        4        CONST                            0011                  23
        8        DATA1                            0020
        9        DATA2                            0021                  22
       13        PATTERN                          C400
       14        SAVE                             C401                  20
       18        START                            C100                  24
       10        STORE                            0023
       11        VALUE                            0026                  18

            Lines Assembled :   26          Assembly Errors :   0
```

Figure 3-5   Assembler listing for a collection of assembler statements.

Layout of the listing.   The assembler listing has several distinct parts. Each part is particularly useful for a certain task. Refer to the boxes on Figure 3-5. The following comments describe the listing by referencing the boxes:

- Box 1 points to the column of decimal numbers that identify the lines on the listing. It is most convenient to talk about the listing by referring to these line numbers.

- Box 2 identifies the address column of the listing. These hexadecimal addresses refer to memory locations in the target computer.

- Box 3 identifies the columns that relate to the memory contents of the target computer. However, some numbers in this column are not memory contents as you will determine from the context of the line. All the numbers in the contents columns are hexadecimal numbers. Since some instructions have five bytes, there must be a large space.

- Box 4 identifies the source statements that were read from the source module by the assembler program. The assembler reproduces the source characters on the listing. Therefore, most people don't print the source listing using the editor. It is almost as easy and certainly more useful to print the assembler listing and use it as a source listing.

- Box 5 points to the beginning of the user symbol table. All the user symbols that the assembler found are listed here with the values that the assembler determined for them. This symbol table also includes a cross reference.

Always remember that the assembler created anything printed on the listing that was not in the source. It is easier to understand the listing if you know what created the information on it.

The assembler listing in detail.   Two software programs (namely, an editor and an assembler) are necessary to create the assembler listing. The program that the listing represents will be put into the target computer. Aspects of all three of these programs are contained in the listing. Consider these programs as you read the following comments about the assembler listing in Figure 3-5. The listing is referenced by line number. Also look at Figure 3-6 to see the contents of memory after the load module is loaded.

- *Line 4.*   The EQU directive creates the user symbol CONST and assigns it the value 17_{10}. The only thing affected by this statement is the assembler symbol table. Nothing in the target computer is affected, so the address column of the listing is left blank by the assembler. The contents column contains the hexadecimal number 0011 which is the 16-bit equivalent of 17_{10}. Be careful! Just because the 0011 is printed in the contents column does not mean it will be loaded into the target computer. Remember that the contents column may contain numbers that do not represent numbers in the memory of the target computer.

- *Line 7.*   The ORG directive tells the assembler the first memory location to be used by the items generated by the following statements. The numerical value usually is a hexadecimal number as illustrated here. The number 0020 was chosen to illustrate some data numbers in the direct addressing range of memory. Instructions referencing these numbers should have direct addressing. Indenting the ORG statement two character positions makes the listing easier to read. Notice that the contents column of the listing is blank to indicate that the memory of the target computer is not affected.

- *Line 8.*   The FCB creates a single-byte number 10 as shown by the contents column. This byte is at address 0020 due to the ORG statement on line 7. Line 8 also defines the address label DATA1. The symbol DATA1 is assigned the value 0020 as the symbol table shows.

  After loading, the number 10 that was created by the FCB is at location 0020 as shown in Figure 3-6.

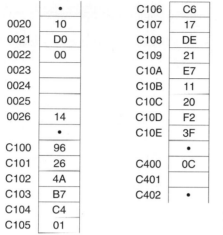

	•
0020	10
0021	D0
0022	00
0023	
0024	
0025	
0026	14
	•
C100	96
C101	26
C102	4A
C103	B7
C104	C4
C105	01

C106	C6
C107	17
C108	DE
C109	21
C10A	E7
C10B	11
C10C	20
C10D	F2
C10E	3F
	•
C400	0C
C401	
C402	•

Figure 3-6 Memory contents after loading the program in Figure 3-5.

- *Line 9.* The FDB directive forms the double-byte number D000 that goes into the next two bytes at addresses 0021 and 0022. The listing shows both bytes on one line. Consequently, the address on the next line is two higher than the address on this line.

  Locations 0021 and 0022 contain D000 in Figure 3-6.

- *Line 10.* This RMB directive tells the assembler to allocate or reserve three memory locations. RMB does not specify any value to be loaded into these locations and the memory of the target computer will not be altered when the program is loaded. To indicate this, the space in the contents column is blank. Since three bytes were allocated, the address on the next line is three higher than on this line. Notice the label STORE appears to be meaningful to the application because the reserved bytes can only be used to store numbers.

  Locations 0023 through 0025 are blank in Figure 3-6 to indicate that the contents are unknown. These locations were not affected by the loader.

- *Line 11.* The FCB directive forms the hexadecimal number 14 that is equivalent to the decimal number 20. The label VALUE is assigned the numerical value 0026.

  Location 0026 contains the number 14 in Figure 3-6.

- *Line 12.* A new ORG statement can be used anywhere in the source program. Here some data numbers are put at locations beyond the direct addressing range because the address C400 is higher than 00FF.

- *Line 13.* This FCB directive generates the number 0C that was specified in binary format. Binary format is especially useful when the individual bits of the number are important to the application. Leading zeros are not necessary, but here they help you visualize the bit pattern in the number.

Location C400 contains 0C in Figure 3-6.

- *Line 14.*   The RMB directive reserves one memory location. The assembler assigned the label SAVE the value C401 as you can see in the symbol table.

Location C401 is shown blank in Figure 3-6 to indicate that the contents are unknown.

- *Line 17.*   Another ORG determines the location of the program section. Usually there will be an ORG at the beginning of both the data and program sections. The addresses specified by the ORGs do not have to be in numerical order.

- *Line 18.*   The first instruction in the program is labeled START to make it easy to find the starting point of the program. The LDAA instruction here has direct addressing. Since the assembly language format of this LDAA refers to either direct or extended addressing, you can only determine the addressing mode by looking at the instruction code the assembler generated. Since the instruction is two bytes long, it must have direct addressing. If the instruction had been three bytes long, it would have had extended addressing.

Locations C100 and C101 contain the instruction code 96 26 in Figure 3-6.

- *Line 19.*   The DECA instruction has only inherent addressing and requires only the one byte 4A in location C102.

- *Line 20.*   This instruction format could specify either direct or extended addressing. By examining the contents columns, the 3-byte form indicates extended addressing. The assembler determined that the value of SAVE is C401 by looking in the symbol table. Therefore, the address is outside the direct addressing range, and the assembler chose extended addressing.

Locations C103, C104, and C105 contain the 3-byte instruction code B7 C4 01 in Figure 3-6.

- *Line 21.*   Since the data values used in immediate addressed instructions are constants, it is often reasonable to put the actual numerical value in the source statement. If the same constant must be used in more than one place, a symbol for it should be defined by an EQU directive. Then changing the EQU statement changes all occurrences of the constant. Here the constant 17 was specified as decimal 23.

Locations C106 and C107 contain the instruction code C6 17 in Figure 3-6.

- *Line 22.*   This LDX instruction references a double-byte number at location DATA2 using direct addressing.

- *Line 23.*   The symbol CONST specifies the constant offset part of this instruction. It is common to use symbols for offsets. Be careful! The offset is an 8-bit unsigned number, so the value of the symbol must fit in eight bits. Many times this offset will be zero, and then it is reasonable to put the actual number in the source statement.

- *Line 24.* The BRA instruction has only program relative addressing. The assembler determined the relative offset to be F2, a negative number, that causes the BRA to branch to a lower address.

- *Line 25.* The SWI instruction stops the program when used in a Motorola trainer. The function of this instruction is described later.

- *Line 26.* The END directive tells the assembler there is no more source code to read. The address C10F printed in the address column has no significance.

Reading an assembler listing and looking at all the details are quite tedious, but necessary to learn what the assembler does. After you learn the details, you will read the listing by focusing only on the parts you need.

The symbol table. The symbol table lists all the information the assembler has about the user symbols that were defined in the program. Here are descriptions of the columns and messages included in the symbol table:

- *Defined*—the line number of the listing line where the symbol was defined. For example, the symbol PATTERN was defined on line 13. Only one line number is possible for each symbol on a correct listing.

- *Symbol name*—the names of the user symbols defined in the source module. You can often find programming errors by looking for misspelled symbol names. Sometimes the erroneous symbol is a hexadecimal number that has the dollar sign missing. The large blank area to the right of the symbols provides space for long symbol names.

- *Value*—the values of the user symbols in hexadecimal number format. The assembler determines these values from the source statements. For example, the value of SAVE is C401 because the ORG said to start assembling at address C400, and then one byte was assembled before the label SAVE was defined.

- *References*—the line number of the lines where each symbol was used or referenced. A long program may reference a symbol hundreds of times making this list very long. In this example, the symbol START was referenced on line 24 by the BRA instruction.

- *Lines assembled*—the number of source lines that the assembler read from the source module. This number must match the number of lines that the editor created. If the numbers don't match, probably there is an erroneous END statement in the source.

- *Assembly errors*—the number of errors detected by the assembler. Unless this number is zero, there is no value in proceeding with the existing program. It will not load and run correctly. Do not be discouraged if the number of errors is very large. For example, it may not seem possible to have approximately one error per line as an average. Large error numbers usually occur when there are many references to the same erroneous symbol. Similarly, one error may cause several other errors, so fixing the one real error may resolve many others.

The symbol table in this example is only marginally useful because this program listing is so short. Practical programs often have listings that are several hundred pages long. Then the symbol table is very valuable for finding symbols, their values, and the instructions that reference them.

Some Bad Assembly Language

Assemblers have many features that enable programmers to create good, useful programs. The same features also can create programs that seem to defy logic. Sometimes programmers use assembler features in clever ways that cause problems for others using the program. This section expresses opinions on some bad ways to use assembly language.

The bad example

Figure 3-7 is a listing containing a collection of statements designed to illustrate some bad ideas. The statements are all valid assembly language statements. The assembler finds no errors. But the organization, ease of use, readability, and statement formats are problems.

As you read the following comments, you should envision a real program, not the small sample shown in the figure. Actual programs usually require a few hundred pages for the listing instead of a few dozen lines. Longer programs magnify the importance of the problems discussed here.

Bad documentation.   Look at the documentation the comments on the listing provide. Most of the documentation is useless as the following points out:

- *Line 1.*   The title is inadequate for an actual program. A good title section will describe the program function, memory requirements, revision history, author, date, and other pertinent items.

- *Line 3.*   The comment on line 3 was too long, so the assembler wrapped part of it to the next line in an unsatisfactory manner. This comment is very difficult to read.

- *Line 5.*   The relevance to the program of the symbol CONST should be stated in the comment field.

- *Line 16.*   The data section ends at line 15 and the program section begins at line 16. No headings or blank lines separate the two parts. Therefore, it is difficult to find the start of the program on the listing. The program and data blur together.

- *Line 18.*   It's not possible to put good comments in this listing that describe the function of the program, because it has no reasonable function—it's only an example of statements. However, there is a problem in the comment on line 18. The comment does not attempt to describe why the STAA instruction is in the program. It only restates the obvious by telling what the machine instruction does. But to make matters worse, the comment is incorrect! The STAA instruction stores the contents

```
  1                                    * THIS LISTING DEMONSTRATES SOME BAD IDEAS
  2                                    *
  3                                    *   NOTE: THIS IS NOT INTENDED TO BE A USEFU
                                       L PROGRAM
  4                                    *
  5            0015                    CONST   EQU    $15
  6                                    *
  7                                    ** DATA SECTION
  8                                    *
  9    0020                                    ORG 32
 10    0020    10                      MARY    FCB    $10
 11    0021    3946                    BOB     FDB    $ABCD/3+2
 12    0023    36                      ABCDEF  FCB    CONST+BOB
 13    0024                            LDAA    RMB    1
 14    0025    0A                      A       FCB    $A
 15    0026    EC                      TWOONES FCB    %11101100
 16    0027    96 24                   START   LDAA   LDAA
 17    0029    4A                              DEC    A
 18    002A    97 45                           STAA   $45        LOAD THE A REGISTER
 19    002C    C6 20                           LDAB   #MARY
 20    002E    D7 25                           STAB   ABCDEF+2
 21    0030    DE 15                           LDX    CONST
 22    0032    E7 20                           STAB   MARY,X
 23    0034    20 F5                           BRA    START+4
 24    0036    3F                              SWI               "STOP" FOR TRAINER
 25    0037                                    END
```

```
  Defined            Symbol Name        Value              References

       14       A                       0025
       12       ABCDEF                  0023           20
       11       BOB                     0021           12
        5       CONST                   0015           12        21
       13       LDAA                    0024           16
```

Figure 3-7 Assembler listing with bad ideas.

of the accumulator—it does not load the accumulator. *Incorrect comments are worse than no comments.* Always strive to write the most clear, most informative, and most useful comments.

Whenever you write a program for any serious use, you should print a listing and then put it aside for a few days. Later, read your comments to see if they make sense. Often you will find that your comments and documentation can be improved.

Bad labels. Most of the address labels are poorly named. The programmer must usually be very creative to select good names for the program labels. Here are some specific problems:

- *Lines 10 through 12.*   People's names as labels may be cute, but they are unlikely to be helpful. The label ABCDEF is equally poor, since it conveys no useful information.

- *Lines 13 and 14.*   The label LDAA is the same as an instruction mnemonic and is very confusing. The label A is easy to confuse with the accumulator A and may cause errors in some assemblers.

- *Line 15.* The label TWOONES seems to mean the number contains two ones, but it doesn't. Labels that try to identify the characteristics of a data number will be troublesome because the data value is likely to change.

Sometimes people conclude that a label on every assembly language line is a good idea—it isn't. Only use labels where they are needed. The reader must examine any unnecessary labels; this extra effort wastes time. Probably the only label that is useful when the program doesn't use it is the label on the first instruction of the program—the starting address.

Bad numbers.   The format of a number should match its application. Normally numbers with different bases should not be mixed in expressions. Here are some examples from Figure 3-7:

- *Line 9.*   The ORG statement specifies an address in decimal format. Addresses should always be hexadecimal numbers. The assembler printed the hexadecimal address in the address column, but the ORG statement is still difficult to read.

- *Line 11.*   The assembler calculates a number in a very complicated way. Generally such calculations should be avoided. If the calculation is necessary, include parentheses in the expression so the precedence of operations is unmistakable. Also, be careful to understand exactly how the assembler does integer division.

Some assemblers will use a default value of zero if a number is omitted. Generally avoid doing this; always state the number exactly as you want it.

Bad expressions.   Most expressions containing more than one symbol are difficult to read and may lead to programming errors. Avoid all complicated expressions. An expression that adds one to a symbol is the most useful and hence most common expression. Here are some problems in Figure 3-7:

- *Line 12.*   The expression CONST+BOB generates a constant number for the FCB directive. The expression uses the address label BOB, which implies a 16-bit number, but the FCB creates only a single-byte number. Adding the symbol CONST to the truncated address is even more confusing. Expressions should use symbols that represent consistent quantities.

- *Line 20.*   The STAB instruction stores a number at an address that is 2 higher than the label ABCDEF. An offset from a label, like the 2, is dangerous. For example, executing the STAA instruction will store to location 0025, which destroys a constant. This must be an error. Probably some changes were made in the data section. A change moved the location where this instruction was supposed to store its data. When you change the data section of a program, it is very difficult to find every instruction that references every data location and correct how they address the data. A much better solution here is to label the location where the number is to be stored and use that label in the STAB instruction. This problem would not occur if the STAB instruction contained a single label instead of an expression.

- *Line 23.* The instruction on line 23 branches in a strange way. The expression START+4 evaluates to 002B, which is not the address of an instruction. Probably the program was changed by removing a 1-byte instruction, which now makes the BRA instruction incorrect. A change in some unrelated part of the program makes the BRA instruction incorrect. The problem would not occur if the expression START+4 were replaced by a label for the correct branch location.

Almost always a complicated expression can be replaced by a single number and a good comment to explain the number.

Bad instructions. Instruction statements should be written to be simple and easy to read. Here are some problems in Figure 3-7:

- *Line 16.* The instruction LDAA LDAA, is correct but quite confusing. It is difficult for people to separate the two meanings of the same symbol. The problem, of course, is caused by the choice of address label.

- *Line 17.* The instruction on line 17 probably is an error. Since line 14 has a label A, this instruction probably intended to decrement location A using extended addressing. But the assembler could not distinguish the label from the A accumulator and generated an inherent addressed instruction of code 4A that decrements the A accumulator. The assembler does not consider this to be an error. Instead, it is a feature that allows people to add a space before the accumulator designator in the instruction mnemonics. The space may improve the readability of the line.

- *Line 18.* The address operand for this STAA instruction is address 0045. Even if the program was moved to a different place, or the data number was moved, this instruction will always store to address 0045. Using a number for the address defeats much of the power of the assembler because the assembler is not determining the address. Also, when changes are made to the program, it will be difficult to find this statement in the listing to determine what is wrong. *Never use a number as the address part of an instruction.* Always use a symbol so the assembler can change the address for you as you modify your program.

- *Line 19.* The instruction on line 19 is probably an error. It is loading the low byte of an address into an accumulator, which is unlikely to be useful.

- *Line 21.* The instruction on line 21 is probably an error, or at least bad practice. The address operand CONST was defined on line 5 using an EQU directive. Using the EQU is a poor way to define this address. Is it obvious to you that a data number is stored at address 0015? It is better to label the item at location 0015 and use that label in the LDX instruction. Then the assembler listing will have an entry in the address column for address 0015 and the use of that location will be apparent. Also, mistakes causing two statements to use the same address will be unlikely. Using the EQU to define addresses defeats much of the usefulness of the assembler. In contrast, sometimes you must link a program to another program that was assembled separately. Then you must use the EQU to define the address label from the other program.

- *Line 22.*   The instruction on line 22 has a poorly chosen offset. The symbol MARY was defined as an address label on line 10. It is unlikely that an address could also be an offset. This instruction can illustrate a good use of the EQU directive. The required offset is a constant that can be defined by an EQU using a meaningful label to name the offset. If the offset must be changed later because the program is changed, a change in the EQU statement reliably changes all occurrences of the offset. Since the same offset usually occurs in many instructions throughout a program, using a symbol for an offset is practical.

Extraneous statements.   The example in Figure 3-7 is not a real program, but it illustrates the following problems anyway:

- *Lines 21 and 26.*   The program never uses the data stored at locations BOB or TWOONES. Never put items in a program that are not used—they waste resources and are very confusing.

- *Line 24.*   The program never uses the SWI instruction on line 24. When editing a program, be careful not to leave unused instructions in the program.

Bad symbol table.   Apparently part of the symbol table was discarded. Some people ignore the symbol table; therefore, some assemblers have an option to suppress printing of the symbol table. Always print and use the symbol table—it is very useful. It will help you find problems and to understand the program.

Assembly Language Copy a Table

A program was written in Chapter 2 to copy a table from one place in memory to another place in memory. That example, in Figure 2-48, is machine language that was coded by hand—you looked at the instruction set table to find the codes. Now let's look at the same program written in assembly language.

The assembler listing is Figure 3-8. The program is identical to the one in Chapter 2 including some programming errors. You can compare the contents columns of the figures to see that the assembler generates the same codes. Of course, it is much easier to use the assembler than to hand code the program.

The documentation in the assembler listing is similar to that in Chapter 2. It could be improved somewhat. Here are some comments on the program listing:

- *Lines 1 through 6.*   These comments title and otherwise document the program.

- *Lines 7 through 10.*   These lines create a user symbol and assign it a value. The comment to the right of the EQU statement gives a brief explanation of the purpose of the symbol. The best place for symbol definitions is at the beginning of the listing so the reader knows the symbols before encountering them in the program.

```
 1                          **********************************************************
 2                          ** COPY TABLE PROGRAM FROM CHAPTER 2
 3                          * NOTE: THIS IS NOT A GOOD PROGRAM
 4                          *
 5                          **********************************************************
 6                          *
 7                          **********************************************************
 8                          ** SYMBOL DEFINITIONS
 9                          **********************************************************
10           0020           SPACE    EQU    $20        SPACING BETWEEN TABLES
11                          *
12                          **********************************************************
13                          ** DATA SECTION
14                          **********************************************************
15   0030                            ORG    $30
16   0030    C110           TABADR   FDB    $C110      ADDRESS OF FIRST TABLE
17   0032    04             INITCT   FCB    4          TABLE LENGTH
18   0033                   WRKCNT   RMB    1          WORKING COUNTER
19                          *
20                          **********************************************************
21                          ** PROGRAM SECTION
22                          **********************************************************
23   C010                            ORG    $C010
24                          * INITIALIZE POINTER TO FIRST TABLE
25   C010    DE 30          START    LDX    TABADR
26                          * INITIALIZE WORKING COUNTER
27   C012    96 32                   LDAA   INITCT     GET INITIAL VALUE
28   C014    97 33                   STAA   WRKCNT     STORE INTO WORKING COUNTER
29                          * WORKING COUNTER EQUALS ZERO?
30   C016    27 0A          AGAIN    BEQ    LAST       BRANCH ON YES
31                          * COPY ONE ENTRY
32   C018    A6 00                   LDAA   0,X        GET ENTRY FROM FIRST TABLE
33   C01A    A7 20                   STAA   SPACE,X    PUT ENTRY INTO SECOND TABLE
34                          * ADVANCE POINTER TO NEXT ENTRY
35   C01C    08                      INX
36                          * COUNT DOWN THE WORKING COUNTER
37   C01D    7A 00 33                DEC    WRKCNT
38   C020    20 F4                   BRA    AGAIN      GO AROUND AGAIN
39                          * STOP THE PROGRAM
40   C022    3F             LAST     SWI               "STOP" FOR MOTOROLA TRAINER
41   C023                            END
```

Defined	Symbol Name	Value		References	
30	AGAIN		C016	38	
17	INITCT		0032	27	
40	LAST		C022	30	
10	SPACE	=	0020	33	
25	START		C010		
16	TABADR		0030	25	
18	WRKCNT		0033	28	37

Lines Assembled : 41   Assembly Errors : 0

Figure 3-8   Assembler listing of the copy-a-table program.

- *Lines 11 through 15.*   The **ORG** statement locates the data section in the direct addressing range. The title identifying the data section makes the listing easier to read. Sometimes the data definitions are put on separate pages of the assembler listing for the same reason.

- *Lines 16 through 18.* These statements allocate memory registers for the data numbers. The symbols used as address labels suggest the use of the associated registers. Comments to the right further document the purpose of each data value. The numbers 4 and 1 on lines 17 and 18 are in decimal format. Use decimal format for small numbers that are the same in both decimal and hexadecimal because they are easier to read.

- *Lines 19 through 22.* These comments title the program section. The blank comment lines improve the readability of the listing by providing white space.

- *Line 23.* The ORG locates the program section. The program section usually is outside the direct addressing range to conserve that space for data values.

- *Lines 24 and 25.* The LDX initializes the X index register as the table pointer. The addressing mode of this instruction is direct because the label TABADR was given a value in the direct addressing range. The comment titling this module of the program was put on a separate line. The comment could be put to the right of the instruction, but the technique used here makes the listing easier to read. Using a separate line for the comment requires more paper to print the listing, but the small extra cost is justified. The label START is not used by the program, but it helps the reader understand where the program starts running.

- *Lines 26 through 28.* The working counter is initialized. The comments in Figure 2-48 are to the right of the instructions. But, in the assembly language listing, the function of the instructions is described by line 26 for clarity. Extra comments to the right of the instructions further explain the instructions.

- *Lines 29 and 30.* This is the beginning of the loop. The label AGAIN was chosen to suggest that something would branch to this place again and again. *The only reason to have a label on an instruction, other than the first instruction, is to support a branch instruction elsewhere in the program.* Names like AGAIN, NEXT, and BACK help the reader recognize loops. Chapter 4 discusses better documentation for loops.

- *Lines 31 through 33.* The program copies one entry from the first table to the second table using two indexed addressed instructions. The comments at the right explain the details. The offset in the STAA instruction was specified symbolically to suggest its effect; namely, that it determines the spacing between the tables.

- *Lines 34 and 35.* Now that an entry has been copied, this instruction advances the pointer to the next entry. The comment is much longer than the instruction, but don't be bothered by this. The instruction does a very important function in the program. The importance justifies the size of the comment.

- *Lines 36 through 38.* The program decrements the working counter and ends the loop. It is important that the DEC instruction affects the Z bit of the condition code register, but this fact is not documented on the listing. The reader must know how

---

Motorola Trainer

Enter the program in Figure 3-8 into the trainer and test it. Read the assembler listing while entering the codes. You may find some aspects of the listing that you don't understand fully.

---

the instructions work. Also, the loop end is primarily documented by the comment on line 34. The label AGAIN in the BRA instruction also suggests the end of the loop. Chapter 4 shows how the loop can be better documented. The technique here makes it difficult to identify the loop.

- *Lines 39 and 40.*   The instruction on line 40 stops the program execution. The label LAST was chosen to suggest the location of the last instruction to be executed in the program. *The STOP instruction should be the last instruction in the listing for good readability.* The comment on line 40 tells you the SWI instruction does the *STOP* function in the Motorola 68HC11 trainer.

- *Line 41.*   The END directive tells the assembler the end of the source has been reached. The address printed in the address column is not useful.

Now consider the symbol table in Figure 3-8. The user symbols that were defined in the program are listed in alphabetical order. The following comments point out some details that are in the symbol table:

- The symbol table shows that the symbol AGAIN was defined on line 30. On line 30 of the listing, you see that AGAIN starts in column one of the source line that defines it as an address label.

- The symbol table shows that the value assigned to AGAIN is C016. The C016 in the address column of listing line 30 confirms this.

- The symbol AGAIN is referenced on line 38 according to the cross reference. Indeed, line 38 contains the BRA AGAIN instruction where the symbol determines the address part of the instruction. Notice the difference between a reference to a symbol and the definition of that symbol. A symbol can only be defined (that is, created and assigned a value) by an EQU statement or by usage as a label. Both techniques require the symbol to start in column one.

- The symbol SPACE was assigned the value 0020 by the EQU directive. An equal sign to the left of the value column indicates that an EQU directive was used for this symbol.

- The symbol table says there are two references to the symbol WRKCNT on lines 28 and 37. Some symbols are referenced hundreds of times in large programs.

Generally, you should look at the symbol table first if there are assembly errors reported on the listing. Incorrectly spelled symbol names are a very common source of errors. If a symbol is doubly defined, many assemblers will list each value and the cross reference will tell you where the definitions are. The symbol table can save you the effort of paging through a long listing when there are errors.

3.4 REVIEW

Why use an assembler? You have seen the copy-a-table program both hand coded and assembled by an assembler. You can develop the program either way. So why use an assembler? Certainly the assembly system is costly. A computer system with a printer is necessary. Both an editor and an assembler program are required. Hand coding requires only an inexpensive instruction set table.

First, using an assembler makes it faster and easier for you to develop new programs. This alone justifies the cost of the assembly system. The assembler generates instruction codes very quickly. During program development, the program will be modified many times. The hand-coding method requires a large amount of time to develop any practical program.

Second, the assembler does error checking. Although most of the errors detected are simply typing errors and misspelled words, the assembler also detects errors in the use of instructions. Errors involving addressing modes and incorrect addressing ranges can be detected by the assembler. Similarly, use of the same locations in memory for more than one purpose can be detected. In large programs developed by a group of people, this error detection is very useful.

Third, the assembler documents the program in the best possible way. Both the source and object code are printed on paper and stored in computer-readable form. The assembly computer system becomes a very sophisticated filing system for storing the program.

The assembler frees you from routine work so you can be more creative and productive in writing programs.

3.5 EXERCISES

3-1. Write an assembly language statement to generate a LDAA instruction that puts the number 33_{10} in the accumulator.

3-2. The last statement in an assembly language program is always _____.

3-3. Why not always use the FCB directive instead of the RMB directive?

3-4. In Figure 3-8, if line 23 was changed to ORG $C022, what would be different about the program? Will it copy the table?

3-5. Fill in the missing parts (a) through (r) in Figure 3-9. Some items have been typed over with Xs.

3-6. After completing question 3-5, assume the object code was loaded into memory and run from location START to the *STOP* instruction. Then consider the following:

    (a) The number 45 was stored in memory location _____.

    (b) The address of the memory location incremented by the instruction on line 19 of the listing is _____.

    (c) The number in the D accumulator is _____.

    (d) The number in the X index register is _____.

    (e) Did the branch instruction branch?

    (f) Would the binary code for the BNE LAST instruction change if the statement on line 10 were changed to ORG $DD00?

    (g) List the line numbers of all the instructions which would have changed binary codes if the statement on line 3 were changed to ORG $D000.

3-7. Fill in the missing parts (a) through (q) in Figure 3-10. Some items have been typed over with Xs.

3-8. Write three distinctly different assembly language program modules that will each add one to a double-byte number in memory without using the A accumulator in any way.

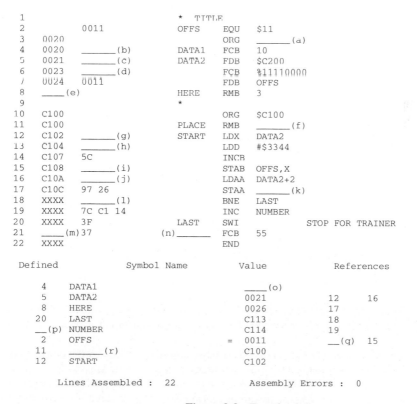

```
 1                              *   TITLE
 2              0011            OFFS    EQU     $11
 3      0020                            ORG     _____(a)
 4      0020    _____(b)      DATA1   FCB     10
 5      0021    _____(c)      DATA2   FDB     $C200
 6      0023    _____(d)              FCB     %11110000
 7      0024    0011                    FDB     OFFS
 8      ____(e)                 HERE    RMB     3
 9                              *
10      C100                            ORG     $C100
11      C100                    PLACE   RMB     _____(f)
12      C102    _____(g)      START   LDX     DATA2
13      C104    _____(h)              LDD     #$3344
14      C107    5C                      INCB
15      C108    _____(i)              STAB    OFFS,X
16      C10A    _____(j)              LDAA    DATA2+2
17      C10C    97 26                   STAA    _____(k)
18      XXXX    _____(l)              BNE     LAST
19      XXXX    7C C1 14                INC     NUMBER
20      XXXX    3F              LAST    SWI             STOP FOR TRAINER
21      ____(m)37         (n)_____    FCB     55
22      XXXX                            END
```

Defined	Symbol Name	Value	References	
4	DATA1	____(o)		
5	DATA2	0021	12	16
8	HERE	0026	17	
20	LAST	C113	18	
__(p)	NUMBER	C114	19	
2	OFFS	= 0011	__(q)	15
11	_____(r)	C100		
12	START	C102		

Lines Assembled :   22   Assembly Errors :   0

Figure 3-9   Exercise 3-5.

```
 1                                * ASSEMBLER EXERCISE
 2                                *
 3           0044                 SYMBOL  EQU   $44
 4     D000                               ORG   $D000
 5     D000    _____(a)         NUMBER  FCB   %1100
 6     D001    _____(b)                 FCB   33
 7     0015                               ORG   $15
 8     0015    _____(c)         DATA2   FDB   SYMBOL
 9     ____(d)1234                        FDB   $1234
10     0019                       WORK    RMB   3
11                                *
12     C100                               ORG   $C100
13     XXXX                       HERE    RMB   1
14     XXXX    _____(e)         START   LDD   NUMBER
15     C104    _____(f)                 STAA  HERE
16     ____(g)5C                          INCB
17     C108    D7 1A                      STAB  WORK+1
18     C10A    _____(h)                 LDX   #WORK
19     ____(i)A7 02                       STAA  2,X
20     ____(j)_____(k)                  BNE   LAST
21     XXXX    FB C1 15                   ADDB  VALUE
22     XXXX    3F                 LAST    SWI          STOP FOR TRAINER
23     XXXX    _____(l)         VALUE   FCB   $55
24     C116                               END
```

```
   Defined            Symbol Name          Value              References

       8       DATA2                        0015
      13       _____(m)                   C100            15
      22       LAST                         ____(n)         __(o)
       5       NUMBER                       D000            14
      14       START                        C101
    __(p)      SYMBOL               =       XXXX             8
      23       VALUE                        C115            21
      10       _____(q)                   XXXX            17     18

         Lines Assembled :  24           Assembly Errors :  0
```

Figure 3-10   Exercise 3-7.

3-9. Figure 3-11 is an assembly language listing of the improved copy-a-table program from Chapter 2. Consider each of the following:
  (a) List the line numbers of the lines that will have altered instruction codes if only the statement on line 19 was changed, and it becomes ORG $C200.
  (b) List the line numbers of the lines that will have altered instruction codes if only the statement on line 9 was changed, and it becomes ORG $C000.

3-10. Modify the program in Figure 3-11 so it adds all the entries of the first table to the corresponding entries of the second table, and stores the sums in the second table.

3-11. Write an assembly language copy-a-table program that copies the entries from the first table to the second table in reverse order. The program must specify the table locations by the addresses of their first entries so the tables can be anywhere in memory. The data section will contain the addresses of the two tables and the single-byte length of the tables. Use only instructions covered by Chapters 1, 2, and 3.

```
 1                              *******************************************************
 2                              ** IMPROVED COPY TABLE PROGRAM FROM CHAPTER 2
 3                              *
 4                              *******************************************************
 5                              *
 6                              *******************************************************
 7                              ** DATA SECTION
 8                              *******************************************************
 9    0020                               ORG    $20
10    0020   C220      TABADR   FDB    $C220      ADDRESS OF FIRST TABLE
11    0022   20        SPACING  FCB    $20        SPACING BETWEEN TABLES
12    0023   04        TABLEN   FCB    4          TABLE LENGTH
13    0024             WRKCNT   RMB    1          WORKING COUNTER
14    0025             WRKPNT   RMB    2          WORKING POINTER SAVE
15                              *
16                              *******************************************************
17                              ** PROGRAM SECTION
18                              *******************************************************
19    C100                              ORG    $C100
20                              * INITIALIZE POINTER TO FIRST TABLE
21    C100   DE 20     START    LDX    TABADR
22    C102   DF 25              STX    WRKPNT
23                              * INITIALIZE WORKING COUNTER
24    C104   96 23              LDAA   TABLEN   GET TABLE LENGTH
25    C106   97 24              STAA   WRKCNT   STORE INTO WORKING COUNTER
26                              * GET TABLE SPACING
27    C108   D6 22              LDAB   SPACING
28                              * WORKING COUNTER EQUALS ZERO?
29    C10A   7D 00 24  AGAIN    TST    WRKCNT
30    C10D   27 11              BEQ    LAST     BRANCH ON YES
31                              * COPY ONE ENTRY
32                              *        GET POINTER TO FIRST TABLE
33    C10F   DE 25              LDX    WRKPNT
34                              *        GET ENTRY FROM FIRST TABLE
35    C111   A6 00              LDAA   0,X
36                              *        POINT TO SECOND TABLE
37    C113   3A                 ABX
38                              *        PUT ENTRY INTO SECOND TABLE
39    C114   A7 00              STAA   0,X
40                              * COUNT DOWN THE WORKING COUNTER
41    C116   7A 00 24           DEC    WRKCNT
42                              * ADVANCE POINTER TO NEXT ENTRY
43    C119   DE 25              LDX    WRKPNT
44    C11B   08                 INX
45    C11C   DF 25              STX    WRKPNT
46    C11E   20 EA              BRA    AGAIN    GO AROUND AGAIN
47                              * STOP THE PROGRAM
48    C120   3F        LAST     SWI             "STOP" FOR MOTOROLA TRAINER
49    C121                      END
```

```
 Defined           Symbol Name        Value          References

    29     AGAIN                       C10A        46
    48     LAST                        C120        30
    11     SPACING                     0022        27
    21     START                       C100
    10     TABADR                      0020        21
    12     TABLEN                      0023        24
    13     WRKCNT                      0024        25     29     41
    14     WRKPNT                      0025        22     33     43     45

        Lines Assembled :  49              Assembly Errors :  0
```

Figure 3-11   Exercise 3-9.

3-12. Write an assembly language program module to do the following: If the number in the A accumulator is −5 or less, replace it with −5, and if the number in A is +5 or greater, replace it with +5. The numbers are two's complement signed numbers.

3-13. Write an assembly language program module to test the number in the B accumulator to determine if it is within or equal to a lower and upper limit in memory locations labeled LOWER and UPPER. If the number is within the limits, the program must place FF for true in location WITHIN; otherwise it puts 00 there. The number in the B accumulator must be unchanged at the end of the program.
   (a) Assume the numbers are 8-bit two's complement signed numbers.
   (b) Assume the numbers are unsigned 8-bit numbers.

Chapter 4

Program Structure and Design

Programming is a topic seldom discussed in engineering and microcomputer textbooks. Many authors assume that people automatically know how to program once they understand what computer instructions are. Such an assumption is unrealistic. Programming is a complicated process—a skill that is most easily developed with guidance from an experienced and thoughtful mentor.

Since this chapter discusses programs and programming, let's begin by defining the following words:

- *Program*—the sequence of instructions, and the associated data values, that the computer hardware uses to carry out an algorithm—the step-by-step procedure required to do something.

- *Programmer*—a person who creates new programs and modifies or maintains existing programs.

- *Programming*—the act of creating programs, which includes initial design and planning, documenting, coding into a language, testing, and debugging.

- *Software*—the programs and related information used by a computer. The word *software* is often used as a synonym for program.

These definitions provide us with some common ground for discussing programming. Don't confuse these definitions with job titles or department names. For example, the person employed as a programmer may have quite different responsibilities from those stated in the definition.

4.1   THE HARD COLD FACTS

Programming is usually taught by discussing the tools used to make programs. The writer assumes that the reader will see the light and understand why these tools are important. But often the light doesn't shine! So let's begin by looking at some issues related to programming before getting to the tools and techniques.

What Does Software Cost?

Software is expensive. Industry studies show that labor cost for program development is about one to one and a half hours per machine instruction. And this is expensive skilled labor. And most useful programs require a minimum of several thousand instructions!

If you are a college student, you certainly believe that software is expensive. Think of the time and effort you put into your last program. You probably felt that the minor task that the program performed was not worth the effort!

Many on-the-job people have personal computers that they have never programmed to do a custom job. Even when advanced application programming languages are available, the effort required to write a custom program is not worthwhile. Usually a program is purchased that is good enough to meet the needs. Also, a large software industry exists to supply people with software tailored to specific applications.

Don't be deluded by the highly sophisticated personal computer program that costs a few hundred dollars or less. Mass market programs selling at that price depend solely upon a large volume of sales to justify their existence. Such programs often cost many hundreds of thousands of dollars to develop. Marketing costs drive the total cost even higher.

What about Software Quality?

The quality of much software and most documentation is poor. Even after extensive testing, software frequently has bugs. Some people say that all programs have at least one bug.

Programmers use the term *bug* to describe a mistake because the word *mistake* devastates their egos. Bugs are not only costly to the supplier, but also to the customer, who relies on the software to do a job.

You might think that good testing and correction will overcome the problem of bugs. Experienced people say that *testing proves the presence of bugs, not the absence of bugs*. Seldom does testing prove the reliability of software because not every possibility can be tested. Since testing has not been very successful, many companies now distribute pre-production copies of software to selected users. They hope to find the bugs before widespread distribution complicates the issue. Despite this effort, bugs frequently show up later.

Testing and debugging of software usually take more time than the original planning and writing. Consequently, most new software is completed later than the planned schedule. It is common for software projects to take two to three times the estimated time that was allotted.

After software has been used for a while, changes are often desired or necessary. Changes can easily introduce new bugs, and the changes are often very difficult to make. Experience at modifying software has led some companies to the following rule: If more than five percent of a program must be changed, throw the program away and start over!

How could this be? How could software quality be so troublesome? Besides the complexity of most software, it's partly due to the way people learn about computers. They must start by learning what a computer is, what instructions are, and what programming is. These are all very detailed efforts that focus the person's attention away from the final goal. As the person learns more, the number of details increases. Unless people make a concerted effort to see the bigger picture, they can become trapped in the habit of seeing only details. The result is poor-quality software. Some people go through an entire career without making an effort to see the final goal.

Programming Is Hard Work

Some people like programming. Others don't! To those who like programming, it is the best expression of creativity. To those who dislike programming, it is tedious, boring work.

Regardless of your feelings about programming, it is a difficult and exacting job. Programs with mistakes usually are nearly worthless. The pressure to be correct is overwhelming. There is no magic that will remove the work from programming.

Starting on the Right Path

Let's make your life easier. Programming can be made easier and you can be more productive if you approach the task properly. Studies of programming and related activities suggest ways to make programming more cost effective and less work, and the programs produced more reliable. This chapter discusses many ideas that have been put into practice and have proved to be useful.

Trial and error is the least effective way to write software. Deliberate and careful design approaches using good tools are necessary for true long-term success that includes maintenance and enhancement of the software.

Two good software development techniques—called *structured programming* and *top/down design*—are widely accepted. They are the starting point for good software design and implementation. They are not the answer to all problems. They are starting points. This book will encourage the use of both of these techniques. The examples in later sections all adhere to these principles.

Structured programming strongly influenced the design of most high-level programming languages developed since about 1970. It took until then for people to understand the programming problem. Since then, even the hardware architecture of computers has been influenced. Top/down design has also changed language design for the better. Many modern languages enforce or encourage these ideas in your programs.

Assembly language, as discussed earlier in this book, has total flexibility. Assembly language does nothing to enforce good programming. Only the discipline of the programmer enforces good programming. So the programmer must understand and embrace the techniques to gain the benefits that structured programming and top/down design promise.

4.2 PROGRAM DESIGN—WHAT'S IMPORTANT

Programming in any language is a human activity. Errors frustrate people and successful working programs cause great joy. Building programs and running a computer system are usually enjoyable activities. Many people work long hours at their home computers as a hobby.

Contrary to this view is the pain of detailed design work that goes into complex software. Program coding requires very exacting work.

Some people who use hobby computers call themselves hackers. This name implies that they use trial and error to get their programs to work as they wish. Hackers usually do little planning or detailed design of their software.

Programmers' Goals

People usually have goals when they start to write a program. Assume that this person is not programming as a hobby, but has a serious reason to do the job. This person may be a college student, working engineer, software developer, or a consultant. Programmer is a useful name for these people, although the job title of programmer may imply quite different duties. Once again, the term *programmer* as used here means the person—usually persons—who designs and writes a program.

Programmers have similar goals as they set out to write programs. Different applications will affect the goals, so assume that microcomputer hardware as discussed in this book is adequate for the application. The list of possible goals is probably very long, so consider only the following five:

- *Write the shortest program.*   The shortest program means the program that occupies the fewest bytes of memory and yet does the required task. There are many reasons for this goal. In product engineering or personal computer applications, the program length may be important because using less memory hardware reduces costs. College students may gain status with other students if their programs are shorter when doing the same assignment. Making the program fit existing resources could be useful if adding more memory is not practical. Many considerations including cost may limit memory size, especially in time-sharing applications.

- *Write the fastest program.*   The fastest program is the one that runs in the shortest time while doing the required task. In product applications, such as automobile engine control, quick processing of complex algorithms is necessary to make the engine run correctly. Personal computers are being used for ever-larger applications, but must quickly interact with the person operating the computer. The fees for using some time-sharing computers are based on the run time of the program.

- *Write an easily understood program.*   People, including the person writing the program, will need to understand the function of the instructions in the program. Understanding is necessary for changing the program, fixing bugs, or coping with changes in the hardware. Complex programs are more difficult to understand than simple programs. The program algorithm may affect the ease of understanding of a program, so the programmer may choose the algorithm accordingly.

- *Write an easily modified program.*   Modifying a program means changing it to cope with changes in the environment. For example, a monitoring computer for several automatic manufacturing machines must monitor more machines if production must increase. The engine control computer for an eight-cylinder engine will require changes if it's to control a four-cylinder engine. A personal computer program may require changes to use a new type of display monitor. Each of these cases involves changes in an existing and functioning program. These examples clearly imply that an entirely new program is not necessary.

- *Meet the schedule.*   Meeting a schedule is usually the goal of the programmer's supervisor or client, or of a college professor. The schedule specifies the date when the software user can do productive work with the program. A contract may dictate the schedule. Release of a new model of a product will enforce a deadline. Remember that microcomputers often are part of a product, and late release will give the competitor's products an advantage. To meet the schedule, people often forget all the other goals discussed and press on as fast as possible.

You probably can add several other goals to this list. What were your goals the last time you wrote a program?

What We Are Working With

The goals of programmers must be put into correct perspective in view of practical market conditions. The cost and performance of microcomputer hardware have changed greatly since microcomputers were first developed. Here are some accomplishments of the integrated circuit and computer manufacturers since the first hardware appeared:

- *Speed.*   Microprocessor speed has increased more than a factor of 10.

- *Cost.*   The cost of chips for equivalent performance has decreased more than a factor of 100.

- *Memory size.*   Usual memory sizes have increased from a few kilobytes to a few megabytes.

- *Secondary storage.*   Secondary storage has evolved beyond slow and small floppy disks with a capacity of a few hundred kilobytes. Hard and optical disks and CD ROMs (Compact Disk read only memory) have hundreds of megabytes of capacity and are much faster than the original floppy disks.

The enormous improvement in computer hardware has also increased its complexity. The complexity of software development has similarly increased. Sometimes additional computing power simplifies the programmer's job through more advanced software, but the complexity is still there.

In product engineering applications with embedded computers, the computer is part of a product and even the electronics will influence the programmer's task. Development software cannot easily hide the hardware complexity, although that is the intention.

The effect of increased complexity has been an ever-increasing cost of software development. Modification and long-term maintenance of software are large problems. The success of microcomputers has made enhancements a necessary marketing device. Competitors will be enhancing their products too!

Assessing the Goals Based on Reality

Let's evaluate each of the programmer's goals in view of the reality of the market and the technology available. Here is some discussion and some opinions about each goal:

- *Write the shortest program.*   This goal emphasizes expensive human resources to reduce the cost of inexpensive hardware. Human resources are an expensive part of product development, and people write programs. Automated factories build computer hardware, so it is low in cost. Thus, this goal is of little practical value. Even if many copies of the program will be used, it is seldom practical to make deliberate efforts to write short programs.

  Effort toward writing short programs also encourages programming tricks to cut memory usage. Tricks usually lead to problems sometime in the lifetime of a product. In contrast, selecting a good algorithm that is particularly efficient in using memory would be practical.

- *Write the fastest program.*   With the high and ever-increasing speed of microcomputer hardware, this is not an important goal for most applications. A big related problem, if speed is important, is knowing how to write the program for fast execution before writing begins. Similarly, determining what to optimize for speed after completing a program that is too slow is difficult. Usually, it is impractical to rewrite an entire program to optimize its speed anyway.

  The speed of a program must be determined under realistic control situations. One testing approach, called *profiling*, is to take data on the frequency of usage of various parts of the program. You find out how often each part of the program runs under realistic circumstances. The usage data reveals which parts have a significant effect on the performance. You then optimize those significant parts. For example, doubling the speed of a part that accounts for one percent of the total processing time does little good. Doubling the speed of a part that accounts for 40 percent of the time makes a large overall improvement.

The realistic goal is to get a good program working, and then optimize the parts that will make a difference. This accomplishes overall cost effectiveness. So deliberate effort to make a fast program from the beginning is usually not practical.

The execution speed of a program is almost independent of the length of the program. Long programs are not necessarily slower than short ones. For example, suppose a short program is written as loops inside loops. An equivalent long program is a sequence of instructions without loops. The short program will certainly run slower than the long one.

- *Write an easily understood program.*   The word *understood* implies understanding by people—including both the programmer and others. Better understanding results from simple straightforward problem solutions as opposed to complex and clever solutions.

Never use programming tricks. For example, never use the op code of an instruction as the data value for another instruction. Clever tricks may slightly shorten or speed up a program. On the other hand, using expensive human resources to save inexpensive computer resources is not cost effective. Therefore, an easily understood program without tricks is a principal goal of realistic programmers.

- *Write an easily modified program.*   Modification of programs happens frequently both during development and after completion. Making a program easy to modify requires planning and effort during the design. However, this small effort is cost effective because it saves very large efforts when making the inevitable changes. Successful programmers focus on long-term goals and not just immediate success.

- *Meet the schedule.*   Many people in the software industry accept late delivery of software as normal, since it happens so frequently. Users of personal computers have coined the term *vaporware* to describe advertised software that is not available for purchase. Good software delivered late is often not profitable.

The best way to meet this goal is to organize carefully and plan for changes. Software written to ease understanding and modification is necessary. Forget about writing short or fast executing programs. Forget about clever programming tricks. Emphasizing the correct goals will get the job done as fast as possible.

The purpose of this section is to emphasize that you should write programs that are easy to understand and easy to modify. No significant effort should go into writing a program so it is fast or short. This does not say that silly things should be done. It says there is little value in spending serious effort to make short or fast programs. This direction is somewhat contrary to human nature. Many people feel that much of the fun of programming is finding clever solutions to programming problems. Instead, that creativity should be applied to bigger problems than the minute details of a program.

4.3   PRACTICAL PROGRAMMING

A set of guidelines will emphasize the important goals in the creative process of programming. Guidelines cannot cover all circumstances and guarantee success—success requires good judgment. The ideas presented here are completely compatible with the goals of easily understood and easily modified programs:

- *Don't use a single resource for multiple purposes.* When an item is used for multiple purposes, compromises will usually be necessary in the use of that item. Instead, create a new resource for each independent purpose. Separate resources will sometimes require a slightly longer program, but the advantages are worth it. For example, don't use a loop counter to form addresses in a pointer. The two uses should be independent of each other; then a change in one use won't affect the other.

- *Use no intimate knowledge of the hardware configuration.* For example, do not use unimplemented bits of a register as default values; they may change later with hardware revisions. Similarly, moving program modules to new memory locations should have no effect on the correctness of the program.

- *Keep the instructions and data separated.* The data numbers should not be scattered between the instructions. Not only is it difficult to understand such a program, but the program will have unnecessary instructions to branch over the data numbers.

- *Use tables.* Collect program parameters and related data together in tables or structures. If the program is designed to interact with a person, provide software that will easily modify the tables.

- *Only put constant data within the instructions.* To change data within instructions, you must have intimate understanding of the instructions in the program. Only when a change in the data also requires the program to be rewritten should data be put inside instructions. For example, immediate and indexed addressed instructions contain constants.

- *Avoid tricks.* Clever use of instructions usually leads to solutions that are not easy to enhance and alter. Tricks usually lead to greater cost.

- *Don't write self-modifying programs.* Programs that change their instructions as they run are very difficult to understand, debug, and modify. If the computer has permanent memory that can't change, as many microcomputers do, the program won't work at all if it must modify itself.

- *Use the instructions in the instruction set well.* The instruction set might be somewhat inconsistent, so you might prefer to avoid some instructions because they are rarely used. However, the design probably includes odd instructions because they make certain functions easy to do. Use all the available resources.

You should always actively strive to write good programs. Don't concentrate only on solving the problem at hand. You will find problem solving will be easier when you search for the simple, straightforward solution instead of the complex and elegant solution.

4.4 FLOWCHARTING

A tool to help organize the programmer's thoughts is valuable when designing and writing programs. Organization will aid in promoting the proper goals. Organizing your thinking with a design tool helps you to include details that you might miss otherwise.

Computer programs are algorithmic processes—they carry out large jobs one small step at a time. Most people understand algorithmic processes best when they are illustrated graphically. Several graphical tools exist, but the one most widely used is the flowchart.

A *flowchart* is a diagram made from several standard symbols connected by flow arrows. The flowchart symbols represent actions to be taken. The arrows direct the reader to follow the progress of the actions of the program.

The flowchart is both a documentation device and a design tool. At the design stage, the programmer usually sketches the flowchart on paper and changes it repeatedly as the design progresses. When the design and program coding are complete, the flowchart becomes a documentation device because it clearly illustrates what the program does and how it does it. Both the programmer and others use the flowchart to understand a program.

Flowchart Symbols

Flowcharts are made from several standard symbols. Let's consider a subset of the standard symbols and their meanings. There are additional specialized symbols, but they often complicate the flowchart and add little in the way of clarity.

Primary flowchart symbols

The primary symbols are necessary for making most flowcharts. With them, you can make any flowchart. All other symbols are optional.

Flow lines and flow arrows. Flow lines with arrow heads guide the reader through the other symbols in the correct order. Several flow lines may come together at an intersection point, and then one line continues from that point as shown in Figure 4-1. Several flow arrows cannot leave an intersection point though, because the reader would not know which line to follow.

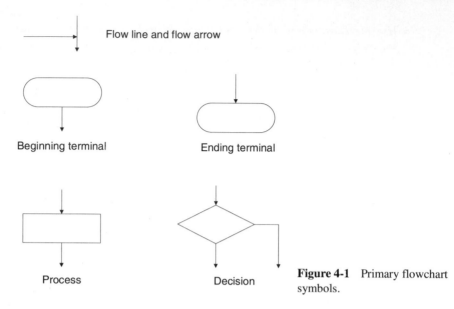

Figure 4-1   Primary flowchart symbols.

Only a single flow line should terminate on a symbol. If two or more flow lines must come together at a symbol, the flow lines should come together before the symbol with only a single flow line terminating at the symbol. This leads to better clarity.

Terminal.   The flowchart begins and ends with a unique symbol called a terminal as shown in Figure 4-1. The beginning terminal tells the reader where to start reading the flowchart. Put the name of the program module associated with this flowchart on the terminal symbol. The ending terminal indicates where the computer stops processing instructions in this program module. The label on the ending terminal is usually END or RETURN.

Process.   The process symbol is a rectangular box that means do something or process some information. Figure 4-1 shows the process symbol. Write the name or description of the process inside the symbol. Most of the symbols in flowcharts are process symbols.

Each process box identifies a group of instructions that together carry out a particular function. This function has a distinct beginning point and a distinct ending point. Hence, the symbol has a single flow arrow entering it and a single flow arrow leaving it. This simple yet important observation, one flow arrow entering and one flow arrow leaving, is discussed further later.

Decision.   The choice between two alternative flow paths is the essence of a decision. Figure 4-1 illustrates the diamond-shaped symbol for a decision. A short word description of the decision followed by a question mark identifies the symbol.

The computer makes binary choices, so the fundamental decision symbol has two flow arrows leaving it and one arrow coming to it. The paths going out usually have two opposite labels, such as YES/NO, UP/DOWN, or TRUE/FALSE. These words answer the question inside the symbol. Decisions made up of more than two alternatives require several fundamental decisions.

Secondary flowchart symbols

The symbols included here are commonly encountered. However, their use is optional and usually unnecessary.

Connector.   Two connectors containing the same identifier indicate the same point in a broken flow line—they connect two parts of a broken flow line. The connector symbol shown in Figure 4-2 is a small circle. Connectors usually contain a letter as an identifier. Each connector will have either one flow arrow coming into it or one flow arrow going out of it. Connectors are seldom used. You should avoid connectors whenever possible because reading broken flow lines is difficult.

Off-page connector.   Figure 4-2 shows the off-page connector symbol—it connects two parts of a broken flow line that are on different sheets of paper. *The off-page connector is never needed and should never be used!* You will understand this very strong statement after reading the next two major sections.

Flowchart Example

A simple flowchart that includes all the primary symbols is shown in Figure 4-3. The symbols are not labeled, because the figure illustrates only the symbols and not a program. However, the logic of the algorithm can be understood even without labels.

Look at the figure carefully to see the individual flowchart symbols. Here are some characteristics of this flowchart that you should observe:

- The flowchart begins with a single terminator symbol.

- Each process box has a single flow arrow coming to it and a single flow arrow leaving it.

- The decision symbol has exactly two flow arrows leaving it.

- When the two flow arrows come together, they meet before the ending terminator so only one arrow meets the ending symbol.

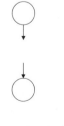

Breaking connector

Continuation connector

Off-page connector

Figure 4-2   Secondary flowchart symbols.

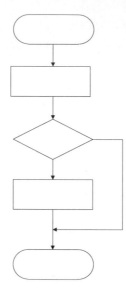
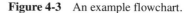

Figure 4-3   An example flowchart.

- The arrow heads clearly show the flow of the algorithm represented by the flow-chart.

- The flowchart has a single ending terminator.

It is good practice to use the flowchart symbols as described here for all flowcharts. Most of these characteristics should seem simple and obvious. However, when an algorithm becomes very complex, and hence its flowchart becomes complex, it is easy to forget these simple rules.

4.5   STRUCTURED PROGRAMMING

One requirement of good programming is simplicity. If programs are very complex, they are difficult to write, to modify, and to understand.

Programs consist of building blocks that flowchart symbols represent. Fortunately, we need only three symbols to make flowcharts: the terminal, the process block, and the decision. This seems simple enough, but there are many ways of connecting these building blocks with flow arrows.

Undisciplined programmers write *spaghetti* programs. The flowchart for a spaghetti program has the flow lines and boxes entangled in ways to make changes or understanding almost impossible. Figure 4-4 illustrates such a flowchart. Try to follow all the possible paths through the flowchart. Some processes have three or four different paths leading to them.

The effort to cope with spaghetti led to research to determine if there are fundamental program building blocks. The research proved there are only three fundamental ways of connecting the flowchart symbols. These three, called *program structures*, are enough to

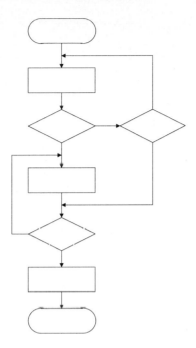

Figure 4-4   The flowchart for a spaghetti program.

build all possible programs. The discipline now called *structured programming* was the result of the research. The purest form of structured programming requires the building of programs from the three fundamental program structures only.

Experience has shown that structured programming leads to better quality software and to more cost-effective software. Of course, programs are only correctly structured if the programmer makes them structured, or the computer language enforces structuring. It is not possible to make an unstructured program look structured on a flowchart. The programmer must design a structured program and then write the program by following the design. It's not possible to write a spaghetti program, get it to work by trial and error, and then make a structured flowchart for it.

Structured programming is just one step in designing good programs and does not guarantee high-quality programs. It is just one necessary ingredient in successful software engineering.

Fundamental Program Structures

The names of the three fundamental program structures are SEQUENCE, IF-THEN-ELSE and DO-WHILE. Look at the three fundamental structures as represented by the flowchart in Figures 4-5 through 4-7. Observe that each structure has a single beginning or entry point and a single exit point. Similarly, each process box on a flowchart has a single entry point and a single exit point. Never draw any additional flow arrows entering or leaving a process box.

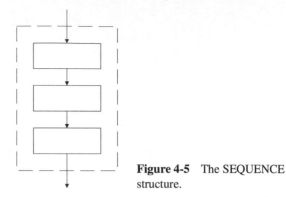

Figure 4-5   The SEQUENCE structure.

Each structure is itself a process—it's correct to draw a rectangular process box around each structure. The fundamental program structure is the basic building block of programs. Structured programming advocates building programs from only these fundamental structures. The phrase *correctly structured program* describes a program built only from fundamental structures.

SEQUENCE structure

The SEQUENCE structure is simply several process boxes strung together one after another. Figure 4-5 shows that this series of boxes begins at one point and ends at one point. Remember this structure by saying that it does one thing after another in a sequence.

IF-THEN-ELSE structure

Figure 4-6 illustrates the binary decision structure called IF-THEN-ELSE. The decision chooses between two alternative processes. The flow arrows must merge at one point after the processes on the two sides. If these two sides do not come back together, you get spaghetti because control is transferred outside the structure.

A common form of this structure has a process that does nothing on one side. The effect is a structure, sometimes called IF-THEN, that does something or bypasses it.

Remember the IF-THEN-ELSE structure by saying that it tests a condition, and IF the condition is satisfied, THEN do something, otherwise do something ELSE.

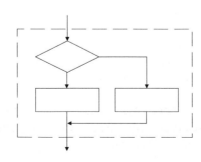

Figure 4-6   The IF-THEN-ELSE structure.

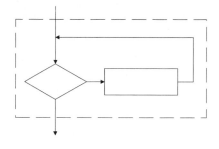

Figure 4-7   The DO-WHILE structure.

DO-WHILE structure

Figure 4-7 illustrates the iterative or loop structure called DO-WHILE. The internal process or body is repeatedly executed until the decision determines that the process should not execute again. That is, it loops until the decision exits the loop.

You can use any kind of condition for the decision. The decision may be based on a number. Alternatively, it could depend upon a complex series of input/output operations. Usually the body of the loop will do something to alter the condition so the loop exits eventually. If the exit never occurs, the loop is an *infinite loop*, meaning that it never ends.

If you are familiar with other kinds of loops, you can easily distinguish the DO-WHILE loop because the DO-WHILE has the decision *before* the body of the loop. The decision may cause the loop to exit without the body of the loop executing even once.

Remember the DO-WHILE structure by saying that it will test for a condition, and then DO something over and over WHILE the condition exists.

Extended Program Structures

A few other structures, called extended structures, meet the general requirements of structured programming. A variety of names have been created for these extra structures. You should look for the fundamental characteristics of structures of other names because they may be the same structures you already know.

Many high-level languages have some extended structures. People also write assembly language versions, although these extra structures are not necessary—the three fundamental structures will carry out all tasks. However, extra structures are sometimes more convenient for the programmer or for the language compiler.

DO-UNTIL structure

The DO-UNTIL loop structure shown in Figure 4-8 is similar to the DO-WHILE. The main difference is that the decision to exit the loop is after the body of the loop rather than before.

A serious limitation of the DO-UNTIL is that the body of the loop always executes at least once. Since the body executes before the decision, it is impossible for the decision to prevent the execution of the body at least once.

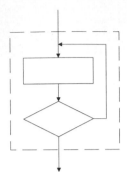

Figure 4-8   The DO-UNTIL structure.

Practical programs often need to execute the body of a loop zero times. So the DO-UNTIL loop is impractical as a general solution. The DO-WHILE loop has no such limitation; it is more flexible and adequate for all programs.

The DO-UNTIL loop can be troublesome if the programmer is not careful. If the loop decrements a numeric counter down to zero to end the loop, an initial counter value of zero causes problems. Probably the loop will execute the maximum number of times that the counter can specify—decrementing a zero value, if unsigned numbers are used, results in the largest possible value. The problem happens because the loop decrements the counter before the decision.

The usual solution to this problem is another decision before the loop that checks for this special case. The decision bypasses the loop to avoid the problem of an initial zero value. This decision adds extra code to the program that is unnecessary and confusing.

The DO-UNTIL loop does reflect normal thought to some extent. That is, people usually think about doing something first and then about making a decision based on the results. By contrast, experienced programmers think of a loop structure and how to get out of the loop. So the DO-WHILE loop seems normal to experienced programmers and odd to others.

IN-CASE-OF structure

Figure 4-9 shows the multiple decision structure with more than two alternatives called IN-CASE-OF. The first distinguishing feature of this structure is that one alternative for each decision is to do nothing. The second feature is that the program exits the structure after a single test is satisfied and the corresponding process is executed.

The IN-CASE-OF structure can be made from fundamental structures. Figure 4-10 shows how multiple IF-THEN-ELSE structures do this. There is also a table lookup technique for making the IN-CASE-OF structure.

The IN-CASE-OF structure is just a program module that has a name because it occurs so often in practical programs. It does meet the basic requirement of a structure in that it has one beginning and one ending point.

Some high-level programming languages have a CASE structure to make programming a little easier. Also, the language compiler may be able to optimize the machine language for fast execution.

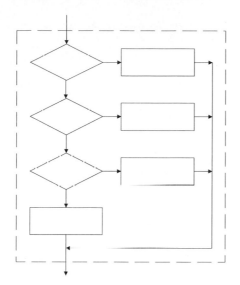

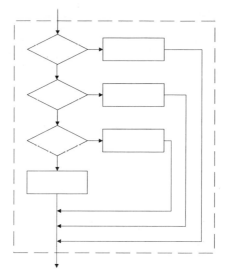

Figure 4-9   The IN-CASE-OF structure.

Figure 4-10   The IN-CASE-OF structure made from IF-THEN-ELSE.

Identifying Structured and Unstructured Programs

The flowchart shown in Figure 4-11 represents a structured program. Dashed lines enclose the fundamental structures. The design uses structures inside structures to build the overall flowchart, and eventually the whole program. Notice that you can study the structure of the program without even knowing the names in the symbols.

To check a flowchart for correct structure, begin by drawing boxes over the flowchart to enclose program structures at all reasonable places. If all the boxes have only a single entry point and a single exit point, the flowchart meets a major requirement of structured programming.

It is not legitimate to enclose a collection of spaghetti with a box and then claim to have a structured program! On the other hand, if each box contains only a fundamental structure, you have met all the requirements.

Look at the unstructured spaghetti flowchart in Figure 4-4. Try to draw boxes on the flowchart that enclose program structures that each have a single entry and a single exit point. Your boxes will make it apparent that the program modules have multiple entry and exit points.

Programs represented by unstructured flow charts usually contain unnecessary branch or jump instructions. Therefore, you can usually identify an unstructured program from its listing by looking at the use of the branch and jump instructions.

Some high-level programming languages have a branch statement called GOTO. Some companies encourage their employees to use *GOTO-less* programming to avoid jumping around in the program. Their goal is to encourage structured programming. However, those

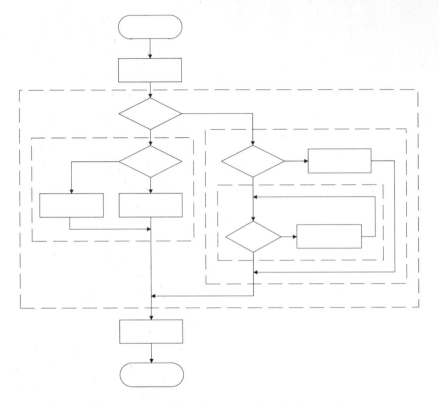

Figure 4-11   A structured flowchart made from fundamental structures.

languages with a GOTO usually require the GOTO statement to make all the fundamental structures. In contrast, other high-level programming languages lack the equivalent of a GOTO statement eliminating any chance for unstructured programs.

Making Structured Loops

If you are unaccustomed to structured programming, making structured DO-WHILE loops may seem difficult. As an example, the loop in Figure 4-12 is clearly unstructured. The loop has two exit points. The problem is caused by the need to terminate the loop prematurely when the program detects an error. The decision in the example sends control out of the loop, effectively making a second exit point.

The alternative flowchart in Figure 4-13 easily handles the premature termination using a structured design. The technique requires that the termination condition for the loop be forced. Then the loop follows its normal course to the end and remains correctly structured.

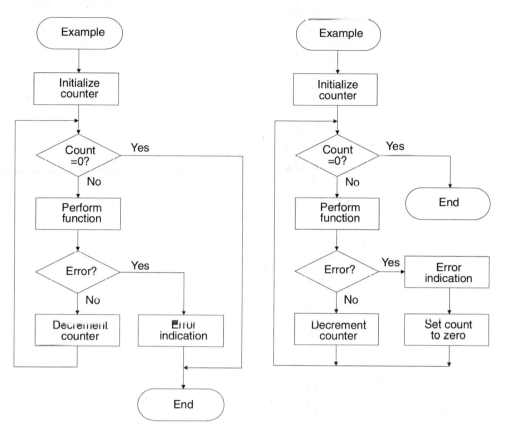

Figure 4-12   Unstructured premature loop termination.

Figure 4-13   Structured premature loop termination.

Complicated loops may need to exit due to several different conditions. These loops are easily implemented in fundamental structures by using a flag that determines whether the loop will exit. The flag is set to an initial value that enables the loop to execute. Then various program conditions alter the flag. The loop exits based on the value of the flag. Sometimes, the value of the flag is used outside the loop. Figure 4-14 illustrates using such a flag to terminate a loop.

A Troublesome Case

There is one problem that often disturbs people when they begin using structured programming. The problem is an error that aborts the program, thus preventing it from going to its end. Figure 4-15 illustrates the case of a program that detects an error that prevents it from continuing.

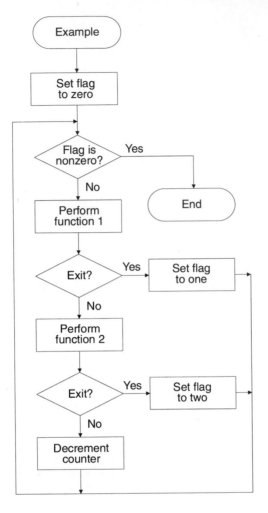

Figure 4-14 Using a flag to terminate a loop.

Aborting the program technically is a violation of structured programming because the program does not come to its normal end. However, it is quite practical to do and it causes no problems. This is true because aborting the program means to leave this execution of the program at some point and not return to continue from that point under any circumstance. So aborting the program prevents it from reaching the normal end of the program.

If a program is run again after being aborted, the new execution starts at the beginning of the program. It never resumes from the point where the program was aborted.

Starting again at the beginning is the reason that aborting a program is allowed within structured programming. Regardless of structuring, the data required by the program may be damaged by running only part of the program. However, running the entire program from the beginning will initialize the program and regenerate any data needed.

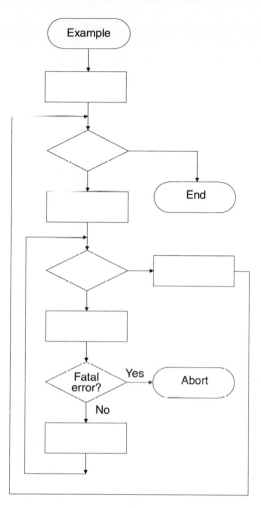

Figure 4-15   A troublesome case for structured programming.

Will You Use It?

If you have experience at writing spaghetti programs, you may decide that creating a structured program is unnecessary and nearly impossible. You will feel very limited by the requirements, which may at times seem artificial. If you persevere, you will learn that structured programming is neither impossible nor confining.

You will often discover that an unstructured program resulted from poor understanding of the problem. Experience shows that forcing a design into proper structure also forces the programmer to think carefully about the problem. When the design meets the requirements of structured programming, other problems are often solved. Thus, structuring is not just a programming tool, but also is an aid to problem solving.

Sometimes people feel that making a structured flowchart limits what can be done in the program code. However, if you cannot solve the problem in the flowchart, you cannot solve the problem in the code.

Making Unstructured Programs Structured

It is almost impossible to make an unstructured program correctly structured by simple changes. Generally, you must write an entirely new program. The logic of the unstructured program must be understood to design the structured equivalent. So it's not possible to illustrate an unstructured flowchart without labels and then make its equivalent. Instead, all the detail of the unstructured program must be understood.

Clearly the only practical approach to structured programs is to design a structured program from the beginning. Then as changes are made, the structuring must be preserved. Experience will show you that this is easier than it may seem. When a program is written in correctly structured form, changes are easier to make.

4.6   TOP/DOWN DESIGN

Top/down design is an old and simple idea that has a new name, since it is now applied to computer program design. Top/down design simply says to get the big picture first, and then consider finer and finer details as the design proceeds. The basic idea is to approach the design of a program by first identifying the major functional parts, or modules, of the program. This collection of major modules is called the top level of the design. Next, each of these parts is further broken into smaller parts, which together are called the second level. The second-level design is equivalent to the top-level module that it expands. The design continues until there is enough detail to write and document the program.

Detail is added to the design by adding more modules at lower levels. It is not correct to alter the top-level modules to make more modules. Doing so would make too many modules, causing the designer to lose sight of the overall design. The result probably would be a spaghetti program.

For example, some second-level modules may be quite complex, so these modules are broken into parts on a lower third level. Again, the parts of the second level are not replaced, but each module is separately broken into parts.

Writing teachers recommend this approach for writing an English composition—another form of software. To write a composition, make an outline with the major sections identified first. Next, add subsections to the outline; the subsections are each equivalent to the major section that they are outlining. This expansion to additional detailed subsections continues until a complete outline results.

The table of contents of a book is an example of an outline of a written document. The design of the book you are reading was done this way. I decided upon the chapter contents by making the table of contents first. Then I determined the sections of each chapter. As I wrote, smaller subsections were designed and added to a detailed table of contents, which served as an outline. The table of contents in the book contains only the upper levels of the detailed table of contents. Some changes in the design were made, but the major modules remained the same as in the original design.

Choosing Program Modules

You must decide how to break the design of a program into practical modules. The programmer must use judgment and experience to do this successfully. You must choose functional parts of the program to be modules. Each module should do something that is immediately recognizable by someone looking at the design. Only related functions should be together in a module.

For example, a program may gather some data and then print a report. The jobs of gathering the data and printing are two separate functions. Probably, these should be thought of separately in tackling the design. There will be details to consider, such as scaling data values for unit conversions. These details can be thought about later after all the top-level design is finished.

Top/Down Design Using Flowcharts

Figure 4-16 illustrates the top/down approach to computer program design using flowcharts. The first step in designing a program is making a top-level flowchart that will segment the total program into its major functional sections. Next, make a second-level flowchart for each process block that requires additional design work. You continue creating additional levels for complex modules. Your judgment determines when you have enough levels. This is when your creativity gets expressed and when you make judgments about the design of the program.

The lower-level flowcharts are equivalent to the higher-level modules they represent. That is, the process blocks each have a single beginning point and a single ending point. This means the expanded flowchart for a block also must have a single beginning point and a single ending point.

Relationship to structured programming

The requirement for a single beginning and single ending point is the same as one requirement of structured programming. Thus, structured programming is perfectly compatible with top/down design. Top/down design requires structured programming.

Number of levels

You must determine the number of levels required. Since this is a creative design process, we can rely only on practical experience to provide guidelines or rules. But there is some justification for the rules.

Maximum number of levels.   The first purpose of a flowchart is to display the function performed by each section of the program. The names placed on the symbols must

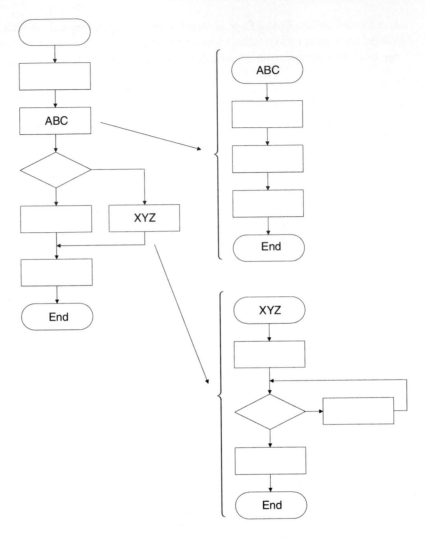

Figure 4-16   Top/down design using flowcharts.

describe these functions. The programming language statements will not appear on the flow-charts, since the language statements comprise the program implementation—not the program function. A listing of the language statements documents the program.

In other words, the flowchart should not have language statements on its symbols. Not placing language statements on the flowchart provides an effective maximum limit on the number of levels of flowcharts. Whenever the only choice is to put language statements on the flowchart, that flowchart is unnecessary.

Similarly, the flowcharts will be independent of the computer architecture and the hardware. Don't put hardware details on the flowchart.

Minimum number of levels.   At the other extreme, the minimum number of levels depends on the size of each flowchart. If there are few levels, it may be necessary to make large flowcharts to provide enough detail. However, large flowcharts destroy most of the advantages of top/down design. Each flowchart should be simple enough that you understand its entire function at a glance without extensive study. This is possible if the flowchart has no more than ten symbols.

Therefore, a rule of thumb is to limit flowcharts to ten symbols. A ten-symbol flowchart is practical because it will easily fit on a single 8 1/2 by 11 inch sheet of paper, making the documentation convenient. Furthermore, *you will never need the off-page connector symbol*, since your flowcharts will each fit on one page. An earlier section encouraged you never to use the off-page connector because of this.

Top/Down Design Summary

Here is a summary of the guidelines for top/down design using flowcharts:

- Make a top-level flowchart first, then make second-level flowcharts, and then other levels if needed. Then start coding. Never start writing code without designing this way first.

- Run a working program as soon as possible to check the design. Don't be concerned if incomplete or dummy modules make the function of the program nonsense.

- Design each program module using structured programming, and then code them in a structured fashion according to the flowchart.

- Put comments in the program that match the flowcharts. Put the comments in the source as you create the source module, not after it has been assembled and tested.

- Use some commenting technique to show the program structure in the listing.

- Put functional names on the flowchart symbols. Don't make any flowcharts so detailed that only language statements can be put on the flowchart.

- Make flowcharts that are independent of the computer architecture and hardware whenever possible. For example, the flowcharts should contain no mention of addressing modes or microprocessor registers.

- Limit the maximum size of each flowchart to ten symbols. This limits the complexity of the flowchart and the flowchart will fit on one sheet of paper.

- Design each flowchart to meet the requirements of structured programming.

These guidelines will help you write good programs, but they do not guarantee success. Only careful and diligent work by a knowledgeable person will result in high-quality software.

4.7 STRUCTURED TOP/DOWN ASSEMBLY LANGUAGE

Assembly language programmers have total flexibility in writing and documenting their programs. The quality of their work varies from excellent to worthless. The following two examples illustrate these extremes. The comments will help you evaluate the ideas presented. Do not assume that the approaches used in the good program are the only good ways to write and document programs. Instead, form your own opinion and use your creativity to make improvements.

A Good Program

The sample program that follows provides an illustration of the techniques of structured programming and top/down design. First, structured flowcharts demonstrate top/down format even though the program is very short and simple. Next, the assembly language program listing illustrates the use of many instructions, addressing modes, and programming techniques. The documentation on the listing is adequate for most purposes. Of course, the documentation assumes the reader has knowledge of the Motorola assembly language.

Example program specifications

The following program searches a table in memory for negative numbers. It both counts and sums these negative numbers and then indicates if all the numbers in the table are negative. The table may represent the inventory of certain parts, and the negative numbers are orders that could not be filled.

The table is specified by the address of its first entry (lowest address) and the length of the table. The table contains single-byte signed numbers. The length (unsigned), negative count, and sum values are double-byte numbers to allow for large tables and large sums. The program does not test for two's complement overflows.

Flowcharts for the example

Flowcharts for this example are shown in Figure 4-17. Though this program is very simple, the top/down design idea is useful. Each flowchart defines a specific function that is independent of the other parts. The title of each flowchart matches exactly the title of the higher-level process that is being expanded.

Documentation on the assembler listing

Documenting the program structure in the listing is very useful. The programmer should use some creativity in deciding upon a format. The format used in the example is only one possibility. It was chosen primarily to make the listing match the flowcharts closely. Here are the details of the format used in the listing:

- *Major sections of the listing.*   The title block, data section, and program section of the listing are labeled with headings surrounded by lines of asterisks. The asterisks

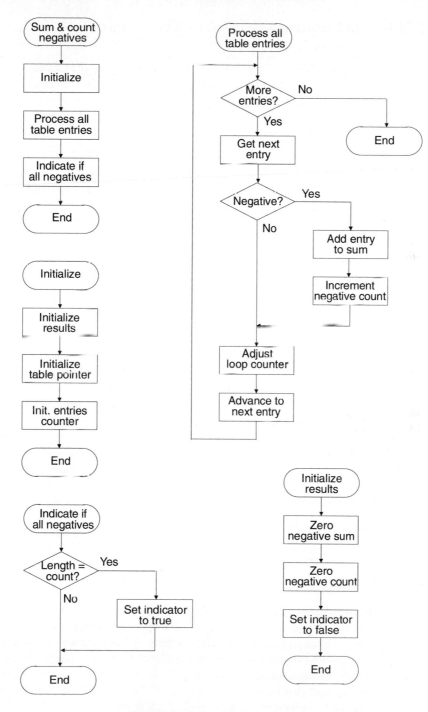

Figure 4-17   Top/down flowcharts.

make the headings easy to find. It is also common to print each of these sections on separate pages of the listing.

- *Top-level format.* The top-level flowchart titles are surrounded by dashed lines as Figure 4-18 shows on lines 36 through 38. The titles on the flowchart must closely match those on the listing. All the in-line programming for this level should be between its title and the title of the next section on the listing that is at the same level. In other words, the program should not jump around on the listing with logical parts of this section within other sections. All the code for the Initialization module should be on the listing before the title for the Process All Entries section.

- *Second-level format.* The titles of the second-level flowcharts have headings without dashed lines as Figure 4-18 shows on lines 39, 47, and 49. These comments mark off the second-level modules. The headings for the second level are less prominent than those for the top level. It is easy to see that the second-level modules are contained within the top-level module.

- *Third-level format.* Indenting of lower-level comments is common practice as Figure 4-18 shows on lines 40, 43, and 45. The indenting makes these comments less prominent on the listing and implies that these modules are within the second-level module.

- *Implementation specific comments.* The last set of comments is at the right of the instructions as Figure 4-18 shows on lines 63 and 64. These comments are not flowchart titles; instead, they explain details of how the instructions were used in writing the program. Sometimes, such comments include specifics of a particular computer architecture and the particular programming approach used. This information is not on the flowchart, since the flowchart describes only the function of the program. Notice that the comment on line 63 was continued on line 64 with two periods that approximate an ellipsis to imply the continuation. The area to the right of instructions is also the perfect place to explain tricky uses of instructions. The explanation is on the line with the instruction, making it easy to understand.

Documentation is an area open to the creativity of the programmer. Some companies attempt to enforce consistency among programmers by mandating the format of the listing.

Editing comments

Since programs change frequently, the comments also will change frequently. You should plan for changes in your comments. The approach used in the example makes these changes easy. For example, changes often require moving sections of the program to new locations. An editor program can easily move a block of lines. If the comments are formatted as shown here, the instructions can be changed or moved without changing the comments. If a change requires that an instruction with a detailed comment at the right be moved, the instruction and its comment can be moved together easily. It is difficult not to move the specific comments with the instruction!

```
 1                         *********************************************************
 2                         ** SUM AND COUNT NEGATIVE TABLE ENTRIES
 3                         ** INDICATE IF ALL NEGATIVE
 4                         *
 5                         * THIS PROGRAM SUMS THE NEGATIVE ENTRIES IN A TABLE,
 6                         * COUNTS THE NUMBER OF NEGATIVES, AND INDICATES IF
 7                         * ALL ENTRIES ARE NEGATIVE.
 8                         *
 9                         * THE TABLE IS SPECIFIED BY ITS ADDRESS AND LENGTH.
10                         * TABLE ENTRIES AND INDICATOR ARE SINGLE-BYTES. THE
11                         * LENGTH, SUM, AND NEGATIVE COUNT ARE DOUBLE-BYTES.
12                         * NO TWO'S COMPLEMENT OVERFLOW CHECKING IS DONE.
13                         *
14                         * AUTHOR: GENE H. MILLER
15                         *
16                         * REVISION HISTORY: VER1.1  4/28/1990
17                         *
18                         *********************************************************
19                         *
20                         *
21                         *********************************************************
22                         ** DATA SECTION
23                         *********************************************************
24      0010                         ORG $10
25      0010               TABADR   RMB    2       PUT ADDRESS OF TABLE HERE
26      0012               TABLEN   RMB    2       NUMBER OF TABLE ENTRIES
27      0014               NEGSUM   RMB    2       PROGRAM PUTS SUM HERE
28      0016               NEGCNT   RMB    2       PROGRAM PUTS COUNT HERE
29      0018               ALLNEG   RMB    1       00=FALSE  FF=TRUE
30      0019               WRKCNT   RMB    2       WORKING LOOP COUNTER
31                         *
32                         *********************************************************
33                         ** PROGRAM SECTION
34                         *********************************************************
35      C100                         ORG $C100
36                         *-------------------------------------------------------
37                         * INITIALIZE
38                         *-------------------------------------------------------
39                         * INITIALIZE RESULTS
40                         *     ZERO NEGATIVE SUM
41      C100  CC 00 00     START    LDD    #0000
42      C103  DD 14                 STD    NEGSUM
43                         *     ZERO NEGATIVE COUNT
44      C105  DD 16                 STD    NEGCNT
45                         *     SET INDICATOR TO FALSE
46      C107  7F 00 18              CLR    ALLNEG
47                         * INITIALIZE POINTER TO TABLE BEGINNING
48      C10A  DE 10                 LDX    TABADR
49                         * INITIALIZE NUMBER OF ENTRIES COUNTER
50      C10C  DC 12                 LDD    TABLEN
51      C10E  DD 19                 STD    WRKCNT
52                         *-------------------------------------------------------
53                         * PROCESS ALL TABLE ENTRIES
54                         *-------------------------------------------------------
55                         * MORE ENTRIES?
56      C110  DC 19        LOOP     LDD    WRKCNT    TEST WORKING LOOP COUNTER
57      C112  27 1B                 BEQ    NEXT      BRANCH ON NO
58                         * GET NEXT ENTRY
59      C114  E6 00                 LDAB   0,X
60                         * NEGATIVE?
61      C116  2A 0D                 BPL    POSITV    BRANCH ON NO
```

Figure 4-18   Assembly language listing for a good program.

```
62                                  * ADD NEGATIVE ENTRY TO SUM
63    C118    4F                        CLRA            EXTEND SINGLE-BYTE NEGATIVE
64    C119    43                        COMA            ..TO DOUBLE-BYTE NEGATIVE
65    C11A    D3 14                     ADDD    NEGSUM
66    C11C    DD 14                     STD     NEGSUM
67                                  * INCREMENT NEGATIVE COUNTER
68    C11E    DC 16                     LDD     NEGCNT
69    C120    C3 00 01                  ADDD    #1
70    C123    DD 16                     STD     NEGCNT
71                                  * ADJUST LOOP COUNTER
72    C125    DC 19            POSITV   LDD     WRKCNT
73    C127    83 00 01                  SUBD    #1
74    C12A    DD 19                     STD     WRKCNT
75                                  * ADVANCE TO NEXT ENTRY
76    C12C    08                        INX
77    C12D    20 E1                     BRA     LOOP
78                                  *------------------------------------------------------
79                                  * INDICATE IF ALL NEGATIVES
80                                  *------------------------------------------------------
81                                  * LENGTH = COUNT?
82    C12F    DC 12            NEXT     LDD     TABLEN
83    C131    93 16                     SUBD    NEGCNT
84    C133    26 04                     BNE     LAST      BRANCH ON NO
85                                  * INDICATE TRUE
86    C135    86 FF                     LDAA    #$FF
87    C137    97 18                     STAA    ALLNEG
88    C139    3F               LAST     SWI               "STOP" FOR MOTOROLA TRAINER
89    C13A                              END
```

Defined		Symbol Name	Value		References			
29	ALLNEG		0018		46	87		
88	LAST		C139		84			
56	LOOP		C110		77			
28	NEGCNT		0016		44	68	70	83
27	NEGSUM		0014		42	65	66	
82	NEXT		C12F		57			
72	POSITV		C125		61			
41	START		C100					
25	TABADR		0010		48			
26	TABLEN		0012		50	82		
30	WRKCNT		0019		51	56	72	74

```
        Lines Assembled :  89              Assembly Errors :   0
```

Figure 4-18 Continued.

A Bad Program

Sometimes people don't recognize the problems caused by poorly written and poorly doc-umented programs. When they know every detail of a program, they have difficulty seeing other people's problems. Usually, the problems become clear to them when they study an-other person's program.

You should study the example bad program in Figure 4-19 to observe some bad prac-tices you should avoid. This program does the same job as the program in Figure 4-18. Notice how simple things become very confusing!

Here are some general problems with this program and the assembler listing shown in Figure 4-19:

```
 1                                    * AN UNACCEPTABLE SUM NEGATIVE TABLE ENTRIES
 2                                    * PROGRAM WRITTEN IN VALID ASSEMBLY LANGUAGE
 3                                    * THAT WORKS CORRECTLY
 4                                    *
 5            0013              R        EQU   $13
 6    0010                               ORG   $10
 7    0010                               RMB   2          ADDRESS OF TABLE
 8    0012              TL               RMB   1          TABLE LENGTH
 9    0013                               RMB   2
10    0015              TL1              RMB   1
11    0016              WCNT1            RMB   1
12    0017              WCNT             RMB   1
13    0018              TEMP             RMB   2
14    001A              NEG              RMB   2
15    001C              *
16    C000                               ORG   $C000
17    C000  7F 00 13                     CLR   R          INIT RESULT TO ZERO
18    C003  96 13                        LDAA  R
19    C005  97 14                        STAA  R+1
20    C007  16                           TAB
21    C008  DD 1A                        STD   NEG        ZERO NEGCNT
22    C00A  7F C0 24                      CLR  ALL
23    C00D  DE 10                        LDX   $10        POINT TO TABLE
24    C00F  96 15                        LDAA  TL1
25    C011  D6 12                        LDAB  TL
26    C013  D7 16                        STAB  WCNT1
27    C015  97 17                        STAA  WCNT
28    C017  7D 00 16    L                TST   WCNT1      TEST LOOP COUNTER
29    C01A  26 16       TH               BNE   XYZ        AND BRANCH
30    C01C  96 17                        LDAA  WCNT1+1
31    C01E  27 06                        BEQ   E
32    C020  20 10                        BRA   XYZ
33    C022  FF          F0               FCB   $FF
34    C023  01          ONE              FCB   $001
35    C024              ALL              RMB   2
36    C026  96 12       E                LDAA  TL
37    C028  D6 15                        LDAB  TL1
38    C02A  93 1A                        SUBD  NEG
39    C02C  26 03                        BNE   F
40    C02E  7A C0 24                     DEC   ALL
41    C031  3F          F                SWI              "STOP"
42    C032  E6 00       XYZ              LDAB  0,X        GET VALUE
43    C034  2B 02                        BMI   RST
44    C036  20 15                        BRA   BILL
45    C038  DB 14       RST              ADDB  R+1        ADD TOTAL
46    C03A  D7 14                        STAB  R+1
47    C03C  F6 C0 22                     LDAB  F0
48    C03F  D9 13                        ADCB  R
49    C041  D7 13                        STAB  R
50    C043  CC 00 00                     LDD   #0
51    C046  5C                           INCB
52    C047  D3 1A                        ADDD  NEG
53    C049  D7 1B                        STAB  NEG+1
54    C04B  97 1A                        STAA  NEG
55    C04D  08          BILL             INX              INCREMENT IND
56    C04E  D6 17                        LDAB  WCNT
57    C050  F0 C0 23                     SUBB  ONE        DECREMENT LOCATIONS
58    C053  D7 17                        STAB  WCNT1+1    17 & 18
59    C055  24 C0                        BCC   L
60    C057  7A 00 16                     DEC   WCNT1
61    C05A  20 BE                        BRA   L+3
62    C05C                               END
```

Figure 4-19 Assembly language listing for a bad program.

- *Program structure.* There is no way to determine the structure of the program by just looking at the listing. Without some study, you probably can't even tell there is a loop in the program. The few comments that are placed to the right of the instructions are little help.

- *Data organization.* The data section seems to be separated from the program section, but closer study will reveal that some data is placed within the program at lines 33 through 35. Careful scrutiny will reveal that the double-byte data numbers are not all stored with the high and then low bytes in adjacent memory locations.

- *Documentation.* There is no title and other identification of the program. The comments that are provided are almost useless because they don't relate to each other well enough. The abbreviations are confusing. Many of the user symbols were poorly named and so cause confusion rather than helping document the program.

Here are some further problems listed by specific line numbers on the listing:

- *Lines 17 through 22.* The instructions here put zero into some memory locations several different ways when one straightforward way would be much better.

- *Line 5.* The address of a data location is defined by the EQU directive, which is confusing. For example, is it obvious to you that the label R is on a double-byte number?

- *Lines 8 and 10.* A double-byte number is stored in two noncontiguous locations. This not only is confusing, but it prevents proper use of the instructions available in the computer.

- *Lines 11 and 12.* The labeling of the two instructions is confusing because they represent a double-byte number that is incorrectly stored with the high byte at the higher address.

- *Line 13.* Two bytes are reserved and assigned a label when they are never used in the program.

- *Line 23.* Never put the numerical address in an instruction. Use a label.

- *Lines 24 through 27.* The instructions here copy the table length to the working counter in a disorganized way. First, the program gets the low byte of the double-byte number into the A accumulator and the high byte into the B accumulator; this order is backward from the normal use of double-byte numbers with the D accumulator. Then it stores the two bytes in the opposite order; the high byte is stored first and the low byte is stored second. These little inconsistencies make it difficult for people to follow the program. Probably a better solution would use the D accumulator.

- *Lines 28 through 32.* The instructions test the double-byte working counter one byte at a time in an unstructured and disorganized manner. Avoid using multiple branches if possible. Here, the number could be loaded into the D accumulator to set the condition code bits.

- *Line 33.*   The number FF created here is a constant that should be in an instruction using immediate addressing.

- *Line 34.*   The number is specified with three digits, which is confusing. Either one or two digits would be much better.

- *Line 35.*   The RMB reserves two memory bytes but only one of them is ever used by the program.

- *Line 40.*   It would be much easier to understand if an instruction sequence stored the number FF into location ALL. The use of the DEC here makes the function unnecessarily dependent upon another part of the program and requires the reader to learn about that other part.

- *Line 41.*   The program stops running due to this instruction that is not at the physical end of the program. This is difficult to find while working with the program.

- *Lines 43 and 44.*   The branch technique on lines 43 and 44 is poor. The two instructions could be replaced by a single DPL BILL, which would be much better.

- *Lines 50 and 51.*   The number one is put into the D accumulator in a long and complicated way. The LDD instruction should load the number one.

- *Lines 53 and 54.*   The instructions here store the D accumulator in a difficult way. Use the available instructions well by using the STD instruction.

- *Lines 56 through 58.*   One byte of the working counter is decremented one way and the other byte is decremented a second way. A better sequence would use the DEC instruction to decrement both bytes.

- *Line 61.*   Don't use expressions for branch addresses—label the branch location instead and use the label in the branch instruction.

Of course, this example was developed to illustrate a large number of problems. Probably no practical program would ever be this bad. However, all of the problems illustrated have been seen by the author in other people's programs.

4.8   LARGE-SCALE TOP/DOWN DESIGN

Teams of people write most programs. Usually the size of a program, and sometimes its complexity, is more than one person can handle in a reasonable period. The team approach is only successful if there is careful coordination between the software written by various people. It is almost impossible to make spaghetti programs work under team circumstances. The top/down design ideas also apply to programming team management.

The Top/Down Team

A programming team will, at least, consist of a team leader and several other programmers. The team leader is an experienced person who has designed software and written programs. The team leader will have the responsibility of designing the top level of the program. This person also may design the second level of the program if it is small enough. Often this design phase will require interactions between the team leader, the team members, and the program users. Both flowcharts and written materials document the design. The documentation of the interactions between program modules is particularly important.

Team members

The team leader gives the upper level flowcharts and documents to other team members. Each person will work on one section of the program. The flowcharts contain only structured modules. Therefore, the team leader is sure that the modules will fit together later unlike those of spaghetti programs.

Each person now makes additional levels of flowcharts to expand the design into lower levels. Each person must meet the requirements of structured programming in designing new program modules.

A problem

Suppose the procedure as described were to continue until everyone on the team completes the design of their sections. Then they do the actual coding of their program modules. When these modules are put together to make the final program, catastrophe will strike! The modules almost certainly won't go together correctly.

Certainly some design work has been incorrect. The program specifications likely have changed. So, much of the design work and coding is useless because they must now be changed.

The problem here occurs because the implementation phase is too late. Detailed coding was done before the design and specifications were proved.

Top/Down Implementation

Top/down implementation helps avoid problems when all the separate program modules developed by different team members are brought together into a single program. The idea is to start writing and running the program soon after starting the design. Start writing the program even before designing the lower levels.

Stubs

At first, writing a program before the design is complete seems impossible, and to some extent it is. So some program modules developed early in the project will be dummy modules called *stubs*. Stubs don't do correct functions, since they are substitutes for the real code. The actual code will be designed and written later. A stub may contain some useful code, but some stubs contain no code at all. Certainly using stubs requires the judgment of a knowledgeable programmer.

An example using stubs

As an example of the use of stubs, consider writing a program that must read some temperature sensors and print a report. The report displays the data collected from the sensors. At the least, the program will have an input section for reading the sensors and a report section for generating the report.

The input program module.   The input program module does three major functions. First, it must read the temperature sensors. Second, it must use an algorithm or table lookup to correct the data for nonlinearity in the sensors. Third, it must scale the data values for useful units.

The temperature sensor program module will probably have three separate parts for these three functions. To write and test all the code for these will be time-consuming. It also may be impossible because the characteristics of the sensors may not yet be known. Also, the sensors may not yet be interfaced to the computer hardware, so they don't yet operate.

These problems should not be a deterrent to writing the program. Instead, the input program can contain a stub that generates phony data from the temperature sensors, a stub that linearizes the data in a phony way, and a stub to scale the data in a phony way.

The report program module.   The report program module will print a report on a printer. The report will need headings, neat columns, titles, time and date, and so on. However, all the details needed on the report probably are not known. The required data to be presented may not even be decided yet. However, these problems should not deter the programmer from writing the report program.

The report program can be written with stubs. The report may contain headings with little information, the time and data may be phony, and the arrangement on the page may be less than desirable. However, the program can be written and made to work.

After the report program module and the input program module are both completed, they can be put together to make a working program. Any bugs can be found easily because the code is still very simple, since much of it is stubs.

The demonstration.   After the program modules have been completed using stubs, a complete working program can be demonstrated. The report generated will contain phony data created in the stubs in the input program. The organization of the report will also need improvements. Regardless of these details, a program has been written that can be demonstrated and evaluated. The team leader, the team members, and maybe the ultimate users of the program can see some results.

Probably this working system will do something that is not right—that is, incorrect, not just missing. Often people will not specify the desired results from a program completely. But when they see it running, they say "See, that is wrong." If what they see is based on stubs, changing the design is still relatively easy and little detailed work is lost. The program design can be changed and the program demonstrated again.

Program testing

Running and demonstrating the program containing stubs checks the design, overall function, and initial coding of the program. The next step is to remove some stubs and replace them with correct modules. The best approach is to replace these one at a time so finding the location of bugs will be easy. Each time a stub is replaced with actual code, a new aspect of the program will perform correctly. Eventually, the entire program will work correctly.

The top/down implementation technique tests most of the program modules to some extent as the program is built and the stubs are replaced. It is valuable that this testing is done within the actual program, and not by a separate test program. You are assured that each program module works in the context of the actual program. This built-in testing significantly reduces the need to write separate test programs.

As the program evolves toward the final design, it should be demonstrated to interested parties several times. If errors occur, they will be caught before further work is completed. Catching errors early reduces the effort needed to correct them. Likewise, if additional features are needed, adding them to the design is easier if the program is not yet completed.

Team member interactions

Usually the team leader will merge new modules into the overall program and test their operation. The other team members do not need to interact with each other. Their individual parts of the program are largely independent of the other programmers' work. The reduced interaction improves the productivity of the team.

Replacing a team member will have little effect on the other team members. New people added to the team need learn only about their part of the program—they do not need to learn all the program.

A major problem of adding new people is the nonproductive time spent informing them about the work completed. Top/down design reduces this time, since the modules are designed to be independent of each other—the design specifications are developed before the modules are written.

The results

Top/down design applied to team programming has been very successful. The goal is to get a system working before coding all the program. The working program demonstrates the design and some working code even if the data is phony. When the entire project is completed, everyone will have confidence that the program works correctly; it has been working and demonstrated from the early stages of design.

The top/down approach to team management is possible only if you have correctly structured programs. Otherwise, the jumping around in spaghetti programs causes different programmers' modules to interact at an intimate level. Changing one person's module will affect another person's module, making it difficult to get the program to function correctly.

Studies of practical programming teams have shown that a combination of structured programming methods and top/down design methods leads to successful projects. Of course, these are techniques that do not exclude other approaches. Usually some bottom/up testing of low-level modules is also done.

4.9   SMALL-SCALE TOP/DOWN DESIGN

An individual programmer also gains from the use of top/down design and top/down implementation. Don't try to design or write all of a program at once. Organize your efforts by making top/down structured flowcharts, and then code the program from the flowcharts. At first, code only the higher-level modules freely using stubs for the lower-level modules. Get your program running as soon as possible so you can do some testing. You may even leave major portions of the program out of the design by making empty stubs. They can be added later. Likewise, you may write the program for hardware that is readily available, and then convert it later for the specific hardware required. Avoid taking on too much at once.

To effectively use top/down design and top/down implementation, you need good editor and assembler programs. The editor will make changes such as replacing a stub easy. After each change, immediately assemble the new program and run it to see the results. Your program will evolve to completion rapidly.

4.10   REVIEW

Good programming approaches have been demonstrated throughout this chapter. Examples have been used to illustrate both good and bad programs. This book may be unique in that it illustrates and labels bad programs. Of course, deciding whether a program is good or bad is a matter of judgment. Not everyone will agree. Therefore, this chapter has given reasons for the judgments that were made. When you write programs, you too will be making such judgments continually. You must decide what is important and set your goals accordingly.

The design of software is an activity that affords people the opportunity to be creative to an extent possible in few other endeavors. Their results can be elegant and beautiful problem solutions or ugly and costly catastrophes.

4.11   EXERCISES

4-1. Name the three fundamental program structures. Sketch flowcharts for each of these structures.

4-2. Explain how to determine whether a loop is a DO-WHILE or a DO-UNTIL structure.

4-3. Figure 4-20 is a structured flowchart that contains only the three fundamental structures. Identify all the structures by drawing boxes around each structure.

4-4. Make a single-level structured flowchart that represents the following algorithm:
Input a number. If this number is within a correct range, print the number. Repeat until four numbers have been input and processed. If a number is out of range, quit without printing the number.

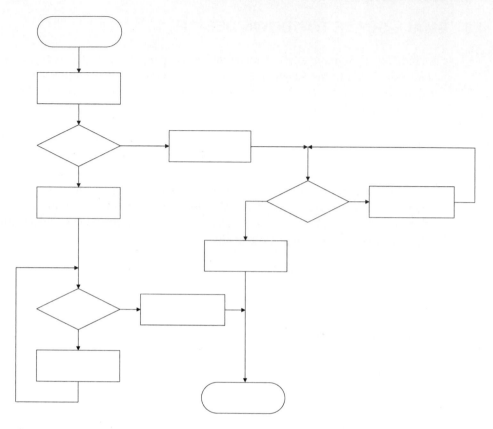

Figure 4-20　Exercise 4-3.

4-5. Make top/down structured flowcharts for the following program:
Input a positive number. Print a report that lists the squares and cubes of all the numbers from zero to the number read. Limit the input number to 100_{10} by printing an error message for incorrect numbers and ending the program. After the report is finished, request a Y or N for repeating the program and respond accordingly. Include messages and headings for the report.

4-6. Make a new structured flowchart using only the three fundamental structures that is equivalent to the incorrectly structured flowchart in Figure 4-21.

4-7. Find a program written in a high-level language such as Basic or Fortran. Study the program to determine if it is built from the three fundamental program structures.

4-8. Make a new structured flowchart using only the three fundamental structures that is equivalent to the incorrectly structured flowchart in Figure 4-22.

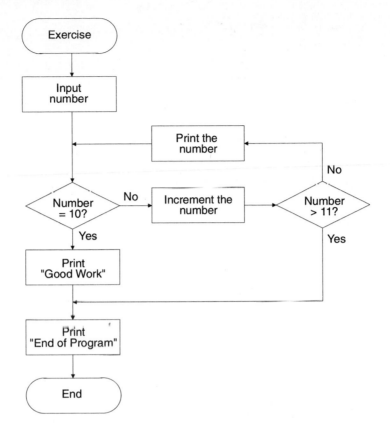

Figure 4-21 Exercise 4-6.

4-9. Make a new structured flowchart using the three fundamental structures and the DO-UNTIL structure that is equivalent to the flowchart in Figure 4-22.

4-10. Modify the program given in Figure 4-18 so it sums and counts both the positive and negative entries found by making new flowcharts. Your program must be properly structured using only the three fundamental structures.

4-11. Write an assembly language program from your flowcharts developed for Exercise 4-10. Your program must follow the flowcharts and the listing must be well documented.

4-12. Name the program structure that starts on line 13 of Figure 5-16.

4-13. Name the program structure that starts on line 38 of Figure 5-17.

4-14. Name the program structure that starts on line 44 of Figure 5-17.

4-15. Name the program structure that starts on line 51 of Figure 5-18.

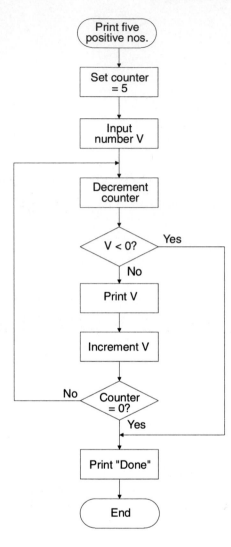

Figure 4-22   Exercises 4-8 and 4-9.

4-16.   Name the program structure that starts on line 56 of Figure 5-18.

———————————————
Chapter 5
———————————————

═══════════════════════════════

Advanced Assembly Language Programming

═══════════════════════════════

The more complicated Motorola 68HC11 instructions that were avoided in previous chapters are introduced in this chapter. Many of the more complex instructions were designed to solve particular programming problems. This chapter discusses both the problems and the use of the instructions to solve the problems. All the examples are presented using assembly language, so memory diagrams are usually omitted.

5.1 MORE INDEXING

The 68HC11 has a Y index register that was avoided in previous chapters. The function of the Y index register is the same in all ways to the function of the X index register. The instruction set has a parallel instruction using the Y index register for every instruction that in any way uses the X register.

The 68HC11 has many instructions that relate to the index registers. Therefore, many instruction op code numbers are needed for these instructions.

Motorola Products

Many of the 68HC11 instructions discussed in this chapter are not available in the Motorola 6800, 6801, 6802, 6803, 6808, and 68701 chips. For example, the 68HC11 has a Y index register that the other chips do not have. Therefore, the 68HC11 has many more instruction codes than the other processors. However, compatible programs written for these other processors will run on the 68HC11. Look in Appendix H for further details.

Consequences of a Large Instruction Set

Many of the Motorola 8-bit microprocessors do not have a Y index register. When the Y index register is included, the required number of instruction op codes exceeds the number of combinations that fit in an 8-bit number. Therefore, some 68HC11 instructions have double-byte op codes.

Prebytes

All the 68HC11 instructions that in any way relate to the Y index register have double-byte op codes. A few other 68HC11 instructions not associated with Y also have double-byte op codes. To make it easy to talk about double-byte op codes, Motorola describes an added op code byte that precedes the normal single op code byte. The added byte is called a *prebyte*. So Motorola literature refers to a prebyte and an op code byte rather than a double-byte op code.

Performance considerations

The use of a prebyte makes the instructions that relate to the Y register one byte longer in length. Consequently, they take one clock cycle longer to fetch from memory. The result is a performance penalty to using the Y index register. Normally, you should use the X index register for all applications that require only a single index register. If you need two index registers, use both X and Y because the program will be better than if you use only the X index register.

Op Code Maps

A table or map of the op code numbers is helpful in understanding the assignment of instruction code values. Appendix G shows the op code maps for the 68HC11.

The instruction set of the 68HC11 has three different prebyte values, so there is a total of four maps. Each of the 256_{10} numerical values on the map corresponds to a box. The box either names the instruction that corresponds to its numerical value or indicates that the code is invalid. Most of the codes were chosen orderly, so the columns of the maps correspond to particular addressing modes. Since the four maps together have room for 1024_{10} possible codes and only 307_{10} of them are valid instructions, most of the codes are invalid.

Index Register Exchange Instructions

The instructions for changing the index registers covered so far allow you to load, store, increment, decrement, or add the B accumulator to the index registers. Here are two instructions that make it easy to manipulate the index registers many other ways:

XGDX, XGDY   *Exchange the D accumulator with the X or Y index register.*
                              These instructions exchange or swap the 16-bit numbers in the
                              two registers. None of the condition code bits are affected.

   Usually, index registers hold addresses and thus act as pointers. For simple manipulation of tables, the load, store, increment, and decrement the index register operations are sufficient. But more complex calculation of addresses is impractical. The exchange instructions XGDX and XGDY make it possible to calculate addresses easily. Move the number in the index register to the D accumulator; then operate on the number using instructions that affect the A, B, and D accumulators. Finally, move the result back to the index register.

   The exchange instructions also make it easy to temporarily save the D accumulator. Use the exchange instruction to save the D accumulator in an index register while using D for other purposes. Using an exchange is easier and faster than storing the D accumulator in memory.

Another Instruction for D

The compare accumulator D to memory instruction, CPD, is unusual. It has only the basic addressing modes, yet it has a prebyte even when Y is not involved. You can see this easily on op code map page 3 in Appendix G.

CPD   *Compare accumulator D to memory.*   Subtract a double-byte
                              number in memory from the D accumulator and discard the
                              answer so the accumulator is unchanged, but make the condi-
                              tion code bits respond.

   Compare the spelling of this CPD instruction to CMPA, CMPB, CPX, and CPY.

5.2   BIT AND BYTE MANIPULATION

All the instructions discussed so far have operated on single-byte or double-byte data numbers. These instructions treat the data as collections of bits that represent a number. This section considers manipulating or using the individual bits within a number and operating on a number as a collection of bits.

Shift Operations

Several instructions can logically shift the bits in an accumulator or a memory register. Shifting means to move a collection of bits to an adjacent position. The shifting of a number is useful as a general programming tool. The meaning of these instructions depends on the context in which they are used.

Rotate instructions

The rotate instructions shift all the bits of an 8-bit register and the carry bit circularly one bit position. The effect is to alter a 9-bit number. Look at the instruction set table in Appendix H as you read about these instructions. Here is a list of the rotate instructions:

ROL, ROLA, ROLB   *Rotate left memory byte or accumulator A or B.* Figure 5-1 illustrates this operation. The name *rotate left* means move bit 7 to the C bit and move the C bit to bit 0 as the other bits are shifted.

ROR, RORA, RORB   *Rotate right memory byte or accumulator A or B.* Figure 5-1 illustrates this operation. The name *rotate right* means move bit 0 to the C bit and move the C bit to bit 7 as the other bits are shifted.

The rotate instructions only move the bits one position. The 68HC11 has no multiple position rotate instructions. However, the inherent addressed versions only require one byte of memory. So four rotates of an accumulator—the maximum number needed for an 8-bit accumulator—only require four bytes of memory. More than four rotates are unnecessary because fewer rotates in the opposite direction do the same job.

The instruction sequence CLC ROLA, or the single instruction ASLA, both do multiply by two for both two's complement signed and unsigned numbers. Following this multiply, the C and V bits correctly indicate overflow information.

Shift instructions

The shift instructions move all the bits of a register one position and insert a 0 at the input end of the register. The bit at the output end of the register moves to the carry bit.

Look at the instruction set table in Appendix H as you read about these instructions. Carefully examine the graphical representations of the instruction operations.

Here is a list of the shift instructions:

ASL, LSL,   *Arithmetic or logical shift left memory byte or accumulator A,*
ASLA, LSLA,   *B, or D.* Each instruction has two different names—use the
ASLB, LSLB,   name, either arithmetic or logical, that fits the application of the
ASLD, LSLD   instruction in the program. Figure 5-1 illustrates the operations with an 8-bit register. Those instructions operating on the D accumulator operate on 16-bit numbers.

LSR, LSRA, LSRB,   *Logical shift right memory byte or accumulator A, B, or D.*
LSRD   Each of these instructions has a single name because the arithmetic meaning, divide by two, applies to unsigned numbers but not to two's complement numbers. Figure 5-1 illustrates these operations with an 8-bit register.

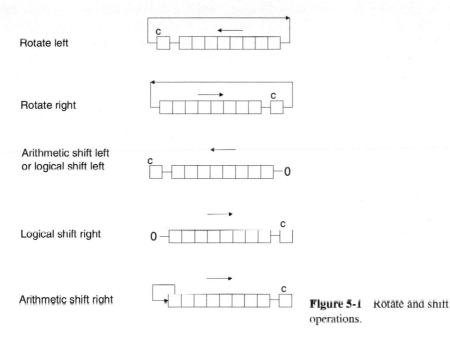

Rotate left

Rotate right

Arithmetic shift left
or logical shift left

Logical shift right

Arithmetic shift right

Figure 5-1   Rotate and shift operations.

ASR, ASRA, ASRB   *Arithmetic shift right memory byte or accumulator A or B.*
These instructions divide an 8-bit two's complement signed
number by two. They are useful for little else. Figure 5-1 illustrates the operation of these instructions.

The shift instructions only move the bits one position. The 68HC11 has no multiple
position shift instructions.

Division by two using ASR.   Table 5-1 illustrates successive divisions by two of
some two's complement numbers. The ASR instruction can do division by two. Carefully
look at the resulting numbers that are all correct! The ASR instruction uses an integer division

TABLE 5-1   SUCCESSIVE DIVISION BY TWO USING ASR

Binary	Decimal	Binary	Decimal
00001010	+10	11110110	−10
00000101	+5	11111011	−5
00000010	+2	11111101	−3
00000001	+1	11111110	−2
00000000	0	11111111	−1
00000000	0	11111111	−1

technique called *floored division*. Floored division rounds the integer quotient to the floor or most negative number. A characteristic of floored division is that a quotient cannot be zero if the original number is negative. Be careful using ASR because floored division is different from the integer division used by some high-level programming languages. For example, Fortran does not do floored division.

Double-precision instructions.   Double-precision shift instructions are only available in the 68HC11 for the D accumulator. It has no double-precision shift instructions that operate on a number in memory. When a program must operate on 16-bit numbers, the double-precision instructions provide significant speed improvement over the 8-bit instructions.

To shift a double-byte number in memory, consider using a logical shift followed by a rotate instruction. These instructions use the C bit so multiple precision shifting is easy.

For review, the 68HC11 has instructions that perform the double-precision operations load, store, add, subtract, and logical shift left and right on the D accumulator.

Read-modify-write instructions

The rotate and shift instructions that operate on a memory register are called *read-modify-write* instructions. To rotate the register, the microprocessor must read the number from memory into the microprocessor, rotate the bits including the C bit, and then write the result back to the memory register. Therefore, read-modify-write instructions are complex. They use more clock cycles than you might expect.

Logical Operations

Instructions are available for the logical operations AND, OR, COMPLEMENT, and EXCLUSIVE OR. Table 5-2 defines these functions. The logical instructions all operate on 8-bit numbers. However, it is unlikely that you would want to AND eight pairs of bits at once as part of an application program! Instead, the logical instructions manipulate bits. Refer to the instruction set table in Appendix H as you read the following.

TABLE 5-2   LOGIC FUNCTIONS

AND			OR			COMPLEMENT		EXCLUSIVE OR		
X	Y	F1	X	Y	F2	X	F3	X	Y	F4
0	0	0	0	0	0	0	1	0	0	0
0	1	0	0	1	1	1	0	0	1	1
1	0	0	1	0	1			1	0	1
1	1	1	1	1	1			1	1	0

$$F1 = X \wedge Y \qquad F2 = X \vee Y \qquad F3 = \overline{X} \qquad F4 = X \veebar Y$$

Bit picking

The normal use of the AND instruction is to pick selected bits from an 8-bit number. Here is the operation of the related AND and BIT instructions:

ANDA, ANDB

And memory byte to accumulator. These instructions AND the corresponding bits in the addressed memory register and the accumulator register and put the result in the accumulator. The N, Z, and V condition code bits are affected.

BITA, BITB

And memory byte to accumulator and discard the result. These instructions AND the corresponding bits in the addressed memory register and the accumulator register and discard the result without altering the accumulator. The N, Z, and V condition code bits are affected.

You can see the effect of the AND instruction by looking at pairs of rows of the truth table for the function. Look at the first two rows of the AND table in Table 5-2 and observe that 0 ANDed with anything is 0. From the third and fourth rows, observe that 1 ANDed with something is the same thing.

This viewpoint helps in understanding how the AND instruction can pick bits from a number. The result from the AND operation contains a 0 at each bit position corresponding to a 0 in the mask. Therefore, a 0 effectively blocks or masks the original bit from the result and a 1 allows the original bit to appear in the result.

Using the AND instruction.   Here are two examples of the ANDA instruction where A designates the number in the A accumulator and M the number in the addressed memory register:

$$
\begin{array}{ll}
\quad 01010101 & \text{A} \\
\wedge\ 11110000 & \text{M} \\
\hline
\quad 01010000 & \text{A}
\end{array}
\qquad\qquad
\begin{array}{ll}
\quad 01011111 & \text{A} \\
\wedge\ 00000100 & \text{M} \\
\hline
\quad 00000100 & \text{A}
\end{array}
$$

In the first example, the four 1s in the memory register allow the bits 0101 from the A accumulator to show in the result. The four 0s in the memory register block the other bits from the result by making the result bits 0s. In the second example, only one bit of the original A accumulator shows in the result and the other bits are 0s.

To continue this viewpoint, let's call the number in the memory register a *mask* because it lets some bits show through and blocks others. Unfortunately, the word *mask* is used to describe several other kinds of numbers.

Testing hardware signals.   Figure 5-2 illustrates a memory register with bits that represent the conditions of some push button switches. Somehow, hardware and software read the conditions of the push button switches and put the bits into the memory register labeled IN1. When a push button switch is pushed, a 1 is in the memory bit. When the push button is released, a 0 is in the bit.

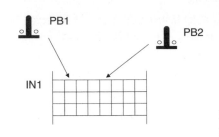
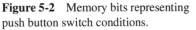

Figure 5-2   Memory bits representing push button switch conditions.

Let's look at a program that executes one program module if both push buttons PB1 and PB2 are pushed, and another program module if they are not both pushed. Figure 5-3 is the assembly language source for the program. Here is the use of each instruction:

- *LDAA.*   The first LDAA instruction copies the conditions of the switches from the memory register labeled IN1 into the A accumulator. Of course, the accumulator has eight bits, not just the two of interest. Assume that other devices such as switches control the other bits.

- *ANDA.*   The first ANDA instruction masks the bit pattern in the A accumulator so only bit 6 shows in the result. Location MASK1 contains the mask bit pattern that selects bit 6. The AND instruction makes the other seven bits of the A accumulator all 0s. The result in A represents the condition of switch PB1. If the number in A is zero, the push button PB1 is not pushed. If the number in A is nonzero, then the push button PB1 is pushed. Observe that the A accumulator is zero or nonzero regardless of which bit PB1 uses. If you connected PB1 to a different bit, you would only need to change the mask.

- *BEQ.*   If the result in the A accumulator is zero because PB1 is not pushed, it is known that the two push buttons are not both pushed. So the BEQ instruction sends program control directly to the module labeled NOT. Testing PB2 would have no value in this case.

```
              •
MASK1    FCB    %01000000
MASK2    FCB    %00001000
              •
              •
         LDAA   IN1
         ANDA   MASK1
         BEQ    NOT
         LDAA   IN1
         ANDA   MASK2
         BEQ    NOT
BOTH          •
              •
              •
NOT           •
```

Figure 5-3   Source program for ANDing two push button switches.

- *LDAA.*   The second LDAA instruction restores the switch conditions to the A accumulator because the AND instruction changed the accumulator.

- *ANDA.*   The second AND instruction uses MASK2 to let the PB2 condition show in the result and to zero the other bits in the A accumulator. If the number in A is zero, the push button PB2 is not pushed. If the number in A is nonzero, then the push button PB2 is pushed.

- *BEQ.*   If the result in the A accumulator is zero because PB2 is not pushed, the BEQ sends program control to the module labeled NOT. If the A accumulator is not zero, then both push buttons are pushed and control goes to the program module labeled BOTH.

The example above ANDs two bits by testing each bit individually and branching to the correct place. Logical operations with bits are usually done this way but there are some variations on the technique. For example, a mask that selects both PB1 and PB2 simultaneously leaves one of four possible patterns in the accumulator. The program then would test for the desired pattern.

Also consider using the BIT instruction in the example in Figure 5-3 to avoid changing the accumulator during the first masking operation. Each of these approaches has good points and bad points.

Bit packing

Selected bits of a register can be forced to known values. Bit packing means to force known bit values into certain bits of a register without changing the other bits. Both the AND and ORA instructions can force bits.

Normally, you will use the ORA instruction to put 1s into selected bits of an 8-bit number. Here is the operation of the ORA instruction:

ORAA, ORAB   *Or memory byte to accumulator A or B.* These instructions OR the corresponding bits in the addressed memory register and the accumulator register. The result is put in the same accumulator.

You can see the effect of the ORA instruction by looking at pairs of rows of the truth table for the OR function. Look at the first two rows of the OR table in Table 5-2 and observe that 0 ORed with something is the same thing. From the third and fourth rows, observe that 1 ORed with something is always 1.

Using the ORA instruction to pack 1s.   Here are two examples of the ORA instruction where A designates the number in the A accumulator and M the number in the addressed memory register:

01010101	A		01100000	A
∨ 11110000	M		∨ 00000100	M
11110101	A		01100100	A

In the first example, the 1s in the memory register force the corresponding bits in the A accumulator to 1s while the 0s leave the other bits unchanged. In the second example, the ORA changes only one bit of the original number in the accumulator.

The number that selects the bits to be operated on is called a *mask* as it was for the AND instruction. The meaning is very different for the two applications but the name is the same. You will find some additional meanings for the word *mask* in later sections, so be careful to avoid being confused by the different but related meanings.

Using the AND instruction to pack 0s.   The following two examples use the AND instruction differently from the earlier example. Here the mask, the number in memory, is opposite the earlier mask because selected bits are forced to 0s.

Look at these examples:

```
      01010101   A              01111111   A
   ∧  11111011   M           ∧  11111101   M
      01010001   A              01111101   A
```

The masks used in these examples contain mostly 1s. Usually only one or a few bits are forced to 0s in practical applications.

Logical instruction example.   The example in Figure 5-4 expands the example in Figure 5-2 to include the control of a light by a memory bit. Figure 5-5 is the source listing of a program that turns the light on if both push button switches are pushed, and turns the light off otherwise. The program uses two additional masks for controlling the light.

Notice that the program can change only the selected bit that controls the light. If other bits in the register labeled OUT control other devices, changing them will cause errors.

Bit reversing

The EXCLUSIVE OR instruction, named EOR, can reverse or complement selected bits of a register. Here is the operation of this instruction:

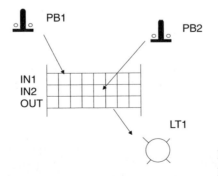

Figure 5-4 Memory bits representing push button switch and light conditions.

```
              .
MASK1   FCB    %01000000
MASK2   FCB    %00001000
MASK3   FCB    %00000100
MASK4   FCB    %11111011
              .
              .
        LDAA   IN1
        ANDA   MASK1
        BEQ    NOT
        LDAA   IN2
        ANDA   MASK2
        BEQ    NOT
BOTH    LDAA   OUT
        ORAA   MASK3
        STAA   OUT
        BRA    NEXT
NOT     LDAA   OUT
        ANDA   MASK4
        STAA   OUT
NEXT          .
              .
```

Figure 5-5   Source program for controlling light with two push button switches.

EORA, EORB   *Exclusive or memory byte to accumulator A or B.* These instructions EXCLUSIVE OR the corresponding bits in the addressed memory register and the accumulator register. The result is put in the same accumulator.

You can see the effect of the EOR instruction by looking at pairs of rows of the truth table for the EXCLUSIVE OR function. Look at the first two rows of the truth table in Table 5-2 and observe that 0 EORed with something is the same thing. From the third and fourth rows, observe that 1 EORed with something results in the opposite value.

Bit set and clear instructions

The 68HC11 has instructions that will set or clear selected bits in a memory register. These instructions contain a mask byte that selects the bits to be operated on. The meaning of the name *mask* in these instructions is different from its meaning when used with the AND and ORA instructions. Here is the operation of the bit set and clear instructions:

BSET   *Set all the bits in a memory byte that correspond to 1s in the mask.* The BSET instruction ORs the mask from inside the instruction to the addressed memory byte and puts the result in the memory byte.

BCLR   *Clear all the bits in a memory byte that correspond to 1s in the mask.* The BCLR instruction ANDs the complement of the mask from inside the instruction to the addressed memory byte and puts the result in the memory byte.

The mask byte selects the bits that the instruction operates on. For all instructions that contain a mask, 1s in the mask enable the operation and 0s disable the operation. Masks that are all 1s or all 0s are seldom used. If the mask contains all 0s, the instruction does nothing.

A BSET instruction with a mask of all 1s is useful, but a BCLR instruction with a mask of all 1s may be replaced by a CLR instruction.

Usually, you will think of the mask as a means to select the bits that the instruction will operate on. However, sometimes you must understand how the instruction uses the mask in computing the result. In particular, some hardware control problems will require this understanding.

Addressing modes for bit instructions. The BSET and BCLR instructions each have two addressing modes for a single instruction. No other instructions in the 68HC11 have two addressing modes. These bit instructions need a memory address of the register to be operated on and a mask byte to select the bits.

The instruction code contains the constant mask byte. Therefore, the mask byte is accessed by immediate addressing. The mask byte makes these instructions one byte longer than expected. Look at the instruction set table for the memory format of these instructions.

The bit instructions can use either direct addressing or indexed addressing to access the memory byte to be operated on. An instruction that can use only direct or indexed addressing has an unusual combination of addressing modes. In particular, the extended addressing mode is not available to these instructions.

To specify the addressing mode for the instructions easily, the instruction set table lists only the addressing mode for the memory byte to be operated on. Since the mask is always accessed by immediate addressing, there is little value in stating this.

The assembly language format. The assembly language for the bit instructions has a new format to accommodate the mask byte. Appendix C shows the format used by the 2500AD assembler. The format is the same as for other direct or indexed addressed instructions, except the mask byte is added at the end of the statement after a comma. For example, the statement

EX1   BSET   LIGHTS,$10

sets bit 4 of the memory location labeled LIGHTS using direct addressing. The value of the mask byte is specified numerically or symbolically; however, the # symbol for immediate addressing is not used.

The order of the symbols in the assembly language—namely, op code, address, and mask—is the same as the order of the instruction bytes in memory. Therefore, the instruction set table gives you the order of the symbols.

Bit testing and branching

Practical programs frequently need to test one or more memory bits and then branch on the outcome of the test. The 68HC11 has instructions that combine the testing and branching operations into one instruction. Here are the bit test-and-branch instructions:

BRSET   *Branch if all the bits in a memory byte that correspond to 1s in the mask are set.* The BRSET instruction ANDs the mask from inside the instruction to the complement of the addressed memory byte and branches if the result is zero.

BRCLR   *Branch if all the bits in a memory byte that correspond to 1s in the mask are clear.* The BRCLR instruction ANDs the mask from inside the instruction to the addressed memory byte and branches if the result is zero.

As in the BSET and BCLR instructions, the mask in the BRSET and BRCLR instructions selects the bits in the memory byte to be tested. All the selected bits must meet the required condition for the branch to occur. The most common mask contains only a single 1, so one bit is tested.

Addressing modes for branch on bit instructions.   The BRSET and BRCLR instructions each have three addressing modes for a single instruction. No other instructions in the 68HC11 have three addressing modes. These two instructions need the address of the memory register to be operated on, a mask byte to select the bits in that memory register, and an offset for the relative addressed branch operation.

The instruction code contains the constant mask byte. Therefore, the mask byte is accessed by immediate addressing. The memory byte tested is accessed by either direct or indexed addressing. The branching operation uses program relative addressing the same as the other branch instructions. The multiple addressing modes make these instructions either four or five bytes long. The instruction set table shows the memory format for these instructions.

The assembly language format.   The assembly language format for these instructions is unique because of the required addressing modes. Appendix C gives the format used by the 2500AD assembler. The format is the same as the BSET and BCLR instructions with a relative address symbol added at the end. For example, the statement

        EX2   BRCLR   1,Y,MASK1,NEXT

creates an instruction using indexed-by-Y addressing with an offset of 1 to access a memory register. The bits in the register that correspond to the 1s in the value of the symbol MASK1 are tested. If all those bits are 0s, then the instruction branches to location NEXT; otherwise execution continues at the next instruction.

The order of the symbols in the assembly language statement is the same as the order of the instruction bytes in memory. Therefore, the instruction set table gives the order of the symbols.

Bit instruction example

Figure 5-6 is the assembly listing for a program that uses the bit instructions. The program tests two memory bits that represent push button switch conditions. If both push buttons are pushed, it turns on a light by putting 1 in a memory bit. Otherwise, it puts a 0 in the bit.

The program uses the same hardware as shown in Figure 5-4 and it performs the same function as the program in Figure 5-5. Look carefully at the hexadecimal codes to see the mask bytes and the multiple addressing modes.

```
 1                           ***********************************************************
 2                           ** DEMONSTRATE BIT INSTRUCTIONS
 3                           **
 4                           * TURN LIGHT ON IF BOTH PUSH BUTTON SWITCHES
 5                           * ARE PUSHED, AND TURN IT OFF OTHERWISE
 6                           *
 7                           ***********************************************************
 8                           *
 9                           ***********************************************************
10                           ** SYMBOL DEFINITIONS
11                           ***********************************************************
12          0040             SW1      EQU    %01000000   SWITCH 1 MASK
13          0008             SW2      EQU    %00001000   SWITCH 2 MASK
14          0004             LT1      EQU    %00000100   LIGHT 1 MASK
15                           *
16                           ***********************************************************
17                           ** DATA SECTION
18                           ***********************************************************
19  D000                              ORG $D000
20  D000                     IOAREA   RMB    1           BEGINNING OF INPUT/OUTPUT AREA
21  D001                              RMB    1           THE MEANING OF THESE LOCATIONS
22  D002                     IN1      RMB    1           ..IS HARDWARE DEPENDENT
23  D003                     IN2      RMB    1
24  D004                     OUT      RMB    1
25                           *
26                           ***********************************************************
27                           ** MAIN PROGRAM
28                           ***********************************************************
29  C100                              ORG    $C100
30                           * CONTROL LIGHT CONTINUOUSLY
31  C100   CE D0 00          START    LDX    #IOAREA   POINT X AT IOAREA
32  C103   1E 02 40 05                BRSET  IN1-IOAREA,X,SW1,TSTSCND
33  C107   1D 04 04                   BCLR   OUT-IOAREA,X,LT1
34  C10A   20 0C                      BRA    NEXT
35  C10C   1E 03 08 05       TSTSCND  BRSET  IN2-IOAREA,X,SW2,LTON
36  C110   1D 04 04                   BCLR   OUT-IOAREA,X,LT1
37  C113   20 03                      BRA    NEXT
38  C115   1C 04 04          LTON     BSET   OUT-IOAREA,X,LT1
39  C118   20 E6             NEXT     BRA    START
40  C11A                              END
```

Figure 5-6 Listing for program using bit instructions.

5.3 ARITHMETIC OPERATIONS

The arithmetic operations covered so far are addition, subtraction, increment, decrement, and multiply or divide by two. The 68HC11 has several more arithmetic instructions that significantly improve the execution speed of programs that do arithmetic.

Multiplication

Programs that implement control systems frequently use multiplication. These programs often need fast execution. The multiply instruction MUL provides very fast multiplication when compared to using a software algorithm to calculate the product. The instruction set table contains further information on the MUL instruction.

Here is the operation of the multiplication instruction:

MUL

Multiply the A accumulator by the B accumulator and put the product in the D accumulator. The multiply instruction multiplies two 8-bit unsigned numbers to make a 16-bit unsigned product. Bit 7 of the product goes to the C bit. The original numbers in the accumulators are lost because the product of the numbers goes to D.

Carefully note that the MUL instruction can only multiply unsigned numbers. The 68HC11 does not have a two's complement number multiplication instruction. Be careful to use the correct type of numbers because the result will be incorrect with signed numbers except in certain special cases.

Arithmetic

One use of the multiply instruction is to multiply two 8-bit numbers to obtain the product of the numbers as an arithmetic result. The biggest product of two 8-bit unsigned numbers is FE01, so there is no possibility of a carry that could affect the C bit. Instead, bit D7 of the result goes to the C bit. Then the C bit can be used for rounding. For example, suppose the product is scaled by using only its most-significant eight bits. If C is set to a 1, it means that the least-significant eight bits are one-half or greater. So, C set to 1 indicates that the 8-bit result should be rounded up to the next highest number.

A program can multiply two's complement signed numbers by converting them to positive numbers before using the MUL instruction. The program must compute the sign of the answer and correct the product as required. The overhead of correcting the sign is easily overcome by the speed of the MUL instruction.

Shifting

If the multiplier is a number containing a single 1, the product from the MUL instruction contains the multiplicand shifted to the position of the 1 in the multiplier. If only the most-significant eight bits of the product are kept, the result is the multiplicand shifted to the right. If the least-significant eight bits are kept, the multiplicand is shifted to the left.

The following examples illustrate using MUL for shifting:

```
        11111111    A              10110101    A
     ×  01000000    B           ×  00001000    B
   0011111111000000 A:B         0000010110101000 A:B
```

The examples both have a number to be shifted in the A accumulator. The B accumulator holds the shift mask. In the first example, the result in the A accumulator is the number shifted right two places while the result in the B accumulator is the number shifted left six places. In the second example, the number is shifted right five places in A and left three places in B. One instruction can shift the number in the A accumulator from zero to seven places with this technique.

Division

The 68HC11 has two integer division instructions that give both a quotient and a remainder after dividing. They use the D accumulator and the X index register. The 68HC11 has no equivalent instructions for the Y register. Here are the divide instructions:

IDIV, FDIV

Divide two 16-bit numbers giving a 16-bit quotient and a 16-bit remainder. All the numbers are 16-bit unsigned numbers. The dividend is the D accumulator, the divisor is the X register, the quotient goes to the X register, and the remainder goes to the D accumulator. The integer divide IDIV expects the quotient to be one or higher. The fractional divide instruction FDIV expects the quotient to be smaller than one.

Carefully select the correct divide instruction because the results obtained from the two instructions are very different.

Arithmetic

The integer divide instruction IDIV expects the quotient to be one or higher. The fractional division instruction FDIV expects the quotient to be smaller than one. The instruction assumes that the binary points of the dividend and the divisor are at the same relative position within the numbers.

The FDIV gives results with the binary points at the left end of the registers. If the quotient is higher than FFFF or there is a divide by zero, the quotient is set to FFFF and the remainder is indeterminate. The C bit indicates divide by zero and the V bit indicates a division overflow—the division was not a fraction, because the denominator was lower or the same as the numerator.

The IDIV instruction gives results with the binary points at the right end of the registers. If the quotient is too big, the case when dividing by zero, the quotient will be FFFF and the remainder is indeterminate. The C bit indicates divide by zero.

Table 5-3 shows the results of dividing several different numbers. Study the examples to see the effects of a division overflow.

Shifting

The division instructions shift a number to the right or left when the divisor contains a single 1. However, using MUL for shifting is usually better because the divide instructions put the quotient in the X register, which is less convenient. The MUL instruction also executes much faster than the divide instructions. The last examples in Table 5-3 illustrate using the divide instructions for shifting.

BCD Operations

The only instruction in the 68HC11 specifically designed for binary-coded decimal numbers is the DAA instruction. Here is the function of the DAA instruction:

TABLE 5-3 DIVISION INSTRUCTION EXAMPLES

Fractional Divide FDIV				Integer Divide IDIV			
D/X; X = Quotient, D = Remainder				D/X; X = Quotient, D = Remainder			
Before (point same)		After (point left)		Before (point same)		After (point right)	
D	X	.X	.D	D	X	X.	D.
0000	0005	0000	0000	000A	0005	0002	0000
000A	0005	FFFF	0000	000B	0005	0002	0001
0005	000A	8000	0000	0005	000A	0000	0005
0005	0009	8E39	0008	0005	0000	FFFF	0005
0001	FFFF	0001	0001	FFFF	0001	FFFF	0000
0123	1000	1230	0000	1234	0100	0012	0034

DAA
Decimal adjust the A accumulator. The DAA instruction correctly decimal adjusts the A accumulator immediately following only an ADDA, ADDB, ADCA, ADCB, or ABA instruction. The DAA corrects any digit that is out of decimal range following the addition and affects the C bit for a BCD result.

The DAA instruction corrects to BCD by adding one of the numbers 00, 06, 60, or 66 to the A accumulator. The algorithm to choose the correct number is complex and depends on the initial values in the C and H bits. The DAA instruction is the only instruction in the 68HC11 that uses the H or half-carry condition code bit.

5.4 THE STACK

Practical programs frequently need to save data generated by a program module. A program module that executes later in the program will retrieve the data. Once the data is retrieved, a copy of the saved data is often no longer needed. Using separate memory registers for each number that is saved and retrieved often requires many registers for large programs. In addition, the organization of these storage places is difficult, making programs more complicated than necessary.

A *stack* is a means of temporarily storing and retrieving numbers that reuses the same memory registers for storage. The stack does not solve all the problems of data storage, but it is very practical for common programming operations.

Stack Operation

A mechanical analogy will help you learn how the stack operates. The stack is a very dynamic device. One common mechanical stack is the plate rack used in some cafeterias. Figure 5-7a

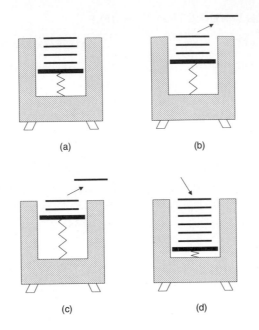

(a)   (b)

(c)   (d)

Figure 5-7   Plate rack analogy to computer stack operation.

illustrates a cross section of a plate rack containing some plates. As hungry customers go through the cafeteria line, each person takes a plate off the top of the rack. When the plate is removed, a mechanism moves the plates upward so the next plate is now at the top of the rack. Figures 5-7b and 5-7c illustrate this. The next customer now can easily access the next plate that is at the top of the rack. When the dishwasher puts clean plates into the rack, the mechanism moves downward. The top plate is again at the top of the rack, as Figure 5-7d illustrates.

If you consider the usage of the plates, you see that the last plate put into the rack is the first plate removed from the rack. The rack is a *last-in-first-out* device, or a LIFO. Notice that a similar effect results from stacking the plates on a table. Then each customer would reach to the top of the pile of plates to get a plate.

A stack in the computer is usually a region of memory allocated by the program. Some computers have registers dedicated to the stack. The 68HC11 has both hardware and instructions for easy use of a stack in memory.

Stack Hardware

A register in the 68HC11 called the *stack pointer* controls the operation of the stack. The stack pointer automatically points to the memory location that is the next available stack location as numbers are stored and retrieved from the stack. The number in the stack pointer is a memory address; that is the reason this register is called a pointer register.

Stack Instructions

Several instructions can manipulate the stack pointer register and the contents of memory pointed at by the stack pointer. The stack instructions were designed for very specific purposes and you should use them only for those specific purposes. Using these instructions for other purposes usually leads to poorly designed programs.

Here are all the stack-related instructions:

INS, DES   *Increment or decrement the stack pointer.* These instructions respectively add one and subtract one from the number in the stack pointer register.

LDS, STS   *Load or store the stack pointer register.* The load the stack pointer instruction creates a stack by placing an address in the stack pointer register. The store the stack pointer instruction is seldom used or needed.

PSHA, PSHB   *Push the A or B accumulator onto the stack.* These PSH instructions store a byte from the accumulator to memory at the address specified by the stack pointer and then decrement the stack pointer by one. The addressing mode is called inherent, but it is a kind of indexed addressing that uses the stack pointer as the index register.

PSHX, PSHY   *Push two bytes from the X or Y index register onto the stack.* These PSH instructions store the double-byte number in the index register to memory at the address specified by the stack pointer and then decrement the stack pointer by two. The addressing mode is called inherent, but it is a kind of indexed addressing that uses the stack pointer as the index register.

PULA, PULB   *Pull a byte from the stack and load it into the A or B accumulator.* These PUL instructions load a byte into an accumulator from memory at the address in the stack pointer and then increment the stack pointer by one. The addressing mode is called inherent, but it is a kind of indexed addressing that uses the stack pointer as the index register.

PULX, PULY   *Pull two bytes from the stack and load them into the X or Y index register.* These PUL instructions load a double-byte number into an index register from memory at the address in the stack pointer and then increment the stack pointer by two. The addressing mode is called inherent, but it is a kind of indexed addressing that uses the stack pointer as the index register.

TSX, TXS, TSY, TYS   *Transfer the stack pointer plus one to the index register or transfer the index register minus one to the stack pointer.* These instructions adjust the number transferred to overcome the automatic adjustment of the stack pointer when it is used for accessing the stack.

Be careful to understand the difference between the stack pointer and the stack. The stack pointer is a register in the microprocessor that holds the memory address of the next available memory byte in the stack. The stack is the collection of memory registers allocated to hold temporary data.

The stack can be any size provided there is enough memory installed in the computer. Most programs require a small stack, generally fewer than 50_{10} bytes. Since the stack pointer holds a 16-bit address, your stack can be anywhere in the memory space. Generally, the stack will be outside the direct addressing range. There is no advantage to placing the stack in the direct addressing range, so placing it elsewhere frees that part of memory for use by direct addressed instructions.

The stack pointer is the last microprocessor register in the 68HC11 to be introduced. You have now seen all the registers that were shown on the programming model in Figure 2-1 in Chapter 2.

Stack Example

A program designed to illustrate the operation of the stack is Figure 5-8. The program creates a stack, creates two data numbers in the accumulators, and then exchanges the two numbers using the stack. A detailed description of the program and the stack operation follows.

```
 1                                 *******************************************************
 2                                 ** DEMONSTRATE STACK OPERATION
 3                                 *
 4                                 * STORE TWO NUMBERS IN STACK AND RETRIEVE THEM IN
 5                                 * REVERSE ORDER EFFECTIVELY EXCHANGING THE VALUES
 6                                 *
 7                                 *******************************************************
 8                                 *
 9                                 *******************************************************
10                                 ** MAIN PROGRAM
11                                 *******************************************************
12   C100                                       ORG    $C100
13                                 * INITIALIZE STACK
14   C100    8E DF FF              START   LDS   #$DFFF    STACK FOR MOTOROLA TRAINER
15                                 * CREATE DATA VALUES FOR DEMONSTRATION
16   C103    86 22                         LDAA  #$22
17   C105    C6 33                         LDAB  #$33
18                                 * STORE DATA IN STACK
19   C107    36                            PSHA
20   C108    37                            PSHB
21                                 * RETRIEVE DATA FROM STACK IN REVERSE ORDER
22   C109    32                            PULA
23   C10A    33                            PULB
24   C10B    3F                            SWI              "STOP" FOR TRAINER
25   C10C                                  END
```

Figure 5-8   Program to demonstrate the stack.

Figure 5-9 shows the stack and the microprocessor registers at each step of the program. The figure shows the memory with higher addresses at the top of the diagram rather than at the bottom, as in previous examples. This order helps in visualizing the stack because the stack builds downward to lower addresses. Drawing the memory this way implies downward movement.

Figure 5-9a shows the memory and microprocessor registers before the program is run. The memory chosen for the stack is at address DFFF and below. The figure shows all the registers without numbers initially because the numbers are unknown. Here is the program description:

- *Lines 14 through 17.*   The LDS instruction on line 14 loads an initial address into the stack pointer register, effectively creating the stack. The initial address locates the highest address used by the stack. Generally, programs will have one and only one LDS instruction because stack operations are automatic after the stack is

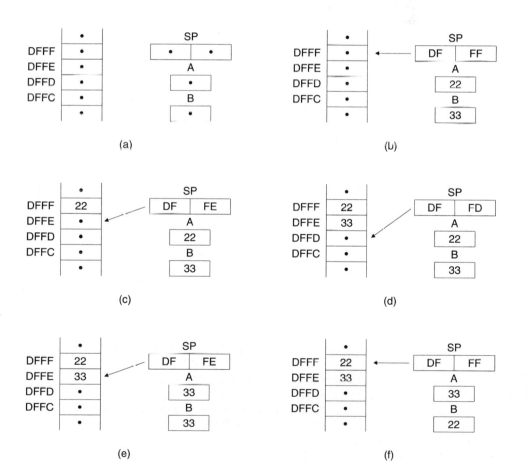

Figure 5-9   Stack diagrams for the program in Figure 5-8.

Motorola Trainer

The monitor program in the trainer will display the contents of the stack pointer register. Use the RM command and look for the S register. The stack pointer always contains the same number if you have just reset the trainer because the monitor program uses the stack pointer. Generally, you should not change the number in the stack pointer from the keyboard. Doing so will likely crash the monitor program when it uses its stack.

The trainer will not interfere with your program if your program uses the stack pointer and a stack. However, since the monitor program uses a stack, it will sometimes use your stack instead of its stack. The monitor program stores exactly nine bytes corresponding to the contents of the microprocessor registers. You must allow room in memory for these extra nine bytes. If the stack is located so it overwrites your program, the computer will crash.

See Appendix D for more information on the use of the trainer.

---

initialized. The next available location in the stack is address DFFF and the stack is now empty. Next, the instructions on lines 16 and 17 load the accumulators with numbers for the demonstration. The stack diagram in Figure 5-9b illustrates the conditions after these instructions have executed.

- *Line 19.*   The PSHA stores the 22 from the A accumulator into memory at the address specified by the stack pointer, namely, address DFFF. Then the PSHA automatically decrements the stack pointer so it now contains the address DFFE. The stack diagram now looks like Figure 5-9c. Notice that the stack pointer always points at the next available stack location. We say that the data number has been *pushed onto the stack.* Also note that the PSHA instruction is only one byte long because the stack pointer holds the address for it.

- *Line 20.*   The PSHB pushes the 33 from the B accumulator onto the stack. The stack diagram now looks like Figure 5-9d. The next available location in the stack is now at address DFFD. Two numbers are now in the stack.

- *Line 22.*   The PULA instruction first increments the number in the stack pointer to DFFE. Second, the PULA loads the number 33 from memory location DFFE into the A accumulator. The stack diagram now looks like Figure 5-9e. The PULA instruction removed the number 33 from the stack so there is only one entry left in the stack. We say that a data number has been *pulled from the stack.* You should observe that the last number put into the stack is the first number taken out of the stack.

- *Line 23.*   The PULB instruction pulls the number 22 from the stack into the B accumulator. The stack diagram now looks like Figure 5-9f. The stack is now empty.

You can tell that this is so because the number in the stack pointer is now the same as its initial value.

At the end of this program, the original numbers in the A and B accumulators have been exchanged. This is a very simple program that stores data in memory. However, no memory locations were permanently devoted to this program module. After it finishes executing, no data locations remain allocated. Other program modules can now use the same memory in the stack.

Using the Stack

You may wonder if the data numbers remain in the memory locations used by the stack. For the example program in Figure 5-8, the numbers 22 and 33 do remain in locations DFFF and DFFE after this program runs. However, the only reasonable point of view is to say that they are gone. Two numbers were pushed onto the stack and two were pulled from the stack, so it must be empty! You must disregard the numbers that remain in the memory registers. To do otherwise defeats the benefits of the stack and leads to elusive programming bugs.

Similarly, a rule to follow when using the stack is *always pull the same number of bytes that were pushed*. To do otherwise is nonsense. If more bytes are pushed than pulled, some bytes are forever left in the stack and are of no value to the program. Likewise, if bytes are pulled that were not pushed, the program will be using garbage numbers obtained from locations outside the stack. The 68HC11 has no hardware that can detect when the stack is used improperly.

Finally, you must determine the maximum depth of your stack and allocate enough memory for it. Be careful that your stack does not overwrite the program at the maximum depth of the stack.

5.5   SUBROUTINES

A *subroutine* is a reusable program module. A main program will call upon it at several locations to do some task. So you only need to write the subroutine code once instead of each time it is needed. However, the memory saved due to subroutines is often less important than the improved program organization that results from the use of subroutines.

Subroutine Concepts

A subroutine is a program module that is logically separate and independent of a main program. To use the subroutine, the main program will transfer program control to the subroutine. The subroutine does its function and then returns control to the main program. The subroutine is independent of the main program, so changes in the main program do not require changes in the subroutine.

The subroutine is not only a powerful programming device, but also a useful conceptual tool. It helps in designing programs because you can think about the function performed by the subroutine without considering the mechanics of doing that function.

It is not surprising that well-written subroutines are perfectly compatible with the structured programming and top/down design ideas. Subroutines were used to achieve many of the advantages of structured programming long before structured programming was formulated.

Instructions for Writing Subroutines

The transfer of control from a main program to a subroutine and from a subroutine back to the main program is very easy. The instruction set includes instructions to do these functions in cooperation with the stack hardware. Here are the instructions:

JSR, BSR   *Jump or branch to subroutine and save the return address in the stack.* These instructions transfer control to the subroutine after pushing the program counter onto the stack. The JSR and BSR instructions differ only in their addressing modes. During the execute phase, these instructions push the double-byte number in the program counter on the stack. The program counter was already incremented during the fetch phase, so the number that is pushed is the address of the next instruction—it is the return address.

RTS   *Return from subroutine by retrieving the return address from the stack.* The RTS instruction pulls a double-byte number from the stack and puts it into the program counter.

To use subroutines, your program must define a stack so the program counter containing the return address can be saved and restored. The body of the subroutine may use the stack to store temporary data. However, when the return point of the subroutine is reached, the stack must be returned to its condition at the entry to the subroutine. If this is not done, the RTS instruction will obtain an erroneous return address. So the body of the subroutine must remove as many bytes from the stack as it adds to it.

Using the subroutine instructions

Figure 5-10 illustrates the instructions to send control to a subroutine and to return control to the main program. In the example, the first JSR instruction jumps to the subroutine at address C400 and puts the return address C103 on the stack. At the end of the subroutine, the RTS sends control to the main program by pulling the address C103 from the stack into program counter. The second JSR instruction at address C18A performs similarly putting the address C18D on the stack. Notice this time the subroutine must return to address C18D, which is different from the first return address. Since the subroutine must return to a different address for each call, the address must be saved at the time of the call. This is the reason the stack is used; it temporarily saves the subroutine return address.

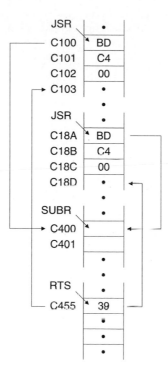

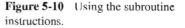

Figure 5-10   Using the subroutine instructions.

You should notice that the stack now has two different purposes. First, a program may save data numbers on the stack. Second, a subroutine will save the return address on the stack. Take care to avoid misusing the two kinds of numbers because both will be in the stack at once. Furthermore, in many practical programs, it is difficult if not impossible to know the position of each number in the stack at any particular time.

The First Subroutine Example

The subroutine in Figure 5-11 demonstrates the subroutine instructions with an example. The subroutine exchanges the low and high four bits of the A accumulator. The main program passes a data value to the subroutine in the A accumulator. The subroutine returns with the result in the A accumulator.

Here is a description of the program details:

- *Line 16.*   Loading an address into the stack pointer creates a stack. The use of subroutines always requires a stack.

- *Line 18.*   The main program gets the data value to be passed to the subroutine into the A accumulator. The main program is passing a parameter to the subroutine.

- *Line 19.*   The JSR instruction sends control to the subroutine and puts the return address C108 onto the stack. The JSR does not affect the accumulators, index

```
 1                      ************************************************************
 2                      ** SUBROUTINE DEMONSTRATION
 3                      * PASS VALUE IN A ACCUMULATOR
 4                      *
 5                      ************************************************************
 6                      ** DATA SECTION
 7                      ************************************************************
 8   0010                      ORG  $10
 9   0010    46        VALUE   FCB  $46        DATA FOR DEMONSTRATION
10                      *
11                      ************************************************************
12                      ** MAIN PROGRAM
13                      ************************************************************
14   C100                      ORG  $C100
15                      * INITIALIZE STACK
16   C100    8E DF FF  START   LDS  #$DFFF    STACK FOR MOTOROLA TRAINER
17                      * DEMONSTRATE SUBROUTINE OPERATION
18   C103    96 10             LDAA VALUE     GET DATA
19   C105    BD C1 09          JSR  SWAPA
20   C108    3F                SWI            "STOP" FOR MOTOROLA TRAINER
21                      *
22                      ************************************************************
23                      ** SUBROUTINE SWAPA
24                      * SWAP HIGH AND LOW 4 BITS OF A ACCUMULATOR
25                      * MODIFIES A,CC
26                      ************************************************************
27                      *----------------------------------------------------------
28                      * SWAP BITS
29                      *----------------------------------------------------------
30   C109    48        SWAPA   LSLA
31   C10A    89 00             ADCA #0
32   C10C    48                LSLA
33   C10D    89 00             ADCA #0
34   C10F    48                LSLA
35   C110    89 00             ADCA #0
36   C112    48                LSLA
37   C113    89 00             ADCA #0
38                      *----------------------------------------------------------
39                      * RETURN FROM SUBROUTINE
40                      *----------------------------------------------------------
41   C115    39                RTS
42   C116                      END
```

Figure 5-11   Main program and subroutine example.

registers, or condition code register. All the information in those registers is effectively passed to the subroutine even if it's not needed. The stack pointer now contains DFFD.

- *Lines 23 through 25.*   This is the minimal documentation required for all subroutines.

- *Lines 30 through 37.*   The body of the subroutine is similar to any other program module. It performs a function on some data; here, it's the data in the A accumulator. Running the body of this subroutine does not alter the stack or stack pointer.

- *Line 41.*   The RTS instruction returns control to the main program without affecting the A accumulator. The result in the accumulator is passed to the main program.

Motorola Trainer

Enter the program in Figure 5-11 into the trainer and single step or Trace the program. Carefully note the numbers in the stack pointer and accumulator as you proceed. Look at the memory in the stack after each instruction. Remember that the monitor program in the trainer will use your stack. So after numbers are pulled from the stack, the monitor program will overwrite your numbers. This can be confusing!

- *Line 20.*   The main program continues running at address C108 because the RTS instruction removed that address from the stack and put it into the program counter. After the RTS, the stack pointer contains DFFF and the stack is empty.

Running the subroutine changes the contents of both the A accumulator and the condition code register from what they were when the JSR instruction was encountered. The other microprocessor registers were not affected. Line 25 documents these changes because the writer of the main program must realize that the subroutine has made these changes.

Flowcharting Subroutines

The flowchart for a subroutine module differs only slightly from the flowchart for any other structured module. Since a structured subroutine will have a single beginning and a single ending point, it is a process. A rectangular process box on the main flowchart represents the subroutine. The subroutine is on a lower level of the top/down flowcharts. The flowchart for the subroutine is independent of the main program as is any lower-level flowchart. To provide some distinction for the subroutine, usually the word RETURN labels the terminator instead of the word END.

Figure 5-12 illustrates the symbol that represents the subroutine on the main program. Usually, a subroutine name represents the function of the subroutine. The name is used as a label in the assembly language program. Most people put the name of the subroutine at the top of the process box. The same name labels the beginning terminal symbol of the subroutine.

Parameter Passing

The difficult part of writing subroutines is choosing and implementing a means of passing parameters or data values between the main program and the subroutine. As a practical matter, the parameters are placed either in microprocessor registers or in memory. The parameter passed can be either the actual data value or a reference to the data value. A *reference* is the memory address of a data value.

When writing subroutines, many details must be considered, including deciding where to put the data in memory and how to access it. Therefore, there are many different techniques for parameter passing. The following sections discuss and illustrate with examples several

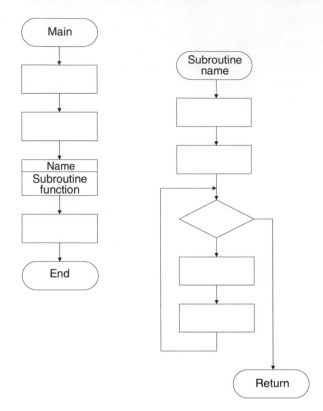

Figure 5-12   Main program and subroutine flowcharts.

parameter passing techniques. Understanding these techniques at the assembly language level will help you understand the characteristics of high-level languages.

Usually, looking at the flowchart will not tell you the parameter passing technique. The flowchart describes the function of the program and not the programming details. Therefore, the flowcharts are omitted for most of the subroutine examples that follow. The emphasis here is on the technique rather than the subroutine function.

A Bad Subroutine Example

Before looking at some good ways to pass parameters to and from subroutines, let's look at an example designed to illustrate the problems caused by bad techniques. The example is a trivial program of no real value except to illustrate some problems. Of course, the same problems occur in useful subroutines.

The listing for the example is Figure 5-13. The main program puts a number into location **NUMBER** and jumps to a subroutine that modifies the number in a trivial way. After control returns to the main program, it puts the result from the subroutine in an answer

```
 1                           ************************************************************
 2                           ** DEMONSTRATE BAD SUBROUTINES
 3                           *
 4                           ************************************************************
 5                           *
 6                           ************************************************************
 7                           ** MAIN PROGRAM
 8                           ************************************************************
 9      C100                            ORG  $C100
10                           *----------------------------------------------------------
11                           * INITIALIZE STACK
12                           *----------------------------------------------------------
13      C100  8E DF FF       START    LDS   #$DFFF    STACK FOR MOTOROLA TRAINER
14                           *----------------------------------------------------------
15                           * USE BAD SUBROUTINES
16                           *----------------------------------------------------------
17                           * MAKE DATA IN MAIN PROGRAM
18      C103  C6 11                   LDAB  #$11
19                           * SET UP DATA FOR SUBROUTINE
20      C105  86 22                   LDAA  #$22
21      C107  B7 C1 25                STAA  NUMBER
22                           * CALL SUBROUTINE TO ADD TWO
23      C10A  BD D0 05                JSR   ADDTWO
24                           * USE RESULT FROM SUBROUTINE
25      C10D  B6 C1 25                LDAA  NUMBER
26      C110  B7 C1 27                STAA  ANSWER2
27                           * SET UP DATA FOR SUBROUTINE
28      C113  86 33                   LDAA  #$33
29      C115  B7 C1 25                STAA  NUMBER
30                           * CALL SUBROUTINE TO ADD TO POSITIVE
31      C118  BD D0 00                JSR   BAD
32                           * USE RESULT FROM SUBROUTINE
33      C11B  B6 C1 25                LDAA  NUMBER
34      C11E  B7 C1 28                STAA  ANSWER3
35                           * STORE MAIN PROGRAM DATA
36      C121  F7 C1 26                STAB  ANSWER1
37      C124  3F                      SWI               "STOP" FOR MOTOROLA TRAINER
38                           *
39                           ************************************************************
40                           ** DATA SECTION
41                           ************************************************************
42      C125               NUMBER   RMB   1
43      C126               ANSWER1  RMB   1
44      C127               ANSWER2  RMB   1
45      C128               ANSWER3  RMB   1
46                           *
47                           ************************************************************
48                           ** SUBROUTINES BAD, ADDTWO, ADDONE
49                           * INCREMENT POSITIVE TWO'S COMPLEMENT NUMBERS, OR
50                           * ADD ONE OR TWO TO ANY NUMBER
51                           ************************************************************
52      D000                            ORG  $D000
53                           * SUBROUTINE BAD--POSITIVE NUMBER?
54      D000  F6 C1 25       BAD      LDAB  NUMBER
55      D003  2A 03                   BPL   ADDONE    BRANCH ON YES
56                           * SUBROUTINE ADDTWO
57      D005  7C C1 25       ADDTWO   INC   NUMBER
58                           * SUBROUTINE ADDONE
59      D008  7C C1 25       ADDONE   INC   NUMBER
60      D00B  39                      RTS
61      D00C                          END
```

Figure 5-13   An example of bad subroutines.

location. This is done twice for different numbers. Here are some problems in the bad example program:

- *Lines 54, 57, and 59.* There is no parameter passing between the main program and the subroutine. Instead, the subroutine directly accesses the location labeled NUMBER to get data and to store the answer. The subroutine is not independent of the main program because it uses a data location owned by the main program. For example, if the main program was changed so there no longer was a location labeled NUMBER, the subroutine could no longer be used—the subroutine also would need changes. You could argue that the subroutine is not a subroutine but just a strange module of the main program. Similarly, if the main program is moved to a new location in memory, the subroutine must be assembled again for the new location. This prevents separate assembly of the main program and the subroutine, which is a useful technique.

- *Lines 21, 25, 29, and 33.* The main program must put the data for the subroutine in the special location labeled NUMBER each time it calls the subroutine. And then the main program must get the result from the location NUMBER each time the subroutine returns. The main program can't choose to use an arbitrary location each time it calls the subroutine. The main program is doing extraordinary things to accommodate the bad subroutine. One advantage of using subroutines is reusing them at many places in a program. However, the extraordinary setup in this example must be repeated each time the main program calls the subroutine. This is inefficient use of memory with nothing gained in return.

- *Lines 18 and 36.* The main program was using the B accumulator before calling the subroutines. However, the BAD subroutine changed the B accumulator without restoring it. So the main program will malfunction at line 36. At the least, the subroutine documentation should list any registers that the subroutine modifies.

- *Lines 48, 54, 57, and 59.* The apparent single subroutine is really three different subroutines merged together with different entry points. The subroutine is incorrectly structured because it does not have a single entry point and a single exit point. Although this makes shorter subroutines, it is confusing and complicated. Changing one subroutine affects the other subroutines as well.

Almost everything about the bad subroutine causes problems in practical programs. The example given is very simple and you may think that the points mentioned are of little importance. But when you write large practical programs, you will discover that the problems discussed are significant.

Some Basic Subroutine Design Considerations

Answering the following questions while writing a subroutine will help you to write good programs:

- *Is your subroutine independent of the main program?* As a test of independence, determine if the main program and its data can be moved to new memory locations without changing the subroutine. Also, can the assembly language labels in the main program be altered without any corrections to the subroutine? You should not even have to assemble the subroutine again after you change the main program.

- *Is your subroutine written in correctly structured code?* A minimum requirement is that your subroutine may have only a single entry point and a single exit point. Always make the first instruction on the subroutine listing the first instruction executed in the subroutine. Likewise, always put the RTS instruction at the physical end of the subroutine listing.

- *Have you determined what data must be passed to and from the subroutine?* You must determine where the data is, how large the numbers are, how many numbers must be passed, and in what order they are to be passed.

- *Does your subroutine restore any microprocessor registers it changed?* If some registers are not restored, the subroutine must have documentation explaining what changes have occurred.

- *Must the main program do much setup to make the subroutine work?* Usually, the parameter passing technique should fit the task done by the subroutine. Then the main program will do little to set up the call to the subroutine. Use of the subroutine will fit into the main program in a natural way. Furthermore, if the main program calls the subroutine at many places, the number of memory locations used by the instructions that set up the subroutine may be unreasonable. A technique requiring little or no set up may be needed.

- *Have you determined where the subroutine will put its local variables?* The numbers that the subroutine works on when doing its function are called *local variables*. Usually, the microprocessor registers will hold these. However, if memory is used, the location of the local variables is a significant decision.

The sections that follow discuss many good parameter passing techniques. The good techniques will satisfy all the questions asked here.

5.6 SUBROUTINE PARAMETER PASSING TECHNIQUES

Parameter passing refers to the method by which data numbers are sent from the main program to the subroutine, or from the subroutine to the main program. Many different techniques are used, although the names for the techniques are not universally agreed upon. The two general categories of techniques considered here are usually named *call-by-value* and *call-by-reference*.

Call-by-Value Technique

The *call-by-value* technique of parameter passing requires the main program to give the subroutine copies of the data values. The subroutine does its function and then may give some data values back to the main program. The main program may keep the original data value in memory, but it does not give the subroutine access to the original data number. This prevents the subroutine from changing it.

The simplest call-by-value technique uses the microprocessor registers to hold the data values. The main program first places the numbers in the registers, and then executes the jump-to-subroutine instruction. So the subroutine has the data when it starts running. The subroutine then places the results in the microprocessor registers and returns to the main program. The results are then available to the main program when it continues running. Using microprocessor registers is the most common technique of passing parameters at the machine and assembly language levels of programming.

The main limitations on passing numbers in the microprocessor registers are the number and size of data values that can be passed. The Motorola 68HC11 can hold data values in both the accumulators and the index registers. The A and B accumulators can each hold one byte and the index registers can each hold two bytes. Therefore, the registers can hold a total of six bytes. Six bytes are enough for many practical applications.

The designs of the main program and the subroutine must be coordinated so the correct numbers are passed in the correct registers. Generally, the main program is designed first. The main program determines the calling sequence for the subroutine. Then the subroutine can be written to be compatible with the calling sequence.

Call-by-value example

The first subroutine example in Figure 5-11 uses the call-by-value technique of parameter passing where the A accumulator holds the value. The next example is a very simple subroutine that illustrates several more characteristics of call-by-value subroutines. In particular, the main program and the subroutine were assembled by separate runs of the assembler program. When you assemble a subroutine separately, you will get assembly errors if the subroutine is not independent of the main program.

Assembling the main and subroutine modules separately has several practical advantages. First, it's convenient because subroutines can be developed independently of the main program—possibly by different people. Second, several subroutines can be grouped together into a library. The library routines can be thoroughly tested to ensure correctness. Then different main programs can use the library subroutines. The programmer can depend on working subroutines in the library without the effort of writing new subroutines.

If the subroutine and the main program are assembled separately, you must provide a means of linking them together. Generally, this linking is not difficult.

Flowcharts.   Flowcharts for the example are in Figure 5-14. The example subroutine provides a time delay by looping for a specified amount of time. The resolution of the time delay is 20_{10} milliseconds because an inner loop provides this delay. An outer loop delays a number of 20_{10}-millisecond periods. The number is determined by the 8-bit value passed

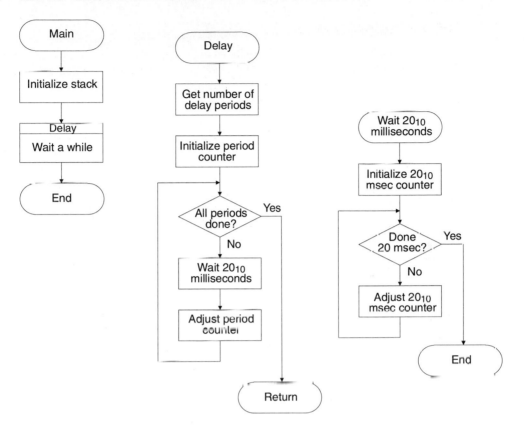

Figure 5-14   Flowcharts for DELAY subroutine and a main program to call it.

from the main program. The 8-bit timing value is an unsigned number, so the maximum time delay is 255_{10} times 20_{10} milliseconds or a little more than five seconds. There are more sophisticated ways to provide timing, but this example illustrates the subroutine principles well.

   The main program.   Figure 5-15 is the listing of the main program. The main program creates a stack, gets the time delay parameter into the A accumulator, and jumps to the subroutine. The statement on line 10 provides the link between the main program and the subroutine. Since the subroutine contains the label DELAY at the beginning of the subroutine, the assembler must know the value of DELAY to assemble line 32. It can't assemble the JSR instruction without knowing the address of the subroutine. Line 10 provides the address manually. The EQU directive tells the assembler the value of DELAY.

   The subroutine.   The subroutine listing is in Figure 5-16. The top/down structured flowcharts show that the subroutine is a loop inside a loop. The following describes the listing in detail:

```
 1                              ************************************************************
 2                              ** DEMONSTRATE DELAY SUBROUTINE
 3                              * PASS DELAY VALUE IN A ACCUMULATOR
 4                              *
 5                              ************************************************************
 6                              *
 7                              ************************************************************
 8                              ** SYMBOL DEFINITIONS
 9                              ************************************************************
10          C150                DELAY   EQU   $C150     LINK TO SUBROUTINE
11                              *
12                              ************************************************************
13                              ** DATA SECTION
14                              ************************************************************
15   0010                               ORG $0010
16   0010                       DELPAR  RMB   1         USER SUPPLIED VALUE
17                              *
18                              ************************************************************
19                              ** MAIN PROGRAM
20                              ************************************************************
21   C100                               ORG $C100
22                              *--------------------------------------------------------
23                              * INITIALIZE STACK POINTER
24                              *--------------------------------------------------------
25   C100    8E DF FF           START   LDS   #$DFFF    STACK FOR MOTOROLA TRAINER
26                              *--------------------------------------------------------
27                              * WAIT SPECIFIED TIME
28                              *--------------------------------------------------------
29                              * GET DELAY PARAMETER
30   C103    96 10                      LDAA  DELPAR
31                              * DELAY
32   C105    BD C1 50                   JSR   DELAY
33   C108    3F                         SWI             "STOP" FOR MOTOROLA TRAINER
34   C109                               END

 Defined            Symbol Name          Value              References

10   DELAY                          =   C150               32
16   DELPAR                             0010               30
25   START                              C100

        Lines Assembled :   34            Assembly Errors :   0
```

Figure 5-15   Main program assembled separately from subroutine.

- *Lines 8 and 9.*   The purpose of the first program module is to get the parameter from the main program. In general, the parameter will be in a microprocessor register or in memory. This example uses the A accumulator, so there is nothing for this module to do and there is no code necessary.

- *Lines 10 and 11.*   The next module initializes the working counter for the outer loop. Since the A accumulator is the working counter, it is already set and no code is necessary.

- *Lines 12 through 25.*   This is the major loop that uses up time for the delay. The outer loop repeatedly uses the 20_{10}-millisecond loop.

- *Line 13.*   The period loop counter is tested to see if all the 20_{10}-millisecond delay periods are finished. The TSTA instruction is necessary because the BEQ instruction

```
 1                           ********************************************************
 2                           ** SUBROUTINE DELAY
 3                           * MODIFIES A,X,CC
 4                           *
 5                           ********************************************************
 6                           *
 7    C150                                    ORG     $C150
 8                           * GET NUMBER OF PERIODS
 9                           *                          NO CODE ALREADY IN A ACC
10                           * INITIALIZE PERIOD COUNTER
11                           *                          USE A ACC FOR PERIOD COUNTER
12                           * ALL PERIODS DONE?
13    C150   4D              DELAY   TSTA
14    C151   27 0B                   BEQ     RT          BRANCH ON YES
15                           * WAIT 20 MILLISECONDS
16                           *     INITIALIZE 20 MILLISECOND COUNTER
17    C153   CE 11 5C                LDX     #$115C  USE X REGISTER FOR COUNTER
18                           *     DONE WITH 20 MILLISECONDS?
19    C156   27 03           AGAIN   BEQ     AHEAD       BRANCH ON YES
20                           *     ADJUST 20 MILLISECOND COUNTER
21    C158   09                      DEX
22    C159   20 FB                   BRA     AGAIN
23                           * ADJUST PERIOD COUNTER
24    C15B   4A              AHEAD   DECA
25    C15C   20 F2                   BRA     DELAY
26                           * RETURN TO MAIN PROGRAM
27    C15E   39              RT      RTS
28    C15F                           END


     Defined           Symbol Name        Value           References

     19    AGAIN                           C156            22
     24    AHEAD                           C15B            19
     13    DELAY                           C150            25
     27    RT                              C15E            14


          Lines Assembled :   28           Assembly Errors :   0
```

Figure 5-16   DELAY subroutine assembled separately from main program.

must have the correct Z bit information. The subroutine must not depend on the main program setting the condition codes correctly before jumping to the subroutine.

- *Lines 15 through 22.*   This 20_{10} millisecond loop uses the index register as a double-byte working counter. You can calculate the number of loops required if you know the number of microprocessor clock cycles necessary to execute the loop. By looking at the instruction set table, you will find that each instruction in this loop requires three clock cycles. If N is the initial number in the X register, the number of clock cycles for this loop is 6+9N. If you know the clock rate, you can determine N. The Motorola trainer uses an 8.0-MHz crystal that gives an E-clock rate of 2.0_{10} MHz or 0.5_{10} microseconds per cycle. To get a loop time of 20_{10} milliseconds with this clock rate, the value of N is 115C.

- *Line 27.*   The RTS instruction gets the subroutine return address C108 from the stack and places it in the program counter, causing execution to continue in the main program. While the body of the subroutine is running, the stack pointer contains

DFFD and the only number in the stack is the return address. After the RTS executes, the stack is empty.

The DELAY subroutine is very simple because it only loops to use the time one data value specifies. However, it illustrates correct principles and is similar to most practical subroutines. It also demonstrates the separate assembly of the main program and subroutine, which is very common.

Position-independent code

The binary instruction codes that form the subroutine in Figure 5-16 have an interesting property. If you change the ORG statement on line 7 to specify any other address, such as ORG $0000, the binary codes will be the same. The binary codes that make up this subroutine can be placed anywhere in memory without alteration and they will work correctly. Therefore, this subroutine has *position-independent* or *binary relocatable* code.

Position-independent code is useful in practical applications. For example, a company can manufacture a permanent memory-integrated circuit containing the binary numbers for a collection of position-independent subroutines. The purchasers of the memory can wire it into their computers without any consideration of the addresses which it will implement, and the subroutines will work correctly.

What makes the subroutine code position independent? In the 68HC11, it is sufficient that the instructions in the subroutine do not use direct or extended addressing. Instructions with other addressing modes don't have addresses within the instructions, so there are no addresses to be considered. For example, the branch instructions which have program relative addressing only have an offset inside the instruction. The branch instructions were designed with this addressing mode to make position-independent code possible.

In a later chapter, a very desirable type of subroutine called a reentrant subroutine is discussed. Since the lack of direct and extended addressed instructions that access data is necessary for reentrant subroutines, it is good practice to avoid their use within all subroutines. Avoiding direct and extended addressing encourages use of the stack to store temporary numbers.

All the remaining subroutine examples in this chapter have position-independent code. In addition, they have *pure procedure* code because the instructions are not altered by using the subroutine. The name *pure procedure* implies that no numbers that are used as data values that change as the program runs are within the instructions.

Call-by-value in memory example

A constant data number can be passed to a subroutine as a value in memory. The value of the constant is determined when the program is loaded into memory. The constant is placed in memory immediately following the JSR instruction. A similar technique can be used for variable data when read/write memory holds the program and the data number.

The example in Figure 5-17 illustrates a subroutine that rotates only the A accumulator to the left a number of positions. The constant passed to the subroutine specifies the number of positions to rotate. An alternative is passing the number of rotates in the B accumulator,

```
 1                                    ***********************************************************
 2                                    ** DEMONSTRATE SUBROUTINE--ROTATE A ACCUMULATOR LEFT
 3                                    ** MULTIPLE POSITIONS
 4                                    * PASS PARAMETER BY VALUE AS MEMORY CONSTANT
 5                                    *
 6                                    ***********************************************************
 7                                    *
 8                                    ***********************************************************
 9                                    ** DATA SECTION
10                                    ***********************************************************
11     0010                                     ORG   $10
12     0010    06                     VALUE   FCB   $06       DATA FOR DEMONSTRATION
13                                    *
14                                    ***********************************************************
15                                    ** MAIN PROGRAM
16                                    ***********************************************************
17     C100                                     ORG   $C100
18                                    * INITIALIZE STACK
19     C100    8E DF FF               START   LDS   #$DFFF    STACK FOR MOTOROLA TRAINER
20                                    * ROTATE A ACCUMULATOR LEFT 4 POSITIONS
21     C103    96 10                          LDAA  VALUE     GET DATA
22     C105    BD C1 0A                        JSR   ROTAL
23     C108    04                              FCB   4         CONSTANT FOR POSITIONS
24     C109    3F                              SWI             "STOP" FOR MOTOROLA TRAINER
25                                    *
26                                    ***********************************************************
27                                    ** SUBROUTINE ROTAL
28                                    * ROTATE ONLY A ACCUMULATOR LEFT  CONSTANT FOLLOWING
29                                    * JSR INSTRUCTION SPECIFIES POSITIONS--MODIFIES A,CC
30                                    ***********************************************************
31                                    *-------------------------------------
32                                    * INITIALIZE SUBROUTINE
33                                    *---------------------------------------------------------
34                                    * SAVE MAIN PROGRAM REGISTERS
35     C10A    3C                     ROTAL   PSHX
36     C10B    37                              PSHB
37                                    * GET NUMBER OF POSITIONS
38     C10C    30                              TSX
39     C10D    EE 03                           LDX   3,X
40     C10F    E6 00                           LDAB  0,X
41                                    *---------------------------------------------------------
42                                    * ROTATE A
43                                    *---------------------------------------------------------
44     C111    5D                     BACK    TSTB
45     C112    27 06                           BEQ   AHEAD
46     C114    5A                              DECB
47     C115    48                              ASLA
48     C116    89 00                           ADCA  #0
49     C118    20 F7                           BRA   BACK
50                                    *---------------------------------------------------------
51                                    * RETURN FROM SUBROUTINE
52                                    *---------------------------------------------------------
53                                    * ADJUST RETURN ADDRESS
54     C11A    30                     AHEAD   TSX
55     C11B    6C 04                           INC   4,X
56     C11D    26 02                           BNE   RET
57     C11F    6C 03                           INC   3,X
58                                    * RESTORE MAIN PROGRAM REGISTERS
59     C121    33                     RET     PULB
60     C122    38                              PULX
61     C123    39                              RTS
62     C124                                    END
```

Figure 5-17   Call-by-value in memory subroutine example.

thus making the main program more complicated and using the B accumulator. In addition, passing the number of rotates in an accumulator treats the number as a variable rather than as a constant.

Here are some details of the program in Figure 5-17:

- *Line 22.*   The constant is placed immediately after the JSR instruction, thus passing it to the subroutine. The subroutine must return to address C109 in this example to avoid executing the data value as an instruction.

- *Lines 35 and 36.*   The subroutine will alter the X and B registers, so they are saved on the stack. Their values are restored at the end of the subroutine. The stack pointer now contains DFFA.

- *Line 38.*   The TSX instruction transfers the number in the stack pointer plus one to the X index register. The index register now contains DFFB, which is the address of the last byte stored in the stack. So the index register points at the entry at the lowest address in the stack.

- *Line 39.*   The index register is loaded with the saved program counter. The JSR instruction saved the program counter in the stack. The saved address, C108, is the subroutine return address. The saved address is now in the X index register. So the index register now points to the constant data value to be passed to the subroutine.

- *Line 40.*   The LDAB instruction gets the data value from the main program into the B accumulator for the subroutine to use. This is the last step in passing the parameter to the subroutine.

- *Lines 44 through 49.*   The body of the subroutine rotates the A accumulator the correct number of positions. This loop uses the value passed from the main program to determine the number of positions to rotate.

- *Line 54.*   The return address for the subroutine must be adjusted so the subroutine returns to the location after the data value. The TSX instruction points the X index register at the last entry in the stack again. Now the saved return address can be accessed.

- *Lines 55 through 57.*   The return address saved in the stack is incremented by one. The first INC instruction adds one to the least-significant byte of the saved address. If there is a carry, the second INC instruction adds one to the most-significant byte. Be careful when adjusting addresses. If the program doesn't check for a carry and increment the most-significant byte when necessary, the program will work for most addresses. But when an address is adjusted that generates a carry, the program will fail. Such a bug could go undetected for a long time.

- *Lines 59 and 60.*   The PUL instructions restore the main program numbers to the B and X registers from the stack.

- *Line 61.*   The RTS instruction sends control to address C109 in this example by pulling this adjusted return address from the stack.

As in this example, subroutines using constant parameters often assume the character of a new instruction in the instruction set of the microprocessor. In this example, the subroutine acts as a rotate-the-A-accumulator-multiple-positions instruction. Some assemblers, called macro-assemblers, allow a new symbol to be defined for this pseudo-instruction. When the assembler encounters this new symbol, it automatically generates the jump to subroutine instruction and constant as required to call the subroutine.

Call-by-Reference Technique

Often the data values that the subroutine must work on are in memory. If this is so, the main program can pass the memory addresses of the data values to a subroutine. The addresses passed to a subroutine are called *references* and the parameter passing technique is named *call-by-reference*. The subroutine does the work to get the data from the locations referenced or addressed. Similarly, the subroutine can pass data back to the main program by directly storing into referenced memory locations. The main program gets the results from memory as it continues running. Usually, the main program will want the results in memory anyway, so it need do nothing to get the results.

Since the subroutine will have the addresses of the data numbers, there is no way to prevent the subroutine from changing the original data. This can make certain errors very troublesome and elusive. However, if you want the subroutine to modify the original data, call-by-reference is a good technique.

The call-by-value technique can be combined with the call-by-reference technique within the same subroutine. It is common to do this. Each parameter should be passed by the technique best suited to its function. For example, a table is usually passed to a subroutine using the call-by-reference technique.

Call-by-reference in microprocessor register example

The reference or address of the data can be passed to the subroutine in a microprocessor register. In the 68HC11, references usually are passed in the index registers. Since there are two index registers, only two references can be passed this way. However, two are enough for many practical subroutines.

Figure 5-18 is the listing of an example program that passes both a reference and a value to the subroutine. The example program uses only the microprocessor registers. A resultant value is passed back to the main program in a microprocessor register.

The example subroutine counts the number of zeros in a table of numbers in memory. The table is at the address specified by the reference. The value determines the length of the table. The subroutine returns the number of zeros in the table as a value. The main program and subroutine were assembled together to shorten the listing. Here are some details about the program:

- *Line 31.*   The value parameter is loaded into the A accumulator in preparation for transfer to the subroutine.

```
 1                                   ***********************************************************
 2                                   ** DEMONSTRATE SUBROUTINE--COUNT ZERO BYTES IN TABLE
 3                                   * PASS VALUE IN A REGISTER AND REFERENCE IN X REGISTER
 4                                   *
 5                                   ***********************************************************
 6                                   *
 7                                   ***********************************************************
 8                                   ** DATA SECTION
 9                                   ***********************************************************
10  0010                                       ORG $10
11  0010    04                  LENGTH  FCB    4           DATA FOR DEMONSTRATION
12  0011                        ANSWER  RMB    1           ANSWER PUT HERE BY MAIN PROGRAM
13                                   *
14  C300                                       ORG $C300
15  C300    45                  TABLE   FCB    $45         TABLE TO BE SEARCHED FOR ZEROS
16  C301    00                          FCB    $00
17  C302    10                          FCB    $10
18  C303    00                          FCB    $00
19                                   *
20                                   ***********************************************************
21                                   ** MAIN PROGRAM
22                                   ***********************************************************
23  C100                                       ORG    $C100
24                                   *-------------------------------------------------------
25                                   * INITIALIZE STACK
26                                   *-------------------------------------------------------
27  C100    8E DF FF            START   LDS    #$DFFF   STACK IN MOTOROLA TRAINER
28                                   *-------------------------------------------------------
29                                   * COUNT NUMBER OF ZERO BYTES IN TABLE
30                                   *-------------------------------------------------------
31  C103    96 10                      LDAA   LENGTH   GET TABLE LENGTH
32  C105    CE C3 00                   LDX    #TABLE   GET TABLE ADDRESS
33  C108    BD C1 0E                   JSR    CTZERO
34  C10B    D7 11                      STAB   ANSWER   SAVE RESULT FROM SUBROUTINE
35  C10D    3F                         SWI             "STOP" FOR MOTOROLA TRAINER
36                                   *
37                                   ***********************************************************
38                                   ** SUBROUTINE CTZERO
39                                   * SEARCH TABLE OF (A) BYTES AT LOCATION (X), RETURN
40                                   * NUMBER OF ZEROS AS (B)--MODIFIES A,B,X,CC
41                                   ***********************************************************
42                                   *-------------------------------------------------------
43                                   * SEARCH TABLE FOR ZEROS
44                                   *-------------------------------------------------------
45                                   * INITIALIZE ZERO COUNTER
46  C10E    5F                  CTZERO  CLRB
47                                   * AT END OF TABLE?
48  C10F    4D                  AGAIN   TSTA
49  C110    27 09                      BEQ    RET      BRANCH ON YES
50                                   * TABLE ENTRY ZERO?
51  C112    6D 00                      TST    0,X
52  C114    26 01                      BNE    AHEAD    BRANCH ON NO
53                                   * INCREMENT ZERO COUNTER
54  C116    5C                         INCB
55                                   * DECREMENT LOOP COUNTER
56  C117    4A                  AHEAD   DECA
57                                   * ADVANCE TO NEXT ENTRY IN TABLE
58  C118    08                         INX
59  C119    20 F4                      BRA    AGAIN
60                                   *-------------------------------------------------------
61                                   * RETURN FROM SUBROUTINE
62                                   *-------------------------------------------------------
63  C11B    39                  RET     RTS
64  C11C                                END
```

Figure 5-18   Passing parameters using call-by-value and reference in microprocessor registers.

- *Line 32.*   The reference parameter is loaded into the X index register. Since a 16-bit address is sent to the subroutine, the data can be anywhere in memory.

- *Line 33.*   The JSR instruction does not alter the accumulators or index registers, so the parameters are effectively passed to the subroutine during this jump.

- *Lines 48 through 59.*   The data passed to the subroutine is used in the body of the subroutine. The result, the number of zeros in the table, is generated in the B accumulator.

- *Line 63.*   The RTS instruction does not alter the microprocessor registers. Therefore, the result is passed to the main program in the B accumulator during the return. Upon return to the main program, the values in the A, B, X, and condition code registers are different from the values at entry to the subroutine.

You should observe that the subroutine has pure procedure, position-independent code. In addition, the subroutine did not need to store any local data in memory to do its function.

Call-by-reference in memory example

The reference or address of a data value can be passed to the subroutine in the memory locations following the JSR instruction. This is a convenient and easily accessible location for the reference, although this is not immediately apparent. In most applications, the location of the data will not change as the program runs. Therefore, the reference passed to the subroutine will be a constant determined when the program is loaded into memory.

The example in Figure 5-19 demonstrates passing parameters by reference in memory. All local variables are kept in the microprocessor registers. The subroutine does the same function as the example in Figure 5-18; only the parameter passing technique is different. The subroutine searches a table of numbers and counts the number of zeros. The subroutine needs the address of the table, the length of the table, and a place to return the number of zeros.

Here are some details about the program in Figure 5-19 and the memory diagram for it in Figure 5-20:

- *Lines 33, 34, and 35.*   The addresses of the memory locations that contain the table address, table length, and resulting zero count are placed following the JSR instruction by the FDB directives. The contents column shows these addresses to be C300, 0025, and C000. Figure 5-20b is a memory diagram that shows the JSR instruction and the references. From this figure, you cannot tell whether each reference is used to pass a value to the subroutine or for it to pass a result back. Sometimes a reference is used for both purposes. Observe that the main program executes no instructions to set up the parameters for the subroutine if the data is already in memory. Usually, the data is already in memory. Then all the work is done inside the subroutine. The setup is not reproduced in the main program each time the subroutine is called. The assembler provides the references to the data values as a list of addresses following the jump to subroutine instruction. However,

```
 1                        *************************************************
 2                        ** DEMONSTRATE SUBROUTINE--COUNT ZERO BYTES IN TABLE
 3                        * PASS PARAMETERS BY REFERENCE IN MEMORY
 4                        * USE MICROPROCESSOR REGISTERS FOR LOCAL STORAGE
 5                        *
 6                        *************************************************
 7                        *
 8                        *************************************************
 9                        ** DATA SECTION
10                        *************************************************
11   0025                          ORG  $25
12   0025  04             LENGTH   FCB  4          DATA FOR DEMONSTRATION
13   C000                          ORG  $C000
14   C000                 ANSWER   RMB  1          ANSWER PUT HERE BY SUBROUTINE
15   C300                          ORG  $C300
16   C300  45             TABLE    FCB  $45        TABLE TO BE SEARCHED FOR ZEROS
17   C301  00                      FCB  $00
18   C302  10                      FCB  $10
19   C303  00                      FCB  $00
20                        *
21                        *************************************************
22                        ** MAIN PROGRAM
23                        *************************************************
24   C100                          ORG   $C100
25                        *-----------------------------------------------
26                        * INITIALIZE STACK
27                        *-----------------------------------------------
28   C100  8E DF FF       START    LDS  #$DFFF    STACK FOR MOTOROLA TRAINER
29                        *-----------------------------------------------
30                        * COUNT NUMBER OF ZERO BYTES IN TABLE
31                        *-----------------------------------------------
32   C103  BD C1 0D                JSR    ZEROCT
33   C106  C300                    FDB    TABLE    ADDRESS OF TABLE
34   C108  0025                    FDB    LENGTH   ADDRESS OF TABLE LENGTH
35   C10A  C000                    FDB    ANSWER   ADDRESS OF ANSWER
36   C10C  3F                      SWI             "STOP" FOR MOTOROLA TRAINER
37                        *
38                        *************************************************
39                        ** SUBROUTINE ZEROCT
40                        * SEARCH A TABLE OF (PAR2) BYTES AT LOCATION PAR1
41                        * RETURN NUMBER OF ZEROS AS (PAR3)--MODIFIES CC
42                        *************************************************
43                        *-----------------------------------------------
44                        * INITIALIZE SUBROUTINE
45                        *-----------------------------------------------
46                        * SAVE MAIN PROGRAM REGISTERS
47   C10D  36             ZEROCT   PSHA
48   C10E  37                      PSHB
49   C10F  3C                      PSHX
50                        * GET TABLE LENGTH
51   C110  30                      TSX             X POINTS TO TOP ENTRY IN STACK
52   C111  EE 04                   LDX    4,X      GET SAVED PROGRAM COUNTER
53   C113  EE 02                   LDX    2,X      GET REFERENCE TO TABLE LENGTH
54   C115  A6 00                   LDAA   0,X      GET TABLE LENGTH
55                        * GET TABLE ADDRESS
56   C117  30                      TSX             X POINTS TO TOP ENTRY IN STACK
57   C118  EE 04                   LDX    4,X      GET SAVED PROGRAM COUNTER
58   C11A  EE 00                   LDX    0,X      GET REFERENCE TO TABLE
59                        * INITIALIZE ZERO COUNTER
60   C11C  5F                      CLRB
61                        *-----------------------------------------------
62                        * SEARCH TABLE FOR ZEROS
63                        *-----------------------------------------------
```

Figure 5-19 Passing parameters by reference in memory.

```
64                              * AT END OF TABLE?
65   C11D   4D          AGAIN   TSTA
66   C11E   27 09               BEQ    RET        BRANCH ON YES
67                      * TABLE ENTRY ZERO?
68   C120   6D 00               TST    0,X
69   C122   26 01               BNE    AHEAD      BRANCH ON NO
70                      * INCREMENT ZERO COUNTER
71   C124   5C                  INCB
72                      * DECREMENT LOOP COUNTER
73   C125   4A          AHEAD   DECA
74                      * ADVANCE TO NEXT ENTRY IN TABLE
75   C126   08                  INX
76   C127   20 F4               BRA    AGAIN
77                      *---------------------------------------------
78                      * RETURN FROM SUBROUTINE
79                      *---------------------------------------------
80                      * SEND RESULT TO MAIN PROGRAM
81   C129   30          RET     TSX               X POINTS TO TOP ENTRY IN STACK
82   C12A   EE 04               LDX    4,X        GET SAVED PROGRAM COUNTER
83   C12C   EE 04               LDX    4,X        GET REFERENCE TO ANSWER
84   C12E   E7 00               STAB   0,X        SEND DATA
85                      * ADJUST RETURN ADDRESS
86   C130   30                  TSX               X POINTS TO TOP ENTRY IN STACK
87   C131   EC 04               LDD    4,X        GET SAVED PROGRAM COUNTER
88   C133   C3 00 06            ADDD   #6         ADVANCE SIX BYTES
89   C136   ED 04               STD    4,X        STORE SAVED PROGRAM COUNTER
90                      * RESTORE MAIN PROGRAM REGISTERS
91   C138   38                  PULX
92   C139   33                  PULB
93   C13A   32                  PULA
94   C13B   39                  RTS
95   C13C                       END
```

Defined	Symbol Name	Value	References
65	AGAIN	C11D	76
73	AHEAD	C125	69
14	ANSWER	C000	35
12	LENGTH	0025	34
81	RET	C129	66
28	START	C100	
16	TABLE	C300	33
47	ZEROCT	C10D	32

Lines Assembled : 95   Assembly Errors : 0

Figure 5-19 Continued.

the subroutine must adjust the return point so the subroutine returns just beyond the list of addresses. You should carefully check your subroutines to be sure they do not return to an incorrect point and execute the addresses as instructions.

- *Lines 46 through 49.*   The main program registers are saved in the stack so they can be restored at the end of the subroutine. The JSR instruction has already saved the program counter in the stack. Since the main program registers are not used for passing parameters, it is usually good practice not to disturb them in the subroutine. Figure 5-20a shows a stack picture at this point in the program. The labels show where the main program registers have been saved in the stack. Also, the stack

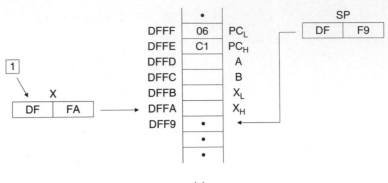

(a)

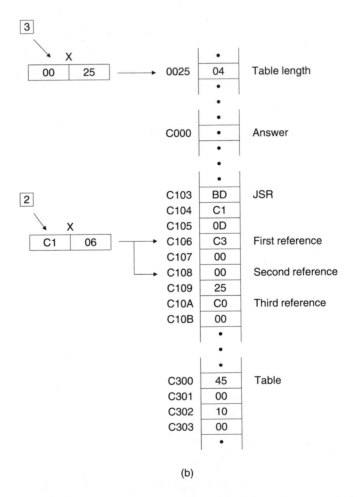

(b)

Figure 5-20 Memory diagram for the program in Figure 5-19.

pointer is shown pointing at the next available stack location because it contains address DFF9.

- *Line 51.*   The TSX instruction points the X index register at the top of the stack—the last entry used in the stack. Carefully note that the TSX instruction transfers the contents of the stack point register *plus one* to the X index register. Remember that the location in memory of the stack is not determined until the subroutine runs. The stack may be at different locations every time the subroutine runs. Therefore, transferring the stack pointer to X allows the subroutine to access the stack contents easily. In this example, the X index register now contains DFFA, as Figure 5-20a shows at box 1.

- *Line 52.*   The number in the program counter was stored in the stack by the JSR instruction. The address stored is the address of the next location in memory after the JSR instruction. In this example, the stored address is the location of the first reference. The LDX instruction loads the X register with the address of the reference by offsetting four bytes from the top of the stack. The X register now contains C106 as Figure 5-20b shows at box 2.

- *Line 53.*   The LDX instruction loads the X register with the second reference, which is the address where the table length is stored. The LDX accesses the second reference due to the offset of 2 in the instruction. The X register now contains 0025, as Figure 5-20b shows at box 3.

- *Line 54.*   The A accumulator is loaded with the data value 04 from location 0025. The first parameter has now been passed into the subroutine.

- *Lines 56 through 58.*   Using the same procedure, these instructions obtain the address of the table to be searched. The X register now contains C300.

- *Lines 59 through 76.*   This is the part of the subroutine that performs the function of counting the zeros in a table. When the loop finishes, the number of zeros is in the B accumulator.

- *Lines 81 through 84.*   The subroutine sends its result to the main program in the same way that it got the data from the main program.

- *Lines 86 through 89.*   The subroutine must adjust the subroutine return address so the subroutine returns to the correct address in the main program. In this example, the return address must be adjusted by six. This accounts for the six bytes of references that follow the JSR instruction. After line 89, the return address is C10C.

- *Lines 91 through 94.*   Removing the saved values from the stack restores the main program registers. When the RTS restores C10C to the program counter, the main program is again in control.

You should observe that this subroutine did not directly store any numbers in memory within the body of the subroutine. All the numbers needed to perform the subroutine function were in the microprocessor registers.

Reference in memory—local variables in stack example

The subroutine example in Figure 5-21 demonstrates passing parameters by reference with the references in memory following the JSR instruction. The subroutine counts the leading zeros in a double-precision number in memory. A hole or working section in the stack holds all the local variables. Since the parameter passing is very similar to the previous example, the following only describes details related to the local variables in the stack:

- *Lines 43 and 44.* The two DES instructions leave two empty bytes at the top of the stack. These bytes form the hole that will hold the local variables.

```
 1                            *****************************************************
 2                            ** DEMONSTRATE SUBROUTINE--COUNT LEADING ZEROS IN
 3                            **   DOUBLE-PRECISION NUMBER
 4                            * PASS PARAMETERS BY REFERENCE IN MEMORY
 5                            * USE STACK FOR LOCAL STORAGE
 6                            *
 7                            *****************************************************
 8                            *
 9                            *****************************************************
10                            ** DATA SECTION
11                            *****************************************************
12    0025                            ORG $25
13    0025    0678            DPNUM   FDB    $0678      DATA FOR DEMONSTRATION
14    C000                            ORG $C000
15    C000                    ANSWER  RMB    1          ANSWER PUT HERE BY SUBROUTINE
16                            *
17                            *****************************************************
18                            ** MAIN PROGRAM
19                            *****************************************************
20    C100                            ORG    $C100
21                            * INITIALIZE STACK
22    C100    8E DF FF        START   LDS    #$DFFF     STACK FOR MOTOROLA TRAINER
23                            * COUNT LEADING ZEROS IN DOUBLE-PRECISION NUMBER
24    C103    BD C1 0B                JSR    LEADZER
25    C106    0025                    FDB    DPNUM      ADDRESS OF DATA NUMBER
26    C108    C000                    FDB    ANSWER     ADDRESS OF ANSWER
27    C10A    3F                      SWI               "STOP" FOR MOTOROLA TRAINER
28                            *
29                            *****************************************************
30                            ** SUBROUTINE LEADZER
31                            * COUNT LEADING ZEROS IN 16-BIT NUMBER AT PAR1,
32                            * RETURN BYTE ANSWER TO (PAR2)--MODIFIES CC
33                            *****************************************************
34                            *---------------------------------------------------
35                            * INITIALIZE SUBROUTINE
36                            *---------------------------------------------------
37                            * SAVE MAIN PROGRAM REGISTERS
38    C10B    3C              LEADZER PSHX
39    C10C    18 3C                   PSHY
40    C10E    36                      PSHA
41    C10F    37                      PSHB
42                            * MAKE HOLE IN STACK FOR LOCAL STORAGE
43    C110    34                      DES               FOR LOOP COUNTER
44    C111    34                      DES               FOR ZERO COUNTER
```

Figure 5-21 Call-by-reference in memory subroutine with local variables in the stack.

```
45                              * INITIALIZE ZERO COUNTER AND LOOP COUNTER
46   C112   30                       TSX               POINT X TO TOP ENTRY IN STACK
47   C113   4F                       CLRA
48   C114   C6 10                    LDAB   #16
49   C116   ED 00                    STD    0,X
50                              * GET NUMBER TO TEST
51   C118   1A EE 08                 LDY    8,X         GET SAVED PROGRAM COUNTER
52   C11B   18 EE 00                 LDY    0,Y         GET REFERENCE
53   C11E   18 EC 00                 LDD    0,Y         GET DATA
54                              *------------------------------------------------------
55                              * COUNT NUMBER OF LEADING ZEROS
56                              *------------------------------------------------------
57                              * 16 BITS TESTED?
58   C121   6D 01            AGAIN   TST    1,X
59   C123   27 0D                    BEQ    RET         BRANCH ON YES
60                              * NEXT BIT A ZERO?
61   C125   05                       ASLD
62   C126   24 04                    BCC    AHEAD       BRANCH ON YES
63                              * TERMINATE ON A ONE
64   C128   6F 01                    CLR    1,X
65   C12A   20 04                    BRA    ENDLOOP
66                              * INCREMENT ZERO COUNTER
67   C12C   6C 00            AHEAD   INC    0,X
68                              * DECREMENT LOOP COUNTER
69   C12E   6A 01                    DEC    1,X
70   C130   20 EF            ENDLOOP BRA    AGAIN
71                              *------------------------------------------------------
72                              * RETURN FROM SUBROUTINE
73                              *------------------------------------------------------
74                              * SEND RESULT TO MAIN PROGRAM
75   C132   A6 00            RET     LDAA   0,X         GET DATA
76   C134   1A EE 08                 LDY    8,X         GET SAVED PROGRAM COUNTER
77   C137   18 EE 02                 LDY    2,Y         GET REFERENCE
78   C13A   18 A7 00                 STAA   0,Y         SEND DATA
79                              * ADJUST RETURN ADDRESS
80   C13D   EC 08                    LDD    8,X
81   C13F   C3 00 04                 ADDD   #4          SKIP TWO REFERENCES
82   C142   ED 08                    STD    8,X
83                              * CLOSE HOLE IN STACK
84   C144   31                       INS
85   C145   31                       INS
86                              * RESTORE MAIN PROGRAM REGISTERS
87   C146   33                       PULB
88   C147   32                       PULA
89   C148   18 38                    PULY
90   C14A   38                       PULX
91   C14B   39                       RTS
92   C14C                            END
```

Defined	Symbol Name	Value	References
58	AGAIN	C121	70
67	AHEAD	C12C	62
15	ANSWER	C000	26
13	DPNUM	0025	25
70	ENDLOOP	C130	65
38	LEADZER	C10B	24
75	RET	C132	59
22	START	C100	

Lines Assembled : 92   Assembly Errors : 0

Figure 5-21   Continued.

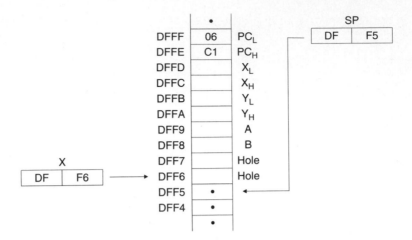

Figure 5-22   Stack diagram for the program in Figure 5-21.

- *Line 46.*   The X index register points at the hole for local variables. All instructions using the hole have indexed by X addressing. The X index register is used for no other purpose. It is left pointing at the top of the stack throughout the subroutine. Therefore, any other indexed addressed instructions use the Y index register. The X index register now contains DFF6 as the stack diagram in Figure 5-22 shows.

- *Lines 47 through 49.*   Initial values are stored in the local variables in the stack. The number 00 is stored in the zero counter and 16_{10} is stored in the loop counter.

- *Lines 51 through 53.*   The first reference is used to pass the double-precision 16-bit data value to the subroutine.

- *Lines 58, 64, 67, and 69.*   The local variables are used in the body of the subroutine. These variables are accessed with indexed addressing because the location of the stack may be different each time the subroutine is called.

- *Lines 84 and 85.*   The hole in the stack is closed, which discards the local variables now that the subroutine no longer needs them. Usually, the subroutine is easier to understand if the hole is opened and closed with the DES and INS instructions instead of the PSH and PUL instructions.

Local variables stored in the stack no longer exist when the subroutine returns to the main program. Sometimes these variables are called *dynamic variables*. Dynamic variables come into existence as the subroutine is entered, and they are discarded before it exits or returns to the main program.

When local variables are in the stack, it is easy to write the subroutine with position-independent code because direct and extended addressing are not needed. All the addressing of data is done with indexed addressing.

5.7   RECURSIVE SUBROUTINES

A *recursive subroutine* calls or jumps to itself. Such a subroutine must contain a decision that ultimately chooses not to call the subroutine again, but instead returns from subroutine—otherwise, the result is an infinite loop. Certain mathematical functions, such as factorial, are easy to calculate using recursion.

Writing a subroutine that can call itself and function correctly is easy if you understand the problem. The problem is with local variables. Consider a subroutine that uses a fixed location in memory for a local variable. When it calls itself, it will overwrite the number in that fixed location and the subroutine fails. Such a fixed location usually is accessed using direct or extended addressing in the 68HC11. However, if the subroutine puts its local variables in the stack, it will create a new hole in the stack each time it is entered. Using a hole in the stack for local variables makes it easy to write recursive subroutines. Although it does not use recursion, the example in Figure 5-21 demonstrates the technique necessary for recursive subroutines.

Recursive subroutines are usually clever programs that use few instructions. However, they are often difficult to understand. Also, they usually require a large stack space to hold a new copy of the local variables and a return address for each call of the subroutine. Since a nonrecursive subroutine can do the function of any recursive subroutine, avoid recursive subroutines.

5.8   REVIEW

Most of the 68HC11 instructions have now been introduced. Only a few instructions remain, and they pertain to input/output hardware. Many instructions in this chapter were designed for specific applications rather than general programming. For example, the stack controlling instructions should be used only for manipulating the stack. To use them for other purposes is to invite programming errors and confusion for anyone reading the listing. In a later chapter, you will find that the stack has further uses that will prevent you from using stack instructions for other purposes.

Subroutines are very important in practical programming. This chapter introduces many parameter passing techniques. Some of these techniques are difficult to implement in the 68HC11. Nevertheless, the techniques are useful. More complex microprocessors have additional addressing modes to make subroutines easier to program. Always, the programmer must make a wise decision about which parameter passing technique to use for each application.

5.9   EXERCISES

5-1.   Write a program module of two instructions that effectively does Arithmetic Shift Right the D accumulator.

5-2. Write a program module to rotate the A accumulator right one place without including the carry bit. This operation is called rotate circular.

5-3. Write a two-instruction program module to rotate the D accumulator left one place without including the carry bit; that is, rotate left circular D.

5-4. Write two program modules to rotate either left or right, including the carry, a double-byte number in memory.

5-5. Does the instruction sequence NEGA, NEGB, SBCA #0 correctly do the operation NEGD?

5-6. If the MUL instruction shifts the number in the A accumulator right three places and puts the result in the A accumulator, what number must be in the B accumulator initially?

5-7. If the MUL instruction shifts the number in the A accumulator left three places and puts the result in the B accumulator, what number must be in the B accumulator initially?

5-8. Write a program module that copies bits 4 through 7 of the A accumulator to bits 0 through 3, respectively, of the B accumulator, and also zeros bits 4 through 7 of the B accumulator. The number in the A accumulator may not be modified.

5-9. Write a program module that copies bits 0 through 3 of the B accumulator to bits 4 through 7, respectively, of the A accumulator without changing bits 0 through 3 of the A accumulator. The number in the B accumulator may be modified.

5-10. Write a program module that interprets the 3-bit number in bits 0 through 2 of the B accumulator as a bit number. The program sets only the bit of the A accumulator numbered in the B accumulator. It must not change any other bits in the A accumulator. Bits 3 through 7 of the B accumulator may be nonzero.

5-11. The program in Figure 5-23 stores a 1 in bit 5 of location RESULT if bits 4 and 5 of location NUMBER1 are both zero or if bit 7 of location NUMBER2 is a one; otherwise, it puts 0 in bit 5 of location RESULT. It does not change any other bits in location RESULT. Supply the missing numbers.

5-12. Write a new program that does the same function as the program in Figure 5-23, but uses the BSET, BCLR, BRSET, and BRCLR instructions instead of ANDA and ORAA.

5-13. Write a subroutine that exchanges the numbers in the A and B accumulators. The subroutine must not use any permanently allocated read/write memory locations.

5-14. Write a subroutine that logical shifts the A accumulator left the number of places specified by the number in the B accumulator. Use the ASLA instruction for all shifting, and limit the maximum number of shifts to the minimum number required. The number in the B accumulator passed to the subroutine must be returned in the B accumulator.

5-15. Write a subroutine that converts a two-digit BCD number in the A accumulator to an 8-bit binary number in the A accumulator. The subroutine must not use any permanently allocated read/write memory locations.

```
                    * BIT MANIPULATION PROGRAM
                              ORG    $C000
          NUMBER1 RMB    1
          NUMBER2 RMB    1
          RESULT  RMB    1
          *
          MASK1   FCB    $_____
          MASK2   FCB    $_____
          MASK3   FCB    $_____
          MASK4   FCB    $_____
          *
                    ORG    $C100
          START   LDAA   NUMBER1
                  ANDA   MASK1
                  BEQ    AHEAD
                  LDAA   NUMBER2
                  ANDA   MASK2
                  BNE    AHEAD
                  LDAA   RESULT
                  ANDA   MASK3
                  STAA   RESULT
                  BRA    LAST
          AHEAD   LDAA   RESULT
                  ORAA   MASK4
                  STAA   RESULT
          LAST    SWI              STOP FOR TRAINER
                  END
```

Figure 5-23   Exercise 5-11.

5-16.   Write a subroutine that converts an 8-bit binary number in the A accumulator to a two-digit BCD number in the A accumulator. The subroutine must not use any permanently allocated read/write memory locations.

5-17.   Write a subroutine that converts an 8-bit two's complement number in the B accumulator to a 16-bit two's complement number in the D accumulator.

5-18.   Write a subroutine that multiplies the two two's complement signed 8-bit numbers in the A and B accumulators and returns the 16-bit product in the D accumulator. Your subroutine must use the MUL instruction to do the multiplication. The subroutine must not use any permanently allocated read/write memory locations.

5-19.   Write a subroutine that forms the absolute value of the two's complement number in the D accumulator and puts the result in the D accumulator. The subroutine must not use any permanently allocated read/write memory locations.

5-20.   Write a copy-a-table program similar to the one in Chapter 2 as a subroutine. The main program must pass the table length in the A accumulator and the addresses of the two tables in the X and Y index registers.

5-21.   Write a subroutine that compares two tables. The references to the tables will be passed in the X and Y registers and the table length will be in the A accumulator. The subroutine will return 00 in the A accumulator if the tables are different and FF if they are the same.

5-22. Write a subroutine named FILL that fills a block of bytes in memory with a number. Pass the number for the fill pattern in the A accumulator, the address of the first byte in the X register, and the 16-bit length of the block in the Y register.

5-23. Write a subroutine that uses bits 0 through 2 of the A accumulator as a bit number and the address in the X index register as a reference to a memory register. The subroutine will set the bit in the referenced memory register as specified by the bit number. Bits 3 through 7 of the A accumulator are unspecified.

5-24. Write a subroutine that finds the largest 16-bit two's complement number in a table. The main program will pass the number of 16-bit numbers in the table in the A accumulator and the first address of the table as a memory reference. The subroutine will return the number found in the D accumulator.

5-25. Change the subroutine in Figure 5-21 so the references are passed between the main program and the subroutine using the stack. Be careful to have the stack pointer always ready to store new information in the stack. This technique of parameter passing is difficult in the 68HC11. Discuss the advantages and disadvantages of this technique of parameter passing.

5-26. Change the program in Figure 5-19 by inserting a BRA instruction in the main program between the JSR instruction and the references. The BRA must branch to the first instruction after the list of references. Change the subroutine so it returns to the BRA instruction. Discuss the advantages and disadvantages of this technique of parameter passing.

Chapter 6

Hardware

Computer hardware is difficult to discuss in a textbook. Usually, specific integrated circuits must be covered. It is especially difficult to use a technique that covers broad principles and applications. However, the Motorola 68HC11 is easier to describe than many products. The hardware that most practical applications require is already in the chip. Memory, input/output hardware, and even a selection of common input/output devices are inside the integrated circuit package.

The 68HC11 is a *single-chip microcomputer* or *microcontroller* because it contains memory and input/output hardware. Many applications require no additional external hardware. Since the hardware devices and the interconnections are all within the chip, you cannot see separate parts and interconnecting wires. It is very difficult to use laboratory instrumentation to observe the internal hardware operation. There is no place to connect the instrumentation! Consequently, you may find it quite abstract to study and use the 68HC11 as a single-chip computer.

Your goal may be to learn to construct microcomputer hardware from a collection of integrated circuits. This is possible when the 68HC11 operates in the expanded mode. In expanded mode, all the internal signals necessary for expansion are available at the integrated circuit pins. When using expanded mode, you must design, construct, and test the hardware. In applying the 68HC11, you would construct your own hardware if the devices available within the package were not appropriate.

This chapter does not discuss the hardware construction. The descriptions avoid the electronic circuit details and concentrate on the logical operation of the hardware and the software necessary to use it. Some examples refer to specific 68HC11 internal input/output hardware. Chapter 7 adds more hardware details.

6.1   HARDWARE/SOFTWARE SYNERGY

People frequently divide computer system development into hardware development and software development. However, computer hardware and software do not operate independently. The operation of a computer in a practical application depends on both. The word *synergy* describes the relationship between hardware and software. The word *synergy* means that each of two things helps to improve the other so the whole is greater than the sum of the parts. This chapter shows that hardware and software are each designed to work with the other to make powerful and useful microcomputers.

If you have used large data processing or scientific computers, learning hardware operation and design may seem unnecessary. Such computers usually isolate the average user from the details of hardware. In many applications of microcomputers, however, the computer is part of the electronic control circuitry. In such applications, it is not possible to remain isolated from the hardware operation.

In most microcomputer applications, there is a tradeoff between software and hardware. Often you can do the same job either in software or with additional hardware. Many considerations come to bear on your decision to use software or hardware. These include cost, complexity of hardware, reliability, size, electrical power consumption, memory space available, and execution speed. Only broad knowledge and experience will lead to the best solution.

6.2   THE HARDWARE BUILDING BLOCKS

You must interconnect several hardware devices to construct a microcomputer. Wires may make the connections between separate integrated circuits. Alternatively, the connections may be within an integrated circuit chip. Where possible, the following discussion implies the first approach with distinct interconnecting wires. However, in principle, there is no difference when the hardware is inside a chip.

Microcomputer

A *microcomputer* is most often a collection of integrated circuits on a circuit board that make a complete functional computer. Typical designs usually include a microprocessor IC, a clock, several memory ICs, and several input/output ICs. When most of these components are in a single integrated circuit, it is called a *single-chip microcomputer*.

Memory

Let's review the signals used by the read/write memory integrated circuit described in Chapter 1. Figure 6-1 is a copy of Figure 1-10.

The figure implies that this integrated circuit contains 64_{10} kilobytes of memory because it has 16_{10} address lines. However, most applications that require 64_{10} kilobytes will need several ICs that each contains fewer than 64_{10} kilobytes of memory. These memory ICs will have fewer address pins. For example, if Figure 6-1 represented a memory IC with 14_{10} address pins, then it would contain $16,384_{10}$ 8-bit registers because 2^{14} is $16,384_{10}$.

Usually the address pins on memory integrated circuits are labeled A_0 through A_{15} and the data lines are labeled D_0 through D_7. The subscripts are the bit numbers that identify the bits in microcomputer registers. In the figure, the IC has eight data pins corresponding to the eight bits in the registers.

The read/write or R/W control line tells the IC to read when the wire is high and to write when the wire is low. When the memory chip writes, it stores the number applied to the data pins in the addressed memory register. When the memory reads, it puts the number in the addressed memory register on the data pins. That is, when the memory is reading, it controls the logic levels on the pins. The R/W signal controls the direction of the data pins. The data pins are called *bidirectional* data pins.

The chip select or CS control line enables the IC to respond to the other signals. When the chip select pin is deasserted, the IC effectively disconnects the pins from the internal hardware. The data pins must have *tri-state* output hardware with three possible conditions— high, low, and disconnected. Tri-state hardware allows another IC control of the levels on the output pins of the IC while the pins are disconnected.

Additional pins not shown in the figure are necessary for the electrical power and ground connections. The power pin is usually labeled V_{CC} or V_{DD} and the ground pin is labeled V_{SS}.

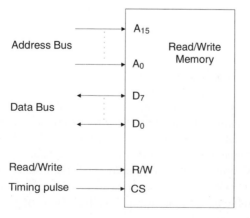

Figure 6-1 Memory signals.

Microprocessor

A *microprocessor* is a single integrated circuit that contains the control unit and processor parts of a microcomputer. Some practical ICs may vary from this definition because they include a few additional hardware items in the chip. The point is that the microprocessor doesn't contain memory or input/output hardware. Therefore, the microprocessor IC must communicate with separate memory and input/output ICs. In most microcomputers, a collection of binary signal wires connects the various ICs.

Buses

A *bus* is a collection of binary signal wires that together carry a binary number. Several electronic devices, often ICs, may connect to the bus to send or receive numbers. Usually a given bus has a particular purpose and has a name indicating that purpose.

Most microprocessors, including those manufactured by Motorola, use three buses to communicate between the microprocessor and other ICs in the microcomputer. First, the *address bus* carries address numbers from the microprocessor to other integrated circuits. Furthermore, the address bus never carries any other kind of number. Second, the *data bus* carries several kinds of data numbers between the microprocessor and other ICs in both directions. Finally, the *control bus* carries control signals between the microprocessor and other ICs. Some control signals go in both directions and some in only one direction.

The 68HC11 has a 16-bit address bus and an 8-bit data bus. The number of control signals depends on whether the design of the computer uses all the signals. Some signals are necessary only for advanced designs.

I/O Integrated Circuits

Input/output ICs transfer data numbers and control signals between the microprocessor and input/output devices. The input/output devices are external to the computer. The input/output ICs connect to both the microprocessor buses and the I/O devices.

Input/output ICs operate at logic signal power levels. Applications requiring higher power levels need additional external hardware. For example, power transistors are necessary to drive devices such as solenoids.

6.3 MEMORY CHARACTERISTICS

Memory technology falls into two broad categories called *read/write memory* and *read only memory*. Read/write memory allows the microprocessor to both write numbers into registers and read back those numbers later. Read only memories hold numbers in registers the microprocessor cannot alter—the numbers are permanent. Although the technologies in these two types of memory are different, the general principles of operation are similar.

Integrated circuit companies manufacture both read/write and read only memories using several different technologies. Memory ICs are available in many configurations with widely differing properties. Consequently, there are many technical terms that describe these ICs.

The following introduces the principles of integrated circuit memory technology and the related terms. The descriptions of the electronic circuits are simplified, and so include only the necessary details.

Memory Terminology

Some very general terms describe the characteristics of memory devices. The terms are independent of the technology used to construct the memory. However, it is common for people to associate certain technologies with the general terms. Sometimes people use the technology name as a replacement for the general term. You may find this confusing.

Here are some general terms that describe memory:

- *Volatile memory.* A volatile memory loses the information stored in it when electrical power is removed from the memory. The information or numbers in a volatile memory evaporate when the power is turned off. Generally, losing information is a disadvantage. However, losing information is unimportant when the volatile memory holds only data numbers a running program uses. In other applications, volatile memory may hold the program instruction numbers if they can be restored easily from another device.

- *Nonvolatile memory.* A nonvolatile memory uses a storage technology that does not require electrical power to retain information. Most nonvolatile memories use a storage technique that makes the stored information permanent and unchangeable. Others use magnetic materials to store information, but few of these are used in practice.

- *Read/write memory.* A read/write memory uses a technology that allows the microprocessor to both store and retrieve numbers electronically at the full speed of the microprocessor. Some technologies are relatively slow, requiring many milliseconds to store a number. Therefore, these are not read/write memories. Most read/write memories are also volatile because an electronic circuit must be active to retain the information. All microcomputers require some read/write memory to store data that changes as the program runs and to make a stack.

- *Read only memory.* A read only memory contains permanent information that cannot be changed by the microprocessor at the full speed of the microprocessor. Some technologies allow the microprocessor to change numbers in the read only memory, but the required time is usually many milliseconds. Most read only memories are also nonvolatile memories. Usually read only memory contains the program instructions in a microcomputer used for a control application. Note that the name *read only* is an oxymoron because something must write to the memory or there would be no information to read! The writing is done either during the manufacture of the memory or by some process that alters the physical characteristics of the memory.

- *Sequential access memory.* A sequential access memory reads and writes its registers in a sequential order. Magnetic tape is an example of sequential access memory because the tape must move to access the numbers. Some registers in a sequential access memory have longer access times than others. For example, the relative tape position affects the access time. A sequential access memory is not practical as the program storage memory of a microcomputer.

- *Random access memory.* Accessing a register in a random access memory takes the same time and effort as accessing any other randomly selected register. Random access memories are electronic memories. They may be either read only memory or read/write memory. Only random access memory is practical for program and data storage in a microcomputer.

The construction of the hardware determines the characteristics of these memories. When you understand the operation of the electronic circuits, the characteristics of the various memories and their uses in practical applications will be clear.

Memory Principles

The operation of the electronic circuits in the integrated circuit determines the characteristics of the memory. It is easy to understand the memory characteristics when you understand the circuit inside. The construction and operation of a simple IC memory can be explained using a diode matrix memory. The diode matrix memory then forms the basis for understanding more complex hardware.

Diode matrix memory

The diode matrix memory is a nonvolatile read only memory. It is constructed from a decoder, a grid of wires, and some diodes. Figure 6-2 shows a simple version of the circuit. The numbers stored in a diode matrix memory depend on the wiring configuration of the circuit. The following describes each of the components.

Decoder. The decoder in Figure 6-2 has two inputs that represent a 2-bit binary number. This decoder has four outputs such that one output is high and the others are low. The input number selects which output has the high level. This decoder is a *one-out-of-four* decoder. Other decoders have more outputs, but the number of outputs is always a power of two.

Diode. The diode in the diode matrix memory is an electronic device that passes electrical current in one direction but not the other direction. A simple but effective model for it is a short circuit of zero resistance when passing current, and an open circuit of nearly infinite resistance when it is blocking current. The arrow head in the diode symbol in the figure indicates the direction of low resistance.

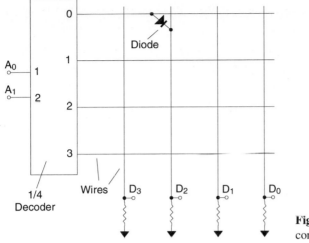

Figure 6-2   Diode matrix memory construction.

Wire grid.   The horizontal wires in the figure connect to the outputs of the decoder; they are not connected to the vertical wires. The vertical wires connect to the ground or common with a resistor to make a complete electrical circuit. The output terminals of the memory connect to the resistors. The terminals are labeled D_0 through D_3 because they provide the output data from the memory.

Operation.   Each horizontal wire in Figure 6-2 forms one register in the memory. The address that selects a register is applied to the two inputs of the decoder. These inputs are labeled A_0 and A_1 because they provide the address to the memory.

As an example, suppose the input number or address is binary 00 because the wires are low. Then horizontal wire number 0 is high, and wires 1, 2, and 3 are low. Assume that high is +5 V_{DC} and low is 0 volts for this example. In Figure 6-2, terminals D_0, D_1, and D_3 are low because there is no source of voltage for these terminals. However, terminal D_2 is high because the diode connected to this vertical wire is passing electric current. Therefore, the terminals D_3 through D_0 are low, high, low, low, which can represent the binary number 0100. The placement of one diode on row 0 or address 0 made a single binary 1 in the output data number. The other horizontal rows did not affect the output.

Next, look at Figure 6-3. Additional diodes are connected to the other rows, but they do not affect the operation of row 0. For the next example, suppose the input address is binary 01, so horizontal wire 1 is now high and the other horizontal wires are low. The diodes connected between horizontal wire 1 and output wires D_0 and D_1 pass current, so terminals D_0 and D_1 are high. The output data number is binary 0011.

Notice that the D_1 vertical wire has a second diode connected to it and then to horizontal wire 2. Making this connection with a wire instead of the diode would allow current to pass from horizontal wire 1 through horizontal wire 2 and make output terminal D_3 high. The diode prevents this because it passes current in only one direction. The diode prevents horizontal wire 1 from affecting terminal D_3. The diodes electrically isolate each horizontal wire from the others so they do not interact.

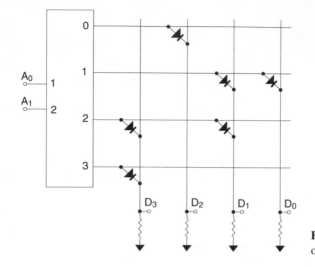

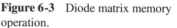

Figure 6-3   Diode matrix memory operation.

Each row or register in the diode matrix memory is programmed with a binary number by connecting diodes at the correct intersections. Figure 6-4 is a memory model using hexadecimal numbers for the memory shown in Figure 6-3. Adding more rows and columns makes a memory that holds more and larger numbers.

Characteristics.   The diode matrix memory is a read only memory. If used with a microprocessor, the microprocessor cannot change the pattern of diodes connected to the wire grid.

The diode matrix memory is also a nonvolatile memory. The information or numbers in the memory are stored by the presence or absence of diodes. If the electrical power is turned off to the memory, the electronic circuits stop working. But the pattern of diodes is unchanged, so the information is not lost.

Using a pattern of diodes is a very reliable way to store information. Information is lost only through mechanical failure of the electronic components. Environmental factors such as electric or magnetic fields do not affect the pattern of diodes.

Flip flop memory

The simplest read/write memory uses flip flops for bit storage. The read/write memory uses a matrix to access the flip flops as the diode matrix memory accesses diodes. The electronics in the read/write memory is much more complicated than in the read only memory. In read/write memory, the matrix must route control signals to the flip flops. However, the diode matrix and read/write memories use the same principles of operation.

Figure 6-4   Memory model for diode matrix memory in Figure 6-3.

Read Only Memory ICs

The acronym for read only memory is ROM. Normally people use the acronym ROM only to name an integrated circuit read only memory. Read only memory usually holds the program and constant data numbers in a microcomputer. Most control applications of microcomputers need the nonvolatile character of the ROM. Such applications need a nonvolatile memory, but people usually call the memory ROM because the ROMs are nonvolatile. They substitute *ROM* for *nonvolatile*.

The diode matrix memory is the basis for integrated circuit read only memories. Many variations of this design, including some with devices other than diodes, provide characteristics useful for a wide range of applications. The following discusses the common ROM integrated circuits including PROMs, EPROMs, and EEPROMs.

Masked ROM

The first practical diode matrix memories were constructed on printed circuit boards. The development of integrated circuit technology quickly replaced the printed circuits with ICs. A *masked ROM* is a custom integrated circuit containing a diode matrix memory. The ROM IC is manufactured with the necessary pattern of diodes in place. This electronic part is very reliable because it is a simple circuit in a highly reliable form; namely, the integrated circuit. Sometimes the memory electronics is incorporated into larger chips such as a single-chip microcomputer.

Usually, a large number of identical ICs are purchased from an integrated circuit manufacturer. The purchase order must document the required numbers. The IC manufacturer must design and manufacture the masks required as part of the manufacturing process. Making the masks is a costly and time-consuming task. After the masks are made, the production of large numbers of ICs can proceed. If many thousands of ICs are manufactured, the cost of the masks and the cost of putting the IC into production are inconsequential. However, if the number is small, the cost of making the masks is prohibitive.

A typical application for a masked ROM is a high-volume product containing a microcomputer. Examples include microwave ovens, cassette tape decks, and other consumer products.

Fusible link PROM

When only a few ROMs are required for laboratory development or for low-volume products, the masked ROM is impractical. It is therefore desirable to have a ROM memory that can be field programmed and used immediately. Such an IC is known by the acronym *PROM*, from field programmable read only memory. The user purchases the PROM as a standard IC and then programs it. If the required number of parts is relatively small, the cost of the ICs and the programming cost compare favorably with the cost of a custom-masked ROM.

Programming.   The first integrated circuit PROM was the fusible link PROM. It is a diode matrix memory with fusible links in series with the diodes. The matrix is completely filled with diodes and links when the integrated circuit is manufactured. The programming process disconnects selected diodes by removing their links.

A suitably large electric current will destroy a link. The links have resistance, so the current causes the selected links within the chip to burn out. Therefore, programming these PROMs is called *burning*. An electronic PROM programmer can selectively burn the correct links when given the hexadecimal numbers for the registers. The chip has circuits to allow access to selected links by the programming device.

Once the PROM is programmed, the numbers are permanent. Certainly the microprocessor will not change the numbers in the PROM. To correct programming errors, you will usually discard the IC and program a new one. If an error leaves links in place, you can program the IC again to remove the incorrect links. You cannot restore a burned link.

EPROM

One disadvantage of the fusible link PROM is that changes in the stored numbers cannot be made. An incorrect IC must be discarded and replaced with a new IC.

The numbers in some ROM memory ICs can be changed. Usually you must erase all the numbers in the chip, and then program all the numbers again. Such an erasable programmable read only memory is known by the acronym EPROM.

Storage mechanism.   The EPROM depends on the charge storage capability of a capacitor. In principle, an FET, or field effect transistor, replaces the diode in the diode matrix memory. The transistor acts either as the diode or as an open circuit. The transistor does one or the other depending on whether its gate is electrically charged. The gate is effectively a capacitor plate encased in a very good electrical insulator similar to glass. Once charged properly, the capacitor will retain its charge for many years.

Programming.   An electronic PROM programmer and the electronics in the chip electrically pulse the selected capacitor to charge it. The pulsing limits the heating of the chip to prevent damage. Usually a microcomputer in the programmer optimizes the charging of each capacitor. The characteristics of the capacitors vary greatly depending on their location on the chip. The PROM programmer is given the hexadecimal numbers needed, and it automatically programs each capacitor. Usually, programming an EPROM IC requires a few minutes. Programming the IC is called *burning*, although the programming process is nondestructive.

Erasing.   Discharging the capacitors erases the IC. Shining ultraviolet light on the surface of the chip causes the charge to leak off the capacitors. The photons of light provide enough energy to allow the charge to pass through the insulator and leak off. Erasing usually takes considerable time, often as long as an hour of exposure to intense ultraviolet light. Incidentally, the photons of white or infrared light do not have enough energy to erase the IC, so ambient light does not affect EPROMs. Sunlight does not affect EPROMs, because the light intensity is too low.

Most EPROMs can be erased and programmed 100 times or more before they fail, but there are wide variations between practical parts. The programming process causes thermal stresses that can lead to eventual failure.

Packaging.   The need to shine light on the chip means that the IC package must have a window to allow light to reach the chip. This window, usually made of quartz, adds to the cost of the IC. In some applications where the EPROM is part of a high-volume product, it is desirable to program the memory during the assembly of the product. Such a product will not change after the customer purchases it, so erasing is unnecessary. Then the EPROM package is made without a window to reduce cost.

The EPROM has an important disadvantage—it must be removed from the microcomputer for erasing or programming. The physical removal and replacement are inconvenient. Furthermore, to allow removal, the EPROM is mounted in a socket. Sockets are costly and less reliable than soldering. And finally, the PROM programmer device required to program the EPROM is costly.

EEPROM

Many applications require the microcomputer to store information in a nonvolatile memory. The device containing the microcomputer needs the information after it is turned off and then on again. For example, a device may measure the total amount of time it has operated so it can recommend timely maintenance. The device must save the accumulated time when the power is turned off. Some devices use a volatile memory with a battery to maintain power to the memory. However, the battery and its associated hardware are costly and unreliable. An alternative is the electrically erasable programmable read only memory IC called the EEPROM. Some companies name these integrated circuits FLASH memory. The microprocessor electrically programs and erases the EEPROM, yet it is a nonvolatile memory.

Storage mechanism.   The storage mechanism in the EEPROM is the same as the EPROM—electrical charge on a capacitor. However, the electronics to program the chip by charging the capacitors must now reside in the memory chip.

Programming.   The microprocessor controls the programming electronics inside the EEPROM IC through software. In addition, programming some EEPROMs requires a separate voltage source. Usually the required programming voltage is higher than the usual +5 VDC power supply. In some applications, the lack of a higher voltage source ensures that the EEPROM is never changed.

Erasing.   The erasing circuit is inside the EEPROM integrated circuit. The microprocessor controls the erasing hardware through software. Some ICs have a complex erasing procedure so accidental erasure is unlikely. Some EEPROMs erase individual bytes; others must erase the entire IC.

Packaging.   The usual integrated circuit package holds the EEPROM. The only distinguishing characteristic is the part number. The control signals are similar to other memory integrated circuits. However, some EEPROMs have a pin devoted to a programming voltage supply. Other ICs create the programming voltage internally.

The EEPROM is not a read/write memory. The EEPROM erasing and programming procedures require times of a few milliseconds—much longer than the response time of flip flops. Furthermore, the lifetime, measured in erase and programming cycles, is limited. The typical lifetime of an EEPROM is many thousands of these cycles. Normal reading of the EEPROM does not affect its lifetime significantly.

Read/Write Memory ICs

Most read/write memory integrated circuits, called RAMs, are volatile memories. They usually hold data numbers that change as the program runs. In some applications, RAMs also may hold the program. Programming techniques such as a stack require the use of read/write memory.

RAM integrated circuits store information using two different technologies. The two types are called *static RAM* and *dynamic RAM*. Usually static RAMs are faster and more expensive than equivalent-size dynamic RAMs.

Static RAM

The static RAM uses flip flops to hold the information. The flip flops require electrical power to operate and thus retain information. The flip flop circuit requires many electronic components, so the flip flops require a relatively large area on a chip.

Dynamic RAM

The dynamic RAM, also called DRAM, uses a tiny capacitor to hold charge that represents the stored information. The capacitor is part of an electronic circuit that both controls the stored charge and reads the voltage on the capacitor. Since the chip must hold thousands of capacitors, each capacitor is very tiny. Therefore, the stored charge is small and is quickly lost through the connected circuitry. Usually the charge becomes unreadable in a matter of a few milliseconds. Therefore, the dynamic RAM requires additional circuitry to periodically *refresh* the capacitors to their original charge levels. The refresh electronics adds complexity to the memory. However, a given area of a chip can hold many more dynamic RAM bits than static RAM bits. This makes the dynamic RAM very attractive. For large memories, the reduced cost of fewer ICs easily offsets the cost of the refresh electronics.

Matching Software to Memory

Most microcomputer designs require parts of the memory to have different characteristics. First, most applications require nonvolatile memory to hold the program instructions and constant data values. Then the program is always available when the power is on. This memory is usually read only memory because it is nonvolatile. However, the program must then have pure procedure code—self-modifying programs are impossible. Furthermore, the selection of the type of ROM may depend on the particular characteristics of the ROM.

Second, most applications require some read/write memory for data that the program changes as it runs. The read/write memory usually is a volatile RAM memory. The program must not depend on volatile information at power up. So most microcomputers have both ROM and RAM memory.

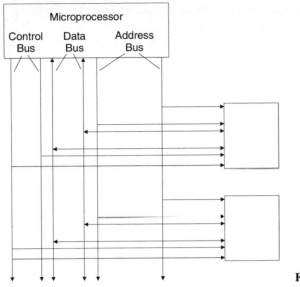

Figure 6-5   Microprocessor buses.

6.4 MICROPROCESSOR BUSES

The microprocessor discussed in this chapter is the 68HC11 operating in a mode that allows access to the buses. Some details were omitted for clarity. Chapter 7 more fully describes the 68HC11 modes and further hardware details.

Bus Characteristics

A *bus* is a collection of binary signal wires used together for a specific purpose. Sometimes a bus carries a binary number from one place to another. Sometimes a bus carries a group of control signals that work together to control a device.

Most microprocessors use three buses to connect the microprocessor integrated circuit to the other integrated circuits in the microcomputer. In particular, the other ICs are mostly memory and input/output ICs. A single-chip microcomputer uses the same buses, but they are inside the chip.

Figure 6-5 illustrates the three buses connecting the parts of the microcomputer. Usually the clock, not shown in the figure, connects directly to the microprocessor. The figure shows only the wires at the extreme left and right of the buses instead of every wire.

Address bus

The purpose of the address bus is to carry addresses from the microprocessor to the memory and input/output ICs. The microprocessor never has an address sent into it. Instead, it always forms the addresses that are on the address bus. The other ICs only use the addresses on the address bus. The figure implies this because arrow heads point from the microprocessor to other ICs.

A 16-bit address bus can carry $65,536_{10}$, or 64K, different addresses. That is, it can directly control memory with addresses from 0000 to FFFF. If a design requires more memory than 64K, a switching technique enables memory in blocks. On the other hand, it is common to install less than 64K of memory to reduce cost. Then some addresses can't be used. Some designs also omit some address wires to further reduce cost.

Data bus

The purpose of the data bus is to carry numbers between the microprocessor and the memory and input/output ICs. The meaning of the numbers can be almost anything, so they are called data numbers. For example, when the microprocessor gets numbers from the memory during the fetch phase of an instruction, the numbers are parts of instructions. When the microprocessor executes a STAA instruction, it sends the number from the accumulator to the memory on the data bus.

The data bus is a *bidirectional* bus because the same wires carry numbers in two different directions. The microprocessor sends a data number on the data bus at one time, and then it receives a number on the data bus at another time. The data bus is *time multiplexed* because its job is different at different times.

Control bus

The control bus contains several signal wires primarily for the microprocessor to control the memory and input/output ICs. However, some ICs send signals to the microprocessor on some control bus lines. The buses for various microprocessors from different companies are similar, but the greatest differences between manufacturers are in the character of these control signals.

Microprocessor Bus Connections

Consider now connecting the microprocessor buses to a read/write memory integrated circuit. As an example, assume that the memory IC contains four kilobytes of static RAM registers. The memory IC has 12_{10} address pins and 8 data pins.

Address bus connections

Figure 6-6 illustrates the connection of the microprocessor to the address pins of the memory IC. The address line notation is the same as the common bit numbering notation. The memory IC has address lines A_0 through A_{11}. The microprocessor controls these lines to select a particular register within the memory IC.

Data bus connections

Figure 6-7 illustrates the address and data buses connected to a memory IC. All the data bus pins on the microprocessor connect to all the data bus pins on the memory IC. When

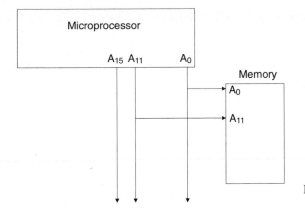

Figure 6-6   Address bus connections.

the microprocessor writes to a memory register, it turns the data bus direction to outgoing from the microprocessor. When the microprocessor reads from the memory, it turns the data bus direction to ingoing to the microprocessor. Notice that the communication to the memory is always eight bits at a time. Again, the figure shows only the left and right bus wires instead of every bus wire.

Control bus connections

The control bus has several individual control wires. First, Figure 6-8 illustrates the connection of the single read/write, or R/W, control signal from the microprocessor to the memory IC. The microprocessor controls the R/W line to tell the memory whether to read or write. Usually the high level means read and the low level means write. The level on the R/W line corresponds to the direction of the data bus. When the microprocessor signals a read operation, the data bus direction is ingoing to the microprocessor. When the microprocessor signals a write operation, the data bus is outgoing from the microprocessor.

Second, Figure 6-8 illustrates the connection of the E-clock signal from the microprocessor to the memory IC. All the operations of the buses must be coordinated in time. The microprocessor sends a high-going pulse called the *E-clock*. The E-clock signal enables the

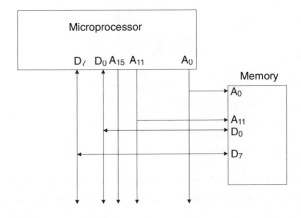

Figure 6-7   Data bus connections are added.

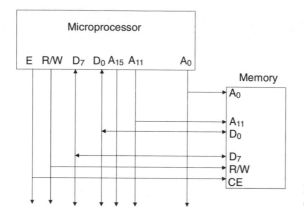

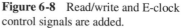

Figure 6-8   Read/write and E-clock control signals are added.

memory IC at the correct time using its chip enable or CE pin. So the memory responds only when the signals on the buses are stable and unchanging. Of course, if the memory responds while the buses are changing, it gets erroneous information.

Bus Operation Example

Let's follow the signals in the computer as it fetches and executes an instruction. Chapter 2 uses this exercise as a block diagram to explain the operation of the microprocessor. This section adds much more detail showing the flow of numbers on the buses. The following accurately describes the operation of the computer.

The instruction

Figure 6-9 shows the read/write memory containing an extended addressed STAA instruction and the number 27 in the A accumulator. The instruction op code is B7 and the extended address is 04FE. This instruction will store the 27 from the A accumulator register into memory register 04FE. The memory register now contains the number 56.

Fetch phase

The numbers in Figure 6-9 are the register contents during the first clock cycle as the microprocessor fetches the instruction. On the first tick, the microprocessor sends the number in the program counter down the address bus. That is, it connects the outputs of the flip flops in the program counter to the microprocessor address bus pins. Since the memory IC has a 12-bit address, only the number on address lines A_0 through A_{11} tell the memory which register to access. So it accesses address 412. Simultaneously, the microprocessor turns its data bus pins inward so it can read a data number supplied by the memory IC. The microprocessor also sends the high or read level on the R/W line to tell the memory IC to do a read operation. When these signals are stable and unchanging, the microprocessor sends a pulse on the E-clock line to tell the memory to respond.

The memory responds by controlling the data bus lines and putting the number B7 on the data bus. The microprocessor routes the number that comes to it on the data bus to the

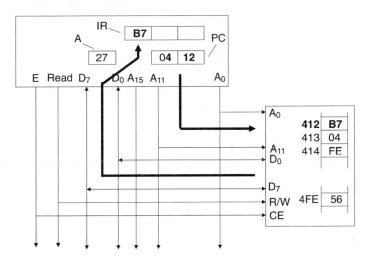

Figure 6-9 Fetching an instruction op code.

instruction register. Then the microprocessor increments the number in the program counter to 0413.

On the next tick of the clock, the same procedure brings the number 04 from address 0413 to the instruction register. Then, on the final tick of the fetch phase, the same procedure brings the number FE from address 0414 to the instruction register.

At the completion of the fetch phase, the three bytes of the instruction code have been transferred over the data bus to the microprocessor. The program counter is pointing to the next instruction because it has been incremented during the fetch phase.

Execute phase

Figure 6-10 illustrates the register contents during the execute phase of the instruction operation. The execute phase of this instruction requires only a single clock cycle.

On the next tick of the clock, the microprocessor examines the B7 op code in the instruction register and learns that it must perform a store operation with the A accumulator. The address of the memory register where the data is to be stored is in the instruction register. The microprocessor connects the 16_{10} instruction register bits that contain the address of the data to the address bus pins. The memory IC receives the 12-bit address 4FE on the address bus.

Simultaneously, the microprocessor turns its data bus outward and connects the outputs of the A accumulator flip flops to the data bus pins. So the microprocessor sends the number 27 on the data bus. The microprocessor also sets the R/W line to the low level to tell the memory IC to perform a write operation.

When the signals are stable and unchanging, the microprocessor sends a pulse on the E-clock line. The E-clock pulse tells the memory to respond to the signals from the microprocessor. When the memory responds, it stores the number 27 in register 4FE.

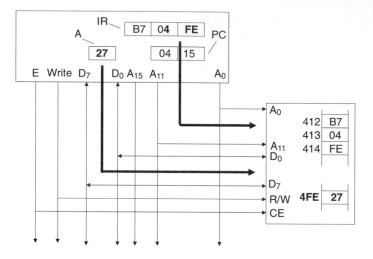

Figure 6-10   Executing a store accumulator instruction.

Computer Failures

Certain failures of the computer hardware may be anticipated. This section simulates some failures that may occur as the microprocessor fetches and executes the instruction discussed above. Of course, many more and very complex failures can occur. We will consider only very simple failures.

Grounded address line

Let's assume that the failure is a short to ground of the address line A_0 as Figure 6-11 shows. The ground simulates a low level or a logic 0 on that line. This failure could occur because some foreign material fell on the circuit, making the undesired connection. Similarly, a failure of the electronics inside the memory chip connected to A_0 could act the same.

Further assume that this failure causes no further failures in the integrated circuits; they continue to operate normally. Return to Figure 6-9 to observe the fetch phase of the instruction.

On the first clock tick, the address sent on the address bus is 0412. The number 0412 has a 0 at bit 0. Therefore, the result with the grounded line is the same as if there was no failure. The microprocessor correctly fetches the instruction op code B7.

On the second clock tick, the address sent on the address bus is 0413, but the ground failure causes the address to be 0412 again. The microprocessor incorrectly fetches the next byte of the instruction from address 0412 and gets B7 again.

On the third clock tick, the address is 0414, which the ground failure does not affect. The microprocessor correctly fetches the number FE. The resulting instruction code in the instruction register is B7B7FE, which is clearly incorrect.

On the fourth tick, the execute phase of the instruction sends the address B7FE on the address bus. The grounded line does not affect this address. So the microprocessor stores 27

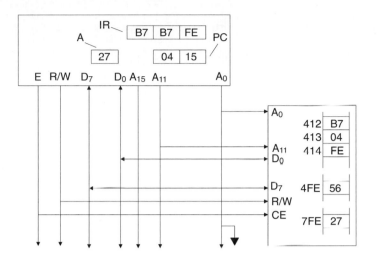

Figure 6-11   Effect of instruction fetched and executed with grounded A_0 line.

from the A accumulator at address B7FE instead of at address 04FE. Figure 6-11 shows the final numbers after fetching and executing the instruction are complete.

It should be clear that any program running in this computer is going to do strange and bizarre things!

Grounded data bus line

Consider another failure similar to the grounded address line; only now let's ground data bus line D_0. Figure 6-12 shows this condition. When the microprocessor fetches the instruction at address 0412, the op code is B6 instead of B7. The complete instruction code fetched is B604FE. This is a LDAA instruction instead of the programmed STAA instruction. Besides doing an incorrect operation, this erroneous instruction alters the number in the A accumulator by loading 88 into it. Figure 6-12 shows the numbers after this instruction is fetched and executed.

As with the grounded address line, a ground on a data bus line can cause both incorrect instructions and data numbers. Again, it should be clear that this computer will do strange and bizarre things.

Other failures

The failures considered here are very simple indeed. Much more complex failures can and do occur. However, if you consider only this instruction, moving the ground to other address or data lines will completely change the effects of the failures. When intermittent failures are also possible, the problem becomes greater yet. This example should clearly illustrate why computers can do things that are almost unexplainable. Such failures are a big problem when a computer controls equipment dangerous to people and other equipment.

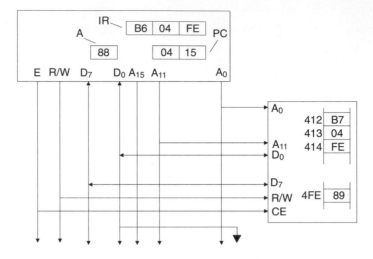

Figure 6-12   Effect of instruction fetched and executed with grounded D_0 line.

Clearly, software in the computer can never check all the computer hardware for failures when the hardware is unpredictable. Safety will require an external hardware solution. Chapter 7 introduces some hardware to check for safe operation of the computer.

Memory Expansion

A single memory IC usually is not enough for a practical microcomputer. Additional ICs provide more memory and different types of memory. However, hardware signals must control each individual memory IC.

Memory chips in parallel

Look at the two RAM memory ICs in Figure 6-13. Each IC has the same connections to the microprocessor. If the two memory ICs contain the same numbers, they will operate in parallel correctly, but the second IC is useless. If the two ICs contain different numbers, there will be conflicts and the hardware will not work correctly. Some failures in computer hardware make multiple ICs operate in parallel, so this exercise is useful.

Both ICs in Figure 6-13 respond to addresses in the range from 0000 to 0FFF. They would be much more useful if the top IC responded to these addresses and the second IC responded to addresses 1000 through 1FFF. That is, we want the first 4K of memory in the first IC and the second 4K in the second IC.

Address decoding

To make the ICs respond to correct addresses, a switch must enable the top IC in the address range 0000 through 0FFF while disabling the second IC in this range. Likewise, the switch must disable the first IC for the range 1000 to 1FFF while enabling the second IC.

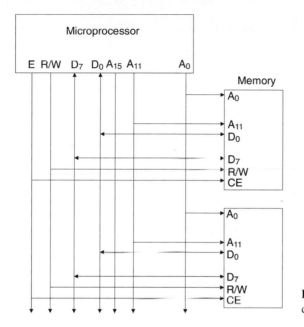

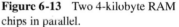

Figure 6-13   Two 4-kilobyte RAM chips in parallel.

Examination of the two address ranges shows that address line A_{12} must control the switch. Bit 12 of the address is the only bit that is different in the two address ranges.

Since the E-clock pulse makes the memory IC respond, the switch must transfer the E pulse to the memory IC only in the correct range of addresses. Figure 6-14 shows a circuit using two AND gates to switch between the two ICs. These gates are called *address decoders* because they determine the range of addresses that can enable the memory IC.

The upper AND gate in the figure passes the E-clock signal to the memory IC if line A_{12} is low. At the same time, the lower AND gate passes the E-clock to the bottom memory IC only when the A_{12} line is high. Therefore, the memory ICs respond only in the correct address ranges.

Adding more memory ICs to the computer in Figure 6-14 requires address decoder gates with many more inputs. A common alternative uses a one-out-of-sixteen decoder IC to divide the memory into 16_{10} ranges. The decoder connects to address lines A_{12} through A_{15}. The selected output of the decoder is a control input to the address decoder gate. A later section on input/output hardware illustrates this technique.

6.5   PARALLEL I/O PRINCIPLES

When hardware transfers all the bits of a number at the same time, the hardware does a *parallel data transfer*. This is the inherent transfer method for the microprocessor, since the data bus transfers all eight bits at once. The following describes hardware that transfers data to I/O devices in parallel.

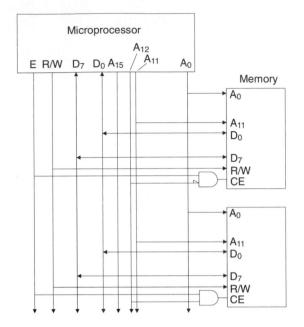

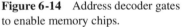

Figure 6-14   Address decoder gates to enable memory chips.

I/O Programming Model

Input/output involves two major operations; namely, *data transfer* and *timing*. Data transfer is the sending of data numbers to output devices or receiving data numbers from input devices. The input and output devices are external to the computer hardware. Timing refers to synchronizing the data transfer to the I/O device with the program running in the computer. The program must cause a data transfer only at the time the I/O device is ready for a data transfer. At other times, the I/O device cannot respond correctly to data transfers.

Data transfer

Figure 6-15 shows a programming model for the I/O section of the computer. Two register boxes represent the data transfer mechanism in the I/O section. The word *port* refers to a place where information enters or leaves the computer. In particular, numbers move between the input and output devices through these 8-bit ports.

Input port.   A transfer of data from the input pins to the microprocessor register occurs at the time an instruction is executed. A LDAA instruction transfers the data to the A accumulator on the E-clock pulse during the execute phase. The input port does not contain a register to hold input data. The data is transferred instantaneously at the time of the E-clock pulse.

Output port or register.   The output port contains a register that controls the pins on the output port hardware. The data transfer is done by an instruction such as STAA. The register is necessary because the data only exists on the data bus during the instruction execution. The data is transferred to the register at the time of the E-clock pulse. The register

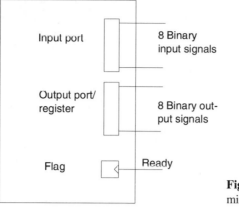

Figure 6-15   Input/output program-ming model.

then holds the signal voltages at the pins so the output device can respond. The register holds the signals until another output operation is executed.

Timing or synchronization

Two methods of synchronizing I/O devices to the computer program are used, but both use the flag device shown in Figure 6-15.

Flag.   The *flag* is a single flip flop that is set to 1 by a ready signal from the I/O device. Setting the flag tells the program that the I/O device is ready for a data transfer.

Polling.   The flowchart in Figure 6-16 illustrates the *polling* technique of input/output device synchronization. The program repeatedly tests or polls the I/O flag to determine when the I/O device is ready for a data transfer. When the program detects that the flag is set, the program clears the flag and controls the I/O hardware to do the data transfer.

The main advantage of the polling technique is its simplicity when used with simple problems. When a sophisticated system using many I/O devices is designed, the polling technique becomes very complex and cumbersome. Polling also may degrade the performance of the I/O devices due to the polling overhead. A more sophisticated technique called *interrupt* is then used. A later section discusses interrupt.

6.6   PARALLEL I/O HARDWARE

The Motorola 68HC11 uses the address, data, and control buses to control input/output hardware as if it were memory. The technique of controlling I/O hardware the same as memory is called *memory mapped* I/O. The input and output ports have memory addresses just as memory registers do. Memory mapped I/O hardware connects to the microprocessor buses the same as does memory.

The same instructions used with memory control the input/output operations. The 68HC11 does not have any instructions specifically for input/output. However, do not assume

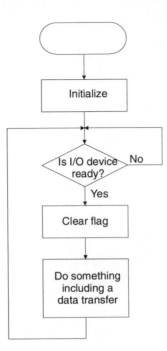

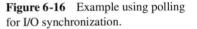

Figure 6-16 Example using polling for I/O synchronization.

that the I/O registers act like memory. Remember that an input port reads binary signals on pins of an IC—it does not read back a number previously stored in a register! For emphasis, certainly a program that fetches instructions from I/O ports will fail.

The example in Figure 6-17 illustrates some consequences of memory mapped I/O. The memory map shows the placement of various kinds of memory and I/O registers in the memory space. It further illustrates that hardware may not be installed for all memory locations, so some addresses are unused.

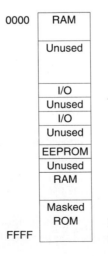

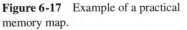

Figure 6-17 Example of a practical memory map.

I/O Circuit Construction

Parallel input/output hardware is built from several different types of integrated circuits. The approach used depends upon the particular application. Sometimes using the least hardware possible reduces cost. The least cost design includes hardware for only the necessary signals. Other applications may require more flexibility because the application is not well known or may change. Flexibility is often gained by adding some redundant hardware.

Output port design

Let's design an 8-bit output port for use with a Motorola 8-bit microprocessor. Assign address 4003 to this port. Additionally, assume that address lines A_2 through A_{11} are not decoded. Further assume no other writable device in the address range from 4000 through 4FFF has binary 11 for bits 0 and 1 of its address.

Figure 6-18 shows the circuit. Not all the address lines are decoded—some are not connected—to reduce cost and complexity. Therefore, more than one address can make the port respond because the unconnected wires make no difference. It is common in discussions of this hardware to assign 0 to the unconnected lines.

Output register. An 8-bit register is the principal component of the output port. The input bus to the register connects to the microprocessor data bus. The register must be clocked when the correct address appears on the address bus, the R/W signal indicates write, and a pulse occurs on the E-clock line. Clocking the register at this time transfers the correct data from the data bus into the output port register. The output register then controls the output pins sending the data to the output device outside the computer.

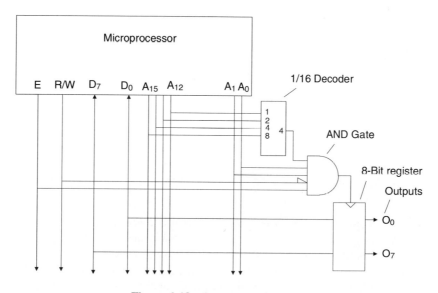

Figure 6-18   Output port circuit.

Address range decoder.   The purpose of the decoder is to indicate when the address on the address bus is within a certain range of addresses. Further decoding is usually necessary so only the correct address makes the port respond.

In Figure 6-18, the four inputs to the one-out-of-sixteen decoder connect to address bus lines A_{12} through A_{15}. Each output of the decoder asserts only when the address is within a certain range. Output 4 asserts when the address is in the range 4000 through 4FFF. Of course, the other decoder outputs correspond to other address ranges. For example, output 15 corresponds to the range F000 to FFFF.

Final decoder.   Output 4 of the decoder is ANDed with the other necessary signals to make the output port register respond correctly. Since bits A_0 and A_1 must both be 1s when the port responds, these address lines are connected to the AND gate. Likewise, to assure that the register only responds on a write signal, the R/W line is connected to a low-asserted input of the AND gate. The E-clock pulse line makes a high-going pulse when the other signals are valid. So the output of the AND gate forms a pulse to clock the register.

In this example, not all the address lines are decoded; address lines A_2 through A_{11} are not connected. This reduces cost and complexity. However, the port responds to more than one address. During discussions of this hardware, and when writing programs, people usually assign 0s to the unconnected address lines. Then the port has only one address.

Read back.   The output port in Figure 6-18 cannot be read by the program. The program can store into the register, but it cannot read the register. Therefore, the program must remember what was last output by saving a copy in memory. Many practical output ports have this limitation. Additional hardware is necessary if the program must read the output port.

Design defect.   A serious defect in this design is the lack of a hardware signal to initialize the output register at power-up. When the electronics is turned on, the flip flops in the register have unknown states. Since the output port may control some dangerous equipment, this is unacceptable in practice. Though software may initialize the output port soon after power-up, it is still unacceptable to depend on the software for initial safety.

Input port design

Now let's design an 8-bit input port for a Motorola 8-bit microprocessor. The design will be similar to the design of the output port. Assign address 4002 to this input port and leave address lines A_2 through A_{11} unconnected. Assume no other readable device will have an address in the range 4000 through 4FFF that also has binary 10 for bits 0 and 1. Figure 6-19 shows the circuit.

Input transfer gates.   The principal component of the input port is a set of eight transfer gates with tri-state outputs. A tri-state output will be high, low, or disconnected. When the device transfers, the output level is the same as the input level. When not transferring, it disconnects the output. The tri-state device is necessary because more than one controlling device connects to the data bus, but only one can control the bus at a time. Those devices not controlling the bus must disconnect from it.

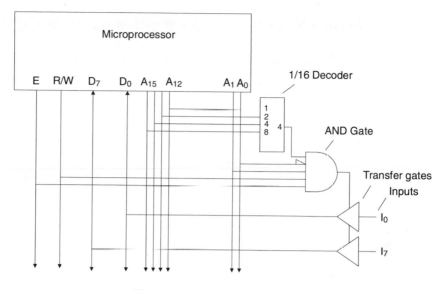

Figure 6-19   Input port circuit.

The transfer gates must transfer the input signals to the data bus at the correct time. The transfer must occur when the correct address appears on the address bus, the R/W signal says read, and the E-clock pulse occurs.

Address range decoder.   The address decoding for the input port example is the same as the output port example. Output 4 asserts when the address on the address bus is in the range 4000 through 4FFF.

Final decoder.   The principle of the final decoder is the same as the decoder for the output example. However, the address it decodes is different because the least-significant two bits must be 10. Therefore, a low-asserted input of the AND gate connects to A_0.

Programming example

Let's use the input and output ports in Figures 6-18 and 6-19. Figure 6-20 shows a high-asserting push button switch connected to input bit 6, and a low-asserting switch connected to bit 2. A high-asserting indicator light is connected to output bit 5. The example program asserts the light only if both push buttons are pushed. The program runs in an infinite loop continually controlling the light.

Figure 6-21 is the listing of the program. Here is a description of it.

- *Line 20.*   The memory register labeled IMAGE holds a copy of the last number sent to the output port. Sometimes the program needs to change only a few of the output bits, but the hardware controls all the bits at once. Therefore, the program must know all the output bits. Since the program cannot read the output port, it must keep a copy of the output bits in memory. The copy provides the unchanged bits. The location IMAGE is in the direct addressing range so the bit instructions can easily access it.

- *Lines 27 through 29.*   Set the output bits to 1s in both the memory register labeled IMAGE and in the output hardware. First, this shows that the output port should be set to some known initial condition. The output port used here has no hardware to initialize it. Second, setting these outputs to 1s implies that we want them to stay 1s. The rest of the program should only modify the output bit for the light. Carefully avoid changing output bits that should remain the same.

- *Line 31.*   Point the index register at the input port. The branch-on-bit-condition instructions can only reach the input port with indexed addressing.

- *Lines 32 and 33.*   Test the two input bits corresponding to the switches. A branch occurs if a switch is released. Since the switch at bit 6 is high-asserted, the branch occurs if the input bit is 0. The switch at bit 2 is low-asserted, so the branch occurs when the input bit is 1.

- *Line 35.*   If a branch did not occur at either line 32 or line 33, then both switches are pushed and control comes to this line. The bit set instruction updates the IMAGE register to assert the light.

- *Line 38.*   If a branch occurs on either line 32 or line 33, at least one switch is released. The bit clear instruction updates the IMAGE register to deassert the light.

- *Lines 40 and 41.*   Transfer the output bit pattern in the IMAGE register to the output port hardware to control the light. Additions to the program that change other IMAGE bits cause no problems, because the program updates all the output bits at once.

- *Line 42.*   The program loops back to run in an infinite loop. Most control programs effectively run in infinite loops.

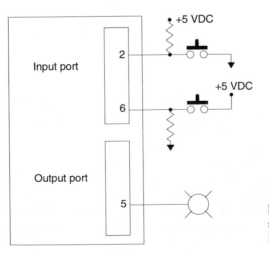

Figure 6-20   Input port connected to switches and output port connected to light.

```
 1                          ********************************************************
 2                          ** ASSERT LIGHT IF TWO PUSH BUTTONS PUSHED
 3                          *
 4                          * LIGHT WIRED TO OUTPUT BIT 5
 5                          * LOW ASSERTING SWITCH WIRED TO INPUT BIT 2
 6                          * HIGH-ASSERTING SWITCH WIRED TO INPUT BIT 6
 7                          *
 8                          ********************************************************
 9                          *
10                          ********************************************************
11                          ** SYMBOL DEFINITIONS
12                          ********************************************************
13          4002            INPORT   EQU   $4002       INPUT PORT
14          4003            OUTPORT  EQU   $4003       OUTPUT PORT
15                          *
16                          ********************************************************
17                          ** DATA SECTION
18                          ********************************************************
19    0010                           ORG   $10
20    0010                  IMAGE    RMB   1           COPY OF OUTPUT BITS
21                          *
22                          ********************************************************
23                          ** PROGRAM SECTION
24                          ********************************************************
25    C100                           ORG   $C100
26                          * INITIALIZE ALL OUTPUTS TO ONES
27    C100   86 FF          START    LDAA  #$FF
28    C102   97 10                   STAA  IMAGE
29    C104   D7 40 03                STAA  OUTPORT
30                          * TEST INPUT SWITCHES
31    C107   CE 40 02       LOOP     LDX   #INPORT
32    C10A   1F 00 40 09             BRCLR 0,X,$40,NEXT1   TEST SWITCH AT BIT-6
33    C10E   1E 00 04 05             BRSET 0,X,$04,NEXT1   TEST SWITCH AT BIT-2
34                          * SET OUTPUT IMAGE TO ASSERT LIGHT
35    C112   14 10 20                BSET  IMAGE,$20        CHANGES ONLY BIT-5
36    C115   20 03                   BRA   OUT
37                          * SET OUTPUT IMAGE TO DEASSERT LIGHT
38    C117   15 10 20       NEXT1    BCLR  IMAGE,$20        CHANGES ONLY BIT-5
39                          * CONTROL OUTPUT PORT
40    C11A   96 10          OUT      LDAA  IMAGE
41    C11C   B7 40 03                STAA  OUTPORT
42    C11F   20 E6                   BRA   LOOP
43    C121                           END
```

Figure 6-21   Program using an input port and an output port.

Flag design

The I/O flag may consist of a single D flip flop as shown in Figure 6-22. The previous figures show the microprocessor to the left of the I/O hardware. Therefore, Figure 6-22 shows the flip flop output signal on the left and the ready signal on the right.

The D lead is always high, so clocking the flip flop always sets it. The ready signal from the input/output device clocks the flip flop to set the flag. The computer tests the output of the flip flop to determine if the I/O device is ready for a data transfer. The computer hardware treats this flag signal as an input bit. The computer controls the direct clear lead on the flip flop to clear the flag. However, common input ports and output ports generate a clear signal for the flag when the program reads or writes the port. Then a separate clear the flag operation is unnecessary.

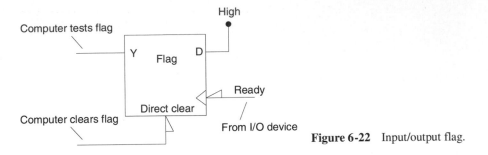

Figure 6-22   Input/output flag.

Programmable I/O Hardware

Input/output circuits are built from integrated circuits. Usually an I/C contains some input ports, output ports, and flags. Whatever the selection of hardware, some customers will find the selection ideal and others will find it unsatisfactory. Some customers will always need a different hardware configuration. The configuration customers need usually changes as a design project proceeds. One fixed design is not adequate for all customers.

The major limitation on integrated circuit design is often the number of pins on the package. The package will hold more electronics than there are pins to use. Therefore, for each pin, the manufacturer may put both input electronics and output electronics in the chip. Then internal electronic switches can connect the correct hardware to the pins. Bits in a control register control the switches. The purchaser of the IC programs it to use the required inputs and outputs by placing numbers in control registers. While using the same IC, each customer can have the unique hardware required for their application. Furthermore, they can adapt to new requirements by changing the numbers in the control registers.

The extra complexity of the programmable I/O hardware does not greatly increase the cost. The cost of ICs decreases as the number sold increases. Since many different customers can use the same programmable hardware, the increased sales volume offsets any extra cost due to its programmability. However, the programmer must learn to program the I/O hardware configuration before using it. The programmability adds a little extra complexity to the program.

6.7 68HC11 PARALLEL I/O HARDWARE

The 68HC11 has five 8-bit I/O ports named PORTA through PORTE. These ports correspond to collections of pins on the 68HC11 IC that carry I/O signals.

The five ports and the buses are all inside the 68HC11 integrated circuit package. The registers related to the I/O hardware have addresses determined by the internal connections. The I/O registers use a block of addresses beginning at address 1000.

One of the internal ports, PORTC, is a programmable parallel I/O port. In contrast, PORTB is an output-only port. The other ports are dedicated to I/O devices in the 68HC11 chip. However, the other ports also can be parallel I/O ports. The following discusses only the PORTB and PORTC ports and the associated control registers called DDRC and PIOC. Chapter 7 discusses all the parallel I/O ports.

The PORTB Register

The 68HC11 port PORTB is an 8-bit output-only port. It is not programmable. The PORTB register is at address 1004. To do output with this port, a program need only store into the PORTB register to control the high-asserted output pins. Usually the store is done with an STAA instruction. If the program reads PORTB, it gets the number last stored into PORTB.

When the computer is powered-up or a hardware reset occurs, the PORTB register contains zeros. Figure 6-23 illustrates the PORTB register with the reset bit values shown below the figure.

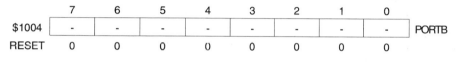

Figure 6-23   PORTB, a parallel output-only register.

The PORTC Register

The 68HC11 I/O port called PORTC is a programmable 8-bit I/O port. The hardware allows each bit in the port to be either an input bit or an output bit. Figure 6-24 illustrates the PORTC register. The figure also shows the values of the bits immediately after a hardware reset of the 68HC11.

After the PORTC register is programmed, some of the bits may be parallel inputs and some may be parallel outputs. The program need only store into PORTC with a STAA instruction to do output, or read PORTC with LDAA to do input. The input operation results in an instantaneous read from the IC pins. The output operation writes into a register that holds the binary signals on the output pins. The pins all are high-asserted for both input and output. So the high level represents logic 1 and the low level represents logic 0.

When the program stores to bits programmed as inputs, the hardware ignores the control signals. When the program reads bits programmed as outputs, it gets the last number stored in PORTC. The same number is read even if the output pins are shorted to ground!

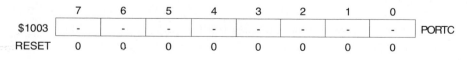

Figure 6-24   PORTC, a programmable parallel I/O register.

The DDRC Register

Any 68HC11 register called a *data direction register* determines whether the bits of a programmable I/O register are inputs or outputs. The data direction register for PORTC is labeled DDRC. Figure 6-25 illustrates the DDRC register, which is at address 1007. The program can read the DDRC register as it would a memory register, but writing into DDRC connects internal hardware in a particular configuration.

The bits in DDRC correspond bit by bit with the bits in PORTC. When a bit in DDRC is 0, it programs the corresponding bit in PORTC as an input bit. A 1 in a DDRC bit makes the corresponding PORTC bit an output. At power-up reset, all the PORTC bits are inputs because reset zeros the DDRC register.

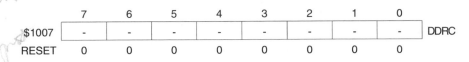

	7	6	5	4	3	2	1	0	
$1007	-	-	-	-	-	-	-	-	DDRC
RESET	0	0	0	0	0	0	0	0	

Figure 6-25   DDRC, the PORTC data direction register.

In most programs, the initialization section stores a number in the DDRC, and then the program never again changes DDRC. However, there are practical applications where the PORTC bits change between inputs and outputs as the program runs.

The PIOC and PORTCL Registers

The 68HC11 register called PIOC is the parallel I/O control register. The PIOC register is at address 1002. The PIOC register controls several hardware options, but it also contains a flag bit. The following discusses only the flag.

The flag bit in PIOC is the output of the flag. A flag is not a memory bit! Therefore, storing into this register bit does not affect the flag.

The flag in PIOC has a ready signal at the 68HC11 pin named STRA for strobe A. The name of the flag is therefore STAF. The program tests the STAF flag by testing bit 7 of PIOC. Figure 6-26 shows the STAF flag in the PIOC register.

The ready signal for the STAF flag, STRA, can be active on either a low-to-high or high-to-low transition. Figure 6-26 shows the EGA bit, bit 1 of PIOC, which is the edge-for-STRA bit. Making EGA a 1 programs the ready signal to respond to low-to-high transitions; making EGA a 0 programs the ready signal for high-to-low transitions. The initialization section of the program must store the needed value into EGA.

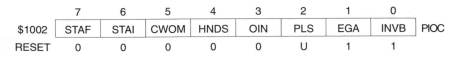

	7	6	5	4	3	2	1	0	
$1002	STAF	STAI	CWOM	HNDS	OIN	PLS	EGA	INVB	PIOC
RESET	0	0	0	0	0	U	1	1	

Figure 6-26   PIOC, the parallel I/O control register.

The STRA pin also does a second function. Besides setting the flag, it clocks or strobes a latch register called PORTCL. In some applications, it is useful to hold an input number in a register or latch at the instant the ready signal occurs. The PORTCL register latches a copy of the number in PORTC at the instant the STRA signal sets the flag. The latching occurs even if the flag was already set. The PORTCL register is at address 1005 as Figure 6-27 illustrates.

	7	6	5	4	3	2	1	0	
$1005	-	-	-	-	-	-	-	-	PORTCL
RESET	0	0	0	0	0	0	0	0	

Figure 6-27   PORTCL, the PORTC input latch register.

Clearing the STAF flag requires the execution of two instructions. The first must read the PIOC register and the second must read the PORTCL register. Use LDAA instructions for both reads.

This may seem a strange way to clear the flag, but remember the flag is not a memory bit. It is a hardware flip flop that is set by a signal on a pin. If you are using input bits, reading the PORTCL register is probably useful anyway.

6.8   PARALLEL I/O EXAMPLE USING POLLING

The 68HC11 has several input/output ports for parallel I/O and several flags. The example that follows uses only the programmable port PORTC and the STAF flag. The example demonstrates the principles of parallel input/output with timing using this hardware and associated software. Look at Figure 6-16 to review the polling technique.

Problem Description

The computer reads a number from a thumbwheel switch, and then displays the number on a display unit. The computer reads the thumbwheel switch only when a person pushes the push button switch. Usually a person sets a number on the thumbwheel switch and then presses the push button. The program updates the display at the time the button is pushed. The thumbwheel switch generates a 4-bit number and the display, which has an internal decoder, displays a 4-bit number.

I/O Hardware

Figure 6-28 illustrates the I/O hardware connections to the 68HC11 input/output ports. Both the thumbwheel switch and the display unit use high-asserted signals. The thumbwheel switch is connected to bits 4 through 7 of PORTC. The display unit is connected to bits 0

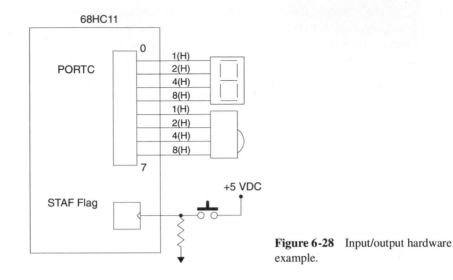

Figure 6-28   Input/output hardware example.

through 3 of PORTC. Therefore, four of the PORTC bits must be inputs, and the other four bits must be outputs.

The push button switch provides the ready signal for the STAF flag. Assume that the switch has no switch contact bounce, or that it makes no difference to the application.

Polling Software

The program in Figure 6-29 illustrates the polling technique of I/O synchronization. The program reads the thumbwheel switch and controls the display only when the push button is pushed. Here is a description of the program.

- *Lines 21 through 24.*   Symbols are defined for the addresses of the input/output control registers.

- *Line 36.*   The PORTC register is set to zero, though it may already contain zeros put there by a hardware reset. The CLR PORTC instruction affects only those PORTC pins that were previously programmed as outputs. If a hardware reset precedes this program, the PORTC pins will be all inputs.

- *Lines 38 and 39.*   The data direction register is set to make four input pins and four output pins. The output pins now respond to the bits in PORTC.

- *Lines 41 through 42.*   The PIOC register, illustrated in Figure 6-26, is initialized. The 1 put into EGA, bit 1 of PIOC, makes the STAF flag respond to a low-to-high transition on the STRA pin. The 0s put into the other bits of PIOC cause no problems. The store to bit 7 does nothing in the hardware.

- *Lines 46 and 47.*   Test the STAF flag and loop until it is set by the ready signal from the push button switch. The STAF flag condition is in bit 7 of the PIOC register.

```
 1                                 *************************************************************
 2                                 ** COPY THUMBWHEEL SWITCH TO DISPLAY WHEN
 3                                 ** PUSHBUTTON IS PUSHED
 4                                 *
 5                                 * USE POLLING TECHNIQUE FOR TIMING
 6                                 *
 7                                 * FOUR BIT THUMBWHEEL SWITCH WIRED TO
 8                                 * ..BITS 4-7 OF PORT C
 9                                 *
10                                 * FOUR BIT DISPLAY WIRED TO BITS 0-3 OF PORT C
11                                 *
12                                 * PUSHBUTTON SWITCH WIRED TO STRA SO
13                                 * ..LOW TO HIGH ON PUSH
14                                 *
15                                 *************************************************************
16                                 *
17                                 *************************************************************
18                                 ** SYMBOL DEFINITIONS
19                                 *************************************************************
20                                 * 68HC11 REGISTERS
21          1002                   PIOC     EQU   $1002      PARALLEL I/O CONTROL REGISTER
22          1003                   PORTC    EQU   $1003      I/O PORT C REGISTER
23          1005                   PORTCL   EQU   $1005      PORT C LATCH REGISTER
24          1007                   DDRC     EQU   $1007      DATA DIRECTION REGISTER C
25          000F                   IOPAT    EQU   $0F        I/O PATTERN, 0=IN 1=OUT
26                                 *
27                                 *************************************************************
28                                 ** PROGRAM SECTION
29                                 *************************************************************
30     C100                                 ORG   $C100
31                                 *-----------------------------------------------------
32                                 * INITIALIZATION
33                                 *-----------------------------------------------------
34                                 * INITIALIZE PORT C
35                                 *     INITIALIZE OUTPUTS TO ZEROS
36     C100    7F 10 03                     CLR   PORTC      0=LOW
37                                 *     SET UP INS AND OUTS
38     C103    86 0F                        LDAA  #IOPAT
39     C105    B7 10 07                     STAA  DDRC       0=IN, 1=OUT
40                                 * SET UP PIOC
41     C108    86 02                        LDAA  #$02       STAF RESPONDS ON LOW TO HIGH
42     C10A    B7 10 02                     STAA  PIOC       ..TRANSITION ON STRA
43                                 *-----------------------------------------------------
44                                 * PUSHBUTTON PUSHED?
45                                 *-----------------------------------------------------
46     C10D    7D 10 02            PBTST    TST   PIOC       TEST STAF FLAG
47     C110    2A FB                        BPL   PBTST      TRICK! FLAG AT SIGN BIT
48                                 *-----------------------------------------------------
49                                 * COPY THUMBWHEEL SWITCH TO DISPLAY
50                                 *-----------------------------------------------------
51                                 * READ THUMBWHEEL SWITCH AND CLEAR I/O FLAG
52     C112    B6 10 02                     LDAA  PIOC       TWO INSTRUCTIONS TO CLEAR STAF
53     C115    B6 10 05                     LDAA  PORTCL     ..FLAG AND INPUT SSSS----
54                                 * POSITION DATA FOR OUTPUT
55     C118    46                           RORA             -SSSS---
56     C119    46                           RORA             --SSSS--
57     C11A    46                           RORA             ---SSSS-
58     C11B    46                           RORA             ----SSSS
59                                 * CONTROL DISPLAY
60     C11C    B7 10 03                     STAA  PORTC      OUTPUT TO PORT C
61     C11F    20 EC                        BRA   PBTST
62     C121                                 END
```

Figure 6-29   Polling program.

Motorola Trainer

You can run the example program in Figure 6-29 on your trainer. The trainer connects both the PORTC pins and the STRA signal to the 60-pin connector at the edge of the printed circuit board. Use a thumbwheel switch and display unit with compatible 0 and +5 volt logic signals. Modify the program for your hardware if it differs from the example.

- *Lines 52 and 53.*   Both the PIOC and PORTCL registers must be read to clear the STAF flag. However, reading the PORTCL register with LDAA inputs the condition of the thumbwheel switch to the accumulator. The bit pattern in PORTCL represents the input bits latched at the instant the STAF flag was set.

- *Lines 55 through 58.*   The bits representing the thumbwheel switch are positioned so they can control the display unit.

- *Line 60.*   Storing the accumulator into PORTC controls the output pins that drive the display unit.

This example program runs in an infinite loop that has complete control of the computer. Most programs for control computers are similar infinite loops.

6.9   INTERRUPT CONCEPTS

The interrupt technique of timing or input/output synchronization is more sophisticated than the polling technique. The performance of the computer is usually better when it uses interrupt rather than polling. The software is also easier to organize when complex I/O programs are necessary.

Figure 6-30 uses flowcharts to illustrate the fundamental concept of interrupt. A main program runs in an infinite loop possibly doing useful work. Sometimes the main program does nothing but run an empty loop. When the input/output device is ready for a data transfer, it sets the I/O flag. The I/O device sets the flag exactly as it did in the polling technique. The hardware interrupt system in the microprocessor responds to the flag by stopping the main program and sending control to the interrupt service routine. The transfer of control is done entirely by hardware. The computer executes no instructions to accomplish the transfer.

The interrupt service routine, or ISR, services the input/output device. The ISR clears the I/O flag, does the data transfer, and completes any other work required. When the I/O device service is complete, the ISR returns control to the main program. The main program continues execution as if nothing had happened. In many practical cases, the main program is completely unaware that the interrupt service routine has run.

The transfer to the ISR occurs only when the I/O device is ready for a data transfer. This synchronizes the program to the I/O device. So interrupt is a timing technique.

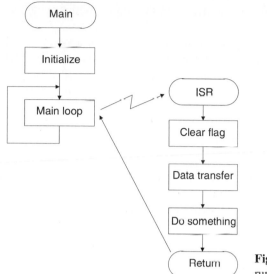

Figure 6-30   Main program and interrupt service routine.

The ISR is similar to a subroutine, but the ISR is not a subroutine. The ISR runs in response to a hardware signal. In contrast, a subroutine runs because an instruction in a program transfers control to it. There are no instructions in the main program to cause the interrupt.

6.10   THE 68HC11 INTERRUPT SYSTEM

The 68HC11 has an interrupt system that can respond to signals from a variety of I/O devices. External I/O devices connected to the microcomputer IC can generate interrupts. In addition, several I/O devices inside the 68HC11 IC also can cause interrupts. The following only discusses using an external device to cause an interrupt.

Interrupt Signal Path

Figure 6-31 is a block diagram of the hardware involved in using interrupt. The figure shows only those signals specifically related to interrupt. The figure omits the address, data, and control bus signals.

The 68HC11 interrupt system hardware receives external interrupt signals through the IRQ interrupt request pin. Driving this pin low requests an interrupt. The I/O flag controls the IRQ line. Therefore, when the ready signal sets the flag, the flag sends a request for an interrupt to the interrupt system.

However, there are two levels of enabling necessary for the signal to reach the interrupt system. First, the flag must have control of the IRQ wire. Usually an electronic switch in the

I/O section connects the flag to the IRQ wire. Programs use this switch to choose whether they will use interrupt.

Second, the IRQ line must have control of the interrupt system. An electronic switch in the microprocessor connects the IRQ pin to the interrupt system. The I bit in the condition code register controls this switch. When the I bit is 0, the switch closes enabling interrupts. When I is 1, the switch opens and masks or disables the interrupt signals. Therefore, the CLI instruction, which puts 0 in the I bit, enables the interrupt system.

Don't be confused by the I bit values that may seem backward. When I is 0, the interrupt system is enabled; when I is 1, the interrupt system is disabled.

Interrupt System Operation

Let's begin this discussion of the interrupt system by assuming the main program initialization enabled the flag to cause an interrupt. Also assume the interrupt system was enabled with the CLI instruction. Now the main program loop is running doing some function. The main program ignores the I/O device connected to the flag.

At some time unknown to the computer, the I/O device gets ready for a data transfer and sets the flag. The flag signals the interrupt system to interrupt by driving the IRQ wire low. The interrupt system hardware then transfers program control to an interrupt service routine program. It does this transfer by placing a new address in the program counter.

The ISR now takes care of the I/O device. In particular, it clears the flag that was the source of the interrupt. Clearing the flag acknowledges that the computer has responded to the interrupt request from the I/O device. Clearing the flag is necessary so the I/O device can set the flag again in the future to request service again. Remember interrupt is a timing technique.

Next, the ISR must do the data transfers necessary for the I/O device and run any other necessary software. When the ISR finishes all this, the ISR returns control to the main program. The main program continues at the point of the interrupt. Usually the main program doesn't know the interrupt occurred.

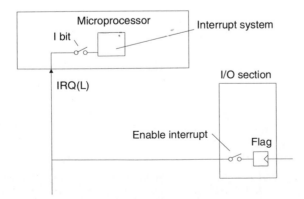

Figure 6-31 Block diagram of interrupt signal path.

Saving status in the stack

When the ISR runs, it will certainly use the microprocessor registers. Usually the ISR modifies the accumulators, index registers, and the condition code register. Transferring control to the ISR also modifies the program counter.

When control returns to the main program, the program can continue execution only if all the microprocessor registers are preserved. The information in these registers at any time is called the *status* of the computer.

To preserve the status, the interrupt system hardware saves the microprocessor registers in the stack. The main program has no instructions to save the status—the interrupt system hardware pushes the registers on the stack.

The interrupt system in the 68HC11 stores nine bytes of information in the stack. At the end of the ISR, all these bytes must be restored. When they are, the main program continues as if nothing happened.

The return from interrupt instruction, RTI, restores the status. The RTI instruction pulls nine bytes from the stack into the microprocessor registers. All interrupt service routines must use the RTI instruction to return to the main program. Returning to the main program any other way makes unstructured spaghetti programs.

Stack use.   A stack is necessary to use interrupt because the interrupt system hardware needs it. The uses of the stack now include storing program data, storing subroutine return addresses, and storing the microprocessor status for the interrupt system.

The interrupt system uses the stack when an I/O device signals that it is ready. Therefore, the computer doesn't know when the interrupt system will use the stack. The main program may be using the stack when the interrupt occurs. Consequently, the main program must always use the stack correctly and orderly. Otherwise, the program crashes when an interrupt occurs.

The status dilemma.   The discussion of the computer status omitted an important point for simplicity—the microprocessor may be fetching an instruction when the interrupt signal arrives at the interrupt system. During the fetch operation, the microprocessor puts the instruction code into the instruction register. However, the interrupt system does not save the instruction register in the stack. If the interrupt system immediately transfers control to the ISR, any bytes already in the instruction register are overwritten and lost. It will not then be possible to continue with the main program execution.

The 68HC11 avoids this dilemma because the interrupt system checks the IRQ signal only at the beginning of each fetch operation. At that point, the previous instruction is completed and there is nothing of value in the instruction register. Therefore, saving the instruction register is unnecessary. However, this delays the response to the interrupt signal by a few E-clock cycles.

The infinite interrupt dilemma.   The way the IRQ line works leads to another dilemma. The I/O flag triggers the interrupt by driving the IRQ wire low. The wire stays low until the flag is cleared in the ISR. However, the interrupt system checks the IRQ wire as it begins to fetch an instruction. Therefore, another interrupt should occur as the microprocessor fetches the first instruction in the ISR! An infinite loop of interrupts is the result.

To prevent this problem, the interrupt system automatically disables itself when it responds to an interrupt. That is, the interrupt system sets the I bit to 1 when it responds to an interrupt request. This allows the ISR to run undisturbed by further interrupt requests. Consequently, the interrupt system ignores the low level that stays on the IRQ line until the I/O flag is cleared. However, the interrupt system must be enabled again when control returns to the main program. Otherwise, the interrupt system would never honor another interrupt request.

The ISR can use the CLI instruction to enable the interrupt system again. However, this is usually unnecessary because the interrupt system saves the status before disabling itself. The status saved in the stack includes the 0 in the I bit. When the RTI instruction restores the status, the I bit is automatically set back to 0. Therefore, the RTI instruction automatically enables the interrupt system at the end of the ISR.

Because the interrupt system disables and enables itself automatically during interrupt service, programs usually contain only one CLI instruction. It enables the interrupt system during the program initialization. Furthermore, programs seldom use the SEI instruction that disables the interrupt system.

Transferring control to the ISR

The interrupt system hardware must know the address of the beginning of the ISR. Remember there are no instructions to send control to the ISR. Therefore, hardware must provide the address. In particular, the 68HC11 uses a block of memory locations at the top of memory to hold addresses for interrupts. For the IRQ interrupt, memory locations FFF2 and FFF3 must contain the address of the interrupt service routine. These locations are called an *interrupt vector* because they contain a pointer or vector to the ISR. When the interrupt system responds to the IRQ wire, it goes to the interrupt vector to get the address of the ISR.

The 68HC11 has many internal devices that can cause interrupts. Each I/O device has a separate interrupt vector. Therefore, each device has its own ISR. Each internal device also has a flag. Each flag has a switch to enable or disable an interrupt from it. The I bit also enables or disables interrupts from these devices.

Using the STAF flag to cause interrupts

The discussion on polling I/O used the STAF flag in an example. The STAF flag in the PIOC register also can cause IRQ interrupts. The ready signal for this flag is the STRA pin.

The STAI bit in PIOC enables the STAF flag to cause IRQ interrupts. Figure 6-26 shows the STAI bit. A 1 in STAI enables interrupts by closing the switch in Figure 6-31. A 0 in STAI prevents the flag from causing an interrupt.

Some people describe the interrupt as *masked* when the enable bit is 0. That is, if an interrupt cannot occur, it is masked.

Since the reset condition of STAI is 0, a program must change STAI before the STAF flag can cause interrupts. Therefore, using the STAF flag in the polling example did not cause any unwanted interrupts. The computer is powered-up in a reset condition with the interrupts masked, so a polling program is not affected by the interrupt system.

Motorola Trainer

You can use the 68HC11 interrupt system with only a small difficulty. The interrupt vectors are in permanent ROM memory in the trainer. So the trainer vectors to an address in the direct addressing range RAM memory. At the proper location, you must put a JMP instruction with extended addressing. The JMP sends control to your interrupt service routine. The monitor program allocates three bytes of space for your JMP instruction. See Appendix D for further details.

6.11   PARALLEL I/O EXAMPLE USING INTERRUPT

The example here is a program that has the same function as the example in Section 6.8 and Figure 6-28. Figure 6-32 shows the interrupt program. The example uses parallel I/O to the thumbwheel switch and display unit. Pushing the push button sets the I/O flag. The flag causes an interrupt to signal that it is time to do the data transfer.

Program Description

The following discusses the operation of the program in Figure 6-32. You also should refer to the polling program in Figure 6-29 because much of this program is the same.

- *Lines 21 through 25.*   Symbols are defined for the addresses of the input/output control registers. All the I/O registers in the 68HC11 are in a block of addresses beginning at address 1000. The symbol REG defines the beginning of this block of addresses.

- *Line 34.*   The interrupt vector is set to the address of the IRQ interrupt service routine. Loading the program into memory sets this vector.

- *Line 44.*   The stack is initialized for use by the interrupt system.

- *Lines 47, 49, and 50.*   The PORTC initialization is the same as in the polling example. Here the DDRC programs four bits as inputs and four as outputs.

- *Lines 52 and 53.*   The PIOC register is initialized. Storing a 1 into bit 6, STAI, of PIOC enables IRQ interrupts from the STAF flag. Storing 1 into bit 1, EGA, makes the STAF flag set on a low-to-high transition of the STRA pin. The 0s put into the other bits of PIOC will cause no problems.

- *Line 55.*   The interrupt system is enabled after all the I/O hardware is initialized. Initializing the interrupt system before this may let the interrupt service routine control uninitialized hardware.

- *Line 59.*   The main program loop does nothing in this example. It only provides an operating program while the computer waits for interrupts.

```
 1                              ************************************************************
 2                              ** COPY THUMBWHEEL SWITCH TO DISPLAY WHEN
 3                              ** PUSHBUTTON IS PUSHED
 4                              *
 5                              * USE INTERRUPT TECHNIQUE FOR TIMING
 6                              *
 7                              * FOUR BIT THUMBWHEEL SWITCH WIRED TO
 8                              * ..BITS 4-7 OF PORT C
 9                              *
10                              * FOUR BIT DISPLAY WIRED TO BITS 0-3 OF PORT C
11                              *
12                              * PUSHBUTTON SWITCH WIRED TO STRA SO
13                              * ..LOW TO HIGH ON PUSH
14                              *
15                              ************************************************************
16                              *
17                              ************************************************************
18                              ** SYMBOL DEFINITIONS
19                              ************************************************************
20                              * 68HC11 REGISTERS
21            1000              REG     EQU   $1000      BASE ADDRESS OF REGISTERS
22            1002              PIOC    EQU   $1002      PARALLEL I/O CONTROL REGISTER
23            1003              PORTC   EQU   $1003      I/O PORT C REGISTER
24            1005              PORTCL  EQU   $1005      PORT C LATCH REGISTER
25            1007              DDRC    EQU   $1007      DATA DIRECTION REGISTER C
26            000F              IOPAT   EQU   $0F        I/O PATTERN, 0=IN 1=OUT
27                              * MASKS
28            0080              BIT7    EQU   %10000000
29
30                              ************************************************************
31                              ** DATA SECTION
32                              ************************************************************
33   FFF2                               ORG  $FFF2
34   FFF2   C113                        FDB  IRQISR   IRQ INTERRUPT VECTOR
35                              *
36                              ************************************************************
37                              ** MAIN PROGRAM
38                              ************************************************************
39   C100                               ORG  $C100
40                              *----------------------------------------------------------
41                              * INITIALIZATION
42                              *----------------------------------------------------------
43                              * INITIALIZE STACK
44   C100   8E DF FF                    LDS   #$DFFF
45                              * INITIALIZE PORT C
46                              *    INITIALIZE OUTPUTS TO ZEROS
47   C103   7F 10 03                    CLR   PORTC    0=LOW
48                              *    SET UP INS AND OUTS
49   C106   86 0F                       LDAA  #IOPAT
50   C108   B7 10 07                    STAA  DDRC     0=IN, 1=OUT
51                              * SET UP PIOC
52   C10B   86 42                       LDAA  #$42     ENABLE STAF INTERRUPT
53   C10D   B7 10 02                    STAA  PIOC     ..LOW TO HIGH ON STRA
54                              * TURN ON INTERRUPT SYSTEM
55   C110   0E                          CLI
56                              *----------------------------------------------------------
57                              * WAIT FOR INTERRUPTS
58                              *----------------------------------------------------------
59   C111   20 FE              HERE     BRA   HERE     DO NOTHING!
60                              *
61                              ************************************************************
62                              ** PUSHBUTTON SWITCH INTERRUPT SERVICE ROUTINE
63                              ************************************************************
```

Figure 6-32 Interrupt program.

```
64                              *---------------------------------------------------
65                              * VALID STAF INTERRUPT?
66                              *---------------------------------------------------
67     C113   CE 10 00          IRQISR   LDX    #REG
68     C116   1F 02 80 0D                BRCLR  PIOC-REG,X,BIT7,RTIRQ    BRANCH ON NO
69                              *---------------------------------------------------
70                              * COPY THUMBWHEEL SWITCH TO DISPLAY
71                              *---------------------------------------------------
72                              * READ THUMBWHEEL SWITCH AND CLEAR I/O FLAG
73     C11A   B6 10 02                   LDAA   PIOC     TWO INSTRUCTIONS TO CLEAR STAF
74     C11D   B6 10 05                   LDAA   PORTCL   ..FLAG AND INPUT SSSS----
75                              * POSITION DATA FOR OUTPUT
76     C120   46                         RORA            -SSSS---
77     C121   46                         RORA            --SSSS--
78     C122   46                         RORA            ---SSSS-
79     C123   46                         RORA            ----SSSS
80                              * CONTROL DISPLAY
81     C124   B7 10 03                   STAA   PORTC    OUTPUT TO PORT C
82                              *---------------------------------------------------
83                              * RETURN TO MAIN PROGRAM
84                              *---------------------------------------------------
85     C127   3B                RTIRQ    RTI
86     C128                              END
```

Figure 6-32   Continued.

- *Lines 67 and 68.*   The STAF input/output flag is tested as a safety measure. A hardware failure could erroneously cause an interrupt. If an erroneous interrupt occurs, the ISR in this example simply returns to the main program. In dangerous situations, other responses would be necessary.

- *Lines 73 through 81.*   These lines of the program clear the STAF flag, read the thumbwheel switch, and control the display. They are the same instructions as in the polling example.

- *Line 85.*   The RTI instruction returns program control to the main program. To do this, the RTI restores all the microprocessor registers with main program data from the stack. The RTI removes nine bytes from the stack. Restoring the registers enables the interrupt system so future interrupts can occur. Execution continues at line 59 in the main program.

The work done by the interrupt service routine is the same as that done by a polling program—only the timing technique is different. Carefully compare lines 73 through 81 of this program to lines 52 through 60 of Figure 6-29.

6.12   SUBROUTINES AND INTERRUPT

Subroutines may not function correctly when a program uses interrupt. A problem may occur when a subroutine is interrupted if the interrupt service routine jumps to the interrupted subroutine. The subroutine must run again from its beginning, though it has not finished the first run. It must be *reentered*. Reentering a subroutine may cause problems. A subroutine

---

Motorola Trainer

If you have hardware connected for the example in Figure 6-29, you can use the same hardware for the example in Figure 6-32. Since the trainer maps the interrupt vector to address 00EE, put a JMP to address C113 there. The JMP sends control to the ISR. Carefully read the Appendix D cautions about using interrupt with the trainer. Don't try to single step or breakpoint a program while the interrupt system is enabled. Appendix D explains how to debug interrupt programs.

---

that is *reentrant* always works correctly, while one that is not reentrant sometimes corrupts the data it is using.

You need to consider reentrancy only if your program uses interrupt. However, most modern applications of microcomputers use interrupt, so reentrancy is important.

The Data Corruption Problem

Let's first look at a good way to prevent a subroutine from being reentrant. To be nonreentrant, a subroutine must store a number in a specific memory location and then retrieve the number later in the subroutine. Suppose an interrupt occurs between the point of saving the number and the point of retrieving the number. When the interrupt service routine uses the subroutine, the data in the specific memory location is overwritten. When the execution of the subroutine continues from the point of interrupt, the subroutine retrieves erroneous data.

The data corruption problem applies only to data stored in memory by the subroutine. Data in the microprocessor registers is never lost due to an interrupt. The interrupt system automatically saves all the microprocessor registers in the stack.

Nonreentrant subroutine example

The program in Figure 6-33 includes a nonreentrant subroutine. It is an example program contrived to show the problems of nonreentrant subroutines. The main program alters a data value that gets corrupted by the nonreentrant subroutine when the interrupt service routine uses it. The subroutine is very simple—it adds two to the A accumulator. The main program tests the altered data value to determine if the subroutine corrupted the data. If so, the program stops.

The example program in Figure 6-33 is almost the same as the program in Figure 6-32. The interrupt service routine reads the thumbwheel switch to get a number for the display. In this example however, the program adds two to the number before displaying it. In addition, the main program loop continually updates a value by adding two to it. This calculation is an example only—it's not a practical program. Here is a description of the program and the problem the nonreentrant subroutine causes.

- *Lines 48 through 61.* The initialization is as before except that it initializes memory location VALUE to 00.

```
1                                    ***************************************************
2                                    ** COPY THUMBWHEEL SWITCH PLUS TWO TO DISPLAY WHEN
3                                    ** PUSHBUTTON IS PUSHED
4                                    *
5                                    * USE NONREENTRANT SUBROUTINE
6                                    *
7                                    * USE INTERRUPT TECHNIQUE FOR TIMING
8                                    *
9                                    * FOUR BIT THUMBWHEEL SWITCH WIRED TO
10                                   * ..BITS 4-7 OF PORT C
11                                   *
12                                   * FOUR BIT DISPLAY WIRED TO BITS 0-3 OF PORT C
13                                   *
14                                   * PUSHBUTTON SWITCH WIRED TO STRA SO
15                                   * ..LOW TO HIGH ON PUSH
16                                   *
17                                   ***************************************************
18                                   *
19                                   ***************************************************
20                                   ** SYMBOL DEFINITIONS
21                                   ***************************************************
22                                   * 68HC11 REGISTERS
23           1000                    REG      EQU   $1000     BASE ADDRESS OF REGISTERS
24           1002                    PIOC     EQU   $1002     PARALLEL I/O CONTROL REGISTER
25           1003                    PORTC    EQU   $1003     I/O PORT C REGISTER
26           1005                    PORTCL   EQU   $1005     PORT C LATCH REGISTER
27           1007                    DDRC     EQU   $1007     DATA DIRECTION REGISTER C
28           000F                    IOPAT    EQU   $0F       I/O PATTERN, 0=IN 1=OUT
29                                   * MASKS
30           0080                    BIT7     EQU   %10000000
31                                   *
32                                   ***************************************************
33                                   ** DATA SECTION
34                                   ***************************************************
35  0010                                     ORG $0010
36  0010                             VALUE    RMB   1         MAIN PROGRAM DATA
37  0011                             SAVE     RMB   1         SUBROUTINE SAVE LOCATION
38                                   *
39  FFF2                                      ORG $FFF2
40  FFF2 C125                                 FDB   IRQISR    IRQ INTERRUPT VECTOR
41                                   *
42                                   ***************************************************
43                                   ** MAIN PROGRAM
44                                   ***************************************************
45  C100                                      ORG $C100
46                                   *---------------------------------------------------
47                                   * INITIALIZATION
48                                   *---------------------------------------------------
49                                   * INITIALIZE STACK
50  C100 8E DF FF                            LDS   #$DFFF
51                                   * INITIALIZE MAIN PROGRAM DATA
52  C103 7F 00 10                            CLR   VALUE
53                                   * INITIALIZE PORT C
54                                   *     INITIALIZE OUTPUTS TO ZEROS
55  C106 7F 10 03                            CLR   PORTC     0=LOW
56                                   *    SET UP INS AND OUTS
57  C109 86 0F                               LDAA  #IOPAT
58  C10B B7 10 07                            STAA  DDRC      0=IN, 1=OUT
59                                   * SET UP PIOC
60  C10E 86 42                               LDAA  #$42      ENABLE STRA INTERRUPT
61  C110 B7 10 02                            STAA  PIOC      ..LOW TO HIGH
62                                   * TURN ON INTERRUPT SYSTEM
```

Figure 6-33   Example program with nonreentrant subroutine.

```
 63   C113   0E                              CLI
 64                           *--------------------------------------------------------
 65                           * WAIT FOR INTERRUPTS
 66                           *--------------------------------------------------------
 67                           * GET VALUE FOR EXAMPLE
 68   C114   96 10            HERE    LDAA   VALUE
 69                           * ADD TWO TO VALUE WITH NONREENTRANT SUBROUTINE
 70   C116   BD C2 00                 JSR    ADDTWO
 71                           * TEST IF VALUE WAS CORRUPTED
 72   C119   D6 10                    LDAB   VALUE
 73   C11B   CB 02                    ADDB   #2
 74   C11D   11                       CBA
 75   C11E   26 04                    BNE    ERROR    BRANCH ON YES
 76                           * SAVE VALUE FOR EXAMPLE
 77   C120   97 10                    STAA   VALUE
 78   C122   20 F0                    BRA    HERE
 79                           * STOP IF DATA GETS CORRUPTED
 80   C124   3F               ERROR   SWI               STOP FOR MOTOROLA TRAINER
 81                           *
 82                           ********************************************************
 83                           ** PUSHBUTTON SWITCH INTERRUPT SERVICE ROUTINE
 84                           ********************************************************
 85                           *--------------------------------------------------------
 86                           * VALID STAF INTERRUPT?
 87                           *--------------------------------------------------------
 88   C125   CE 10 00         IRQISR  LDX    #REG
 89   C128   1F 02 80 10              BRCLR  PIOC-REG,X,BIT7,RTIRQ    BRANCH ON NO
 90                           *--------------------------------------------------------
 91                           * COPY THUMBWHEEL SWITCH TO DISPLAY
 92                           *--------------------------------------------------------
 93                           * READ THUMBWHEEL SWITCH AND CLEAR I/O FLAG
 94   C12C   B6 10 02                 LDAA   PIOC     TWO INSTRUCTIONS TO CLEAR
 95   C12F   B6 10 05                 LDAA   PORTCL   ..FLAG AND INPUT SSSS----
 96                           * POSITION DATA FOR OUTPUT
 97   C132   46                       RORA            -SSSS---
 98   C133   46                       RORA            --SSSS--
 99   C134   46                       RORA            ---SSSS-
100   C135   46                       RORA            ----SSSS
101                           * ADD TWO TO DISPLAY NUMBER
102   C136   BD C2 00                 JSR    ADDTWO   MAY CORRUPT DATA IN MAIN!
103                           * CONTROL DISPLAY
104   C139   B7 10 03                 STAA   PORTC    OUTPUT TO PORT C
105                           *--------------------------------------------------------
106                           * RETURN TO MAIN PROGRAM
107                           *--------------------------------------------------------
108   C13C   3B               RTIRQ   RTI
109                           *
110                           ********************************************************
111                           ** NONREENTRANT SUBROUTINE ADDTWO
112                           * ADD 2 TO A ACCUMULATOR--MODIFIES CC
113                           ********************************************************
114   C200                            ORG    $C200
115                           * INCORRECTLY STORE DATA IN FIXED MEMORY LOCATION
116   C200   97 11            ADDTWO  STAA   SAVE
117                           * GET NUMBER TWO
118   C202   86 02                    LDAA   #2
119                           * RETRIEVE INCORRECTLY STORED DATA
120   C204   9B 11                    ADDA   SAVE
121                           * RETURN FROM SUBROUTINE
122   C206   39                       RTS
123   C207                            END
```

Figure 6-33 Continued.

- *Lines 66 through 68.*   The main program loop gets the number in location VALUE into the A accumulator. Let's assume the data number is 22. At line 68, control goes to the nonreentrant subroutine.

- *Line 116.*   The subroutine stores the 22 passed in the A accumulator in memory location SAVE. This is the data number the subroutine corrupts.

- *Line 118.*   Assume an interrupt occurs at the completion of the instruction on line 116 or line 118. The interrupt must occur at these points or the problem will not occur. Therefore, the chances of the interrupt occurring at this exact point are small. Control next goes to the instruction on line 88.

- *Lines 88 through 100.*   When an interrupt occurs, the interrupt system hardware transfers control here. This part of the interrupt service routine clears the flag, reads the thumbwheel switch, and positions the data.

- *Line 102.*   The interrupt service routine calls the subroutine to add two to the number from the thumbwheel switch. Assume we set the thumbwheel switch to 5.

- *Line 116.*   The subroutine stores the number 05 in memory location SAVE. This destroys the number 22 that the subroutine stored at SAVE on the last run. This problem makes the subroutine nonreentrant!

- *Lines 118 through 122.*   The subroutine correctly adds two and returns the correct result 07

- *Lines 104 through 108.*   The interrupt service routine finishes correctly and returns control to the main program loop.

- *Line 118.*   The subroutine continues the first run. However, the ADDA instruction adds two to the incorrect number 07 in location SAVE. The subroutine returns the incorrect result 09 to the main program.

- *Lines 72 through 75.*   In this example program, the main program checks for a reentrancy error. If it finds one, it branches to line 80 and stops.

- *Lines 77 and 78.*   If the interrupt did not occur at a point that causes a reentrancy error, the program stores the updated number in location VALUE. It then sends control to the beginning of the main program loop.

Reentering a subroutine is only a problem if the interrupt occurs at the correct time when the subroutine is at the correct point. Even if the chances of this are small, it will eventually happen and the program will fail.

The chances for error

Many circumstances must converge to make a program fail due to reentrancy problems. Consider the nonreentrant subroutine example in Figure 6-33. The subroutine corrupts data because it stores a number in memory location SAVE.

Now consider the coincidence of events that must happen for the subroutine to cause a problem. First, the main program must have jumped to the subroutine that is nonreentrant. Next, an I/O device must cause an interrupt after the STAA SAVE instruction is executed but before the LDAA SAVE instruction executes. Remember, the I/O device is external to the computer. There is no way to know when it will set the I/O flag. And, finally, the interrupt service routine must jump to this subroutine.

All these events must occur to make the program fail. The chance of every one of these events happening is small. Therefore, the problem occurs infrequently and at random times. If you were testing this program, you may run the computer for hours and hours without a problem. But, eventually, the series of events will occur and the program will malfunction. Often the failure is very surprising. You may have run the program for months without a problem.

Such behavior frequently baffles people. They sometimes dismiss the failure as a one-time occurrence due to electrical noise. Sometimes they load the program into memory again assuming that something changed the program code. They may replace memory ICs believing there must be an intermittent failure in an IC. How else could a program that works perfectly for hours to months suddenly fail? You should now understand that such failures can occur due to incorrectly written and nonreentrant subroutines.

The nonreentrant subroutine solution

The nonreentrant subroutine problem has only one solution—don't write subroutines that allow it to happen. Write only good programs that don't have problems. Testing your program cannot prove that it works correctly!

Data Corruption Solutions

The best way to make a subroutine reentrant is to avoid storing data numbers so the subroutine overwrites them upon reentry. The following discusses several techniques that avoid the problem of data corruption.

Use the stack

Saving data in the stack is the best solution to the reentrancy problem! Then, when the subroutine is reentered, it uses new locations in the stack and does not destroy any saved data. Figure 6-34 shows a new version of the nonreentrant subroutine from Figure 6-33. The subroutine makes a working location in the stack. The stack location replaces location SAVE in the original program. The program in Figure 6-33 looks very difficult when it does such a simple job, but its purpose is to illustrate the programming technique.

The Motorola 68HC11 instruction set makes reentrant subroutines possible. The instruction set has instructions to save the registers A, B, X, and Y in the stack. Therefore, the subroutine can store all the temporary data in the stack. Furthermore, all the data manipulation instructions, by using indexed addressing, can reach the data values inside the stack. For example, a subroutine that uses a loop counter can put the counter in the stack.

```
 1                              ************************************************************
 2                              ** REENTRANT SUBROUTINE ADDTWO
 3                              * ADD 2 TO A ACCUMULATOR--MODIFIES CC
 4                              ************************************************************
 5                              *
 6   C200                                   ORG  $C200
 7                              * STORE DATA IN STACK
 8   C200   3C                 ADDTWO  PSHX
 9   C201   34                         DES
10   C202   30                         TSX
11   C203   A7 00                      STAA   0,X
12                              * ADD TWO
13   C205   86 02                      LDAA   #2
14   C207   AB 00                      ADDA   0,X
15                              * CLEAR STACK
16   C209   31                         INS
17   C20A   38                         PULX
18                              * RETURN FROM SUBROUTINE
19   C20B   39                         RTS
20   C20C                              END
```

Figure 6-34   Reentrant subroutine that uses the stack.

Some Motorola 8-bit microprocessors do not have instructions to save the index register in the stack or to transfer the index register to another microprocessor register. Therefore, when using such a microprocessor, any subroutine that needs to save the index register and then restore it later cannot be reentrant. The subroutine must store the index register in a dedicated memory location.

Put no data in memory

The subroutine can use only data values in microprocessor registers as a solution to the reentrancy problem. Storing no data in memory registers avoids the data corruption problem.

Figure 6-35 shows another variation of the subroutine from Figure 6-33. This new subroutine that uses only the microprocessor registers is very simple. However, complex subroutines usually need more storage space than the microprocessor registers. If not, using only the microprocessor registers avoids many problems.

```
 1                              ************************************************************
 2                              ** REENTRANT SUBROUTINE ADDTWO
 3                              * ADD 2 TO A ACCUMULATOR--MODIFIES CC
 4                              ************************************************************
 5                              *
 6   C200                                   ORG  $C200
 7                              * ADD TWO
 8   C200   8B 02              ADDTWO  ADDA   #2
 9                              * RETURN FROM SUBROUTINE
10   C202   39                         RTS
11   C203                              END
```

Figure 6-35   Reentrant subroutine that uses microprocessor registers.

Motorola Trainer

Run the example program in Figure 6-33 to investigate the effects of nonreentrant subroutines. Remember to put a JMP to the interrupt service routine at address 00EE. See Appendix D for information about using interrupts in the trainer. Using an oscillator to cause periodic interrupts is a good way to test the program. A 555 integrated circuit makes a practical oscillator. A fast oscillator increases the chances of error. Also run the program after substituting the reentrant subroutines in Figures 6-34 and 6-35.

Prevent interrupts

Preventing interrupts while the subroutine runs is another solution to the reentrancy problem. The main program disables the interrupt system using the SEI instruction before jumping to the subroutine. When control returns to the main program, it enables the interrupt system again.

Preventing interrupts to solve the reentrancy problem has a serious disadvantage. The computer will not service the I/O devices while the subroutine is running. Therefore, the I/O devices operate more slowly because they must wait for the subroutine to finish before getting service. The I/O device cannot interrupt until the subroutine returns and the main program enables the interrupt system again.

Alternatively, the subroutine can enable and disable the interrupt system. Then the subroutine can disable the interrupt system for the minimum amount of time. That is, the subroutine disables the interrupt system only during the part of the subroutine that may cause a problem. However, use this technique with caution. The subroutine may enable the interrupt system when it should not. For example, if the interrupt service routine runs with the interrupt system disabled, the subroutine would enable it prematurely.

Don't reenter

Using multiple copies of the subroutine that each store data in different memory locations avoids the reentrancy problem. Each program that can enter the subroutine uses a different copy. Of course, this solution defeats much of the advantage of using a subroutine.

More Examples of Reentrant Subroutines

For more examples of subroutines, return to Chapter 5. The subroutine examples in Figures 5-11, 5-17, 5-18, 5-19, and 5-21 are good reentrant subroutines. Use those subroutines as examples of good technique. They keep temporary subroutine data in microprocessor registers or in the stack.

Also look at the discussion of recursive subroutines in Chapter 5. A recursive subroutine also is reentrant.

6.13   REVIEW

Chapter 6 introduced the basic hardware in the microcomputer. The microprocessor connects to the memory and input/output hardware with the address, data, and control buses. Memory mapped I/O treats the I/O parts the same as memory using the same bus signals. Therefore, identical wiring connects the microprocessor to the memory and the I/O hardware. However, the I/O hardware does not function the same as memory. In practical applications, load and store instructions transfer data to and from I/O devices. Timing or synchronizing those transfers to the program requires an I/O flag and a means of testing that flag. The I/O device sets the flag to indicate it is ready for a data transfer. The computer clears the flag to indicate that it is responding to the request for a data transfer. The computer detects the flag condition using either polling or interrupt. Interrupt is the most common and effective timing technique. When using interrupt, be careful to write reentrant subroutines.

6.14   EXERCISES

6-1. What word best describes a memory IC that loses its information when the power to the IC is turned off?

6-2. What terminology best describes a memory IC that prevents the microprocessor from changing its numbers due to its storage technique?

6-3. Is an EEPROM a read/write memory?

6-4. Will sunlight shining on an EPROM erase it?

6-5. Is the lifetime of an EEPROM measured in erase/program cycles approximately equal to the lifetime of a RAM measured in read/write cycles?

6-6. A RAM memory IC has 10_{10} address pins. How many registers does this IC contain?

6-7. During the execute phase of a STAA instruction, is the direction of the data bus into or out of the microprocessor? What is it during the fetch phase?

6-8. Does the data bus ever carry instruction op codes?

6-9. While an instruction op code is fetched from a RAM memory, is the R/W line high or low?

6-10. How many bytes are there in the largest memory that the 68HC11 can directly address?

6-11. When does the address bus carry a number into the microprocessor?

6-12. Is it true that the execution of a ROL memory instruction uses the data bus to both read a data number from memory and to store a data number into memory?

6-13. Why does the instruction in Figure 6-12 load 88 into the A accumulator?

6-14. Which addresses will make the output port in Figure 6-18 respond?

6-15. In Figure 6-18, if the AND gate were connected to output 2 instead of output 4 of the decoder, what range of addresses would make the output port respond?

6-16. In Figure 6-18, if the inputs to the AND gate now connected to A_1 and A_0 were instead connected to A_7 and A_5, what range of addresses would make the output port respond?

6-17. How can the circuit in Figure 6-19 be changed so the input port has the same address as the output port in Figure 6-18? Can both ports be used in the same computer when they have the same address?

6-18. Change the circuit in Figure 6-18 so the output register can be read by the microprocessor with the same address used to write it.

6-19. Using the fewest number of logic devices, change the circuit in Figure 6-18 by adding a second output port that responds to address 4007.

6-20. Suppose two output ports respond to addresses 6006 and 6007. Can they be used as a 16-bit output port with address 6006? Can the STD instruction be used to output to this port?

6-21. What is the effect of changing the instruction on line 38 of Figure 6-21 to CLR IMAGE?

6-22. Discuss the pros and cons of input and output ports with addresses in the direct addressing range.

6-23. Design a circuit with both a RAM and a ROM memory at the same addresses with hardware to switch between them under program control.

6-24. Write a polling program to read two 4-bit thumbwheel switches and display the results on two seven-segment displays each time a push button is pushed. Use the PORTB and PORTC registers and the STAF flag.

6-25. Refer to the program in Figure 6-29. Describe what will be seen on the display unit if the push button is pushed and held while the thumbwheel is changed?

6-26. Refer to the program in Figure 6-32. Assume the flag is always set because the clearing hardware failed. Describe how the program will perform including what the thumbwheel switch and the display do.

6-27. Refer to the program in Figure 6-32. Assume the flag is always cleared because the flag hardware failed. Describe how the program will perform including what the thumbwheel switch and the display do.

6-28. Refer to the program in Figure 6-32. Describe how the program performs if a CLI instruction is inserted at line 69 and the existing lines 69 and higher are moved down one line.

Chapter 7

Advanced 68HC11 Hardware

The 68HC11 integrated circuit contains many input/output devices and several types of memory. The I/O devices are those frequently required for control applications. The 68HC11 can be expanded by adding external input/output devices and memory. If a change in an application requires additional hardware, expanding the hardware is easy.

This chapter discusses the hardware devices inside the 68HC11 chip. Example programs illustrate their operation. Furthermore, this chapter discusses 68HC11 expansion using the microprocessor buses and the SPI bus.

This chapter also introduces techniques of event timing, waveform generation, serial communications, and fail-safe operation. All these techniques are important to control applications of microcomputers. The 68HC11 internal devices are used in examples of these techniques.

7.1 THE HARDWARE CONFIGURATION

The 68HC11 hardware is programmable. Both the microcomputer hardware configuration and the input/output devices are programmable. Numbers in registers control how each hardware device operates. The design of the 68HC11 allows a wide range of applications.

Operating Modes

The 68HC11 operates in one of two modes called the *single-chip microcomputer mode* and the *expanded mode*. Hardware signals decide the operating mode as the microcomputer is powered-up. Software can never change the operating mode, because doing so would be dangerous.

In the single-chip mode, the 68HC11 uses only the resources inside the chip. These resources are primarily memory and input/output devices. The address, data, and control buses are not available for expanding the computer. However, considerable expansion is possible using the high-speed SPI serial bus with ICs designed to communicate serially.

In the expanded mode, the 68HC11 connects the internal address, data, and control buses to pins. Consequently, in expanded mode, some internal I/O devices cannot be used. The pins those devices use in the single-chip mode are used for bus signals in the expanded mode. The devices lost are two parallel I/O ports and a flag. However, having the buses available outside the chip makes it possible to expand the microcomputer with external memory and I/O chips. Later sections of this chapter discuss 68HC11 expansion.

The operating mode of the microcomputer affects the programmer little. Only the character of the hardware affects the program.

The 68HC11 Chip Versions

The 68HC11 chip is available in several versions. Most versions differ principally in the amount and kind of memory inside the chip. Some versions omit part of the memory and some I/O devices. Others, such as the 68HC11A1, are the same part as another, but are shipped with internal programming to disable the internal ROM.

The 68HC11A8 and 68HC11E9 versions accurately represent the entire 68HC11 family. The A8 version has eight kilobytes of masked ROM and 256_{10} bytes of RAM. The E9 version has 12_{10} kilobytes of masked ROM and 512_{10} bytes of RAM. An additional version, the 68HC711, substitutes EPROM for the masked ROM in the E9 version. The A8 and E9 versions have a full complement of I/O devices.

Each of the 68HC11 ICs is functionally the same—the differences are mainly in the amount of memory in the chip. However, some versions have larger hardware differences. For example, some can operate only in the expanded mode.

The examples in this book assume the A8 or E9 versions. However, all the examples apply to other versions that have functionally equivalent hardware.

Block Diagram of the 68HC11

Figure 7-1 is the block diagram of the 68HC11 operating in the single-chip mode. All the input/output devices built into the chip are available in this mode. Figure 7-2 is the block diagram for the expanded mode.

The block diagrams show the pins on the 68HC11 package and some of the pin functions. The pins connect the microcomputer to other devices, so they are most visible to the

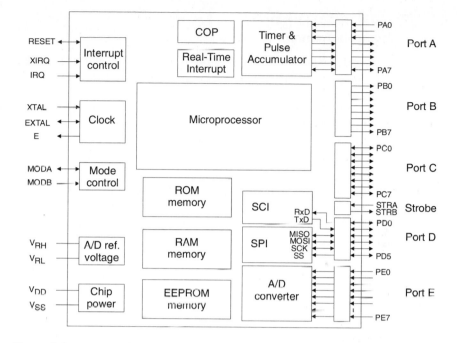

Figure 7-1   Block diagram of the 68HC11A8 hardware while in single-chip mode.

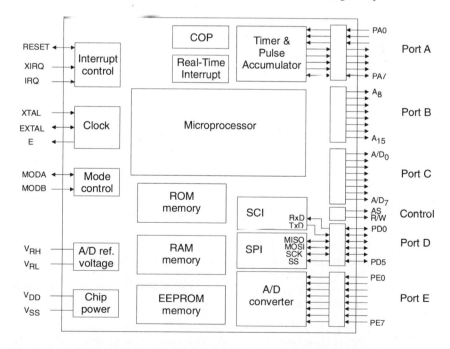

Figure 7-2   Block diagram of the 68HC11A8 hardware while in expanded mode.

Motorola Trainer

The Motorola trainer contains either the 68HC11A8 or 68HC11E9 integrated circuit. Some may have the 68HC11A1, but it is the same as the 68HC11A8 with the internal EEPROM register programmed differently. Other than the size and location of the memory, you should not discern a difference between these parts until you are very experienced with them.

user of the computer. The collections of pins called ports A through E are input/output, address bus, and data bus signals.

The block diagrams also show the internal organization of the chip. Here is a description of the hardware in the IC package:

- *The 68HC11 microprocessor.* The 68HC11 microprocessor executes a total of 307_{10} instruction codes.

- *ROM memory.* The A8 chip has eight kilobytes of masked ROM and the E9 chip has 12_{10} kilobytes of masked ROM. The ROM addressing places it at the high end of memory so the ROM includes address FFFF. A programmable control register can disable the internal ROM so that other memory can use these addresses.

- *RAM memory.* The A8 chip has 128_{10} bytes of static RAM, and the E9 chip has 512_{10} bytes of static RAM. The RAM addressing places it at the low end of the memory space including address 0000. The RAM is thus in the direct addressing range. A programmable control register can move the memory to other addresses.

- *EEPROM memory.* Both the A8 and E9 versions contain 512_{10} bytes of EEPROM memory. The E9 chip has a control register that prevents erroneous changing of the EEPROM.

- *Internal clock oscillator.* Only a crystal and two capacitors are necessary to build the clock for the 68HC11.

- *SCI serial communications interface.* The SCI asynchronous serial device allows communication to remote serial I/O devices.

- *SPI serial peripheral interface.* The SPI interface allows both control of other ICs in the microcomputer and communications to another nearby circuit board.

- *Parallel input/output ports.* Several parallel I/O ports, including some programmable ports, allow communication to external I/O devices.

- *Programmable timer.* The timer device allows measurement of timing intervals and timed control of outputs. Quantities such as RPM are easily measured. Accurate output waveforms, such as pulse-width modulated waveforms, are easily generated.

- *Analog-to-digital converter.*   Eight channels of the A/D converter measure DC voltages. Including analog hardware in the chip allows sensors of many kinds to interface easily to the 68HC11.

- *Pulse accumulator.*   The pulse accumulator can both count pulses and measure the duration of pulses from I/O devices outside the computer.

- *Computer operating properly, clock monitor, and illegal instruction devices.*   Each of these devices forces a safe hardware response when certain computer hardware or software has failed.

A block of registers, usually mapped to address 1000, controls all the internal I/O devices. Appendix J contains a summary of all these control registers. These registers are described throughout this chapter.

68HC11 Pin Connections

Look at the pins in Figures 7-1 and 7-2. Here is a brief description of the pin functions:

- *V_{DD} and V_{SS}.*   The power and ground pins are called V_{DD} and V_{SS}. The 68HC11 operates with V_{DD} at +5 V_{DC}.

- *XTAL and EXTAL.*   The crystal for the clock connects to the pins named XTAL and EXTAL. The crystal usually operates near 8 MHz.

- *MODA and MODB.*   The MODA and MODB pins determine the operating mode of the 68HC11 chip.

- *RESET.*   The RESET pin initializes the microcomputer hardware.

- *IRQ and XIRQ.*   The interrupt system has two external interrupt lines called IRQ and XIRQ. The internal STAF flag connects to the IRQ interrupt line.

- *Ports A through E.*   In single-chip mode, all the ports illustrated in Figure 7-1 support input/output. In the expanded mode, ports B and C, as illustrated in Figure 7-2, carry address and data bus signals while the other ports support input/output.

Some 68HC11 pins have multiple functions. For example, the MODB pin also provides standby power for the internal RAM memory. It can power the RAM while the rest of the chip is powered down.

7.2   MEMORY SPACE

Figure 7-3 illustrates the memory space in the 68HC11. The figure shows the internal memory addresses after the 68HC11 has been powered-up in the single-chip microcomputer mode. The figure shows the differences between the A8 and E9 versions of the integrated circuit.

Any unlabeled area of memory can be external memory when the 68HC11 is in expanded mode. In single-chip microcomputer mode, the unlabeled areas are unused.

Internal ROM

The internal masked ROM is always located so the high end includes address FFFF. The ROM therefore contains the interrupt vectors. Usually, the program and constant data values are stored in this ROM.

Internal RAM

The internal static RAM is usually located so its lowest address is 0000. Therefore, the RAM is in the direct addressing range. Since the ROM memory is usually much smaller than 64_{10} kilobytes to reduce cost, using the shorter direct addressed instructions to reach data is important. So normally it is desirable to have RAM in the direct addressing range.

A separate pin on the 68HC11 powers the internal RAM. Therefore, the rest of the IC can be off while the RAM memory retains its information. Usually the RAM gets its power from a backup battery while the rest of the IC is off. Retaining information during power down is very valuable when the computer stores diagnostic information in the RAM. The standby voltage supply is connected to the MODB/V$_{STBY}$ pin.

When the RAM has a standby voltage supply, the RAM is called *keep-alive* memory. The battery does not make the RAM a nonvolatile memory, but does enable it to retain information while the computer is off.

Internal EEPROM

The internal EEPROM is always at address B600. The microprocessor reads EEPROM registers the same as any other memory registers. However, programming the EEPROM

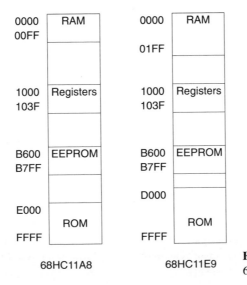

Figure 7-3 Internal memory of the 68HC11A8 and 68HC11E9 ICs.

requires a setup procedure that reduces the chance of accidental changes to the EEPROM. The programming is done one byte at a time.

Programming the EEPROM changes 1s to 0s. Therefore, programming a register with 1s if 0s are already programmed requires erasing the registers first. The erased state is all 1s. The erasing hardware erases either the entire EEPROM, groups of registers, or individual registers. Erasing larger groups requires less time than erasing multiple individual bytes.

Registers

A block of memory addresses is reserved for the hardware control registers. These are all the registers for control of memory and the input/output devices. Appendix J lists all the hardware control registers in the 68HC11. Look at the table in Appendix J to get an overview of all the control registers. The purpose of these registers becomes clear as various hardware devices are introduced. Generally, you need only think about one or two of these registers at a time. Don't be discouraged by the many registers and the many control bits.

Memory configuration and mapping

The internal RAM and hardware control registers can be moved to different addresses by software. Similarly, software can disable the internal memory.

The INIT register. Figure 7-4 shows the INIT register which determines the addresses of the internal RAM and hardware control registers block. The INIT register specifies the most-significant four bits of the addresses. The reset condition makes the RAM start at address 0000 and the registers start at address 1000. For example, if software changed the INIT register to 20, the RAM would begin at address 2000 and the registers at address 0000.

	7	6	5	4	3	2	1	0	
$103D	RAM3	RAM2	RAM1	RAM0	REG3	REG2	REG1	REG0	INIT
RESET	0	0	0	0	0	0	0	1	

Figure 7-4 RAM and I/O mapping register.

If moved from the reset locations, the RAM or control registers can conflict with the ROM or with each other. If so, the RAM has precedence over the ROM and the registers have precedence over the RAM.

The CONFIG register. The functions of the CONFIG register include enabling and disabling the internal ROM and EEPROM memories. Other bits in the CONFIG register control other options.

Figure 7-5 shows the bits in the CONFIG register. The ROMON bit enables the ROM memory when it is 1 and disables it when it is 0. Read the name ROMON as *ROM on*. However, the ROM can never be disabled in the single-chip mode, because the computer must have the ROM to operate. If the ROM is disabled, its memory space is available on the external buses.

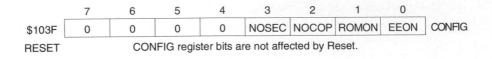

Figure 7-5 is illustrated by the following table:

	7	6	5	4	3	2	1	0	
$103F	0	0	0	0	NOSEC	NOCOP	ROMON	EEON	CONFIG
RESET				CONFIG register bits are not affected by Reset.					

Figure 7-5 System configuration register.

The EEON bit in the CONFIG register enables the EEPROM memory when it is 1, and disables it when it is 0. If the EEPROM is disabled, its memory space is externally available in the expanded mode. Read the name EEON as *EE on*.

The CONFIG register is an EEPROM register. It is programmed as the EEPROM memory is programmed. Since the CONFIG register is a nonvolatile register, it determines the configuration of the microcomputer hardware when the 68HC11 is powered-up.

7.3 HARDWARE RESET

The reset procedure determines the way much of the hardware in the 68HC11 operates. Usually the RESET pin is used when the power is turned on to the computer, so it affects all the future operation of the computer. For example, the MODA and MODB pins are read during reset to determine whether the 68HC11 operates in expanded mode or single-chip mode.

Reset Operation

The block diagrams in Figures 7-1 and 7-2 show the RESET pin. The RESET signal forces a hardware initialization of all the hardware devices in the microcomputer—including the 68HC11. Most, but not all, of the control bits in the internal 68HC11 registers are forced to 0 by RESET. A low signal voltage on the RESET pin resets the hardware.

Reset sources

Many hardware devices can drive the RESET pin low. Some of these are inside the 68HC11 IC and others are outside it. Figure 7-1 shows the RESET pin as bidirectional to indicate that devices inside or outside the 68HC11 can cause the reset. Some common reasons for reset are turning on the computer or detecting a hardware error.

Software effects

Normally, the RESET pin is used at program start time to ensure that the electronic circuits in the computer start at a known condition. First, the reset initializes the electronics in the microprocessor and the rest of the microcomputer. Then the microprocessor gets an address from the reset vector and puts it in the program counter. The computer starts running at this address. The reset vector for all Motorola 8-bit microprocessors is at addresses FFFE and FFFF.

Motorola Trainer

The reset button on the trainer board causes a hardware reset. The trainer normally vectors to the monitor program on a reset. However, if you move the jumper J4 from pins 1 and 2 to pins 2 and 3, a reset can send control to your program. Your program must now start at location B600—the first location in the EEPROM. You may put a JMP instruction there to send control to a program in the RAM. Move the jumper back to the original position to use the monitor program again.

Reset is not an interrupt. The reset vector is not an interrupt vector. The reset vector only determines the starting address of the program. If something forces a reset while a program is running, the computer stops running that program and begins again at the address specified in the reset vector. The status of the microprocessor is not saved in the stack, so there is nothing to restore.

Power-on reset

The DC power supply for the 68HC11 requires a little time to stabilize the voltage after it is turned on. A circuit outside the 68HC11 keeps RESET low while the voltage stabilizes. After the voltage is stable, the circuit changes the level on the RESET pin to high. The microcomputer responds by loading the program counter with the address stored at the reset vector and starts running.

The 68HC11 also has an internal power-on timer. The internal circuit senses when the supply voltage V_{DD} changes from low to high. The power-on circuit forces an internal reset for the next 4064_{10} E-clock cycles, and then responds to the RESET pin. In typical applications, this causes a delay of about two milliseconds even if the power supply stabilizes faster. Therefore, the 68HC11 will always require a small time after power-on before it starts operating.

Hardware Programmable Options

The operating mode of the 68HC11, either single-chip mode or expanded mode, is selected during a hardware reset. When the RESET pin is low, the MODA and MODB pins select one of four modes. Two of these are test modes—not normal operating modes.

Table 7-1 lists the modes and the pin values. The pins use high-asserted signals. For example, if both MODA and MODB are connected to V_{DD} with pull-up resistors, a reset puts the 68HC11 into the expanded mode.

After reset, software cannot change the mode of the 68HC11. If software could change the operating mode, an errant program could accidentally change the mode. This could lead to dangerous operation.

TABLE 7-1   MODE SELECTION

MODB Pin	MODA Pin	Mode Selected
1	0	Single-chip
1	1	Expanded
0	1	Special test
0	0	Special bootstrap

Timed-Write-Once Programmable Options

Many hardware options in the 68HC11 chip are programmable. Numbers in control registers determine the configuration of the programmable hardware. Reset initially configures the programmable hardware. Following reset, the program usually changes the configuration once in the initialization. Only rarely does a program change the configuration many times as the program runs.

Erroneous changes to certain programmable hardware could cause unsafe operation. To avoid errors, some 68HC11 programming bits only respond to one write after a reset. Thereafter, these special bits are read-only bits; further writes cannot change them. Call these special control bits *timed-write-once* bits.

Besides the write-once feature, the timed-write-once bits also will not change after 64_{10} E-clock cycles after the RESET pin goes high. Therefore, if the reset condition of the timed-write-once bits is incorrect, the program must initialize them immediately after the RESET. Thereafter, the program cannot change them.

The timed-write-once bits add a measure of safety to the computer. They reduce the chance of an incorrect hardware configuration. The effects of hardware failures that cause errant programs are reduced if the hardware configuration cannot change.

7.4   INTERRUPT SYSTEM

Chapter 6 introduced the operation of the interrupt system. Chapter 7 adds many more details. The interrupt system in the 68HC11 supports several types of interrupts from many input/output devices. The 68HC11 also has a hardware reset function that is similar to an interrupt. Hardware signals trigger both interrupts and resets. The hardware signals may originate both within and outside the chip. Before examining the many input/output devices in the 68HC11, let's look at the details of the interrupt system.

Most of the interrupts in the 68HC11 have separate interrupt vectors that send control to separate interrupt service routines. The interrupt vectors contain the addresses of the interrupt service routines for each device.

The following discussion mentions only the interrupt vectors not associated with particular input/output devices. Later sections devoted to specific I/O devices discuss the interrupts for those devices.

Refer to Table 7-2. It lists the many interrupt vectors in the 68HC11. The interrupts from the various I/O devices all operate similarly. Looking at the table gives an overview of the details to follow.

IRQ Interrupt

The IRQ interrupt is named from the phrase "interrupt request." The IRQ interrupt is the interrupt discussed in Chapter 6. The example there uses the STAF flag inside the 68HC11 to cause interrupts. However, the IRQ line also connects to a pin so external devices can cause interrupts. Only the STAF flag connects to the IRQ line inside the 68HC11 chip.

TABLE 7-2   INTERRUPT VECTOR ADDRESSES AND MASK BITS

Vector Address	Interrupt Device	Condition Code Mask Bit	Local Device Mask Bit
FFC0, C1 through FFD4, FFD5	Reserved	None	None
FFD6, FFD7	SCI Receive Data Register Full	I	RIE
	SCI Receiver Overrun	I	RIE
	SCI Idle Line Detect	I	ILIE
	SCI Transmit Data Register Empty	I	TIE
	SCI Transmit Complete	I	TCIE
FFD8, FFD9	SPI Serial Transfer Complete	I	SPIE
FFDA, FFDB	Pulse Accumulator Input Edge	I	PAII
FFDC, FFDD	Pulse Accumulator Overflow	I	PAOVI
FFDE, FFDF	Timer Overflow	I	TOI
FFE0, FFE1	Timer Output Compare 5	I	OC5I
FFE2, FFE3	Timer Output Compare 4	I	OC4I
FFE4, FFE5	Timer Output Compare 3	I	OC3I
FFE6, FFE7	Timer Output Compare 2	I	OC2I
FFE8, FFE9	Timer Output Compare 1	I	OC1I
FFEA, FFEB	Timer Input Capture 3	I	IC3I
FFEC, FFED	Timer Input Capture 2	I	IC2I
FFEE, FFEF	Timer Input Capture 1	I	IC1I
FFF0, FFF1	Real Time Interrupt	I	RTII
FFF2, FFF3	IRQ (External Pin or Parallel I/O)	I	None
	IRQ Parallel I/O	I	STAI
FFF4, FFF5	XIRQ Pin	X	None
FFF6, FFF7	SWI	None	None
FFF8, FFF9	Illegal Opcode Trap	None	None
FFFA, FFFB	COP Timeout	None	NOCOP
FFFC, FFFD	Clock Monitor Timeout	None	CME
FFFE, FFFF	RESET	None	None

The IRQ interrupt is the principal external interrupt line in the 68HC11. It has a single interrupt vector to send control to a single interrupt service routine. The IRQ interrupt in the 68HC11 is nearly the same as the IRQ interrupt in other Motorola 8-bit microprocessors.

Multiple IRQ interrupt devices

More than one external device may have a flag connected to the IRQ pin. The flags must connect with open-collector or open-drain hardware so the various flags are wire-ORed. This connection allows any device connected to the IRQ pin to pull the voltage to the low level without interference from the others.

The multiple devices that control the IRQ line share the IRQ interrupt vector. All the devices send control to the same interrupt service routine. The program determines which device interrupted by examining each flag to find which is set.

Figure 7-6 shows the flowchart for an interrupt service routine that polls two flags to determine which caused the interrupt. The string of decisions is called a *polling chain*.

The overhead to poll the flags is much smaller than the overhead of the polling I/O technique. With interrupt, the polling occurs only once each time a device sets a flag. In the polling technique, the polling must happen continually so the computer can respond quickly when a flag gets set.

IRQ example

The example using interrupt is an expansion of the interrupt example in Chapter 6. There, the computer reads a thumbwheel switch and displays the number when a push button is pushed. In the following example, a second device also can interrupt, so the interrupt service routine follows the flowchart in Figure 7-6.

Operation. A push button switch sends a ready signal to the STAF flag to cause an interrupt. In responding to the IRQ interrupt request, the program reads a number from a

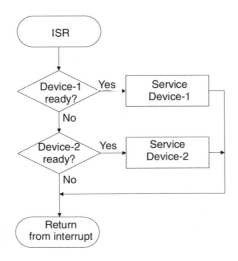

Figure 7-6 Flowchart of ISR for multiple interrupting devices.

thumbwheel switch and controls a display. In addition, an external free-running oscillator causes periodic interrupts. At each oscillator interrupt, the program reverses the state of a light to make a flasher. Both the display control and the light flasher operate concurrently.

Hardware.   Figure 7-7 illustrates the input/output hardware. The push button switch connects to the STRA pin to control the STAF flag. The thumbwheel switch connects to PORTC bits 4 through 7. The display connects to PORTB bits 4 through 7. PORTB is an output only port. This part of the hardware is similar to the connections in Chapter 6; however, the display unit now connects to PORTB instead of PORTC.

In addition, an external flag is made from a D flip flop. Another flag inside the 68HC11 could be used, but this example uses an external flag. The D lead of the flip flop is connected to the high level. A transition of the flip flop clock lead by the oscillator sets the flag. Bit 0 of PORTB makes a clear signal for the flag. Driving bit 0 low clears the flag. The output of the flag drives the IRQ line through an open drain driver. The IRQ pin must have an external pull-up resistor as shown. The external flag and the internal STAF flag are therefore wire-ORed on the IRQ line. That is, if either flag is set, it will pull the IRQ line to the low level.

Program operation.   Figure 7-8 shows the program for the IRQ example. Here is a description of it.

- *Line 43,*   Loading the program into memory initializes the IRQ interrupt vector.

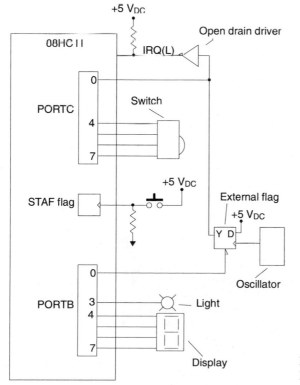

Figure 7-7   Hardware for multiple IRQ interrupt example.

```
 1                                        ********************************************************
 2                                        ** COPY THUMBWHEEL SWITCH TO DISPLAY WHEN
 3                                        ** PUSHBUTTON IS PUSHED AND FLASH A LIGHT
 4                                        *
 5                                        * USE INTERRUPT TECHNIQUE FOR TIMING
 6                                        *
 7                                        * FOUR BIT THUMBWHEEL SWITCH WIRED TO
 8                                        * ..BITS 4-7 OF PORT C
 9                                        *
10                                        * FOUR BIT DISPLAY WIRED TO BITS 4-7 OF PORT B
11                                        *
12                                        * PUSHBUTTON SWITCH WIRED TO STRA SO
13                                        * ..LOW TO HIGH ON PUSH
14                                        *
15                                        * EXTERNAL FLAG WITH OSCILLATOR CONNECTED TO IRQ
16                                        *
17                                        * LIGHT WIRED TO BIT 3 OF PORT B
18                                        *
19                                        * FLAG DIRECT CLEAR WIRED TO BIT 0 OF PORT B
20                                        *
21                                        ********************************************************
22                                        *
23                                        ********************************************************
24                                        ** SYMBOL DEFINITIONS
25                                        ********************************************************
26                                        * 68HC11 REGISTERS
27            1000                        REG      EQU   $1000   BASE ADDRESS OF REGISTERS
28            1002                        PIOC     EQU   $1002   PARALLEL I/O CONTROL REGISTER
29            1003                        PORTC    EQU   $1003   I/O PORT C REGISTER
30            1004                        PORTB    EQU   $1004   OUTPUT PORT B REGISTER
31            1005                        PORTCL   EQU   $1005   PORT C LATCH REGISTER
32            1007                        DDRC     EQU   $1007   DATA DIRECTION REGISTER C
33            00F1                        IOPAT    EQU   $F1     I/O PATTERN, 0=IN 1=OUT
34                                        * MASKS
35            0001                        BIT0     EQU   %00000001
36            0008                        BIT3     EQU   %00001000
37            0080                        BIT7     EQU   %10000000
38                                        *
39                                        ********************************************************
40                                        ** DATA SECTION
41                                        ********************************************************
42     FFF2                                        ORG   $FFF2
43     FFF2   C118                                 FDB   IRQISR   IRQ INTERRUPT VECTOR
44                                        *
45                                        ********************************************************
46                                        ** MAIN PROGRAM
47                                        ********************************************************
48     C100                                        ORG   $C100
49                                        *----------------------------------------------------
50                                        * INITIALIZATION
51                                        *----------------------------------------------------
52                                        * INITIALIZE STACK
53     C100   8E CF FF                              LDS   #$CFFF
54                                        * INITIALIZE PORT B
55     C103   86 01                                LDAA  #BIT0    DON'T CLEAR EXTERNAL FLAG, AND
56     C105   B7 10 04                              STAA  PORTB    ..ZEROS FOR LIGHT AND DISPLAY
57                                        * INITIALIZE PORT C
58                                        *    INITIALIZE OUTPUTS TO ZEROS
59     C108   7F 10 03                              CLR   PORTC    0=LOW
60                                        *   SET UP PORTC INS AND OUTS
61     C10B   86 F1                                LDAA  #IOPAT
62     C10D   B7 10 07                              STAA  DDRC     0=IN, 1=OUT
```

Figure 7-8   IRQ Interrupt program.

```
 63                      * SET UP PIOC
 64    C110   86 42             LDAA   #$42       ENABLE STAF INTERRUPT
 65    C112   B7 10 02          STAA   PIOC       ..LOW TO HIGH ON STRA
 66                      * TURN ON INTERRUPT SYSTEM
 67    C115   0E                CLI
 68                      *------------------------------------------------------
 69                      * WAIT FOR INTERRUPTS
 70                      *------------------------------------------------------
 71    C116   20 FE      HERE    BRA    HERE      DO NOTHING!
 72                      *
 73                      ********************************************************
 74                      ** INTERRUPT SERVICE ROUTINE
 75                      ********************************************************
 76                      *------------------------------------------------------
 77                      * INTERRUPT POLLING CHAIN
 78                      *------------------------------------------------------
 79                      * INTERRUPT FROM PUSH BUTTON?
 80    C118   CE 10 00   IRQISR  LDX    #REG
 81    C11B   1E 02 80 06        BRSET  PIOC-REG,X,BIT7,COPY     BRANCH ON YES
 82                      * INTERRUPT FROM OSCILLATOR?
 83    C11F   1E 03 01 12        BRSET  PORTC-REG,X,BIT0,FLASH   BRANCH ON YES
 84                      * ILLEGAL INTERRUPT
 85    C123   20 1E             BRA     RTIRQ     IGNORE ILLEGAL INTERRUPT
 86                      *------------------------------------------------------
 87                      * COPY THUMBWHEEL SWITCH TO DISPLAY
 88                      *------------------------------------------------------
 89                      * READ THUMBWHEEL SWITCH AND CLEAR I/O FLAG
 90    C125   B6 10 05   COPY    LDAA   PORTCL    CLEAR STAF FLAG, INPUT SSSS
 91                      * FORM OUTPUT VALUE
 92    C128   84 F0             ANDA    #$F0      KEEP SWITCH BITS
 93    C12A   F6 10 04          LDAB    PORTB     GET LAST OUTPUT TO PORT B
 94    C12D   C4 0F             ANDB    #$0F      REMOVE DISPLAY BITS
 95    C12F   1B                ABA               MERGE OUTPUT BITS
 96                      * CONTROL DISPLAY
 97    C130   B7 10 04          STAA    PORTB     OUTPUT TO PORT B
 98                      * RETURN TO MAIN PROGRAM
 99    C133   20 0E             BRA     RTIRQ
100                      *------------------------------------------------------
101                      * FLASH LIGHT
102                      *------------------------------------------------------
103                      * CLEAR OSCILLATOR FLAG
104    C135   1D 04 01   FLASH   BCLR   PORTB-REG,X,BIT0         DRIVE PIN LOW
105    C138   1C 04 01          BSET    PORTB-REG,X,BIT0         DRIVE PIN HIGH
106                      * TOGGLE LIGHT BIT
107    C13B   B6 10 04          LDAA    PORTB
108    C13E   88 08             EORA    #BIT3
109    C140   B7 10 04          STAA    PORTB
110                      * RETURN TO MAIN PROGRAM
111    C143   3B         RTIRQ   RTI
112    C144                      END
```

Figure 7-8 Continued.

- *Lines 53 through 67.*   The program initializes the computer hardware and enables the interrupt system.

- *Line 71.*   The main program loop does nothing but wait for interrupts.

- *Lines 80 and 81.*   Using indexed addressing, the **BRSET** instruction tests the STAF flag. If the flag is set because the push button was pushed, control is sent to line 90.

Motorola Trainer

The example in Figures 7-7 and 7-8 can be run on the trainer. The hardware arrangement is slightly different from the arrangement used in Chapter 6. However, only small changes are necessary. The changes make it possible to use only the internal I/O ports in the 68HC11. An external pull-up resistor on the IRQ pin is not needed, because one is on the trainer board. The program needs only the interrupt vector changed. Put a JMP to C118 instruction at address 00EE to send control to the interrupt service routine.

- *Line 83.*   The external flag is connected to bit 0 of PORTC so the flag can be tested. The BRSET instruction tests the flag. If the flag is set because the oscillator time has expired, control is sent to line 104.

- *Line 85.*   If neither flag was set, an erroneous interrupt was detected. The program returns to the main program ignoring the error.

- *Line 90.*   Reading the PORTCL latch register clears the STAF flag. Remember that both the PIOC and PORTCL registers must be read to clear the STAF flag. However, the BRSET instruction on line 81 already read PIOC. Reading PORTCL also inputs the number from the thumbwheel switch.

- *Lines 92 through 95.*   The bits read from PORTC are masked so only bits 4 through 7, the data from the thumbwheel switch, are retained. The bits last output to PORTB are read and the display bits are masked. The remaining bits from the two ports are merged.

- *Lines 97 and 99.*   The new output bits are stored in PORTB to update the display. Bits 0 through 3 remain the same. Then control returns to the main program.

- *Lines 104 and 105.*   The direct clear lead of the external flag flip flop is first driven low and then driven high. This clears the flip flop and then allows it to respond to the normal clock lead.

- *Lines 107 through 111.*   Toggle bit 3 of PORTB to reverse the state of the flashing light. Control then returns to the main program.

You should observe that the interrupt system is disabled for the entire time that the ISR runs. Therefore, if both input/output devices interrupt at the same time, the display is updated first and then the oscillator interrupts to control the light.

Hardware failures

Let's look at the effects of a hardware failure on the program in Figure 7-8. Flags and input/output ports connect to external devices. Therefore, they are susceptible to damage. The connections may be made with lengthy cables and to devices with different power supply voltages. An improper voltage on the cable could damage some hardware. The following describes the effects of some failures:

- *STAF flag fails set.*   When the flag fails, the IRQ wire goes low and requests an interrupt so control goes to the interrupt service routine. The ISR tries to clear the flag; however, the flag does not clear, because it failed and the IRQ wire will remain low. The ISR does not enable the interrupt system with a CLI instruction, so the ISR cannot be interrupted and will continue running. The ISR copies the thumbwheel switch to the display and continues running until it executes the RTI instruction.

  The RTI instruction restores the main program registers and enables the interrupt system. Remember, the IRQ line is still low because the failed flag is still set. As the microprocessor starts to fetch an instruction from the main program, the interrupt system causes another interrupt. Control goes to the ISR again and the same sequence repeats. The result is an infinite loop because control always returns to the ISR immediately after the RTI instruction.

  The effects of this failure can now be determined. The main program will never run again—not even a single instruction. On the other hand, the ISR runs repeatedly as fast as the computer can go.

  The effect of the ISR quickly and repeatedly servicing an I/O device depends on the kind of device it is. In the example, the computer continually reads the thumbwheel switch and updates the display without anyone pushing the push button. If someone changes the thumbwheel to a new position, the display updates as the input number changes.

  Next consider the effect on the flashing light. When the oscillator sets the second flag, the flag has no effect on the IRQ line because it is already low. Furthermore, the polling chain does not detect that the second flag is set, so the light stops flashing and it remains at the state it was in when the STAF flag failed.

  Such behavior from a computer can be baffling. One hardware device continues working and another stops working. It may not seem possible that a computer could do such strange things.

- *The external flag fails set.*   If the external flag is always set, the IRQ line will always be low. The oscillator has no effect on the IRQ line. The ISR is in an infinite loop servicing the flashing light repeatedly. The light flashes as fast as the ISR can toggle the output bit. A person will see only a dim light.

  The STAF flag continues to work normally and the polling chain responds to it. So the display is updated only when the push button is pushed. The main program never runs again.

- *The STAF flag fails clear.*   If the STAF flag fails clear, the push button can never cause an interrupt. The computer ignores the thumbwheel switch and the display. If the thumbwheel switch is changed, the display remains the same.

The polling chain detects the external flag, so the oscillator continues to interrupt and the light flashes normally. The main program runs normally.

- *The external flag fails clear.*   If the external flag stays clear, the oscillator can never cause an interrupt. The ISR will completely ignore the light, so the light stays in the state it was when the flag failed.

The polling chain detects the STAF flag, so the thumbwheel switch and display work normally. The main program continues to operate normally.

- *Both flags fail set.*   If both flags fail set, the IRQ line is always low and the main program never runs again. The polling chain tests the STAF flag first, so it sends control to the thumbwheel switch and display routine. When the ISR finishes updating the display, the ISR returns control to the main program. Therefore, the interrupt service routine does not test the external flag and the computer ignores the oscillator.

Immediately after the RTI instruction, another interrupt occurs and the ISR sends control to the thumbwheel switch and display routine again. So, as when the STAF failed alone, the display is updated continually and the light does not flash.

- *The IRQ wire is grounded.*   The IRQ wire is always low, so the main program will never run, because interrupts will occur continually. However, the polling chain will detect when the flags set, so the display and flashing light work normally.

- *Noise pulse on IRQ wire.*   If electrical noise causes a very short duration low-going pulse on the IRQ wire, it may trigger an interrupt. If none of the flags are set, the polling chain in this example simply returns control to the main program. The computer ignores the false interrupt signal. If a flag is set at the time of the pulse, the polling chain will respond normally to the flag. The main program is not affected.

This failure could occur in a computer controlling something that is very dangerous. If the polling chain does not detect a set flag, the ISR should then respond to the failure instead of returning control to the main program. For example, the program may somehow force a hardware reset. Alternately, it may signal a warning to a person.

Many other failures are possible. The consequences depend both on the design of the hardware and the software. These examples should help you to better understand the interrupt system.

Level or edge triggering for IRQ

The IRQ interrupt pin can be programmed to interrupt at either the low level or on a high-to-low transition. Figure 7-9 shows the OPTION control register. The IRQE bit, bit 5 of the OPTION register, determines which condition triggers the interrupt. When IRQE is 0, the IRQ pin is programmed for low-level assertion. Normally, the IRQ pin is used in a wired-OR circuit. When IRQE is 1, the pin is programmed for the high-to-low transition. When the

Motorola Trainer

The trainer programs the IRQ interrupt for level-sensitive operation. A pull-up resistor on the trainer board prevents accidental interrupts if external hardware is not connected.

68HC11 is reset, IRQE is set to 0, so IRQ is level-sensitive if the program does not change it. The IRQE bit is a timed-write-once bit.

The level-sensitive interrupt is the most commonly used. It is also the only choice in other Motorola 8-bit microprocessors. Therefore, this book uses the level-sensitive interrupt for all example programs.

Software Interrupt

An instruction can cause an interrupt. The SWI or *software interrupt* instruction triggers an interrupt. The software interrupt acts like an IRQ interrupt, except it is triggered by an instruction and there is a separate interrupt vector. Furthermore, the software interrupt cannot be disabled; if the instruction is fetched, the interrupt occurs. However, the SWI instruction disables the interrupt system with the I bit as other interrupts do. When the interrupt service routine returns control to the main program, it continues at the next instruction after SWI.

The SWI instruction may be used when the program detects a fatal error. Instead of branching to an error routine, it may be necessary to reset the computer quickly for safety. The software interrupt can vector to a routine that forces a hardware reset through additional hardware. A later section shows an example of this use along with the COP timer.

XIRQ Interrupt

The 68HC11 has an external nonmaskable interrupt; that is, an interrupt that cannot be disabled. The I bit does not disable the XIRQ interrupt. Usually the application requiring a nonmaskable interrupt involves safety.

An application for XIRQ

The most common application of the XIRQ interrupt requires an interrupt when "the world is coming to an end!" That is, if it makes no difference what else is happening, it is best to interrupt from it and respond to the nonmaskable interrupt.

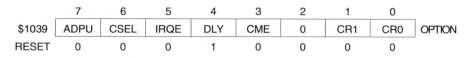

	7	6	5	4	3	2	1	0	
$1039	ADPU	CSEL	IRQE	DLY	CME	0	CR1	CR0	OPTION
RESET	0	0	0	1	0	0	0	0	

Figure 7-9 Configuration options register.

Motorola Trainer

Programs similar to the monitor program in the trainer are most likely to use the SWI instruction. For example, in this book, the instruction called *STOP* that stops programs is the SWI instruction. The SWI stops the user's program in the trainer by saving the registers in the stack and then sending control to the monitor program. The monitor program then knows the status of the user's program because it is in the stack.

Furthermore, the SWI transfers control to the monitor program with a single-byte instruction that cannot be stopped. Also, the SWI disables the interrupt system so external interrupts cannot affect the monitor program without its control.

The classic example is a microcomputer powered from the power line. When the power fails, it makes no difference what the computer is doing. Soon, the computer will stop running because the power is off—an interrupt can't hurt anything. Generally, the power supply for a microcomputer will continue to work for a few milliseconds after a power failure. The microcomputer can use this time to save important information in a nonvolatile memory. A circuit in the power supply must detect the power failure and trigger the nonmaskable interrupt.

XIRQ interrupt system operation

The XIRQ interrupt line connects only to a pin. So only input/output devices external to the 68HC11 can cause nonmaskable interrupts. An XIRQ signal causes an interrupt even if another interrupt service routine is executing. The interrupt vector for XIRQ is at addresses FFF4 and FFF5.

The X bit. The XIRQ interrupt has an interrupt-enable bit, called X, in the condition code register. The X bit is very different from the I bit because XIRQ is nonmaskable.

The 68HC11 disables the XIRQ interrupt at reset by forcing the X bit to 1. The program, at the correct point in the initialization, puts 0 in the X bit to enable the XIRQ interrupt. However, the X bit is a *sticky bit* that the program cannot change back to 1. Only an interrupt signal at the XIRQ pin or a hardware reset can set X to 1; only hardware can set X to 1. Therefore, once the nonmaskable interrupt is enabled, it remains enabled and is nonmaskable for the rest of the time the program runs.

The TAP instruction. Only the TAP and RTI instructions can make the X bit 0. The TAP enables XIRQ interrupts by transferring a number from the A accumulator to the condition code register. The TAP instruction usually enables both the XIRQ interrupt and interrupts under control of the I bit.

The TAP instruction cannot change X to 1. Look at the TAP instruction in the instruction set table in Appendix H. The effect on the X bit is shown with a downward arrow. This symbol means that X can be changed only from 1 to 0.

Motorola Trainer

The XIRQ interrupt vectors to address 00D9 in the trainer. An external pull-up resistor is necessary on the XIRQ pin because the trainer board does not provide one.

Be careful because the TAP instruction controls the other condition code bits while it zeros X and I. Generally, use the TAP instruction only in the initialization part of an interrupt-driven program. Don't use it in an interrupt service routine.

XIRQ interrupt operation.   When an XIRQ interrupt occurs, the XIRQ interrupt system hardware sets both the X bit and the I bit to 1 disabling further XIRQ and IRQ interrupts. The RTI instruction returns both the X bit and the I bit to their previous states. So, return from the interrupt service routine enables the XIRQ again. In most ways, the XIRQ interrupt is identical to the IRQ interrupt.

XIRQ interrupt signal.   The XIRQ pin on the 68HC11 is a level-sensitive pin, so connect hardware to the XIRQ pin as you would to the IRQ pin. The XIRQ pin is not programmable; it is only level-sensitive. If both the IRQ and XIRQ pins request interrupts simultaneously, the 68HC11 responds to the XIRQ interrupt request. That is, XIRQ has priority over IRQ. The XIRQ also can interrupt an IRQ interrupt service routine that is in progress.

Other microprocessors.   Some other Motorola 8-bit microprocessors have a similar interrupt named NMI for *nonmaskable interrupt*. The NMI interrupt in some processors can truly never be disabled, and therefore must use a transition-sensitive signal. However, if an interrupt occurs soon after a program starts and before the initialization is completed, the program could crash. The nonmaskable interrupt in the 68HC11 is more sophisticated.

Illegal Instruction Interrupt

An illegal instruction op code is a number that does not represent an instruction implemented in the microprocessor. Illegal instruction codes represent either programming errors or hardware failures. The 68HC11 microprocessor detects if an illegal instruction code is fetched.

When the 68HC11 detects an illegal instruction code, it generates an internal interrupt. The microprocessor vectors through addresses FFF8 and FFF9 to an interrupt service routine. Usually the illegal instruction interrupt service routine somehow forces a reset on the computer.

The illegal instruction interrupt is a nonmaskable interrupt that has priority over the IRQ interrupt because it sets the I bit to 1. The illegal instruction interrupt does not set the X bit, but if the XIRQ interrupt service routine fetches an illegal instruction, it will be interrupted. An illegal instruction interrupt is more important than the XIRQ because the microprocessor is not executing valid instructions.

If the illegal instruction results from a memory failure, the illegal instruction interrupt service routine also may have illegal instructions. This may cause an infinite loop of illegal

---

Motorola Trainer

The illegal instruction interrupt vectors to address 00F7 in the trainer. You can put a JMP instruction there that sends control to your own interrupt service routine. If you don't, the monitor program sets the vector to direct control to a STOP instruction that stops the trainer from operating. You must press the reset button to continue using the trainer. It can be confusing that the trainer completely stops working due to an illegal instruction in a program.

---

instruction interrupts. Other safety measures should detect this problem, but the stack probably will overflow and may destroy important data in RAM. Therefore, the illegal instruction interrupt may reset the stack pointer to avoid the stack overrun. Of course, the rest of the program must then account for this.

Most of the possible 2-byte op codes and a few of the possible 1-byte op codes are not valid instructions. Therefore, there is a good chance the microprocessor can detect failures. For example, if a memory chip fails, it's likely an incorrect instruction will be fetched. The computer can respond to this failure if the hardware detects the incorrect instruction.

Many other Motorola 8-bit microprocessors use only single-byte op codes. Most of their possible op code numbers are valid, so there is little value in detecting an illegal instruction code. Those processors do not have illegal instruction detection. When they fetch and execute an illegal code, the operation of the microprocessor is unpredictable.

Interrupt Priority

If two or more devices all request an interrupt simultaneously, the interrupt system hardware must choose one to respond to first. The 68HC11 uses a strict priority system—the device with the highest priority is serviced first. In the 68HC11, the device with an interrupt vector at the highest address is also at the highest priority. When the interrupt service routine returns to the main program, the device with the highest priority at that time is serviced next.

Interrupt priority is important only when two or more devices interrupt at the same time. In most applications, it is of little importance. However, it can be important when the program must know which of two related devices is serviced first.

7.5 PARALLEL I/O PORTS

The block diagrams in Figures 7-1 and 7-2 show ports A through E and two associated pins that are not part of a port. The ports have different functions depending on the operating mode of the 68HC11.

The ports are collections of signal wires or pins that the 68HC11 uses to communicate with devices outside the chip. The port names are arbitrary because each port has several functions.

Software can program the 68HC11 hardware to connect ports A, D, and E to input/output devices, such as an analog-to-digital converter, inside the 68HC11. People often associate the ports with those hardware devices, though the ports also do other functions. Later sections of this book discuss the special associations of the ports with particular I/O devices.

Let's begin by describing the parallel input/output capability of the ports. All the I/O port pins have either digital input or digital output capability. However, the parallel I/O capability is different for the single-chip mode and the expanded mode. For example, the ports B and C used in examples in this book have an additional function.

Hardware Initialization

A hardware reset initializes the input/output hardware in the 68HC11. The reset also puts the chip into the correct operating mode—either single-chip mode or expanded mode.

A hardware reset disables all the input/output devices inside the 68HC11. The effect is to program all available I/O ports as parallel I/O ports. The reset clears all the input and output registers. Also, reset clears the data direction register bits making any programmable port bits inputs. All data direction register bits make an input when they are 0 and make an output when they are 1.

Parallel I/O

Most of the parallel input/output pins function the same in both the single-chip mode and the expanded mode. Table 7-3 lists the port pins and their parallel input/output functions for both modes. It also lists the data direction register control bits for the programmable I/O pins.

The functions of the various bits of a port may seem disorganized. For example, port A has input only, output only, and programmable I/O pins. The variety results because these pins can connect to an internal I/O device that requires this configuration of input and outputs. Only ports B and C have the same functions regardless of internal programming.

Table 7-3 shows the reset condition of the ports before any software control of them. The table does not show that the electrical characteristics of the various pins differ somewhat. Some ports can be programmed for different electrical characteristics. Consult a Motorola manual for details of the electronics.

Single-chip mode parallel I/O

When a reset puts the 68HC11 into the single-chip mode, ports B and C become parallel I/O ports. In particular, port B is an output only port so it does not have a data direction register. Port C is a programmable input/output port with a data direction register named DDRC.

There are two pins associated with the ports that are not part of any port. In single-chip mode, these pins are named STRA and STRB. The pin STRA is the *strobe A* or clock or ready

TABLE 7-3   PARALLEL INPUT/OUTPUT PIN FUNCTIONS

Port	Single-chip Mode			Expanded Mode		
Bit Name	Pin Name	Pin Function	DDR Bit	Pin Name	Pin Function	DDR Bit
A-0	PA0	In only		PA0	In only	
A-1	PA1	In only		PA1	In only	
A-2	PA2	In only		PA2	In only	
A-3	PA3	Out only		PA3	Out only	
A-4	PA4	Out only		PA4	Out only	
A-5	PA5	Out only		PA5	Out only	
A-6	PA6	Out only		PA6	Out only	
A-7	PA7	In/Out	DDRA7	PA7	In/Out	DDRA7
B-0	PB0	Out only		A8	Address bus	
B-1	PB1	Out only		A9	Address bus	
B-2	PB2	Out only		A10	Address bus	
B-3	PB3	Out only		A11	Address bus	
B-4	PB4	Out only		A12	Address bus	
B-5	PB5	Out only		A13	Address bus	
B-6	PB6	Out only		A14	Address bus	
B-7	PB7	Out only		A15	Address bus	
C-0	PC0	In/Out	DDRC0	A0/D0	Address/Data bus	
C-1	PC1	In/Out	DDRC1	A1/D1	Address/Data bus	
C-2	PC2	In/Out	DDRC2	A2/D2	Address/Data bus	
C-3	PC3	In/Out	DDRC3	A3/D3	Address/Data bus	
C-4	PC4	In/Out	DDRC4	A4/D4	Address/Data bus	
C-5	PC5	In/Out	DDRC5	A5/D5	Address/Data bus	
C-6	PC6	In/Out	DDRC6	A6/D6	Address/Data bus	
C-7	PC7	In/Out	DDRC7	A7/D7	Address/Data bus	
D-0	PD0	In/Out	DDRD0	PD0	In/Out	DDRD0
D-1	PD1	In/Out	DDRD1	PD1	In/Out	DDRD1
D-2	PD2	In/Out	DDRD2	PD2	In/Out	DDRD2
D-3	PD3	In/Out	DDRD3	PD3	In/Out	DDRD3
D-4	PD4	In/Out	DDRD4	PD4	In/Out	DDRD4
D-5	PD5	In/Out	DDRD5	PD5	In/Out	DDRD5
None	STRA	Strobe A		AS	Address strobe	
None	STRB	Strobe B		R/W	Read/Write	
E-0	PE0	In only		PE0	In only	
E-1	PE1	In only		PE1	In only	
E-2	PE2	In only		PE2	In only	
E-3	PE3	In only		PE3	In only	
E-4	PE4	In only		PE4	In only	
E-5	PE5	In only		PE5	In only	
E-6	PE6	In only		PE6	In only	
E-7	PE7	In only		PE7	In only	

signal for the STAF flag. Both STRA and STRB, strobe B, have additional programmable functions.

Expanded mode parallel I/O

When a reset puts the 68HC11 into expanded mode, ports B and C become address and data bus pins. Therefore, the port B and port C input/output functions are lost. The STRA signal for the STAF flag is also lost. Table 7-3 lists the pin functions for expanded mode.

Port C is multiplexed with both address and data bus signals, so an external latch IC is necessary. All the address, data, and control bus signals are available when the port B, port C, AS, and R/W pins are used.

7.6 INTERNAL FLAGS

Most I/O devices inside the 68HC11 have flags. An I/O device sets a flag to indicate completion of an operation; the flag usually causes an interrupt. The program, in responding to the flag, must clear the flag. However, not all the flags in the 68HC11 clear the same way.

The STAF Flag

The STAF flag discussed earlier is cleared in an indirect way. In particular, instructions must read two registers to clear the STAF flag that is in a third register. A few other flags are cleared in a similar indirect way, but most of the other flags in the 68HC11 are cleared a different and direct way.

Direct-Clearing Flags

All the direct-clearing flags in the 68HC11 are cleared when an instruction writes a 1 into the flag bit! It may seem strange to write a 1 to something that is in the 1-state to make it go to the 0-state, but that is how the hardware works. The reason is that several flags are grouped together in a single register. Writing 0s into flag bits does nothing. So only those bits containing 1s in the number written clear a flag.

BSET instruction problems

It may seem that a BSET instruction is the perfect instruction to clear one of these direct-clearing flags, but it won't clear the flags correctly! Here is an example of the problem. Suppose a memory register is all flags with bit 7 and bit 5 now set. If a BSET instruction is to clear the bit 7 bit only, the mask in the instruction is 80. The BSET instruction ORs the mask to the memory register and writes the result back to the memory register. So when it reads memory, it gets A0 because two flags are set. Then it ORs 80 and gets A0, which it writes back to memory. When it does, it clears both flags! Of course, this is incorrect. The BSET instruction clears all flags that are set, not just the one selected.

BCLR for clearing flags

The BCLR instruction can correctly clear flags; however, the complement of the normal mask is used. The BCLR instruction ANDs the complement of the mask to the memory register, and writes the result back to the memory register. To clear the flag at bit 7 in a flags register, use a mask of 7F. If the flags at bit 7 and at bit 5 are set, the AND instruction reads A0 from the flags register, ANDs the complement of 7F getting 80, and writes the 80 back to the flags register. Writing the 1 at bit 7 clears the flag at bit 7 correctly, and the 0 at bit 5 does not affect the bit 5 flag. Therefore, the BCLR instruction with a complemented mask will correctly clear flags. Be careful to use the BCLR instruction, not the BSET instruction.

7.7   REAL-TIME CLOCK

It is sometimes desirable for a computer to perform certain I/O operations at specified times. One way for a computer to track time is to use an I/O device that causes interrupts periodically. An oscillator sets a flag at the end of each period. The interrupt service routine then can count interrupts to track time.

The RTI Device

When a computer is used as a control device, periodic timing is usually necessary. The example in the previous section included a flashing light. The time base for the timing was an external oscillator and a flag.

Since the need for periodic timing is common, the 68HC11 has an internal I/O device called the real-time interrupt device, or the RTI. The real-time interrupt device is simply an oscillator with a flag that can cause periodic interrupts. The interrupt service routine that responds to these interrupts can do data transfers at precise times determined by the interrupts.

The frequency of the oscillator that sets the flag is dependent on the E-clock rate of the 68HC11. A programmable counter driven at the E-clock rate provides four interrupt rates. The E-clock runs at one-fourth the rate of the crystal.

Figure 7-10 shows a block diagram of the RTI hardware. The control bits for the timer are in various 68HC11 control registers.

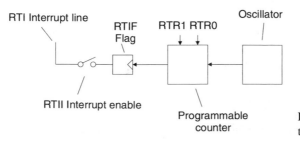

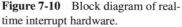

Figure 7-10   Block diagram of real-time interrupt hardware.

RTI flag

The real-time interrupt device causes an interrupt by setting a flag named RTIF for real-time interrupt flag. A program can examine this flag by testing bit 6 of the TFLG2 register at address 1025. Figure 7-11 shows the TFLG2 register.

The RTIF flag is set periodically by the real-time interrupt oscillator. A program clears the RTIF flag by writing a 1 to bit 6 of the TFLG2 register. Writing a 0 to the RTIF bit does nothing to it. Similarly, writing 0s to the other bits of this register will not affect any other I/O hardware. Normally, you will use the STAA instruction to write the 1 to clear the flag. Section 7.6 discusses using bit instructions with flags.

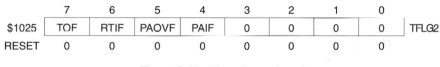

	7	6	5	4	3	2	1	0	
$1025	TOF	RTIF	PAOVF	PAIF	0	0	0	0	TFLG2
RESET	0	0	0	0	0	0	0	0	

Figure 7-11   Timer flag register 2.

If you choose not to use interrupt, the RTI device flag can be polled. Most applications use interrupt, so the device is named accordingly.

RTI control bits

Bit 1 and bit 0 of the PACTL register at address 1026 program the rate of interrupts. Figure 7-12 illustrates the PACTL register. The name of this register does not relate to the real-time interrupt device.

The control bits are named RTR1 and RTR0, respectively. The two control bits determine which one of four divide factors is applied to the E-clock in generating the interrupts. That is, they select one of four interrupt rates. Table 7-4 shows the interrupt rates for several different E-clock rates.

The real-time interrupt is enabled or disabled by a switch controlled by bit 6 of the TMSK2 register at address 1024. This interrupt-enable bit is named RTII. Figure 7-13 shows the TMSK2 register and the RTII bit. A 0 in the RTII bit disables the RTI interrupt and a 1 enables the RTI interrupt.

When using only the real-time interrupt device, avoid problems caused by other bits in the PACTL, TMSK2, and TFLG2 registers by only storing 0s to those bits.

The real-time interrupt has its own interrupt vector at address FFF0. The real-time interrupt is under control of the I bit.

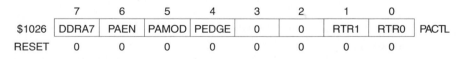

	7	6	5	4	3	2	1	0	
$1026	DDRA7	PAEN	PAMOD	PEDGE	0	0	RTR1	RTR0	PACTL
RESET	0	0	0	0	0	0	0	0	

Figure 7-12   Pulse accumulator control register.

TABLE 7-4   REAL-TIME INTERRUPT RATE

RTI Control Bits		Rate is E Divided by	Crystal Frequency		
RTR1	RTR0		8.3886 MHz	8.0 MHz	4.9152 MHz
			Interrupt Period (milliseconds)		
0	0	2^{13}	3.91	4.10	6.67
0	1	2^{14}	7.81	8.19	13.33
1	0	2^{15}	15.62	16.38	26.67
1	1	2^{16}	31.25	32.77	53.33
		E =	2.0971 MHz	2.0000 MHz	1.2288 MHz

RTI Programming Example

The following example uses the real-time interrupt as a time base to toggle the bits of PORTC every 8.19 milliseconds. Each time the interrupt service routine runs, all the output bits in the PORTC are complemented. Figure 7-14 shows the listing of the program. Here is a description of the program:

- *Line 27.*   The RTI vector at address FFF0 sends control to the interrupt service routine at address C118. No other device shares this interrupt vector.

- *Line 37.*   The program initializes the stack because the interrupt system will use it to store the microprocessor status when an interrupt occurs.

- *Lines 40 through 43.*   The program initializes PORTC for all outputs with the outputs all cleared.

- *Lines 46 and 47.*   The interrupt rate of the real-time interrupt oscillator is set. The rate after reset is the fastest rate because reset clears the rate control bits. Here the RTR1 and RTR0 bits are set to 01 to choose the 8.19-millisecond interrupt rate.

- *Lines 49 and 50.*   The real-time interrupt is enabled to cause interrupts. Be careful because other bits in the TMSK2 register can enable other interrupts.

- *Lines 65 and 66.*   The interrupt vector sent control here because the RTI device interrupted. At this point, the interrupt system is disabled because a 1 is in the I bit. The RTIF flag is checked to see if it is set. If not, an error caused an invalid interrupt. Checking for invalid interrupts is good practice in practical programs.

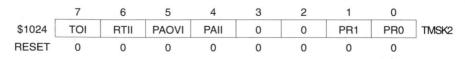

	7	6	5	4	3	2	1	0	
$1024	TOI	RTII	PAOVI	PAII	0	0	PR1	PR0	TMSK2
RESET	0	0	0	0	0	0	0	0	

Figure 7-13   Timer interrupt mask register 2.

```
  1                             ***********************************************************
  2                             ** REVERSE ALL PORTC BITS EVERY 8.19 MILLISECONDS
  3                             *
  4                             * USE REAL TIME INTERRUPT AS TIME BASE
  5                             *
  6                             * USE 8.0 MHZ CRYSTAL FOR 68HC11 CLOCK
  7                             *
  8                             ***********************************************************
  9                             *
 10                             ***********************************************************
 11                             ** SYMBOL DEFINITIONS
 12                             ***********************************************************
 13                             * 68HC11 REGISTERS
 14          1003              PORTC    EQU    $1003     I/O PORT C REGISTER
 15          1007              DDRC     EQU    $1007     DATA DIRECTION REGISTER C
 16          1024              TMSK2    EQU    $1024     TIMER MASK REGISTER
 17          1025              TFLG2    EQU    $1025     TIMER FLAG REGISTER
 18          1026              PACTL    EQU    $1026     PULSE ACCUMULATOR CONTROL REG
 19          00FF              IOPAT    EQU    $FF       I/O PATTERN, 0=IN 1=OUT
 20                             * MASKS
 21          0040              BIT6     EQU    %01000000
 22                             *
 23                             ***********************************************************
 24                             ** DATA SECTION
 25                             ***********************************************************
 26    FFF0                             ORG $FFF0     RTI INTERRUPT VECTOR
 27    FFF0   C118                      FDB    RTIISR
 28                             *
 29                             ***********************************************************
 30                             ** MAIN PROGRAM
 31                             ***********************************************************
 32    C100                             ORG $C100
 33                             *----------------------------------------------------------
 34                             * INITIALIZATION
 35                             *----------------------------------------------------------
 36                             * INITIALIZE STACK
 37    C100   8E CF FF         START    LDS    #$CFFF
 38                             * INITIALIZE PORT C
 39                             *     INITIALIZE OUTPUTS TO ZEROS
 40    C103   7F 10 03                  CLR    PORTC     0=LOW
 41                             *     SET UP PORTC INS AND OUTS
 42    C106   86 FF                     LDAA   #IOPAT
 43    C108   B7 10 07                  STAA   DDRC      ALL OUTPUTS
 44                             * INITIALIZE REAL TIME INTERRUPT
 45                             *     SET INTERRUPT RATE TO 8.19 MS
 46    C10B   86 01                     LDAA   #1        ZEROS IN OTHER BITS
 47    C10D   B7 10 26                  STAA   PACTL     ..CAUSE NO PROBLEMS
 48                             *     ENABLE RTI INTERRUPT
 49    C110   86 40                     LDAA   #BIT6     ZEROS IN OTHER BITS
 50    C112   B7 10 24                  STAA   TMSK2     ..CAUSE NO PROBLEMS
 51                             * TURN ON INTERRUPT SYSTEM
 52    C115   0E                        CLI
 53                             *----------------------------------------------------------
 54                             * WAIT FOR INTERRUPTS
 55                             *----------------------------------------------------------
 56    C116   20 FE            HERE     BRA    HERE      DO NOTHING!
 57                             *
 58                             ***********************************************************
 59                             ** INTERRUPT SERVICE ROUTINE
 60                             ***********************************************************
 61                             *----------------------------------------------------------
 62                             * INTERRUPT POLLING CHAIN
 63                             *----------------------------------------------------------
```

Figure 7-14   Interrupt program for real-time interrupt.

```
64                      * INTERRUPT FROM REAL TIME INTERRUPT DEVICE?
65    C118   CE 10 25   RTIISR  LDX    #TFLG2
66    C11B   1F 00 40 08        BRCLR 0,X,BIT6,RTRTI  IGNORE ILLEGAL INTERRUPT
67                      *-----------------------------------------------------
68                      * CONTROL PORT C OUTPUTS
69                      *-----------------------------------------------------
70                      * CLEAR REAL TIME INTERRUPT FLAG
71    C11F   86 40              LDAA   #BIT6    STORE 1 TO CLEAR FLAG!
72    C121   B7 10 25           STAA   TFLG2    ..ZEROS DO NOTHING
73                      * COMPLEMENT PORT C OUTPUTS
74    C124   73 10 03           COM    PORTC
75                      * RETURN FROM INTERRUPT
76    C127   3B         RTRTI   RTI
77    C128                      END
```

Figure 7-14   Continued.

- *Lines 71 and 72.*   Storing a 1 to the RTIF flag bit clears the real-time interrupt flag.

- *Line 74.*   The PORTC outputs are complemented. This happens every 8.19 milliseconds because this interrupt service routine runs every 8.19 milliseconds. That is, it runs every time the RTI flag is set.

- *Line 76.*   Control returns to the main program and the interrupt system is enabled again.

To change this program for longer times, first change the RTI rate control bits. If even longer times are necessary, the interrupt service routine can count multiple interrupts before performing an action.

7.8   THE PROGRAMMABLE TIMER

Control applications of computers usually require measurements of time. The performance of control systems is usually time-dependent. The 68HC11 contains a hardware timer. The timer can measure time for both inputs and outputs. The timing schemes are different for inputs and outputs.

The timer in the 68HC11 is very flexible. It will accurately measure times from microseconds to centuries! The characteristics of the timer are programmable with software. The timer uses the interrupt system and it has several interrupt vectors. However, the accuracy of the timer does not depend on the software.

Timer Principles

The timer consists of three logical parts: a free-running counter, input-capture hardware, and output-compare hardware. Because there are many programmable options, this hardware is very complex. However, the fundamental principles of its operation are quite simple. Let's begin with an overview of the operation of the timer.

Motorola Trainer

The real-time interrupt program in Figure 7-14 only needs the interrupt vector corrected before it will run on the trainer. You can examine the effects of this program by looking at the output voltage on any PORTC pin using an oscilloscope. Similarly, an analog DC voltmeter connected to a PORTC pin should read about 2.5 volts.

The free-running counter

An up-counter is a special register that counts up by one each time it is clocked. The free-running counter in the 68HC11 is a 16-bit up-counter driven or clocked by an accurate oscillator. The free-running counter counts up by one on each cycle of the oscillator. The counter continually counts whenever the 68HC11 is powered-up —thus the name free-running counter. The free-running counter is the time base for all the timer functions.

The free-running counter counts from 0000 to FFFF, and then rolls over to 0000 again. Rolling over to zero is called an *overflow*. The number in the counter and the overflow can be used for timing. For example, if the oscillator operates at 1.0 MHz, the counter rolls over every $65,536_{10}$ microseconds, or about every 65_{10} milliseconds. By checking the number in the counter and the rolling over of the counter, timing with a resolution of 1.0 microsecond can be done. The accuracy of the timing depends on the accuracy of the oscillator only.

Input capture for timing events

Figure 7-15 shows the free-running counter connected to another register. A parallel transfer from the counter to the register occurs when the register is clocked. So clocking the register captures a copy of the number in the counter.

For example, suppose the capture register is clocked, and it contains the number 0100. A little later, it is clocked again, and then it contains 0200. Assuming the counter did not overflow, we conclude that 100_{16} microseconds elapsed between the captures. Therefore, we have determined that the time between captures was 256_{10} microseconds.

By using input signals to clock the capture register, and reading the capture register and noting overflows, any event outside the computer can be accurately timed. The times between events can range from microseconds to years!

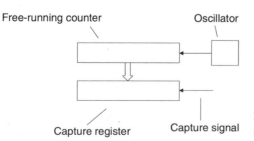

Figure 7-15   Free-running counter and capture register.

Output compare for controlling events

Figure 7-16 shows the free-running counter, an output-compare register, and a comparison circuit. The comparator looks at the numbers in the counter and the compare register, and signals whenever the two numbers are the same.

As a simple example, if the number in the compare register doesn't change, the numbers will match every $65,536_{10}$ counts. If the oscillator runs at 1.0 MHz, the comparator indicates a match every 65.536_{10} milliseconds.

A more practical example requires the program to change the number in the compare register. For example, suppose the compare register contains 0100 and a match was just indicated. The program responds by reading the compare register, adding 0100, and storing the result 0200 into the compare register. The comparator indicates the next match exactly 256_{10} microseconds after the first.

If the match signal complements an output bit, the bit is changed every 256_{10} microseconds. The timing is very accurate. The time the software takes to change the compare register does not affect the accuracy of the timing.

Free-Running Counter

The free-running counter in the 68HC11 is a 16-bit up-counter. The time base for the counter is the crystal in the 68HC11 clock. The free-running counter is the basis for all the timing functions of the programmable timer system.

The counter hardware

Figure 7-17 shows the free-running counter and its clock. The oscillator runs at the E-clock rate and is driven by the crystal. The prescaler is a programmable counter that divides the E-clock rate by one of four factors; namely, 1, 4, 8, or 16_{10}.

Prescaler control.   The prescaler control bits are shown in Table 7-5 with typical clock rates. The control bits called PR1 and PR0 are in the timer mask register called TMSK2. Figure 7-12 shows this register.

The prescaler control bits are timed-write-once bits. Therefore, they must be set by the program within 64_{10} E-clock cycles after reset.

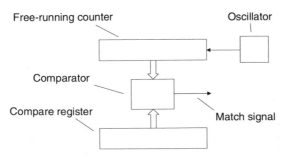

Figure 7-16   Free-running counter, compare register, and compare circuit.

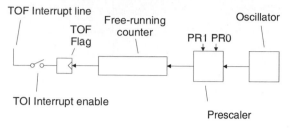

Figure 7-17   Block diagram of free-running counter hardware.

Timer-overflow flag.   When the free-running counter overflows from FFFF to 0000, it sets the timer-overflow flag called TOF. Writing a 1 into the TOF bit clears the TOF flag. The TOF flag is in the timer flag register called TFLG2. Figure 7-10 shows the TFLG2 register.

The timer-overflow flag can cause an interrupt. The enable bit for this interrupt is the TOI bit in the TMSK2 register. The timer-overflow interrupt vector is at address FFDE. This interrupt is under control of the I bit.

Reset condition.   Reset clears the free-running counter. After that, it is a read only register that is unaffected by instructions. Reads are buffered so an instruction that reads a double-byte number gets the correct number. The least-significant byte is not out of date.

Example program

Figure 7-18 is the listing for a program that uses the timer-overflow interrupt. The program is similar to the example in Figure 7-14. The program does the same function, but it uses the timer overflow as the time base.

The example uses an 8.0-MHz crystal and programs the prescaler for a divide-by-eight rate. The free-running counter then overflows every 262.1_{10} milliseconds. Remember that the prescaler is programmed by timed-write-once bits.

This example is a simple use of the timer-overflow interrupt. More often, timer overflow is used with other timing functions to extend their time range.

TABLE 7-5   FREE-RUNNING COUNTER RATE AND RANGE

Prescaler Control Bits		Divide Factor	Crystal Frequency		
			8.3886 MHz	8.0 MHz	4.9152 MHz
PR1	PR0		One Count(μs) / Overflow Range(ms)		
0	0	1	0.477 / 31.25	0.5 / 32.77	.814 / 53.33
0	1	4	1.91 / 125	2 / 131.1	3.26 / 213.3
1	0	8	3.81 / 250	4 / 262.1	6.51 / 426.7
1	1	16	7.63 / 500	8 / 524.3	13.02 / 853.7
		E =	2.0971 MHz	2.0000 MHz	1.2288 MHz

```
 1                      **********************************************************
 2                      ** REVERSE ALL PORTC BITS EVERY 262.1 MILLISECONDS
 3                      *
 4                      * USE TIMER OVERFLOW AS TIME BASE
 5                      *
 6                      * USE 8.0 MHZ CRYSTAL FOR 68HC11 CLOCK
 7                      *
 8                      **********************************************************
 9                      *
10                      **********************************************************
11                      ** SYMBOL DEFINITIONS
12                      **********************************************************
13                      * 68HC11 REGISTERS
14         1003         PORTC    EQU    $1003     I/O PORT C REGISTER
15         1007         DDRC     EQU    $1007     DATA DIRECTION REGISTER C
16         1024         TMSK2    EQU    $1024     TIMER MASK REGISTER
17         1025         TFLG2    EQU    $1025     TIMER FLAG REGISTER
18         00FF         IOPAT    EQU    $FF       I/O PATTERN, 0=IN 1=OUT
19                      * MASKS
20         0040         BIT7     EQU    %01000000
21                      *
22                      **********************************************************
23                      ** DATA SECTION
24                      **********************************************************
25  FFDE                         ORG $FFDE     TOF INTERRUPT VECTOR
26  FFDE   C113                  FDB  TOFISR
27                      *
28                      **********************************************************
29                      ** MAIN PROGRAM
30                      **********************************************************
31  C100                         ORG $C100
32                      *-------------------------------------------------------
33                      * INITIALIZATION
34                      *-------------------------------------------------------
35                      * INITIALIZE STACK
36  C100   8E CF FF     START    LDS    #$CFFF
37                      * INITIALIZE PORT C
38                      *     INITIALIZE OUTPUTS TO ZEROS
39  C103   7F 10 03              CLR    PORTC     0=LOW
40                      *     SET UP PORTC INS AND OUTS
41  C106   86 FF                 LDAA   #IOPAT
42  C108   B7 10 07              STAA   DDRC      ALL OUTPUTS
43                      * INITIALIZE TIMER OVERFLOW INTERRUPT
44  C10B   86 82                 LDAA   #$82      PR1:PR0=10 FOR 262.1 MS
45  C10D   B7 10 24              STAA   TMSK2     ..ENABLE TOF INTERRUPT
46                      * TURN ON INTERRUPT SYSTEM
47  C110   0E                    CLI
48                      *-------------------------------------------------------
49                      * WAIT FOR INTERRUPTS
50                      *-------------------------------------------------------
51  C111   20 FE        HERE     BRA    HERE      DO NOTHING!
52                      *
53                      **********************************************************
54                      ** INTERRUPT SERVICE ROUTINE
55                      **********************************************************
56                      *-------------------------------------------------------
57                      * INTERRUPT POLLING CHAIN
58                      *-------------------------------------------------------
59                      * INTERRUPT FROM TIMER OVERFLOW?
60  C113   CE 10 25     TOFISR   LDX    #TFLG2
61  C116   1F 00 40 08           BRCLR  0,X,BIT7,RTTOF  IGNORE ILLEGAL INTERRUPT
62                      *-------------------------------------------------------
63                      * CONTROL PORT C OUTPUTS
```

Figure 7-18   Interrupt program for timer-overflow interrupt.

```
64                              *-----------------------------------------------------
65                              * CLEAR TIMER OVERFLOW FLAG
66      C11A    86 40                   LDAA   #BIT7    STORE 1 TO CLEAR FLAG!
67      C11C    B7 10 25                STAA   TFLG2    ..ZEROS DO NOTHING
68                              * COMPLEMENT PORT C OUTPUTS
69      C11F    73 10 03                COM    PORTC    OUTPUT TO PORT C
70                              * RETURN FROM INTERRUPT
71      C122    3B              RTTOF   RTI
72      C123                            END
```

Figure 7-18   Continued.

Input Capture

Input capture can measure the time between events external to the computer. A signal sent to the computer must make a proper transition at the time of the event to trigger the capturing hardware. An input-capture flag is set when a capture takes place; the flag may cause an interrupt.

If the input signal is periodic, the time between identical events is the period of the waveform. When the period is known, the frequency of the input signal can be calculated. Many kinds of applications that require timing can use input capture.

The hardware

The 68HC11A8 IC has three sets of input-capture hardware, and the 68HC11E9 has four sets. The E9 version shares a pin and other hardware between an optional input-capture device and an optional output-compare device. The input-capture signals are part of the port A pins. In all details, each input-capture functions the same. Therefore, the following discussion describes the hardware for all the input captures.

Figure 7-19 shows the parts of the input-capture hardware. The edge control hardware determines the active edge or transition of the pin.

Input-capture registers.   The timer input-capture registers are each 16-bit registers that can hold numbers from the 16-bit free-running counter. The three registers are named TIC1, TIC2, and TIC3 and are at addresses 1010, 1012, and 1014 respectively. A program can only read these registers—writing to them has no effect.

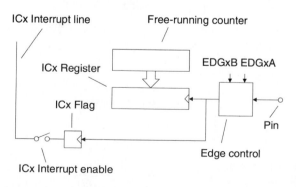

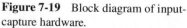

Figure 7-19   Block diagram of input-capture hardware.

Motorola Trainer

The timer-overflow example program in Figure 7-18 does not run correctly in the trainer if you use the monitor program. The problem is due to the timed-write-once prescaler control bits. The monitor program in the trainer sets the prescaler for the fastest count rate. Your program cannot change the control bits, because too many cycles have passed while the monitor program runs. You should try the program to see that the rate at which PORTC changes is eight times faster than Figure 7-18 says. Put a JMP to address C113 at address 00D0 to fix the timer overflow interrupt vector in the trainer.

It is possible to make the trainer go directly to your program instead of the monitor program. Then the example program can work correctly. See Appendix D for details.

The E9 version of the 68HC11 has a fourth input capture that shares a pin and other hardware with an output-compare device. Then the corresponding input-capture register is called TI4O5 and is at address 101E. Storing 0s in bit 2 and bit 3 of the PACTL register programs TI4O5 for input capture, and 1s program it for output compare.

Port signals.   The input-capture pins are part of port A. The pins are called input captures 1, 2, and 3. IC1 connects to pin PA2, IC2 connects to pin PA1, and IC3 connects to pin PA0. When IC4 exists, it connects to pin PA3. Refer to Figures 7-1 and 7-2 to clarify these connections.

Edge control.   Table 7-6 shows the edge control bits for the input-capture pins. The control bits called EDGxB and EDGxA are in the timer-control register called TCTL2. Figure 7-20 shows this register. The figure shows the register for the A8 version of the 68HC11, which has three input captures. The program may change the edge control bits at any time.

Table 7-6 shows that an input capture may be disabled. While an input capture is disabled, the corresponding pin is available as an input-only pin. Refer to Table 7-3 for the parallel I/O functions of the ports.

If the pin is enabled for input captures, the capture register and the flag are clocked on a low-to-high transition, a high-to-low transition, or both transitions. These transitions are also called *rising edge*, *falling edge*, and *any edge*, respectively.

Flags.   Figure 7-21 shows the input-capture flags in the timer-flag register called TFLG1. The flags are named IC1F, IC2F, and IC3F to correspond to the input captures named

TABLE 7-6   INPUT CAPTURE EDGE

EDGxB Bit	EDGxA Bit	Active Pin Transition
0	0	Capture disabled
0	1	Capture on low-to-high
1	0	Capture on high-to-low
1	1	Capture on both transitions

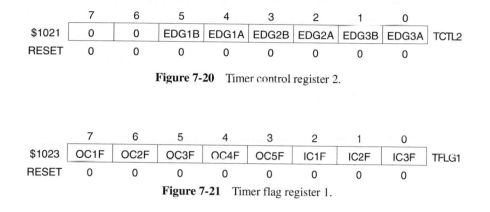

	7	6	5	4	3	2	1	0	
$1021	0	0	EDG1B	EDG1A	EDG2B	EDG2A	EDG3B	EDG3A	TCTL2
RESET	0	0	0	0	0	0	0	0	

Figure 7-20   Timer control register 2.

	7	6	5	4	3	2	1	0	
$1023	OC1F	OC2F	OC3F	OC4F	OC5F	IC1F	IC2F	IC3F	TFLG1
RESET	0	0	0	0	0	0	0	0	

Figure 7-21   Timer flag register 1.

IC1, IC2, and IC3, respectively. The input-capture flags are set by active transitions on the associated input-capture pins. Writing a 1 to an input-capture flag clears it; writing a 0 does not affect it.

In the E9 version of the 68HC11, bit 3 of TFLG1 is called I4/O5F. A 0 in bit 2 of the PACTL register makes I4/O5F an input-capture flag.

Interrupts.   Each input capture flag can trigger an interrupt. The interrupt-enable bits for IC1, IC2, and IC3, respectively, are called IC1I, IC2I, and IC3I. They are in the timer mask register called TMSK1. A 1 in an interrupt-enable bit enables the flag to cause an interrupt, and a 0 disables it. Figure 7-22 shows the TMSK1 register. The reset condition shows that a hardware reset disables all the input-capture interrupts.

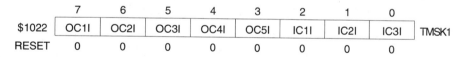

	7	6	5	4	3	2	1	0	
$1022	OC1I	OC2I	OC3I	OC4I	OC5I	IC1I	IC2I	IC3I	TMSK1
RESET	0	0	0	0	0	0	0	0	

Figure 7-22   Timer interrupt mask register 1.

In the E9 version of the 68HC11, the interrupt from the fourth input capture is enabled by bit 3 of TMSK1 called I4O5I. Zeros in bit 2 and bit 3 of the PACTL register enables the input-capture function.

Measuring short elapsed times

A short time is any time less than the time between overflows of the free-running counter. If the time is longer, then overflows must be counted and the complexity is greater. If the E-clock runs at 2.0 MHz and the timer prescaler is set for the fastest free-running counter, the overflow time is 32.77_{10} milliseconds with a resolution of 0.5 microsecond.

Figure 7-23 is an example program that illustrates the use of input capture. Assume that the input signal connects to port A at pin PA0. This pin corresponds to input capture 3. Further assume that the elapsed time is measured between low-to-high transitions of the signal. The program repeatedly measures the elapsed time between these transitions. It puts 1 in bit 0 of PORTC only if the time is at or below a limit, and it puts 1 in bit 1 of PORTC only if the time is over the limit; otherwise, these bits are 0s. If the input signal stops changing, the time will certainly be over the limit. Here is a description of the program:

- *Line 35.* The time limit is the data number the program compares to the elapsed time to determine if the time is out of limits. The limit is a double-byte number of free-running counter periods.

- *Line 37.* The elapsed time between input captures in free-running counter periods.

- *Lines 58 through 62.* Input capture 3 is programmed to respond to low-to-high transitions on the PA0 pin and to cause an interrupt.

- *Lines 75 through 85.* The main program loop continually checks the elapsed time and updates the two indicator bits in PORTC. If the elapsed time is higher than the time limit, bit 1 is set to a 1; otherwise, bit 0 is set to a 1. When an interrupt occurs, the interrupt service routine updates the elapsed time.

- *Lines 100 and 101.* The external signal that is being timed set the flag, which caused the interrupt. The flag is now cleared by storing a 1 into the flag bit.

- *Lines 103 through 105.* The input-capture register is read and then the last value read from the input-capture register is subtracted from it. The difference is the elapsed time in free-running counter periods. So the result is stored in the elapsed time location. The numbers in the capture register are unsigned 16-bit numbers. The subtraction gives the correct elapsed time even if the free-running counter has overflowed. Convince yourself that this calculation is correct by trying several different numbers.

- *Lines 107 and 108.* The current number in the input-capture register is saved in the last time register.

- *Line 110.* Control returns to the main program loop that now uses the updated elapsed time.

You can use this program as a go/no-go frequency meter. If the frequency of the input signal is too low, the program indicates an out of limit time. If the frequency is high enough, it indicates the time is within the limit. If the input signal comes from a pulse transducer on a rotating device, the program can indicate if the RPM is above or below a limit.

Measuring long elapsed times

If the time to be measured may be longer than the overflow time for the free-running counter, the program must count overflows. Therefore, both the input capture interrupt and

```
  1                                     ******************************************************
  2                                     ** MEASURE ELAPSED TIME BETWEEN EVENTS AND INDICATE
  3                                     ** IF OUT OF ACCEPTABLE RANGE
  4                                     *
  5                                     * USE INPUT CAPTURE 3 TO MEASURE TIME
  6                                     *
  7                                     * USE 8.0 MHZ CRYSTAL FOR 68HC11 CLOCK AND RUN
  8                                     * ..FREE-RUNNING COUNTER AT MAXIMUM RATE
  9                                     *
 10                                     * MAXIMUM ELAPSED TIME MUST BE LESS THAN FREE-RUNNING
 11                                     * ..COUNTER OVERFLOW TIME OF 32.77 MILLISECONDS
 12                                     *
 13                                     ******************************************************
 14                                     *
 15                                     ******************************************************
 16                                     ** SYMBOL DEFINITIONS
 17                                     ******************************************************
 18                                     * 68HC11 REGISTERS
 19          1003                       PORTC    EQU    $1003     I/O PORT C REGISTER
 20          1007                       DDRC     EQU    $1007     DATA DIRECTION REGISTER C
 21          1014                       TIC3     EQU    $1014     TIMER INPUT CAPTURE 3 REGISTER
 22          1021                       TCTL2    EQU    $1021     TIMER CONTROL REGISTER
 23          1022                       TMSK1    EQU    $1022     TIMER MASK REGISTER
 24          1023                       TFLG1    EQU    $1023     TIMER FLAG REGISTER
 25          0003                       IOPAT    EQU    $03       I/O PATTERN, 0=IN 1=OUT
 26                                     * MASKS
 27          0001                       BIT0     EQU    %00000001
 28          0002                       BIT1     EQU    %00000010
 29          0001                       IC3F     EQU    BIT0
 30                                     *
 31                                     ******************************************************
 32                                     ** DATA SECTION
 33                                     ******************************************************
 34   0010                                       ORG    $0010
 35   0010   9000                       TLIMIT   FDB    $9000     MAX ALLOWED ELAPSED TIME
 36   0012                              LASTTIM  RMB    2         COUNTER AT LAST IC3 CAPTURE
 37   0014                              ELAPSED  RMB    2         ELAPSED TIME SINCE LAST CAPTURE
 38                                     *
 39   FFEA                                       ORG $FFEA        IC3 INTERRUPT VECTOR
 40   FFEA   C135                                FDB    IC3ISR
 41                                     *
 42                                     ******************************************************
 43                                     ** MAIN PROGRAM
 44                                     ******************************************************
 45   C100                                       ORG $C100
 46                                     *----------------------------------------------------
 47                                     * INITIALIZATION
 48                                     *----------------------------------------------------
 49                                     * INITIALIZE STACK
 50   C100   8E CF FF                   START    LDS    #$CFFF
 51                                     * INITIALIZE PORT C
 52                                     *     INITIALIZE OUTPUTS TO ZEROS
 53   C103   7F 10 03                            CLR    PORTC      0=LOW
 54                                     *     SET UP PORTC INS AND OUTS
 55   C106   86 03                               LDAA   #IOPAT
 56   C108   B7 10 07                            STAA   DDRC       TWO OUTPUT PINS
 57                                     * INITIALIZE INPUT CAPTURE 3
 58   C10B   86 01                               LDAA   #$01       EDG3B:EDG3A=01 FOR LOW-TO-HIGH
 59   C10D   B7 10 21                            STAA   TCTL2      ..CAPTURE
 60                                     * ENABLE IC3 INTERRUPT
 61   C110   86 01                               LDAA   #BIT0
 62   C112   B7 10 22                            STAA   TMSK1
 63                                     * INITIALIZE ELAPSED TIME
```

Figure 7-23 Input capture 3 example.

```
 64    C115    CC 00 00              LDD     #0
 65    C118    DD 14                 STD     ELAPSED
 66                           * INITIALIZE LAST TIME
 67    C11A    FC 10 14              LDD     TIC3
 68    C11D    DD 12                 STD     LASTTIM
 69                           * TURN ON INTERRUPT SYSTEM
 70    C11F    0E                    CLI
 71                           *-----------------------------------------------------
 72                           * MAIN PROGRAM LOOP
 73                           *-----------------------------------------------------
 74                           * ELAPSED TIME OVER LIMIT?
 75    C120    DC 14         HERE    LDD     ELAPSED
 76    C122    1A 93 10              CPD     TLIMIT
 77    C125    22 07                 BHI     AHEAD      BRANCH ON YES
 78                           * SET TIME OK INDICATOR
 79    C127    86 01                 LDAA    #BIT0    1 IN BIT0 = OK
 80    C129    B7 10 03              STAA    PORTC
 81    C12C    20 05                 BRA     AGAIN
 82                           * SET TIME OVERLIMIT INDICATOR
 83    C12E    86 02         AHEAD   LDAA    #BIT1    1 IN BIT1 = OVERLIMIT
 84    C130    B7 10 03              STAA    PORTC
 85    C133    20 EB         AGAIN   BRA     HERE
 86                           *
 87                           *************************************************************
 88                           ** INTERRUPT SERVICE ROUTINE
 89                           *************************************************************
 90                           *-----------------------------------------------------
 91                           * INTERRUPT POLLING CHAIN
 92                           *-----------------------------------------------------
 93                           * INTERRUPT FROM IC3?
 94    C135    CE 10 23      IC3ISR  LDX     #TFLG1
 95    C138    1F 00 01 10           BRCLR   0,X,IC3F,RTIC3   IGNORE ILLEGAL INTERRUPT
 96                           *-----------------------------------------------------
 97                           * SERVICE INPUT CAPTURE 3
 98                           *-----------------------------------------------------
 99                           * CLEAR IC3 FLAG
100    C13C    86 01                 LDAA    #BIT0    STORE 1 TO CLEAR FLAG!
101    C13E    A7 00                 STAA    0,X      ..ZEROS DO NOTHING
102                           * CALCULATE ELAPSED TIME
103    C140    FC 10 14              LDD     TIC3
104    C143    93 12                 SUBD    LASTTIM
105    C145    DD 14                 STD     ELAPSED
106                           * SAVE CURRENT CAPTURE TIME
107    C147    FC 10 14              LDD     TIC3
108    C14A    DD 12                 STD     LASTTIM
109                           * RETURN FROM INTERRUPT
110    C14C    3B            RTIC3   RTI
111    C14D                          END
```

Figure 7-23   Continued.

the timer overflow interrupt are used. Each time an overflow occurs, a separate overflow counter is incremented if timing is in progress.

The most difficult part of extending the time range is deciding whether to count an overflow. If the input capture happens close to the overflow, both the input capture flag and the timer overflow flag will be set when a timer interrupt service routine runs. However, the overflow interrupt service routine must increment the overflow counter only if the overflow happened before the input capture. Since the input capture has higher interrupt priority, its interrupt will be serviced before the overflow interrupt, which makes it possible to resolve the problem. Then, if the captured value has a 1 in its most-significant bit, the capture was before the overflow. If the captured value has a 0 in its most-significant bit, the capture was after the overflow.

When determining whether to increment the overflow counter, the timer interrupts must be serviced within half the time of an overflow of the free-running counter. If this is not so, the free-running counter may have another overflow before the relative capture time is determined.

Output Compare

The output-compare hardware normally controls the timing of changes in output bits. Usually the output signal is nearly periodic; for example, a pulse-width modulated waveform. However, almost any kind of timing can be achieved.

The 68HC11 has five output-compare registers. Output compare 1 has characteristics very different from those of output compares 2 through 5. Since output compares 2 through 5 share some similarity with the input captures, let's begin with them.

Output compares 2 through 5

The 68HC11A8 and 68HC11E9 ICs each has five sets of output-compare hardware. The E9 version shares a pin and other hardware between an optional input-capture device and output compare 5. The output-compare signals are part of the port A pins.

In all details, each of the output compares OC2 through OC5 functions the same. The other output compare, OC1, has additional functions that are discussed later. Therefore, the following describes the hardware for the OC2 through OC5 devices.

Output-compare registers. Figure 7-24 shows four output-compare registers labeled as TOCx. They are each 16-bit registers so they can be compared to the free-running counter. The four output-compare registers are named TOC2, TOC3, TOC4, and TOC5 and are at addresses 1018, 101A, 101C, and 101E, respectively. A program may both read and write these registers; normally it will write to them only.

The output compare 5 register in the E9 version of the 68HC11 is called TI4O5. Storing 1s in bit 2 and bit 3 of the PACTL register programs TI4O5 for output-compare functions.

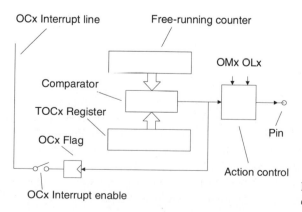

Figure 7-24 Block diagram of output-compare hardware.

Port signals.   Port A includes the pins that the output-compare hardware controls. The pins are named PA3, PA4, PA5, PA6, and PA7. Output compare OC2 connects to PA6, OC3 to PA5, OC4 to PA4, and OC5 to PA3. Remember that pin PA3 is shared by an input-capture and an output-compare.

Comparator.   The comparator hardware looks for a match between the number in a compare register and the number in the free-running counter. When the match occurs, which it inevitably will, the comparator triggers an output action and sets a flag.

Action control.   When the comparator in Figure 7-24 detects a match between a compare register and the free-running counter, it triggers some action that takes place at an output pin. Table 7-7 lists the possible actions taken when a match occurs. Two control bits determine the actions. The control bits are called OM and OL for *output mode* and *output level*. By looking at the table, you can see that a 1 in OM makes the OL bit directly control the output bit when the match occurs. When OM is 0, the output pin is either disconnected from the timer or is toggled. The program must set OM and OL for the correct action.

TABLE 7-7   OUTPUT COMPARE ACTION

OMx Bit	OLx Bit	Successful Compare Action
0	0	Disconnect timer from output pin
0	1	Complement output pin
1	0	Set output pin low
1	1	Set output pin high

Figure 7-25 shows the TCTL1 register that contains the OM and OL bits for the output-compares. The action of output compare 1 is not controlled by TCTL1.

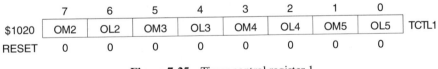

	7	6	5	4	3	2	1	0	
$1020	OM2	OL2	OM3	OL3	OM4	OL4	OM5	OL5	TCTL1
RESET	0	0	0	0	0	0	0	0	

Figure 7-25   Timer control register 1.

Flags.   Figure 7-21 shows the output-compare flags in the timer-flag register called TFLG1. The flags are named OC1F through OC5F corresponding to the output compares called OC1 through OC5. Matches between the free-running counter and the associated output-compare register set the respective flags. A flag is cleared when a 1 is written to the flag. Writing 0s to these flags does not affect them.

In the E9 version of the 68HC11, bit 3 of TFLG1, the flag for output compare 5, is called I4/O5F. A 1 in bit 2 of the PACTL register makes I4/O5F an output-compare flag.

Motorola Trainer

The monitor program in the trainer uses output compare 5. Be careful because interactions between the monitor program and your program can be very confusing.

Interrupts.   Each output-compare flag can cause an interrupt. The interrupt-enable bits corresponding to OC1 through OC5 are called OC1I through OC5I. They are in the timer mask register called TMSK1. Figure 7-22 shows this register. A 1 in an interrupt-enable bit enables the flag to cause an interrupt. The reset condition disables all the output-compare interrupts.

The output compare 5 flag in the E9 version of the 68HC11 can cause an interrupt. Set bit 3 of TMSK1, called I4O5I, to 1 to enable the OC5 interrupt.

Instructions.   Usually, the program will change the number in the compare register to determine the time when the next output action will occur. Use a double-byte instruction to write to the 16-bit compare register or the comparison circuit may not function correctly. A match may occur at the wrong time if only one byte of the compare register is updated at a time.

Direct pin control.   While the output-compare hardware controls a pin, direct software control of the pin is not possible. Be careful because the timer may not control the output pins if the output-compare action disables the timer. When all the timer output functions for a pin are disabled, the port A pins are controlled by the PORTA register. The timer does not affect the PORTA register.

Pulse-width modulation using OC2

A common digital-to-analog conversion technique is to pulse-width modulate a digital output pin. The pin is switched between low and high rapidly. Controlling the low and high times adjusts the average value of the waveform, which is used as an analog output. A measure of the average value, called the *duty cycle*, is the time the pin is high as a percentage of the period.

The example in Figure 7-26 uses output compare 2 to control the duty cycle of port A pin PA6. The output pin is driven high after a time delay, and then is driven low after another time delay. Repeating this procedure generates the waveform. Here is a description of the program:

- *Lines 43 and 44.*   The OC2 is programmed to make the output low on the first compare. A hardware reset disconnects the timer from the output pin and clears port A. Therefore, after reset, the OC2 pin is also low.

  After reset, the free-running counter contains 0000 and the output-compare registers contain FFFF. Therefore, the first compare, after a reset, happens only after the full

```
 1                              ********************************************************
 2                              ** PULSE WIDTH MODULATE PORT A BIT 6
 3                              *
 4                              * USE OUTPUT COMPARE 2 TO CONTROL DUTY CYCLE
 5                              *
 6                              ********************************************************
 7                              *
 8                              ********************************************************
 9                              ** SYMBOL DEFINITIONS
10                              ********************************************************
11                              * 68HC11 REGISTERS
12           1000              REG     EQU    $1000    BEGINNING OF REGISTERS
13           1018              TOC2    EQU    $1018    OUTPUT COMPARE 2 REGISTER
14           1020              TCTL1   EQU    $1020    TIMER CONTROL REGISTER
15           1022              TMSK1   EQU    $1022    TIMER MASK REGISTER
16           1023              TFLG1   EQU    $1023    TIMER FLAG REGISTER
17                              * MASKS
18           0040              BIT6    EQU    %01000000
19           0040              OC2F    EQU    %01000000
20                              *
21                              ********************************************************
22                              ** DATA SECTION
23                              ********************************************************
24    0020                              ORG  $20
25    0020   C000              PWMLO   FDB    $C000    LOW OUTPUT TIME
26    0022   4000              PWMHI   FDB    $4000    HIGH OUTPUT TIME
27                              *                      ..RATIO OF PWMLO AND
28                              *                      ..PWMHI SET DUTY CYCLE
29                              *
30    FFE6                              ORG $FFE6
31    FFE6   C110                       FDB OC2ISR     OC2 INTERRUPT VECTOR
32                              *
33                              ********************************************************
34                              ** MAIN PROGRAM
35                              ********************************************************
36    C100                              ORG $C100
37                              *------------------------------------------------------
38                              * INITIALIZATION
39                              *------------------------------------------------------
40                              * INITIALIZE STACK
41    C100   8E CF FF          START   LDS    #$CFFF
42                              * INITIALIZE OUTPUT COMPARE OC2
43    C103   86 80                      LDAA   #$80     OM2:OL2=10 FOR SET TO LOW
44    C105   B7 10 20                   STAA   TCTL1    ..ON COMPARE
45                              * ENABLE OC2 INTERRUPT
46    C108   86 40                      LDAA   #$40
47    C10A   B7 10 22                   STAA   TMSK1
48                              * TURN ON INTERRUPT SYSTEM
49    C10D   0E                         CLI
50                              *------------------------------------------------------
51                              * WAIT FOR INTERRUPTS
52                              *------------------------------------------------------
53    C10E   20 FE             HERE    BRA    HERE
54                              *
55                              ********************************************************
56                              ** INTERRUPT SERVICE ROUTINE
57                              ********************************************************
58                              *------------------------------------------------------
59                              * INTERRUPT POLLING CHAIN
60                              *------------------------------------------------------
61                              * INTERRUPT FROM OC2?
62    C110   CE 10 00          OC2ISR  LDX    #REG
```

Figure 7-26   Pulse-width modulation using output compare 2.

```
63   C113   1F 23 40 1C              BRCLR TFLG1-REG,X,OC2F,RTOC2    IGNORE ILLEGAL
64                              *                       ..INTERRUPT
65                              *-----------------------------------------------------
66                              * SERVICE OUTPUT COMPARE 2
67                              *-----------------------------------------------------
68                              * CLEAR OC2 FLAG
69   C117   86 40                     LDAA  #OC2F     STORE 1 TO CLEAR FLAG
70   C119   A7 23                     STAA  TFLG1-REG,X  ..ZEROS DO NOTHING
71                              * WAS LAST OUTPUT HIGH?
72   C11B   1E 20 40 0B               BRSET TCTL1-REG,X,BIT6,LASTHI  BRANCH ON YES
73                              * PROGRAM NEXT OUTPUT TO BE HIGH
74                              *    SET OC2 OUTPUT ACTION
75   C11F   1C 20 40                  BSET  TCTL1-REG,X,BIT6  OM2:OL2=11
76                              *    SET HIGH OUTPUT COMPARE TIME
77   C122   EC 18                     LDD   TOC2-REG,X
78   C124   D3 20                     ADDD  PWMLO
79   C126   ED 18                     STD   TOC2-REG,X
80   C128   20 09                     BRA   RTOC2
81                              * PROGRAM NEXT OUTPUT TO BE LOW
82                              *    SET OC2 OUTPUT ACTION
83   C12A   1D 20 40          LASTHI  BCLR  TCTL1-REG,X,BIT6  OM2:OL2=10
84                              *    SET LOW OUTPUT COMPARE TIME
85   C12D   EC 18                     LDD   TOC2-REG,X
86   C12F   D3 22                     ADDD  PWMHI
87   C131   ED 18                     STD   TOC2-REG,X
88                              * RETURN FROM INTERRUPT
89   C133   3B                RTOC2   RTI
90   C134                             END
```

Figure 7-26   Continued.

range of the free-running counter. The program may initialize the output-compare register if this is unacceptable.

- *Lines 46 through 53.*   The rest of the hardware is initialized and the main program loop starts running waiting for interrupts.

- *Lines 62 and 63.*   The OC2 flag is tested for a valid interrupt. The X register is used as a pointer to the first hardware control register. Bit-oriented instructions with indexed addressing access the control registers.

- *Lines 69 and 70.*   Writing 1 to the flag bit clears the OC2 flag.

- *Line 72.*   The program tests the OL bit to determine if the output pin was high after the last interrupt. If so, it must be changed to low on the next interrupt. Otherwise, it must be changed to high. Since this instruction can only be executing if an interrupt has occurred, this is a sure test of the last state of the output pin.

- *Line 75.*   Set the output level or OL bit so the next compare makes the output pin high.

- *Lines 77 through 79.*   The number in the output-compare register is advanced by a count that represents the low time of the output pin. Overflows from the addition cause no problems.

- *Lines 83 through 87.* These lines set up the output to go low after the proper high time.

- *Line 89.* Control returns to the main program. The low and high times must be long enough for the return and another interrupt to complete before the next output change is required.

The longest high and low time appropriate to the application should be used. Shorter times cause more frequent interrupts and greater software overhead. Very short times could cause the interrupt service overhead to be so great that nothing else could be done. The computer could spend most of its time in the interrupt service routine.

Output compare 1

Output compare 1 controls the output pin differently from the other four output compares. In addition, OC1 may control all five output compare pins at once, although four of them may also be under control of their output-compare hardware. The output-compare signals are part of the port A pins. Figure 7-27 shows the parts of the output-compare 1 hardware.

Output-compare 1 register. The output-compare 1 register that Figure 7-27 shows is a 16-bit register because it is compared to the free-running counter. The output-compare register is named TOC1 and is at address 1016. A program may both read and write this register; normally the program only writes to it.

Port signals. Port A includes the pins that the output-compare hardware controls. The pins are named PA3, PA4, PA5, PA6, and PA7. Output compare OC1 may control all these output pins even if other output compares also control them.

Pin PA7 shares functions between output compare 1 and the pulse accumulator device. Pin PA7 is a programmable I/O pin. The program must make pin PA7 an output when the output-compare device uses it. Figure 7-12 shows the PACTL register and the data direction register bit DDRA7. The program puts a 1 in DDRA7 to make PA7 an output pin.

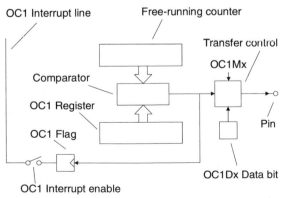

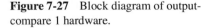

Figure 7-27 Block diagram of output-compare 1 hardware.

Transfer control.   When the comparator in Figure 7-27 detects a match between the output-compare 1 register and the free-running counter, it triggers the transfer of a data bit to the output pin. A mask bit called OC1Mx enables or disables the transfer, and a data bit called OC1Dx determines the output pin level. If the program has set the mask to 1, the transfer takes place when the match occurs. The program must store the value into the data bit before the match occurs. Therefore, the timing of the transfer to the pin is independent of the software overhead.

Figure 7-28 shows the OC1 mask register called OC1M. Bits 3 through 7 of OC1M correspond to pins PA3 through PA7 of port A. A 1 in a mask bit enables OC1 to control the corresponding port A pin.

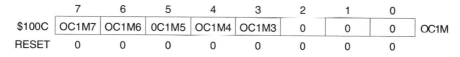

	7	6	5	4	3	2	1	0	
$100C	OC1M7	OC1M6	0C1M5	OC1M4	OC1M3	0	0	0	OC1M
RESET	0	0	0	0	0	0	0	0	

Figure 7-28   Output-compare 1 mask register.

If a mask bit enables a transfer, the transfer occurs on the next match despite other hardware actions. For example, suppose both OC2 and OC1 control port A pin PA6. If both try to affect the pin on the same E-clock cycle, OC1 overrides the other hardware

Figure 7-29 shows the OC1 data register called OC1D. Bits 3 through 7 of OC1D correspond to pins PA3 through PA7 of port A. If the mask enables a transfer, a 1 in a data bit makes the corresponding port A pin high when the transfer occurs, and a 0 makes it low.

	7	6	5	4	3	2	1	0	
$100D	OC1D7	OC1D6	OC1D5	OC1D4	OC1D3	0	0	0	OC1D
RESET	0	0	0	0	0	0	0	0	

Figure 7-29   Output-compare 1 data register.

Flag.   Figure 7-21 shows the output-compare flags in the timer flag register called TFLG1. The OC1 flag is set by matches between the free-running counter and the output-compare 1 register. Writing a 1 to an output-compare flag bit clears the flag. Writing a 0 to the flag bit does not affect it.

Interrupt.   The output compare 1 flag, OC1F, can cause an interrupt. The interrupt-enable bit OC1I corresponding to OC1 is in the timer mask register called TMSK1. Figure 7-22 shows the TMSK1 register. Writing a 1 into an interrupt-enable bit enables the flag to cause an interrupt. The reset condition disables all the output-compare interrupts.

Instructions. Always use a double-byte instruction, such as STD, to write to the 16-bit output compare 1 register or the comparison circuit may not function correctly. A match may occur at the wrong time if only one byte of the compare register is updated at a time.

Direct pin control. When the output-compare hardware controls a pin, direct software control of the pin is not possible. Two output-compare devices must be disabled to enable direct control of a pin. First, the corresponding OC1 mask bit must be 0 to disable OC1 from controlling the pin. Second, if another output-compare corresponds to the pin, it must be disconnected. Then the port A output pins are controlled by the PORTA register. The timer does not affect the PORTA register.

Pulse-width modulation using OC1

The program in Figure 7-30 uses output compare 1 to control the duty cycle of port A pin PA7. This example that uses OC1 is very similar to the example in Figure 7-26 that uses OC2. The output pin is driven high after a time delay, then driven low after another time delay. Repeating this procedure rapidly generates the waveform with a specified duty cycle.

The example uses port A pin PA7 because this pin is more complicated than the other port A outputs. Here is a description of the program that highlights only the differences from Figure 7-26:

- *Lines 46 and 47.* A 1 is put in the OC1 mask register to enable it to control port A pin PA7. Hardware reset disables all the mask bits and disables all the other output compares from controlling port A pins.

- *Line 49.* Clearing the output data register will make the initial state of the output pin the low level.

- *Lines 51 and 52.* Port A pin PA7 has several functions including both input and output operations, so it has a data direction bit. To use an output-compare to control this pin, the data direction must be set to output. Storing 1 in the DDRA7 bit in the PACTL register makes PA7 an output.

- *Line 80.* Reading the last data value that OC1 used indicates the state of the output pin. If the pin is low, control goes to line 83.

- *Line 83.* The output data bit is set to 1 so the pin goes high on the next match between the free-running counter and the TOC1 output-compare register.

- *Lines 85 through 87.* Since the output pin went low when this interrupt occurred, the time the output must be low is added to the compare register. When the next compare occurs, the output pin will go high.

Most of this example appears similar to the example using OC2. However, the operation of the two output-compares is very different. OC2 has more functions that it can do to the output pin than does OC1.

```
 1                                  ***********************************************************
 2                                  ** PULSE WIDTH MODULATE PORT A BIT 7
 3                                  *
 4                                  * USE OUTPUT COMPARE 1 TO CONTROL DUTY CYCLE
 5                                  *
 6                                  ***********************************************************
 7                                  *
 8                                  ***********************************************************
 9                                  ** SYMBOL DEFINITIONS
10                                  ***********************************************************
11                                  * 68HC11 REGISTERS
12            1000                  REG       EQU    $1000    BEGINNING OF REGISTERS
13            100C                  OC1M      EQU    $100C    OUTPUT COMPARE 1 MASK REGISTER
14            100D                  OC1D      EQU    $100D    OUTPUT COMPARE 1 DATA REGISTER
15            1016                  TOC1      EQU    $1016    OUTPUT COMPARE 1 REGISTER
16            1020                  TCTL1     EQU    $1020    TIMER CONTROL REGISTER
17            1022                  TMSK1     EQU    $1022    TIMER MASK REGISTER
18            1023                  TFLG1     EQU    $1023    TIMER FLAG REGISTER
19            1026                  PACTL     EQU    $1026    PULSE ACCUMULATOR CONTROL REG
20                                  * MASKS
21            0080                  BIT7      EQU    %10000000
22            0080                  OC1F      EQU    %10000000
23                                  *
24                                  ***********************************************************
25                                  ** DATA SECTION
26                                  ***********************************************************
27    0020                                    ORG    $20
28    0020    C000                  PWMLO     FDB    $C000    LOW OUTPUT TIME
29    0022    4000                  PWMHI     FDB    $4000    HIGH OUTPUT TIME
30                                  *                        ..RATIO OF PWMLO AND
31                                  *                        ..PWMHI SET DUTY CYCLE
32                                  *
33    FFE8                                    ORG    $FFE8
34    FFE8    C118                            FDB    OC11SR   OC1 INTERRUPT VECTOR
35                                  *
36                                  ***********************************************************
37                                  ** MAIN PROGRAM
38                                  ***********************************************************
39    C100                                    ORG    $C100
40                                  *----------------------------------------------------------
41                                  * INITIALIZATION
42                                  *----------------------------------------------------------
43                                  * INITIALIZE STACK
44    C100    8E CF FF              START     LDS    #$CFFF
45                                  * INITIALIZE OUTPUT COMPARE OC1 MASK
46    C103    86 80                           LDAA   #$80
47    C105    B7 10 0C                        STAA   OC1M     ENABLE PIN CONTROL
48                                  * INITIALIZE OUTPUT COMPARE OC1 DATA
49    C108    7F 10 0D                        CLR    OC1D
50                                  * INITIALIZE DATA DIRECTION BIT FOR PA7 PIN
51    C10B    86 80                           LDAA   #$80
52    C10D    B7 10 26                        STAA   PACTL    DDRA7=1
53                                  * ENABLE OC1 INTERRUPT
54    C110    86 80                           LDAA   #$80
55    C112    B7 10 22                        STAA   TMSK1
56                                  * TURN ON INTERRUPT SYSTEM
57    C115    0E                              CLI
58                                  *----------------------------------------------------------
59                                  * WAIT FOR INTERRUPTS
60                                  *----------------------------------------------------------
61    C116    20 FE                 HERE      BRA    HERE
62                                  *
```

Figure 7-30   Pulse-width modulation using output compare 1.

```
63                          ****************************************************
64                          ** INTERRUPT SERVICE ROUTINE
65                          ****************************************************
66                          *----------------------------------------------------
67                          * INTERRUPT POLLING CHAIN
68                          *----------------------------------------------------
69                          * INTERRUPT FROM OC1?
70   C118   CE 10 00        OC1ISR LDX   #REG
71   C11B   1F 23 80 1C            BRCLR TFLG1-REG,X,OC1F,RTOC1   IGNORE ILLEGAL
72                          *                        ..INTERRUPT
73                          *----------------------------------------------------
74                          * SERVICE OUTPUT COMPARE 1
75                          *----------------------------------------------------
76                          * CLEAR OC1 FLAG
77   C11F   86 80                  LDAA   #OC1F    STORE 1 TO CLEAR FLAG
78   C121   A7 23                  STAA   TFLG1-REG,X  ..ZEROS DO NOTHING
79                          * WAS LAST OUTPUT HIGH?
80   C123   1E 0D 80 0B            BRSET OC1D-REG,X,BIT7,LASTHI   BRANCH ON YES
81                          * PROGRAM NEXT OUTPUT TO BE HIGH
82                          *     SET OC1 OUTPUT DATA FOR HIGH OUTPUT
83   C127   1C 0D 80               BSET   OC1D-REG,X,BIT7
84                          *     SET HIGH OUTPUT COMPARE TIME
85   C12A   EC 16                  LDD    TOC1-REG,X
86   C12C   D3 20                  ADDD   PWMLO
87   C12E   ED 16                  STD    TOC1-REG,X
88   C130   20 09                  BRA    RTOC1
89                          * PROGRAM NEXT OUTPUT TO BE LOW
90                          *     SET OC1 OUTPUT DATA FOR LOW OUTPUT
91   C132   1D 0D 80        LASTHI BCLR   OC1D-REG,X,BIT7
92                          *     SET LOW OUTPUT COMPARE TIME
93   C135   EC 16                  LDD    TOC1-REG,X
94   C137   D3 22                  ADDD   PWMHI
95   C139   ED 16                  STD    TOC1-REG,X
96                          * RETURN FROM INTERRUPT
97   C13B   3B              RTOC1  RTI
98   C13C                          END
```

Figure 7-30   Continued.

Forcing output compares

A program can force the output-compare action to take place without a match between the free-running counter and the output-compare register. Therefore, the program can advance the time when the output action takes place.

Output-compare initialization.   Programs often force output-compares to initialize the output hardware to a known condition. Software cannot directly control an output pin while an output-compare has control of the pin. Therefore, forcing the compare hardware is the only way the program can initialize the level on the pin.

The CFORC register.   Figure 7-31 shows the output-compare-force register named CFORC. To force or trigger an output action, a program writes a 1 to a FOCx force-bit in the CFORC register. Writing 0s into force-bits does nothing. Furthermore, forcing the action does not set the flag! So forcing cannot make an interrupt occur earlier.

Each output compare can be forced by the corresponding bit in CFORC. Since the CFORC register is a hardware trigger register, reading CFORC is meaningless.

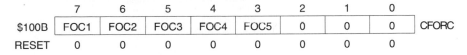

	7	6	5	4	3	2	1	0	
$100B	FOC1	FOC2	FOC3	FOC4	FOC5	0	0	0	CFORC
RESET	0	0	0	0	0	0	0	0	

Figure 7-31   Timer compare force register.

Forcing toggle actions.   Forcing the output action does not prevent the normal output action when a match occurs. Be careful using the force register if the output action is to toggle the output pin. The forced toggle of the output pin may be immediately followed by a normal toggle of the pin causing confusing results.

Using Input Capture with Output Compare

When input capture and output compare are used together, it is possible to synchronize a timed output function to a timed input function. The synchronization is very accurate without dependence on latency time of software.

Make delayed pulse using IC1 and OC3

The example program in Figure 7-32 shows the use of both input-capture hardware and output-compare hardware together. The program uses OC3 to make a pulse on the port A pin PA5 that is delayed from the time a trigger from input capture 1 occurs. The programmable timer controls the delay time before the pulse starts and the duration of the pulse. The output pin is normally low, so the pulse is a high-going pulse.

The program is very similar to previous examples. The following describes only those parts related to the programmable timer:

- *Lines 61 through 63.*   The output compare 3 is programmed to make the pin go low on the next match between the free-running counter and the output-compare register. Then the instruction on line 63 writes to the compare-force register to initialize the pin to the low level.

  This initialization may not be necessary. If a hardware reset precedes this program, the reset forces the pin low. Furthermore, if this is not so, the pin will go low on the next match between the free-running counter and the output-compare 3 register. The match will occur sometime within the next 32.77_{10} milliseconds. Even if a reset doesn't precede the program, initializing the pin within 32.77_{10} milliseconds may be acceptable.

- *Lines 65 and 66.*   Both the IC1 and OC3 devices use interrupt, but only the IC1 interrupt is enabled here. Otherwise, OC3 will interrupt every time the output-compare register matches the free-running counter.

- *Lines 78 and 79.*   When the input signal for IC1 triggers a capture, the IC1F flag is set causing the interrupt. The IC1F flag is now cleared.

```
 1                                 ****************************************************************
 2                                 ** MAKE DELAYED TRIGGERED PULSE
 3                                 *
 4                                 * USE INPUT CAPTURE 1 TO TRIGGER ON LOW-TO-HIGH
 5                                 * ..TRANSITION AT PORT A BIT2
 6                                 *
 7                                 * USE OUTPUT COMPARE 3 TO MAKE HIGH-GOING PULSE
 8                                 * ..AT PORT A BIT5
 9                                 *
10                                 * USE 8.0 MHZ CRYSTAL FOR 68HC11 CLOCK AND RUN
11                                 * ..FREE-RUNNING COUNTER AT MAXIMUM RATE
12                                 *
13                                 * MAXIMUM DELAY IS 32.77 MS AND MAXIMUM DURATION
14                                 * ..IS 32.77 MS
15                                 *
16                                 ****************************************************************
17                                 *
18                                 ****************************************************************
19                                 ** SYMBOL DEFINITIONS
20                                 ****************************************************************
21                                 * 68HC11 REGISTERS
22            1000                 REG      EQU    $1000     BEGINNING OF 68HC11 REGISTERS
23            100B                 CFORC    EQU    $100B     COMPARE FORCE REGISTER
24            1010                 TIC1     EQU    $1010     INPUT CAPTURE 1 REG
25            101A                 TOC3     EQU    $101A     OUTPUT COMPARE 3 REG
26            1020                 TCTL1    EQU    $1020     TIMER CONTROL REG 1
27            1021                 TCTL2    EQU    $1021     TIMER CONTROL REG 2
28            1022                 TMSK1    EQU    $1022     TIMER INT MASK 1
29            1023                 TFLG1    EQU    $1023     TIMER INT FLAG 1
30                                 * MASKS
31            0004                 BIT2     EQU    %00000100
32            00FB                 BBIT2    EQU    %11111011
33            0020                 BIT5     EQU    %00100000
34            00DF                 BBIT5    EQU    %11011111
35                                 *
36                                 ****************************************************************
37                                 ** DATA SECTION
38                                 ****************************************************************
39   0000                                  ORG    $0000
40   0000    4000                 DELCNT   FDB    $4000     DELAY TIME IN COUNTER PULSES
41   0002    6000                 PWCNT    FDB    $6000     PULSE HIGH TIME IN PULSES
42                                 *
43   FFE4                                  ORG    $FFE4
44   FFE4    C132                          FDB    OC3ISR    OC3 INTERRUPT VECTOR
45   FFEE                                  ORG    $FFEE
46   FFEE    C118                          FDB    IC1ISR    IC1 INTERRUPT VECTOR
47                                 *
48                                 ****************************************************************
49                                 ** MAIN PROGRAM
50                                 ****************************************************************
51   C100                                  ORG    $C100
52                                 *--------------------------------------------------------
53                                 * INITIALIZATION
54                                 *--------------------------------------------------------
55                                 * INITIALIZE STACK
56   C100    8E CF FF             START    LDS    #$CFFF
57                                 * INITIALIZE IC1 ACTIVE EDGE
58   C103    86 10                         LDAA   #$10      LTOH RISING EDGE ONLY
59   C105    B7 10 21                      STAA   TCTL2
60                                 * INITIALIZE OC3 OUTPUT TO LOW
61   C108    86 20                         LDAA   #$20      OM3:OL3=10 FOR SET TO LOW
62   C10A    B7 10 20                      STAA   TCTL1     ..ON COMPARE
```

Figure 7-32   Delayed pulse using IC1 and OC3.

```
63   C10D   B7 10 0B              STAA    CFORC     FORCE OC3 ACTION
64                        * ENABLE IC1 AND DISABLE OC3 INTERRUPTS
65   C110   86 04                 LDAA    #BIT2
66   C112   B7 10 22              STAA    TMSK1
67                        * TURN ON INTERRUPT SYSTEM
68   C115   0E                    CLI
69                        *----------------------------------------------------
70                        * WAIT FOR INTERRUPTS
71                        *----------------------------------------------------
72   C116   20 FE         HERE    BRA     HERE
73                        *
74                        *******************************************************
75                        ** INPUT CAPTURE 1 INTERRUPT SERVICE ROUTINE
76                        *******************************************************
77                        * CLEAR IC1 FLAG
78   C118   CE 10 00      IC1ISR  LDX     #REG
79   C11B   1D 23 FB              BCLR    TFLG1-REG,X,BBIT2  STORE 1 TO CLEAR FLAG
80                        * SET TIME FOR OUTPUT PULSE TO GO HIGH
81   C11E   FC 10 10              LDD     TIC1
82   C121   D3 00                 ADDD    DELCNT
83   C123   FD 10 1A              STD     TOC3
84                        * PROGRAM OC3 TO GO HIGH ON NEXT MATCH
85   C126   86 30                 LDAA    #$30      OM3:OL3=11
86   C128   B7 10 20              STAA    TCTL1
87                        * CLEAR OC3 FLAG
88   C12B   1D 23 DF              BCLR    TFLG1-REG,X,BBIT5  STORE 1 TO CLEAR FLAG
89                        * ENABLE OC3 INTERRUPT
90   C12E   1C 22 20              BSET    TMSK1-REG,X,BIT5
91                        * RETURN FROM IC1 INTERRUPT
92   C131   3B                    RTI
93                        *
94                        *******************************************************
95                        ** OUTPUT COMPARE 3 INTERRUPT SERVICE ROUTINE
96                        *******************************************************
97                        * DISABLE FURTHER OC3 INTERRUPTS
98   C132   CE 10 00      OC3ISR  LDX     #REG
99   C135   1D 22 20              BCLR    TMSK1-REG,X,BIT5   NO NEED TO CLEAR FLAG
100                       * SET TIME FOR PULSE TO GO LOW
101  C138   FC 10 1A              LDD     TOC3
102  C13B   D3 02                 ADDD    PWCNT
103  C13D   FD 10 1A              STD     TOC3
104                       * PROGRAM OC3 TO GO LOW ON NEXT MATCH
105  C140   86 20                 LDAA    #$20      OM3:OL3=10
106  C142   B7 10 20              STAA    TCTL1
107                       * RETURN FROM OC3 INTERRUPT
108  C145   3B                    RTI
109  C146                         END
```

Figure 7-32   Continued.

- *Lines 81 through 83.* The time to start the output pulse with OC3 is set. First, the IC1 capture register is read to get the time when the input signal triggered an input capture. The latency time for processing the interrupt has no effect because the trigger time is in the capture register. Note that reading the free-running counter will give errors in the timing, so always read the capture register. Second, the delay time in counts of the free-running counter is added to the capture time and stored in the output-compare register. Therefore, the output pin will be affected at the time of the next match. The maximum possible delay in this program is the time between free-running counter overflows.

Motorola Trainer

The example programs for the programmable timer in Figures 7-23, 7-26, 7-30, and 7-32 can all be run in the trainer. In all cases, the interrupt vector in the trainer must be fixed to send control to the interrupt service routine. A 555 timer-integrated circuit can provide a periodic input signal. An oscilloscope is the best tool to observe the input and output waveforms. You can easily observe the effects of the pulse-width modulated outputs with an indicator light such as an LED.

- *Lines 85 and 86.* The initialization programmed OC3 to go low, so now it's programmed to go high on the upcoming match. Therefore, OC3 will generate a high-going pulse.

- *Line 88.* While waiting for an input signal, or while processing the interrupt and running the interrupt service routine, a match for OC3 may have occurred. If a match set the OC3F flag, it must be cleared. Otherwise, an interrupt from OC3 will occur immediately instead of after the delay.

- *Line 90.* The OC3 interrupt is enabled. After the delay, the OC3 match will make the output pin high, set the OC3F flag, and cause an interrupt to signal that the delay is complete.

- *Line 92.* Control returns to the main program after servicing the interrupt from input capture 1. The main program and other interrupts run during the delay time.

- *Lines 98 and 99.* The delay period is over and OC3 caused an interrupt to send control here. Usually when a device interrupts, the interrupt service routine must clear flag so it is ready for future interrupts. But that is not so here. There is no need to know when the output pulse is complete. Furthermore, OC3 continues to set OC3F repeatedly as the free-running counter causes further matches. So OC3 must be prevented from causing further interrupts by disabling its interrupt.

- *Lines 101 through 103.* The time at which OC3 must change the output pin is set. The high-going time is read from the compare register, the duration in counts is added, and the compare register is updated.

- *Lines 105 and 106.* Output compare 3 is programmed to make the pin go low after the proper pulse duration. The timer continues to operate from now on independent of the program. Therefore, the pin goes low at an accurate time, independent of the program.

The time between free-running counter overflows is 32.77_{10} milliseconds in this example. Therefore, the maximum delay time and maximum pulse time are both 32.77_{10} milliseconds. Longer times require use of the timer-overflow interrupt.

The example assumes that an input signal will not trigger a new pulse before the last pulse is complete. You should investigate the consequences of the input signal triggering a new pulse before the last one is finished. Also, consider the effects of other interrupt service routines that may delay the running of the timer interrupt service routines.

An application for a delayed pulse

Consider a gasoline engine that uses electronic fuel injection synchronized to the engine rotation. A fuel injector allows fuel flow in pulses. The pulses must occur only when the engine is at a particular point in a crankshaft revolution. A sensor on the engine makes a pulse as the crankshaft rotates to a reference position. The injector must supply fuel at some time beyond the occurrence of the sensor pulse. The program in Figure 7-32 can use the pulse from the sensor to make the control pulse for the injector.

As the engine runs at higher speeds, the delay time must be reduced. Furthermore, the duration of the injector pulse must be adjusted under different engine running conditions to deliver the correct fuel flow. A feedback control system determines the delay and pulse length. The control system program runs independently of the timer interrupt service routines. The program example here only makes the injector pulse.

Timer Flag Applications

Some applications may not need some or all of the input-capture functions. If this is true, the input-capture flags are available as general-purpose flags. Each flag has a separate interrupt vector. Ignore the input-capture register if you want to use only the flag.

Because the input-capture flags are available, the 68HC11, when using the STAF flag, has from one to five flags. Therefore, many applications will not need an external flag.

7.9 PULSE ACCUMULATOR

The pulse accumulator either counts pulses on a pin or it counts cycles of an oscillator to make a timer. The pulse accumulator operates in two modes called the *external-event-counting* mode and the *gated-time-accumulation* mode.

The primary hardware in the pulse accumulator is an 8-bit up-counter. The port A pin PA7 controls the counter. Figure 7-33 shows the pulse-accumulator counter called PACNT. The program may both read and write the PACNT register.

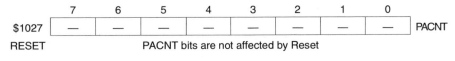

Figure 7-33   Pulse-accumulator count register.

The mode of operation of the pulse accumulator is controlled by three bits in the pulse-accumulator-control register called PACTL. Figure 7-34 is a copy of Figure 7-12 that shows the PACTL register.

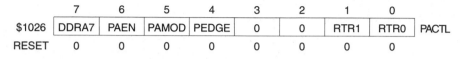

	7	6	5	4	3	2	1	0	
$1026	DDRA7	PAEN	PAMOD	PEDGE	0	0	RTR1	RTR0	PACTL
RESET	0	0	0	0	0	0	0	0	

Figure 7-34   Pulse-accumulator control register.

The pulse-accumulator-enable bit, PAEN, in the PACTL register enables the pulse accumulator while it is 1. The program may make the PAEN bit 0 to disable the pin from affecting the pulse accumulator. Usually, programs disable the pulse accumulator if pin PA7 is programmed for output. The DDRA7 bit in the PACTL register controls whether pin PA7 does input or output.

The pulse-accumulator-mode bit, PAMOD, in the PACTL register selects one of the two primary modes of operation. The program selects the external-event-counting mode by making the PAMOD bit 0, and it selects the gated-time-accumulation mode by making the PAMOD bit 1. The purpose of the PEDGE bit in PACTL depends on the mode of operation.

Event-Counting Mode

The pulse accumulator counts active transitions on port A pin PA7 while the pulse accumulator is in the event-counting mode. Figure 7-35 is a block diagram of the parts of the pulse accumulator in this mode. The hardware is very flexible; it is used for many kinds of applications.

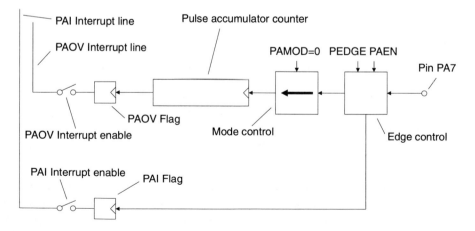

Figure 7-35   Pulse accumulator in event-counting mode.

Hardware operation

Active transitions of signals applied to the PA7 pin clock the 8-bit counter register. The counter increments by one each time it is clocked.

Flags and interrupts.   When the counter rolls over from FF to 00, it sets the pulse-accumulator overflow flag, PAOVF, in the TFLG2 register. Setting the PAOVF flag while the pulse-accumulator-overflow interrupt is enabled causes an interrupt if the interrupt system is on. The pulse-accumulator-overflow-interrupt-enable bit, PAOVI, in the TMSK2 register must be 1 to enable overflow interrupts. The overflow interrupt has an interrupt vector at address FFDC and FFDD as Table 7-2 shows.

While the pulse accumulator is in event-counting mode because PAMOD is 1, the hardware transfers the active transition from the PA7 pin to the counter. Figure 7-35 shows this transfer with a bold arrow. The active transition at pin PA7 also sets the pulse-accumulator input flag, PAIF. If the pulse-accumulator-input-interrupt-enable bit, PAII, is 1, setting the flag causes an interrupt. The interrupt vector is at addresses FFDA and FFDB as Table 7-2 shows.

Active transitions.   The PEDGE bit in the PACTL register determines whether the active transition at pin PA7 is high-to-low or low-to-high. While PEDGE is 0, the high-to-low transition is active. While PEDGE is 1, the low-to-high transition is active. However, if the pulse-accumulator-enable bit PAEN is 0, the input signal at the pin has no effect on any of the pulse-accumulator hardware.

Summary.   While the pulse accumulator is enabled, each active transition of the PA7 pin increments the pulse-accumulator counter and sets the pulse-accumulator-input flag. If the counter rolls over to 00, it sets the pulse-accumulator-overflow flag. If the flags are enabled to cause interrupts, setting the flags cause interrupts to unique interrupt vectors.

Programming example

Consider an application where a toothed wheel, magnetic sensor, and electronic interface make pulses as a mechanical device rotates. Each tooth generates a pulse as it passes the magnetic sensor. The pulses cause interrupts so the computer responds to the rotation. However, the pulses may occur so frequently that the computer spends too much time responding to the pulses. If the application does not require the computer to respond to every pulse, some pulses can be skipped. Suppose we want the computer to respond to every fifth pulse. Rather than built an electronic circuit to generate an interrupt signal after five pulses, let's use the pulse accumulator.

For simplicity, the example program only complements port B every fifth pulse. Figure 7-36 is the listing of the example program. The following is a description of the program.

- *Lines 42 and 43.*   The program enables the pulse accumulator and puts it in the event-counting mode. It also programs pin PA7 to respond to low-to-high transitions. The data direction bit for pin PA7, DDRA7, makes the pin an input so the pulse accumulator responds to external pulses at the pin.

- *Lines 45 and 46.* The program enables interrupts from the pulse-accumulator-overflow flag. The counter generates an interrupt each time it overflows from FF to 00. These instructions also disable the pulse-accumulator-input-flag interrupt. This flag gets set on each input pulse, but this application doesn't need it.

- *Lines 48 and 49.* These instructions set the pulse-accumulator counter to FF so it overflows to 00 on the very first input pulse. After the first pulse, overflows occur every fifth pulse.

- *Lines 64 and 65.* This test of the pulse-accumulator-overflow flag ensures that a valid interrupt occurred. The program ignores illegal interrupts. This is good programming practice.

- *Lines 71 and 72.* These instructions clear the pulse-accumulator-overflow flag so it can respond to the next input pulse.

- *Lines 74 and 75.* The pulse-accumulator counter now contains 00 because an overflow occurred that sent control to this interrupt service routine. Here the counter is set to FB so another overflow will occur after five more input pulses.

```
 1                              ***********************************************************
 2                              ** COMPLEMENT PORT B ON EVERY FIFTH INPUT PULSE
 3                              *
 4                              * USE PULSE ACCUMULATOR INPUT AT PIN PA7
 5                              *
 6                              ***********************************************************
 7                              *
 8                              ***********************************************************
 9                              ** SYMBOL DEFINITIONS
10                              ***********************************************************
11                              * 68HC11 REGISTERS
12           1000               REG    EQU    $1000      BEGINNING OF REGISTERS
13           1004               PORTB  EQU    $1004      PORTB REGISTER
14           1024               TMSK2  EQU    $1024      TIMER MASK REGISTER
15           1025               TFLG2  EQU    $1025      TIMER FLAG REGISTER
16           1026               PACTL  EQU    $1026      PULSE ACCUMULATOR CONTROL REG
17           1027               PACNT  EQU    $1027      PULSE ACCUMULATOR COUNTER REG
18                              * MASKS
19           0010               BIT4   EQU    %00010000
20           0020               BIT5   EQU    %00100000
21           0040               BIT6   EQU    %01000000
22                              *
23                              ***********************************************************
24                              ** DATA SECTION
25                              ***********************************************************
26    FFDC                                    ORG $FFDC
27    FFDC   C118                              FDB    PAOVISR  PAOV INTERRUPT VECTOR
28                              *
29                              ***********************************************************
30                              ** MAIN PROGRAM
31                              ***********************************************************
32    C100                                    ORG $C100
```

Figure 7-36   Example program for event counting.

```
33                              *-----------------------------------------------------
34                              * INITIALIZATION
35                              *-----------------------------------------------------
36                              * INITIALIZE STACK
37    C100    8E CF FF          START   LDS    #$CFFF
38                              * INITIALIZE PORT B
39    C103    7F 10 04                  CLR    PORTB
40                              * INITIALIZE PULSE ACCUMULATOR
41                              *   EVENT COUNTING MODE
42    C106    86 50                    LDAA   #$50      DDRA7:PAEN:PAMOD:PEDGE=0101
43    C108    B7 10 26                 STAA   PACTL     INPUT:ENABLE:EVENT:L-TO-H
44                              *   ENABLE PULSE ACCUMULATOR OVERFLOW INTERRUPT
45    C10B    86 20                    LDAA   #BIT5     PAOVI=1
46    C10D    B7 10 24                 STAA   TMSK2
47                              *   INITIALIZE COUNTER FOR IMMEDIATE INTERRUPT
48    C110    86 FF                    LDAA   #$FF      ONE COUNT TO OVERFLOW
49    C112    B7 10 27                 STAA   PACNT
50                              * TURN ON INTERRUPT SYSTEM
51    C115    0E                       CLI
52                              *-----------------------------------------------------
53                              * WAIT FOR INTERRUPTS
54                              *-----------------------------------------------------
55    C116    20 FE             HERE    BRA    HERE
56                              *
57                              ***************************************************
58                              ** INTERRUPT SERVICE ROUTINE
59                              ***************************************************
60                              *-----------------------------------------------------
61                              * INTERRUPT POLLING CHAIN
62                              *-----------------------------------------------------
63                              * INTERRUPT FROM PULSE ACCUMULATOR OVERFLOW?
64    C118    CE 10 00          PAOVISR LDX    #REG
65    C11B    1F 25 20 0A               BRCLR  TFLG2-REG,X,BIT5,RTPAOV   IGNORE ILLEGAL
66                              *                            INTERRUPT
67                              *-----------------------------------------------------
68                              * SERVICE PULSE ACCUMULATOR OVERFLOW
69                              *-----------------------------------------------------
70                              * CLEAR PULSE ACCUMULATOR OVERFLOW FLAG
71    C11F    86 20                    LDAA   #BIT5     STORE 1 TO CLEAR FLAG
72    C121    A7 25                    STAA   TFLG2-REG,X  ..ZEROS DO NOTHING
73                              * SET UP PULSE ACCUMULATOR COUNTER FOR NEXT INTERRUPT
74    C123    86 FB                    LDAA   #$FB      WILL INTERRUPT ON FIFTH PULSE
75    C125    A7 27                    STAA   PACNT-REG,X
76                              * COMPLEMENT PORTB
77    C127    63 04                    COM    PORTB-REG,X
78                              * RETURN FROM INTERRUPT
79    C129    3B                RTPAOV  RTI
80    C12A                              END
```

Figure 7-36   Continued.

- *Line 77.*   This example program simply complements port B in response to the fifth input pulse.

Gated-Time-Accumulation Mode

The pulse accumulator, while in the gated-time-accumulation mode, counts active transitions of an oscillator while enabled by port A pin PA7. Figure 7-37 is a block diagram of the

---

Motorola Trainer

The example program for the pulse accumulator in Figure 7-36 can be run in the trainer. The interrupt vector in the trainer must be fixed to send control to the interrupt service routine. A 555 timer integrated circuit can provide a periodic input signal. An oscilloscope is the best tool to observe the input and output waveforms.

---

parts of the pulse accumulator in this mode. The counter accumulates time or counts while the signal at the pin is asserted; the PA7 pin is level-sensitive for this function.

Hardware operation

In the gated-time-accumulation mode, an oscillator based on the E-clock for the microprocessor drives the 8-bit counter. The frequency of the oscillator is always the E-clock frequency divided by 64_{10}. The signal at pin PA7 enables and disables the counter so it responds to the oscillator at the correct times. The terminology *gated* means the counter can be enabled and disabled. While the counter is enabled, it increments on each oscillator cycle. While the counter is disabled, it holds the last count. Therefore, the counter accumulates the number of oscillator cycles that occur while the counting is enabled—the pulse accumulator is a timer.

Flags and interrupts.　When the counter rolls over from FF to 00, it sets the pulse accumulator overflow flag, PAOVF, in the TFLG2 register. Setting the PAOVF flag causes an interrupt if the pulse-accumulator-overflow interrupt is enabled and the interrupt system is on. The pulse-accumulator-overflow-interrupt-enable bit, PAOVI, in the TMSK2 register must be 1 to enable overflow interrupts. The overflow interrupt has an interrupt vector at address FFDC and FFDD as Table 7-2 shows.

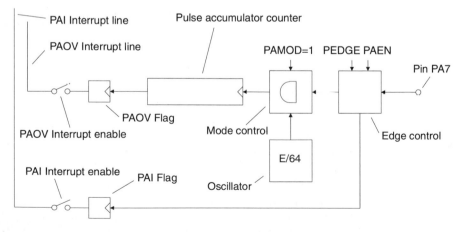

Figure 7-37　Pulse-accumulator gated-time-accumulation mode.

If the pulse accumulator is in gated-time-accumulation mode because the PAMOD bit is 0, the hardware transfers the active transitions from the oscillator to the counter while the PA7 pin is asserted. That is, the counter increments while pin PA7 is asserted. Pin PA7 is level-sensitive for this operation. Figure 7-37 shows the transfer of the oscillator signal to the counter with an AND-gate that acts as a transfer gate. However, when pin PA7 is changed to the deasserted level, this transition at pin PA7 sets the pulse accumulator-input flag, PAIF. If the pulse-accumulator-input-interrupt-enable bit, PAII, is 1, setting the PAIF flag causes an interrupt. The interrupt vector is at addresses FFDA and FFDB as Table 7-2 shows.

Active levels and transitions.   The PEDGE bit in the PACTL register determines which logic level is the active or asserted level at pin PA7. While PEDGE is 0, the high level is the asserted level. While PEDGE is 1, the low level is the asserted level. However, if the pulse-accumulator-enable bit PAEN is 0, the input signal at the pin has no effect on any of the pulse-accumulator hardware.

Remember that pin PA7 is level-sensitive while enabling the counter to respond to oscillator cycles. However, pin PA7 is transition sensitive when setting the flag.

Summary.   In the gated-time-accumulation mode, if the pulse accumulator is enabled, the counter accumulates a count of the oscillator cycles while pin PA7 is asserted. The counter holds the last count while the PA7 pin is deasserted, although the program may write a new number into the counter. A transition from asserted to deasserted at pin PA7 sets the PAIF flag. When the counter rolls over to 00, it sets the pulse-accumulator-overflow flag. If the flags are enabled to cause interrupts, setting a flag causes an interrupt to a unique interrupt vector.

Timing resolution and range

The oscillator that makes the pulse-accumulator counter increment is based on the microprocessor E-clock. The oscillator always runs at the E-clock rate divided by 64_{10}. This rate determines both the resolution of the timing and the counter overflow time.

If the crystal clock operates at the common frequency of 8.0_{10} MHz, the E-clock rate is 2.0 MHz. This rate gives a resolution of 32_{10} microseconds and an overflow time of 8.192_{10} milliseconds. Therefore, the pulse accumulator can easily measure times of approximately eight milliseconds. Longer times are measured by tracking overflows of the counter using the overflow flag, but the complexity of the program is much greater.

Programming example

Consider an application where a toothed wheel, magnetic sensor, and electronic interface make pulses as a mechanical device rotates. The pulse length in time is dependent on the physical length of the tooth and the rotation rate of the device. If the time for the tooth to pass is measured, the rotational velocity of the device can be calculated.

The example program measures the duration of a pulse in pulse-accumulator counts. If the pulse duration is long enough to allow the counter to overflow, the program indicates an error. The duration is not used for any purpose in this example.

Figure 7-38 is the listing of the example program. The example uses a pulse that is high, so the transition at the trailing edge is from high-to-low. The following is a description of the program.

- *Line 44.*   The program creates a stack because the interrupt system requires it.

- *Lines 46 and 48.*   The program variables are initialized.

- *Lines 51 and 52.*   These instructions program the pulse accumulator to operate in the gated-time-accumulation mode. They also make the high level the asserted condition of the PA7 input pin.

- *Lines 54 and 55.*   Both the pulse-accumulator input and overflow interrupts are enabled. An overflow interrupt indicates an error because the interrupt occurs only if the duration of the input pulse is too long.

- *Line 57.*   The pulse-accumulator counter is set to zero so the first pulse will be accurately timed. The counter starts incrementing when the input signal enables it. In this example, the counter accumulates time while the input signal is high. When the input changes to low at the end of the pulse, the transition sets the PAIF flag which causes an interrupt.

- *Lines 78 and 79.*   At the end of the input pulse, the interrupt system sends control here. The PAIF flag is tested for an illegal interrupt as good programming practice.

- *Lines 81 and 82.*   The pulse-accumulator counter is no longer incrementing because the pulse has ended. While the input is low, the counter retains the last count. The program reads the counter to determine the duration of the last pulse.

- *Line 84.*   The pulse-accumulator counter is set to zero so the counter correctly measures the duration of the next input pulse.

- *Lines 94 and 95.*   The interrupt system sends control here if the pulse accumulator overflows. The overflow may interrupt during the pulse-accumulator-input interrupt service routine because the overflow vector has a higher priority than the input vector. The overflow flag is tested for illegal interrupts as good programming practice.

- *Lines 101 and 102.*   The program clears the overflow flag to remove the source of overflow interrupts. However, if the input pulse is long enough, multiple overflows can occur. There is no indication of multiple overflows.

- *Lines 104 and 105.*   The program indicates an overflow error because an overflow interrupt occurred. The pulse-accumulator hardware determined that the error occurred.

Nothing in this program example uses the pulse duration or error indication. Therefore, the error indication is permanent because nothing resets the error.

```
 1                                    *****************************************************
 2                                    ** MEASURE THE DURATION OF AN INPUT PULSE
 3                                    *
 4                                    * USE PULSE ACCUMULATOR INPUT AT PIN PA7 TO DETECT
 5                                    * ..HIGH PULSE
 6                                    *
 7                                    * MAXIMUM PULSE DURATION IS $FF PULSE ACCUMULATOR
 8                                    * ..COUNTS. ERROR INDICATION PROVIDED.
 9                                    *
10                                    *****************************************************
11                                    *
12                                    *****************************************************
13                                    ** SYMBOL DEFINITIONS
14                                    *****************************************************
15                                    * 68HC11 REGISTERS
16            1000                    REG      EQU    $1000    BEGINNING OF REGISTERS
17            1024                    TMSK2    EQU    $1024    TIMER MASK REGISTER
18            1025                    TFLG2    EQU    $1025    TIMER FLAG REGISTER
19            1026                    PACTL    EQU    $1026    PULSE ACCUMULATOR CONTROL REG
20            1027                    PACNT    EQU    $1027    PULSE ACCUMULATOR COUNTER REG
21                                    * MASKS
22            0010                    BIT4     EQU    %00010000
23            0020                    BIT5     EQU    %00100000
24                                    *
25                                    *****************************************************
26                                    ** DATA SECTION
27                                    *****************************************************
28   0010                                      ORG    $0010
29   0010                             PULDUR   RMB    1        PULSE DURATION IN PA COUNTS
30   0011                             ERROR    RMB    1        PULSE OVERTIME ERROR INDICATOR
31                                    *
32   FFDA                                      ORG    $FFDA
33   FFDA   C119                               FDB    PAIISR   PAI INTERRUPT VECTOR
34   FFDC   C12B                               FDB    PAOVISR  PAOV INTERRUPT VECTOR
35                                    *
36                                    *****************************************************
37                                    ** MAIN PROGRAM
38                                    *****************************************************
39   C100                                      ORG    $C100
40                                    *--------------------------------------------------
41                                    * INITIALIZATION
42                                    *--------------------------------------------------
43                                    * INITIALIZE STACK
44   C100   8E CF FF                  START    LDS    #$CFFF
45                                    * INITIALIZE PULSE DURATION
46   C103   7F 00 10                           CLR    PULDUR
47                                    * INITIALIZE PULSE OVERTIME ERROR INDICATOR
48   C106   7F 00 11                           CLR    ERROR    00=FALSE, FF=TRUE
49                                    * INITIALIZE PULSE ACCUMULATOR
50                                    *   GATED TIME ACCUMULATION MODE
51   C109   86 60                              LDAA   #$60     DDRA7:PAEN:PAMOD:PEDGE=0110
52   C10B   B7 10 26                           STAA   PACTL    INPUT:ENABLE:TIME:H-TO-L
53                                    *   ENABLE PULSE ACC OVERFLOW AND INPUT INTERRUPTS
54   C10E   86 30                              LDAA   #$30     PAOVI:PAII=11
55   C110   B7 10 24                           STAA   TMSK2
56                                    *   INITIALIZE COUNTER FOR FIRST MEASUREMENT
57   C113   7F 10 27                           CLR    PACNT
58                                    * TURN ON INTERRUPT SYSTEM
59   C116   0E                                 CLI
60                                    *--------------------------------------------------
61                                    * WAIT FOR INTERRUPTS
62                                    *--------------------------------------------------
```

Figure 7-38   Example program for gated-time accumulation.

```
63    C117    20 FE              HERE      BRA    HERE
64                               *
65                               ******************************************************
66                               ** PULSE ACCUMULATOR INPUT INTERRUPT SERVICE ROUTINE
67                               ******************************************************
68                               *-----------------------------------------------------
69                               * ILLEGAL INTERRUPT?
70                               *-----------------------------------------------------
71    C119    CE 10 00           PAIISR LDX    #REG
72    C11C    1F 25 10 0A               BRCLR  TFLG2-REG,X,BIT4,RTPAI    IGNORE ILLEGAL
73                               *                           ..INTERRUPT
74                               *-----------------------------------------------------
75                               * SERVICE PULSE ACCUMULATOR INPUT
76                               *-----------------------------------------------------
77                               * CLEAR PULSE ACCUMULATOR INPUT FLAG
78    C120    86 10                      LDAA   #BIT4     STORE 1 TO CLEAR FLAG
79    C122    A7 25                      STAA   TFLG2-REG,X  ..ZEROS DO NOTHING
80                               * READ PULSE ACCUMULATOR COUNTER FOR PULSE DURATION
81    C124    A6 27                      LDAA   PACNT-REG,X
82    C126    97 10                      STAA   PULDUR
83                               * INITIALIZE COUNTER FOR NEXT PULSE
84    C128    6F 27                      CLR    PACNT-REG,X
85                               * RETURN FROM INTERRUPT
86    C12A    3B                 RTPAI    RTI
87                               *
88                               ******************************************************
89                               ** PULSE ACCUMULATOR OVERFLOW INTERRUPT SERVICE ROUTIN
90                               ******************************************************
91                               *-----------------------------------------------------
92                               * ILLEGAL INTERRUPT?
93                               *-----------------------------------------------------
94    C12B    CE 10 00           PAOVISR LDX    #REG
95    C12E    1F 25 20 08               BRCLR  TFLG2-REG,X,BIT5,RTPAOV   IGNORE ILLEGAL
96                               *                           ..INTERRUPT
97                               *-----------------------------------------------------
98                               * SERVICE PULSE ACCUMULATOR OVERFLOW
99                               *-----------------------------------------------------
100                              * CLEAR PULSE ACCUMULATOR OVERFLOW FLAG
101   C132    86 20                      LDAA   #BIT5     STORE 1 TO CLEAR FLAG
102   C134    A7 25                      STAA   TFLG2-REG,X  ..ZEROS DO NOTHING
103                              * INDICATE OVERTIME ERROR
104   C136    86 FF                      LDAA   #$FF
105   C138    97 11                      STAA   ERROR
106                              * RETURN FROM INTERRUPT
107   C13A    3B                 RTPAOV   RTI
108   C13B                                END
```

Figure 7-38   Continued.

Pulse-Accumulator Flag Applications

Many applications will not need to use the pulse accumulator. If so, the pulse-accumulator-input flag can be used as a general-purpose flag. The PAIF can respond to either transition of the input signal, and can generate an interrupt with a unique interrupt vector. The pulse-accumulator-overflow flag is less useful as a general-purpose device.

Remember that the flags associated with the programmable timer can also be used as general-purpose flags when they are not used for timing purposes. When all these flags are used with the STAF flag, many flags are available without constructing custom hardware.

Motorola Trainer

The example program for the pulse accumulator in Figure 7-38 can be run in the trainer. The interrupt vectors in the trainer must be fixed to send control to the proper interrupt service routines. A 555 timer integrated circuit can provide a periodic input signal. Adjust the pulse width and frequency with pulses between 1 and 10_{10} milliseconds. The example program must be stopped with the trainer reset button before the results can be seen. The program can be modified to give better outputs. See the pertinent exercise at the chapter end for ideas.

7.10   SERIAL COMMUNICATIONS INTERFACE

The serial communications interface, SCI, inside the 68HC11 makes serial transmission and reception easy. The SCI device is very flexible so it can adapt to most applications. However, its sophistication means that the program must select many control options and control many data bits. Most programs for controlling the SCI use interrupt, so the examples in this chapter only use interrupt.

Data Transmission

Typical digital systems must send data numbers from one device to another. For example, the microprocessor must send data numbers to the memory chips. The address, data, and control buses serve this purpose. In similar applications, the distance between the two devices is small—usually a few centimeters. Therefore, using many wires as in the address, data, and control buses poses little difficulty. Transmitting the bits over many wires at the same time is called *parallel* transmission.

Other applications require data transmission over much larger distances. For example, data sent between a computer and a keyboard/display terminal, a computer and a printer, or two microcomputers may require 10 or 20 feet of cabling. Figure 7-39a illustrates sending 8-bit data between two such devices. The input and output ports of the computer could be port C and port B of a 68HC11 microcomputer. The figure makes it clear that parallel transmission requires many wires to connect the two devices—16_{10} data wires, two timing wires, and a common wire. If the distance between the two devices exceeds 20 feet, it's likely to be impractical to use so many wires. Even distances of a few feet may be inconvenient and costly with so many wires.

The inconvenience of a large cable makes it attractive to compromise the transmission system if fewer wires are necessary. At least two wires are necessary for sending a binary signal. When using only two wires, only a single bit can be sent at once. This is the principal characteristic of a *serial* transmission path—it transmits one bit at a time. Figure 7-39b illustrates a common wire and two signal wires for two directions of serial transmission at once, which is equivalent to the system in Figure 7-39a.

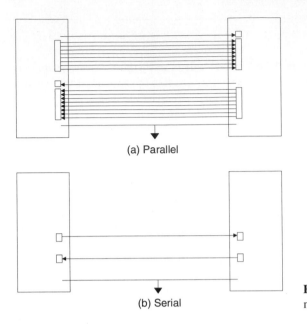

(a) Parallel

(b) Serial

Figure 7-39   Parallel and serial transmission.

Some compromises are necessary to use serial transmission compared to parallel transmission. First, there are no signal wires for the timing or ready signals. Therefore, the bit stream must contain the timing information. Second, if equivalent hardware for transmitting 8-bit numbers is compared, the serial transmission must be at least eight times slower than the parallel transmission. Since the serial system uses only one signal path instead of eight paths, the information transmission rate must be slower. In practice, due to the timing encoding, the transmission rate is even slower. Therefore, the advantages gained from serial transmission must be greater than the disadvantage of slower speed. For example, if the transmission distance is very long, the cost of parallel transmission is prohibitive.

Communication Terminology

Several variations of the serial communication system shown in Figure 7-39b are practical. The communication industry developed terminology for each variation long before computer technology influenced communication. Telegraph, telephone, and radio communication preceded computer communication. Because of its origin, the terminology is sometimes strange to people who work with computers. For example, logical terms using 1s and 0s can describe the serial signal without referring to the electrical characteristics of the hardware. However, the communication terminology calls a logical 1 a *mark* and a logical 0 a *space*.

Simplex communication

A *simplex* communication system supports communication in one direction only. There is no way for the system to support a response to a message. Figure 7-40a illustrates the hardware necessary for simplex serial communication between a computer and another device.

Simplex communication is very common—it is the typical radio and television broadcasting system. Furthermore, computers frequently control serial printers that cannot return information to the computer.

Duplex communication

A duplex communication system can support communication in both directions between two devices. However, there are two variations of duplex communication called *half-duplex* and *full-duplex.*

Half-duplex communication.   A half-duplex system supports communication in two directions, but only in one direction at a time. The same hardware communicates in both directions. Figure 7-40b illustrates the hardware for half-duplex serial communications between two devices such as two microcomputers.

A half-duplex system can switch the signal wire between the transmitter and receiver at each end of the path. Controlling the switching between transmitter and receiver is complicated. Usually one device will transmit until both devices agree to switch roles. After switching, the second device transmits.

If something goes wrong, both devices may try to transmit at once causing a *collision* between messages. The system *protocol* or agreement between the devices must specify how to recover from such errors.

The advantage of half-duplex communication is the reduced cost of using the same wire to transmit in both directions. Often the cost of the electronic switching hardware is much less than the cost of additional wiring.

A possible disadvantage of half-duplex communication is the need for one device to wait until the other device finishes transmitting. The waiting may slow the communication process. However, in many applications, the first device interrogates the second device asking for particular information. The first device may continue only after receiving the information from the second device, so little speed is lost by using half-duplex communication.

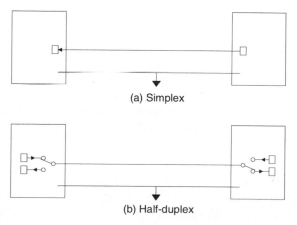

(a) Simplex

(b) Half-duplex

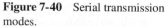

Figure 7-40   Serial transmission modes.

Full-duplex communication. A full-duplex system supports communication in both directions at the same time. The hardware in Figure 7-39b is typical of a full-duplex serial system. It is the most general system and is also the most costly. However, in many applications, the cost is very small.

A typical application of full-duplex communication is the connection between a CRT terminal and a computer system. The keyboard device in the terminal transmits character codes to the computer at the same time the computer transmits to the display device. Serial communication is commonly used in this application because only a very small cable is required, and the transmission does not need to be very fast because the terminal is operated by a person.

The terminology used with commercial CRT terminals connected to mainframe computers is sometimes confusing. In this application, the terminology full-duplex usually means that the computer transmits each character received from the keyboard to the display. Similarly, half-duplex means that the computer does not transmit a received character back to the display. The terminal must be set to operate in the mode that is compatible with the computer. Incorrect half-duplex and full-duplex settings result either in no display when keys are pressed or two copies of each key pressed. The mode settings on the terminal determine whether the terminal will internally copy the character from the keyboard to the display.

ASCII Communication Codes

This section discusses character transmission codes because most character-oriented devices use serial communication. However, many other applications besides character transmission use serial communication.

Binary codes can represent the alphabetic and numeric characters found on the typical keyboard. Most small computers use the character codes defined by the American Standards Committee for Information Interchange. Therefore, these character codes are called the *ASCII codes*. Pronounce the acronym ASCII *ask-key*.

Character codes

The ASCII code is a 7-bit code though serial systems usually transmit an 8-bit binary number. A 7-bit code can represent 128_{10} different characters.

The ASCII code is a weighted code. Therefore, the code numbers corresponding to the letters of the alphabet and the numerical characters are in numerical order. If you remember that the code 1000001 represents the capital letter A and the code 0110000 represents the digit 0, you can reproduce the codes for other letters and numbers by counting. Using hexadecimal numbers, the ASCII code for A is 41 and the code for 5 is 65.

Error detection

When a transmission system transmits character information over long distances, electrical interference may cause errors in the received codes. Interference can change ones to zeros and zeros to ones. The receiving system must detect such errors to prevent use of the erroneous information. One response to an error may be a message requesting the transmitting device to transmit the information again.

Parity bits.   Probably the simplest of many available error-detection algorithms is the *parity* scheme. When using parity, an eighth bit is added to the 7-bit ASCII code in the most-significant position. Both the transmitting device and the receiving device must know the algorithm used to select the bit. The receiving device checks received codes with the algorithm to detect erroneous codes. However, the addition of a single bit is not sufficient to detect all possible errors. Therefore, parity checking is not an adequate error-checking scheme for most applications.

Parity algorithms.   There are four algorithms for adding the parity bit. The two that provide the most useful error-checking ability are called *even parity* and *odd parity*. Even parity means add a 1 or a 0 so the number of 1s in the 8-bit code is even. Odd parity means add a 1 or a 0 so the number of 1s in the 8-bit code is odd.

Less useful are the algorithms that specify that the parity bit will always be 1 or will always be 0. Because of the communication heritage of the terminology, these are called *mark parity* and *space parity*. Table 7-8 shows some ASCII codes with parity bits added.

Even and odd parity schemes cannot detect certain multiple-bit errors. For example, suppose the system transmits an odd-parity A with a code of 11000001. If transmission errors change the code to 11001101, parity checking fails to detect an error because the code still contains an odd number of 1s. Thus, parity checking has limited value for detecting errors.

Serial Communication Principles

The serial bit stream used to transmit binary numbers contains both data bits and timing information. Both the format of the bit stream and the electrical characteristics of the hardware are well established because many manufacturers' equipment must be compatible.

Serial signals

Binary signals in electronic systems usually represent the logical values 1 and 0 with two different voltage levels usually called high and low. Most serial transmission systems

TABLE 7-8   SELECTED ASCII CODES

Character	Even Parity	Odd Parity	Mark Parity	Space Parity
A	01000001	11000001	11000001	01000001
B	01000010	11000010	11000010	01000010
C	11000011	01000011	11000011	01000011
D	01000100	11000100	11000100	01000100
•	•	•	•	•
0	00110000	10110000	10110000	00110000
1	10110001	00110001	10110001	00110001
2	10110010	00110010	10110010	00110011
•	•	•	•	•

use voltage levels for the electronic signals; however, many serial systems instead use two different current levels. Most commercial equipment meets the requirements of a standard. The standard specifies the signals so the equipment is compatible with other equipment. The two most common standards are called *20-milliamp current loop* and *RS232*.

20-milliamp current loop.   Teletype machines made by Teletype Corporation use this type of logic signal. The equipment turns a source of 20-milliamps of direct current on and off to make a binary signal. A mechanism in the machine uses solenoids. The strength of the magnetic field in the solenoid is current dependent. Therefore, the amount of current in the signal is significant.

Few Teletype machines are now used with computer equipment. However, some electronic equipment still uses the signal format because it has greater immunity to interference from electrical noise than some voltage-level signal systems.

RS232D.   The most common standard for serial communication signals is the Electronic Industries Association standard RS232 which is now in revision D. The standard describes the characteristics of the transmitter and receiver hardware, and the connections between them. The signal levels at the receiving end of the cable must be between +3 and +25 VDC for the high level, and between −3 and −25 VDC for the low level. Using nonzero voltages for each level provides greater immunity to electrical interference. The wide range of possible voltages makes it easy to build compatible equipment. In practice, however, most manufacturers use +12 and −12 VDC signals.

Assertion designation.   An association between the logical value of a binary signal and the physical electrical signal must be made. For the sake of compatibility, serial transmission systems use only a single definition. In the 20-milliamp current loop system, 20-milliamps of current is a logical 1 and no current is a logical 0. In the RS232 system, the negative voltage is a logical 1 and the positive voltage is a logical 0.

Serial signal format

Whatever the meaning of the numbers transmitted, or the number of bits in the numbers transmitted, the format or arrangement of the bits is the same. Since the numbers transmitted are frequently 8-bit ASCII character codes, the following describes character transmission. Many people speak of the data number as a character even if the code does not represent a character. Figure 7-41 illustrates the waveform for an even parity character *M*. Remember that only one bit at a time is transmitted, so the time axis shows how the bits are spaced in time.

The format of the serial signal described here is called *non-return-to-zero*, or NRZ. The name means that the signal does change within the bit time and that the signal value during the bit time determines the bit value. Other systems determine the bit values by using various kinds of transitions of the signal either during or between the bit times.

Start bit.   Before the transmission begins, the serial transmission system is idle and the signal is a binary one or mark as Figure 7-41 shows. At the beginning of the transmission of any character code, the signal changes to a binary zero or space. From this beginning,

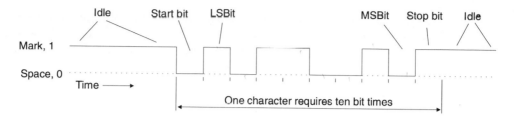

Figure 7-41   Serial signal format for an even-parity ASCII M character.

each bit is allocated a fixed amount of time until the end of the current character. The first time period or bit is called the *start bit*. The transmitter hardware automatically creates the start bit.

Data bits.   Usually eight data bits are used, so the next eight bits in Figure 7-41 represent the data for the character M. The data bits are transmitted least-significant bit first and most-significant bit last. In this example, the last data bit sent is the parity bit.

It is common to find systems that transmit five, seven, or nine data bits. For example, the system uses nine bits when an 8-bit number and a parity bit are sent.

Stop bit.   Following the data bits, the transmitter always sends a 1 called the *stop bit*. The stop bit usually lasts for one bit time, but some systems use two stop periods or two stop bits. The number of data bits and the time for the stop bit may vary from one system to another.

At the end of the stop period, the system is again idle. The start bit of the next character may begin immediately after the stop period of the current character. Sometimes the system may remain idle for a while.

Serial transmitter operation

A serial transmitter is a digital electronic circuit usually in an integrated circuit. The transmitter automatically generates the waveform when given the data number to transmit. It also creates the start and stop bits that are not part of the data.

A separate clock or time base enables the transmitter to control the timing of the bits. Usually, it is easy for the transmitter to change to different bit times.

Serial receiver operation

The serial receiver is a digital electronic circuit that samples the incoming signal to extract the data from it. The receiver does not know when a character will arrive; it must determine all its information from the received waveform. The receiver must operate with the same bit time as the transmitter or this is impossible. Furthermore, the receiver must know how many data bits were transmitted.

Figure 7-42 illustrates the principle of sampling the received waveform. The Xs show the samples that are taken at a rate much higher than the bit rate of the waveform. A typical rate is 16_{10} times faster than the bit rate—it is difficult to show such a rate in the figure.

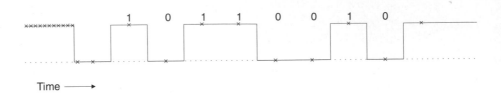

Time ⟶

Figure 7-42   Serial receiver sampling points for one character.

When the receiver detects the first 0 beyond the idle signal, it suspects that a character is being received—this is the start bit. To detect the start bit as early as possible, the sampling rate must be much faster than the bit rate in the serial stream. However, electrical noise may make a pulse that leads to a false start. So most receivers sample the start bit at least once more to determine if a correct start bit has arrived. The simplest algorithm is to sample again after one-half bit time as the figure shows.

When a valid start bit occurs, the receiver waits one time period before sampling the waveform again. Successive samples occur every period until the stop bit is sampled. Therefore, the receiver can retrieve the data number from the bits within one character.

Most receivers use a more sophisticated algorithm than described here to detect errors due to electrical noise. For example, the sample near the middle of the bit time may consist of three successive samples at the 16_{10} times rate. Then a voting algorithm determines the actual value of the bit.

UART hardware

Serial transmitters and receivers are available in integrated circuits. The most common IC is known by the acronym UART for Universal Asynchronous Receiver Transmitter. A UART contains all the electronics for both a receiver and a transmitter. The receiver and transmitter are independent so the UART can implement a full-duplex system.

Usually a UART requires a clock signal to determine the transmission rate. It also requires additional electronics to control the relatively high positive and negative signal voltages required for many serial systems.

Serial errors

A variety of situations can cause erroneous reception of the data value. Electrical noise is a major cause of erroneous reception. However, other problems related to operating the receiver can lead to errors.

Timing errors.   Timing errors always occur because the transmitter and the receiver will not run at identical rates. They are two separate pieces of equipment. It is impossible to make two independent devices operate at the same rate. There is not a common clock signal between the two devices. Therefore, the serial communication system described here is called *asynchronous serial communication*.

The timing error between the transmitter and receiver would always lead to errors if the error accumulated from one character to the next. After enough characters were sent, an error would occur. However, this does not happen, because the receiver synchronizes to each incoming character by detecting the beginning of the start bit. Since the timing error accumulates only within one character, the receiver accommodates small timing errors without data errors.

Figure 7-43 will help in determining an upper limit on the allowable timing error. In Figure 7-43a, the receiver runs faster than the transmitter, which causes the samples to occur too early. At the limit, the sample could be one-half bit time early at the end of 10_{10} bit times and still get the correct result. Similarly, Figure 7-43b shows the receiver running more slowly than the transmitter. Here the sample could be one-half bit time late at the end and still be correct. Therefore, the maximum allowable timing error between the transmitter and receiver is plus or minus five percent. In practice, this theoretical limit is not achieved and the allowable error is somewhat smaller. Practical electronic circuits seldom have difficulty achieving the required accuracy.

Framing errors.   Each character begins with a start bit that is 0 and ends with a stop bit that is 1. A *framing error* occurs when the received character does not end with the correct stop bit. That is, the start and stop bits do not properly frame the character.

Other than when caused by electrical noise, a framing error occurs when the receiver is out of synchronization and interprets a data bit as a start bit. Figure 7-44 illustrates sampling beginning at an incorrect point and the detection of the framing error.

If the receiver erroneously starts a character at the point where a data bit changes from 1 to 0, a 1 may not be found where the stop bit should be. Then the receiver detects the framing error. If the receiver finds a 1, it cannot detect the error. In such a case, it is likely that a framing error will occur within the next few characters. In the example, the receiver is effectively making data numbers by using bits from two different characters.

Most serial receivers automatically check the bit stream for framing errors. The receiver sets a flag bit to indicate a framing error.

Overrun errors.   Immediately after the receiver has received a character, the receiver transfers the data bits to a data register for the computer to read. With a data register, the receiver can receive another character immediately even if there is a short delay before

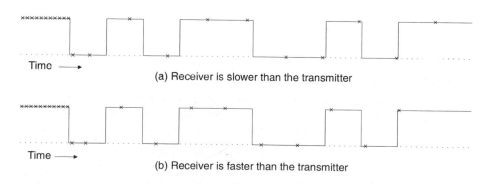

Time ⟶

(a) Receiver is slower than the transmitter

Time ⟶

(b) Receiver is faster than the transmitter

Figure 7-43   Effects of timing errors on sampling points.

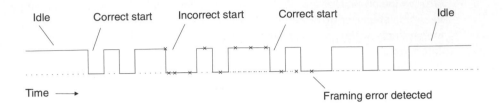

Figure 7-44   Framing error.

the computer reads the previous character. Remember that the receiver cannot control when the transmitter sends a character. If the computer is too slow, the receiver may receive another character and transfer it to the data register overwriting or overrunning the last character. The last character is then lost. This problem is called an *overrun error*. The receiver hardware must detect the overrun error and indicate it.

Serial transmission rate

The time allocated for each bit determines the rate at which data bytes are transmitted. Usually we prefer the fastest possible rate of transmission. However, several factors limit the maximum rate of transmission. These include both limitations of the devices sending and receiving information and limitations of the transmission medium that carries the signals. Furthermore, the rate usually must be a standard rate so communication with commercial equipment is possible.

Bit rate.   The rate of serial information transmission is usually specified in bits per second or in characters per second. The rate in bits per second is also called the *baud rate*. This name comes from the work of a mathematician named Baudot, who worked in the area of communication theory. Unfortunately, correct application of Baudot's work does not result in a baud rate exactly equal to the number of bits per second. However, the number is close so people in the computer industry define baud rate as bits per second.

When determining baud rate, consider all the bits required for a character. The example in Figure 7-41 uses 10_{10} bits for each 8-bit character when you include the necessary start and stop bits. A system that can transmit a maximum of 240_{10} of these characters per second has a rate of 2400 baud.

Several standard baud rates are used by manufacturers of equipment that must communicate with other manufacturers' equipment. Table 7-9 lists the common baud rates—note that K or kilo is 1000_{10} when used in this context. The table is based on use of 8-bit characters or numbers. The table also lists the time for each bit. At the higher rates, the short bit times make it difficult for the hardware to respond properly.

A practical view of transmission rate.   It is valuable to get a physical feel for the standard transmission rates. Since serial communication systems often send text, let's use text as an example. A CRT terminal can display text as it receives the characters serially. Ideally, filling the screen with characters will be instantaneous.

TABLE 7-9   COMMON STANDARD BAUD RATES

Baud Rate	Number of Stop Bits	8-bit Numbers per Second	Bit Time (milliseconds)
110	2	10	9.09
150	1	15	6.67
300	1	30	3.33
1200	1	120	0.83
2400	1	240	0.42
4800	1	480	0.21
9600	1	960	0.10
19.2 K	1	1920	0.05

If the transmission is at 300 baud, most people can easily read the text as the CRT prints the characters on the screen. This is a slow rate that is unacceptable to most people unless there is no alternative. At 1200 baud, the display speed is much better. But even at 1200 baud, the screen will fill with characters so slowly that it will irritate most people. At 9600 baud, the screen will fill quickly enough to be acceptable to most people, but the delay is still noticeable. The printing of the lines of text can still be seen. At 19.2 kilobaud, the screen fills quite rapidly—most people would say the screen is printed instantaneously.

Speeds higher than 19.2 kilobaud are much more difficult to achieve. However, for filling screens with text, there is not much reason to go faster because the added expense will gain little. Most people would not perceive a significant improvement in speed.

Waveform distortion.   Let's consider increasing the baud rate of a serial system since faster speeds are better than slow speeds. Unfortunately, there are physical limitations on the transmission medium that make it impractical to increase the speed. Figure 7-45 illustrates the problem.

When the voltage applied to the transmitter end of a cable changes abruptly, the voltage at the other end of the cable does not follow exactly. Instead, the capacitance, inductance, and resistance of the wires alter the waveshape. The top drawing in Figure 7-45 illustrates how the cable rounds the signal voltage.

Now consider changing the baud rate of a serial waveform. The top two drawings in Figure 7-45 show the effects of doubling the baud rate. The cable characteristics and rounding remain the same, but the effect on a pulse is to distort it a greater amount. The third drawing shows the effects of doubling the baud rate again. Now the distortion is so severe that the received waveform is likely to be useless. Doubling the baud rate again as in the bottom drawing results in almost no output at all.

The effects of different cables on the waveshape depend on the cable characteristics. Some cable types have a smaller effect or rounding than others. However, for a given cable, the rounding effect is independent of the signals sent through it. The characteristics of the transmitter and receiver electronics also affect the waveshape.

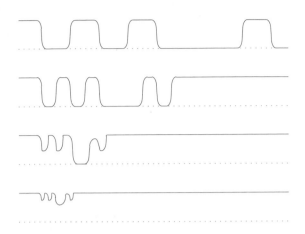

Figure 7-45 Effects of serial cable on voltage waveform as baud rate changes from a normal rate at the top to eight times faster at the bottom.

Clearly, the characteristics of the transmission medium limit the speed of serial transmission. Furthermore, rounding of the signal makes it more difficult for the receiver to correctly sample the waveform. Rounding also makes timing errors more severe. Practical systems usually require a timing error of less than plus or minus 1.5 percent. Also, if the receiver is near its limit of recognition of the bits, any noise on the signal has a greater effect.

Receiver wake-up

Some receivers have special hardware features to improve the performance of multiple receiver networks. Figure 7-46 shows a typical connection of one transmitter and two receivers. Let's consider the case of the transmitter sending messages to the two receivers.

Messages.   A message simply means a block of data numbers. Each message may begin with a message identifier number. Some messages may be pertinent to both receivers, and others may be of interest to only one receiver. The receiver can decide whether the message is of interest by inspecting the message identifier.

Whenever the transmitter begins a message, both of the receivers respond by receiving characters. If a receiving device decides that the message is of no interest, it must still receive all the characters in the message. Usually, each incoming character causes an interrupt, and the interrupt service routine reads and discards the unwanted character. These interrupts use considerable processing time. At 9600 baud, the interrupts occur about every millisecond.

Purpose of wake-up.   If the receiver has wake-up hardware, the receiving computer can put the receiver to sleep so it no longer responds to incoming characters. The computer will not have to waste time discarding characters. However, the receiver must be awake when a new message is transmitted.

Wake-up triggering.   Some special condition must trigger the receiver to wake up. The simplest wake-up condition is an idle transmission line. An idle condition means the transmitter has stopped transmitting. When the transmitter starts transmitting again, the receiver responds normally. If the transmitter stops for a short time at the end of each message,

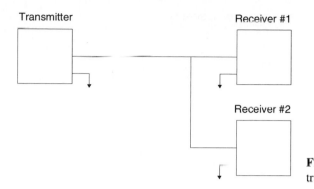

Figure 7-46 Multiple receiver serial transmission system.

all the receivers wake up. One character time is enough idle time to trigger wake-up, so little time is lost triggering the receivers. However, the transmitter must not hesitate during the transmission of a message.

SCI Serial I/O Hardware

The 68HC11 contains a complete serial receiver and transmitter system. This serial system is called the SCI for serial communications interface. The many control and data registers for the SCI are in the memory block beginning at address 1000. The program needs only to use these registers to operate the SCI. One pin of the 68HC11 chip is the receiver input and another is the transmitter output. The signal levels are 0 and +5 VDC, so external hardware is necessary to make a compatible RS232 interface.

Baud rate control

The SCI transmitter and receiver can operate at a wide range of baud rates. The baud rate for the transmitter is always the same as for the receiver. The timing for the SCI is derived from the microprocessor's crystal-controlled clock. Therefore, you must choose the correct frequency of the crystal for the 68HC11 clock if a standard baud rate is necessary. The crystal also controls the E-clock frequency.

Baud rate divider chain.   The E-clock signal passes through two dividers to generate the correct clock rate for the SCI. Figure 7-47 illustrates the divider chain.

The first programmable divider circuit is called the *prescaler*. It divides the E-clock rate by one of four different factors. The output of the prescaler drives another programmable divider called the rate control. This second divider reduces the prescaler rate by one of eight different factors. The output of the rate-control divider determines the sampling rate of the serial receiver. The receiver samples at a rate 16_{10} times higher than the baud rate. Therefore, a fixed divider with a factor of 16_{10} divides the receive clock to form the transmit clock. The prescaler and rate control dividers together provide many different baud rates for a given E-clock rate.

One divide factor for the rate control divider is 1. That is, the output rate equals the input rate. Therefore, the output of the prescaler is called the *highest baud rate*. In other

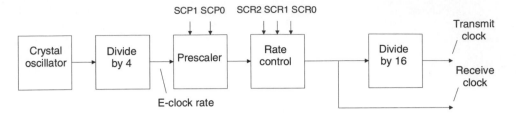

SCP1 SCP0   SCR2 SCR1 SCR0

Transmit clock

Receive clock

E-clock rate

Figure 7-47   SCI baud rate divider chain.

words, the rate control divider can only make the baud rate equal to or smaller than the rate from the prescaler.

BAUD register.   The control bits for the programmable dividers are in the BAUD register at address 102B. Figure 7-48 illustrates the BAUD register. The program must store into the SCP bits to control the prescaler for a baud rate other than is obtained at reset. Notice the SCP bits are set to 0s at reset. Since reset leaves the SCR bits undefined, the program must always store a number in the SCR bits to control the rate-control divider.

Table 7-10 shows the divide factors and the required SCP bits for the prescaler. In addition, the table shows examples of the highest baud rate obtained with three different crystal frequencies.

Table 7-11 shows the divide factors and the required SCR bits for the rate-control divider. The table also shows examples of the final baud rate with three given baud rates from the prescaler.

Consider an example using both tables together. If the crystal operates at 8.0 MHz, the number 32 in the BAUD register sets the transmitter and receiver baud rates at 2400_{10} baud.

SCI data registers

The program transmits data or reads data through the serial interface by writing or reading a data register in memory. The serial hardware sets flags when it receives or transmits a character or discovers an error. The flags can trigger interrupts.

The SCI can use either 8-bit or 9-bit data numbers or characters. A control bit must be set to use 9-bit characters. The following discussion assumes 8-bit characters. A later section discusses 9-bit characters.

Receive data register.   As a character is received, the data bits are moved into a receiver shift register that connects to the receive pin on the 68HC11. When all the bits have

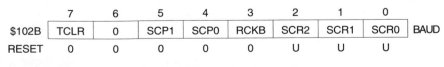

	7	6	5	4	3	2	1	0	
$102B	TCLR	0	SCP1	SCP0	RCKB	SCR2	SCR1	SCR0	BAUD
RESET	0	0	0	0	0	U	U	U	

Figure 7-48   SCI baud rate register.

TABLE 7-10   SCI PRESCALER HIGHEST BAUD RATE

Prescaler Control Bits		Prescaler Divide Factor	Crystal Frequency		
			8.3886 MHz	8.0 MHz	4.9152 MHz
SCP1	SCP0		Highest Baud Rate (kilobaud)		
0	0	1	131.072	125.000	76.80
0	1	3	43.690	41.666	25.60
1	0	4	32.768	31.250	19.20
1	1	13	10.082	9.6000	5.907

arrived, the receiver automatically transfers the data bits to the receive data register. The data register is called SCDR for serial communications data register and is at memory address 102F.

Figure 7-49 shows most of the serial communications interface hardware. The figure includes both the transmitter and receiver hardware. The receiver input is shown at the most significant position of the shift register because the bits are received least-significant bit first.

Transmit data register.   The transmitter has a transmit data register and a transmitter shift register. The shift register controls the transmit pin that connects to the serial line. To transmit a character, the program stores the data number into the SCDR at address 102F.

It appears that the transmitter and receiver both use the same data register named SCDR. This is not true; the name and the address refer to two registers. Figure 7-49 clearly shows separate receiver and transmitter data registers. The interface hardware uses the read/write signal to distinguish the receiver register from the transmitter register.

TABLE 7-11   SELECTED SCI OUTPUT BAUD RATES

Rate-Control Control Bits			Rate-Control Divide Factor	Baud Rate from Prescaler (kilobaud)		
				131.072	76.80	9.600
SCR2	SCR1	SCR0		Output Baud Rate (kilobaud)		
0	0	0	1	131.072	76.80	9.600
0	0	1	2	65.536	38.40	4.800
0	1	0	4	32.768	19.20	2.400
0	1	1	8	16.384	9.600	1.200
1	0	0	16	8.192	4.800	0.600
1	0	1	32	4.096	2.400	0.300
1	1	0	64	2.048	1.200	0.150
1	1	1	128	1.024	0.600	0.075

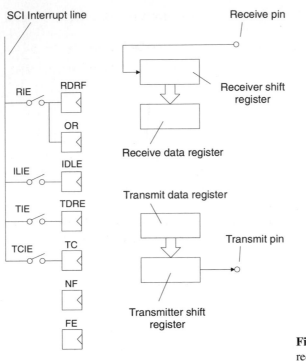

Figure 7-49 Block diagram of SCI
receiver and transmitter hardware.

After the program stores the data number in the SCDR, the transmitter transfers the
number to the transmit shift register when the shift register is empty. If the shift register is
already empty, the transfer occurs immediately. This transfer scheme means that the program
can easily keep the transmitter operating at full speed. While the current character is being
transmitted, the program can obtain the next character and put it in the data register.

SCI flags and interrupts

All the flags for the devices in the SCI are in the serial communications status register
called SCSR. Figure 7-50 shows seven flags in this register. Bit 0 of SCSR is not used and
always is 0. The names of the flags in SCSR do not end with the letter F as do most of the
other 68HC11 flag names.

Clearing SCI flags. All the flags associated with the receiver are cleared by the
program reading the SCSR status register followed by reading the SCDR data register. All

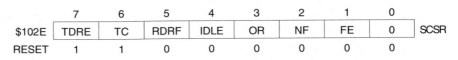

	7	6	5	4	3	2	1	0	
$102E	TDRE	TC	RDRF	IDLE	OR	NF	FE	0	SCSR
RESET	1	1	0	0	0	0	0	0	

Figure 7-50 Serial communications status register.

the flags associated with the transmitter are cleared by reading the SCSR followed by writing to the SCDR.

The program cannot clear a single receiver flag or a single transmitter flag. All the receiver flags are cleared at once and all the transmitter flags are cleared at once.

Only the flags set at the time the SCSR is read are cleared. When reading the SCSR to determine if a flag is set, be cautious because an additional flag could be set before the clearing is completed.

Receiver data flags.   The SCI receiver has two flags related to data reception. The receiver sets a receive flag when it transfers an incoming character from the shift register to the data register. The receiver flag is called RDRF for receiver data register full. The RDRF flag is in the SCSR register as Figure 7-50 shows. A program can read the SCDR to obtain the incoming character when the RDRF flag is set.

The SCI receiver also detects the incoming line becoming idle after receiving one or more characters without stopping. When the line changes to idle for one full character time, the receiver sets the IDLE flag in the SCSR register.

Receiver error flags.   The SCI receiver detects three kinds of reception errors, which it indicates by setting associated flags. The three errors are called overrun error, noise error, and framing error.

The receiver sets the overrun error flag OR when a character is received and the RDRF flag is already set. Since the flag is already set, a previous character must be in the data register, This happens when the program has not yet read the last character when another arrives. When an overrun occurs, the previous character remains in the data register and the incoming character is lost.

The receiver detects electrical noise on any of the received bits including the start and stop bits. It detects noise by sampling the bit at three consecutive sampling times. The receiver sets the noise flag called NF if the three samples do not yield the same results.

The receiver also detects framing errors. If the receiver does not detect a stop bit at the end of a character, it sets the framing-error flag called FE. Since the framing error occurs at the end of a character, the FE flag is set at the same time the RDRF flag is set. If the receiver detects both an overrun error and a framing error on the same character, it only recognizes the overrun error. Furthermore, a set FE flag inhibits transfers to the SCDR.

Transmitter flags.   The SCI transmitter uses two flags to indicate when a transmit operation is complete. When a program uses the transmitter, it stores into the transmit data register called SCDR. The transmitter transfers the number in the data register to the transmit shift register when the transmit shift register is empty. The shift register may not be empty for a while after SCDR is written.

At the time of the transfer to the shift register, the transmitter sets the transmit-data-register-empty flag called TDRE. The actual transmission that makes the transmit pin respond begins when the transfer to the shift register occurs. After the TDRE flag is set, the program may immediately store the next character into the SCDR.

Usually, the program assumes the character has been transmitted when TDRE is set, although the transmission will take some time. If the program must know when the transmit pin becomes idle, it must use the transmit complete flag called TC. For normal transmission, the transmitter sets TC when the transmit shift register finishes sending a character and another character has not been placed in the SCDR register.

In half-duplex applications, the serial line must be switched from transmitting to receiving at the end of a transmission. The program must know when the transmission is complete so the switching does not cause loss of the last character. When the transmitter sets the TC flag, the switching may be done.

SCI interrupts.   All the SCI flags except the noise flag NF and the framing error flag FE can cause an interrupt. The five interrupting flags are all connected to a single interrupt line with an interrupt vector at address FFD6. Figure 7-49 shows the flags and the interrupt line.

Interrupt-enable bits control whether a flag can cause an interrupt. The four interrupt-enable bits for the SCI are in the second serial communications control register called SCCR2. Figure 7-51 shows this register.

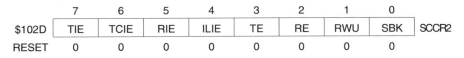

	7	6	5	4	3	2	1	0	
$102D	TIE	TCIE	RIE	ILIE	TE	RE	RWU	SBK	SCCR2
RESET	0	0	0	0	0	0	0	0	

Figure 7-51   Serial communications control register 2.

The receiver data flag RDRF and the overrun flag OR share a single interrupt-enable bit called RIE for receiver interrupt enable. The ILIE or idle line interrupt-enable bit controls the idle flag interrupt. The TIE or transmitter interrupt-enable bit controls the interrupts from the transmitter flag. And finally, the TCIE or transmit complete interrupt-enable bit controls interrupts from the transmission complete flag.

Since the SCI has only a single interrupt vector, the interrupt service routine must poll the SCI flags to determine which one caused the interrupt. The overhead of polling these flags is small because the SCI is a relatively slow device. For the same reason, the SCI interrupt is at the lowest address and thus the lowest priority of all the 68HC11 interrupts.

SCI character length

The SCI can use either 8-bit or 9-bit characters. The program selects the character length by controlling the M bit in the serial communications control register called SCCR1. Figure 7-52 shows the SCCR1 register. The program must put a 1 in the M bit to change to 9-bit operation. The reset condition of M is 0, so the SCI defaults to 8-bit characters in response to a power-up reset.

The serial data registers are 8-bit registers. When using 9-bit characters, the extra bit must go elsewhere. The SCI uses the bits in SCCR1 named R8 and T8 to hold bit 8 of the received or transmitted 9-bit characters, respectively.

As the program transmits characters, it needs to update the T8 bit only if a change is required. If successive characters use the same bit value for bit 8, the program need not

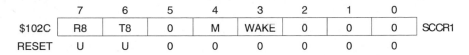

	7	6	5	4	3	2	1	0	
$102C	R8	T8	0	M	WAKE	0	0	0	SCCR1
RESET	U	U	0	0	0	0	0	0	

Figure 7-52   Serial communications control register 1.

change it. This reduces the work the program must do to transmit 9-bit characters. However, using 9-bit characters is more complex than using 8-bit characters.

Receiver wake-up

Multiple receiver applications as shown by Figure 7-46 can easily use the SCI receiver because it has wake-up hardware. The receiver can be put to sleep so the receiving computer can ignore certain messages. While the receiver is asleep, all five SCI receiver flags are inhibited from being set. The receiver returns to normal operation after wake-up is triggered.

The SCI receiver has two ways of triggering wake-up. The WAKE bit in the SCCR1 register selects the wake-up method. Figure 7-52 shows this bit. When WAKE is 0, wake up is triggered when the receiver line is idle for one full character time. That is, the receiver must detect either 10_{10} or 11_{10} consecutive 1s—depending on the state of the M bit—to trigger wake-up. The reset condition of WAKE is 0, so the SCI defaults to idle line wake-up in response to a power-up reset.

If the program sets WAKE to 1, wake-up is triggered by reception of a character code with a 1 in its most-significant bit. This wake-up method may reduce the time lost during the idle time of the first method.

The RWU bit in the SCCR2 register is the receiver wake-up bit. The program puts the SCI receiver to sleep by storing a 1 in the RWU bit. The SCI hardware clears the RWU bit whenever wake-up is triggered. The program also may store 0 in the RWU bit, although this is unusual.

When using the wake-up hardware, it is unlikely that a program would also use the IDLE flag and interrupt. The IDLE flag can be used to implement software wake-up.

Transmitter and receiver control

The pins associated with the serial communications interface are in port D. Pin PD0 is the receiver line and pin PD1 is the transmitter line. While the serial transmitter and receiver are disabled, these port D pins may be used for general purpose I/O. Port D has a data direction register at address 1008. When used for I/O, the program reads or writes the PORTD data register at address 1007. While the SCI transmitter and receiver are enabled, they control the associated port D pins.

The program can independently enable and disable the SCI receiver and transmitter. The receiver is enabled by storing 1 in the RE or receiver enable bit in the SCCR2 register. Figure 7-51 shows the SCCR2 register. While the receiver is enabled, bit DDRD0 is forced

Motorola Trainer

The SCI transmitter is connected to both a pin on the ribbon cable connector and a pin in the host port. The host port connection of the transmitter is through jumper J6. The SCI receiver connects through an electronic switch to either the host port or the ribbon cable connector. The switch is controlled by the write-only bit 0 of address 4000. When this bit is 1, the connection is to the host port. Reset sets the control bit to 0 so the connection is to the ribbon cable connector. To use the SCI through the host port, you can use the monitor program to change the control bit, but the monitor program may put it back. It is better to include the following instructions in your program initialization: LDAA #$01, STAA $4000.

to a 0 to make the PD0 pin an input pin. While the receiver is disabled, the five receiver flags are inhibited.

The serial transmitter is enabled by storing 1 in the TE or transmitter enable bit in the SCCR2 register. While the transmitter is enabled, bit DDRD1 is forced to a 1 to make port D bit 1 an output.

At the time the transmitter is enabled, it automatically transmits one character time of all 1s. The initial string of 1s is called an *idle character*. Sending an idle character helps receivers accurately determine the beginning of a transmission following a period when the transmitter is disabled.

If the TE bit is changed to 0 while the shift register is transmitting a character, that character is finished before the transmitter stops controlling the output pin. Therefore, the program can disable the transmitter as soon as the TDRE flag is set for the last character.

Programming the SCI

Using the serial communications interface with practical programs is often difficult. The program must account for interactions between the serial I/O device and the computer. Usually interrupt is used with the SCI because the computer may be running other program modules between the reception and transmission of serial data bytes.

Receiver ISR

When using interrupts, the receiver interrupt service routine runs each time a character arrives. The ISR must read the character immediately in response to the interrupt so an overrun doesn't happen. Usually the ISR stores the character in a memory buffer and then tells some other program module that a character has come in. The ISR may instead examine the received characters and only tell the other program when a particular character is received. Similarly, the number of received characters may trigger notification.

The receiver ISR must also deal with reception errors such as overruns, framing errors, and noise errors. The strategy of dealing with errors depends on the application using the serial communications.

Transmitter ISR

Usually the serial transmitter uses interrupt. The interrupt service routine does most of the transmission work. The ISR usually sends a character string that it gets from a memory buffer. Some other program module creates the character string in the buffer before transmission begins.

Interrupt response.   Consider the work the ISR must do in response to an interrupt. The ISR gets a character from the buffer, sends it to the transmitter, which clears the transmitter flag, and then returns from the interrupt. When the transmitter finishes with that character, it sets its flag causing an interrupt back to the ISR. The ISR gets the next character from the buffer and sends it to the transmitter. At each interrupt, the ISR transmits another character. The transmission is somewhat automatic as the ISR responds to each interrupt.

Stopping the transmitter.   Eventually, all the characters in the buffer are transmitted. But when the transmitter finishes the last character, the transmitter sets its flag and interrupts again. On this interrupt, the ISR has nothing more for the transmitter to do. However, the transmitter's flag is set causing the request for service. Clearing the flag is done only by transmitting a character, but there are no more characters. Returning from the interrupt immediately causes another interrupt from the transmitter.

To prevent this dilemma, the ISR must disable the transmitter interrupt or disable the transmitter when sending the last character. Usually the ISR must tell the controlling program when the transmission is finished.

Kick-starting the transmitter.   Transmission of characters is automatic once the transmitter is started. But how is the transmitter started in the first place? The ISR can't start it because it only responds to interrupts after characters are transmitted. So the program module that controls the transmitter must kick-start the transmitter by sending the first character. The controlling program can then ignore the transmitter until all the characters have been transmitted by the ISR.

Before beginning a new transmission, the program must enable both the transmitter and its interrupt. The sequence in which this is done must not trigger an interrupt before the first character is sent.

SCI Programming Example

The serial communications interface is often used with character-oriented devices such as a CRT terminal. A CRT terminal transmits ASCII characters serially from a keyboard, and receives and displays characters on a screen. The following example program shows using the SCI in such an application. The example hardware is common so experimentation is easy.

The example program reads a character from the keyboard when a key is pressed, inserts the character into a message, and then transmits the message to the display. The program uses the SCI receiver and transmitter with interrupts from both devices. Testing the program is simplified by displaying the received character within the message.

Figure 7-53 is the listing of the example program. The following text describes the program.

- *Lines 4 and 5.*   The crystal for the 68HC11 clock operates at 8.0 MHz. The crystal is the time base for the SCI that controls the baud rate.

- *Line 28.*   This data location holds the count of characters that have been transmitted so far. This counter determines when the last character in the message is sent.

- *Lines 32 to 35.*   These lines define the ASCII characters in the message. The program stores the received character in location INCHAR at line 33. The carriage return and line feed characters format the displayed message in a single line.

- *Line 38.*   A single interrupt vector is set because the SCI uses only one vector though it has five flags that cause interrupts.

- *Line 48.*   A stack is created because the interrupt system requires it.

- *Line 51.*   Clearing the SCCR1 register sets the SCI mode to 8-bit characters and disables the wake-up hardware. A power-up reset also clears the SCCR1 register, so this initialization may be unnecessary.

- *Lines 53 and 54.*   The SCI receiver and transmitter baud rates are set to 1200 baud by controlling the prescaler and rate-control dividers with the BAUD register. The baud rate is unknown after reset, so the program must always initialize the BAUD register. Remember that the baud rate also depends on the crystal frequency.

- *Lines 56 and 57.*   The SCCR2 register is set to enable the receiver and its interrupt while disabling the transmitter and its interrupt. Disabling the transmitter interrupt is particularly important because the power-up reset condition of the transmitter flag is 1. At power-up, the transmitter flag correctly indicates that the transmit data register is empty. However, if the transmitter interrupt was enabled here, an erroneous transmitter interrupt would occur as soon as the interrupt system is turned on. The receiver causes no such problem. The reset condition of the receiver flag is 0, which means that a character has not been received.

- *Lines 59 and 63.*   The interrupt system is enabled and the main program loop does nothing while waiting for an interrupt.

- *Line 72.*   The interrupt system sends control here whenever any interrupt from the SCI occurs. This is the beginning of the interrupt service routine. The index register is set to point to the 68HC11 registers so bit instructions with indexed addressing can control the SCI hardware.

- *Lines 73 to 77.*   The SCI device has only a single interrupt vector, so software must determine which SCI device caused the interrupt. The BRSET instruction on line 73 sends control to the receiver service routine if the receiver flag is set. If the receiver

```
 1                            ********************************************************
 2                            ** TRIGGER OUTPUT MESSAGE WITH INPUT CHARACTER
 3                            *
 4                            * USE SCI SERIAL COMMUNICATIONS INTERFACE WITH 8.0 MHZ
 5                            * ..CRYSTAL FOR 68HC11 CLOCK
 6                            *
 7                            ********************************************************
 8                            *
 9                            ********************************************************
10                            ** SYMBOL DEFINITIONS
11                            ********************************************************
12                            * 68HC11 REGISTERS
13         1000               REG     EQU   $1000     BEGINNING OF REGISTERS
14         102B               BAUD    EQU   $102B     BAUD RATE REGISTER
15         102C               SCCR1   EQU   $102C     CONTROL REGISTER 1
16         102D               SCCR2   EQU   $102D     CONTROL REGISTER 2
17         102E               SCSR    EQU   $102E     STATUS REGISTER
18         102F               SCDR    EQU   $102F     DATA REGISTER
19                            * MASKS
20         0008               BIT3    EQU   %00001000
21         0020               BIT5    EQU   %00100000
22         0080               BIT7    EQU   %10000000
23                            *
24                            ********************************************************
25                            ** DATA SECTION
26                            ********************************************************
27  0010                              ORG   $0010
28  0010                      CHARCNT RMB   1         NUMBER OF CHARS TRANSMITTED
29                            *
30  C500                              ORG   $C500
31                            * MESSAGE TABLE
32  C500  54 48 45 20 49      BEGMSG  FCC   'THE INPUT CHARACTER WAS '
    C505  4E 50 55 54 20
    C50A  43 48 41 52 41
    C50F  43 54 45 52 20
    C514  57 41 53 20
33  C518                      INCHAR  RMB   1         INPUT CHARACTER INSERTED IN MSG
34  C519  0D                          FCB   $0D       CARRIAGE RETURN
35  C51A  0A                  ENDMSG  FCB   $0A       LINE FEED
36                            *
37  FFD6                              ORG   $FFD6
38  FFD6                              RMB   SCIISR    SCI INTERRUPT VECTOR
39                            *
40                            ********************************************************
41                            ** MAIN PROGRAM
42                            ********************************************************
43  C100                              ORG   $C100
44                            *------------------------------------------------------
45                            * INITIALIZATION
46                            *------------------------------------------------------
47                            * INITIALIZE STACK
48  C100  8E CF FF            START   LDS   #$CFFF
49                            * INITIALIZE SCI SERIAL COMMUNICATIONS INTERFACE
50                            *    INITIALIZE SCI MODE
51  C103  7F 10 2C                    CLR   SCCR1     8-BIT CHARACTERS, NO WAKE UP
52                            *    INITIALIZE SCI BAUD RATE TO 1200 BAUD
53  C106  86 33                       LDAA  #$33      SCP1:SCP0=11 SCR2:SCR1:SCR0=011
54  C108  B7 10 2B                    STAA  BAUD
55                            *    ENABLE SCI RECEIVER AND ITS INTERRUPT
56  C10B  86 24                       LDAA  #$24      DISABLES SCI TRANSMITTER AND
57  C10D  B7 10 2D                    STAA  SCCR2     ..ITS INTERRUPT
58                            * TURN ON INTERRUPT SYSTEM
59  C110  0E                          CLI
```

Figure 7-53   Example program for serial communications interface.

```
60              *-------------------------------------------------------
61              * WAIT FOR INTERRUPTS
62              *-------------------------------------------------------
63   C111  20 FE        HERE     BRA    HERE
64              *
65              ************************************************************
66              ** SCI INTERRUPT SERVICE ROUTINE
67              ************************************************************
68              *-------------------------------------------------------
69              * INTERRUPT POLLING CHAIN
70              *-------------------------------------------------------
71              * INTERRUPT FROM SCI RECEIVER?
72   C113  CE 10 00     SCIISR   LDX    #REG
73   C116  1E 2E 20 06           BRSET  SCSR-REG,X,BIT5,SCIRCV
74              * INTERRUPT FROM SCI TRANSMITTER?
75   C11A  1E 2E 80 10           BRSET  SCSR-REG,X,BIT7,SCITX
76              * ILLEGAL INTERRUPT
77   C11E  20 27                 BRA    RTSCI     IGNORE
78              *-------------------------------------------------------
79              * SERVICE SCI RECEIVER
80              *-------------------------------------------------------
81              * READ INPUT CHARACTER
82   C120  A6 2F        SCIRCV   LDAA   SCDR-REG,X  FINISH CLEARING FLAG
83              * PUT INPUT CHARACTER INTO OUTPUT MESSAGE
84   C122  B7 C5 18              STAA   INCHAR
85              * INITIALIZE MESSAGE BYTE COUNT
86   C125  7F 00 10              CLR    CHARCNT
87              * START MESSAGE - ENABLE SCI XMTR AND ITS INTERRUPT
88   C128  1C 2D 88              BSET   SCCR2-REG,X,BIT7+BIT3  SENDS IDLE CHAR
89              * RETURN TO MAIN PROGRAM
90   C12B  7E C1 47              JMP    RTSCI
91              *-------------------------------------------------------
92              * SERVICE SCI TRANSMITTER
93              *-------------------------------------------------------
94              * AT END OF MESSAGE?
95   C12E  86 1B        SCITX    LDAA   #ENDMSG-BEGMSG+1  MESSAGE LENGTH
96   C130  91 10                 CMPA   CHARCNT
97   C132  22 05                 BHI    MORE      BRANCH ON NO
98              * TERMINATE MESSAGE - DISABLE XMTR AND ITS INTERRUPT
99   C134  1D 2D 88              BCLR   SCCR2-REG,X,BIT7+BIT3
100  C137  20 0E                 BRA    RTSCI
101             * TRANSMIT NEXT CHARACTER
102             *    GET CHARACTER FROM TABLE
103             *       POINT TO MESSAGE TABLE
104  C139  CE C5 00     MORE     LDX    #BEGMSG
105             *       ADJUST POINTER TO NEXT CHARACTER
106  C13C  D6 10                 LDAB   CHARCNT
107  C13E  3A                    ABX
108             *       GET NEXT CHARACTER ASCII CODE
109  C13F  A6 00                 LDAA   0,X
110             *    OUTPUT NEXT CHARACTER
111  C141  B7 10 2F              STAA   SCDR   FINISH CLEARING XMTR FLAG
112             *    INCREMENT COUNT OF CHARACTERS SENT
113  C144  7C 00 10              INC    CHARCNT
114             *-------------------------------------------------------
115             * RETURN FROM SCI INTERRUPT
116             *-------------------------------------------------------
117  C147  3B           RTSCI    RTI
118  C148                        END
```

Figure 7-53   Continued.

flag is not set, the BRSET instruction on line 75 sends control to the transmitter service routine if the transmitter flag is set. If neither flag is set, there was an error and the program ignores the interrupt by returning to the main program at line 77.

- *Line 82.*   Control comes to this receiver routine before it can go to the transmitter routine because a key must be pressed to trigger an output message. The LDAA instruction reads the input character code from the receiver data register. This instruction also completes the clearing of the receiver flag RDRF. Clearing the receiver flag requires a sequence of two read operations while the flag is set. The first was the read of SCSR done by the BRSET instruction on line 73. The second is the read of the data register by the LDAA instruction.

- *Line 84.*   The input character from the receiver data register is stored in memory within the predetermined character string that defines the output message.

- *Line 86.*   The character counter tracks the number of characters from the message that have been transmitted. The counter is cleared so it's ready for the start of a new message.

- *Line 88.*   This receiver service routine now enables the transmitter and its interrupt—the receiver effectively triggers the output message. Enabling the transmitter makes it control the output pin. Upon enable, the transmitter automatically sends an idle character consisting of 10_{10} consecutive 1s. This operation does not clear the TDRE flag. Therefore, a transmitter interrupt occurs immediately when the RTI instruction at the end of this ISR turns on the interrupt system. The transmitter interrupt service routine then transmits the message.

- *Lines 90 and 117.*   The interrupt service routine returns control to the main program. The interrupt service routine ran with the interrupt system off, but the RTI instruction now turns it on again. Since the transmitter flag is already set, the transmitter interrupts immediately.

- *Lines 72 to 75.*   The interrupt system sends control here. The receiver flag is clear because the receiver could not have received another character in such a short time. Therefore, control goes to the transmitter service routine because the transmitter flag is set. The transmitter service routine sends one character of the message to the serial transmitter.

- *Lines 95 to 97.*   The number of characters previously transmitted is in location CHARCNT. This count is compared to the length of the message, which is 1B in this example. If there are more characters to transmit, control goes to line 104. The first time the transmitter routine runs following an input character, the number in location CHARCNT is zero.

- *Lines 104 to 109.*   The character code for the next character in the message is gotten from the message table. The character count in location CHARCNT acts as the offset from the beginning of the message table to the next character.

- *Line 111.*   The character code is stored in the transmitter data register to transmit the character. This also finishes clearing the transmitter flag TDRE. Clearing the transmitter flag requires both a read and a write operation. The BRSET instruction on line 74 read the SCSR register for the first part of clearing the flag. Writing to the SCDR register completes the clearing function. The transmitter flag remains clear until the character has effectively been transmitted by the transfer of the character from the data register to the shift register. This may take some time if the shift register is now transmitting another character. When the transfer occurs, the transmitter sets its flag to request another interrupt.

- *Line 113.*   The interrupt service routine increments the character counter because the ISR has sent another character.

After the transmitter sends the last character in the message, the transmitter interrupt sends control to the transmitter service routine. Now the ISR must stop the transmitter instead of transmitting another character.

- *Lines 95 to 97.*   The interrupt system, in response to the transmitter interrupt, and the polling chain send control here. The character count is tested to determine if the last character was sent. If the transmitter has sent the complete message, control goes to line 99.

- *Line 99.*   The SCI transmitter and its interrupt are both disabled. This prevents further interrupts from the transmitter, effectively ending the transmission of the message.

This example ignores several important issues. The program does not use the receiver framing error and noise flags, so the program treats erroneous characters the same as any other character.

The program does not test for overrun errors, because they are not possible—the computer is fast enough to always read a character before another is received. However, receiving a new character before the message is finished starts the message again from the beginning because the character count is set to zero.

7.11   ANALOG-TO-DIGITAL CONVERTER

The analog-to-digital converter in the 68HC11 makes 8-bit unsigned numbers representing external DC voltages. The A/D converter, by using an 8-channel multiplexer, can read voltages from eight different pins on the 68HC11 package. Port E is the collection of the eight input pins for the A/D converter. Port E also can be read as a parallel digital input-only port using the PORTE register.

An A/D converter normally reads signals from analog sensors. Typical sensors measure temperature, pressure, or position.

Analog-to-Digital Conversion Principles

An analog-to-digital converter makes a binary number that is proportional to an unknown DC voltage. A digital-to-analog converter makes a DC voltage proportional to a binary number. Generally an A/D converter is much more complex than a D/A converter, which is relatively simple and inexpensive.

Most A/D converters operate by comparing the unknown voltage to a voltage controlled by a D/A converter. The D/A output is varied according to some algorithm. When the two voltages are nearly the same, the number currently controlling the D/A converter becomes the digital output of the A/D converter.

Figure 7-54 shows the parts of an A/D converter. An unknown voltage and the voltage from the D/A converter are applied to an analog comparator. The comparator asserts its output while the D/A voltage is greater than the unknown voltage. The controller changes the number in the D/A register according to some algorithm until it detects a correct change in the comparator output.

Up-counting converter

The simplest algorithm for the controller starts the D/A at zero volts and then counts the register up until the D/A voltage crosses the unknown voltage. At the crossing, the counting stops and the flag is set indicating that the A/D converter has completed the conversion.

The up-counting algorithm is very simple, but it has several disadvantages. The major disadvantage is that the converter takes a different amount of time to reach the result for each different voltage. If the voltage is small, the result is reached quickly, but if the voltage is large, the time is very long.

Successive-approximation converter

Another control algorithm for the A/D converter is more complex, but the performance is much better than the up-counting algorithm. Here the controller first sets the D/A register

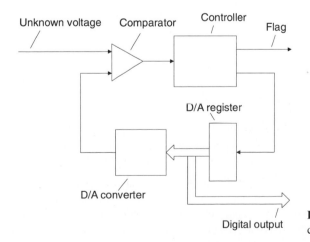

Figure 7-54   Block diagram of A/D converter hardware

to binary 10000000 to make a voltage that is one-half of the maximum. The comparator indicates whether the unknown voltage is higher than or lower than the D/A voltage. If the unknown voltage is higher than the D/A voltage, the D/A is set to a voltage halfway between this one and the maximum. That is, the binary number is made 11000000. If now the unknown voltage is lower than the D/A voltage, the D/A is set to a value halfway between the previous two values; namely, 10100000. The converter determines all eight bits by following this procedure eight times. This algorithm is called *successive-approximation*.

One advantage of the successive-approximation algorithm is that eight trials always determine the result whatever the unknown voltage. The conversion time is always known for all voltages. Also, the average successive-approximation conversion time is many times smaller than the up-counting conversion time. However, the controller is more complex.

Multiplexer

An A/D converter is a complex device using many analog electronic components. Therefore, its cost is relatively high. If a computer must read many different analog voltage signals, using one A/D converter for each signal usually is prohibitively expensive. In such applications, it is often practical to compromise the speed at which the signal voltage can be read to reduce cost.

A *multiplexer* is an electronic switch that connects one of several analog signals to a single A/D converter. Typical multiplexers switch between either eight or 16_{10} different signals. A multiplexer enables the A/D converter to read many different signals, but it reduces the system performance. The computer must control the multiplexer telling it which signal to pass to the A/D converter.

The multiplexer takes a small amount of time to operate before the A/D can read the incoming voltage. Since the A/D converter can read only one voltage at a time, the rate at which all the voltages can be read is greatly reduced. In many applications, the lower cost makes the performance reduction with a multiplexer acceptable.

68HC11 A/D Converter

The 68HC11 chip contains an 8-bit successive-approximation A/D converter. There is no other analog input or output device in the chip. It is noteworthy that the 68HC11 chip contains both digital and analog circuits on the same chip.

Converter hardware

The A/D converter in the 68HC11 chip includes a single A/D converter, a sample-and-hold circuit, and a 16-channel multiplexer. The converter can read a voltage over a 5-volt range with a maximum error of plus or minus one least-significant bit.

A/D converter.   The A/D converter is an 8-bit successive-approximation converter. The power supply for the 68HC11 must provide the A/D converter both a high and a low analog reference voltage. These voltage supplies connect to the 68HC11 pins named V_{RH} and V_{RL}. Typically +5 V_{DC} and 0 V_{DC} are used, but other positive voltages are allowable if V_{RH}

is 2.5 to 5.0 volts greater than V_{RL}. Normally V_{RH} and V_{RL} also supply the voltage for the analog sensor.

A measured voltage equal to V_{RL} returns the 8-bit number 00 and a voltage equal to or greater than V_{RH} returns FF. Such a converter is called a *ratiometric* A/D converter.

Each conversion requires the time of exactly 32_{10} E-clock cycles for usual applications. With an 8.0-MHz crystal, the conversion time is 16_{10} microseconds.

Sample-and-hold.   An analog sample-and-hold circuit measures the unknown voltage at the beginning of a conversion. During the conversion, the sample-and-hold maintains a constant voltage for the A/D converter. Use of the sample-and-hold avoids conversion errors caused by a changing voltage during the conversion process.

Multiplexer.   The multiplexer has 16_{10} channels, although only eight channels connect to pins on the 68HC11 chip. Therefore, the multiplexer makes it possible to measure eight different analog voltage signals. Of the other eight channels, four are used for internal testing and four are unused.

Certain varieties of the 68HC11 integrated circuit have fewer pins than required by the hardware in the chip. These chips can use only four channels of the multiplexer because the other four channels do not connect to pins.

A/D control

Software controls the A/D converter in ways similar to other I/O devices in the 68HC11. However, the way the A/D operates and its speed of conversion leads to some unique programming approaches.

A/D control register.   Figure 7-55 shows the A/D control register called ADCTL. It's unusual that control bits are unknown after a power-up reset as are most of the ADCTL bits.

The A/D converter starts a conversion within one E-clock cycle after the program writes a number into the ADCTL register. The number written into the control register selects one of several options on how the converter reads and stores conversion results.

A/D flag.   Starting the converter clears the conversions-complete flag, which is called CCF. When a conversion sequence is complete, the A/D converter sets the flag.

If the program writes to ADCTL while a conversion is in progress, the current conversion stops and a new conversion sequence begins.

A/D interrupt.   The A/D converter cannot cause an interrupt. The conversion is so fast that the overhead of servicing an interrupt makes polling attractive. However, since the exact number of E-clock cycles needed for a conversion is known, the program may execute instructions to delay 32_{10} E-clock cycles while the conversion takes place. Then the program can read the A/D immediately and it need not poll the flag.

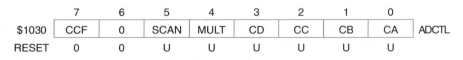

	7	6	5	4	3	2	1	0	
$1030	CCF	0	SCAN	MULT	CD	CC	CB	CA	ADCTL
RESET	0	0	U	U	U	U	U	U	

Figure 7-55   Analog-to-digital control register.

Channel selection and scanning

When the program starts the analog-to-digital converter, the converter always does four consecutive A/D conversions as fast as it can. There is no choice to do only a single conversion. The four conversions may be either on a single channel of the multiplexer or on four different channels. Furthermore, the A/D can operate continuously by repeating the conversions without the program starting it each time.

The A/D converter sets the CCF flag only after four conversions are complete. Few programs use the flag because the A/D converter is so fast and its conversion time in E-clock cycles is known exactly.

Result registers.   The A/D converter puts the numbers from the four conversions in four A/D result registers. These registers are called ADR1, ADR2, ADR3, and ADR4. The addresses of these registers are 1031, 1032, 1033, and 1034, respectively. The result of the first conversion goes to ADR1 and the last result to ADR4. The program may only read the result registers; writes to them do nothing.

The A/D puts the conversion results into the result registers as each conversion finishes. Therefore, the program may read the results as they are stored rather than waiting until all four conversions are complete. Reading the results early may be an advantage if very fast response is necessary.

Single-channel reading.   When the MULT bit in the ADCTL register is 0, the A/D converter reads a single channel. The channel is selected by the number in the CD, CC, CB, and CA bits of the ADCTL register. Only the first eight channels can read external voltages, so the CD bit is set to 0 by most programs. If the program needs only a single reading of a single channel, the result is available in the ADR1 register 34_{10} E-clock cycles after the write to the control register.

Multiple-channel reading.   When the MULT bit in the ADCTL register is 1, the A/D converter reads four channels in succession. Only the first eight channels of the multiplexer can read external voltages, so the CD bit is usually 0. The CC bit then selects the first group of four channels or the second group of four channels. That is, when the CD:CC bits are 00, channels 0 through 3 are read; when the CD:CC bits are 01, channels 4 through 7 are read. The CB and CA bits have no effect when MULT is 1. No other grouping of four channels is possible.

Continuous and single-channel scanning.   The A/D converter reads four times according to two different scanning methods. The program sets the SCAN bit to 1 to choose the continuous-scan mode. In the continuous-scan mode, the converter repeats the four readings continuously without program intervention. When four conversions are complete, the A/D converter immediately begins reading the four voltages again. Therefore, the four result registers are updated continually. The flag serves no purpose in this mode.

In the single-scan mode, the program starts the conversions. When the four conversions are complete, the A/D converter stops. So the result registers are updated once each time the program starts the converter. When the four conversions are complete, the A/D sets its CCF flag.

A/D power control

The program can turn off the electrical power to the A/D converter if the converter is not needed. Power can be restored when the A/D is again needed. The power savings may be especially important if a battery powers the 68HC11. Look at the electrical specifications to find the details of the power saved.

Figure 7-56 shows the OPTION register. The OPTION register was first shown by Figure 7-9. The ADPU bit in the OPTION register controls the power to the A/D converter.

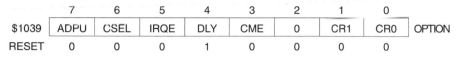

	7	6	5	4	3	2	1	0	
$1039	ADPU	CSEL	IRQE	DLY	CME	0	CR1	CR0	OPTION
RESET	0	0	0	1	0	0	0	0	

Figure 7-56   Configuration options register.

The reset condition of the A/D is off. The program must write a 1 to the ADPU bit to power-up the A/D converter. When the program turns on the A/D, it must wait at least 100_{10} microseconds before using the converter to allow the electronics to stabilize.

By changing the ADPU bit, the program can turn the A/D power on or off at any time. Some other control bits in the OPTION register are timed write-once bits.

A/D clock options

Either one of two clocks within the 68HC11 chip may drive the A/D converter. Normally the E-clock is the clock source for the A/D converter. A power-up reset selects the E-clock.

Another clock controlled by an internal resistor-capacitor oscillator is necessary when the E-clock rate is below 750_{10} KHz. Such a low E-clock rate reduces the power consumption of the 68HC11 chip. To select the R-C clock for the A/D, the program must write a 1 to the clock select bit CSEL in the OPTION register.

The R-C oscillator runs at about 1.5 MHz; it is not as accurate as the E-clock. It takes about 10 milliseconds after selecting the R-C clock before the A/D stabilizes so the program can use it. When using the R-C clock, the program should poll the CCF flag to determine when the conversions are complete.

By changing the CSEL bit, the program can select a different clock source for the A/D at any time. Some other control bits in the OPTION register are timed-write-once bits.

The CSEL bit also enables a resistor-capacitor oscillator used in programming the EEPROM in the 68HC11 chip. Be careful to avoid problems caused by interactions due to programming the A/D clock option.

Analog Input Example

Every 8.19_{10} milliseconds, the example program reads the A/D converter and controls two digital output bits. One bit indicates if the voltage is above some specified limit. The other bit indicates if the voltage is too high for the A/D converter—it actually indicates if the A/D reading is exactly FF. The program uses the real-time interrupt device with interrupts to determine the timing. This program is based on the RTI program in Figure 7-14, so only the new parts are discussed below.

- *Lines 52 and 53.*   The reset state of the A/D converter is powered-down, so first the program powers it up and selects the E-clock to drive the converter hardware. The A/D requires about 100_{10} microseconds to stabilize after it is powered-up, so the first reading taken by this program may be erroneous.

- *Lines 81 through 88.*   The real-time interrupt service routine runs after a time delay of 8.19 milliseconds.

- *Lines 90 and 91.*   A subroutine reads the A/D converter. The main program sends the channel number to the subroutine in the A accumulator. The channel number should be in the range of zero through seven.

- *Lines 111 through 113.*   Inside the subroutine, the channel number is masked to ensure that it is in a valid range for the A/D converter. The masking also sets the SCAN and MULT bits so the A/D reads four times and stops and the four readings are all of the same channel. Storing into the ADCTL register starts the A/D conversion in the correct mode. It also clears the CCF flag, but the flag is not used in this example.

- *Lines 115 through 120.*   Since the CCF flag is not used here, the program executes a few instructions to use at least 33_{10} E-clock cycles while the A/D converter operates. After this time, the converter has completed only one A/D conversion.

- *Line 122.*   The program reads the A/D converter results from the first conversion result register. The first register must be read because only one conversion is complete at this time.

- *Line 124.*   The subroutine returns to the calling program inside the interrupt service routine.

- *Lines 93 through 100.*   The program tests the reading from the A/D converter the subroutine returned in the A accumulator. It also puts the bit pattern in accumulator B indicating the range value and the overload bit.

- *Line 102.*   The output pattern is sent to port C indicating the range and overload condition.

- *Line 104.*   The RTI instruction returns control to the main program loop, which waits for another interrupt. The next interrupt occurs 8.19 milliseconds after the previous one.

This program causes the output bit to flicker between 0 and 1 when the analog voltage is near the limit. A simple digital filter added to the program would reduce or prevent the flickering.

```
 1                              ***************************************************
 2                              ** READ ANALOG VOLTAGE EVERY 8.19 MILLISECONDS AND
 3                              ** INDICATE VOLTAGE RANGE AND OVERLOAD (A/D READS FF)
 4                              *
 5                              * USE REAL TIME INTERRUPT AS TIME BASE
 6                              *
 7                              * PORTC BIT0 IS 1 FOR UPPER HALF OF VOLTAGE RANGE
 8                              * PORTC BIT1 IS 1 FOR OVERLOAD
 9                              *
10                              * USE 8.0 MHZ CRYSTAL FOR 68HC11 CLOCK
11                              *
12                              ***************************************************
13                              *
14                              ***************************************************
15                              ** SYMBOL DEFINITIONS
16                              ***************************************************
17                              * 68HC11 REGISTERS
18            1003              PORTC    EQU    $1003       I/O PORT C REGISTER
19            1007              DDRC     EQU    $1007       DATA DIRECTION REGISTER C
20            1024              TMSK2    EQU    $1024       TIMER MASK REGISTER
21            1025              TFLG2    EQU    $1025       TIMER FLAG REGISTER
22            1026              PACTL    EQU    $1026       PULSE ACCUMULATOR CONTROL REG
23            1030              ADCTL    EQU    $1030       A/D CONTROL REGISTER
24            1031              ADR1     EQU    $1031       A/D RESULT REGISTER
25            1039              OPTION   EQU    $1039       HARDWARE OPTION CONTROL REG
26                              * MASKS
27            0001              BIT0     EQU    %00000001
28            0002              BIT1     EQU    %00000010
29            0040              BIT6     EQU    %01000000
30            0080              BIT7     EQU    %10000000
31            00FF              IOPAT    EQU    $FF         I/O PATTERN, 0=IN 1-OUT
32                              * SYMBOLS
33            0003              CHNO     EQU    3           A/D CHANNEL NUMBER
34            0060              VLIMIT   EQU    $60         ANALOG VOLTAGE RANGE LIMIT
35                              *
36                              ***************************************************
37                              ** DATA SECTION
38                              ***************************************************
39   FFF0                                ORG   $FFF0    RTI INTERRUPT VECTOR
40   FFF0     C11D                        FDB  RTIISR
41   FFF2                       *
42                              ***************************************************
43                              ** MAIN PROGRAM
44                              ***************************************************
45   C100                                 ORG  $C100
46                              *--------------------------------------------------
47                              * INITIALIZATION
48                              *--------------------------------------------------
49                              * INITIALIZE STACK
50   C100     8E CF FF          START    LDS   #$CFFF
51                              * INITIALIZE A/D CONVERTER
52   C103     86 80                      LDAA  #BIT7       POWER-UP A/D USING E-CLOCK
53   C105     B7 10 39                    STAA OPTION      ..ADPU:CSEL=0:0
54                              * INITIALIZE PORT C
55                              *    INITIALIZE OUTPUTS TO ZEROS
56   C108     7F 10 03                    CLR  PORTC      0=LOW
57                              *    SET UP PORTC INS AND OUTS
58   C10B     86 FF                       LDAA #IOPAT
59   C10D     B7 10 07                    STAA DDRC        ALL OUTPUTS
60                              * INITIALIZE REAL TIME INTERRUPT
61                              *    SET INTERRUPT RATE TO 8.19 MS
62   C110     86 01                       LDAA #BIT0       ZEROS IN OTHER BITS
63   C112     B7 10 26                    STAA PACTL       ..CAUSE NO PROBLEMS
```

Figure 7-57   Example program for A/D converter.

```
64                              *     ENABLE RTI INTERRUPT
65    C115    86 40                   LDAA   #BIT6     ZEROS IN OTHER BITS
66    C117    B7 10 24                STAA   TMSK2    ..CAUSE NO PROBLEMS
67                              * TURN ON INTERRUPT SYSTEM
68    C11A    0E                      CLI
69                              *-------------------------------------------------------
70                              * WAIT FOR INTERRUPTS
71                              *-------------------------------------------------------
72    C11B    20 FE             HERE    BRA    HERE      DO NOTHING!
73                              *
74                              ************************************************************
75                              ** INTERRUPT SERVICE ROUTINE
76                              ************************************************************
77                              *-------------------------------------------------------
78                              * INTERRUPT POLLING CHAIN
79                              *-------------------------------------------------------
80                              * INTERRUPT FROM REAL TIME INTERRUPT DEVICE?
81    C11D    CE 10 25          RTIISR  LDX    #TFLG2
82    C120    1F 00 40 1A               BRCLR  0,X,BIT6,RTRTI  IGNORE ILLEGAL INTERRUPT
83                              *-------------------------------------------------------
84                              * CONTROL PORT C OUTPUTS
85                              *-------------------------------------------------------
86                              * CLEAR REAL TIME INTERRUPT FLAG
87    C124    86 40                    LDAA   #BIT6     STORE 1 TO CLEAR FLAG!
88    C126    B7 10 25                 STAA   TFLG2    ..ZEROS DO NOTHING
89                              * READ A/D CONVERTER
90    C129    86 03                    LDAA   #CHNO
91    C12B    BD C1 3F                 JSR    ADREAD
92                              * DETERMINE VOLTAGE RANGE BIT
93    C12E    5F                       CLRB
94    C12F    81 60                    CMPA   #VLIMIT
95    C131    25 02                    BLO    NEXT
96    C133    C8 01                    EORB   #BIT0     SET BIT0
97                              * DETERMINE OVERLOAD BIT
98    C135    81 FF             NEXT    CMPA   #$FF
99    C137    26 02                     BNE    NEXT1
100   C139    C8 02                     EORB   #BIT1     SET BIT1
101                             * CONTROL OUTPUT BITS
102   C13B    F7 10 03          NEXT1   STAB   PORTC
103                             * RETURN FROM INTERRUPT
104   C13E    3B                RTRTI   RTI
105                             *
106                             ************************************************************
107                             ** READ ANALOG-TO-DIGITAL CONVERTER SUBROUTINE
108                             * PASS CHANNEL NUMBER IN A, RETURNS READING IN A
109                             ************************************************************
110                             * ACCEPT ONLY VALID CHANNEL NUMBERS
111   C13F    84 07             ADREAD  ANDA   #$07      ALSO SELECT SINGLE SCAN, ONE CH
112                             * START A/D CONVERSION
113   C141    B7 10 30                  STAA   ADCTL     SCAN:MULT=00
114                             * WASTE AT LEAST 33 CLOCK CYCLES WHILE A/D OPERATES
115   C144    37                        PSHB              DO NOT ALTER REGISTERS
116   C145    33                        PULB              USE MINIMUM STACK SPACE
117   C146    37                        PSHB
118   C147    3D                        MUL
119   C148    3D                        MUL
120   C149    33                        PULB
121                             * READ A/D CONVERSION RESULTS
122   C14A    B6 10 31                  LDAA   ADR1      USE FIRST RESULT REGISTER
123                             * RETURN FROM SUBROUTINE
124   C14D    39                        RTS
125   C14E                              END
```

Figure 7-57 Continued.

Motorola Trainer

The port E pins for the A/D converter connect directly to the ribbon cable connector on the trainer. Port E is both the analog input port and a digital input port. At reset, the trainer reads port E bit 0 as a digital input bit. A 1 tells it to run the monitor program normally and a 0 tells it to execute the program at the beginning of the EEPROM without any initialization. Jumper J4 connects pin PE0 to a 10K-ohm resistor, which goes to either ground or +5 VDC to provide a default input bit. When you use port E, you must account for the 10K-ohm resistor and the program start-up procedure. If the jumper bypasses the monitor program, the OPTION register remains at the reset condition, so the A/D converter is powered-down. The monitor program powers-up the A/D converter and selects the E-clock to drive it.

The A/D example program in Figure 7-57 will run in the trainer with only the interrupt vector changed. The RTI interrupt is mapped to address 00EB.

7.12   FAIL-SAFE OPERATION

Many microcomputers control dangerous devices. The danger may be to people or to equipment and machinery. Therefore, the computer must respond to failures that hardware and software can detect. Certain failures cannot be detected without extraordinary complication and cost.

Watchdog Timer

Many control systems, including computers, use a device called a *watchdog timer* to ensure that the system is operating. Motorola calls the timer in the 68HC11 the *computer-operating-properly timer*, or COP.

Principles of watchdog timer

A watchdog timer is a hardware device that can reset a system after a time period has expired. The system will restart the timer periodically if it is working correctly. If the system fails, it will likely not restart the timer. Then the timer will expire and reset the system. The reset must force everything to a safe condition. The reset may also cause the system to start operating again and it may then continue operating correctly. If the system cannot recover from the failure, the safe condition continues.

Watchdog operation.   In a computer system, the watchdog timer is reset by a program that runs in a loop. When the program repeats the loop, it restarts the timer. If the program fails to complete the loop and restart the timer, the timer forces a system reset. The watchdog timer hardware can reset the system even when other hardware has failed.

Failures detected.   Many kinds of failures can lead to timeout of the timer. Program errors that occur only under unusual circumstances may crash the program so it cannot restart the timer. Failure of a memory bit can change an instruction in a program leading to a crash and a timeout. Certain interrupt failures may prevent a part of the program from executing and thus restarting the timer. Therefore, a watchdog timer detects and responds to a wide range of software and hardware errors and failures that are difficult to predict.

Computer-operating-properly timer

The 68HC11 chip contains a watchdog timer called the *computer-operating-properly*, or COP, timer. When the COP times out, it forces a reset on the 68HC11 chip and other chips connected to its reset pin. Figures 7-1 and 7-2 show the reset pin as a bidirectional signal pin. The reset signal may originate within the 68HC11 due to the COP.

COP period.   The program sets the COP timeout period to one of four times based on the E-clock rate. Figure 7-58 shows the COP divider chain and the control bits CR1 and CR0. Figure 7-56 shows the OPTION register that contains the control bits. At reset, the COP time is set to the shortest and thus safest time.

The CR1 and CR0 bits are timed-write-once bits. Therefore, the program must set the COP timeout time within 64_{10} E-clock cycles of reset. Thereafter, the program cannot change the COP time. This provides improved security that the COP will operate correctly even if failed programs try to alter it.

Table 7-12 shows typical timeout periods for several crystal frequencies. Usually the timeout period is small because the COP is used in control applications. Many control systems require sections of the program to execute periodically at a rapid rate. If the program does not execute at the correct time, damage to equipment may result. Therefore, short COP times confirm that the system is updating the control information in a timely way.

Enabling the COP.   Most control applications of the 68HC11 use the COP to provide safety. A bit in the CONFIG register enables the COP. Figure 7-5 shows the NOCOP bit in the CONFIG register. When the NOCOP bit is 0, the COP operates.

The CONFIG register is made of EEPROM cells, so it is programmed permanently as part of the control system. The program cannot affect whether the COP is active.

During software development for control system applications, the programmer usually disables the COP. This avoids resets during software debugging and testing. Likewise, applications that have no need of the COP leave it disabled.

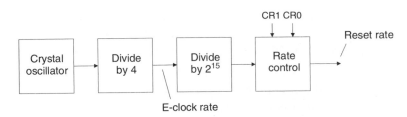

Figure 7-58   COP timer divider chain.

TABLE 7-12   COP TIMEOUT PERIOD

COP Control Bits		Rate is E Divided by	Crystal Frequency		
			8.3886 MHz	8.0 MHz	4.9152 MHz
CR1	CR0		Timeout Period (milliseconds)		
0	0	2^{15}	15.625	16.384	26.667
0	1	2^{17}	62.5	65.536	106.67
1	0	2^{19}	250	262.14	426.67
1	1	2^{21}	1000	1049	1707
		E =	2.1 MHz	2.0 MHZ	1.2288 MHz

Restarting the COP timer.   The principal purpose of the COP timer is to detect software failures. Failed software must not easily restart the timer. Consequently, restarting the timer is deliberately difficult.

Restarting the timer requires two distinct operations by the program. First, the program must store the number 55 into the COP-reset register called COPRST. The COPRST register is at memory address 103A. Second, the program must store the number AA into the COPRST register.

The program must complete the two stores into COPRST before the COP times out to prevent the COP from resetting the system. Each time the reset sequence is completed, a new COP timeout period begins.

The program may execute any number of instructions between the two stores into COPRST. The program can obtain no useful information by reading the COPRST register. Furthermore, reading it has no affect on the COP.

The 8-bit number 55 is the complement of the number AA. Using these two numbers to reset the COP reduces the possibility of a program resetting it in error. For example, if a failure of the data bus has grounded a bus line, the COP cannot be reset.

Program strategy.   Clever programming of the COP reset can improve the safety provided by the COP. Usually it is good to separate the two store instructions into different parts of a program. Then failure of one part alone prevents the COP from being reset. Similarly, if a part of the memory fails, separating the reset instructions improves the likelihood of detecting a problem.

If a certain I/O device is particularly critical to an application, part or all the COP reset may be placed in the interrupt service routine. For example, the COP can test the real-time interrupt device by using its ISR to do part of the COP reset.

COP reset.   Following a reset of the computer system by the COP, the 68HC11 continues normal operation with one exception. After the reset, the microprocessor uses a reset vector at addresses FFFA and FFFB. Therefore, the program can detect that a COP reset has occurred and take appropriate action. For example, the program may record the number of times a COP reset occurred. The number of failures may aid a service person.

Motorola Trainer

The trainer as supplied by Motorola does not use the COP timer, because the CONFIG register is programmed to disable the COP. Since the CONFIG register is made of EEPROM cells, special procedures are necessary to change it. Regardless, the monitor program sets the OPTION register for the longest COP timeout period. To use another period, your program must bypass the monitor program because the COP rate bits are timed-write-once bits.

Forcing a reset with COP

Programs that detect fatal errors may attempt to recover by forcing a hardware reset on the entire computer system. The microprocessor has no instructions to force reset, so the reset must be done by hardware. Usually, the program disables interrupts and then goes into an infinite loop. Soon the COP times out and forces the desired reset of all the hardware in the computer system.

A typical example of forcing a reset is a response to an illegal instruction interrupt. If an illegal instruction code was fetched, the integrity of the entire computer system is in doubt. The erroneous program may have incorrectly programmed I/O hardware and destroyed information in volatile memory. Therefore, using the COP to force a reset of the system is appropriate following an illegal instruction interrupt.

Clock Failure Detection

All the many functions of the 68HC11 microprocessor and internal I/O devices depend on proper operation of the crystal clock. If the crystal clock fails completely or operates at a grossly incorrect frequency, the computer system may cause unsafe operation in certain applications.

Clock monitor

The 68HC11 contains hardware to detect if the clock is operating below a certain rate that includes a complete failure. When the clock monitor detects a clock failure, the clock monitor forces a system reset through the 68HC11 reset pin. The reset puts all devices in the computer system into the reset condition so the system is safe.

Minimum clock rate.   The clock monitor need not be accurate, since its principal purpose is to detect failed clocks. The specifications for the 68HC11 state that clock rates above 200 KHz will not trigger a reset. Furthermore, clock rates below 10 KHz always force a reset. Special applications that use slow or changeable clock rates may have difficulty using the clock monitor.

Motorola Trainer

The monitor program in the trainer disables the clock monitor, although its interrupt vector is mapped to address 00FD. Your program may enable the clock monitor by changing the OPTION register. You also must provide a reset routine for the clock monitor vector that is mapped to address 00FD.

Enabling the clock monitor.   The program enables the clock monitor by storing 1 in the clock monitor enable bit called CME. Figure 7-56 shows the OPTION register containing the CME bit. The reset condition of CME disables the clock monitor.

The program can change the CME bit at any time. Some bits in the OPTION register are timed-write-once bits.

Clock monitor reset.   If the clock is operating following a clock monitor reset, the 68HC11 operates normally except for the use of a different reset vector. The clock monitor reset vector is at addresses FFFC and FFFD. The program module that handles the reset thus knows that a clock failure occurred.

COP clock

The computer-operating-properly timer derives its time from the crystal clock for the 68HC11. If the clock fails to operate, or operates at a low frequency, the COP is nearly useless! Therefore, the COP must always be used in conjunction with the clock monitor. Then if the clock does not operate correctly, the computer system will be reset even if the COP cannot respond correctly.

7.13   I/O PORT SUMMARY

All the pins of all the input/output ports in the 68HC11 are digital input bits, digital output bits, or programmable digital I/O bits. There are restrictions on some bits because other I/O hardware uses them.

Port A

The programmable timer and pulse accumulator use port A pins in addition to the parallel I/O functions. The PORTA register at address 1000 controls the digital input and output functions. Pins PA0, PA1, and PA2 are input-only pins. Pins PA3 through PA6 are output-only pins. Pin PA7 is bidirectional using the data direction bit DDRA7 in the PACTL register to control the direction.

In the E9 version of the 68HC11 chip, pin PA3 is also bidirectional. Then, bit 3 of the PACTL register is called data direction bit DDRA3.

The PORTA register may be read at any time, but information from bits corresponding to timer and pulse-accumulator functions read their information, which is not always input pin information. Writing to the PORTA register controls the corresponding output pins only if they are not being controlled by the timer. The bits written into PORTA are remembered and will control the output pins later if the timer function is disabled.

Port B

In single-chip-computer mode, port B is always an output-only digital port. The PORTB register at address 1004 controls the output pins. No other devices use the port B pins. In expanded mode, the output function of port B is lost.

Port C

In single-chip-computer mode, port C is always a programmable I/O port. The data direction register DDRC at address 1007 determines whether a pin is an input or an output. The program may either write or read the PORTC register at address 1003. No other devices use these port C pins. In expanded mode, the I/O functions of port C are lost.

In single-chip mode, the port C outputs can be either CMOS compatible or open-drain outputs. The port C wired-OR mode bit in the PIOC register controls the mode. While CWOM is 0 as it is after a reset, the port C outputs are CMOS compatible. While CWOM is 1, the outputs are open-drain outputs.

Port D

Port D is a 6-bit programmable I/O port. The PORTD register at address 1008 is used to read or write to the port. The data direction register DDRD at address 1009 controls the direction of each pin.

The outputs are affected by the DWOM bit in the SPCR register. When DWOM is 0, the outputs are CMOS compatible. When DWOM is 1, the outputs are open-drain drivers.

Two serial I/O devices also use the port D pins. When those devices are enabled, they override some of the functions specified by the DDRD and PORTD registers. Due to the multiple functions of these pins, several considerations in the electronics also come into play, so consult a Motorola manual for additional details.

Port E

The port E pins are both an input-only digital input port and the inputs to the analog-to-digital converter. The pins serve both functions simultaneously, though one function is analog and the other digital! The digital input port is read by reading the PORTE register at address 100A.

Motorola Trainer

At reset, the trainer reads port E bit 0 as a digital input bit. A 1 tells it to run the monitor program normally and a 0 tells it to execute the program at the beginning of the EEPROM without any initialization. Jumper J4 connects pin PE0 to a 10K-ohm resistor, which goes to either ground or +5 VDC to provide a default input bit. When you use port E, you must account for the 10K-ohm resistor and the program start-up procedure.

7.14   HARDWARE EXPANSION

Many applications of the 68HC11 require additional I/O hardware beyond that available within the chip. If the chip is operating in expanded mode, the microprocessor buses allow expansion, although using the buses may be too costly for some applications. Regardless, in the single-chip mode, the buses are not available! To provide for expansion in either mode, the 68HC11 chip contains a serial interface for communicating with I/O chips. An alternative application is to provide communication between two 68HC11 chips.

Serial Peripheral Interface

The 68HC11 I/O hardware can be expanded using a synchronous serial I/O bus called the serial peripheral interface, or the SPI bus. Input/output chips communicate with the 68HC11 over the SPI bus. The SPI bus does not communicate with I/O devices directly. Many commercial chips are available for serial communication over the SPI bus.

The SPI bus operates at a high baud rate, so the I/O chips must be close to the 68HC11 chip—usually both chips are on the same circuit board. Using the SPI bus leads to modest compromises in input/output speed when compared to using the microprocessor buses. This speed reduction is of little concern in many applications.

Serial communication principles

The serial peripheral interface is, in principle, a simple device based on two shift registers. Chapter 1 showed a serial communication system similar to the SPI in Figure 1-15. Figure 7-59 is a simpler version of that figure, which illustrates the principles of the SPI device.

The shift registers in the two SPI devices are in a circular connection. A common clock signal clocks both the shift registers. By definition, the master device contains the controlling clock. The slave device receives its clock signal from the master device.

When a clock pulses the shift leads of both the devices, one bit from the master device goes to the slave device and one bit from the slave device goes to the master device. After eight clock pulses, the numbers in the two registers have been exchanged.

The transmission and reception of bytes occur simultaneously over the SPI bus. Therefore, the SPI is a full-duplex communication system. Furthermore, the common clock makes

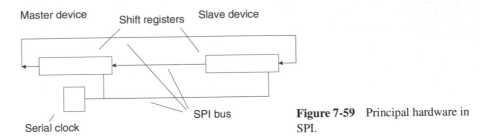

Figure 7-59   Principal hardware in SPI.

the SPI a synchronous serial device because both devices respond in synchronism. The SCI serial device is asynchronous because there is no common clock. Therefore, the SCI receiver must periodically sample the input signal—the SPI does not require sampling.

SPI hardware operation

The SPI contains a single data shift register, a control register, and a status register. The SPI hardware may operate in either the master mode or the slave mode. Three pins on the 68HC11 connect the SPI bus lines to the other device. More than two devices may connect to the SPI bus. However, only one device can be the master.

Hardware connections.   Three wires form the SPI bus between a master and a single slave device that have a circuit common. One wire carries the serial clock signal between the pins labeled SCK on each device. The other two wires carry the data signals between master and slave devices.

On each device, one pin is labeled MOSI for master-out-slave-in and the other is labeled MISO for master-in-slave-out. These labels imply that you should connect bus wires between pins with the same label on both the master and slave devices. These connections do not depend on which of the devices acts as the master.

To complete the connections, the low-asserted slave-select pin must be low on the slave device to enable it for responding to the SPI bus. There is no need for a slave-select pin on the master device, so the pin performs other functions. First, it is the input to the bus contention detection hardware. Second, it is a digital output bit.

Mode selection.   Selecting one of the two modes of operation makes the hardware operate differently. The master-mode select bit called MSTR determines the mode of operation. The MSTR bit is in the serial peripheral control register called SPCR. Figure 7-60 shows the SPCR register which is at address 1028.

Usually the computer chip is the master unless it is a slave to another computer chip. The master device generates the serial clock and therefore controls all the data transfers over the SPI bus. The slave device cannot initiate communication. The slave receives data from

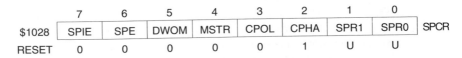

	7	6	5	4	3	2	1	0	
$1028	SPIE	SPE	DWOM	MSTR	CPOL	CPHA	SPR1	SPR0	SPCR
RESET	0	0	0	0	0	1	U	U	

Figure 7-60   Serial peripheral interface control register.

the master and can transmit data to the master. However, the master must still initiate the transmission.

Baud rate.   The rate of the serial clock determines the baud rate of the SPI. The program sets the baud rate by controlling the SPR1 and SPR0 bits in the SPCR register. Figure 7-61 shows the divider chain that drives the SPI clock. Table 7-13 shows typical baud rates for the SPI.

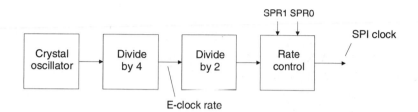

Figure 7-61   SPI clock divider chain.

Data register.   When the program stores into the shift register of the master, the SPI controller automatically generates eight pulses to complete the transfer of a byte between the master and slave devices. The shift register is called SPDR for serial peripheral data register. The SPDR register is at address 102A.

Flags and interrupts.   Whether operating in the master or slave mode, when a transmission is complete, the SPI sets the SPIF flag. The SPIF flag is in the serial peripheral status register called SPSR. Figure 7-62 shows the SPSR at address 1029.

If the 68HC11 is operating in the slave mode, the program should store into the SPI data register immediately after the flag is set. In the master mode, the program can store into the data register any time after the flag is set. In either case, if a store occurs while a transmission is in progress, a *write collision* occurs and the store has no effect.

TABLE 7-13   SPI BAUD RATE

SPI Control Bits		Rate-Control Divide Factor	Crystal Frequency		
			8.3886 MHz	8.0 MHz	4.9152 MHz
SPR1	SPR0		SPI Baud Rate (kilobaud)		
0	0	1	1049	1000	614.4
0	1	2	5243	500.0	307.2
1	0	8	131.1	125.0	76.80
1	1	16	65.54	62.50	38.40
		E =	2.0971 MHz	2.0000 MHz	1.2288 MHz

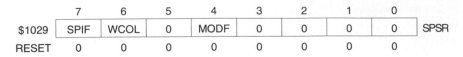

	7	6	5	4	3	2	1	0	
$1029	SPIF	WCOL	0	MODF	0	0	0	0	SPSR
RESET	0	0	0	0	0	0	0	0	

Figure 7-62 Serial peripheral interface status register.

The write-collision bit called WCOL in the SPSR register indicates if a write collision happened. The WCOL flag is cleared by reading the SPSR register followed by reading or writing the SPDR register.

The SPIF flag can cause an interrupt when it is set. The interrupt-enable bit is called SPIE for serial peripheral interrupt enable. The interrupt vector for the SPI device is at addresses FFD8 and FFD9.

If the SPI bus is operating at a high baud rate, it may not be practical to use the flag—especially with an interrupt. The transmission time may be short enough that the program may simply delay long enough to allow the transmission to complete. Using the interrupt may cause greater overhead rather than less.

SPI control

The serial peripheral interface control register called SPCR contains several bits that control the SPI hardware. The program enables the SPI by writing 1 to the SPI enable bit called SPE in the SPCR register. While enabled, the SPI controls the appropriate port D output pins overriding the PORTD register.

Also in the SPCR register are the clock polarity bit called CPOL and the clock phase bit CPHA. These bits control the timing of the serial clock. Four different timing patterns make the 68HC11 compatible with most commercially available I/O chips that use the SPI bus.

The electrical characteristics of the port D output pins are programmed by the DWOM bit in the SPCR register. The name DWOM means port D wired-OR mode selection bit. While DWOM is 0 as it is following a reset, the port D outputs are CMOS compatible. While DWOM is 1, the port D outputs are open-drain drivers. This electrical difference may be important when more than two devices are on a single SPI bus.

SPI bus with multiple slaves

The SPI bus can communicate with several I/O chips or other devices with a single bus. Most applications use one of two fundamental configurations. The first configuration is a simplex system where the master device broadcasts data to multiple slave devices. This system is similar to the system described with the SCI interface.

The second configuration is a full-duplex system with multiple slave devices. In this case, only one slave device can send data to the master at a time; otherwise the signals would collide. While the slave is transmitting, all other slave devices must be disabled.

Motorola Trainer

The SPI bus is not used within the trainer. The port D pins are connected to the ribbon cable connector and the interrupt vector is mapped to address 00C7.

The slave-select pin labeled SS enables or disables the slave devices. Usually, digital output pins on the 68HC11 control the slave select pins of the slave devices. Then the program in the master 68HC11 controls the slave devices enabling them as needed.

Microprocessor Bus Expansion

The 68HC11 can be expanded by adding additional memory and I/O chips. To do this, the chip must be operated in expanded mode so the microprocessor buses are available external to the chip. In the single-chip computer mode, the buses are not available externally, so the only expansion means is the SPI bus.

Mode selection

The operating mode of the 68HC11 chip is determined by high-asserted signals applied to the MODA and MODB pins during a hardware reset. Table 7-1 shows the modes selected. It's important that the operating mode is selected by hardware and not software. This prevents dangerous operation of the computer due to erroneous programs.

The single-chip computer mode and the expanded mode are the normal operating modes. Two other special modes are for testing and other purposes and are not normal operating modes. Only the normal modes are discussed here. Figure 7-63 shows the HPRIO register; the bits RBOOT, SMOD, MDA, and IRV relate to the special modes. Consult a Motorola manual for further details.

Expanded mode

When the 68HC11 chip operates in the expanded mode, the pins of port B and port C become address and data bus pins. Figure 7-2 is a block diagram for the expanded mode. The port C pins carry both address and data signals at different times—this does not slow the computer's operation.

To separate the address and data bus information, an external latch is necessary. In expanded mode, the STRA pin becomes a strobe for the latch so it captures the address information. The STRA pin is then named AS for address strobe. Similarly, the STRB pin

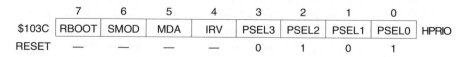

	7	6	5	4	3	2	1	0	
$103C	RBOOT	SMOD	MDA	IRV	PSEL3	PSEL2	PSEL1	PSEL0	HPRIO
RESET	—	—	—	—	0	1	0	1	

Figure 7-63 Highest-priority I-interrupt register.

becomes the read/write control line and is named R/W for the expanded mode. Figure 7-64 shows a block diagram of the hardware necessary to complete the address and data buses in expanded mode.

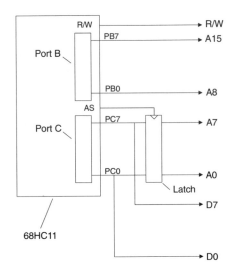

Figure 7-64   Expanded mode bus expansion using external latch.

When the 68HC11 is used with the external latch and operated in the expanded mode, the buses are compatible with the buses of other Motorola 8-bit microprocessors. Expansion with memory and I/O chips is straightforward. However, the use of port B and port C for I/O is lost. Table 7-14 shows all the pin connections for the ports in each of the normal operating modes.

Port replacement unit

In expanded mode, port B and port C no longer function as I/O ports. To regain the same I/O functions that the 68HC11 has in single-chip computer mode, additional hardware is necessary. The 68IIC24 chip, known as the Port Replacement Unit, or PRU, replaces the lost ports. The PRU connects to the buses and fully implements the port B and port C input/output functions. When using the PRU chip, all the single-chip functions, including the memory addresses, are the same as those of the single-chip mode.

It is very helpful to use the PRU during development of a system that will use single-chip mode in the final design. During development, all the internal signals can be seen on the external buses when expanded mode with a PRU is used. When all development of the software is complete, the same software operates the chip in single-chip mode.

The PRU also makes it practical to upgrade a product design. When changing a design that uses the 68HC11 in single-chip mode, the PRU makes it easy to add memory or I/O devices. All the original design is retained when more hardware is added.

TABLE 7-14   PORT SIGNAL SUMMARY FOR 68HC11A8

Pin Designation Port-Bit	Pin Function in Single-chip Mode	Pin Function in Expanded Mode
A-0	PA0/IC3	PA0/IC3
A-1	PA1/IC2	PA1/IC2
A-2	PA2/IC1	PA2/IC1
A-3	PA3/OC5/and-or OC1	PA3/OC5/and-or OC1
A-4	PA4/OC4/and-or OC1	PA4/OC4/and-or OC1
A-5	PA5/OC3/and-or OC1	PA5/OC3/and-or OC1
A-6	PA6/OC2/and-or OC1	PA6/OC2/and-or OC1
A-7	PA7/PAI/and-or OC1	PA7/PAI/and-or OC1
B-0	PB0	A8
B-1	PB1	A9
B-2	PB2	A10
B-3	PB3	A11
B-4	PB4	A12
B-5	PB5	A13
B-6	PB6	A14
B-7	PB7	A15
C-0	PC0	A0/D0
C-1	PC1	A1/D1
C-2	PC2	A2/D2
C-3	PC3	A3/D3
C-4	PC4	A4/D4
C-5	PC5	A5/D5
C-6	PC6	A6/D6
C-7	PC7	A7/D7
D-0	PD0/RxD	PD0/RxD
D-1	PD1/TxD	PD1/TxD
D-2	PD2/MISO	PD2/MISO
D-3	PD3/MOSI	PD3/MOSI
D-4	PD4/SCK	PD4/SCK
D-5	PD5/SS	PD5/SS
None	STRA	AS
None	STRB	R/W
E-0	PE0/AN0	PE0/AN0
E-1	PE1/AN1	PE1/AN1
E-2	PE2/AN2	PE2/AN2
E-3	PE3/AN3	PE3/AN3
E-4	PE4/AN4	PE4/AN4
E-5	PE5/AN5	PE5/AN5
E-6	PE6/AN6	PE6/AN6
E-7	PE7/AN7	PE7/AN7

Motorola Trainer

The trainer uses a 68HC11 chip operating in expanded mode. A PRU chip provides the lost ports so the trainer can simulate the single-chip computer mode. Furthermore, by using expanded mode, the monitor program is in an external EPROM chip. The user may choose to replace or alter the monitor program by changing the code in the EPROM. The RAM memory for user programs is also external memory connected to the buses.

7.15 SPECIAL HARDWARE OPERATION

Several instructions and control register bits alter the normal behavior of the 68HC11. Most of these special operations involve changing the performance of the interrupt system and lowering power consumption. Some bits are for factory test functions.

Highest-Priority Interrupt

The priority of interrupts is of little concern in many applications. However, certain applications require very quick response to a particular device. Often, the device has critical timing requirements and the delay caused by the processing of higher-priority interrupts is a problem. To overcome this difficulty, the 68HC11 can promote a single I-bit controlled interrupt to the highest priority. Promoting the priority of one interrupt does not affect the relative priorities of the remaining interrupts.

Four priority-select bits named PSEL3, PSEL2, PSEL1, and PSEL0 choose an interrupt to promote to the high-priority level. These priority-select bits are in high-priority register called HPRIO. Figure 7-63 shows the HPRIO register at address 103C. The PSEL bits choose an interrupt according to the values in Table 7-15.

The program can change the PSEL bits only while the I-bit is 1. That is, while the interrupt system is disabled, the program can select a new high-priority interrupt. Usually, the program sets the high-priority register during its initialization. However, an interrupt service routine also can modify the HPRIO register so software can create a sophisticated priority interrupt system.

The reset condition of the HPRIO register puts 0101 in the PSEL bits. Therefore, normally the reserved high-priority interrupt defaults to the IRQ interrupt. This is consistent with the address order of the interrupt vectors, which places IRQ at the highest address.

Wait Mode

Through program control, the microprocessor can enter a wait mode where program execution ceases. The processor exits the wait mode in response to an interrupt. The wait instruction WAI first puts the microprocessor status on the stack and then enters the wait state.

TABLE 7-15   HIGHEST-PRIORITY INTERRUPT SELECT BITS

PSEL3	PSEL2	PSEL1	PSEL0	Highest Interrupt
0	0	0	0	Timer Overflow
0	0	0	1	Pulse-Accumulator Overflow
0	0	1	0	Pulse-Accumulator Input Edge
0	0	1	1	SPI Serial Transfer Complete
0	1	0	0	SCI Serial System
0	1	0	1	Reserved (Default to IRQ)
0	1	1	0	IRQ (External pin or Parallel I/O)
0	1	1	1	Real-Time Interrupt
1	0	0	0	Timer Input Capture 1
1	0	0	1	Timer Input Capture 2
1	0	1	0	Timer Input Capture 3
1	0	1	1	Timer Output Compare 1
1	1	0	0	Timer Output Compare 2
1	1	0	1	Timer Output Compare 3
1	1	1	0	Timer Output Compare 4
1	1	1	1	Timer IC4/OC5

During the wait, the clocks continue to operate, but the microprocessor does not execute instructions.

There are two purposes to the wait mode. First, the microprocessor can respond very quickly to an interrupt. Since the microprocessor status is already on the stack at the time of an interrupt, the interrupt response is much quicker than for other interrupts. Of course, the price for this response is that no instructions are executed while the microprocessor waits for the interrupt.

Second, while the microprocessor is not executing instructions, the power consumption of the chip is reduced. Power reduction may be very important for a device operated by a battery.

Stop Mode

The STOP instruction puts the microprocessor into the stop mode, which stops all the clocks. The purpose of the stop mode is to reduce power consumption to the minimum possible. Recovery from the stop mode requires a hardware reset or an XIRQ or IRQ interrupt.

The response to an XIRQ interrupt request is unusual when the processor is in the STOP mode. An XIRQ interrupt forces recovery from the stop mode whatever the state of the X bit. However, if X is 0, a normal XIRQ interrupt sequence follows an XIRQ interrupt. If the X bit is 1, an XIRQ interrupt causes execution to continue with the instruction after the STOP instruction without requesting an XIRQ interrupt.

A STOP instruction is only effective if the S bit in the condition code register is 0. Otherwise, STOP acts as a NOP instruction. Only the TAP instruction can change the stop

---

Motorola Trainer

The program *STOP* used to stop programs in the trainer is not the STOP instruction, which stops the 68HC11 clock. The program stop is a SWI instruction that sends control to the monitor program. The STOP instruction can be used in the trainer.

---

disable or S bit. Stopping the microprocessor may be dangerous in some applications—all bit values, including the I/O bits, are retained. The S bit locks out the STOP instruction to make it less likely the microcomputer will execute a STOP instruction by accident.

Since the STOP instruction stops the clock oscillator, recovery from the stop mode requires time for the oscillator to stabilize. Normally, the processor will begin operation only after 4064_{10} clock cycles to allow the clock to reach normal operation. If an application uses a separate clock instead of the internal clock, this delay is unnecessary. Making the DLY bit in the OPTION register 0 disables the delay. The DLY bit is a timed-write-once bit.

Factory Tests

The register named TEST1 at address 103E is used only during factory testing of the 68HC11 chip. Several bits in other registers are also useful only for factory testing. These include the TCLR and RCKB bits in the BAUD register.

The TEST instruction is used only in factory testing when the 68HC11 chip is in a special mode. In normal operating modes, it is an illegal instruction and will cause an illegal instruction interrupt.

7.16 REVIEW

The 68HC11 chip is available in several variations. Most of the variations are quite similar in principle and vary mostly in details such as the amount of memory and the number of input/output signals. The reset and interrupt systems are nearly the same as are the many input/output devices within the 68HC11 chip. The various I/O devices provide parallel and serial input/output; timing of inputs, outputs, and program execution; counting of external events; measurement of analog voltages; and detection of failures of hardware and software.

7.17 EXERCISES

7-1. What effect does a hardware reset have on the stack if the reset occurs while a program is running?

7-2. In Figure 7-1, why is the reset signal shown with a double-headed arrow?

7-3. How much time following reset does a 68HC11 computer with an 8.0-MHz clock have to program the timed-write-once bits?

7-4. How does a program clear the STAF flag bit?

7-5. Refer to the program listing in Figure 7-8. If the programmer erroneously entered a NOP instruction instead of the CLI instruction, what will the program do? Explain what each output does.

7-6. Refer to the program listing in Figure 7-8. What is the effect of putting the instructions on lines 104 and 105 in the opposite order?

7-7. Using the hardware in Figure 7-7, change the program in Figure 7-8 to make the BCD display count up by one periodically. Use the oscillator interrupts as the time base. Read the thumbwheel switch to determine the rate at which counting should take place. The number on the switch multiplied by five is the number of oscillator interrupts between updates of the display. Also make the light toggle each time the push button is pushed.

7-8. Using the hardware in Figure 7-7, change the program in Figure 7-8 to display the number of times the button is pushed during each 10_{10} periods of the oscillator. Assume a hexadecimal display unit. If the number is too big, saturate at the highest number. Also assume that the switch has no contact bounce.

7-9. Following a hardware reset, are the IRQ and XIRQ pins level-sensitive or transition-sensitive?

7-10. In an application that uses the XIRQ interrupt, beyond enabling the interrupt, is there any purpose to the X bit?

7-11. Does a 1 in the I bit prevent an interrupt from the SWI instruction? Does executing the SWI instruction affect the I bit?

7-12. Refer to Figure 7-14. If the instruction on line 71 was written incorrectly so it loaded the accumulator with zero, what is the effect on the port C bits? How frequently will the instruction on line 56 be executed?

7-13. Modify the program in Figure 7-14 so the port C bits are toggled every 65.54_{10} milliseconds.

7-14. Using the RTI device as a time base, write a polling program to pulse-width modulate output bits. That is, change the output between low and high to make an average level that is a percentage of the high level—this percentage is called a duty cycle. Use PORTB for the output bits. The duty cycle for bit 0 is 10%, for bit 1 is 30%, for bit 2 is 70%, and for bit 3 is 90%. The total cycle should be 10_{10} periods of the RTI.

7-15. Using the RTI device as a time base, write an interrupt program to pulse-width modulate four output bits. That is, change the output between low and high to make an average level that is a percentage of the high level—this percentage is called a duty cycle. Use

PORTC for the output bits. The duty cycle for bit 0 is 20%, for bit 1 is 40%, for bit 2 is 60%, and for bit 3 is 80%. The total cycle should be 10_{10} periods of the RTI.

7-16. Modify the program in Figure 7-23 to indicate OK if the length of the pulse from the input signal is less than 10_{10} milliseconds. The length here is defined as the elapsed time from the low-to-high transition until the high-to-low transition. To measure this time only, the capture edge will be changed after each capture.

7-17. Modify the program in Figure 7-26 to pulse-width modulate port A bit 5. The duty cycle will vary from 1 to 99_{10} percent in increments of 1 percent based on an 8-bit number in the range 1 to 99_{10} stored in location DUTYCYC. The full cycle of the output must always be 10_{10} milliseconds. Why does the program in Figure 7-26 not work correctly if the low or high times are nearly zero?

7-18. Which pins can output compare 1 control? Can the PORTA register control an output pin at the same time that OC1 is also controlling it?

7-19. Modify the program in Figure 7-26 to pulse-width modulate port A bit 7 using OC1 instead of OC2.

7-20. Modify the program in Figure 7-8 to use the pulse-accumulator input flag PAIF instead of the STAF flag. The push button switch will be connected to port A pin 7.

7-21. Write the 8-bit ASCII codes for the letter M and the digit 9 using even, odd, mark, and space parity.

7-22. If a serial cable is much too long for your application, is it a good idea to coil the excess cable around a cable spool to prevent the cable from getting tangled?

7-23. Change the SCI serial message program in Figure 7-53 so pressing a key can only start a new message after the current message is finished. After the completion of the message, the next key pressed determines the character inserted in the next message.

7-24. Write a program to read an analog voltage approximately once a second using the real-time interrupt as a time base. Output the binary number for the lowest voltage read on port B and the number for the highest voltage read on port C. If the STAF flag is set, reset the lowest value to FF and the highest value to 00.

7-25. Write a program to read an analog voltage and send the 8-bit number to another device using the SCI at 1200 baud. The program must transmit approximately once a second using the real-time interrupt device as the time base.

Appendix A

Using MSDOS Computers

The most common type of computer used with the Motorola 68HC11 trainer is an IBM PC compatible personal computer (PC). It can run both an editor and an assembler program. The PC can also be used as a terminal for the trainer if no other terminal is available. The most common system software used in these computers is an MSDOS compatible operating system. For example, your computer may use MSDOS® from Microsoft or PCDOS® from IBM or DRDOS® from Digital Research.

The computer hardware can exist in a variety of configurations. This makes it difficult to cover all possibilities. So this appendix assumes a particular configuration, and then refers to it in the most generic way possible. If your system is substantially different, you may need to consult other documentation for further help. The configuration assumed here includes a hard disk drive called C, one floppy disk drive called A, and a printer. The names *hard disk*, *Winchester disk*, and *fixed disk* are used interchangeably.

The hard disk should contain the MSDOS-compatible operating system and the editor and assembler programs. Assume the floppy disk holds all your other files. These may include assembly language source and object files. The hard disk will be called the *system disk*, since it holds the operating system and other software. The floppy disk will be called the *data disk*. The type and capacity of each disk drive makes no difference to the discussion.

411

The following sections repeatedly refer to the disk drives. If your computer system uses different disk drives or uses the hard disk for both purposes, you must substitute the correct drive name at the appropriate places.

You may have some difficulty following the discussion if your computer system has only a single floppy disk drive. It will be necessary for you to swap disks frequently, which will be more difficult. However, it will usually be clear when you need to swap disks.

A.1   HOW TO GET STARTED

Here is a list of things you must learn to do so you can use the personal computer for assembly language programming:

- Install or adjust the paper in the printer so it is correctly positioned. Many dot matrix impact printers expect fan-fold paper to be positioned so the perforations are initially just above the print head. These printers usually allow the paper to be adjusted with the power turned off. Each type of printer has some unique controls.

- Turn the power on by reading and following the section below on turning on the computer.

- Format a floppy disk as described in the MSDOS commands section on using the FORMAT command.

- Look at the directory of a disk as described in the MSDOS commands section on using the DIR command.

- Learn to use the editor program on your computer system. See Appendix B for information on the SPF/PC editor.

- Learn to use the assembler program on your computer system. See Appendix C for information on the 2500AD assembler.

- Turn off the computer as described in the section below on turning off the computer.

A.2   TURNING ON THE PC AND RUNNING MSDOS

Unless there is a master power switch provided, begin by turning on the peripheral devices connected to the personal computer. Turn on the printer, the monitor display screen, and then the personal computer.

Now consider how the personal computer starts up assuming no intervention from you. There is a monitor program in permanent ROM memory that automatically starts running when the computer is turned on. The monitor program first tests the entire computer system including the memory and disk drives. As this occurs, you may hear the hard disk drive working and lights on the disk drives may turn on for a while. In addition, a message may be printed on the screen during the tests.

If the hardware fails no tests, the monitor program automatically loads the MSDOS operating system from the system disk into the computer memory. If the load was successful, it then starts the MSDOS program. MSDOS will then display some messages that end with the prompt C> and the cursor. The prompt means that MSDOS is ready to use.

A.3   TURNING OFF THE PC

When you have finished using your application program that ran under control of MSDOS, the monitor should again display the MSDOS C> prompt. If you were using the editor program, you will use the command that exits the editor to reach MSDOS. Most assembler programs will automatically return control to MSDOS after the assembly process is complete.

If the C> prompt is displayed, you should remove your floppy disk and then turn the power to the computer off. This procedure will ensure that all your information will be stored correctly on your disks and nothing will be lost. On the contrary, if you turn the power off while a program is running, you may destroy the data on all the disks.

A.4   USING THE PRINTER

There is little for you to do to use most printers. Usually, turning the printer on initializes it to the correct settings. If your printer has an *On Line* or *Select* light, it must be illuminated. When the printer is on line, the personal computer controls it instead of the manual control buttons.

Check the paper to be sure it is installed correctly and positioned correctly. Some printers will not print if the paper jams or there is no paper. This may cause MSDOS to display a message and request a response. One response may be *Abort*. This will completely cancel the program that was running, so it used only in catastrophic situations. Another response may be *Retry*. Type this response after correcting the printer problem, and probably the program will continue without error.

If you suspect that the printer is not working correctly, turn it off and back on again to reset it. If it continues to malfunction, the printer may have a self-test that will identify the problem independent of the computer.

A.5   USING THE CRT DISPLAY MONITOR

Normally no adjustments to the CRT display monitor will be necessary. If the screen is difficult to read, adjustment of the brightness or contrast controls probably will solve the program. Bigger problems such a tearing of the image or severe narrowing of the display will require servicing of the monitor. The MSDOS operating system does not provide error messages about the condition of the monitor.

A.6   RESTARTING MSDOS AFTER A PROBLEM

Certain problems may cause you to lose control of the personal computer. Usually the keyboard will not respond correctly or the monitor screen may stop displaying new information or go blank. Similarly, you may want to stop your program and return to MSDOS, but it will not respond to the keyboard.

In these cases, you can completely restart the personal computer as if the power was turned on. Of course, you will lose anything that you have developed unless you saved it on the disk. To restart, press the Control, Alternate, and Delete keys simultaneously. This requires much less effort than turning the computer off and back on, but does the same thing. However, there are situations where the problem prevents this technique from working. Then the only recourse is to turn the computer off and back on again.

A.7   USING A FLOPPY DISK

The two common types of floppy diskettes include the 5 1/4 inch and 3 1/2 inch diskettes. Each of these diskettes has more than one possible data density, but these differences do not affect the discussion here. Both types of diskettes have a protect notch or hole that is read by the disk drive. If the disk is protected, the disk drive cannot alter information on the disk, but it can read the information.

5 1/4 Inch Floppy Diskette

Caution! Never touch the surface of the disk that is exposed through the diskette cover. Also, discard the disk if any dirt or liquid gets on the disk. When they are not in use, keep your diskettes in a paper cover in a suitable box to protect them. They are very fragile.

The outer cover of the diskette has a write protect notch in one side. The disk is write protected if this notch is covered with a protect tape. In normal use, the notch will be uncovered so the disk can store new information.

To install a diskette, first open the door of the disk drive and pull out any diskette already in it. Then insert your diskette in the disk drive slot. Position the disk with the openings in the cover for the heads to contact the disk installed first. If the disk slot is horizontal, the protect notch must be on the left. Close the disk drive door.

3 1/2 Inch Floppy Diskette

Caution! Never open the sliding door in the diskette cover or touch the disk if you do. Also, discard the diskette if any dirt or liquid gets on the disk.

The outer cover of the diskette has a protect hole that may be covered by a sliding tab. If you can see through the protect hole, the disk is write protected. In normal use, the tab covers the hole so you cannot see through it; this enables the disk to store new information.

To install a diskette, first push the eject button on the drive and pull out any diskette already in it. Then push the end of the diskette with the sliding cover into the drive slot. If the drive is horizontal, the protect hole will be on the left. Keep pushing the diskette into the slot until it snaps into place.

A.8   USING THE MSDOS OPERATING SYSTEM

Since MSDOS is a disk operating system, most of the operating system commands relate to operations performed on disks. Probably most of your work will require the use of files stored on floppy disks. Although floppy disks can have subdirectories, the following discussion assumes only a root directory. The root directory is adequate for most assembly language work.

Disk Filename Conventions

Most disk drives have either a fixed hard disk or a removable floppy disk. The MSDOS operating system refers to a disk drive by name. Although the names may differ, the most common name is C for the first hard drive and A for the first floppy drive. You can put different floppy disks into the A drive, but the drive retains its name.

The operating system program works on one drive by default so the system commands are simpler. The current or default drive name is displayed on screen as part of the prompt. When a computer system with a hard drive is turned on, it usually loads the operating system from the C drive. Thus, the prompt usually reads C>, which identifies C as the default drive. The format of the prompt can be modified, so your prompt may be slightly different.

Files

A file is a collection of information stored on a disk under a name. The disk directory of a disk contains the names of the files on that disk. The directory also contains information that tells MSDOS where to find the file on the disk. The information stored in a file may be characters of text or the binary numbers of a program. Regardless of the meaning, the information in the file is just a list of binary numbers.

Filenames

The name of a file has two parts separated by a period. To the left of the period is the part called the filename, and to the right is the part called the extension. The filename is one to eight characters and the extension is one to three characters. In effect, the filename part identifies a file while the extension specifies the kind of file. Some programs require a specific extension while others allow you to create your own.

When the MSDOS operating system refers to a file, it must know the name of the disk drive, the filename, and the extension. Therefore, operating system commands must provide all this information unless some default is possible. For example, the drive name is not necessary if the disk is in the default disk drive as identified by the prompt.

Disk Subdirectories

The MSDOS operating system allows disks to be divided into sections called subdirectories. Each subdirectory acts like a separate disk drive. Subdirectories on your floppy disk are unnecessary for any of the examples in this book. However, if you use a hard disk as your system disk, you likely have a subdirectory devoted to assembly language programming. This subdirectory should hold your editor and assembler programs. Tell MSDOS to change to that subdirectory before using the personal computer for anything else. Then all the examples in this book are correct for your computer and require no changes. For example, if the subdirectory is on the default disk drive and you have named it ASSEMBLY, the command

CD \ASSEMBLY

changes the attention of MSDOS to this subdirectory only. The effect is to make a new hard drive that contains only assembly language related files. The C> prompt now refers to this new drive that is a subdirectory.

MSDOS Operating System Commands

The following is a list of the most commonly used operating system commands. A short description identifies the operation performed by the command. Some parts of commands can be omitted when a default value is acceptable. The system commands are always typed immediately to the right of the MSDOS prompt.

Copy disk files   COPY *drive:filename.ext drive:filename.ext*

This command copies the first file named into the second file. The files may be on the same or different disk drives and may have the same or different filenames and extensions. If the file exists on the destination disk, it will be overwritten. An example of this command is

COPY C:LEARN.ASM A:WHO.NOS

which copies one file into another as follows:

COPY	the disk file copy command
C:	copy source disk drive—if this drive name is omitted, the default drive is used
LEARN.ASM	copy source filename and extension
A:	copy destination disk drive—if this drive name is omitted, the default drive is used
WHO.NOS	destination filename and extension—if omitted, they default to the source filename and extension.

The asterisk character is a wildcard character that stands for anything. If asterisk is used as the source filename, the command copies all files with the specified extension regardless of the filename. If used as the source extension, the command copies all files with filename regardless of the extension. If used for the source filename and the extension, the command copies all files.

For example, the command:

$$COPY\ C:*.ASM\ A:$$

copies all the files with an ASM extension on the C disk drive to identically named files on the A disk drive.

Display disk filenames   DIR *drive:*

The directory command displays a disk directory on the personal computer screen. An example of this command is

$$DIR\ A:/W$$

which displays a directory in wide format as follows:

DIR	the directory display command
A:	the disk drive containing the disk for which the directory listing will be made
/W	an optional parameter that says print in wide format.

The wide or horizontal format of the directory leaves out the file length and date information making a compact listing. If the /W is omitted, the command gives a vertical format listing with file lengths and dates included. At the end of the listing, the number of bytes of free space on the disk is printed.

It is sometimes useful to print the directory of a disk on paper using the printer, Printing the directory of the disk in disk drive A: is done by typing

$$DIR\ A:\ >PRN:$$

which uses the >PRN: to redirect the output from the screen to the printer.

Copy a floppy disk   DISKCOPY *drive: drive:*

Copy an entire floppy disk to another floppy disk using either one or two disk drives. The DISKCOPY command cannot be used with hard disks. The destination disk does not need to be formatted before making the copy. Follow the directions on the screen that tell you which disk to install in the disk drive. An example of this command is

$$DISKCOPY\ A:\ B:$$

which copies the floppy disk in the A drive to the floppy disk in the B drive as follows:

DISKCOPY	the command to copy an entire floppy disk without alteration
A:	the source disk drive—reads the floppy disk to be copied
B:	the destination floppy disk drive—if there is only one disk drive, omit this and the same drive will be used for both source and destination.

You should use the protect mechanism on your original disk while using DISKCOPY to prevent accidental erasing of it! Note that an accidental copy from the destination to the source disk will erase the entire source disk!

Make backup copies of your floppy disks regularly, since it is easy to damage a disk and lose your information.

Erase disk files   ERASE *drive:filename.ext*

Removes individual files, groups of files, or all the files from the specified disk. The name DEL for delete can be substituted for ERASE. An example of this command is

ERASE A:MYFILE.S19

which erases a single file from a floppy disk as follows:

ERASE	the erase or delete command
A:	disk drive containing the disk with the file to be erased—if omitted, the default drive is used
MYFILE.S19	filename and extension of the file to be erased.

The asterisk character is a wildcard character that stands for anything. If asterisk is used as the filename, the command erases all files with the specified extension regardless of the filename. If used as the extension, the command erases all files with filename regardless of the extension. If used for the filename and the extension, the command erases all files. For example, the command

ERASE A:*.S19

erases all the files with the extension S19 from the disk in the A disk drive.

Format a new disk   FORMAT *drive:*

Format or prepare a new disk for use by the MSDOS operating system. The formatting process creates a directory on the disk and tests the disk for flaws. If there are minor flaws, portions of the disk are marked as defective. MSDOS will automatically avoid defective areas of the disk. Any information on a used disk will be destroyed by the formatting process. An example of the command is

FORMAT A:

which formats the floppy disk in the A drive as follows:

FORMAT	the command to start the formatting process
A:	the disk drive containing the disk to be formatted.

Once formatted, your disk will never need formatting again unless you destroy the information on it. Information can be destroyed if you place your floppy disk near strong magnetic fields such as those near transformers. So don't lay your disks on any electronic equipment or on speakers. Of course, any mechanical damage such as a small fold or a drop of liquid on the disk medium will destroy the disk.

Since a hard disk usually contains a large amount of information, replacing the information is time-consuming. So be careful not to format a hard disk accidentally. Some versions of the FORMAT command prevent accidental formatting of the hard disk.

Display file contents   TYPE *drive:filename.ext*

This command prints or types the text stored in a file on the personal computer screen. The file must be in ASCII format to be entirely readable. Most programming editors make ASCII files.

An example of this command is

TYPE A:LEARN.ASM

which displays the text as follows:

TYPE	the command to display text on the screen
A:	disk drive containing the disk with the file to be displayed
LEARN.ASM	filename and extension of the file to be displayed.

The command will scroll the text rapidly up the screen. Typing Control S will stop the scrolling and pressing the space bar will continue the scrolling. Typing Control C will abort the type command. Generally, using an editor program to view text files is much easier.

It is sometimes useful to print the text from a disk file on paper using the printer. Printing the same file used above is done by typing

TYPE A:LEARN.ASM >PRN:

which uses the >PRN: to redirect the output from the screen to the printer.

The TYPE command is useful for displaying the contents of object files made by an assembler. The binary numbers must be coded as ASCII characters or the information displayed will be garbage. The S-Record format used with the Motorola trainer is an ASCII format that can be displayed and read easily. Appendix C discusses the S-Record format.

Set the date   DATE *mm-dd-yy*

This command sets the date kept by the operating system. Many programs read the date from the operating system and print it as part of their output.

The month *mm* is a one- or two-digit number. The day *dd* is a one- or two-digit number. The year *yy* can be either a two-digit number or a four-digit number.

If the date is omitted, the command will display the current date and ask for a new date. The required input format will be displayed. Press the Enter key to leave the date unchanged.

An example of this command is

DATE 4-23-1991

which sets the date to April 23 of 1991.

Set the time   TIME *hh:mm:ss.hh*

This command sets the time of day kept by the operating system. Many programs read the time from the operating system and print it as part of their output. The time is kept in a 24-hour format.

The hour *hh* and minute *mm* are one- or two-digit numbers. The second *ss* and hundredths of seconds *hh* are optional and can be either one- or two-digit numbers.

If the time is omitted, the command will display the current time and ask for a new time. The required input format will be displayed. Press the Enter key to leave the time unchanged.

An example of this command is

$$\text{TIME 13:4}$$

which sets the time to four minutes after one o'clock in the afternoon.

Appendix B

Using the SPF/PC Editor Program

An editor program can create a text file on a disk that can be the source file for an assembler. The editor can create, change, insert, delete, copy, or move text. Programming editors make editing easy. They treat the text line by line like computer programs are written. Although you can use a word processor program as an editor, you will find that a programming editor is much easier to use.

This appendix is an abbreviated manual for the SPF/PC® Version 2.0 editor sold by Command Technology Corporation in Oakland, California. The commands covered are those essential to simple editing of assembly language programs. The SPF/PC editor has many more commands and features. See your SPF/PC manual for further details.

Much of this appendix assumes that you are running SPF/PC as you are reading. Seeing the screens as they are described will help you. A tutorial section leads you through a hands-on editing session. A hands-on session is the easiest way to learn to use an editor. Also see Appendix A for help with the MSDOS operating system.

SPF/PC has many options that configure how the program works. The options can be chosen and the choices saved with the program. Then each time the program is run, the options are predetermined. This appendix assumes that you have set the options as described in Appendix F on setting up a lab. Some keys will not work as described here if you have not set the options correctly. The options used here are different from the options that are set when the program is supplied by the manufacturer.

B.1 INTRODUCTION TO THE EDITOR

The editor program described here is the SPF/PC editor from Command Technology Corporation. It is a very powerful editor for IBM PC personal computer compatibles. SPF/PC runs on IBM PC compatible personal computers and emulates the IBM editor used on IBM mainframe computers.

The editor program resides on your system disk and your text files on your data disk. Using a floppy disk as your data disk is convenient. When you remove it from the computer, it also is protected from other people's mistakes.

The editor program should be on a hard disk if you have one. Otherwise, use a second floppy disk if you have two floppy disk drives. A single floppy disk drive can be used, and then the system disk and the data disk will be the same disk. The discussion here uses system disk and data disk as generic terms for whatever kind of disks you are using. See Appendix A for further discussion of the system and data disks.

The SPF/PC editor will operate in full screen mode without line numbers in the text file. Most of your editing can be done by moving the cursor to the point of the edit and typing the new text.

The editor has commands to do various functions such as delete an entire line. The commands consist of two sets called the Primary Commands and the Line Commands. You enter Primary Commands on a command line at the top of the screen. You enter Line Commands at the left of the line of text. The function keys also issue certain commands.

Most of the following discussion assumes that you will run the editor program as you read. Practice using the editor as you learn.

B.2 LOADING AND STARTING THE EDITOR PROGRAM

If you are using a floppy disk as a data disk, place your formatted disk in the floppy disk drive and close the drive door; then you can start the editor program. The data disk will hold the text files you create and edit with SPF/PC.

SPF/PC runs under control of the MSDOS operating system program. To use the editor, you must have MSDOS running first. You know that MSDOS is running correctly if a prompt such as C> is the last item on the screen. To begin editing, type SPF to the right of the MSDOS prompt and then press the Enter or Return key. The command SPF means load and run the editor program from the disk file named SPFPC.EXE. The SPF command invokes a batch file to do this.

When the editor starts, it places a menu on the screen. The cursor will be in the command position at the top of the screen. Select an item from the menu by typing the number of the operation that you want and press Enter. In this case, you want the number 2, which means edit a file. Do this even if the file of interest does not exist yet. If you selected the wrong menu function, press F3 and try again.

During the following discussion, use the Delcte, Backspace, Insert, and cursor keys to edit your entries if you make mistakes.

Selecting menu item 2 causes a new menu to appear that specifies which file on your disk to edit. Many of the choices are predetermined or blank. You can leave them unchanged by pressing Enter or by moving the cursor with the cursor control keys. For example, the first two choices for the disk drive and subdirectories are predetermined, so press Enter twice.

The next choice is the name of your file, which you must determine. So type a name of up to eight characters and press Enter.

The rest of the choices are predetermined, so press the Enter key three more times. Pressing the Enter key after the last entry causes editing to start and the edit screen to appear.

Here is an alternative and sometimes shorter approach to selecting the file and starting editing. Whenever the information for all the entries is correct, press the large + key on the numeric keypad. The position of the cursor makes no difference. The + key causes the edit screen to appear with fewer key strokes.

B.3   IDENTIFYING THE EDIT SCREEN AREAS

What you see in the central area of the edit screen depends on whether the specified disk file exists. If the file does not exist, you will see dots down the left side of the screen. If the file already exists, you will see the text in that file.

If you are creating a new file, the dots tell you that the editor has started in continuous text entry mode. This is not a very useful mode for assembly language work, so immediately change it. As an experiment, type the word TEXT and press the F2 function key. Now the editor has made one line of text for your file and has entered its normal edit mode.

If you are editing an existing file, the editor starts in normal edit mode. Regardless, you now have a normal edit screen. Let's identify the important areas of the screen. The very top line of the screen identifies the disk file you are editing. It will match the name you specified on the menu in starting the editor. The next line down is the Primary Command entry line. The right end of this line indicates the scroll mode; it was predetermined to be half-page scrolling.

Down the left side of the screen are one or more line numbers. The line number part of a line is also the Line Command field. You type Line Commands over the line numbers overwriting some of the digits! To the right of the line number is the text to be edited. If you created a new file as discussed above, your text is the word TEXT. Note the line numbers are not part of the text—they are for your reference only.

An information line is at the bottom of the screen. The left end of the information line lists some predetermined options and memory usage; these are of little interest here. The most important part of this line is the now blank central part where SPF/PC displays messages. Some messages displayed here confirm that certain operations have taken place, such as BACKUP SUCCESSFUL. Others are error messages like INVALID PRIMARY COMMAND.

The right end of the blank area will say INSERT MODE if the editor is in character insert mode. Character insert means that characters typed at the cursor will be inserted rather than typed over existing characters. At the far right of the information line is an indication of the current row and column position of the cursor.

B.4   EXITING THE EDITOR

At any time with the cursor at any position, you can safely exit the editor program and return to MSDOS. Do this by pressing the F3 function key three times. All your work will be saved on your disk.

Actually, the F3 key returns the editor to the previously used menu, or exits the editor if at the top-level menu. So when editing, pressing F3 three times will move the editor back through the menus and exit the program.

Caution! After SPF/PC exits and returns control to MSDOS, pressing F3 once again will put the characters SPF after the MSDOS prompt. Then you can restart SPF by pressing only the Enter key. This is a feature of later versions of MSDOS. It restores the last command you typed when you press F3. Don't be confused if you press F3 too often when exiting SPF/PC.

Notice that the editor does not save your text on your disk until you press F3 the first time. So be sure to exit the editor orderly. Turning the computer off in the middle of editing will destroy your text.

Whenever you change an existing file and save it, the original file is retained. To distinguish the new file from the original file, the editor changes the extension part of the original filename to BAK.

B.5   RESTARTING THE EDITOR

To restart the editor and continue editing a file, type SPF followed by a space and the name of the file to be edited.

B.6   THE EDITOR COMMANDS

The editor commands fall into groups including the cursor control keys, the Primary Commands, the Line Commands, and the function keys. The cursor determines the location and thus the type of command. You can type a Primary Command only on the command line at the top of the edit screen. You can type a Line Command over any digit of a line number. You delimit or process the Primary and Line commands by pressing Enter. Correct typing errors with the Backspace and Delete keys, or by typing over. The function keys issue certain commands, although some depend on the cursor position. Also, some functions require other commands before they become active. That is, some commands work in pairs.

Cursor Control Commands

The following is a list of the cursor control commands with the word name of the key that causes the operation. Each command is associated with a key on the keyboard.

Cursor Up

The cursor up key moves the cursor up the screen. If the cursor is at the top of the text area of the screen, it causes the text window to move upward over the text—the text scrolls downward. When the cursor reaches the top end of the text, it will jump to the command line. Next it jumps to the bottom of the screen.

Cursor Down

The cursor down key moves the cursor down the screen. If the cursor is at the bottom of the text area of the screen, it causes the text window to move downward over the text—the text scrolls upward. When the cursor reaches the bottom end of the text, it will jump to the command line. Next it jumps to the top of the screen.

Cursor Left

In the text or line number areas, the cursor left key moves the cursor to the left. If the cursor runs off the left side of the screen, it will wrap around to the right side. In other areas of the screen, the cursor left key moves the cursor to the left and jumps it over certain items. If the text has too many columns to fit on the screen, the text may scroll sideways. If the text was scrolled to the left by the cursor right key, the cursor left key will scroll the text to the right when needed.

Cursor Right

In the text or line number areas, the cursor right key moves the cursor to the right. If the cursor runs off the right side of the screen, it will wrap around to the left side. In other areas of the screen, the cursor right key moves the cursor to the right and jumps it over certain items. If the text has too many columns to fit on the screen, the text may scroll sideways. If the text doesn't fit on the screen, the cursor right key will scroll the text to the left when needed.

Home

The Home key moves the cursor to the left end of the primary command line.

End

When the cursor is in the text area, the End key moves the cursor to the right end of the line. When the cursor is in the line number area, it moves the cursor to the right end of the line number.

Page Up

The Page Up key moves the text window upward over the text by one-half page—the text scrolls downward. The cursor moves with the window.

Page Down

The Page Down key moves the text window downward over the text by one-half page—the text scrolls upward. The cursor moves with the window.

Tab

Whether the cursor is in the line number area or the text area, the Tab key moves the cursor to the right to the next predetermined tab position. If the cursor goes beyond the rightmost tab position, the cursor wraps down to the next line.

Shift Tab

Whether the cursor is in the line number area or the text area, Shift Tab moves the cursor to the left to the next predetermined tab position or to the left of the line number. If it goes beyond the line number, the cursor wraps up to the next line.

Enter

The Enter key moves the cursor to the beginning of the next line number when the cursor is on text while the editor is not in line insert mode. The same is true if the cursor is on a blank command line or on a line number. If the editor is in line insert mode, the Enter key moves the cursor to the position on the next line that matches the position of the first character on the current line. Also, the next line is a new line.

Primary Commands

The following is a subset of the Primary Commands. The discussion includes the format for typing each command on the command line. The Enter key delimits or processes the Primary Commands. The cursor can be moved to the command line by pressing the Home key. Edit the command with the Backspace and Delete keys and by typing over.

Locate a line   L linenumber

Locates or positions the text so the line specified by the line number is the first line on the edit screen. For example, the command L 257 puts line 257 at the top of the screen. If the line number is greater than the last line number, the last line is made the first line on the screen.

Print the text   PRINT ALL

Prints all the text on the printer. If you omit the ALL, only the current screen of text is printed.

Save text on disk   S

Saves the current text in your disk file. Only use this command if you want to force a save. Normally, the editor saves your text automatically when it exits the edit mode. You may fear a power failure or other problem and want to save during a lengthy editing session.

Find a character string   F characterstring

Finds the first occurrence of the character string by placing the cursor on its first character. The search begins at the first line of text displayed on the screen. For example, the command

F LADA will find the first occurrence of the characters LADA even if they are embedded within other characters. If your character string contains spaces, you must enclose it with single quotation marks. To find subsequent occurrences of the same string, press the F5 key. Each press will take you to the next occurrence. The F5 key does nothing if the find command has not been issued. If the character string is not found, the editor displays a message at the bottom of the screen.

Change a character string   C oldchars newchars firstcol lastcol ALL

Finds and changes all occurrences of the old character string to the new character string. The search includes only the first column through the last column. This command is often described as search and replace. For example, the command C SUM TOTAL 1 72 ALL changes the characters SUM to TOTAL if they occur within columns 1 through 72. If a character string contains spaces, the string must be enclosed with single quotation marks. The editor puts *chg* in the line number field of every line that was changed. The cursor is positioned after the first new character string. If you omit ALL, only the first occurrence beginning at the first line on the screen is changed. If you omit the column numbers, the search includes columns 1 through 80. Also see F2 key.

Cancel editing changes   CAN

Cancel all changes made since the last time the disk file was updated. That is, exit editing and trash the current text without saving to the disk.

Line Commands

The following is a subset of the SPF/PC Line Commands that work on a single line or a block of lines. You may type the Line Commands anywhere within the line number field of the lines of interest. The line on which a command is entered is called the current line. The command characters will temporarily replace the digits of the line number of the current line. The Enter key delimits or processes the Line Commands. When more than one line must have a Line Command, the order of entry is unimportant—the function takes place immediately when you enter the last of the required commands.

After   A

Marks a line after which another function will occur. A command on another line specifies the function. The After command is mutually exclusive with the Before command. Also see C, CC, M, and MM.

Before   B

Marks a line before which another function will occur. A command on another line specifies the function. The Before command is mutually exclusive with the After command. Also see C, CC, M, and MM.

Copy   C   or   F7

Inserts a copy of the current line before or after a line marked by a Before or After command. Copy does not delete the current line.

Move   M or F8

Inserts a copy of the current line before or after a line marked by a Before or After command, and then deletes the current line.

Block Copy   CC

Inserts copies of the lines through and including the first and second CC commands before or after a line marked by a Before or After command. Block Copy does not delete the lines in the block marked by the two CC commands.

Block Move   MM

Inserts copies of the lines through and including the first and second MM commands before or after a line marked by a Before or After command. Block Move deletes the lines in the block marked by two MM commands.

Delete a Line   D or F10

Deletes the current line of text.

Block Delete   DD

Deletes all the lines through and including the first and second DD commands.

Exclude   X

The X command excludes the current line from viewing on the screen. Use this to compare lines that precede and follow this line because the Exclude command displays them as adjacent lines. The F2 key restores the excluded line to the screen.

Block Exclude   XX

Excludes from viewing on the screen all the lines through and including those marked by the first and second XX commands. Use this command to examine lines of text that are widely separated but logically related. The F2 key restores the excluded block of lines to the screen.

Repeat   R number

Repeats or copies the current line the number of times specified by the number. The copies of the line are next to the current line. The lack of a number defaults to one.

Function Key Commands

The keyboard for an IBM PC compatible computer has several keys labeled with function names. Some are labeled only with F and a number. Many of these keys provide new commands to SPF/PC and others duplicate some of the functions described above. Since the F function keys can be programmed in SPF/PC, the following assumes you have used the setup described in Appendix F.

Help   F1

Places the editor in help mode. Follow the screen directions for the various help functions.

Reset   F2

After you use some line commands, the display of the text and line numbers is altered. The reset function clears these changes. Reset also cancels any outstanding commands.

Exit   F3

Exits the current editor mode and returns to the previously used menu. If the editor was editing text, F3 also saves the text in your disk file. If already at the top menu, it exits the editor and returns control to MSDOS.

Tabs   F4

Displays the current tab positions on the line on which the cursor resides. Also allows the tabs to be changed by normal editing of the line. Also see F2 key.

Find   F5

Repeats the find operation specified by the last Find command. See the Primary Command called Find.

Columns   F6

Displays a temporary line with column numbers on the line on which the cursor resides. Also see F2 key.

Copy Command   F7

Places a Copy Line Command on the line on which the cursor resides. A C will replace the first line number digit at the beginning of the line.

Move Command   F8

Places a Move Line Command on the line on which the cursor resides. An M will replace the first line number digit at the beginning of the line.

Line Insert Mode   F9

Places the editor in line insert mode. A blank line is displayed following the line on which the cursor resides when entering this mode. You enter text on the blank line. Then press Enter to create another new blank line. Pressing Enter with no new characters on a line cancels the line insert mode. Also see F2 key.

Delete a Line   F10

Deletes the entire line of text on which the cursor resides.

Delete Key   Delete

Deletes the character at the cursor position and moves the text left to fill the gap.

Insert Key   Insert

Switches the character insert mode between on or off. When character insert mode is on, characters typed at the cursor are inserted into the text. When character insert mode is off, characters typed at the cursor overwrite existing characters. The information line at the bottom of the screen will say INSERT MODE if character insert mode is on. It will be blank otherwise.

B.7 A SESSION WITH THE EDITOR PROGRAM

The following leads you through an editing session using the SPF/PC editor. You will first make a text file and then edit that file. It is assumed that the editor program is on your system disk and your text file will be on your data disk.

Getting Started

In the following discussion, you will enter many things to control the editor program. If something goes wrong, you can recover from any catastrophe by pressing the F3 function key until you recognize something or you have left the editor program and returned to the MSDOS operating system.

Let's begin by starting the editor program and creating a file on your data disk. Start the editor program by typing SPF at the MSDOS prompt. When SPF/PC starts, choose 2 from the menu to enter edit mode. Fill in the items on the next menu for your computer system. If your system was set up according to Appendix F, all but one entry will have default values that are correct. However, you must choose a filename for your text file. Let's choose TRIAL as this name. Use the Delete, Backspace, and cursor control keys to correct the entries on the menu. When they are all correct, press the large + key on the numeric keypad to enter edit mode.

If you are beginning, the file TRIAL.ASM will not exist on your data disk. The editor will start with dots down the left side of the edit area. If you see the dots, the editor is in continuous text entry mode, which is not the normal edit mode. If there are no dots, the file you selected already exists and you see the text in the edit area with line numbers on the left side.

If you have the dots, type TEXT and press the F2 function key. The editor will change to the normal edit mode. The dots will be replaced by line numbers and a top and bottom of file message will appear.

The editor is now ready for editing a file. If you want to stop at this point, press the F3 function key three times to return to MSDOS. The editor program will automatically save your file on your disk with the filename TRIAL.

Now let's make some text that can be used for further experimentation. Access your file TRIAL.ASM and move the cursor to any place on the first line that says TEXT. Press the F9 function key to put the editor into the line insert mode. A blank line will be displayed with the cursor at the left. Now type LINE 2 and press Enter. The cursor will jump to line 3. Type LINE 3, press Enter, and continue until you reach line 25. Then press the F2 function key to exit the line insert mode. Don't worry about typing errors; you can edit them soon.

Learning Cursor Control

Let's begin at a common point. Press your Home key and the cursor will jump to the command line if it was not already there. Now, think of the editor as working on a long scroll of paper where you are looking through a small window at the text it contains. The central area of the screen is the window, so it's called the text area of the screen. The text that you can see is called a page of text.

Let's move your cursor into the text area. Press the Enter key and watch the cursor. It will move to the beginning of the line of asterisks. Press it again and it moves to the first line number. Now press cursor right and the cursor will move into the text area. Play with the cursor keys to see the cursor move down, left, right, and up the screen. Notice how it jumps to the command line when you go too far. Also move it around on the command line and over the line numbers. Carefully observe what happens. You should note that it displays a message TOP OF DATA when it reaches the beginning of the test. When it reaches the end, it displays BOTTOM OF DATA.

The edit window can also be moved over the text with the Page Up and Page Down keys. Each press of these moves the window by a half page.

Now move the cursor to the Primary Command line by pressing the Home key. The Home key always moves the cursor back to the command line so new commands can be typed if desired.

Now position the cursor at the beginning of line 5 and we will experiment with the Tab key. Press the Tab key several times to see that it causes the cursor to jump to predetermined positions on the line, or to the next line. Also try Shift Tab because this moves the cursor to the left and is very useful.

Finally, move the cursor to a line number and press the End key. It moves the cursor to the end of the line number it is on. Then move the cursor onto some text and press the End key. Now it moves the cursor to the end of the line.

Editing Existing Text

Typing errors made in the following section can be corrected using the Backspace key and then typing over existing characters.

Editing means to change existing text or add new text. Let's begin by changing the existing text. Place the cursor at the beginning of the text on line 6. Type XYZ over the existing text. You have changed the text by typing over it. Pressing Enter now will move the cursor to the next line. Notice that the Enter key never modifies anything; it just moves the cursor. Experiment now by typing over lines 7 and 8.

Deleting lines

Now let's delete lines 7 and 8. Move the cursor to any place on line 7 and press the F10 function key twice. Each time you press F10 it deletes one full line. Notice that the remaining lines are updated with new line numbers.

Inserting lines

Next you will insert a new line 7. The line insert function always inserts a line immediately after the line that contains the cursor. To insert a new line 1, move the cursor to the line above line 1. Place the cursor anywhere on line 6 and press the F9 key. The editor is now in line insert mode and you can enter as many lines as you want. So type ABC, press the Tab key, type XYZ, and press Enter. Press the Tab key, then type NEWLINE to insert the new text at the second tab position. Now press Enter and observe that the cursor is positioned at the second tab position. This is a feature of SPF/PC that encourages good program documentation by making it convenient to indent multiple lines to the same position. So type NEXTLINE and press Enter. The cursor will again jump to the second tab position. Now just press Enter and the line insert mode will be ended. Shift Tab will move the cursor to the next position left if you don't want the automatic indenting.

Inserting characters

Next let's add some new characters within an existing line. Press the Insert key to turn on the character insert mode. The information line at the bottom of the screen will say insert mode. Now move the cursor to some text and type ABC. You should see the ABC inserted with the other characters moved to the right. In other words, the original characters were not overwritten. Now turn the character insert mode off by pressing the Insert key again.

Deleting characters

Now let's delete the ABC that was just inserted. Move the cursor to the A and press the Delete key. Each time it is pressed, a character is deleted and the remaining text is moved to the left one position. Remember this key because it is often more useful than the Backspace key which leaves spaces where the characters are deleted. Finish deleting the ABC before proceeding.

Editing multiple lines

Now let's observe that the order you enter multiple line commands makes no difference. First, put a Move command on line 20 and press Enter. Second, put an After command on line 10 and press Enter. The line 20 is moved to the line 11 position. Now, first put an After command on line 9 and press Enter. Second, put a block move on line 15 and press Enter. And third, put a block move on line 12 and press Enter. When Enter is pressed the third time, the block is correctly moved.

This practice session has not covered all the commands, so you should try your own examples for all the other commands.

Leaving the Editor

To exit from the editor program and automatically save your edited file, press the F3 function key several times until the MSDOS prompt appears. Since the F3 function returns to the next higher menu, the number of times you will need to press F3 depends on the operation you are currently doing.

If you want to leave the editor without saving your changes, move the cursor to the command line with the Home key and then type the CAN or Cancel command before using the F3 key to exit.

Appendix C

Using the 2500AD Assembler Program

The 2500AD cross-assembler program translates standard Motorola symbolic source programs into binary object code. The assembler described here runs on IBM compatible personal computers. The 2500AD assembler was chosen for this book because it is a good assembler that is easy to use. The listing format and error message handling are very good. 2500AD Software, Inc. in Buena Vista, CO is a well-established company. You should find it easy to buy a copy of their 68c11® assembler. The examples in this book were made with Version 4.02 of this assembler.

The following discussion assumes you are using a personal computer with one hard disk drive and one floppy disk drive. The hard disk holds the system software and the assembler program. A floppy disk will hold all the files for your assembly language program. Other configurations are easy to use with only minor variations from the approach discussed.

The assumed configuration is very convenient and yet provides you with security. For maximum security, remove your floppy disk from the disk drive when you finish using the personal computer and store your disk in a safe place.

Your assembly language source file must be on the floppy disk in the ASCII format required by the assembler. Appendix B discusses the SPF/PC editor and its use in creating or editing a source file. You may use another editor if it provides the correct file format.

Furthermore, you must use the batch files provided in Appendix F to run the personal computer. These files provide complete control of the personal computer system as described in this appendix.

C.1   USING THE 2500AD ASSEMBLER

The XASM batch file will control the assembly process. The assembler program will read a source file from your floppy disk and create an object file on your floppy disk and a listing on the printer. You will create the source file using an editor program.

The editor program must add the extension ASM to your filename so it is ready for use by the assembler. The assembler creates an object file with the same name as the source file, but it adds the extension OBJ to the filename. The assembler also prints a listing that documents both the source and object code and includes a cross-reference symbol table.

The assembler erases an existing object file with the same name, and the download erases an existing S-Record file with the same name. If the assembler detects any errors, it prints them on the screen and on the listing. You will know immediately if you have an error.

Loading and Running the Assembler

To load and run the assembler program, type the following at the MSDOS C> prompt:

XASM LAB2

where XASM means load and run the cross-assembler program with all the options predetermined. LAB2 is the name of your source file that the editor program created, and it must be on your floppy disk in the A disk drive. The disk drives will operate and the listing will be printed.

Exiting the 2500AD Assembler

Whenever you wish to stop the assembler before its normal end, type Control C at the keyboard. Type the Control C character by holding the Control key down while pressing the C key. Your Control key may be labeled Ctrl. Doing this will not harm your source file, but the object file will be garbage.

Assembler Problems

If nothing happens after the floppy disk drive runs, probably the printer is off line or turned off. Simply push the button on the printer to put it on line—on line means controlled by the computer—and the assembly process will continue. If you specify an incorrect filename, a file not found error will be displayed on the screen and you must enter the XASM command correctly. An *Abort, Retry, Ignore, Fail?* message probably means that the printer is not ready for printing for some reason. Some printer problems may require you to fix the problem, and then turn the printer off and on again to reset it. After this, press R for Retry.

Other problems can cause MSDOS to display an *Abort, Retry, Ignore, Fail?* message. It occurs when you have not correctly installed your floppy disk in the floppy disk drive and closed the floppy drive door. If this is the problem, fix it and then press R for Retry. If all else fails, press A for abort and start over!

C.2   THE 2500AD ASSEMBLER SOURCE FORMAT

Chapter 3 contains a detailed discussion of the source format. The 2500AD assembler requires statements in the format discussed there. It has other characteristics that you must know to use it correctly. In particular, two more directives are necessary. This section points out other differences and omissions. See Chapter 3 for the basic characteristics of numbers, user symbols, expressions, and the source statement format.

Numbers

Numbers are specified exactly as discussed in Chapter 3. Remember that the assembler always forms 16-bit numbers internally. The leading bits are filled with either leading 0s or leading 1s as needed. Directives are then used to specify the size of the number required in the program.

User Symbols

User symbols can be up to 31_{10} characters long. Special characters such as punctuation marks and underscores can be used within symbols. It is unlikely that you will want to use symbols with 31_{10} characters very often—these are very long symbols.

Expressions

Expressions are written as discussed in Chapter 3. Use parentheses within expressions to make the precedence of operations clear.

Source Statement Format

Chapter 3 omitted some of the addressing modes. Table C-1 lists the format of source statements for all the addressing modes. The operand formats do not allow spaces between the operands. The indexed modes allow either the X or Y register. The operand type column lists the purpose of the operand. The operand is usually designated by a symbol. Use numeric values only for data numbers, offsets, and masks. Addresses are always represented by symbolic address labels.

Table C-2 contains examples for each of the addressing mode formats. Of course, not all addressing modes are available for every instruction, so the table contains representative instructions.

TABLE C-1 OPERAND FORMATS

Addressing Mode	Operand Format	Operand Type
Inherent		None
Immediate	#operand	data number
Extended	operand	address
Direct	operand	address
Indexed	operand,X	offset
Program relative	operand	address
Direct, Inherent	operand,operand	address—mask byte
Indexed, Immediate	operand,X,operand	offset—mask byte
Direct, Immediate, Relative	operand,operand,operand	address—mask—address
Indexed, Immediate, Relative	operand,X,operand,operand	offset—mask—address

C.3 THE 2500AD ASSEMBLER DIRECTIVES

The 2500AD assembler has many features that the following does not discuss. For example, it can be used as either an absolute assembler or as a relocatable assembler. This book only discusses the absolute assembler. Everything in Chapter 3 applies correctly to the 2500AD assembler when you use absolute mode.

Two directives are necessary to tell the assembler to operate in absolute mode. First, put the ABSOLUTE directive before any lines that generate data values. Second, put the RELATIVE directive before the lines of the program section that generate instructions. The example listings in Chapter 3 were made this way, and then the ABSOLUTE and RELATIVE directives were changed to comment lines on the listing before it was printed.

Failure to use these two directives causes two kinds of errors. First, the branch instructions will have incorrect relative offsets. Second, no instructions will have direct addressing

TABLE C-2 INSTRUCTION FORMAT EXAMPLES

Addressing Mode	Example 1	Example 2
Inherent	ABA	INX
Immediate	LDAA #$4A	LDX #INITPT
Extended	STAA TEMP	STAB PRESS
Direct	LDAB COUNT	INC COUNT
Indexed	LDAA 2,X	LDX SPACE,X
Program relative	BRA LOOP	BVS ERROR
Direct, Immediate	BSET OUTS,$40	BCLR FLAGS,ERROR1
Indexed, Immediate	BCLR OUTS,X,BIT1	BSET PORTB,X,BIT2
Direct, Immediate, Relative	BRSET FLAGS,$02,ERROR	BRCLR IMAGE,TEMP,HOT
Indexed, Immediate, Relative	BRCLR PORTC,Y,BIT7,UP	BRSET 0,X,$F0,HEXF

because the assembler will always choose extended addressing. The first error will prevent the program from running correctly. The second will only make the program longer.

Number formation

Chapter 3 covers all the basic Motorola number formation directives except the following one.

FCC directive.   Form constant character string. The FCC directive creates ASCII character codes and puts them into consecutive memory registers. The format of the statement is

        [label]   FCC   delimiterstringdelimiter

where two delimiter characters surround the string of alphanumeric characters. Any of the printable ASCII characters can be contained in the string. The first nonblank character after the FCC directive is the delimiter. The delimiter can be any printable ASCII character, but a quotation mark is the most common.

For example, the statement

        WORDS   FCC   "THE MACHINE IS ON FIRE!"

creates a table of 23_{10} bytes beginning at the address WORDS. The quotation marks are not part of the string.

Assembler control

Chapter 3 covers the basic Motorola control directives. NAM, PAGE, and $ are also standard Motorola directives. The ABSOLUTE, RELATIVE, and PW directives are unique to the 2500AD assembler.

ABSOLUTE directive.   Set the assembler mode to absolute. The ABSOLUTE directive should occupy a separate line for clarity. Always use the ABSOLUTE directive before the definition of labels that represent memory locations in the direct addressing range. For simplicity, use it before the definition of the data section of all your programs. Note that the RELATIVE directive must precede the program section when the ABSOLUTE directive is used. Programs without an ABSOLUTE directive will never have direct addressed instruction codes.

NAM directive.   NAM assigns the program a name that the assembler prints at the top of each page of the listing. The format of the statement is

        NAM   string

where the character string is the name to be printed on the listing. For example,

        NAM   COPY A TABLE

prints COPY A TABLE on each page of the listing. Usually make this directive the first statement of an assembly language source program. Its use is optional and more than one NAM directive can be in a program.

PAGE directive.   Advance the printer paper to the top of the next page. The assembler does not print the directive PAGE on the assembler listing.

PW directive.   The PW or page width directive sets the number of columns used in printing the listing. The format of this statement is

                    PW   number

where the number is the number of columns available for printing the listing. For example, 80 columns is a good choice if the size of the printer paper is 8 1/2 by 11 inches.

PL directive.   The PL or page length directive sets the number of lines printed on each page of the listing. The format of this statement is

                    PL   number

where the number is the number of lines available for printing on each page. The default page length is 61 lines.

RELATIVE directive.   Set the assembler mode to relative. The RELATIVE directive should occupy a separate line for clarity. In relative mode, the 2500AD assembler can correctly generate relative addresses in the branch instructions. In absolute mode, the assembler makes errors. It is easiest to put a RELATIVE directive before the beginning of the program section of all programs.

∗ and $ directives.   The dollar sign directive is different from the dollar sign that denotes hexadecimal numbers. When a dollar sign is used alone as a single character, it takes on the value of the address of the current location. When an asterisk is used outside column one as a directive, it is identical to the dollar sign directive. Don't be confused by this alternative function of the asterisk character. Consider the following example:

        START   EQU   ∗
                        LDAA   DATA

where the label START is defined as the address of the LDAA instruction. These two statements have the same effect as the statement

        START   LDAA   VALUE

but require two statements instead of one. With two statements, you can change the instruction without the need to move the label. This technique is best used at the beginning of a program module where the extra line makes the listing easier to read.

C.4   AN EXAMPLE FROM THE 2500AD ASSEMBLER

A program was written in Chapter 2 to copy a table in memory. Figure 2-48 is the machine language that was coded by hand—you looked at the instruction set table to find the codes. Then in Chapter 3, the same program was written in assembly language and the listing shown in Figure 3-8. That is an edited assembler listing. Items were removed that are unique to the 2500AD assembler. Figure C-1 is the same listing from the 2500AD assembler with nothing removed.

Here are some comments on this complete listing:

- The listing begins with a title section that does not have line numbers at the left. The date, time, and page number are at the top of the page. The assembler gets the date and time from the MSDOS operating system in the personal computer. Next is the name and version code for the assembler. And finally the symbolic source file and binary object filenames are identified. The assembler calls these the input file and the output file respectively with the extensions ASM and OBJ. If you tell the assembler to print to a disk file, it uses the source filename and the extension LST as the name of the listing file.

- Lines 1 through 41 document both the source code and the object code. The only differences from Figure 3-8 are on lines 11 and 19. Figure C-1 shows the directives as they were used.

- The assembler printed the text that follows line 41 on a second page that has the date, time, and page number at the top. The second page of the listing was included in this single figure.

- The last section of the listing is the symbol table. Three lines were removed from Figure 3-8 because they were of no concern. They are the three lines in Figure C-1 that have symbols identified by the prefix *Pre* in the defined column. The Pre means that these symbols are predefined by the assembler. These three symbols always exist in the 2500AD assembler. You will not use them when using the assembler in absolute mode.

- The symbol table also indicates which symbols were defined by EQU directives. The symbol SPACE was defined by an EQU, so an equal sign is printed to the left of its value.

Be careful to avoid using the symbols CODE, DATA, and PAGE0 in your programs because you will obtain multiple definition errors. These errors can be confusing because the first definition will not appear in your program.

C.5   ASSEMBLER ERROR MESSAGES

The listing in Figure C-2 illustrates most of the errors detected by the 2500AD assembler. The listing is the result of assembling a source file that contains errors. This listing fully documents the response of the assembler. That is, it shows both the error messages and the object code generated by the assembler.

If you are trying to find information on a particular error message, scan Figure C-2 for that message. Then read the comments for the lines containing that error.

The 2500AD assembler generates error messages as English statements that are very descriptive. The assembler prints a message on the line following the line in which an error occurred. Sometimes an error message at one line may be due to an error on another line. You must interpret the error messages carefully!

```
                 2500 A.D. 68c11 Macro Assembler  -  Version 4.02a
                 ------------------------------------------------
                        Input  Filename : copytab.asm
                        Output Filename : copytab.obj

 1                                   ***********************************************************
 2                                   ** COPY TABLE PROGRAM FROM CHAPTER 2
 3                                   * NOTE: THIS IS NOT A GOOD PROGRAM
 4                                   *
 5                                   ***********************************************************
 6                                   *
 7                                   ***********************************************************
 8                                   ** SYMBOL DEFINITIONS
 9                                   ***********************************************************
10           0020                    SPACE   EQU   $20       SPACING BETWEEN TABLES
11  0000                                     ABSOLUTE
12                                   ***********************************************************
13                                   ** DATA SECTION
14                                   ***********************************************************
15  0030                                     ORG $30
16  0030     C110                    TABADR  FDB   $C110     ADDRESS OF FIRST TABLE
17  0032     04                      INITCT  FCB   4         INITIAL COUNTER VALUE
18  0033                             WRKCNT  RMB   1         WORKING COUNTER
19  0034                                     RELATIVE
20                                   ***********************************************************
21                                   ** PROGRAM SECTION
22                                   ***********************************************************
23  C010                                     ORG $C010
24                                   * INITIALIZE POINTER TO FIRST TABLE
25  C010     DE 30                   START   LDX   TABADR
26                                   * INITIALIZE WORKING COUNTER
27  C012     96 32                           LDAA  INITCT    GET INITIAL VALUE
28  C014     97 33                           STAA  WRKCNT    STORE INTO WORKING COUNTER
29                                   * WORKING COUNTER EQUALS ZERO?
30  C016     27 0A                   AGAIN   BEQ   LAST      BRANCH ON YES
31                                   * COPY ONE ENTRY
32  C018     A6 00                           LDAA  0,X       GET ENTRY FROM FIRST TABLE
33  C01A     A7 20                           STAA  SPACE,X   PUT ENTRY INTO SECOND TABLE
34                                   * ADVANCE POINTER TO NEXT ENTRY
35  C01C     08                              INX
36                                   * COUNT DOWN THE WORKING COUNTER
37  C01D     7A 00 33                        DEC   WRKCNT
38  C020     20 F4                           BRA   AGAIN     GO AROUND AGAIN
39                                   * STOP THE PROGRAM
40  C022     3F                      LAST    SWI             "STOP" FOR MOTOROLA TRAINER
41  C023                                     END
```

Thu Jan 4 1990 13:58   Page   2
Defined   Symbol Name   Value   References

Defined	Symbol Name	Value	References
30	AGAIN	C016	38
Pre	CODE	0030	15 23
Pre	DATA	0000	
17	INITCT	0032	27
40	LAST	C022	30
Pre	PAGE0	0000	
10	SPACE	= 0020	33
25	START	C010	
16	TABADR	0030	25
18	WRKCNT	0033	28 37

```
        Lines Assembled :  41          Assembly Errors :  0
```

Figure C-1   A complete listing from the 2500AD assembler.

The following comments describe the error and the response of the assembler. The comments are keyed to the line number of the listing.

- *Lines 8 and 9.*   Line 9 defines the same symbol that was defined on line 8. The assembler displays the error message MULTIPLE DEFINED SYMBOL when it encounters the second definition. The symbol occurs twice in the symbol table but the assembler uses the first definition in later references to the symbol.

- *Line 15.*   This line defined the symbol DATA a second time because the 2500AD assembler has a predefined symbol DATA. The symbol table lists both definitions. The assembler uses the first definition in later references.

- *Line 19.*   The number was omitted from the FCB statement. The assembler defaulted to a value of zero and did not print an error message.

- *Line 20.*   The number was omitted from the RMB statement, which the assembler detected as a syntax error. Apparently this error caused the assembler to change the location counter. You can see the following addresses are out of sequence.

- *Line 21.*   The number was omitted from the FDB statement. The assembler defaulted to a value of zero and did not print an error message.

- *Line 22.*   The invalid user symbol A was used as a label. The assembler puts the symbol A into the symbol table, but does not use it in subsequent statements where its usage is incorrect. The assembler did not print an error message.

- *Line 23.*   Here the assembler uses the invalid user symbol A to form a double-byte number correctly. However, an incorrect error message says the number is too large. Also, the invalid user symbol Y is used as a label and Y is entered in the symbol table. There is no error message for this problem.

- *Lines 27 through 30.*   In each of these cases, the statement requires a number that fits in one byte when the value of the symbol requires two bytes. The error messages TOO LARGE accurately describe the problem. In each case, the assembler used the least-significant byte of the number specified and generated code accordingly.

- *Line 31.*   The STA instruction does not have immediate addressing as the message states. The assembler generated no code here.

- *Line 32.*   The instruction mnemonic was incorrectly spelled with a space before the accumulator designator. However, the assembler generated the correct code as if there was no error.

- *Line 33.*   The instruction mnemonic was incorrectly spelled and the assembler did not generate any code.

- *Line 34.*   The operand symbol was omitted. However, the assembler used the word MISSING as the operand. Fortunately MISSING was not a valid symbol name, so the assembler generated an UNDEFINED SYMBOL error message. You can see that

```
 1                              ********************************************************
 2                              * SOURCE TO GENERATE ASSEMBLER ERROR MESSAGES
 3                              *
 4                              ********************************************************
 5                                          PW     90       SET PAGE WIDTH
 6                              *
 7     0000                                 ABSOLUTE
 8           1122               LGCON   EQU     $1122
 9           9876               LGCON   EQU     $9876       REDEFINITION ERROR
       ***** MULTIPLE DEFINED SYMBOL *****
10          00F0               MASK    EQU     $F0
11                              *
12     0050                                 ORG   $50
13     0050                     HERE    RMB     2
14     0052  4567               THERE   FDB     $4567
15     0054                     DATA    RMB     1           REDEFINITION ERROR
       ***** MULTIPLE DEFINED SYMBOL *****
16                              *
17     C123                                 ORG   $C123
18     C123  0A                 NUMBER  FCB     10
19     C124  00                         FCB
20     C125                             RMB
       ***** SYNTAX ERROR *****
21     0E77  0000                       FDB
22     0E79                     A       RMB     1           INCORRECT SYMBOL
23     0E7A  0E79               Y       FDB     A           INCORRECT SYMBOL
       ***** # TOO LARGE *****
24                              *
25     0E7C                             RELATIVE
26     C000                             ORG   $C000
27     C000  23                         FCB     NUMBER    SIZE ERROR
       ***** # TOO LARGE *****
28     C001  86 22                      LDAA    #LGCON    SIZE ERROR
       ***** # TOO LARGE *****
29     C003  A6 22                      LDAA    LGCON,X   SIZE ERROR
       ***** # TOO LARGE *****
30     C005  A6 FE                      LDAA    -2,X      SIZE ERROR
       ***** # TOO LARGE *****
31     C007                             STAA    #THERE    ILLEGAL ADDRESSING MODE
       ***** ILLEGAL ADDRESSING MODE *****
32     C007  B9 C1 23                   ADC A NUMBER      ILLEGAL MNEMONIC
       ***** SYNTAX ERROR *****
33     C00A                             LADA    NUMBER    ILLEGAL MNEMONIC
       ***** ILLEGAL MNEMONIC *****
34     C00A  B6 00 00                   LDAA              MISSING OPERAND
       ***** UNDEFINED SYMBOL *****
35     C00D  B6 44 4C                   LDAA
       ***** SYNTAX ERROR *****
36     C010  B6 00 00                   LDAA    A         INCORRECT OPERAND
       ***** SYNTAX ERROR *****
37     C013  86 4C                      LDAA    #         MISSING OPERAND
       ***** SYNTAX ERROR *****
38     C015  86 4C                      LDAA    #
       ***** SYNTAX ERROR *****
39     C017  7C 00 00                   INC     0,A       INCORRECT REGISTER
       ***** EXTRA CHARACTERS AT END OF OPERAND *****
40     C01A  96 00                      LDAA    0,        MISSING X OR Y
       ***** EXTRA CHARACTERS AT END OF OPERAND *****
41     C01C  96 00                      LDAA    0, X      MISSING X OR Y
       ***** EXTRA CHARACTERS AT END OF OPERAND *****
42     C01E  A6 00                      LDAA    ,X        MISSING NUMBER
43     C020  A6 00                      LDAA    X         CORRECT STATEMENT
44     C022  A6 00                      LDAA    A,X       INCORRECT OPERAND
```

Figure C-2   Assembler error messages.

```
45    C024   A6 00                      LDAA   X,X
      ***** UNDEFINED SYMBOL *****
46    C026                              MISSING ASTERISK TO MAKE LINE A COMMENT
      ***** ILLEGAL MNEMONIC *****
47    C026   B7 00 00                   STAA   HOLE      UNDEFINED SYMBOL
      ***** UNDEFINED SYMBOL *****
48    C029   20 FE                      BRA    $         CORRECT STATEMENT
49    C02B   86 2B                      LDAA   #$        MISSING NUMBER
      ***** # TOO LARGE *****
50    C02D   7C 00 00                   INC    DATA      INCORRECT SYMBOL
51    C030   F6 00 50                   LDAB   FORWARD   NOT DIRECT ADDRESSED
52    C033                              LDAD   THERE
      ***** ILLEGAL MNEMONIC *****
53    C033   20 6A                      BRA    AHEAD     OUT OF RANGE
      ***** RELATIVE JUMP TOO LARGE *****
54    C035   20 03                      BRA    ι3        USELESS
55    C037   20 50                      BRA    HERE      HERE IS ABSOLUTE
56    C039   1B             THERE       ABA              REDEFINITION ERROR
      ***** MULTIPLE DEFINED SYMBOL *****
57    C03A   26 52                      BNE    THERE     THERE IS ABSOLUTE
58                              *
59    D678                              ORG    $D678
60    D678   1D 33 F0                   BCLR   $33,X,MASK           CORRECT STATEMENT
61    D67B   1D 33 F0                   BCLR   $33,X MASK           MAKES CORRECT CODE
      ***** SYNTAX ERROR *****
62    D67E   1D 33 00                   BCLR   $33,X               MISSING OPERAND
      ***** SYNTAX ERROR *****
63    D681   15 50 F0                   BCLR   HERE,MASK           CORRECT STATEMENT
64    D684   15 50 F0                   BCLR   HERE MASK           MAKES CORRECT CODE
      ***** SYNTAX ERROR *****
65    D687   1E 33 F0 14                BRSET $33,X,MASK,AHEAD     CORRECT STATEMENT
66    D68B   1E 33 F0 10                BRSET $33,X MASK AHEAD     MAKES CORRECT CODE
      ***** SYNTAX ERROR *****
67    D68F   1E 33 F0 00                BRSET $33,X,MASK           MISSING OPERAND
      ***** SYNTAX ERROR *****
68    D693   12 33 7A F0                BRSET $33 X MASK           SYNTAX ERROR
      ***** SYNTAX ERROR *****
69    D697   12 50 F0 04                BRSET HERE,MASK,AHEAD      CORRECT STATEMENT
70    D69B   12 50 F0 00                BRSET HERE MASK AHEAD      MAKES CORRECT CODE
      ***** SYNTAX ERROR *****
71    D69F   86 44          AHEAD       LDAA   #$44
72                              *
73    D6A1                              ABSOLUTE
74    0050                              ORG    $50
75    0050   66             FORWARD FCB $66
76    0051                              END
```

Defined	Symbol Name	Value	References			
22	A	0E79	23			
71	AHEAD	D69F	53	65	66	69
			70			
Pre	CODE	0050	12	17	26	59
			74			
15	DATA	0054				
Pre	DATA	0000	50			
75	FORWARD	0050	51			
13	HERE	0050	55	63	64	69
			70			
9	LGCON	= 9876				
8	LGCON	= 1122	28	29		
10	MASK	= 00F0	60	61	63	64
			65	66	67	68

Figure C-2   Continued.

```
                                                            69        70
     18      NUMBER                        C123            27        32
     Pre     PAGE0                         0000
     56      THERE                         C039
     14      THERE                         0052            31        57
     23      y                             0E7A            45        68

            Lines Assembled :   76          Assembly Errors :   33
```

Figure C-2   Continued.

MISSING is not in the symbol table. The assembler generated code using a value of zero for the erroneous symbol.

- *Line 35.*   The operand symbol is missing and there are no other characters on the line. The assembler printed an appropriate error message, but also generated garbage code.

- *Line 36.*   This statement uses the invalid user symbol A in the operand. The assembler generates an appropriate error message. The assembler apparently did not use the value of A from the symbol table!

- *Lines 37 and 38.*   The operand is missing. The assembler printed an appropriate error message. However, it also generated strange code.

- *Lines 39 through 41.*   Apparently indexed addressing was intended in each of these cases. However, the assembler interpreted the operand as address 0000 with some extra characters at the end. Hence the assembler generated code with extended or direct addressing.

- *Line 42.*   The offset number was omitted. The assembler defaulted to the value zero and did not print an error message.

- *Line 43.*   The assembler accepts this as a correct statement for an indexed instruction with a default offset of zero.

- *Line 44.*   The offset is an invalid user symbol. The assembler ignored it and defaulted to a value of zero without printing an error message.

- *Line 45.*   The predefined symbol X was used as an offset. The assembler looked for user symbols and did not fine X and printed an UNDEFINED SYMBOL message. The assembler used a default value of zero for the symbol in generating the code.

- *Line 46.*   This was intended as a comment but the asterisk in column one was omitted. The assembler used the word MISSING as an instruction mnemonic and printed an ILLEGAL MNEMONIC message.

- *Line 47.*   The symbol HOLE was not defined. The assembler generated code using a default value of zero for the symbol.

- *Line 48.*   The assembler interprets the symbol $ as the current address in the location counter, so this is a correct statement.

- *Line 49.*   The assembler interprets the symbol $ as the current address in the location counter, so the immediate value is TOO LARGE. The assembler generated code using the least-significant byte of the immediate value.

- *Line 50.*   The symbol DATA is an invalid user symbol because the assembler predefined this symbol. The assembler generated code using the predefined value of DATA and did not print an error message.

- *Line 51.*   The problem here is named a *forward reference*. The value of the symbol FORWARD is 0050, but the assembler generated an extended addressed instruction when a direct addressed instruction is expected. This happened because a line forward of this reference defines the symbol referenced. Here is the problem. The assembler passes over the source twice to generate code. On the first pass, it makes the symbol table. Note the length of an instruction code affects the value of labels forward from that instruction. If, as on line 51, an instruction operand symbol has not been defined when the assembler encounters the instruction, the assembler cannot decide whether direct or extended addressing is appropriate. The choice determines whether the instruction will occupy two or three bytes. The assembler must therefore choose extended addressing to be safe. As pass one continues, the symbol is defined. On the second pass, the assembler generates the code using the symbols found in the first pass. When line 51 is encountered again, the operand suggests direct addressing. But now it is too late to generate a direct addressed instruction because a shorter instruction would make the symbol table incorrect. This problem is not an error.

- *Line 52.*   The instruction mnemonic is incorrect. It probably should have been LDD. Here the assembler identifies the problem, but does not generate any code.

- *Line 53.*   The relative addresses in branch instructions are one byte long, which limits the distance that an instruction can branch. Here the relative address was not large enough to reach the location of the referenced address. The code generated is erroneous.

- *Line 54.*   This statement generates correct code, but the code is generally useless. The operand number was used as the offset in the instruction. Rarely you would know what relative offset number to put in an instruction.

- *Line 55.*   This statement generates correct code, but is useless. The operand symbol was defined as an absolute symbol. Therefore, the assembler used the value of the symbol as the relative offset in the instruction. The assembler did not calculate the correct relative offset to the referenced location. This is not an error to the assembler.

- *Line 56.*   The symbol THERE has already been defined on line 14. The assembler lists both occurrences of THERE in the symbol table.

- *Line 57.*   The first definition of the symbol THERE made it absolute. Since THERE is absolute, the assembler used its value as the relative offset in the branch instruction. This is not an error, but the code is useless. Look at the code the assembler generated to see that this instruction will not branch to location THERE on the line above.

- *Lines 60 and 61.* The assembler interprets both lines correctly, but line 61 causes an error message because the comma is missing.

- *Line 62.* The operand to define the mask is missing. The assembler generated code using zero for the missing operand.

- *Lines 63 through 66.* The assembler interprets these lines correctly, but lines 64 and 66 cause error messages because the commas are missing.

- *Line 67.* The assembler substituted zero for the missing operand in generating the instruction code.

- *Line 68.* The missing comma caused the assembler to use direct addressing and to generate erroneous code.

- *Line 70.* The missing comma caused the assembler to use direct addressing, which was accidentally correct, so the code generated is correct. However, the assembler generated a syntax error because the comma was missing.

The example and the comments describe most of the errors you are likely to encounter with the 2500AD assembler. For additional information, refer to your manual, which is supplied with the assembler.

C.6   S-RECORDS

The personal computer system must transmit binary numbers to the Motorola trainer in S-Record format. The purpose of the transmission is to load numbers into the memory of the trainer. The 2500AD linker program can convert a 2500AD assembler object file into an S-Record format load module. The download batch file discussed in Appendix D section D.5 includes running the linker as part of the download sequence.

S-Record Format

The S-Record format was developed for transmitting binary numbers between computers in character format. Not all computer systems can easily transmit 8-bit numbers to other systems. However, most computer systems can control printers and therefore can transmit S-Records.

S-Records use the characters 0 to 9 and A to F to represent hexadecimal digits. The hexadecimal digits are easily converted to binary numbers. Two characters together represent one 8-bit binary number. There is a drawback to this scheme. Two numbers representing the characters must be sent to convey a single 8-bit number. Thus, the format is convenient but not very efficient. For short programs, this is no problem at all.

There is an additional benefit of the character format. The binary information is easily printed in hexadecimal format that people can easily read. An editor program is convenient for viewing S-Records. The editor also can change the S-Records. However, this editing is not nearly as useful as changing the assembly language source program and running the assembler again.

S-Record Definition

There are ten kinds of S-Records. However, the Motorola 68HC11 trainer and the 2500AD linker program only use types S1 and S9. Each string of information, or record, begins with the character S followed by a 1 or a 9. An S1 means the information that follows consists of numbers to be placed in the memory of the 68HC11 trainer. An S9 means that all the information has been sent; that is, this is the end.

The 2500AD linker program creates multiple S-Records where each record is a maximum of 42_{10} characters long. These S-Records will fit on one line of any printer.

One complete S-Record contains the following items in the order given:

- Two characters, either S1 or S9, to identify the record type.

- Two characters for the hexadecimal number of bytes yet to come in this record.

- Four characters to specify the beginning load address in the trainer.

- A variable number of pairs of characters to specify the data bytes.

- Two characters as a checksum byte.

The checksum is an 8-bit number formed by first adding the individual bytes of the byte count, the address, and the data. Second, complement the result. Any higher-order bits are discarded. The actual numbers are added, not the character codes. Finally, the checksum is converted into two characters.

The trainer uses the checksum byte to detect if any transmission errors occurred. As the trainer receives an S-Record, it forms a checksum on the received data and compares it to the checksum that was received. A discrepancy indicates an error in transmission.

S-Record Example

Here is an example of three S-Records:

                    S1070012447E31A54E
                    S109C020FFDD1620E63FDF
                    S9030000FC

In the first S1 record, the S1 is followed by 07 because seven bytes follow in this record. Next is the load address 0012 that tells the loader program where to start loading the bytes into memory. Next there are four data bytes that the loader program loads into memory; namely the 44, 7E, 31, and A5. Figure C-3 illustrates the memory after these bytes are loaded. Finally, the record ends with the checksum 4E. The checksum is formed by first adding the bytes 07, 00, 12, 44, 7E, 31, and A5; second, this sum is complemented; and third, the least-significant byte of this result is converted to the characters 4E.

In the second record, the S1 is followed by 09 to indicate that nine bytes follow. Next is the load address C020 followed by the data bytes FF, DD, 16, 20, E6, and 3F. And finally, the checksum is DF.

The last record is always an S9 record, the termination record, which always has three bytes. The S9 is followed by the 03 to indicate that three bytes follow. An address field is still used, but the address always is 0000 so the checksum FC is the complement of 03.

Figure C-3 illustrates all the numbers loaded into memory as a result of these three S-Records.

C.7 ASSEMBLER FILES

The 2500AD assembler reads the source file and then creates several files. The XASM batch file controls the use and creation of these files. Appendix F discusses this file.

The source file made by the editor program is an ASCII file named with a filename with the extension ASM. The XASM batch file runs the assembler. The assembler reads the source file and makes an object file with the same filename and the OBJ extension.

The XASM batch file may also run the 2500AD linker program. In this book, the linker only converts the OBJ file to a load file with the same filename and extension S19. The S19 file is compatible with the Motorola trainer.

If a printer is available, the XASM file may print the listing. If a printer is not available, the XASM file can send the listing to a disk file with the extension LST. Another program, such as the SPF/PC editor, can be used to view the listing on the monitor screen.

	•
0012	44
0013	7E
0014	31
0015	A5
	•
	•
	•
C020	FF
C021	DD
C022	16
C023	20
C024	E6
C025	3F
	•
	•

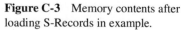

Figure C-3   Memory contents after loading S-Records in example.

Appendix D

The Motorola Microcomputer Trainer

The Motorola trainer, part number M68HC11EVB, is a single-board computer that requires a DC power supply and a cathode ray tube (CRT) terminal. The EVB in the name is an abbreviation for evaluation board. The board contains sufficient read/write RAM memory to hold practical programs. It has a monitor program in permanent ROM memory so you can control the computer easily. This computer board is a very practical tool for experimenting with and learning the 68HC11 computer. It is called a *trainer* because most people will design custom hardware for their applications rather than incorporating this board into the design.

D.1 INTRODUCTION TO THE MOTOROLA TRAINER

Motorola designed the M68HC11EVB microcomputer trainer for making a prototype of a device that will contain a 68HC11 single-chip microcomputer. Learning to use a microcomputer and developing a prototype of a device can both be done with this board.

Many other trainers are available for Motorola products. All trainers have similar features, but this appendix concentrates on the Motorola 68HC11 trainer. References are made to this trainer throughout this book. Boxes enclose the references to separate them from the text. Those people using other trainers can easily ignore the references to the Motorola trainer.

The Trainer Components

A working trainer consists of the microcomputer printed circuit board, a DC power supply, and a CRT terminal—screen display and keyboard. An IBM PC compatible computer can act like a CRT terminal.

The computer circuit board contains the 68HC11 microcomputer, both read/write and read only memory, and input/output hardware. The read only memory is permanent memory that contains a monitor program named BUFFALO. The monitor program makes the hardware act as a microcomputer trainer. The read/write memory allows the user to put a program into memory.

Always remember that you are interacting with a program when you are operating the trainer. The microcomputer responds to the keyboard and controls the screen only if the monitor program is running. The monitor program prompts the human operator by placing a right arrow character at the left side of the screen. The prompt means that the monitor program is ready to do something.

Starting the Computer in the Trainer

The microcomputer must be running in an orderly fashion to make the trainer operational. Turning the power on causes an automatic hardware reset that starts the microcomputer. After the power is on, pushing the reset button on the trainer board forces a hardware reset that acts as if the power was just turned on. Use the button only to simulate turning the power on; reset can cause problems if used in other situations.

Pushing and releasing the reset button also starts the monitor program, which prints a message on the screen. Following reset, pressing the Enter or Return key on the keyboard causes a prompt to be printed on the screen. You can feel confident that almost everything in the trainer is working properly if the prompt appears.

Crashing the Monitor Program

It is easy to crash the monitor program. A *crash* means that the program stops operating correctly because something is wrong. A crash causes no harm to the trainer—pressing the reset button causes it to recover.

A bug in your program is the likely cause of a crash. Your program probably changes something in memory. Your program may destroy itself and the monitor program; therefore, you must check your program carefully before proceeding after a crash.

Don't blame the monitor program for changing your program! After you press the reset button, your program may be gone due most likely to errors in your program. Pressing the reset button does not destroy your program.

D.2   MONITOR PROGRAM CAPABILITIES

The microcomputer trainer will help you write and debug programs. Most microcomputer trainers have similar features regardless of the manufacturer. The monitor program determines most of the characteristics of the trainer. The following lists the principal characteristics of most trainers.

Single-Step

A feature called single-step or trace executes your program one instruction at a time. After the trainer executes your instruction, the monitor program regains control. You can then single step again, run the program at full speed, or do other things.

Single-step is an excellent tool for learning how instructions work, since it shows the effects of the instruction immediately. Seeing the details of how a program works also helps you debug programs easily.

Unfortunately, executing a large group of instructions with single-step requires too many keystrokes even if you have already checked the instructions. Breakpoints solve this problem.

Breakpoint

A breakpoint takes control away from your program and gives it to the monitor program. Your program runs normally up to the breakpoint and then breaks out to the monitor. You can then use all the monitor commands to check and debug your program. You will frequently want to single step after a breakpoint is encountered. There is a command to tell the monitor program to return control to your program continuing it from the current point until the next breakpoint.

When using breakpoints, you run segments of your program individually to prove that each segment works correctly. Each segment may contain only a few instructions or hundreds of instructions. Using breakpoints will save you from much tedious work.

Downloading

Downloading is the transmission of binary numbers from a host computer to the memory of the trainer. The word *down* implies that the host computer, probably a personal computer system, is a bigger computer than the trainer. The most common communications medium is a cable connected from the personal computer to the trainer. Programs run on the host computer will generate the binary program and data information for the trainer.

Help Screen

A help screen is one CRT screen of information that describes the program that is in use. Help screens usually document the commands that the program recognizes. The operator of the trainer must request the help information through a command. A help screen is a kind of computer manual.

D.3   WRITING PROGRAMS FOR THE MOTOROLA TRAINER

You must follow a few rules when writing programs to run in the Motorola M68HC11EVB trainer. Your program must correctly use the trainer hardware, and it must avoid memory used by the monitor program. The monitor program resides at memory addresses E000 through FFFF inclusively. It also uses read/write memory addresses 0036 through 00FF to hold data that it needs in responding to your commands.

Stopping Your Program

Your program must stop in a way compatible with the monitor program. A *STOP* instruction, op code 3F, at the end of your program will stop your program most easily. The *STOP* instruction is actually an SWI instruction, but is called *STOP* in italics to emphasize its function in the trainer. The *STOP* instruction transfers control from your program to the monitor program, which then displays the registers. This transfer effectively stops your program but does not stop the computer.

Using Available Memory

Your program may only use the read/write memory locations with addresses 0000 through 0035 and C000 through DFFF. If your trainer has the optional extra memory installed, you also may use locations 6000 through 7FFF.

Don't use memory locations where there isn't any memory installed. If you use non-existent memory for data, your program may run but the results will be meaningless. Your program will read and use unknown data values from the nonexistent memory locations.

Do not ignore the memory restrictions and assume that you can use memory locations 0036 *through* 00FF; *these locations do exist but the monitor program uses them.*

Changing the contents of memory locations 0036 through 00FF probably will crash the monitor program, or, worse yet, cause it to work incorrectly without crashing.

D.4   OPERATING THE MICROCOMPUTER TRAINER

The keyboard for the trainer controls all the trainer functions other than start up. The trainer responds with messages on the CRT screen.

Communicating With the Monitor Program

The Motorola trainer requires either a CRT terminal or an IBM PC compatible computer used as a CRT terminal. Choose the section below that fits your equipment.

Using a CRT terminal

A CRT terminal consists of a keyboard and CRT display device that are independent of each other. The keyboard generates character codes in response to key presses; the codes can be transmitted to a computer. The CRT display receives character codes from a computer and forms character patterns on the screen. Some terminals also can send characters directly from the keyboard to the display.

Incidentally, a CRT terminal display is different from a personal computer monitor. The monitor is essentially just a TV screen that responds to the signals sent to it. The CRT terminal contains the electronics to form the characters on the screen.

Terminal characteristics. Many CRT terminals have special keys beyond those on a common QWERTY keyboard. Some of these may be special function or F keys. You only need the normal keys so ignore the special keys.

Most CRT terminals have many programmable options. Some designs use a menu screen to set the options. Others use switches located on the back panel. Your terminal may require some changes if the screen prints strange characters or the screen does not respond correctly.

Screen blanking. Some CRT terminals automatically blank or turn off the screen if it is idle for a few minutes. Screen blanking improves the lifetime of the screen. Blanking causes no loss of information. The screen immediately activates when it prints new characters. Press the space bar on the keyboard to activate a blanked screen; spaces have no effect on the trainer so the same information returns to the screen.

CRT problems. Some CRT terminals get locked up if the computer sends improper information. Such a lock up may make you think that the microcomputer trainer has stopped operating. You must reset the terminal to correct the problem; resetting usually requires turning the power to the terminal off and then back on again.

Using a personal computer as a terminal

A communications program is necessary to make the personal computer act as a CRT terminal. This discussion assumes you are using PROCOMM, which is available both as a shareware program and as a commercial program. See Appendix A for help on running programs on an IBM PC compatible personal computer.

Options and connections. Starting PROCOMM causes its options to be set to predetermined default values. The defaults should have been previously set to correspond to the equipment you are using. The personal computer hardware also must be connected to the trainer hardware correctly. A proper serial cable must connect the serial port on the personal computer to the terminal port on the Motorola trainer. Appendix F provides the details of these connections and the software installation.

Using PROCOMM.   Start the PROCOMM program by typing PROCOMM following the MSDOS prompt. When PROCOMM starts running, you will get a screen display that acts just like a CRT terminal. That is, when you type characters, those characters are transmitted to the trainer; any characters returned by the trainer are displayed on the monitor screen.

If you turned on the power to the trainer before starting the PROCOMM program, the initial BUFFALO message from the trainer was lost. To assure that everything is working correctly, press the reset button on the trainer. Look for the BUFFALO message on the personal computer monitor screen to confirm that everything is working correctly.

Entering Monitor Program Commands

Commands entered on the CRT terminal keyboard control the Motorola trainer. The general format of a command is a character string followed by a space followed by one or more numbers separated by spaces. Some commands do not require any numbers. All numbers entered at the keyboard or printed on the screen by the monitor program are hexadecimal numbers. You can omit leading zeros in numbers. Type commands immediately to the right of the prompt and, for most commands, end them with the Enter key.

Seeing the help screen

Pressing the Enter key twice immediately after the BUFFALO message appears displays the help screen. At all other times, the H command displays the help screen. The help screen lists all the possible commands.

Command format

A command is a symbolic name followed by symbolic modifiers or numbers. Spaces normally separate the symbols and numbers, but commas work too. The spaces are necessary for all commands so the discussion below omits mention of the required spaces.

Canceling commands

Pressing the delete key will immediately cancel the function of any command. Some keyboards may have two delete keys, but only one of them will work correctly.

Freezing the screen

Typing Control W—hold the Control key while pressing W—for wait will freeze the screen so it quits printing new characters. Press any key to continue displaying new information.

Repeating commands

Pressing the Enter key without typing anything else will repeat the last command entered. This is very confusing if misunderstood, and very useful otherwise.

The Monitor Program Commands

This section describes some of the BUFFALO monitor commands. The commands covered here are the only commands you should need. The help screen displays more commands than listed here, but the other commands are unnecessary if you have the equipment assumed in this book. The required equipment is an assembler program and an IBM PC compatible computer with a cable connection to the trainer.

Assembler/Disassembler   ASM *address*

This very limited assembler/disassembler command is unnecessary because a complete assembler program should be available on your host computer.

Block Fill   BF *address1 address2 data*

Block fill puts the *data* value into all memory locations specified by the range from *address1* through and including *address2*. If there is no read/write memory at the locations specified, you will get a *rom-* error message.

Breakpoint Insert   BR *address*

Enters a breakpoint *address* into the breakpoint address table and then lists the current four breakpoint addresses.

Run your program after you have inserted breakpoints at addresses containing instruction op codes. If your program encounters a breakpoint location during the fetch of an instruction, the break occurs. Control goes to the monitor program that displays the microprocessor registers. Then use the monitor commands to check your program. To continue from the breakpoint, use the P command.

When a break occurs, the instruction at the breakpoint location has not yet been executed.

The breakpoint will be transparent to the user. That is, examination of the breakpoint location shows no change when you insert or remove a breakpoint.

Whenever a prompt is displayed, the Breakpoint Insert or Breakpoint Remove commands will modify the breakpoint addresses.

Only put breakpoints at read/write memory locations. Don't use the P command to proceed from a breakpoint set on an SWI or *STOP* instruction—op code 3F.

Pressing the reset button while breakpoints are in place will remove all breakpoints.

Be careful when you use the reset button because the monitor program may alter the numbers at the breakpoint locations.

Reset will be necessary if your program gets into an infinite loop that does not correctly include the breakpoint location.

Breakpoints set at locations that do not contain instruction op codes may cause your program to malfunction.

Breakpoint Remove   BR – or BR *–address*

The Breakpoint Remove command followed by a minus sign removes all breakpoints. The Breakpoint Remove command followed by a minus sign and an *address* removes only that address from the breakpoint table.

Bulk Erase EEPROM   BULK

Erases the entire EEPROM memory that is inside the 68HC11 chip. The EEPROM is memory locations B600 through and including B7FF. After erasing, these locations will contain FF. In some versions of the monitor program, this command is of little use because erasing is not necessary to reprogram the EEPROM. In other versions, the EEPROM must be erased using Bulk before the Move command will correctly program it.

Bulk Erase All   BULKALL

WARNING: DO NOT USE BULKALL, since it is not useful for training purposes. In some versions of the monitor program, it will switch the trainer to a version of the monitor program in internal memory that is probably obsolete. To check this, carefully read the BUFFALO message after pressing the reset button. If (INT) follows the word BUFFALO, reprogram the CONFIG register, address 103F, to contain 0D. See the Memory Modify command.

Call   CALL *address*

The trainer executes a subroutine only. The *address* is the execution address of the subroutine. A return from subroutine instruction in your subroutine returns control to the monitor program.

Go   G *address*

Run the program starting at the *address* specified. If you omit the *address*, the monitor program uses the current value of the program counter it displays with a Register Modify command.

The program will not proceed if the location specified by the address has a breakpoint or contains a *STOP* instruction—op code 3F.

Starting the computer at an address of nonexistent memory probably will crash the computer.

Help   H

Display the help screen that lists all the monitor commands.

Load   LOAD FILE

Download a binary program into the memory of the trainer from the host computer system. The monitor program prints the word FILE on the next line after the command and puts the cursor on the word FILE. The trainer will wait for the host computer to start the download. After the download is complete and correct, the trainer prints the word *done* on the following line. See the download procedures in Appendix C.

If the download does not occur for some reason, press the reset button to regain control of the trainer. The trainer continues to wait for a download otherwise.

The trainer cannot download directly to the EEPROM. See the Move command.

The information downloaded must be in the Motorola S19 format. The 2500AD assembler (and linker) can generate a file in the correct format.

If the file contains load information that specifies an invalid memory location, the monitor program displays an error message.

Memory Display   MD *address1 address2*

Show the contents of a block of memory from *address1* through and including *address2*. The display format is lines of three regions that contain addresses, data numbers, and characters. First, each line starts with a memory address. Second, the data is 16_{10} bytes that are the numbers in 16_{10} memory registers beginning with the address at the left. Third, there are 16_{10} ASCII characters corresponding to the memory bytes. The monitor program substitutes a space if there is no corresponding ASCII character.

If you omit *address2*, the screen displays nine lines beginning at *address1*.

If you omit both addresses, the screen displays nine lines beginning at the last memory location accessed.

Memory Modify   MM *address*

Display the contents of the memory location specified by *address* and leave the cursor at the right of the number. Whether hardware for that memory location exists is not considered, so the number displayed could be garbage.

Three subcommands can follow Memory Modify. First, the Enter key will stop the Memory Modify. Second, Control J, or cursor down, will examine the next memory location. Third, Control H, or backspace, will examine the previous memory location. Typing a number following *address* and before a subcommand puts that number into the memory location specified.

Always check your entries before proceeding. Since the Enter key repeats the last command, it is easy to restart the Memory Modify from the beginning by pressing Enter. After restarting the command, use Control J to inspect and correct your entries.

If you try to enter numbers into nonexistent or permanent read only memory, you will get a *rom-* error message.

Memory Modify will erase and reprogram individual memory locations in the EEPROM.

Move Memory   MOVE *address1 address2 address3*

Copies the block of memory locations *address1* through and including *address2* to the locations beginning at *address3*. Omitting *address3* moves the block one location higher.

Move Memory programs the EEPROM by copying read/write memory to it. In some versions of the monitor program, it will be necessary to erase the EEPROM using the Bulk command before Move will work correctly.

Moving to nonexistent or permanent read only memory does not cause an error message.

Do not modify the CONFIG register (address 103F). See the Bulkall command.

Proceed   P

Proceed or continue program execution after encountering a breakpoint. If P is used after a Trace command, it works the same as the G command.

Register Display   RD

Register Display is a second name for the Register Modify command.

Register Modify   RM

Modify the contents of the internal 68HC11 registers P, X, Y, A, B, C, and S. The command displays two lines. The first lists the contents of the 68HC11 internal registers. The second line is P-*number* where *number* is the contents of the program counter.

After Register Modify displays the registers, two subcommand keys are effective. First, the Enter key ends the command. Second, each press of the space bar shows the next register on the next line. Typing a number before the subcommand changes the contents of the register most recently displayed to that value.

A variation of the Register Modify command is RM *register*, which displays *register* initially. *Register* is the single character designation of a register including P, X, Y, A, B, C, and S.

Trace   T *number*

Single step or trace the *number* of instructions. Execution begins at the location specified by the program counter; use Register Modify to see or change the program counter. After each instruction execution, Trace displays two lines. The first line displays Op- *number* where *number* is the first byte of the op code of the instruction that was executed. The second line lists the contents of the 68HC11 internal registers P, X, Y, A, B, C, and S.

Omitting *number* causes the number to default to one and T single steps only one instruction. You can then repeat Trace by pressing only the Enter key.

After single stepping, you can continue the program at full speed by using the G or P commands.

Messages Generated by the Monitor Program

When error conditions occur, the monitor program will print a message on the next line following the command. The message often requires considerable interpretation to understand how it applies to your circumstances.

What?

You typed an invalid command. Type a new and correct command.

rom-

You have tried to change read only memory that cannot change. The message implies that the monitor program did not store your number—this is not what happens. Actually, the monitor program stores your number and then reads it back. The *rom-* message is displayed if the number read back is different from the number stored. The monitor program stores all the bits of your number that the hardware can accept.

Many different situations cause this message including an actual read only memory register and a register that has some read/write bits and some permanent bits. A defective bit in a read/write memory register that reads incorrectly for the desired number also causes the error message. If the defective bit read correctly, no message would result.

You can confirm this method of error checking. Examine an actual read only memory location, and then store the same value into it.

Command?

Incorrectly entered hexadecimal digits are the usual cause for this message. For example, entering FZ as a hexadecimal number causes the monitor program to ask if you are trying to input a command.

Bad argument

Usually the error will be apparent. You probably entered a command with incorrect arguments or parameters. Be careful because many commands substitute default values for omitted arguments. Such substitution is not an error to the monitor program.

Too Long

You probably entered a command name with more than eight characters. This message may occur for other reasons also, but the problem is usually obvious.

done

The download from the host computer system finished. You may now use the program, which is in the trainer memory.

error *address*

An error occurred at the *address* during downloading from the personal computer. The error was probably due to a download into nonexistent memory, read only memory, or to the EEPROM. If so, rewrite your program and download the corrected version.

checksum error

An error occurred during the downloading of information from the personal computer system. Check the cable connections between the computers and try again.

No host port available

A hardware failure has occurred.

D.5   DOWNLOADING FROM A HOST COMPUTER

To *download* means to transmit binary numbers from a personal computer to the Motorola trainer. The personal computer supplies the information so it is called the host. The following downloading procedures assume the information to be downloaded exists in a disk file named *filename.S19*. Also, you must use the batch files in the personal computer that Appendix F describes.

The downloading procedures are different if you are using a CRT terminal or if you are using the personal computer as a CRT terminal. Choose the section below that is appropriate to your configuration.

Downloading When Using a CRT Terminal

Before you try a download, both serial connectors on the Motorola trainer must have correctly connected cables. One goes to the CRT terminal and the other to the personal computer.

Appendix F describes the necessary connections. Begin at the trainer by typing LOAD FILE on the CRT keyboard. The monitor program prints the word FILE the next line and puts the cursor on the word FILE. The trainer is now waiting for the personal computer to start transmitting information. The download process can be interrupted from now on only by pressing the reset button on the trainer.

Next, type DLOAD *filename* on the personal computer keyboard. The *filename* is the name of the file generated by the assembler program. The DLOAD command invokes a batch file that handles all the details to complete the download. When the download is complete, the trainer will display *done* on the CRT screen to indicate that a correct transfer has occurred.

If the word *done* is missing after the personal computer prompt has returned, the download transfer was unsuccessful. The only way to recover is to press the reset button on the trainer.

Stopping a download

You can press the reset button on the trainer to stop a download. This will not affect the personal computer, which continues to transmit over the cable. You can then press Control C on the personal computer to stop it. Usually, it is easier to do nothing; just wait until the download is completed.

Downloading errors

During a download, an *Abort, Retry, Ignore, Fail?* message probably means that you have not installed your floppy disk containing the load file in the disk drive correctly. If so, fix the problem and press R for Retry.

If the download fails, the CRT will not display *done* or will display an error message. If there are no messages, there probably is a bad connection in the cable from the personal computer to the trainer. If the cable connects to a switch box, check the switch settings.

Downloading With PC Used as Terminal

Before you do a download, a cable must correctly connect the terminal port serial connector on the Motorola trainer to the personal computer. Appendix F describes the necessary connections.

The following assumes that the PROCOMM communications program makes the personal computer act like a CRT terminal. Appendix A describes how to start programs in the personal computer.

If PROCOMM is running and communications with the trainer have been established, begin by typing LOAD T on the keyboard. The trainer will not respond; it is waiting for the personal computer to start the download through the terminal port on the trainer. Now you can transmit the load file to the trainer two ways.

Caution! Following a download using LOAD T, be careful not to type a carriage return because it will repeat the load command. Then the trainer will wait for a download to begin when you don't expect it. This can be very confusing!

Downloading with PROCOMM ASCII file transfer.   The first way to download uses the PROCOMM ASCII file transfer. Press the PAGE UP key, choose ASCII from the menu, and type the complete filename of the S-Record file. For example, type A:MYPROG.S19. When the transfer is complete, the trainer responds with *done*.

If the trainer does not display *done*, the transfer was unsuccessful; the only way to recover is to press the reset button on the trainer. The trainer may respond with other error messages. Any errors relating to disk files result in error messages from PROCOMM.

Downloading with MSDOS commands.   The second way to transmit the load file uses the DOS gateway in PROCOMM. Press Alternate F4 to tell PROCOMM that you want to enter MSDOS commands; then type DLOAD *filename* where *filename* is the name of the file generated by the assembler program. The DLOAD command will invoke a batch file that handles all the details to complete the transfer. When the download is complete, type EXIT to return to PROCOMM, and then press Alternate H to restore normal communications with the trainer.

You will not see the message returned by the trainer using this transfer technique. If there was a transmission error, the trainer will not respond. The only way to recover is to press the reset button on the trainer.

D.6   SUGGESTIONS ON USING THE TRAINER

Debugging programs is easy if you use the features available in the trainer. You must be patient and use the trainer effectively. Testing begins with the assumption that your program has errors; then you must check its performance orderly. Running a faulty program over and over with poorly thought out changes inserted periodically will waste time.

The single-step and breakpoint features make it easy to check the operation of a program and to find problems. Check every new program with these tools.

The fastest approach to get a program working is to begin by single stepping it. You must examine the memory and microprocessor registers that are important to the program after each step. If the program has a loop, you may have some confidence in the loop after single stepping around it once. If so, put a breakpoint at the beginning of the loop. Then use the P command to run the loop once at full speed. If the results are good, continue to run the loop with the P command. When the loop exits, you can single step through the next section.

The loop may require too many iterations for this to be practical. If so, remove the breakpoint and put a new one just beyond the loop. Then use P again to run the rest of the loop at full speed.

By using single-step and breakpoint, you can check the entire program in a few minutes and find the mistakes. You will waste no time at all. On the contrary, just starting up a new program and finding out that it doesn't work provides almost no information—you knew it wouldn't work, but you still don't know the problem. Running it probably will destroy the information that you entered and crash the monitor program in the trainer. So running it is a waste of time. Slow, careful, and orderly techniques to programming and testing programs is the quickest way to success.

Using Interrupts

If you have not yet learned about the hardware interrupt system, skip this section and return to it when you want to use interrupts.

It is very difficult to run a program using interrupts and use the monitor program at the same time. For example, tracing or single stepping a program while interrupts are occurring is troublesome. However, you can avoid any problems by executing parts of your program with the interrupt system disabled and using breakpoints.

For example, you can run the initialization part of your program with a breakpoint set at the CLI instruction. The breakpoint prevents the CLI from enabling the interrupt system, but the initialization will be correct. Do not proceed with the P command, because that will execute the CLI instruction. Instead, you can run the main program loop using the G command with breakpoints set in the loop. Next, you can run an interrupt service routine with a breakpoint at the RTI instruction. The breakpoint prevents the RTI from executing, but the entire interrupt service routine can be executed and tested. The goal here is to avoid enabling the interrupt system. Therefore, if your interrupt service routine contains a CLI instruction, replace it with a NOP during this test.

The recommendations here avoid using the Trace feature because it uses interrupt and the programmable timer device. If your program uses the timer, interactions will occur that can be very confusing. The timer is also used by the Proceed command, so it too must be avoided.

The section on trainer hardware provides further information on setting up the interrupt vectors for your program. Read it carefully before using interrupts.

D.7   A PRACTICE SESSION WITH THE TRAINER

The following step-by-step tutorial teaches you to use the Motorola M68HC11EVB trainer. It assumes very little knowledge of the microcomputer instructions. Therefore, you can learn to use the trainer before learning much about the 68HC11 computer.

This tutorial discusses using the trainer only with a CRT terminal. If you are using an IBM PC compatible computer as a terminal, read the section on the terminal before beginning. Then when the tutorial refers to the terminal, interpret terminal to mean the personal computer used as a terminal.

Turn on the Trainer

Begin by turning on the power to the CRT terminal; then turn on the power to the trainer. The DC power supply may have an indicator light to show that it is working.

When the trainer powers up, it will print a message on the CRT screen identifying the BUFFALO monitor program. It then positions the cursor at the right end of this character string.

You next need the carriage return key that is usually labeled Enter. Some keyboards label the Enter key with the word Return or with a bent arrow. Others have both a Return and an Enter key. On most keyboards, these two keys will have the same effect on the monitor program.

Press the Enter key on the keyboard to cause the monitor program to begin normal operation. The monitor program shows that it is responding by printing a right arrow character at the left side of the screen. The right arrow character, called a *prompt*, alerts or prompts the operator. The prompt means that the trainer is ready for a command. The appearance of the prompt also means that most of the trainer works properly.

Some mistakes crash the monitor program and the trainer will apparently stop working. You recover from these mistakes by pressing the reset button on the trainer circuit board. A reset acts like you just turned on the power. Press the reset button now, and then press the Enter key again.

Next, press the Enter key a second time. This time, and this time only, pressing the Enter key causes the monitor program to display the help screen. The help screen is a command summary. It shows all the commands that the monitor program understands; you won't need all of them.

The prompt should have returned at the left side of the screen. You may now type in other commands.

Displaying and Changing Memory Contents

You need to access memory to examine and change the numbers. Consider read/write memory—called RAM—first. Initially, there are unknown numbers in the RAM memory. During power up, the flip flops in the memory ICs will flip and flop however they like. This leaves a strange pattern of ones and zeros in the memory accurately called *garbage*. The pattern is not random, since it depends on the characteristics of the transistors in the memory ICs. If the trainer is turned off and then back on, most of the bits will come back to the same pattern. Some bits will change because the heat generated due to the operation of the memory chip changes the transistor characteristics.

Display memory

The trainer displays the contents of memory in several different ways. Let's begin with the simplest. Type the memory display command MD C000 and press Enter; always press Enter to delimit the commands discussed here. The MD command prints nine lines of information with three regions to each line. First, the number at the left of each line is a beginning address for the next region. The second region is 16_{10} bytes of memory contents in hexadecimal format. The third region is 16_{10} ASCII characters corresponding to the memory bytes. If there is no character for a byte value, the monitor program substitutes a space.

Remember, pressing only the Enter key repeats this command. Try it now.

You select a different size block of memory by specifying a beginning and ending address. Type MD C005 C103. The display now contains more locations than you requested, but it includes all the specified locations.

Now let's try a different way to display memory. Type MM C100. Next press the cursor down key if you have one, or hold the Control key down and press J to make a Control J.

Doing this repeatedly shows successive locations in a vertical format. End this command by pressing the Enter key. If you forget to use cursor down and press Enter too soon, remember to repeat your original command by pressing the Enter key.

The MM command also allows you to go backward through locations; that is, show the contents of successively lower addresses. Type MM C100 again. Next, repeatedly press the backspace key or Control H and end with the Enter key.

You can display memory that doesn't exist, but be careful. The values you get may be garbage because the memory isn't there. However, it's more complicated than that. The hardware in the trainer cannot distinguish all the possible addresses. Therefore, several different addresses actually access the same memory location. If you type MD 200, you will get values that include ASCII characters for the alphabet. Now type MD 300, and then MD 400. You get the same values because the hardware cannot distinguish these addresses; they all refer to the same memory hardware.

Change memory

The MM command will also change the contents of memory registers. Type MM C100 to display the contents of memory location C100. The cursor will be at the right end of the contents. Now type 23 and press the Enter key. The number 23 will be stored at location C100. Demonstrate this by typing MM C100 once again to look at the contents.

Displaying and Changing Microprocessor Registers

The trainer displays the microprocessor registers together, and then modifies them individually. The values displayed are the values put into the registers when the monitor program transfers control to your program. So, if you run your program, it will start with the displayed values in the microprocessor registers. The number in the program counter register determines where your program must be in memory.

If you have already run your program and it stopped, the register values that are displayed were the numbers in the registers when your program stopped and returned control to the monitor program. They are not the values in the registers at the instant that you type the command. The monitor program is running and using the registers, so it saves a copy of your program registers.

Enter a Register Modify command by typing RM and look at the message on the display. The first line shows seven registers, each identified by a single letter name, and the numbers in those registers. Since some registers hold 8-bit numbers and others hold 16-bit numbers, the numbers have either two or four hexadecimal digits.

The next line shows the program counter register and its contents. If you now press the Enter key, the RM command is finished. If instead you type a new number and then press Enter, the RM command puts that number into the program counter. Change the program counter to C100, and then type RM again to see the new value.

Now let's put a number into the X register. Type RM X. The first line will look the same as before, but the second line shows the X register and its contents. Type 321 and press Enter to put this number in the X register. Type RM to see the results.

Entering a Practice Program

Now let's enter a simple program to demonstrate some features of the trainer. The example assumes that you have just started learning the microcomputer instructions and addressing modes. You do not need to understand the instructions to follow this example.

The first example program has four instructions. The program loads the A accumulator with 22, loads the A accumulator with 33, loads the A accumulator with 44, and then jumps back to the beginning. So it's an infinite loop that never stops.

Always carefully check entered codes, since errors are likely and incorrect codes might destroy your program when you run it.

Enter the program in Figure D-1 using the Memory Modify command. Type MM C100, and then each number followed by cursor down or Control J to access the next sequential memory location. When you have reached the end of the required values, press the Enter key to end the Memory Modify command.

After entering the program, use the MD command to look at all your numbers to be sure that they are perfectly correct. Correct any errors with the Memory Modify command.

Running the First Practice Program

Running a program means placing the address of the first instruction into the program counter and then starting the computer. The GO or G command runs a program. It puts a number into the program counter and transfers control from the monitor program to your program, effectively starting the computer.

When using the G command to run a program, carefully check what you have typed before you press Enter. If you have typed the command incorrectly, your program may be destroyed.

Type G C100 to run your program starting at address C100. Correct typing errors by backspacing and reentering characters. Backspacing does not erase the original character, but typing a new character will overwrite the old one.

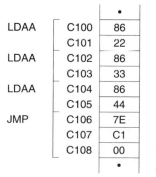

		•
LDAA	C100	86
	C101	22
LDAA	C102	86
	C103	33
LDAA	C104	86
	C105	44
JMP	C106	7E
	C107	C1
	C108	00
		•

Figure D-1   Practice program.

While the example program is running, the keyboard and display will not respond, because your program is an infinite loop and it has complete control of the computer. The monitor program is not running, so the terminal does not respond. To regain control of the trainer by making the monitor program run again, press the reset button. You should get the BUFFALO message.

You should learn an important lesson from running this infinite loop program. The infinite loop prevents the CRT terminal from responding while the program is working properly. So, if you ever have the trainer stop working, you should investigate the chance that you have a program with an infinite loop. Don't immediately assume that the trainer has failed.

Resetting the trainer will not change your program numbers. Use the memory display command to see that your program still is in memory; type MD C100. If your program is gone, you made a mistake. Don't blame the trainer or the monitor program.

Here is a second way to run your program. First, manually enter the address of the first instruction into the program counter register using the Register Modify command; type RM, press Enter, and then type C100. Now type G alone to run your program. The G command without a number starts the computer at the address that is already in the program counter.

Running the Second Practice Program

Enter the program in Figure D-2 into the trainer memory. This program has a *STOP* instruction at the end instead of the jump in the previous example. The *STOP* instruction transfers control from your program back to the monitor program. It does not stop the computer from running—it stops your program from running.

When the *STOP* instruction sends control to the monitor program, the program automatically displays the microprocessor registers as the Register Modify command does. The display after a *STOP* shows the program counter containing the address of the *STOP* instruction. Normally the address in the program counter advances to the next instruction.

Run your program by typing G C200 and read the register contents. The first instruction in the program put the number 22 in the A accumulator, the second put 33 in the A

		•
LDAA	C200	86
	C201	22
LDAA	C202	86
	C203	33
LDX	C204	CE
	C205	12
	C206	34
STOP	C207	3F
INVALID	C208	00
		•

Figure D-2   Practice program.

accumulator, and the third put 1234 in the X index register. The program counter P should have C207, which is the address of the *STOP* instruction. You should look carefully at the numbers listed for each register.

Experiment with this program by changing the data numbers in the instruction codes. For example, change the program so it ends with 44 in A and 6789 in X.

Using Single-Step

The Single-Step or Trace command requires that the program counter be set to the address of the instruction to be executed. Let's use the program in Figure D-2. Enter the program into memory or check it if you already have it in memory.

Use the Register Modify command to put C200 in the program counter to set up the single-step. Then type the T command and press the Enter key. The T command executes only one instruction and then it displays the instruction op code and the 68HC11 internal registers. After using T once, you should have an op code of 86, the number C202 in the program counter, and 22 in the A register. The program counter is ready for the next instruction at address C202.

Continue by executing two more instructions using the Trace command twice more. You could do this by typing T, Enter, T, and Enter again. However, remember that pressing Enter by itself repeats the last command. So type T, Enter, and then Enter again. Now the program counter should contain C207.

Next, single step the *STOP* instruction by typing T again. Single stepping the *STOP* does nothing but advance to the next instruction in order, so be careful. You can easily single step beyond the end of your program, which can cause problems. For example, the number in the next register after the *STOP* instruction is an invalid instruction code. Use T to single step once more. The trainer will go dead because the invalid instruction physically stops the trainer from running. You must press the reset button to restart the trainer. However, this error will not cause anything in memory to be lost.

Let's do a multiple Trace from the beginning of the program. First, load the program counter with C200 using the Register Modify command. Then type T 3 to single step three instructions at once.

Using Breakpoints

Breakpoints make your program transfer control to the monitor program at selected places. By breaking out of your program, you can check if it is working correctly up to the breakpoint.

Let's use the program in Figure D-1 again. Set a breakpoint on the second instruction by typing BR C102. The monitor program will display the breakpoint table, which contains four addresses. The first will be C102, the address of your breakpoint, and then three zeros, which mean there are no more breakpoints. If this is not true, press reset and try again. The reset will remove any breakpoints that have been left in place.

Now run the program from the beginning by typing G C100. When the program gets to the breakpoint, the monitor program gets control and displays the Register Modify message. The program counter should contain C102, which is the location of the breakpoint. Notice that the instruction at location C102 has not yet been executed, because the program counter contains C102.

Now continue running your program by typing the P command for proceed from breakpoint. The program will run through the loop and come back to the breakpoint; the monitor program displays the same message again. It will appear that nothing has happened, but the loop did run.

Let's add a second breakpoint to make the operation easier to observe. Put a breakpoint at address C106 by typing BR C106. Now type P and see that a break occurs at address C106. Type P again and a break will occur at address C102. Look at the contents of all the registers as you continue to use the P command several times.

To prove that it can be done, single step a few instructions with the T command and then type P to proceed to the next breakpoint.

Next let's remove the breakpoints. First, remove the breakpoint at address C102 by typing BR –C102. The minus sign means remove that breakpoint. To see the effect, type BR alone to display the breakpoint table. Now type BR – without a number to remove all breakpoints. Again type BR alone to see the breakpoint table.

Breakpoint problems

All trainers that have breakpoint capability can cause problems and confusion if you make certain errors. So let's look more carefully at breakpoints.

Use the program in Figure D-2 and put breakpoints at addresses C200 and C204. To be sure the breakpoints are correctly in place, type BR alone and check the breakpoint table. Now type MD C200 and look at memory locations C200 and C204. Your instructions should be shown as if the breakpoints did nothing.

The monitor program makes a breakpoint by putting a 1-byte instruction at the breakpoint address. The breakpoint instruction replaces your instruction, but the monitor program saves a copy of your instruction. However, the monitor program puts the breakpoint instruction in place only when you run the program, and it puts your instruction back when the program stops due to a breakpoint or *STOP* instruction. This is why you don't see any changes when using the Memory Display command when breakpoints are set. The breakpoints are transparent to the user.

Incorrectly located breakpoint.   Unfortunately transparent features can be very confusing when something goes wrong. To demonstrate this, remove any breakpoints by typing BR – and then BR alone to be sure. Now put a breakpoint at address C203. This is an incorrect breakpoint because location C203 does not contain the op code of an instruction.

Now run the program by typing G C200 and observe that the program stops at address C207 and the breakpoint appears to do nothing. However, the breakpoint instruction was put in place as you can see by looking at the contents of the A accumulator register. The LDAA instruction loaded 3F into the A register instead of the correct data 33.

		•
LDAA	C100	86
	C101	22
LDAA	C102	86
	C103	33
LDAA	C104	86
	C105	44
JMP	C106	7E
	C107	C1
	C108	06
		•

Figure D-3 Practice program.

To be sure that the problem is clear, type MD C200 and look at the second LDAA instruction to see that the instruction appears to be correct even though it loaded the number 3F into the A register.

If you ever have a program that seems to work correctly until you put in the break-points, an incorrectly located breakpoint is likely to be the problem.

An incorrectly located breakpoint is a serious problem because it prevents your program from working correctly. The problem is also very difficult to find because the instruction appears to be correct, but it works incorrectly when the program runs. Of course, if the breakpoint is erroneously located outside your program and data area, then it will not affect your program and a break will never occur.

Reset while breakpoint is in place.   Use the program in Figure D-3 for this example, but press reset before entering it into memory to be sure that the monitor program is initialized. The program is the same as that in Figure D-1 except that the jump instruction jumps to itself making a tight infinite loop.

Put in a correct breakpoint by typing BR C102. Now run the program by typing G C100 and then type the P command to continue from the breakpoint. The program will go into the infinite loop. The only way out of the loop is to press the reset button, so press it. Now display the program by typing MD C100 and then look carefully at the codes. You should see that your instruction at the breakpoint location was not put back and that the breakpoint instruction 3F is still at address C102. Your instruction is permanently lost. You must reenter your instruction using the Memory Modify command.

The problem is caused by a reset while a breakpoint instruction is in place. The trainer could not put your instruction back. The breakpoint instruction was left in place because the infinite loop did not encounter a *STOP* or breakpoint.

If you must use the reset button while also using breakpoints, always check to see that your program has not been modified.

When this problem is combined with an incorrectly located breakpoint in a long program, you may have difficulty recognizing it. Always be very careful when entering breakpoints so you enter them at the correct addresses.

D.8 TRAINER HARDWARE

In using the microcomputer trainer, you always need to know which memory addresses are occupied and what kind of memory is present at each address. In addition, you may need to know the interrupt vector addresses and how the trainer uses these interrupt vectors. The following sections tabulate this information. It also points out details about the input/output ports and the connections to these ports that may cause problems if you ignore certain hardware on the trainer board.

Trainer Memory Map

Table D-1 shows the memory addresses used by the hardware in the Motorola trainer. Each region of memory is designated by a range of addresses. The table lists the type of memory or I/O hardware at those addresses. Regions listed as *not used* have no hardware installed in the trainer.

Trainer Interrupts

Table D-2 shows the mapping of the 68HC11 interrupt vectors. Since the vector locations in the trainer are in permanent ROM memory, the vector addresses are mapped into a region of read/write RAM memory. Type MD FFD6 to do a Memory Display that shows the addresses of the interrupt vectors.

Each vector in read/write memory has three bytes of room allocated. You may put jump instructions in these locations to redirect the interrupts to your interrupt service routines. Unless you are using interrupts in the trainer, you need not be concerned with these jump instructions.

Reset state of jump table

If you have put a jump instruction in the jump table so you can use an interrupt, the trainer reset will not affect your jump instruction. However, when the trainer is reset and the monitor program finds something other than a jump instruction in the jump table, the monitor program replaces it with a new jump instruction. This occurs when the trainer is powered up. Any new jumps provided by the monitor program all send control to a hardware STOP instruction. So, if you don't change the jump instruction and a corresponding interrupt occurs, the STOP instruction will be executed. The STOP instruction physically stops the microprocessor from running, so the trainer will no longer respond to the keyboard. A reset or an interrupt restarts the computer.

Don't confuse a hardware STOP instruction with the trainer *STOP* function that stops a program.

Breakpoints and STOP

The trainer implements the breakpoint feature by replacing your instruction op code with a software interrupt instruction or SWI. The monitor program saves a copy of the op

TABLE D-1 TRAINER MEMORY MAP

Address Range	Function
0000	
	54_{10} bytes user RAM in 68HC11
0035	
0036	
	Monitor RAM in 68HC11
00FF	
0100	
	Not used
0FFF	
1000	
	Port replacement and register decode
17FF	
1800	
	Not used
3FFF	
4000	
	Flip flop decode—switches SCI input port
5FFF	
6000	
	Optional 8K RAM
7FFF	
8000	
	Not used
B5FF	
B600	
	EEPROM in 68HC11
B7FF	
B800	
	Not used
BFFF	
C000	
	8K bytes user RAM
DFFF	
E000	
	Monitor program EPROM
FFFF	

TABLE D-2   TRAINER INTERRUPT JUMP ADDRESSES

Vector Address	Jump Address	Interrupt Device
FFD6	00C4	SCI Receive Data Register Full
		SCI Receiver Overrun
		SCI Idle Line Detect
		SCI Transmit Data Register Empty
		SCI Transmit Complete
FFD8	00C7	SPI Serial Transfer Complete
FFDA	00CA	Pulse-Accumulator Input Edge
FFDC	00CD	Pulse-Accumulator Overflow
FFDE	00D0	Timer Overflow
FFE0	00D3	Timer Output Compare 5
FFE2	00D6	Timer Output Compare 4
FFE4	00D9	Timer Output Compare 3
FFE6	00DC	Timer Output Compare 2
FFE8	00DF	Timer Output Compare 1
FFEA	00E2	Timer Input Capture 3
FFEC	00E5	Timer Input Capture 2
FFEE	00E8	Timer Input Capture 1
FFF0	00EB	Real Time Interrupt
FFF2	00EE	IRQ (External Pin or Parallel I/O)
FFF4	00F1	XIRQ Pin
FFF6	00F4	SWI
FFF8	00F7	Illegal Opcode Trap
FFFA	00FA	COP Timeout
FFFC	00FD	Clock Monitor Timeout
FFFE	None	Hardware Reset

code and replaces it after the break occurs. The *STOP* instruction used to stop your programs is the SWI instruction, so the *STOP* is effectively a breakpoint. Since the SWI instruction causes the microprocessor registers to be saved in the stack, the monitor program knows all the register contents from your program whenever a break occurs.

Illegal instruction execution

If you have not modified the interrupt jump table and then execute an illegal instruction in a program, the illegal op code interrupt will lead to a hardware STOP instruction. The trainer will go dead. Pressing the reset button will restart it.

User Reset Vector

You may want to use the reset button on the trainer to perform a reset to your program instead of the monitor program. The monitor program can simulate the reset by jumping to your program upon reset.

At the very beginning of the monitor program, the port E bit 0 is examined as an input bit. If the input is logic 0, the monitor program continues normally. If the input is logic 1, control is sent to the beginning of the EEPROM. So you can use the reset button to send control to your program in the EEPROM. Jumper J4 on the trainer board determines which program will operate upon reset.

Analog-to-Digital Converter

The A/D converter input pins connect directly to the ribbon cable connector with one exception. Port E bit 0 is used by the monitor program to decide whether to run the monitor program or a user program following a reset. Jumper J4 connects a 10K-ohm resistor to either ground or +5 VDC to indicate which program to run. When using channel 0 of the A/D converter, you must account for this resistor. The jumper can be removed to disconnect the resistor if you properly take care of selecting the correct program following reset.

SCI Receiver Connection

The input signal to the SCI serial receiver connects to pin PD0 of the 68HC11. In the Motorola trainer, the signal to pin PD0 passes through an electronic switch. The switch allows two different sources of serial input; namely, the host port serial connector or the 60-pin I/O connector. The switch is controlled by a flip-flop that implements bit 0 of memory location 4000.

Address 4000 consists of only a single bit that can be written but not read. When 1 is stored in this bit, the SCI serial input comes from the host serial port. When 0 is stored in the bit, the SCI serial input comes from the 60-pin I/O connector.

The monitor program sets this switch-controlling bit to 0 when reset is pressed and at other times. Therefore, if you want to use the host port connector with the SCI receiver, your program must put a 1 into bit 0 of address 4000. Using the monitor program to control the bit before running your program won't work.

Furthermore, setting the electronic switch incorrectly can cause confusing problems. Suppose you connect a serial input device to the host port and nothing to the 60-pin connector. The incorrect switch position directs input from the 60-pin connector. However, crosstalk from the host port may cause noise and framing errors in the receiver. This problem can lead you to think your input device is correctly connected but defective!

Trainer Ribbon Cable Connector

The 60-pin ribbon cable connector on the trainer board makes it possible to directly connect external devices to all the 68HC11 input/output port pins. Some other pins on the chip also connect to the cable connector. One pin connects directly to the +5 VDC power supply for the trainer. Therefore, power for the external hardware can be obtained through the ribbon cable connector.

When using the A/D converter, the external circuits must supply its reference voltage because the V_{RH} and V_{RL} pins are not connected on the trainer board. The IRQ pin has an on-board pull-up resistor, but the XIRQ pin connects directly to the cable connector. The reset pin can reset external circuits as the computer hardware is reset, but jumper J1 can disconnect this signal.

The MODA and MODB pins have pull-up resistors to select expanded mode. Usually jumper J2 will select the on-board crystal clock and the EXTAL pin on the cable connector will not be connected.

Figure D-4 shows the pin locations for the various signals. Pin 1 is the ground or common for all the other signals. Be careful with pin 26 because it connects to the +5 VDC power supply for the board—incorrect connections could easily damage your hardware.

GND	1	● ●	2	MODB
MODA	3	● ●	4	STRA
E	5	● ●	6	STRB
EXTAL	7	● ●	8	XTAL
PC0	9	● ●	10	PC1
PC2	11	● ●	12	PC3
PC4	13	● ●	14	PC5
PC6	15	● ●	16	PC7
RESET	17	● ●	18	XIRQ
IRQ	19	● ●	20	PD0
PD1	21	● ●	22	PD2
PD3	23	● ●	24	PD4
PD5	25	● ●	26	V_{DD}
PA7	27	● ●	28	PA6
PA5	29	● ●	30	PA4
PA3	31	● ●	32	PA2
PA1	33	● ●	34	PA0
PB7	35	● ●	36	PB6
PB5	37	● ●	38	PB4
PB3	39	● ●	40	PB2
PB1	41	● ●	42	PB0
PE0	43	● ●	44	PE4
PE1	45	● ●	46	PE5
PE2	47	● ●	48	PE6
PE3	49	● ●	50	PE7
V_{RL}	51	● ●	52	V_{RH}
NC	53	● ●	54	NC
NC	55	● ●	56	NC
NC	57	● ●	58	NC
NC	59	● ●	60	NC

Figure D-4   Ribbon cable connector pin assignments.

Appendix E

Laboratory Exercises

This appendix contains laboratory projects that can be completed using a microcomputer trainer. Some require input/output hardware such as switches or indicator lights. Freely select from the projects because some of them require efforts similar to others. Modify as you desire, but realize that some requirements have been chosen to force you to think about important programming details. Therefore, a project may sometimes seem academic rather than practical. Unfortunately, practical programs are usually too long for beginning exercises.

E.1 LAB PROJECTS

You can use the Motorola 68HC11EVB trainer for all the projects that follow. In particular, the addresses chosen in the specifications are appropriate to this trainer. Usually data locations are specified in the direct addressing range because every trainer should have memory in that range. The program locations must be altered for other trainers. Since many trainers have memory at address 0100, the suggested addresses start at address D100 so changing the addresses requires only that the Ds be changed to 0s in the addresses!

Of course, not all trainers have the same hardware, so some innovation is required. For example, not all trainers have access to the EEPROM, and I/O addresses will be different.

Project 1:   Microprocessor Registers Exercise

Complete the mnemonic and data address columns of the program listing in Figure E-1. Use the reverse instruction set to find the instruction mnemonics.

Make up some data numbers for the program and put the program and your data numbers into a microcomputer trainer. If your trainer does not have the addresses specified, change them to suitable numbers. In many trainers, the program can be put at address 0100; just change the Ds to 0s in the addresses. The 3F code is the *STOP* instruction used by Motorola trainers.

Now run the program. Practice using all the trainer features such as memory and microprocessor register examine and change, single-step, and breakpoints.

Next, predict the contents of the program counter, A and B accumulators, and condition code bits after each instruction. Use the chart in Figure E-2 to record your results. Note that *unknown* is sometimes the correct answer. Single step the program using the trainer to check your predictions.

What number is at address 0023 at the end of the program? What does your trainer do when you single step the *STOP* instruction?

Address	Content	Mnemonic	Address of data	Addressing mode	Data number
D100	96				
D101	20				
D102	D6				
D103	21				
D104	1B		—		
D105	BB				
D106	D2				
D107	22				
D108	97				
D109	23				
D10A	3F	*STOP*	—	—	—

Figure E-1   Program listing.

Step	PC	A	B	H	N	Z	V	C
1								
2								
3								
4								
5								
6								

Figure E-2   Chart for recording single-step results.

Project 2: Machine Language Copy-a-Table Anywhere

Write a machine language program that copies a source table of data numbers to a destination table. The two tables may be anywhere in memory. The length of the tables exceeds hexadecimal FF entries, but will always be less than 64_{10} kilobytes.

The program must be given three data numbers—the addresses of the first entries of each table and the length of the tables. Put the address of the source table at address 0010, the address of the destination table at address 0012, and the table length at address 0014.

Your program must use a loop with a counter to determine the loop exit condition. The program must not test addresses to determine the loop exit condition. The program should not consider the location of the tables even if they overlap other information.

Document your program with a handwritten listing of the hexadecimal instruction codes, addresses, mnemonic instruction names, addressing modes, and enough comments to make the documentation easy to understand.

Project 3: Machine Language Memory Search

Write a machine language program that searches through a block of memory counting the number of negative, zero, and nonzero positive single-byte two's complement numbers. The length of the block of memory exceeds hexadecimal FF entries, but the largest block is always a little less than 64_{10} kilobytes long.

The program must be given two numbers—the lowest address and the highest address of the locations in the block of memory to be searched. The search includes the first and last locations specified, and tests only one number if the addresses are equal. The three counters for the negative, zero, and nonzero positive numbers must be double-byte numbers. Put the address of the lowest entry of the block of memory at location 0000 and the address of the highest entry at location 0002. The program must put the number of negative numbers at address 0004, the number of zero numbers at address 0006, and the number of nonzero positive numbers at address 0008.

The program must test that the higher address is larger or equal to the lower address, and make all results zero if this is not so. Furthermore, the program must use a loop with a loop counter to determine the loop exit condition. Do not terminate the loop by testing or comparing addresses—this is part of the exercise! The loop counter must be a double-byte number.

Document your program with a handwritten listing of the hexadecimal instruction codes, addresses, mnemonic instruction names, addressing mode indication, and enough comments to make the documentation easy to read.

Project 4: Assembly Language Memory Search

Write an assembly language program that searches through a block of memory counting the number of negative, zero, and nonzero positive single-byte two's complement numbers. The length of the block of memory exceeds hexadecimal FF entries, but the largest block is always a little less than 64_{10} kilobytes long.

The program must be given two numbers—the lowest address and the highest address of the locations in the block of memory to be searched. The search includes the first and last locations specified, and tests only one number if the addresses are equal. The three counters for the negative, zero, and nonzero positive numbers must be double-byte numbers.

Put the address of the lowest entry of the block of memory at location 0000 and the address of the highest entry at location 0002. The program must put the number of negative numbers at address 0004, the number of zero numbers at address 0006, and the number of nonzero positive numbers at address 0008.

The program must test that the higher address is larger or equal to the lower address, and make all results zero if this is not so. Furthermore, the program must use a loop with a loop counter to determine the loop exit condition. Do not terminate the loop by testing or comparing addresses—this is part of the exercise! The loop counter must be a double-byte number.

Design your program by making top/down structured flowcharts using at least two levels. Write and assemble a structured assembly language program that follows the flowcharts. The listing must include comments for documentation that show the structure and the function of the parts of the program. Choose assembly language symbols to make the program easy to understand.

Project 5:   Subroutine for Table Lookup

A one-dimensional table is one way of representing a function of a single variable. The independent variable locates an entry in the table and the number at that location is the value of the function. Write an assembly language table lookup subroutine to evaluate a function represented by a table.

The table holds 16_{10} single-byte unsigned numbers that are values of the function. The independent variable is a single-byte unsigned number. The values in the table represent the function when the independent variable has the values hexadecimal 00, 10, 20, etc.

The main program will pass the independent variable to the subroutine using the A accumulator and the subroutine will return the value of the function in the A accumulator. The main program will pass the memory address of the first table entry to the subroutine using a reference in the X index register. The subroutine must restore all appropriate main program registers before it returns control to the main program.

The subroutine must truncate the independent variable to the values hexadecimal 00, 10, 20, etc. The subroutine will not interpolate between the values in the table.

Figure E-3 shows a listing of part of the main program and a sample table. Figure E-4 shows a graph of the function. In this example, if the independent variable is 30, the subroutine returns the value 37. If the independent variable is 60, the result is 25.

Write and assemble a main program module with the subroutine to test it. The listing must include comments for documentation that show the structure and the function of the

```
** MAIN PROGRAM FOR PROJECT 5
            •
XVALUE     RMB    1
YVALUE     RMB    1
            •

            •
* GET REFERENCE TO TABLE
           LDX    #TABLE1
* GET INDEPENDENT VARIABLE
           LDAA   XVALUE
* EVALUATE FUNCTION
           JSR    LOOKUP
* SAVE DEPENDENT VARIABLE
           STAA   YVALUE
           SWI              STOP FOR TRAINER
            •

            •
TABLE1     FCB    $0        X=$0
           FCB    $12       X=$10
           FCB    $20       X=$20
           FCB    $37       X=$30
           FCB    $35       X=$40
           FCB    $55       X=$50
           FCB    $25       X=$60
            •

            •
```

Figure E-3 Example of part of main program and table for Project 5.

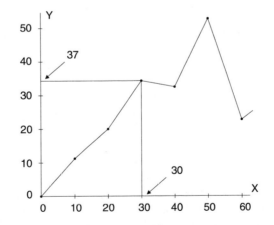

Figure E-4 Graph of function represented in Figure E-3 for Project 5.

parts of the program. Choose assembly language symbols to make the program easy to understand.

Project 6:   Subroutine for Table Lookup With Interpolation

A one-dimensional table is one way of representing a function of a single variable. The independent variable locates two entries in the table. Through interpolation between the two entries, the value of the function is calculated. Write an assembly language table lookup subroutine that uses linear interpolation to evaluate a function represented by a table.

Use a table that holds 17_{10} single-byte unsigned numbers that are given values of the function. Make the independent variable a single-byte unsigned number. The values in the table represent the function when the independent variable has the values hexadecimal 00, 10, 20, and so on through 100.

The main program must pass the independent variable to the subroutine using the A accumulator and the subroutine must return the value of the function in the A accumulator. The main program must pass the memory address of the first table entry to the subroutine using a reference in the X index register. The subroutine must restore all appropriate main program registers before it returns control to the main program. If any local storage is needed, use a hole in the stack.

Figure E-5 shows a listing of part of the main program and a sample table. Figure E-6 shows a graph of the function. In this example, if the independent variable is 43, the subroutine returns the value 3B. If the independent variable is 53, the result is 4C.

Design your subroutine by making top/down structured flowcharts using at least two levels. Write and assemble a structured assembly language program that follows the flowcharts. The listing must include comments for documentation that show the structure and the function of the parts of the program. Choose assembly language symbols to make the

```
** MAIN PROGRAM FOR PROJECT 6
                 •
XVALUE      RMB    1
YVALUE      RMB    1
                 •
                 •
* GET INDEPENDENT VARIABLE
            LDAA   XVALUE
* EVALUATE FUNCTION
            JSR    LOOKUP
               FDB TABLE
* SAVE DEPENDENT VARIABLE
            STAA   YVALUE
            SWI                   STOP FOR TRAINER
                 •
                 •
TABLE       FCB    $0         X=$0
            FCB    $12        x=$10
            FCB    $20        X=$20
            FCB    $37        X=$30
            FCB    $35        X=$40
            FCB    $55        X=$50
            FCB    $25        X=$60
                 •
                 •
```

Figure E-5   Example of part of main program and table for Project 6.

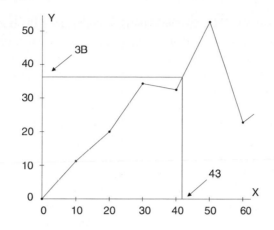

Figure E-6 Graph of function represented in Figure E-5 for Project 6.

program easy to understand. Also make a stack diagram that shows the use of each location in the stack.

Project 7:   Toggle Bit Using Real-Time Interrupt

Write an assembly language program that toggles an output bit periodically using the real-time interrupt device as the time base, and concurrently echoes the terminal keyboard to the screen. That is, immediately print on the screen any character typed at the keyboard.

Begin by writing a program using polling to sense the keyboard flag. Each time the keyboard flag is set, read the keyboard and immediately send the character to the screen. In the Motorola trainer, the keyboard flag is bit 0 of location 9801 and this flag is cleared by reading the character code from location 9800. The character is transmitted to the screen by storing into memory location 9800. The monitor program initializes the I/O hardware so your program does not need to. This program will run in an infinite loop.

Test your program by typing various characters on the keyboard and observing the screen. Notice that functions such as carriage return and line feed or down arrow are actually separate characters. Most trainers will exit the infinite loop only when you press the reset button.

Next, enhance the polling program by adding an interrupt service routine for the 68HC11 internal real-time clock. Your interrupt service routine must toggle or reverse bit 4 of PORTC periodically while leaving the other bits of PORTC unchanged. The interrupt service routine will time the output changes by counting real-time interrupts. The number of interrupts between toggles is determined by the character typed at the keyboard. In particular, use the least-significant four bits of the ASCII character code as the number RATE. Make the time between toggles of the output bit five times RATE times 32.77_{10} milliseconds. The echo keyboard to screen program must continue working concurrently with the interrupts so new RATEs can be entered while the program runs.

If you are using the Motorola trainer, demonstrate the operation of your program by connecting an analog DC voltmeter to pins 1 and 13 of the 60-pin connector. Pin 13 corresponds to bit 4 of PORTC. Pin 1 is ground. If a 4 is entered, the voltmeter needle should move every 655_{10} milliseconds, which is an easily observed rate for most voltmeters.

Here are some suggestions. First, carefully read the cautions about using the Motorola trainer with interrupts. These cautions apply to most other trainers as well. Second, be sure your program initializes the real-time interrupt and port C hardware. Third, develop your program carefully because interrupt programs are especially easy to crash. Attention to detail will be necessary for success. Fourth, you should check the other port C outputs to be sure they are not changing.

Design your program by making top/down structured flowcharts. Write, assemble, and demonstrate a structured assembly language program that follows the flowcharts. The listing must include comments for documentation that show the structure and the function of the parts of the program. Choose assembly language symbols to make the program easy to understand.

Project 8:   Time-of-day Clock Using Programmable Timer

Make a 12-hour time-of-day clock using interrupts from the programmable timer as the time base. Use output compare 2 to generate periodic interrupts. Interface four BCD displays to ports B and C to display hours and minutes. Set the time by entering numbers into memory before starting the program.

Design your program by making top/down structured flowcharts. Write, assemble, and demonstrate a structured assembly language program that follows the flowcharts. The listing must include comments for documentation that show the structure and the function of the parts of the program. Choose assembly language symbols to make the program easy to understand.

Enhancement 1:   Add two input signals to make your clock run forward at two fast rates to enable you to set the time easily.

Enhancement 2:   Add a.m. and p.m. indicators.

Project 9:   Electronic Stopwatch Using Programmable Timer

Make an electronic stopwatch using interrupts from the programmable timer as the time base. Use output compare 2 to generate an interrupt every 10_{10} milliseconds, and count interrupts to determine elapsed time.

Interface four BCD displays to ports B and C to display seconds and tenths of seconds. Use switches connected to two input bits for the start and stop signals. Start timing when the start input goes low-to-high and stop when the stop input goes low-to-high. Use input capture flags for the start and stop inputs. Timing should not begin if both the start and stop inputs are high. A third input bit resets the elapsed time to zero while it is high.

Design your program by making top/down structured flowcharts. Write, assemble, and demonstrate a structured assembly language program that follows the flowcharts. The listing must include comments for documentation that show the structure and the function of the parts of the program. Choose assembly language symbols to make the program easy to understand. Also make a wiring diagram showing how the I/O signals are connected.

Project 10:   Overspeed Detector Using Programmable Timer

Make an electronic overspeed detector that indicates if a rotating wheel has exceeded 4000_{10} revolutions per minute. This may be used to indicate if a gasoline engine is exceeding its design speed. Assert bit 0 of port C while the wheel is over the design speed.

A sensor on the wheel generates one pulse per revolution. Use an input capture with interrupt to measure the time between low-to-high transitions of the pulses. Be sure to consider the effects of the free-running counter overflowing if the time between pulses is long.

Design your program by making top/down structured flowcharts. Write, assemble, and demonstrate a structured assembly language program that follows the flowcharts. The listing must include comments for documentation that show the structure and the function of the parts of the program. Choose assembly language symbols to make the program easy to understand. A laboratory oscillator or a 555 timer IC can make the input pulses for testing the program.

Project 11:   PWM Output Bit Using OC4

Modify the program in Figure 7-26 to pulse-width modulate port A bit 4 using output compare 4. The duty cycle will vary from 0 to 100 percent based on a 4-bit number read from a BCD thumbwheel switch connected to port C. Measure the average output voltage level with an analog DC voltmeter.

Design your program by making top/down structured flowcharts. Write, assemble, and demonstrate a structured assembly language program that follows the flowcharts. The listing must include comments for documentation that show the structure and the function of the parts of the program. Choose assembly language symbols to make the program easy to understand. Also make a wiring diagram showing how the I/O signals are connected.

Project 12:   Display Analog Voltage Using CRT and SCI

Write a program to display the voltages read from A/D converter channels 4, 5, 6, and 7 on a CRT display. The display must be updated every 131_{10} milliseconds using interrupts from the real-time interrupt as the time base. The message must include a heading and the hexadecimal numbers read from the A/D converter. Use the SCI serial transmitter with interrupts to display the message. Be careful to connect the CRT terminal to the correct pins when using the SCI interface.

Design your program by making top/down structured flowcharts. Write, assemble, and demonstrate a structured assembly language program that follows the flowcharts. The listing must include comments for documentation that show the structure and the function of the parts of the program. Choose assembly language symbols to make the program easy to understand.

Explain any special programming required to use the SCI interface in the Motorola trainer. Also make a wiring diagram showing how the I/O signals are connected.

Project 13:   PWM Output Bit With Analog Control

Write a program to pulse-width modulate port A bit 4 using output compare 4. The duty cycle will vary from 0 to 100 percent based on the analog voltage read from port E bit 7. Use a 5-volt source for a potentiometer and read the analog voltage at pin PE7. Vary the duty cycle from 0 to 100 percent for an input voltage of 0 to 5 volts. Measure the input voltage and the average output voltage level with an analog DC voltmeter. The two voltages should be equal.

Project 14:   DC Voltmeter Using A/D Converter

Write a program to make a simple DC voltmeter. The voltmeter will measure voltages between 0 and +5 VDC. The display for the voltmeter is an array of eight light-emitting diodes, so the voltage range must be broken into eight segments. All the LEDs representing voltages within that segment must light. For example, a voltage of 2.6_{10} volts will light the first five lights.

Your voltmeter should read the analog voltage and update the display every 32.77_{10} milliseconds using interrupts from the real-time interrupt device as the time base. If you change the input voltage rapidly, you should detect the delay in the readings.

Also make an overload indicator that lights an LED. Define the overload condition as an A/D reading of FF. This reading indicates the largest possible voltage, or a voltage that is greater than the high-reference voltage.

Drive the eight display LEDs with port B, and drive the overload indicator with port C bit 0. Use the power supply voltage and common for the A/D converter reference voltages. Use A/D converter channel 7 to read the unknown voltage.

Appendix F

Setting Up a Computer Lab

Several other appendixes in this book discuss using software and hardware for hands-on experience with the 68HC11 microcomputer. This appendix explains how to set up a computer lab using the Motorola Trainer along with an IBM PC compatible personal computer system. People interested in using the equipment after it has been set up need not read further in this appendix.

The material in this book assumes an IBM PC compatible computer for use in a lab setting. A Motorola 68HC11EVB trainer with cabling to the personal computer is also desirable. A CRT terminal for use with the trainer is also useful.

F.1 SET UP PERSONAL COMPUTER

Several programs are necessary to support the examples, exercises, and lab projects in various appendixes. The software includes an editor, an assembler, and batch files to control this software and to transmit the object code to the trainer.

Editor Program

The editor program that Appendix B discusses is the SPC/PC editor. This editor operates completely in character mode so it works with any IBM compatible personal computer including palmtop computers with enough memory. No mouse or other devices are required.

Any ASCII text editor may be used. Furthermore, a word processor that makes standard ASCII files may also be used, but editing computer programs is much easier with an editor designed for this purpose. The word processor is less costly if you already own the software.

Install your editor program according to the manufacturer's instructions. Be sure it is set up to make ASCII disk files. Then set tabs at reasonable points for the op code, operand, and comment fields. The examples in this book were made with tabs set at columns 9, 15, and 24 with the first column called column 1. These settings allow space for seven-character labels. You may want to allow more room for longer labels.

The examples in this book use all capital letters for good readability with small type. Careful use of uppercase and lowercase characters can improve the readability of actual listings. Your editor may be able to force all capitals if you prefer.

Assembler Program

Appendix C discusses the 2500AD assembler program. Other assembler programs may also be used. However, you are encouraged to investigate the quality of the error messages provided an assembler. Furthermore, investigate the compatibility with Motorola source language before acquiring an assembler. Assemblers that deviate from the Motorola format significantly make it very difficult to use Motorola manuals for reference material.

Batch Files

Batch files can control your software to make it very easy to use. The batch files suggested here are those used in Appendix C and Appendix D. They assume that all files will be kept on floppy disks. This is most convenient when a computer is used by many different people. It also provides the greatly level of security. The batch files therefore provide defaults to disk drive A and therefore reduce the amount of typing required to run the software.

Figure F-1 shows the batch file to control the 2500AD assembler. The first line is a remark that prints on the personal computer screen to indicate that the assembler is being used. The second line runs the assembler program. Most assemblers, including this one, have many options. The options chosen specify that only error messages are displayed on the screen, the object file has the same name as the source file, and a listing with a cross-reference symbol table is sent to the printer.

Figure F-2 shows a batch file to transmit the binary code to the Motorola trainer—this is called downloading. This file uses the 2500AD linker program to make an S-record file

```
rem ASSEMBLE PROGRAM
X68C11 -q A:%1.ASM -px
```

Figure F-1 XASM.BAT file to control the 2500AD assembler program.

from the object file before sending it to the trainer. It assumes that the source file is on the floppy disk in disk drive A.

The first line of the file DLOAD is a remark that displays on the personal computer screen. The software will display further messages as it runs. The second line sets the serial port on the personal computer to the correct baud rate and format for the Motorola trainer. The third line erases any previous version of the S19 file because the linker program will not overwrite an existing file. The third line runs the linker program with options to display a load map and to output in the correct Motorola file format. The fourth line transmits the S-records to the trainer using the serial port named COM1 on the personal computer.

The DLOAD batch file operates correctly even if old versions of the files exist on the floppy disk. If there is no .S19 file, ignore the FILE NOT FOUND error message the ERASE command displays on the personal computer.

F.2   SET UP MOTOROLA TRAINER

Motorola has supplied at least three versions of the 68HC11EVB trainer board with an even greater number of versions of the BUFFALO monitor program. If you use any of these versions, you should find only small discrepancies from the information in this book, which is based on the revision C board with version 2.5 software The part number on the circuit board includes the hardware revision level. The Buffalo message that follows a hardware reset includes the revision level of the program.

Several jumpers on the trainer board determine how the hardware operates. The factory settings of most of the jumpers will likely correspond to your needs. The jumper of greatest concern at the initial setup of the trainer is jumper J5. It sets the baud rate the trainer uses to communicate with a CRT terminal or the personal computer used as a CRT terminal. If the jumper doesn't match the terminal, garbage will be displayed on the screen. Since different versions of the trainer allow different baud rates, consult your manual for the correct setting.

Correctly connecting a CRT terminal or a personal computer to the trainer can be challenging. When the connection is made with an incorrect serial cable, no response is obtained from the trainer.

If an actual CRT terminal is used, connect a straight-through cable from the CRT to the terminal port called P2 on the trainer. The serial port on the CRT terminal is a DTE or data terminal equipment port. The terminal port on the trainer is configured as a DCE or data communication equipment serial port to facilitate this connection.

```
rem DOWNLOAD FILE TO MOTOROLA TRAINER
MODE COM1:9600,n,8,1
ERASE A:%1.S19
LINK -c A:%1.OBJ -1
COPY A:%1.S19 COM1:
```

Figure F-2   DLOAD.BAT file for downloading 2500AD object files to the Motorola trainer.

A personal computer used as a terminal can be connected to the terminal port on the trainer. Then the serial port on the computer must be configured as a DTE serial port if a straight-through serial cable is used. Most computers use this configuration. If your computer does not, a null-modem cable is required instead. This cable reverses the connections of two pins so the transmit and receive signals are on the proper pins.

Instead, a personal computer used both as a terminal and for downloading programs to the trainer can be connected to the host port on the trainer. The host port is configured as a DTE serial port, so a null-modem cable must be used to connect to a computer with a serial port configured as a DTE port.

If you have doubt about which is the terminal and which is the host port, do not assume that you have the correct one if you get a BUFFALO message. At reset, the trainer transmits the message to both ports!

Appendix G

The 68HC11 Op Code Maps

The op code maps or tables display the mnemonic name of the instructions at the coordinates specified by the hexadecimal digits of the numeric op code. Since there are instructions without a prebyte and others with one of three prebyte values, there are four op code maps. On a given map, you can find the mnemonic name of an instruction from its numeric op code. You must find the row corresponding to the least-significant digit and the column corresponding to the most-significant digit. A gray scale entry means there is no instruction corresponding to that number. One of the best uses for these maps is finding out which op codes are invalid—those with a gray scale entry.

G.1 OP CODE PAGES

Motorola refers to each op code map as a page of op codes. Page 1 corresponds to those instructions that do not have a prebyte—those with a single-byte op code. The other pages list those instructions with double-byte op codes. Pages 2, 3, and 4 correspond to prebyte values of 18, 1A, and CD.

Most of the columns of the maps correspond to one addressing mode. However, there are exceptions for pages 1 and 2 noted at the bottom of the tables. The mnemonics for the exceptions are shown in italics.

	INH	INH	REL	INH	ACCA	ACCB	IND,X	EXT	IMM	DIR	IND,X	EXT	IMM	DIR	IND,X	EXT	
	0	1	2	3	4	5	6	7	8	9	A	B	C	D	E	F	
0	TEST	SBA	BRA	TSX	NEG				SUB								0
1	NOP	CBA	BRN	INS					CMP								1
2	IDIV	*BRSET*	BHI	PULA					SBC								2
3	FDIV	*BRCLR*	BLS	PULB	COM				SUBD				ADDD				3
4	LSRD	*BSET*	BCC	DES	LSR				AND								4
5	ASLD	*BCLR*	BCS	TXS					BIT								5
6	TAP	TAB	BNE	PSHA	ROR				LDA								6
7	TPA	TBA	BEQ	PSHB	ASR						STA				STA		7
8	INX	PAGE2	BVC	PULX	ASL				EOR								8
9	DEX	DAA	BVS	RTS	ROL				ADC								9
A	CLV	PAGE3	BPL	ABX	DEC				ORA								A
B	SEV	ABA	BMI	RTI					ADD								B
C	CLC	*BSET*	BGE	PSHX	INC				CPX				LDD				C
D	SEC	*BCLR*	BLT	MUL	TST				BSR	JSR			PAGE4		STD		D
E	CLI	*BRSET*	BGT	WAI			JMP		LDS				LDX				E
F	SEI	*BRCLR*	BLE	SWI	CLR				XGDX		STS		STOP		STX		F
	0	1	2	3	4	5	6	7	8	9	A	B	C	D	E	F	

Codes 12 through 15 = DIR
Codes 1C through 1F = IND,X

Op Code Map Page 1 — No prebyte

	INH	IND,Y		INH			IND,Y		IMM	DIR	IND,Y	EXT	IMM	DIR	IND,Y	EXT	
	0	1	2	3	4	5	6	7	8	9	A	B	C	D	E	F	
0				TSY			NEG		SUB						SUB		0
1									CMP						CMP		1
2									SBC						SBC		2
3							COM		SUBD						ADDD		3
4							LSR		AND						AND		4
5				TYS					BIT						BIT		5
6							ROR		LDA						LDA		6
7							ASR		STA						STA		7
8	INY			PULY			ASL		EOR						EOR		8
9	DEY						ROL		ADC						ADC		9
A				ABY			DEC		ORA						ORA		A
B									ADD						ADD		B
C		*BSET*		PSHY			INC		CPY				LDD				C
D		*BCLR*					TST		JSR				STD				D
E		*BRSET*					JMP		LDS				LDY				E
F		*BRCLR*					CLR		XGDY		STS		STY				F
	0	1	2	3	4	5	6	7	8	9	A	B	C	D	E	F	

Codes 1C through 1F = IND,Y

Op Code Map Page 2 — Prebyte = 18

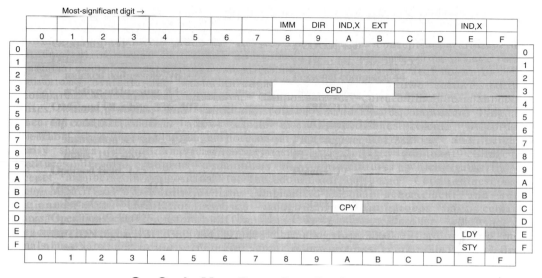

Op Code Map Page 3 — Prebyte = 1A

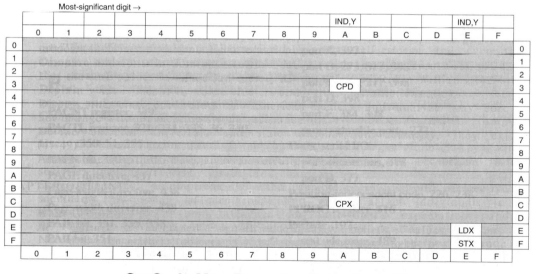

Op Code Map Page 4 — Prebyte = CD

G.2   ASSEMBLER PAGE DESIGNATION

Some assemblers print an op code page indication for instructions that are on page 2, 3, or 4 of the op code maps. The prebyte code is then printed on a separate line of the listing with the page designation printed at the op code position on the line.

Figure G-1 illustrates the assembly listing when the page designation is included. This format for the listing adds little to understanding, since the assembler generates the correct instruction code whether the page number is printed or omitted.

```
19   C100   97 24                    STAA   THERE
20   C102   18                       PG2
            CE 00 22          START   LDY    #DATA2
21   C106   DC 20                     LDD    DATA1
22   C108   CD                        PG4
            A3 00                     CPD    0,Y
23   C10B   27 0E                     BEQ    LAST
24   C10D   18                        PG2
            1D 02 80                  BCLR   OFF,Y,MASK
25   C111   18                        PG2
            1E 02 02 04               BRSET  OFF,Y,MASK1,NEXT
26   C116   18                        PG2
            1C 02 04                  BSET   OFF,Y,MASK2
27   C11A   4F                NEXT    CLRA
28   C11B   96 25             LAST    LDAA   VALUE
29   C11D   1B                        ABA
```

Figure G-1   Partial assembler listing with op code page designations.

Appendix H

The 68HC11 Instruction Set

The instruction set of a computer is the collection of all the codes that are recognized as valid instructions by the microprocessor. The 68HC11 recognizes 307_{10} op codes. Not many invalid single-byte codes are possible, because 235_{10} of the possible 256_{10} values for the first byte of the op code are valid. But a valid page switch code that forces a double-byte op code results in many possible invalid codes in the second byte. The op code maps in Appendix G illustrate the valid and invalid codes graphically.

The instruction set table lists all the valid op codes and the details of the corresponding instruction. The instruction set table is the principal aid to machine language and assembly language programmers. Almost any detail needed to code a program is contained in the instruction set table.

The instruction set table lists the instructions in alphabetical order by mnemonic name. Unfortunately, this means that you must know the name of an instruction before you can find it in the table. However, the names of most instructions strongly imply the operation performed, so a little creative guessing will help you find the desired instruction quickly.

H.1   INSTRUCTION SET TABLE

Columns of instruction set table

Source form	instruction mnemonic and any operands required
Operation	word description of the function performed
Addr. mode	microprocessor register if appropriate and memory addressing mode
Op code	one or two byte op codes in hexadecimal format
Operand	format and use of the operand bytes
Bytes	number of bytes of memory occupied by the instruction
Cycles	number (decimal) of E-clock cycles required by the Motorola 68HC11 to fetch and execute the instruction
Condition codes	operation performed on the condition code bit during instruction execution

Source form operand notation

(opr)	operand—data, data address, or offset for a memory reference instruction
(msk)	mask byte—1s in the mask select operand bits
(rel)	relative offset of program relative addressed branch instruction

Operation notation

s	instruction intended for two's complement signed numbers only
u	instruction intended for unsigned numbers only

Boolean Expression

+	add
∨	or
−	subtract
∧	and
∀	exclusive or
×	8-bit by 8-bit unsigned multiply
/	16-bit by 16-bit divide
( )	the contents of
→	make the contents of destination register the same as the contents of the source register
:	concatenate two registers
0	1-bit number zero
00	8-bit number zero
$FF	8-bit hexadecimal number FF
1	1-bit number 1
+1	add one to the contents of the register
−1	subtract one from the contents of the register

Address	address formed by the instruction
A	the 8-bit contents of accumulator A
B	the 8-bit contents of accumulator B
BCD	Binary Coded Decimal
C	the 1-bit contents of carry/borrow bit
CCR	the 8-bit contents of the Condition Code Register
D	the 16-bit contents of double accumulator D
D7	contents of bit 7 of the double accumulator D
I	the 1-bit contents of the interrupt mask bit
mm	8-bit mask byte—1s in the mask select operand bits
$\overline{mm}$	the complement of the 8-bit mask byte
M	the contents of the memory register addressed by the instruction
$\overline{M}$	the complement of the contents of the memory register
(M + 1)	the contents of the next higher memory register
PC	contents of program counter register
r	16-bit remainder from division
SP	the contents of the stack pointer register
Stk	the contents of the memory register at the top of the stack
V	the 1-bit contents of the two's complement overflow bit
X	the 16-bit contents of index register X
Y	the 16-bit contents of index register Y

Addressing mode

A	The instruction accesses the A accumulator.
B	The instruction accesses the B accumulator.
D	The instruction accesses the D accumulator.
DIR	direct addressing
EXT	extended addressing
IMM	immediate addressing
IND,X	indexed by X addressing
IND,Y	indexed by Y addressing
INH	inherent addressing
REL	program relative addressing
S	The instruction accesses the stack pointer register.
X	The instruction accesses the X index register.
Y	The instruction accesses the Y index register.

Instruction operand notation

ii	8-bit immediate data
dd	low byte of a direct address
hh ll	high and low bytes of an extended address
ff	unsigned 8-bit offset in indexed addressed instruction
jj kk	high and low bytes of 16-bit immediate data
mm	8-bit mask byte—1s in the mask select operand bits
rr	signed 8-bit relative offset in branch instruction

Cycles

3	requires three E-clock cycles for fetch and execute
?	depends on external hardware signals

Condition code bit notation

-	Bit is unaffected by this instruction.
0	Bit is always cleared to 0 by instruction.
1	Bit is always set to 1 by instruction.
↕	Bit is set or cleared depending on instruction.
↓	Bit can change from 1 to 0 but not 0 to 1, or can remain at either 1 or 0.

Motorola 68HC11 Instruction Set

Source Form	Operation	Boolean Expression	Addr. Mode	Op Code	Operand	Bytes	Cycles	S	X	H	I	N	Z	V	C
ABA	Add Accumulators	A + B → A	INH	1B		1	2	-	-	↕	-	↕	↕	↕	↕
ABX	Add B to X	X + 00:B → X	INH	3A		1	3	-	-	-	-	-	-	-	-
ABY	Add B to Y	Y + 00:B → Y	INH	18 3A		2	4	-	-	-	-	-	-	-	-
ADCA (opr)	Add with Carry to A	A + M + C → A	A IMM	89	ii	2	2	-	-	↕	-	↕	↕	↕	↕
			A DIR	99	dd	2	3								
			A EXT	B9	hh ll	3	4								
			A IND,X	A9	ff	2	4								
			A IND,Y	18 A9	ff	3	5								
ADCB (opr)	Add with Carry to B	B + M + C → B	B IMM	C9	ii	2	2	-	-	↕	-	↕	↕	↕	↕
			B DIR	D9	dd	2	3								
			B EXT	F9	hh ll	3	4								
			B IND,X	E9	ff	2	4								
			B IND,Y	18 E9	ff	3	5								
ADDA (opr)	Add Memory to A	A + M → A	A IMM	8B	ii	2	2	-	-	↕	-	↕	↕	↕	↕
			A DIR	9B	dd	2	3								
			A EXT	BB	hh ll	3	4								
			A IND,X	AB	ff	2	4								
			A IND,Y	18 AB	ff	3	5								
ADDB (opr)	Add Memory to B	B + M → B	B IMM	CB	ii	2	2	-	-	↕	-	↕	↕	↕	↕
			B DIR	DB	dd	2	3								
			B EXT	FB	hh ll	3	4								
			B IND,X	EB	ff	2	4								
			B IND,Y	18 EB	ff	3	5								
ADDD (opr)	Add Memory to D	D + M:(M+1) → D	D IMM	C3	jj kk	3	4	-	-	-	-	↕	↕	↕	↕
			D DIR	D3	dd	2	5								
			D EXT	F3	hh ll	3	6								
			D IND,X	E3	ff	2	6								
			D IND,Y	18 E3	ff	3	7								
ANDA (opr)	And Memory to A	A ∧ M → A	A IMM	84	ii	2	2	-	-	-	-	↕	↕	0	-
			A DIR	94	dd	2	3								
			A EXT	B4	hh ll	3	4								
			A IND,X	A4	ff	2	4								
			A IND,Y	18 A4	ff	3	5								
ANDB (opr)	And Memory to B	B ∧ M → B	B IMM	C4	ii	2	2	-	-	-	-	↕	↕	0	-
			B DIR	D4	dd	2	3								
			B EXT	F4	hh ll	3	4								
			B IND,X	E4	ff	2	4								
			B IND,Y	18 E4	ff	3	5								
ASL (opr)	Arithmetic Shift Left Memory		EXT	78	hh ll	3	6	-	-	-	-	↕	↕	↕	↕
			IND,X	68	ff	2	6								
			IND,Y	18 68	ff	3	7								
ASLA	Arithmetic Shift Left A		A INH	48		1	2	-	-	-	-	↕	↕	↕	↕
ASLB	Arithmetic Shift Left B		B INH	58		1	2	-	-	-	-	↕	↕	↕	↕
ASLD	Arithmetic Shift Left D		D INH	05		1	3	-	-	-	-	↕	↕	↕	↕

Motorola 68HC11 Instruction Set

Source Form	Operation	Boolean Expression	Addr. Mode	Op Code	Operand	Bytes	Cycles	S	X	H	I	N	Z	V	C
ASR (opr)	Arithmetic Shift Right Memory[S]		EXT	77	hh ll	3	6	-	-	-	-	$\updownarrow$	$\updownarrow$	$\updownarrow$	$\updownarrow$
			IND,X	67	ff	2	6								
			IND,Y	18 67	ff	3	7								
ASRA	Arithmetic Shift Right A[S]		A INH	47		1	2	-	-	-	-	$\updownarrow$	$\updownarrow$	$\updownarrow$	$\updownarrow$
ASRB	Arithmetic Shift Right B[S]		B INH	57		1	2	-	-	-	-	$\updownarrow$	$\updownarrow$	$\updownarrow$	$\updownarrow$
BCC (rel)	Branch if Carry Clear	? C = 0	REL	24	rr	2	3	-	-	-	-	-	-	-	-
BCLR (opr) (msk)	Clear Memory Bit(s)	M $\wedge$ $\overline{mm}$ → M	DIR	15	dd mm	3	6	-	-	-	-	$\updownarrow$	$\updownarrow$	0	-
			IND,X	1D	ff mm	3	7								
			IND,Y	18 1D	ff mm	4	8								
BCS (rel)	Branch if Carry Set	? C = 1	REL	25	rr	2	3	-	-	-	-	-	-	-	-
BEQ (rel)	Branch if = Zero	? Z = 1	REL	27	rr	2	3	-	-	-	-	-	-	-	-
BGE (rel)	Branch if Gr. Than or Equal[S]	? N $\veebar$ V = 0	REL	2C	rr	2	3	-	-	-	-	-	-	-	-
BGT (rel)	Branch if Greater Than[S]	? Z $\vee$ (N $\veebar$ V) = 0	REL	2E	rr	2	3	-	-	-	-	-	-	-	-
BHI (rel)	Branch if Higher[U]	? C $\vee$ Z = 0	REL	22	rr	2	3	-	-	-	-	-	-	-	-
BHS (rel)	Branch if Higher or Same[U]	? C = 0	REL	24	rr	2	3	-	-	-	-	-	-	-	-
BITA (opr)	Bit(s) Test A with Memory	A $\wedge$ M	A IMM	85	ii	2	2	-	-	-	-	$\updownarrow$	$\updownarrow$	0	-
			A DIR	95	dd	2	3								
			A EXT	B5	hh ll	3	4								
			A IND,X	A5	ff	2	4								
			A IND,Y	18 A5	ff	3	5								
BITB (opr)	Bit(s) Test B with Memory	B $\wedge$ M	B IMM	C5	ii	2	2	-	-	-	-	$\updownarrow$	$\updownarrow$	0	-
			B DIR	D5	dd	2	3								
			B EXT	F5	hh ll	3	4								
			B IND,X	E5	ff	2	4								
			B IND,Y	18 E5	ff	3	5								
BLE (rel)	Branch if Less Than or Equal[S]	? Z $\vee$ (N $\veebar$ V) = 1	REL	2F	rr	2	3	-	-	-	-	-	-	-	-
BLO (rel)	Branch if Lower[U]	? C = 1	REL	25	rr	2	3	-	-	-	-	-	-	-	-
BLS (rel)	Branch if Lower or Same[U]	? C $\vee$ Z = 1	REL	23	rr	2	3	-	-	-	-	-	-	-	-
BLT (rel)	Branch if Less Than[S]	? N $\veebar$ V = 1	REL	2D	rr	2	3	-	-	-	-	-	-	-	-
BMI (rel)	Branch if Minus[S]	? N = 1	REL	2B	rr	2	3	-	-	-	-	-	-	-	-
BNE (rel)	Branch if Not = Zero	? Z = 0	REL	26	rr	2	3	-	-	-	-	-	-	-	-
BPL (rel)	Branch if Plus[S]	? N = 0	REL	2A	rr	2	3	-	-	-	-	-	-	-	-
BRA (rel)	Branch Always	? 1 = 1	REL	20	rr	2	3								
BRCLR(opr) (msk) (rel)	Branch if Memory Bit(s) Clear	? M $\wedge$ mm = 00	DIR	13	dd mm rr	4	6	-	-	-	-	-	-	-	-
			IND,X	1F	ff mm rr	4	7								
			IND,Y	18 1F	ff mm rr	5	8								
BRN (rel)	Branch Never	? 1 = 0	REL	21	rr	2	3	-	-	-	-	-	-	-	-
BRSET(opr) (msk) (rel)	Branch if Memory Bit(s) Set	? $\overline{M}$ $\wedge$ mm = 00	DIR	12	dd mm rr	4	6	-	-	-	-	-	-	-	-
			IND,X	1E	ff mm rr	4	7								
			IND,Y	18 1E	ff mm rr	5	8								
BSET (opr) (msk)	Set Memory Bit(s)	M $\vee$ mm → M	DIR	14	dd mm	3	6	-	-	-	-	$\updownarrow$	$\updownarrow$	0	-
			IND,X	1C	ff mm	3	7								
			IND,Y	18 1C	ff mm	4	8								
BSR (rel)	Branch to Subroutine	See Text	REL	8D	rr	2	6	-	-	-	-	-	-	-	-

Motorola 68HC11 Instruction Set

Source Form	Operation	Boolean Expression	Addr. Mode	Machine Code Op Code	Operand	Bytes	Cycles	S	X	H	I	N	Z	V	C
BVC (rel)	Branch if Overflow Clear	? V = 0	REL	28	rr	2	3	-	-	-	-	-	-	-	-
BVS (rel)	Branch if Overflow Set	? V = 1	REL	29	rr	2	3	-	-	-	-	-	-	-	-
CBA	Compare A to B	A – B	INH	11		1	2	-	-	-	-	$\updownarrow$	$\updownarrow$	$\updownarrow$	$\updownarrow$
CLC	Clear Carry Bit	0 → C	INH	0C		1	2	-	-	-	-	-	-	-	0
CLI	Clear Interrupt Mask	0 → I	INH	0E		1	2	-	-	-	0	-	-	-	-
CLR (opr)	Clear Memory Byte	00 → M	EXT	7F	hh ll	3	6	-	-	-	-	0	1	0	0
			IND,X	6F	ff	2	6								
			IND,Y	18 6F	ff	3	7								
CLRA	Clear Accumulator A	00 → A	A INH	4F		1	2	-	-	-	-	0	1	0	0
CLRB	Clear Accumulator B	00 → B	B INH	5F		1	2	-	-	-	-	0	1	0	0
CLV	Clear Overflow Flag	0 → V	INH	0A		1	2	-	-	-	-	-	-	0	-
CMPA (opr)	Compare A to Memory	A – M	A IMM	81	ii	2	2	-	-	-	-	$\updownarrow$	$\updownarrow$	$\updownarrow$	$\updownarrow$
			A DIR	91	dd	2	3								
			A EXT	B1	hh ll	3	4								
			A IND,X	A1	ff	2	4								
			A IND,Y	18 A1	ff	3	5								
CMPB (opr)	Compare B to Memory	B – M	B IMM	C1	ii	2	2	-	-	-	-	$\updownarrow$	$\updownarrow$	$\updownarrow$	$\updownarrow$
			B DIR	D1	dd	2	3								
			B EXT	F1	hh ll	3	4								
			B IND,X	E1	ff	2	4								
			B IND,Y	18 E1	ff	3	5								
COM (opr)	Complement Memory Byte	$FF – M → M	EXT	73	hh ll	3	6	-	-	-	-	$\updownarrow$	$\updownarrow$	0	1
			IND,X	63	ff	2	6								
			IND,Y	18 63	ff	3	7								
COMA	Complement A	$FF – A → A	A INH	43		1	2	-	-	-	-	$\updownarrow$	$\updownarrow$	0	1
COMB	Complement B	$FF – B → B	B INH	53		1	2	-	-	-	-	$\updownarrow$	$\updownarrow$	0	1
CPD (opr)	Compare D to Memory	D – M:(M + 1)	D IMM	1A 83	jj kk	4	5	-	-	-	-	$\updownarrow$	$\updownarrow$	$\updownarrow$	$\updownarrow$
			D DIR	1A 93	dd	3	6								
			D EXT	1A B3	hh ll	4	7								
			D IND,X	1A A3	ff	3	7								
			D IND,Y	CD A3	ff	3	7								
CPX (opr)	Compare X to Memory	X – M:(M + 1)	X IMM	8C	jj kk	3	4	-	-	-	-	$\updownarrow$	$\updownarrow$	$\updownarrow$	$\updownarrow$
			X DIR	9C	dd	2	5								
			X EXT	BC	hh ll	3	6								
			X IND,X	AC	ff	2	6								
			X IND,Y	CD AC	ff	3	7								
CPY (opr)	Compare Y to Memory	Y – M:(M + 1)	Y IMM	18 8C	jj kk	4	5	-	-	-	-	$\updownarrow$	$\updownarrow$	$\updownarrow$	$\updownarrow$
			Y DIR	18 9C	dd	3	6								
			Y EXT	18 BC	hh ll	4	7								
			Y IND,X	1A AC	ff	3	7								
			Y IND,Y	18 AC	ff	3	7								
DAA	Decimal Adjust A	Adjust Sum to BCD	A INH	19		1	2	-	-	-	-	$\updownarrow$	$\updownarrow$	$\updownarrow$	$\updownarrow$
DEC (opr)	Decrement Memory Byte	M – 1 → M	EXT	7A	hh ll	3	6	-	-	-	-	$\updownarrow$	$\updownarrow$	$\updownarrow$	-
			IND,X	6A	ff	2	6								
			IND,Y	18 6A	ff	3	7								

Motorola 68HC11 Instruction Set

Source Form	Operation	Boolean Expression	Addr. Mode	Op Code	Operand	Bytes	Cycles	S	X	H	I	N	Z	V	C
DECA	Decrement Accumulator A	A − 1 → A	A INH	4A		1	2	-	-	-	-	↕	↕	↕	-
DECB	Decrement Accumulator B	B − 1 → B	B INH	5A		1	2	-	-	-	-	↕	↕	↕	-
DES	Decrement Stack Pointer	SP − 1 → SP	S INH	34		1	3	-	-	-	-	-	-	-	-
DEX	Decrement Index Register X	X − 1 → X	X INH	09		1	3	-	-	-	-	-	↕	-	-
DEY	Decrement Index Register Y	Y − 1 → Y	Y INH	18 09		2	4	-	-	-	-	-	↕	-	-
EORA (opr)	Exclusive OR A with Memory	A ⊻ M → A	A IMM	88	ii	2	2	-	-	-	-	↕	↕	0	-
			A DIR	98	dd	2	3								
			A EXT	B8	hh ll	3	4								
			A IND,X	A8	ff	2	4								
			A IND,Y	18 A8	ff	3	5								
EORB (opr)	Exclusive OR B with Memory	B ⊻ M → B	B IMM	C8	ii	2	2	-	-	-	-	↕	↕	0	-
			B DIR	D8	dd	2	3								
			B EXT	F8	hh ll	3	4								
			B IND,X	E8	ff	2	4								
			B IND,Y	18 E8	ff	3	5								
FDIV	Fractional Divide 16 by 16[U]	D/X → X; r → D*	INH	03		1	41	-	-	-	-	-	↕	↕	↕
IDIV	Integer Divide 16 by 16[U]	D/X → X; r → D*	INH	02		1	41	-	-	-	-	-	↕	0	↕
INC (opr)	Increment Memory Byte	M + 1 → M	EXT	7C	hh ll	3	6	-	-	-	-	↕	↕	↕	-
			IND,X	6C	ff	2	6								
			IND,Y	18 6C	ff	3	7								
INCA	Increment Accumulator A	A + 1 → A	A INH	4C		1	2	-	-	-	-	↕	↕	↕	-
INCB	Increment Accumulator B	B + 1 → B	B INH	5C		1	2	-	-	-	-	↕	↕	↕	-
INS	Increment Stack Pointer	SP + 1 → SP	S INH	31		1	3	-	-	-	-	-	-	-	-
INX	Increment Index Register X	X + 1 → X	X INH	08		1	3	-	-	-	-	-	↕	-	-
INY	Increment Index Register Y	Y + 1 → Y	Y INH	18 08		2	4	-	-	-	-	-	↕	-	-
JMP (opr)	Jump	Address → PC	EXT	7E	hh ll	3	3	-	-	-	-	-	-	-	-
			IND,X	6E	ff	2	3								
			IND,Y	18 6E	ff	3	4								
JSR (opr)	Jump to Subroutine	See Text	DIR	9D	dd	2	5	-	-	-	-	-	-	-	-
			EXT	BD	hh ll	3	6								
			IND,X	AD	ff	2	6								
			IND,Y	18 AD	ff	3	7								
LDAA (opr)	Load Accumulator A	M → A	A IMM	86	ii	2	2	-	-	-	-	↕	↕	0	-
			A DIR	96	dd	2	3								
			A EXT	B6	hh ll	3	4								
			A IND,X	A6	ff	2	4								
			A IND,Y	18 A6	ff	3	5								
LDAB (opr)	Load Accumulator B	M → B	B IMM	C6	ii	2	2	-	-	-	-	↕	↕	0	-
			B DIR	D6	dd	2	3								
			B EXT	F6	hh ll	3	4								
			B IND,X	E6	ff	2	4								
			B IND,Y	18 E6	ff	3	5								

* FDIV and IDIV: Z is set if quotient is zero; C is set if denominator is zero

FDIV: V is set if denominator is lower or same as numerator

Motorola 68HC11 Instruction Set

Source Form	Operation	Boolean Expression	Addr. Mode	Op Code	Operand	Bytes	Cycles	S	X	H	I	N	Z	V	C
LDD (opr)	Load Accumulator D	M:(M + 1) → D	D IMM	CC	jj kk	3	3	-	-	-	-	↕	↕	0	-
			D DIR	DC	dd	2	4								
			D EXT	FC	hh ll	3	5								
			D IND,X	EC	ff	2	5								
			D IND,Y	18 EC	ff	3	6								
LDS (opr)	Load Stack Pointer	M:(M + 1) → SP	S IMM	8E	jj kk	3	3	-	-	-	-	↕	↕	0	-
			S DIR	9E	dd	2	4								
			S EXT	BE	hh ll	3	5								
			S IND,X	AE	ff	2	5								
			S IND,Y	18 AE	ff	3	6								
LDX (opr)	Load Index Register X	M:(M + 1) → X	X IMM	CE	jj kk	3	3	-	-	-	-	↕	↕	0	-
			X DIR	DE	dd	2	4								
			X EXT	FE	hh ll	3	5								
			X IND,X	EE	ff	2	5								
			X IND,Y	CD EE	ff	3	6								
LDY (opr)	Load Index Register Y	M:(M + 1) → Y	Y IMM	18 CE	jj kk	4	4	-	-	-	-	↕	↕	0	-
			Y DIR	18 DE	dd	3	5								
			Y EXT	18 FE	hh ll	4	6								
			Y IND,X	1A EE	ff	3	6								
			Y IND,Y	18 EE	ff	3	6								
LSL (opr)	Logical Shift Left Memory Byte	c ← [□□□□□□□□] ← 0	EXT	78	hh ll	3	6	-	-	▪	▪	↑	↑	↑	↑
			IND,X	68	ff	2	6								
			IND,Y	18 68	ff	3	7								
LSLA	Logical Shift Left A		A INH	48		1	2	-	-	-	-	↕	↕	↕	↕
LSLB	Logical Shift Left B		B INH	58		1	2	-	-	-	-	↕	↕	↕	↕
LSLD	Logical Shift Left D	c ← [□□□□ - □□□□] ← 0	D INH	05		1	3	-	-	-	-	↕	↕	↕	↕
LSR (opr)	Logical Shift Right Memory Byte	0 → [□□□□□□□□] → c	EXT	74	hh ll	3	6	-	-	-	-	0	↕	↕	↕
			IND,X	64	ff	2	6								
			IND,Y	18 64	ff	3	7								
LSRA	Logical Shift Right A		A INH	44		1	2	-	-	-	-	↕	↕	↕	↕
LSRB	Logical Shift Right B		B INH	54		1	2	-	-	-	-	↕	↕	↕	↕
LSRD	Logical Shift Right D	0 → [□□□□ - □□□□] → c	D INH	04		1	3	-	-	-	-	0	↕	↕	↕
MUL	Multiply A by B[U]	A × B → D, D7 → C	INH	3D		1	10	-	-	-	-	-	-	-	↕
NEG (opr)	Negate Memory Byte[S]	00 − M → M	EXT	70	hh ll	3	6	-	-	-	-	↕	↕	↕	↕
			IND,X	60	ff	2	6								
			IND,Y	18 60	ff	3	7								
NEGA	Negate Accumulator A[S]	00 − A → A	A INH	40		1	2	-	-	-	-	↕	↕	↕	↕
NEGB	Negate Accumulator B[S]	00 − B → B	B INH	50		1	2	-	-	-	-	↕	↕	↕	↕
NOP	No Operation		INH	01		1	2	-	-	-	-	-	-	-	-

Motorola 68HC11 Instruction Set

Source Form	Operation	Boolean Expression	Addr. Mode	Op Code	Operand	Bytes	Cycles	S	X	H	I	N	Z	V	C
ORAA (opr)	OR A with Memory	A ∨ M → A	A IMM	8A	ii	2	2	-	-	-	-	↕	↕	0	-
			A DIR	9A	dd	2	3								
			A EXT	BA	hh ll	3	4								
			A IND,X	AA	ff	2	4								
			A IND,Y	18 AA	ff	3	5								
ORAB (opr)	OR B with Memory	B ∨ M → B	B IMM	CA	ii	2	2	-	-	-	-	↕	↕	0	-
			B DIR	DA	dd	2	3								
			B EXT	FA	hh ll	3	4								
			B IND,X	EA	ff	2	4								
			B IND,Y	18 EA	ff	3	5								
PSHA	Push A onto Stack	A→Stk,SP-1→SP	A INH	36		1	3	-	-	-	-	-	-	-	-
PSHB	Push B onto Stack	B→Stk,SP-1→SP	B INH	37		1	3	-	-	-	-	-	-	-	-
PSHX	Push X onto Stack	X→Stk,SP-2→SP	X INH	3C		1	4	-	-	-	-	-	-	-	-
PSHY	Push Y onto Stack	Y→Stk,SP-2→SP	Y INH	18 3C		2	5	-	-	-	-	-	-	-	-
PULA	Pull A from Stack	SP+1→SP,Stk→A	A INH	32		1	4	-	-	-	-	-	-	-	-
PULB	Pull B from Stack	SP+1→SP,Stk→B	B INH	33		1	4	-	-	-	-	-	-	-	-
PULX	Pull X from Stack	SP+2→SP,Stk→X	X INH	38		1	5	-	-	-	-	-	-	-	-
PULY	Pull Y from Stack	SP+2→SP,Stk→Y	Y INH	18 38		2	6	-	-	-	-	-	-	-	-
ROL (opr)	Rotate Left Memory Byte		EXT	79	hh ll	3	6	-	-	-	-	↕	↕	↕	↕
			IND,X	69	ff	2	6								
			IND,Y	18 69	ff	3	7								
ROLA	Rotate Left A		A INH	49		1	2	-	-	-	-	↕	↕	↕	↕
ROLB	Rotate Left B		B INH	59		1	2	-	-	-	-	↕	↕	↕	↕
ROR (opr)	Rotate Right Memory Byte		EXT	76	hh ll	3	6	-	-	-	-	↕	↕	↕	↕
			IND,X	66	ff	2	6								
			IND,Y	18 66	ff	3	7								
RORA	Rotate Right A		A INH	46		1	2	-	-	-	-	↕	↕	↕	↕
RORB	Rotate Right B		B INH	56		1	2	-	-	-	-	↕	↕	↕	↕
RTI	Return from Interrupt	See Text	INH	38		1	12	↕	↓	↕	↕	↕	↕	↕	↕
RTS	Return from Subroutine	See Text	INH	39		1	5	-	-	-	-	-	-	-	-
SBA	Subtract B from A	A – B → A	INH	10		1	2	-	-	-	-	↕	↕	↕	↕
SBCA (opr)	Subtract with Carry from A	A – M – C → A	A IMM	82	ii	2	2	-	-	-	-	↕	↕	↕	↕
			A DIR	92	dd	2	3								
			A EXT	B2	hh ll	3	4								
			A IND,X	A2	ff	2	4								
			A IND,Y	18 A2	ff	3	5								
SBCB (opr)	Subtract with Carry from B	B – M – C → B	B IMM	C2	ii	2	2	-	-	-	-	↕	↕	↕	↕
			B DIR	D2	dd	2	3								
			B EXT	F2	hh ll	3	4								
			B IND,X	E2	ff	2	4								
			B IND,Y	18 E2	ff	3	5								
SEC	Set Carry	1 → C	INH	0D		1	2	-	-	-	-	-	-	-	1
SEI	Set Interrupt Mask	1 → I	INH	0F		1	2	-	-	-	1	-	-	-	-
SEV	Set Overflow Flag	1 → V	INH	0B		1	2	-	-	-	-	-	-	1	-

Motorola 68HC11 Instruction Set

Source Form	Operation	Boolean Expression	Addr. Mode	Op Code	Operand	Bytes	Cycles	S	X	H	I	N	Z	V	C
STAA (opr)	Store Accumulator A	A → M	A DIR	97	dd	2	3	-	-	-	-	↕	↕	0	-
			A EXT	B7	hh ll	3	4								
			A IND,X	A7	ff	2	4								
			A IND,Y	18 A7	ff	3	5								
STAB (opr)	Store Accumulator B	B → M	B DIR	D7	dd	2	3	-	-	-	-	↕	↕	0	-
			B EXT	F7	hh ll	3	4								
			B IND,X	E7	ff	2	4								
			B IND,Y	18 E7	ff	3	5								
STD (opr)	Store Accumulator D	D → M:(M + 1)	D DIR	DD	dd	2	4	-	-	-	-	↕	↕	0	-
			D EXT	FD	hh ll	3	5								
			D IND,X	ED	ff	2	5								
			D IND,Y	18 ED	ff	3	6								
STOP	Stop Internal Clocks		INH	CF		1	2	-	-	-	-	-	-	-	-
STS (opr)	Store Stack Pointer	SP → M:(M + 1)	S DIR	9F	dd	2	4	-	-	-	-	↕	↕	0	-
			S EXT	BF	hh ll	3	5								
			S IND,X	AF	ff	2	5								
			S IND,Y	18 AF	ff	3	6								
STX (opr)	Store Index Register X	X → M:(M + 1)	X DIR	DF	dd	2	4	-	-	-	-	↕	↕	0	-
			X EXT	FF	hh ll	3	5								
			X IND,X	EF	ff	2	5								
			X IND,Y	CD EF	ff	3	6								
STY (opr)	Store Index Register Y	Y → M:(M + 1)	Y DIR	18 DF	dd	3	5	-	-	-	-	↕	↕	0	-
			Y EXT	18 FF	hh ll	4	6								
			Y IND,X	1A EF	ff	3	6								
			Y IND,Y	18 EF	ff	3	6								
SUBA (opr)	Subtract Memory from A	A − M → A	A IMM	80	ii	2	2	-	-	-	-	↕	↕	↕	↕
			A DIR	90	dd	2	3								
			A EXT	B0	hh ll	3	4								
			A IND,X	A0	ff	2	4								
			A IND,Y	18 A0	ff	3	5								
SUBB (opr)	Subtract Memory from B	B − M → B	B IMM	C0	ii	2	2	-	-	-	-	↕	↕	↕	↕
			B DIR	D0	dd	2	3								
			B EXT	F0	hh ll	3	4								
			B IND,X	E0	ff	2	4								
			B IND,Y	18 E0	ff	3	5								
SUBD (opr)	Subtract Memory from D	D − M:(M+1) → D	D IMM	83	jj kk	3	4	-	-	-	-	↕	↕	↕	↕
			D DIR	93	dd	2	5								
			D EXT	B3	hh ll	3	6								
			D IND,X	A3	ff	2	6								
			D IND,Y	18 A3	ff	3	7								
SWI	Software Interrupt	See Text	INH	3F		1	14	-	-	-	1	-	-	-	-
TAB	Transfer A to B	A → B	INH	16		1	2	-	-	-	-	↕	↕	0	-
TAP	Transfer A to Condition Codes	A → CCR	INH	06		1	2	↕	↓	↕	↕	↕	↕	↕	↕
TBA	Transfer B to A	B → A	INH	17		1	2	-	-	-	-	↕	↕	0	-
TEST	Test (Only in Test Modes)	Addr. Bus Counts	INH	00		1	?	-	-	-	-	-	-	-	-

Motorola 68HC11 Instruction Set

Source Form	Operation	Boolean Expression	Addr. Mode	Machine Code Op Code	Machine Code Operand	Bytes	Cycles	S	X	H	I	N	Z	V	C
TPA	Transfer Condition Codes to A	CCR → A	INH	07		1	2	-	-	-	-	-	-	-	-
TST (opr)	Test Memory Byte	M − 00	EXT	7D	hh ll	3	6	-	-	-	-	$\updownarrow$	$\updownarrow$	0	0
			IND,X	6D	ff	2	6								
			IND,Y	18 6D	ff	3	7								
TSTA	Test Accumulator A	A − 00	A INH	4D		1	2	-	-	-	-	$\updownarrow$	$\updownarrow$	0	0
TSTB	Test Accumulator B	B − 00	B INH	5D		1	2	-	-	-	-	$\updownarrow$	$\updownarrow$	0	0
TSX	Transfer Stack Pointer to X	SP + 1 → X	INH	30		1	3	-	-	-	-	-	-	-	-
TSY	Transfer Stack Pointer to Y	SP + 1 → Y	INH	18 30		2	4	-	-	-	-	-	-	-	-
TXS	Transfer X to Stack Pointer	X − 1 → SP	INH	35		1	3	-	-	-	-	-	-	-	-
TYS	Transfer Y to Stack Pointer	Y − 1 → SP	INH	18 35		2	4	-	-	-	-	-	-	-	-
WAI	Wait for Interrupt	Stack Regs, Wait	INH	3E		1	?	-	-	-	-	-	-	-	-
XGDX	Exchange D with X	X → D, D → X	INH	8F		1	3	-	-	-	-	-	-	-	-
XGDY	Exchange D with Y	Y → D, D → Y	INH	18 8F		2	4	-	-	-	-	-	-	-	-

H.2   PROGRAMMING MODEL

The programming model is a graphic illustration of the registers in the microprocessor. It shows the sizes of the registers, the symbolic register names, and the register word names. The instruction set table contains many references to these registers.

68HC11 Programming Model

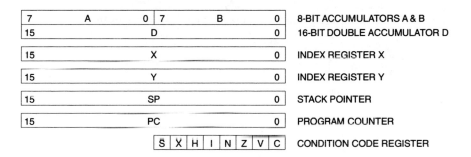

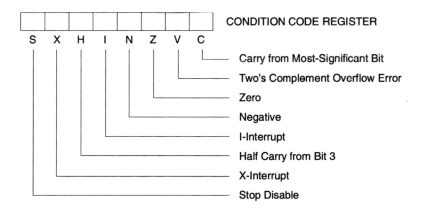

H.3 MOTOROLA INSTRUCTION SETS

The 68HC11 evolved from several other Motorola products. It is compatible with those earlier products in that the same binary instruction codes will work in the 68HC11. The 68HC11 has many more instructions and an additional addressing mode as compared to the earlier products. The following lists provide a practical comparison to those products.

6800, 6802, 6808

The instruction set table for the 68HC11 can be used for these microprocessors if the following changes are made:

- Remove any instruction that in any way involves the Y index register.

- Remove any instruction that in any way involves the D accumulator.

- Remove any prebyte or instruction that has a 2-byte op code.

- Remove any instruction that contains a mask.

- Remove the following instructions: ABX, BHS, BLO, BRN, IDIV, FDIV, LSL, MUL, PSHX, PULX, STOP, TEST, XGDX.

- Remove direct addressing from the JSR instruction.

- Change the N and V bits for the CPX instruction to affected by the subtraction of only the most-significant bytes.

- The number of cycles is greater for a few instructions.

6801, 68701, 6803

The instruction set table for the 68HC11 can be used for these single-chip microcomputers if the following changes are made:

- Remove any instruction that in any way involves the Y index register.

- Remove any prebyte or instruction that has a 2-byte op code.

- Remove any instruction that contains a mask.

- Remove the following instructions: BRN, CPD, IDIV, FDIV, STOP, TEST, XGDX.

Appendix I

68HC11 Reverse Instruction Set

The reverse instruction set lists the instructions in the numerical order of the instruction op codes. The usual instruction set is in alphabetical order by instruction mnemonic or instruction description.

The reverse instruction set is valuable for analyzing a program. For example, if you entered erroneous codes into memory and ran them as a program, strange things may have happened. To determine what did happen, trace the program by determining what each number did when it was used as an instruction. You can find each code in the reverse instruction set table. Of course, if the sequence is too long to trace, this is not very helpful.

Some numbers are not in the table, because they are not valid instruction codes. If the microprocessor tries to execute an illegal code, an illegal instruction interrupt occurs. The response to the interrupt depends on the software in the computer.

I.1 INSTRUCTION SET TABLE

Columns of instruction set table

Op code	the 1-byte op codes followed by the 2-byte op codes in hexadecimal format
Operands	those bytes of the instruction code beyond the op code
Mnemonic	symbolic instruction op code
Addr. Mode	memory addressing mode

Instruction operand notation

ii	8-bit immediate data
dd	low byte of a direct address
hh ll	high and low bytes of an extended address
ff	unsigned 8-bit offset in indexed addressed instruction
jj kk	high and low bytes of 16-bit immediate data
mm	8-bit mask byte—1s in the mask select operand bits
rr	signed 8-bit relative offset in branch instruction

Reverse Instruction Set Table

Op Code	Operands	Mnemonic	Addr. Mode	Op Code	Operands	Mnemonic	Addr. Mode
00		TEST	INH	10		SBA	INH
01		NOP	INH	11		CBA	INH
02		IDIV	INH	12	dd mm rr	BRSET	DIR
03		FDIV	INH	13	dd mm rr	BRCLR	DIR
04		LSRD	INH	14	dd mm	BSET	DIR
05		ASLD/LSLD	INH	15	dd mm	BCLR	DIR
06		TAP	INH	16		TAB	INH
07		TPA	INH	17		TBA	INH
08		INX	INH	18		Page 2 Switch	
09		DEX	INH	19		DAA	INH
0A		CLV	INH	1A		Page 3 Switch	
0B		SEV	INH	1B		ABA	INH
0C		CLC	INH	1C	ff mm	BSET	IND,X
0D		SEC	INH	1D	ff mm	BCLR	IND,X
0E		CLI	INH	1E	ff mm rr	BRSET	IND,X
0F		SEI	INH	1F	ff mm rr	BRCLR	IND,X

Reverse Instruction Set Table

Op Code	Operands	Mnemonic	Addr. Mode	Op Code	Operands	Mnemonic	Addr. Mode
20	rr	BRA	REL	47		ASRA	INH
21	rr	BRN	REL	48		ASLA/LSLA	INH
22	rr	BHI	REL	49		ROLA	INH
23	rr	BLS	REL	4A		DECA	INH
24	rr	BCC/BHS	REL	4C		INCA	INH
25	rr	BCS/BLO	REL	4D		TSTA	INH
26	rr	BNE	REL	4F		CLRA	INH
27	rr	BEQ	REL	50		NEGB	INH
28	rr	BVC	REL	53		COMB	INH
29	rr	BVS	REL	54		LSRB	INH
2A	rr	BPL	REL	56		RORB	INH
2B	rr	BMI	REL	57		ASRB	INH
2C	rr	BGE	REL	58		ASLB/LSLB	INH
2D	rr	BLT	REL	59		ROLB	INH
2E	rr	BGT	REL	5A		DECB	INH
2F	rr	BLE	REL	5C		INCB	INH
30		TSX	INH	5D		TSTB	INH
31		INS	INH	5F		CLRB	INH
32		PULA	INH	60	ff	NEG	IND,X
33		PULB	INH	63	ff	COM	IND,X
34		DES	INH	64	ff	LSR	IND,X
35		TXS	INH	66	ff	ROR	IND,X
36		PSHA	INH	67	ff	ASR	IND,X
37		PSHB	INH	68	ff	ASL/LSL	IND,X
38		PULX	INH	69	ff	ROL	IND,X
39		RTS	INH	6A	ff	DEC	IND,X
3A		ABX	INH	6C	ff	INC	IND,X
3B		RTI	INH	6D	ff	TST	IND,X
3C		PSHX	INH	6E	ff	JMP	IND,X
3D		MUL	INH	6F	ff	CLR	IND,X
3E		WAI	INH	70	hh ll	NEG	EXT
3F		SWI	INH	73	hh ll	COM	EXT
40		NEGA	INH	74	hh ll	LSR	EXT
43		COMA	INH	76	hh ll	ROR	EXT
44		LSRA	INH	77	hh ll	ASR	EXT
46		RORA	INH	78	hh ll	ASL/LSL	EXT

Reverse Instruction Set Table

Op Code	Operands	Mnemonic	Addr. Mode
79	hh ll	ROL	EXT
7A	hh ll	DEC	EXT
7C	hh ll	INC	EXT
7D	hh ll	TST	EXT
7E	hh ll	JMP	EXT
7F	hh ll	CLR	EXT
80	ii	SUBA	IMM
81	ii	CMPA	IMM
82	ii	SBCA	IMM
83	jj kk	SUBD	IMM
84	ii	ANDA	IMM
85	ii	BITA	IMM
86	ii	LDAA	IMM
88	ii	EORA	IMM
89	ii	ADCA	IMM
8A	ii	ORAA	IMM
8B	ii	ADDA	IMM
8C	jj kk	CPX	IMM
8D	rr	BSR	REL
8E	jj kk	LDS	IMM
8F		XGDX	INH
90	dd	SUBA	DIR
91	dd	CMPA	DIR
92	dd	SBCA	DIR
93	dd	SUBD	DIR
94	dd	ANDA	DIR
95	dd	BITA	DIR
96	dd	LDAA	DIR
97	dd	STAA	DIR
98	dd	EORA	DIR
99	dd	ADCA	DIR
9A	dd	ORAA	DIR
9B	dd	ADDA	DIR
9C	dd	CPX	DIR
9D	dd	JSR	DIR
9E	dd	LDS	DIR

Op Code	Operands	Mnemonic	Addr. Mode
9F	dd	STS	DIR
A0	ff	SUBA	IND,X
A1	ff	CMPA	IND,X
A2	ff	SBCA	IND,X
A3	ff	SUBD	IND,X
A4	ff	ANDA	IND,X
A5	ff	BITA	IND,X
A6	ff	LDAA	IND,X
A7	ff	STAA	IND,X
A8	ff	EORA	IND,X
A9	ff	ADCA	IND,X
AA	ff	ORAA	IND,X
AB	ff	ADDA	IND,X
AC	ff	CPX	IND,X
AD	ff	JSR	IND,X
AE	ff	LDS	IND,X
AF	ff	STS	IND,X
B0	hh ll	SUBA	EXT
B1	hh ll	CMPA	EXT
B2	hh ll	SBCA	EXT
B3	hh ll	SUBD	EXT
B4	hh ll	ANDA	EXT
B5	hh ll	BITA	EXT
B6	hh ll	LDAA	EXT
B7	hh ll	STAA	EXT
B8	hh ll	EORA	EXT
B9	hh ll	ADCA	EXT
BA	hh ll	ORAA	EXT
BB	hh ll	ADDA	EXT
BC	hh ll	CPX	EXT
BD	hh ll	JSR	EXT
BE	hh ll	LDS	EXT
BF	hh ll	STS	EXT
C0	ii	SUBB	IMM
C1	ii	CMPB	IMM
C2	ii	SBCB	IMM

Reverse Instruction Set Table

Op Code	Operands	Mnemonic	Addr. Mode
C3	jj kk	ADDD	IMM
C4	ii	ANDB	IMM
C5	ii	BITB	IMM
C6	ii	LDAB	IMM
C8	ii	EORB	IMM
C0	ii	ADCD	IMM
CA	ii	ORAB	IMM
CB	ii	ADDB	IMM
CC	jj kk	LDD	IMM
CD		Page 4 Switch	
CE	jj kk	LDX	IMM
CF		STOP	INH
D0	dd	SUBB	DIR
D1	dd	CMPB	DIR
D2	dd	SBCB	DIR
D3	dd	ADDD	DIR
D4	dd	ANDB	DIR
D5	dd	BITB	DIR
D6	dd	LDAB	DIR
D7	dd	STAB	DIR
D8	dd	EORB	DIR
D9	dd	ADCB	DIR
DA	dd	ORAB	DIR
DB	dd	ADDB	DIR
DC	dd	LDD	DIR
DD	dd	STD	DIR
DE	dd	LDX	DIR
DF	dd	STX	DIR
E0	ff	SUBB	IND,X
E1	ff	CMPB	IND,X
E2	ff	SBCB	IND,X
E3	ff	ADDD	IND,X
E4	ff	ANDB	IND,X
E5	ff	BITB	IND,X
E6	ff	LDAB	IND,X
E7	ff	STAB	IND,X

Op Code	Operands	Mnemonic	Addr. Mode
E8	ff	EORB	IND,X
E9	ff	ADCB	IND,X
EA	ff	ORAB	IND,X
EB	ff	ADDB	IND,X
EC	ff	LDD	IND,X
ED	ff	STD	IND,X
EE	ff	LDX	IND,X
EF	ff	STX	IND,X
F0	hh ll	SUBB	EXT
F1	hh ll	CMPB	EXT
F2	hh ll	SBCB	EXT
F3	hh ll	ADDD	EXT
F4	hh ll	ANDB	EXT
F5	hh ll	BITB	EXT
F6	hh ll	LDAB	EXT
F7	hh ll	STAB	EXT
F8	hh ll	EORB	EXT
F9	hh ll	ADCB	EXT
FA	hh ll	ORAB	EXT
FB	hh ll	ADDB	EXT
FC	hh ll	LDD	EXT
FD	hh ll	STD	EXT
FE	hh ll	LDX	EXT
FF	hh ll	STX	EXT
18 08		INY	INH
18 09		DEY	INH
18 1C	ff mm	BSET	IND,Y
18 1D	ff mm	BCLR	IND,Y
18 1E	ff mm rr	BRSET	IND,Y
18 1F	ff mm rr	BRCLR	IND,Y
18 30		TSY	INH
18 35		TYS	INH
18 38		PULY	INH
18 3A		ABY	INH
18 3C		PSHY	INH
18 60	ff	NEG	IND,Y

Reverse Instruction Set Table

Op Code	Operands	Mnemonic	Addr. Mode
18 63	ff	COM	IND,Y
18 64	ff	LSR	IND,Y
18 66	ff	ROR	IND,Y
18 67	ff	ASR	IND,Y
18 68	ff	ASL/LSL	IND,Y
18 69	ff	ROL	IND,Y
18 6A	ff	DEC	IND,Y
18 6C	ff	INC	IND,Y
18 6D	ff	TST	IND,Y
18 6E	ff	JMP	IND,Y
18 6F	ff	CLR	IND,Y
18 8C	jj kk	CPY	IMM
18 8F		XGDY	INH
18 9C	dd	CPY	DIR
18 A0	ff	SUBA	IND,Y
18 A1	ff	CMPA	IND,Y
18 A2	ff	SBCA	IND,Y
18 A3	ff	SUBD	IND,Y
18 A4	ff	ANDA	IND,Y
18 A5	ff	BITA	IND,Y
18 A6	ff	LDAA	IND,Y
18 A7	ff	STAA	IND,Y
18 A8	ff	EORA	IND,Y
18 A9	ff	ADCA	IND,Y
18 AA	ff	ORAA	IND,Y
18 AB	ff	ADDA	IND,Y
18 AC	ff	CPY	IND,Y
18 AD	ff	JSR	IND,Y
18 AE	ff	LDS	IND,Y
18 AF	ff	STS	IND,Y
18 BC	hh ll	CPY	EXT
18 CE	jj kk	LDY	IMM

Op Code	Operands	Mnemonic	Addr. Mode
18 DE	dd	LDY	DIR
18 DF	dd	STY	DIR
18 E0	ff	SUBB	IND,Y
18 E1	ff	CMPB	IND,Y
18 E2	ff	SBCB	IND,Y
18 E3	ff	ADDD	IND,Y
18 E4	ff	ANDB	IND,Y
18 E5	ff	BITB	IND,Y
18 E6	ff	LDAB	IND,Y
18 E7	ff	STAB	IND,Y
18 E8	ff	EORB	IND,Y
18 E9	ff	ADCB	IND,Y
18 EA	ff	ORAB	IND,Y
18 EB	ff	ADDB	IND,Y
18 EC	ff	LDD	IND,Y
18 ED	ff	STD	IND,Y
18 EE	ff	LDY	IND,Y
18 EF	ff	STY	IND,Y
18 FE	hh ll	LDY	EXT
18 FF	hh ll	STY	EXT
1A 83	jj kk	CPD	IMM
1A 93	dd	CPD	DIR
1A A3	ff	CPD	IND,X
1A AC	ff	CPY	IND,X
1A B3	hh ll	CPD	EXT
1A EE	ff	LDY	IND,X
1A EF	ff	STY	IND,X
CD A3	ff	CPD	IND,Y
CD AC	ff	CPX	IND,Y
CD EE	ff	LDX	IND,Y
CD EF	ff	STX	IND,Y

Appendix J

Hardware Control Registers

The 68HC11 microcomputer chip assigns a section of memory for hardware control registers. Most of the registers control input/output hardware. Others control the internal operation of the microcomputer. For example, the highest-priority interrupt is programmable by a control register.

J.1 REGISTER ADDRESSES

The block of memory devoted to hardware control registers extends from address 1000 through address 103F in the 68HC11A8 and 68HC11E9 chips. Other variations may use additional addresses. Since these registers use memory addresses, physical memory cannot also use these addresses.

Software can move the hardware control registers to new locations. Address 1000 is the beginning address of the block of addresses because a reset sets this address. However, the block of control registers can start at any 4K boundary in the memory space. The least-significant four bits of the INIT register at address 103D set the most-significant four bits of the block address. Similarly, the program can move the internal RAM memory to any 4K boundary using the most-significant four bits of INIT. Normally, the RAM begins at address 0000. Therefore, the reset value in INIT is 01.

The INIT register contains only timed-write-once bits that must be set within the first 64_{10} E-clock cycles of a hardware reset. The timed-write-once bits prevent erroneous programs from changing the location of the hardware control registers, which could be dangerous.

J.2 CONTROL REGISTERS AND BITS

The following quick-reference table shows all the control registers and bits. The addresses are those resulting from a hardware reset.

The registers are generally grouped according to the device they are associated with. Some registers are input/output registers while others perform only control functions. Still others contain collections of control bits and flags. Some registers are read only and others are write only. Reference the appropriate text material to use these bits correctly.

All the assigned names and acronyms for both the registers and bits are in the index to this book to facilitate quick reference to the text.

Hardware Control Registers and Bits

Address	Bit 7	Bit 6	Bit 5	Bit 4	Bit 3	Bit 2	Bit 1	Bit 0	Name	Description
$1000	—	—	—	—	—	—	—	—	PORTA	I/O Port A
$1001										Reserved
$1002	STAF	STAI	CWOM	HNDS	OIN	PLS	EGA	INVB	PIOC	Parallel I/O Control Register
$1003	—	—	—	—	—	—	—	—	PORTC	I/O Port C
$1004	—	—	—	—	—	—	—	—	PORTB	Output Port B
$1005	—	—	—	—	—	—	—	—	PORTCL	Alternate Latched Port C
$1006										Reserved
$1007	—	—	—	—	—	—	—	—	DDRC	Data Direction for Port C
$1008			—	—	—	—	—	—	PORTD	I/O Port D
$1009			—	—	—	—	—	—	DDRD	Data Direction for Port D
$100A	—	—	—	—	—	—	—	—	PORTE	Input Port E
$100B	FOC1	FOC2	FOC3	FOC4	FOC5	0	0	0	CFORC	Compare Force Register
$100C	OC1M7	OC1M6	OC1M5	OC1M4	OC1M3	0	0	0	OC1M	OC1 Action Mask Register
$100D	OC1D7	OC1D6	OC1D5	OC1D4	OC1D3	0	0	0	OC1D	OC1 Action Data Register

Hardware Control Registers and Bits

Address	Bit 7	Bit 6	Bit 5	Bit 4	Bit 3	Bit 2	Bit 1	Bit 0	Name	Description
$100E	—	—	—	—	—	—	—	—	TCNT	Timer Counter Register
$100F	—	—	—	—	—	—	—	—		
$1010	—	—	—	—	—	—	—	—	TIC1	Input Capture 1 Register
$1011	—	—	—	—	—	—	—	—		
$1012	—	—	—	—	—	—	—	—	TIC2	Input Capture 2 Register
$1013	—	—	—	—	—	—	—	—		
$1014	—	—	—	—	—	—	—	—	TIC3	Input Capture 3 Register
$1015	—	—	—	—	—	—	—	—		
$1016	—	—	—	—	—	—	—	—	TOC1	Output Compare 1 Register
$1017	—	—	—	—	—	—	—	—		
$1018	—	—	—	—	—	—	—	—	TOC2	Output Compare 2 Register
$1019	—	—	—	—	—	—	—	—		
$101A	—	—	—	—	—	—	—	—	TOC3	Output Compare 3 Register
$101B	—	—	—	—	—	—	—	—		
$101C	—	—	—	—	—	—	—	—	TOC4	Output Compare 4 Register
$101D	—	—	—	—	—	—	—	—		
$101E	—	—	—	—	—	—	—	—	TOC5	Output Compare 5 Register
$101F	—	—	—	—	—	—	—	—		
$1020	OM2	OL2	OM3	OL3	OM4	OL4	OM5	OL5	TCTL1	Timer Control Register 1
$1021	0	0	EDG1B	EDG1A	EDG2B	EDG2A	EDG3B	EDG3A	TCTL2	Timer Control Register 2
$1022	OC1I	OC2I	OC3I	OC4I	OC5I	IC1I	IC2I	IC3I	TMSK1	Timer Interrupt Mask Reg 1
$1023	OC1F	OC2F	OC3F	OC4F	OC5F	IC1F	IC2F	IC3F	TFLG1	Timer Interrupt Flag Reg 1
$1024	TOI	RTII	PAOVI	PAII	0	0	PR1	PR0	TMSK2	Timer Interrupt Mask Reg 2
$1025	TOF	RTIF	PAOVF	PAIF	0	0	0	0	TFLG2	Timer Interrupt Flag Reg 2
$1026	DDRA7	PAEN	PAMOD	PEDGE	0	0	RTR1	RTR0	PACTL	Pulse Accumulator Control Reg
$1027	—	—	—	—	—	—	—	—	PACNT	Pulse Accumulator Count Reg

Hardware Control Registers and Bits

Address	Bit 7	Bit 6	Bit 5	Bit 4	Bit 3	Bit 2	Bit 1	Bit 0	Name	Description
$1028	SPIE	SPE	DWOM	MSTR	CPOL	CPHA	SPR1	SPR0	SPCR	SPI Control Register
$1029	SPIF	WCOL	0	MODF	0	0	0	0	SPSR	SPI Status Register
$102A	—	—	—	—	—	—	—	—	SPDR	SPI Data Register
$102B	TCLR	0	SCP1	SCP0	RCKB	SCR2	SCR1	SCR0	BAUD	SCI Baud Rate Control
$102C	R8	T8	0	M	WAKE	0	0	0	SCCR1	SCI Control Register 1
$102D	TIE	TCIE	RIE	ILIE	TE	RE	RWU	SBK	SCCR2	SCI Control Register 2
$102E	TDRE	TC	RDRF	IDLE	OR	NF	FE	0	SCSR	SCI Status Register
$102F	—	—	—	—	—	—	—	—	SCDR	SCI Data (Rd RDR/ Wr TDR)
$1030	CCF	0	SCAN	MULT	CD	CC	CB	CA	ADCTL	A/D Control Register
$1031	—	—	—	—	—	—	—	—	ADR1	A/D Result Register 1
$1032	—	—	—	—	—	—	—	—	ADR2	A/D Result Register 2
$1033	—	—	—	—	—	—	—	—	ADR3	A/D Result Register 3
$1034	—	—	—	—	—	—	—	—	ADR4	A/D Result Register 4
$1035 to $1038										Reserved
$1039	ADPU	CSEL	IRQE	DLY	CME	0	CR1	CR0	OPTION	Sytem Configuration Options
$103A	—	—	—	—	—	—	—	—	COPRST	Arm/Reset COP Timer Circuitry
$103B	ODD	EVEN	0	BYTE	ROW	ERASE	EELAT	EEPGM	PPROG	EEPROM Programming Control
$103C	RBOOT	SMOD	MDA	IRV	PSEL3	PSEL2	PSEL1	PSEL0	HPRIO	Highest Priority I-Bit Int and Misc
$103D	RAM3	RAM2	RAM1	RAM0	REG3	REG2	REG1	REG0	INIT	RAM and I/O Mapping Register
$103E	TILOP	0	OCCR	CBYP	DISR	FCM	FCOP	TCON	TEST1	Factory Test Control Register
$103F	0	0	0	0	NOSEC	NOCOP	ROMON	EEON	CONFIG	COP, ROM, EEPROM Enable

Appendix K

Answers to Selected Exercises

K.1 CHAPTER 1 ANSWERS

1-1.   (a)   00000011 + 10011100 = 10011111   No overflow
        (b)   11110110 + 11110100 = 11101010   No overflow
        (e)   01001011 − 01100100 = 11100111   No overflow
        (i)   10110100 + 10101110 = 01100010   Overflow

1-2.   (a)   FF   (e)   149
        (b)   00100101   (f)   303
        (c)   1001001   (g)   48

1-3.   (b)   00000100
        (e)   10000000   Overflow
        (f)   1000000100000000
        (j)   00100100

1-4.   (b)   −4   (g)   −128
        (c)   +15   (i)   +78
        (e)   −32768   (j)   −1
        (f)   +127

1-5.   (b)   A5   (f)   C3
          (c)   3C   (g)   8E
          (e)   EB7C   (j)   6AEF

1-9.   No conclusions possible.

1-10.   The number D is higher than or larger than number C. Don't use the words greater than because the numbers are unsigned.

1-11.   32,767

1-13.   The numbers 00 through 7F are positive and 80 through FF are negative.

1-15.   negative

1-19.   You must convert the 8-bit number to a 16-bit number before adding to get 1001101001001101.

1-20.   000100010101

1-22.   4

1-24.   Low is −10 volts and high is 0 volts.

1-26.   START = 1 if A = 1 and B = 0.

1-30.

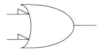 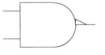

1-31.

TERMINAL VOLTAGES

Inputs		Output
T1	T2	T3
L	L	H
L	H	H
H	L	H
H	H	L

1-35.   A small change in the circuit, such as that caused by temperature variations, may push the system into failure.

K.2   CHAPTER 2 ANSWERS

2-6. 7F C234, which is the CLR instruction with extended addressing.

2-7. Signed numbers.

2-8. positive

2-10. For number 80: N=1, Z=0, V=1, C=1. For number 00: N=0, Z=1, V=0, C=0.

2-12. Branch on nonzero positive.

2-15. The branch instructions do not affect the condition code bits so multiple branches can be done without resetting the condition codes.

2-16. After a subtraction of unsigned numbers, the C bit is meaningful and the V bit isn't. After a subtraction of signed numbers, the V bit is meaningful and the C bit isn't.

2-18. In general, no. The C bit may be different.

2-19. Unless the number is needed in the A accumulator, use the TST instruction.

2-29. Use the ADDD instruction with immediate addressing and data of 0001.

2-34. There is neither an advantage nor a disadvantage to this order.

2-36. Yes, the program would not work correctly because the condition code bits would not be set correctly for the BEQ instruction.

2-37. The first instruction of a program can never have indexed addressing because the index register will contain an unknown number.

2-38. A table of FF entries.

2-43. The maximum spacing is FF.

2-48. Yes. To prove this, use the circular representation of numbers, but interpret the numbers as unsigned numbers.

K.3   CHAPTER 3 ANSWERS

3-1. LDAA #33

3-2. END

3-3. In most practical programs, the FCB could be used instead of the RMB. However, using RMB conveys the intent that the number in memory after the program is loaded is of no significance. FCB implies that a useful number is to be loaded into memory at the specified location. Be careful to distinguish between load time and run time.

3-4. The same binary instruction codes would be loaded at the new address. The program would function the same as it did. It would work on the same data numbers.

3-5.

(a)	$20	(b)	0A	
(c)	C200	(d)	F0	
(e)	0026	(f)	2	
(g)	DE 21	(h)	CC 33 44	
(i)	E7 11	(j)	96 23	
(k)	HERE	(l)	26 03	
(m)	C114	(n)	NUMBER	
(o)	0020	(p)	21	
(q)	7	(r)	PLACE	

3-6.

(a)	C211	(b)	C114	
(c)	F045	(d)	C200	
(e)	Yes	(f)	No	
(g)	12, 16, 17, 19			

K.4   CHAPTER 4 ANSWERS

4-2. Determine whether the decision to exit the loop is executed before or after the body of the loop.

4-12. DO-WHILE

4-13. SEQUENTIAL

4-14. DO-WHILE

4-15. IF-THEN-ELSE

K.5   CHAPTER 5 ANSWERS

5-1. ASRA, RORB

5-5. No, the condition code bits are incorrect.

5-7. 04

5-11. 30, 80, DF, 20

5-13. PSHA, TBA, PULB, RTS

5-14.

```
 1                                  ** EXERCISE 5-14
 2                                  * DON'T CHANGE B ACCUMULATOR
 3                                  *
 4    C100                                    ORG    $C100
 5    C100     37          SHIFTA   PSHB
 6    C101     C1 08                CMPB   #8
 7    C103     23 02                BLS    LOOP
 8    C105     C6 08                LDAB   #8
 9    C107     5D          LOOP     TSTB
10    C108     27 04                BEQ    LAST
11    C10A     48                   ASLA
12    C10B     5A                   DECB
13    C10C     20 F9                BRA    LOOP
14    C10E     33          LAST     PULB
15    C10F     39                   RTS
16    C110                          END
```

K.6   CHAPTER 6 ANSWERS

6-1.   Volatile.

6-2.   Read only memory or ROM.

6-3.   No, because the microprocessor cannot read and write it at full speed.

6-4.   No, the light intensity is not great enough.

6-5.   No, EEPROMs wear out in relatively few erase and program cycles.

6-7.   During the fetch of any instruction, the data bus carries numbers into the microprocessor. During execute of STAA, the data bus carries a number out of the microprocessor.

6-9.   High.

6-10.   The 68HC11 can directly address 64 KB of memory without using any switching or paging techniques.

6-11.   Never.

6-12.   Yes, this instruction is a read-modify-write instruction.

6-15.   Any address from 2003 to 2FFF that has 1s in the least-significant two bits.

6-20.   Yes for both questions. Also, STX and STY can output with this port.

6-21.   All eight bits of the output will be cleared instead of only a single bit. The effects depend on the hardware, if any, controlled by those bits, but good practice is to control only the bits that are in use.

6-25. The computer responds only to the change in the push button because the flag input responds only to transitions. Thereafter, holding the push button does nothing so the program will not read the thumbwheel switch again.

6-26. The main program never again executes even a single instruction. The ISR runs repeatedly as fast as it can continuously reading the thumbwheel switch and updating the display. The push button switch has no effect.

6-27. The main program runs forever. The ISR never runs so the display is never updated. The push button switch has no effect.

6-28. The CLI at line 69 causes continuous interrupts after the flag is set because the flag is never cleared. The main program never again runs. The ISR never runs beyond the CLI, so the display is never updated. The push button switch has no effect.

K.7   CHAPTER 7 ANSWERS

7-1. None.

7-2. The reset pin is a bidirectional signal pin. External devices can reset the 68HC11 chip and I/O devices inside the 68HC11 chip can reset external devices.

7-3. The timed-write-once bits must be programmed within 64_{10} E-clock cycles, or 32_{10} microseconds with an 8.0-MHz crystal.

7-4. The program must read the PIOC register and then read the PORTCL register.

7-5. The main program loop runs forever. The ISR never runs so the display is never updated from its initial state. The push button switch has no effect.

7-12. The flag will not be cleared, so the main program loop never again executes even a single instruction. The port C bits will toggle as fast as the computer can repeatedly execute the interrupt service routine.

7-18. Output compare 1 can control the five port A pins PA3 through PA7. The PORTA register has no effect while the output compare hardware is enabled to control the output pins.

7-21. The codes for the letter M are 01001101, 11001101, 11001101, and 01001101, respectively. The codes for the digit 9 are 00111001, 10111001, 10111001, 00111001, respectively.

7-22. Making a coil of the excess cable is a bad idea because the electrical characteristics of the cable will be changed and the signal may be distorted enough to prevent proper operation of the serial transmission system.

Glossary

Accumulator   A register within a microprocessor that is the source or destination of data for machine instructions.

Acronym   A word formed from the initial letters of each part or word of a compound term. Common practice is to pronounce some acronyms as a word, such as PROM. For others, pronounce the individual letters, such as CPU.

Active-High   The active, true, one, or asserted case of a binary signal is the high—most positive—voltage level. See asserted-high.

Active-Low   The active, true, one, or asserted case of a binary signal is the low—less positive—voltage level. See asserted-low.

Address   The binary number that represents the collection of binary signals used by memory hardware to determine which memory register to access.

Aliasing   The introduction of false lower frequency components in a reconstructed sampled signal due to too slow sampling rate.

ASCII   An acronym for American Standards Committee for Information Interchange. Usually names the weighted code for the letters, numbers, and punctuation marks created by the committee. Pronounce it *ask-key*.

Assembler   A computer program that converts symbolic assembly language programs into equivalent binary machine language programs. Each symbolic instruction is converted to a single machine instruction.

Asserted-High   The asserted, true, one, or active case of a binary signal is the high—most positive—voltage level.

Asserted-Low   The asserted, true, one, or active case of a binary signal is the low—less positive—voltage level.

Big-Endian   A byte ordering system where the most-significant byte of a multiple-byte number is placed in memory at the lowest address.

Bit   A contraction for binary digit.

Bug   A mistake or problem in software or hardware. An incident with an early vacuum tube computer that failed when insects got into the computer cabinet resulted in this term.

Bus   A group of binary signal wires that collectively carry a binary number from one device to another. Bus is also spelled buss.

Byte   A group of eight bits that collectively represents a single number.

Calling sequence   The sequence of instructions that handle parameter passing to a subroutine and the jump to subroutine.

Checksum   A number formed by an algorithm, possibly addition, applied to a data record. A communications system will transmit the record and the checksum for error detection by the receiver.

Chip   The piece of semiconductor material that contains the electronic circuit within an integrated circuit.

Clock   The electronic device that provides timing pulses for a microprocessor.

Code   When used as a verb, code means to write a program. As a noun, code refers to the binary instructions of a program.

Compiler   A computer program that translates high-level language statements to machine language. Making a complete program may require other software besides the compiler.

Complement   Change all the bits of a binary number so ones become zeros and zeros become ones.

Concatenate   To link together or place end to end. Two 8-bit binary numbers can be concatenated to make a 16-bit number.

CPU   Originally an acronym for central processing unit. Now vaguely used to name anything from a microprocessor to a mainframe computer. Pronounce the letters *C*, *P*, and *U*.

Crash   Slang used to describe a program with errors that cause it to stop functioning correctly. "The program crashed."

Cross assembler An assembler program that runs on a different kind of computer than that for which it generates code.

CRT terminal An electronic device including both a keyboard and a cathode ray tube display. Most CRT terminals transmit and receive ASCII character codes using asynchronous serial communication.

Cursor A bright figure used as a pointer on a computer screen. Some cursors blink.

Debug To correct mistakes in both software and hardware.

Delimit To determine the limits of something, such as the end of a computer command character string.

Download To transmit binary numbers from a large central or host computer to a smaller satellite computer.

Editor A program used to create, edit, store, and retrieve text files on disk or other storage media. The text files are generally used as computer programs, so an editor has commands to make editing of programs easy.

EEPROM Acronym for electrically erasable programmable read only memory. Pronounce the letters *E*, *E*, and then *prom*. A type of memory integrated circuit.

Effective address The final memory address used by an instruction. The instruction may require the microprocessor to perform several operations to generate the effective address.

EPROM Acronym for erasable programmable read only memory, originally UVEPROM for ultraviolet erasable PROM. Pronounce it *E*, and then *prom*. A type of memory integrated circuit.

Execute The complete operation by which the microprocessor carries out an instruction.

Fetch The complete operation by which the microprocessor reads an instruction code from memory.

Floating point number A number represented in the computer in mantissa and exponent form.

Greater than Used when comparing two two's complement signed binary numbers. The number that is more positive than the other is said to be greater than the other. For example, the binary number equivalent to -10_{10} is greater than the number equivalent to -50_{10}.

Hardware The physical parts of a computer as opposed to numbers or software.

Hard disk A memory device using a rotating rigid metal or glass disk with a magnetic coating. Physically small sealed units are called Winchester disks.

Hexadecimal The base 16 number system that has 0 through 9 and A through F as the digits. In spoken language, pronounced Hex. Usually used as a condensed notation for binary numbers. Hexadecimal is often incorrectly spelled hexidecimal.

Higher   Used when comparing two unsigned binary numbers. The number that is numerically greater than the other is said to be higher than the other.

High-level language   A computer language with commands that do not directly represent the machine instructions. Usually the commands resemble English statements.

IC   Acronym for integrated circuit. Pronounce the letters I, C.

Index register   A microprocessor register that holds part of or all the effective address used by an instruction.

Instruction   A binary code number that directs the control unit of a computer to perform a certain operation. Each operation has a unique instruction code.

Instruction set   The collection of the instruction codes recognized by the control unit of a computer.

Integer number   A whole number represented in the computer as a fixed number of binary bits. Methods of representing both signed and unsigned numbers exist. Contrast integer number with floating point number.

Integrated circuit   An electronic circuit assembly containing a chip that performs a complete function. Standard packages make mounting them on a printed circuit board convenient. See IC and chip.

Interrupt   A technique of input/output timing or synchronization that uses hardware to stop the current program and transfer control to another program. A signal from the I/O device determines when this transfer occurs.

Kilobit 1024_{10} bits. Abbreviated Kb.

Kilobyte 1024_{10} bytes. Abbreviated KB.

Less than   Used when comparing two two's complement signed binary numbers. The number that is less positive than the other is said to be less than the other. For example, the binary number equivalent to -50_{10} is less than the number equivalent to -10_{10}.

Level-sensitive   Describes the input hardware in an electronic digital circuit that responds to the high level or low level of the binary signal applied to it. See transition-sensitive.

Little-Endian   A byte ordering system where the least-significant byte of a multiple-byte number is placed in memory at the lowest address.

Lower   Used when comparing two unsigned binary numbers. The number that is numerically less than the other is said to be lower than the other.

Memory   A large collection of electronic registers that the microprocessor can access quickly and randomly one at a time. The bit storage technology of the memory determines its characteristics.

Memory location   A memory register as specified by its address. The word location implies physical position.

Microcomputer   One integrated circuit or a collection of integrated circuits including a microprocessor that make a computer. These components usually reside on a single printed circuit board.

Microprocessor   The single integrated circuit or the portion of a single-chip microcomputer that implements the processor and control unit of a microcomputer.

Minicomputer   A small computer package built from a manufacturer's standard components. It requires no additional components or assembly. The manufacturer will usually supply operating system software and peripheral hardware devices to make a computer system.

Minuend   A number from which another number is to be subtracted.

Modular number system   A number system represented best by numbers on a circle because the numbers repeat. The numbers on a clock face are an example.

Monitor program   A simple program permanently stored in a computer that usually can start other programs, control the computer hardware, or test the hardware. It usually starts running automatically when the power to the computer is turned on.

Nonmaskable interrupt   A hardware interrupt that software cannot disable.

Nonvolatile memory   A type of memory that retains information without electrical power. Most ROM memories are also nonvolatile memories.

Op code   Operation code. The part of a binary machine instruction that directs the control unit of a computer to perform a certain operation.

Parallel transfer   A transfer of multiple bits from one register to another simultaneously. Parallel transfers require multiple bit paths.

PC   The nearly universal acronym that has meanings including program counter, personal computer, process controller, programmable controller, and printed circuit. People using computers prefer personal computer.

Personal computer   A microcomputer based computer system intended for operation by a single person. The smallest system includes a CRT monitor, a disk drive, and a keyboard. Often such a system will include several microcomputers within its components.

Pointer   A register that holds an address of data rather than the data.

Position-independent code   Binary program code that runs correctly when moved to a new place in memory. Also called binary relocatable code.

Program counter   A microprocessor register that holds the memory address of the next instruction to be fetched.

PROM   An acronym for programmable read only memory. PROM is a common name for several types of field programmable nonvolatile memory integrated circuits. Pronounced like the word *prom*.

Protocol   The set of conventions that govern the treatment and formatting of data in an electronic communications system.

Pure procedure code   Program code that does not modify itself as it runs.

RAM   A misnomer for read/write memory integrated circuit that originally was an acronym for random access memory. RAM is a common name for several types of memory integrated circuits. Pronounced like the word *ram*.

Random access memory   A memory in which the access of each register takes the same time and effort. This is still true when the access of a randomly selected register follows the access of any register. Contrast this with a sequential access memory.

Real time   Describes a computer system that responds fast enough to make a difference. The time scale depends upon the application.

Reentrant   A term that describes subroutines that are interrupted and reentered without failure. The response to the interrupt can include calling the same subroutine.

Register   An electronic device that holds a binary number.

Reset   In digital systems, to force the system to a known starting point, such as the power-up condition.

ROM   An acronym for read only memory. Read only means that the microprocessor can only read from this kind of memory because writing is impossible. A common name used for several types of memory integrated circuits. Often used to imply that the memory is also nonvolatile. Rhymes with *prom*.

RS232   The identification number of a standard published by the Electronic Industries Association. This standard specifies the electrical characteristics of a serial communications system.

Sampling theorem   The original frequencies in a sampled signal can be reproduced when the signal is reconstructed only if the sampling rate is greater than twice the highest frequency in the original signal.

Sequential access memory   A memory in which access of the registers must be in sequential order. Magnetic tape is an example.

Serial communications   Transmission of binary data from one device to another one bit at a time. This requires only a single bit path—an advantage in many applications.

Software   The numbers in a computer memory that represent instructions and data.

Subroutine   A program module independent of the main program that is designed to be used repeatedly. A main program transfers control to the subroutine; the subroutine performs a function; and then the subroutine returns control to the main program so it continues. People speak of jumping to or calling the subroutine when transferring control to it. Similarly, they speak of returning from the subroutine. The main program usually calls the subroutine at many places.

Subtrahend   A number that is to be subtracted from another number.

Structured programming   The discipline of writing programs using only the three fundamental program structures called SEQUENCE, IF-THEN-ELSE, and DO-WHILE.

"The registers"   In spoken language, this phrase refers to the registers inside the microprocessor, such as accumulators. It does not include the memory registers.

Timed-write-once bit   A hardware control bit that a program can alter only once, and the alteration must occur within a short time after the computer hardware is reset. Further efforts to change the bit will be ineffective. Such a bit prevents erroneous programs, possibly due to hardware failures, from modifying the hardware operation.

Toggle   A word meaning to reverse or complement the state of something. This jargon probably comes from the operation of a toggle switch that only has two positions.

Top/down design   A software design philosophy that advocates an overall design with only a few major pieces first. Next, each piece is broken into smaller pieces with more detail. This continues until there is enough detail to write the program. Structured programming makes this practical.

Transition-sensitive   Describes the input hardware in an electronic digital circuit that responds to a change of the binary signal applied to it. Most transition-sensitive inputs respond to either the low-to-high transition or the high-to-low transition, but not both transitions. See level-sensitive.

Two's complement numbers   Binary numbers that are members of the two's complement number system. This modular number system represents signed integer numbers (positive and negative).

Two's complement overflow   A sign error that occurs when arithmetic operations performed on two's complement numbers result in an answer that needs a number with more bits.

Upload   To transmit binary numbers from a small satellite computer to a larger central or host computer.

Volatile memory   A type of memory that loses the numbers stored in it when electrical power is removed from it. Most RAM memories are also volatile memories.

Weighted code   A code made up of items that are assigned a numerical coefficient based on the position of the item within the code. For example, Arabic numbers are weighted but Roman numbers are not. Weighted codes are desirable because computers can easily sort the codes into numerical order to determine other orders. For example, sorting weighted character codes puts them into alphabetical order.

General Index